NAMES

AND

THEIR HISTORIES

A Handbook of

HISTORICAL GEOGRAPHY

and

TOPOGRAPHICAL NOMENCLATURE

BY

ISAAC TAYLOR, M.A., Litt. D., Hon. LL.D.

CANON OF YORK

AUTHOR OF 'WORDS AND PLACES'

SECOND EDITION, REVISED

RIVINGTONS

KING STREET, COVENT GARDEN

LONDON

1898

REPUBLISHED BY GALE RESEARCH COMPANY, BOOK TOWER, DETROIT 1969

Library of Congress Catalog Card Number 68-17936

PREFACE

THE favour accorded for more than thirty years to successive editions of a volume entitled *Words and Places* has encouraged me to undertake another work on the same subject, but written on a different plan, and with a different intention.

The object of the former book was to show how an acquaintance with the etymology of local names may be of use to students of such sciences as Ethnology, Mythology, or History.

Regret has frequently been expressed that I did not venture beyond the definite plan I had proposed to myself, and especially that I had left several classes of local names without explanation. The object of the present book is to supply some of these omissions by giving an account of certain names, especially those of philological interest or of geographical importance, whose origin or etymology has been ascertained, and then tracing historically the changes which have taken place in their forms or in their geographical significance. Such names, for example, as America, Austria, Scotland, Saxony, Africa, or Peru have now a very different application from that which they originally possessed, and the history of their migrations, extensions, or transformations is a subject of investigation not destitute of interest.

Changes of this class are legitimate, being due to the regular operation of natural causes ; but it is otherwise with Ghost-names, which owe their existence to the blunders, conjectures, misconceptions, or perversities of scribes, map-makers, or explorers. Among the more notable Ghost-names are Madagascar, the Hebrides, the Grampians, San Remo, Morocco, Mogador, Moldavia, Ararat, Ceylon, Canton, Texas, Yucatan, California, Canada, and Young Island; with the rivers Congo, Cam, Isis, Rom, Penk, Eden, Lett, and Nogoa. The study of geographical names might have supplied the materials for a noteworthy chapter in Mr. Caxton's great History of Human Error.

In order not to add to geographical perplexities I have carefully endeavoured to avoid that common and fertile source of error, mere etymological guesswork based upon the modern forms of names. I have therefore made it a rule to exclude from consideration names whose earlier forms are unknown, and whose signification cannot therefore be historically determined. In a few important cases, such as London, Britain, or Berlin, where the meaning is not ascertainable, an exception has been made, and it has seemed expedient to enumerate the more probable conjectures which have been made by competent authorities. On the other hand, in order not needlessly to swell the bulk of the book, I have left unnoticed thousands of obscure places mentioned in Cartularies and similar documents, as being more suited for discussion in local monographs. Such, for instance, are the Icelandic farms and hamlets whose origin is recorded in that unique document, the *Landnáma-bók* of Iceland, which tells the story of the first settlement of the Island by emigrants from Norway. But a typical selection of English village names, as they appear in early Charters or in Domesday, has been given in the Appendix.

I have treated with great brevity classes of names

which have been discussed in competent and accessible monographs, such as those of Förstemann, Grandgagnage, Gatschet, Joyce, and Sibree, writers who have systematically explained the local nomenclature of Germany, Belgium, Switzerland, Ireland, and Madagascar.

I have also omitted many recent names in the Arctic regions and in Australia, whose significance is known from the published journals of explorers, as they will mostly be found in Egli's *Nomina Geographica*, a valuable though not always trustworthy work. Useful as this compilation has proved, I have, in most cases, thought it best to refer directly to the books he quotes, and to which his work serves as a sort of Index. For this reason it has seemed needless to increase the size of this volume by constant references to authorities, since they are usually cited by Egli, whose book will naturally be consulted by the few readers who may have occasion to go more deeply into the history of any particular place. But I have appended for the use of students a bibliographical note enumerating a few standard works on the subject. I have also drawn up a prologue or short introduction pointing out some of the more curious and interesting names, which, to facilitate reference, have been arranged in alphabetical order in the Glossary which follows.

I have to render my warm thanks to Mr. Cecil Bendall, of the British Museum, who has revised the notices of Indian names, and to Mr. Henry Bradley, the joint-editor of the new Oxford Dictionary, who has performed the same service for the remainder of the book, and to whom I am indebted for numerous corrections, and many valuable suggestions, only a few of which have been acknowledged in the text.

I. T.

SETTRINGTON, *November* 1895.

ADVERTISEMENT TO THE SECOND EDITION

THIS Edition has been carefully corrected and revised; also in compliance with numerous requests, an Index has been added, chiefly of the names (2059) which occur in England.

CONTENTS

NAMES AND THEIR HISTORIES

THE PROLOGUE

THE investigation of the etymology of local names is beset with peculiar difficulties, arising from the fact that, unlike other words, they constantly outlive the languages from which they are derived, while successive races transform the old names which they have received so as to make them significant to themselves. Hence speculation as to the meaning of a name, without reference to its primitive form or to its subsequent history, is always futile, and frequently misleading, as it may have been orally transmitted from people to people, continuing in vernacular use long after the language in which it was significant has been altered by dialectic change, or has been supplanted by some other tongue.

Italy is the only land in which language and civilisation have been so continuous as to permit any considerable number of names to be transmitted, practically unchanged, for two thousand years. Roma, Capua, Mantua, Ravenna, Nola, Ostia, Cortona, are still called by the names which they bore in the time of the republic, and in other cases the change has been very slight. Thus Perugia was Perusia, Chiusi was Clusium, Rimini was Ariminum, Sorrento was Surrentum, Salerno was Salernum, but even in Italy the difficulty is not wholly removed, as many of these names are not significant in Latin, but must be referred to the lost languages of prehistoric races.

In other lands names have rarely come down to us with so

A

little change. Even in the countries of neo-Latin speech, barbarian invasion, followed as usual by dialectic change, has curiously transformed names derived from Latin sources. In France, for instance, it would be difficult, without documentary evidence, to recognise in the village name Glisolles a corruption of *ecclesiola*, the 'little church,' or to understand how *silvagium* has been converted into Servais, *basilicæ* into Bazolles, *podium* into Le Puy, *tres viæ* into Treviers, or *mutationes* into Muison. In France, moreover, numerous Celtic and Teutonic names have survived the effacement of Celtic and Teutonic speech ; Vernon and Vernay, for instance, being from the Celtic *wernos*, an alder tree, Condé from *condate*, a confluence, while Quillebeuf answers to our English Kilby, Quittebeuf to Whitby, and Cherbourg to Scarborough.

In England we have the same descent of local names from languages or dialects no longer vernacular. In Welsh *afon* means a 'river,' and *cwm* a 'hollow,' and the fact that we have an Avon and a Combe in Hampshire proves that Welsh was once spoken in that part of England. Cornishmen now speak English, and have forgotten that the name of Garrick signified a 'rock' in the old Cornish speech. Even names of undoubted Anglo-Saxon or Scandinavian origin cannot usually be explained off-hand from the resources of modern English. It is not obvious, for instance, that the first syllable of Redbridge referred to 'reeds,' or that of Redriff to 'oxen,' much less that such forms as Howsham, Welham, and Welwyn are really due to dative plurals.

In some parts of Germany Celts have been succeeded by Wends, and Wends by Teutons, with the result that Celtic, Slavonic, and Teutonic names are strangely intermixed. Without some knowledge of historical ethnology, it would be difficult to explain the fact that many names in Germany, such as Ratisbon, Mainz, Bonn, and Trier, can only be explained from Celtic sources, that others, such as Dresden, Leipzig, or Mecklenburg Strelitz, are of Slavonic origin ; while for a few, such as Cologne, Coblentz, or Cassel, we have to resort to the speech of an Italian city. Sometimes, as in the case of Brandenburg, a name apparently Teutonic proves to be a Celtic or Slavonic designation which has assumed a Teutonic shape so as to become significant in German ears, just as in Wales a name like Barmouth, apparently English, is really Welsh, while in Ireland Money-sterling is partly Greek and partly Gaelic, and in Scotland Loch Long is a Celtic name accommodated so as to bear an English signification.

How rapidly such a stratification of names can be effected is shown in the case of North America, where we find a layer of Indian names, like Massachusetts, Niagara, Canada, Quebec, Erie, or Ontario, overlaid by Franco-Indian terms like Huron or Illinois, or pure French names such as Vermont, Lake Superior, or Montreal, by Dutch names like Brooklyn or Hoboken, with a Spanish stratum such as Florida, Colorado, Montana, or Rio Grande, and the whole overlaid by such pure English names as Westpoint, Maryland, or Springfield.

Even when the etymology of a name is manifest, a knowledge of historical geography is often needed in order to explain its modern application. France, for instance, is named from the Franks, a German tribe who only obtained a footing in a portion of the country; Burgundy, Lombardy, and Andalusia from three other German tribes now completely absorbed. For more than a thousand years there have been no Huns in Hungary, and Saxony has never been inhabited by men of Saxon race. Russia, a typically Slavonic land, owes its name to a band of Swedish vikings, and Prussia, typically German, to a remote Lithuanian province which was conquered by an order of Teutonic knights. A Celtic tribe which has long vanished from history has bestowed a name on Bohemia, which is peopled by Slaves, and on Bavaria, inhabited by men of German speech. No less difficult would it be to discover the origin of names which have been derived from the heraldic bearings of medieval lords, as in the case of the old French province of Dauphiny, or of the town of Leonberg in Würtemberg. Some knowledge of history is needed to understand how it is that an insignificant village has been able to give its name to Switzerland, or how the vast region which we call Siberia was named from another village which has totally vanished from our maps.

The vitality of a name is lost when the meaning is no longer generally understood. It then becomes specially liable to corruption, which frequently results in an assimilation of the form to that of other names which are more familiar, or which still remain significant. It follows that names apparently similar or identical often prove to have different etymologies ; while dissimilar names may come from the same source, as in the case of Terni and Teramo in Italy, both of which are corruptions of Interamna, 'between the rivers.' It might be supposed that the first syllable of the county names Carmarthen, Cardigan, and Carlow, all of which are of Celtic origin, are from the same source. The *Car* in Carmarthen and Carlisle is the Celtic *caer*, a 'fortress' or 'city,' in Cardigan it is part of a personal name, while in Carlow it is the numeral *cether*, 'four.' Or, to take a French example, Châlons-sur-Marne is a tribal name, a corruption of the dative plural *Catalaunis*, while Chalon-sur-Saône is from *Cabillonum*, a name of totally different origin. Again, Holland, Holstein, and Holderness have nothing to do with hollows, and it is only by research in obscure archives, without which the most ingenious speculation as to the meaning of these names would be futile, that scholars have ascertained the ancient forms, which prove that they all refer to districts of primeval forest.

In the same way English names have frequently been so perverted or obscured by corruption or assimilation, that without the aid of documentary evidence it would be impossible to arrive at correct conclusions as to their significations. Thus Alton in Hants is not, as we might expect, the 'old tun,' but, as is proved by the Anglo-Saxon name *Æweltun*, the 'tun

at the *æwel,'* the source of water from which the celebrated Alton
ales are brewed, but Aldborough in Yorkshire, occupying the
site of the Brigantine city of Isurium, was rightly named the
'old burgh,' and Aldborough in Suffolk is the burgh on the
River Alde. Aldershot and Alresford in Hants are named
from the alder tree, while Alderbury in Wilts and the Isle of
Alderney are both from personal names.

The suffix -*ham*, so common in English village names, has
two distinct significations, the meaning to be assigned to it
depending on the quality of the vowel in Anglo-Saxon, which
was lost as early as the Norman Conquest; while *Ham-* as a
prefix is usually derived from an adjective of entirely different
signification. So the common suffixes -*ton*, -*don*, -*den* and
-*stone* are constantly assimilated or interchanged, and the same
has frequently occurred with -*ford* and -*worth*, -*head* and -*hithe*,
-*grove* and -*grave*, -*ham* and -*holm*; Durham, to take a well-
known example, being a corruption of Dunholm, while the
meaning of such common names as Hampton, Hinton, Burton,
Bolton, Grafton, Harley, and many more, can only be determined with certainty by early documentary evidence. In the
case of Whittlesea, Mersea, and Hornsea, the last syllable
means in one case, 'lake,' in another, 'island,' while in the third
it is derived from an obsolete grammatical inflexion denoting
the dative singular. In like manner the sign of the dative plural
has frequently lapsed into -*holm* or -*ham*. Whether the first
syllable of such names as Fulbeck, Fulmere, and Fulham signifies
full, foul, or fowl, can only be determined by a knowledge of
the primitive forms, which is also requisite to enable us to determine whether such a name as Wotton or Wootton refers to
woods, weeds, width, or wheat; whether Widford and Widcombe
refer to willows, width, or whiteness; Linton to limes or flax;
Shipton and Skipton to ships or sheep; Hambledon or Himble-
don to sheep or hops; Ashton and Aston to the ash or to the
east; and Gatton, Gaddesden, and Gateshead to gates or goats.
Melbourne may be the mill burn or the middle burn, an

ambiguity which applies also to Milton and Melton, while the names of Harrow, Harrogate, and Harrowby are all derived from entirely different sources. Such ambiguities may suffice to show how useless, or rather how misleading, it is to guess at the meaning of a name unless the ancient form can be recovered from charters or similar evidence. Unfortunately not a few names, and those often of considerable importance, have been handed down in popular parlance from times so remote that their primitive forms can only be matters of ingenious conjecture. Thus a considerable but mostly futile literature has gathered round the name of Berlin, which has been explained in turn from Celtic, Slavonic, and Teutonic sources. It is doubtful whether the name of Spain is Phœnician or Basque, the etymologies usually accepted of Rome and London are probably wrong, while as to the name of Britain scholars are hopelessly at variance.

Historical materials have sometimes come to light, which have made it possible to unravel, with greater or less success, the meaning of names whose etymology had been given up as hopeless, or of which an erroneous interpretation had been usually accepted. This has been the case with Lichfield and Maidenhead, where myths originating in popular etymologies have taken graphic form on the corporation seals. In the case of Madagascar, a hearsay report of Malay or Arab sailors, misunderstood by Marco Polo, or by the scribes who took down the great traveller's tale, has had the effect of transferring a corrupt form of the name of a portion of the African continent to the great African island; while the modern names of the Hebrides, the Grampians, and Iona are due to the adoption of erroneous readings of manuscript texts by the editors of early editions of Latin writers. To errors in the interpretation of ancient authors we owe such blunders as the names of Odessa, Pomona, and Morecambe Bay, while the names of the Cam and the Isis must be attributed to erroneous philological speculation. Glerawly, the second title of Lord Annesley, is a name due to the blunder of a clerk, who, in making out the patent

for the peerage, wrote Glerawly by mistake for Glenawly, originally Clanawley, the family estate in Fermanagh.

The names of imaginary saints have occasionally been evolved
out of geographical names by popular etymology. Thus a
village in Belgium called Saint-Fontaine appears in a document
of 1313 as Centfontaines, evidently from *terra de centum fontanis*, the land of a hundred springs; while Saint Plovoir, a
place in Limburg, is a corruption of *simplex via*. Sentiniacus,
which signified the estate of Sentinius, has become Saint Igny,
S. Petrus de Villa is now St. Peraville, S. Petrus in Via is now
St. Peravy, while S. Remigii Mons has become St. Remimont.
The reverse process may occasionally be detected. In the
duchy of Luxemburg there is a place called Sandweiler, which
would ostensibly signify a dwelling on the sand, but which is
really a corruption of S. Valerius, while S. Nectarius has become
Senneterre, and S. Casius is now Sommecaise.

Owing to the mistakes of explorers, clouds or icebergs have
been entered on maps as islands or mountain ranges, and have
sometimes remained on the charts for centuries, to the confusion
of geographers and sailors. Peninsulas have been marked as
islands, and land-locked bays as the mouths of rivers, as in the
case of Rio, the capital of Brazil, which is not situated on a
river, as the name would lead us to suppose. The most endur-
ing of these errors are the names of the West Indies and of the
State of Indiana, both ultimately due to the delusion of Columbus, who died in the belief that the lands he had discovered
formed a part of Asia.

The origin of other names which seem inappropriate or
absurd is explained when the history of the name is known.
Sometimes an essential portion of the name has fallen into disuse, as with the names of Hull, Leith, Thame, and Frome, all
of which are properly names of rivers, and not, in the first
instance, of the towns by which the river names have been
appropriated. The name of Honduras is derived from a Spanish
word meaning 'deep,' which was originally given to a river;

and Brazil is from a Portuguese word denoting glowing coals; Penang is the Malay name of a certain tree, and Canada is an Indian word signifying a collection of huts or wigwams. The huge mountain mass of the Camaroons bears a Portuguese name which means shrimps, while in the case of the Congo a native word which signifies mountains has been transferred to a great African river.

Not unfrequently, as in the case of Africa, Asia, India, Borneo, Italy, Greece, or Portugal, names have received an enormous extension of their original significance, while others, as Peru, Saxony, Westphalia, or Northumberland, have been shifted far from the district to which they originally referred.

Imaginary names of another class have been derived from popular legend, or from works of fiction supposed at the time to be veracious narratives. Bimini, described in the fictitious travels of Mandeville as a land containing the fountain of perpetual youth, in search of which the adventurous expedition which led to the discovery of Florida was equipped, has found a local habitation in one of the Bahamas; and it is now known that the 'golden State' derived its name from a romance whose author invented the name of California for the long-sought El Dorado whose discovery he described. Manitoba is so called from an Indian legend which there localised the habitation of the spirits of the dead, and to a similar Cornish legend of a land of Goire, the bourne from which no one could return, we may probably attribute the name of Gower, the peninsula seen dimly looming across the Severn Sea.

Old Greek legends are embodied in names which remain upon the map. On the south coast of the Black Sea we find a Cape Yason, which represents the Greek Iasonion, where the myth of Jason and the Argonauts was localised by Milesian sailors. Odessa was founded on a site wrongly supposed to be that of the Greek city of Odessus, which may have been so named to give a local habitation to a legend of the hero of the Odyssey, whose visit to Circe was localised on the coast near Naples at a place marked on our modern maps as Cape Circeo. On the same lovely shores we find the islands of the Sirens, where it requires no great amount of imagination to transform the white surf playing round the rocks awash with the waves into the white shoulders of maidens floating in the sea. The islands of the Hesperides with their golden apples are known to all winter visitors to the Riviera, the spear of Polyphemus is the name given to a pointed rock which stands erect beside a cave at the back of Capri, and the name of Acis will be found on the Sicilian coast not far from Scylla and Charybdis. Plato's account of the island of Atlantis may have helped to give currency to the name of the Atlantic Ocean, while the Greek myth of Atlas, the giant who bore the heavens on his shoulders, is recalled to mind when the traveller who approaches Gibraltar sees a low belt of cloud resting on the shoulders of the hill called Atlas by the Greeks, which is itself an outlier of the chain to which we have transferred the name. When the ancient legend tells us how Europa, a Phœnician damsel, was carried by a bull across a strait which still bears the name of the Bosphorus, the 'passage of the bull,' it is impossible to determine how far the name arose from the legend or the legend from the name, but it would seem that the legend points to the remote period, when, owing to astronomical causes, the constellation which was the leader in the procession of the Zodiacal signs was not Pisces or Aries, but Taurus, in which capacity he would conduct Europa, the 'broad-faced moon, in the diurnal progress from the Eastern land of Asia to the region of the sunset. In any case the names of Europe and Asia for the two great continents could only have arisen when the land connection was unknown, and the Ægean and the Euxine were believed to divide the world into two parts. To the same mythical era we must assign the old name of the River Po, to which the Greeks gave the name of the constellation Eridanus, apparently identifying the earthly river with the heavenly river of the Babylonian astronomy. Another astronomical name is that of the Arctic

Ocean, which reminds us that the Greek term for the north was derived from the constellation of the Great Bear. It may also be noted that in the Swedish district of Thielemarken we may probably find a local habitation for the extreme northern land dimly known by hearsay as Ultima Thule to the ancient world.

In the names upon the map we find a host of survivals of various kinds—ethnological, historical, ecclesiastical, biographical, and philological.

Bygone institutions or jurisdictions are commemorated in such names as Dingwall, Walsoken, Galton, or Buckrose; and forgotten tenures or ancient modes of tillage in Theale, Oundle, Huish, Buckland, Fifehead, Sixpenny Handley, Pennygown, and Unganab.

But what we may call ethnological survivals are of greater value, since local names may furnish valuable evidence as to the geographical position of races or tribes now vanished or absorbed.

The name of Venice long remained a solitary memorial of the Veneti, an ancient tribe whose affinities were unknown, and it is only within the last few years that the prehistoric cemeteries of Este and Padua have yielded inscriptions from which we gather that the Veneti were an Illyrian people, who must have crossed the Adriatic and taken possession of lands previously held by the Etruscans, to whom we assign the names of Mantua and Ravenna, while Milan, Como, and Genoa are among the names due to the Celtic inroad which transformed Northern Etruria into Cisalpine Gaul. The names of Florence, Piacenza, and the Emilia speak of the Roman dominion, Lombardy of the latest Teutonic invasion, while Cimiez and the Ciminian mountains are believed to be vestiges of the pre-Aryan population of the Italian peninsula. The names of Rumelia, Roumania, and perhaps of Erzeroum remind us that the New Rome founded on the Bosphorus became the capital of the Roman Empire, the province of Romagna being so called because for a time it remained the sole Italian possession of the Roman Emperors in the East. Austria is a name which carries us back to the time when an Eastern marquisate had to be erected as a frontier to resist the Magyar horsemen, and the Bavarian province still called the Pfalz is a record of the dismembered fief once held by the Count of the Palace, one of the great official dignitaries of the Holy Roman Empire of the West.

It sometimes happens that the names of kingdoms, provinces, or tribes survive only in the name of some physical feature, or of an insignificant village. The Pentland Firth and possibly the Pentland Hills bear witness to the extent and position of the great kingdom of the Picts, and the kennels of the Pytchley hounds remind us that in one of their destructive inroads they penetrated as far south as the county of Northampton. The situation of the seven provinces of the Pictish realm, and of the earldoms into which they merged, are also indicated by obscure names. Braemar and Cromar, both in Aberdeenshire, belonged to the great prehistoric earldom of Mar, while the position of the earldom of Buchan is indicated by Buchan Head : that of Moray by the Moray Firth, and of Athole by Blair-Athole. The earldom of Angus is now miscalled Forfarshire from the county town of Forfar, but the older name is retained by Coupar-Angus and Fetter-Angus. The county of Fife preserves the old name of one of the Pictish provinces, but if, as in other cases, the name had been changed, the position of the province would still be marked by Cupar-Fife and Fifeness, as has happened in the case of the province of Caith, where the name is preserved by Caithness, the curious Picto-Scandinavian name of its northern promontory which has been adopted for an existing county. The position and extent of Fidach, another of the Pictish provinces, is historically unknown. The name is believed to have meant the 'forest' (Gaelic *fid*, Welsh *gwydd*), and the province seems to have been part of the territory afterwards included in the earldoms of Mar, Moray, and Buchan, and hence we may probably recognise the name in Glen Fiddich in Banffshire. In like manner the position of the district called Manu (genitive, *mannann*) is indicated by the names of Clackmannan, the 'stone of Manu,' and Slamannan, the 'mountain of Manu.'

Dunmyat, a hill near Stirling, is believed to have been the 'dun' or fort of the Meatæ, a Caledonian tribe mentioned by Tacitus. Dumbarton and Dumfries are also the names of tribal fortresses. Dumfries was the fort of Frisian settlers, while Dumbarton, formerly called Dunbretane and Dumbriton, the 'fort of the Britons,' was a northern outpost of the British kingdom of Strathclyde, a part of which has retained the name of Cumberland, the 'land of the Cymry,' the more southern portion being overlooked by Ingleborough, the border fortress of the Angles, which crowns a commanding summit of the Pennine chain. The further progress of Anglian conquest is marked by the name of Englefield, formerly called Englafield, a Berkshire battlefield between Angles and Saxons, the most southern point at which the English, as distinguished from the Saxons, can be traced. There are a few similar records of intrusion or extrusion, such as Britford in Wiltshire, the 'ford of the Britons,' doubtless a ford by which Welsh cattle-raiders invaded Wessex; or Exton, in Hampshire, a corruption of East-Sexna-tun, which shows that a body of East Saxons must have migrated from Essex to this West-Saxon village. Conderton in Worcestershire is a still more singular name, being a corruption of Cantwara-tún, the 'tun of the Cantware' or men of Kent, whose capital was at Cantwarabyrig, now Canterbury.

Similar migrations or conquests, but on a much larger scale, have, from historical causes, had the curious result that the names of large countries are frequently derived from a small portion of the inhabitants. The name of France is a case in point, though not so extreme as those of Germany, Russia, and Africa. Scotland is an excellent instance of the way in which the extension of a national name may be due to dynastic causes. In early documents the terms Scoti and Scotia always refer to Ireland. This Irish sept, having crossed the narrow sea, conquered for themselves a new home in Argyle, which then, as the name implies, became the borderland of the Gaelic invaders. The kings of the Scots, having obtained the Pictish throne by marriage, became powerful enough to incorporate the northern part of the Welsh kingdom of Strathclyde, and to annex the English district of the Lothians in the South, and in the North the Scandinavian earldoms of Caithness and Orkney. Hence it has come to pass that we apply the inappropriate name of Scotland to a composite realm, of which only a small part has ever, except in a dynastic sense, been a land of the Irish adventurers who alone can properly be called Scots. Somewhat similar is the history of the dynastic extension of the Frankish name to ancient Gaul, or of the English name to ancient Britain. Owing to the succession of Eadgar, an Anglian king, to the throne of Wessex, it has come to pass that the Angles, and not the Saxons, have given their name to England, though it might easily have been otherwise, as is shown by the fact that the Welsh still give to all Englishmen the name of Saesneg, from the name of the foes they first encountered.

In numerous instances a tribal name has become territorial, the name of the tribe or people being used as the designation of the land they occupy. A simple case is that of the northern and southern divisions of the East-Anglian folk, whose territories we now call Norfolk and Suffolk, without noticing that such names must originally have designated not a district, but its inhabitants. In like manner Essex, Middlesex, Sussex, and Wessex, as well as Somerset and Dorset, are plural forms, denoting primarily the settlers, and not the district in which they settled, the changed usage being probably due to the alderman or earl of the tribe acquiring territorial jurisdiction, and so becoming the alderman or earl of the district.

Wales, the modern form of the Anglo-Saxon word *Wealas*, which means 'foreigners,' still retains the sign of the plural, which has disappeared in the name of Cornwall, owing to its name having been derived from Cornweala, the genitive plural, and not from the nominative plural Cornwealas, which would have given Cornwales, the 'Welsh of the horn,' as the name of the county.

These tribal names distinguish from the shires those counties which are not shires. We do not speak of Essexshire or Cornwallshire; and Dorsetshire and Somersetshire, though sometimes used, are incorrect. The distinction is still kept up in peasant parlance; an Essex labourer, for instance, will talk of going 'into the shires.' While such counties as Northumberland, Cumberland, Norfolk, Suffolk, Essex, Middlesex, Sussex, Kent, Somerset, Dorset, or Cornwall were originally kingdoms or tribal settlements, the shires, which take their names from towns, were administrative districts, into which such larger kingdoms as Wessex and Mercia were divided by Alfred and his successors.

We have an historical distinction of the same sort in Scotland, where Argyle and Fife are properly counties, while Invernessshire, Stirlingshire, and Dumfriesshire are shires. In Ireland, Meath, Kerry, Tyrone, and Fermanagh belong to one class, Sligo, Waterford, and Wexford to the other; but here, unfortunately, owing to the policy of the English conquerors in breaking up the authority of the tribal chiefs, the names of the old sub-kingdoms, such as Thomond, Desmond, Ormonde, Ossory, Tirconnel, Offaly, or Oriel, have disappeared, or survive only in the titles of Irish peerages.

In England we have in local names a few such memorials of kingdoms or of tribal dominions which did not survive as counties. When the great Northumbrian kingdom, which at one time extended from the Humber to the Forth, had shrunk into the narrow limits of the present county of Northumberland, the severed southern portion, to which by right the name North-Humberland should have appertained, became the kingdom of Deira, with its capital at York, and this kingdom of Deira has bequeathed a curious memorial of its existence in the name of the earldom or county of Hol-der-ness, which signifies the ness or promontory of the Deira holt or forest. The British kingdoms of Elmet and Loidis, which for a time remained independent of the kings of Deira, are localised by the names of Sherburn in Elmet and Leeds, while Skipton in Craven and Nether Hallam preserve the memory of Cravenshire and Hallam-shire, the old name of Howdenshire being happily revived for one of the new electoral divisions. Henley-in-Arden localises the forest of Arden, while at Bridgenorth, a corruption of Bridgemorfe, was the bridge over the Severn which led to the great forest of Morfe.

Many of the old French provinces, like the English counties, bore tribal names. Armorica obtained the name of Brittany when it became the refuge of the Britons who fled across the channel from the Saxon invasion. Burgundy was the land settled by the Burgundians, a Teutonic tribe who had marched with the Goths from the shores of the Baltic across the Danube and the Alps. Normandy was the coast land ceded to the Northmen who came from the same region by another route. The Pictavi or Pictones, a Celtic tribe, left their name in Poictou, the Andecavi in Anjou, the Cenomani in Maine, the Petracorii in Périgord, and the Bituriges in Berri. It is worthy of note that while in Southern Gaul the great cities have, as a rule, retained their ancient names, Toulouse, for instance, being Tolosa, Lyons being Lugdunum, and Marseille being Massilia, in the north they have frequently acquired the names of the Gaulish tribes whose capitals they were, the chief town of the Ambiani becoming Amiens, that of the Remi becoming Rheims, of the Seni becoming Sens; while Lutetia, the capital of the Parisii, is now Paris.

In Germany the shiftings of population have seldom permitted the retention of the tribal names. We have, however, a memorial of the Celtic Treviri in Trier or Trèves, of the Boii in Bavaria and Bohemia, of the Chatti in Hesse, of the Eastern Franks in Franconia, of the Suevi in Swabia, of the Thurings in Thuringia, and of the Huns in Hungary.

Among religious and ecclesiastical survivals the foremost

place must be assigned to the rare records of pre-Christian heathendom. How the name of Athens came to be associated with that of the virgin goddess is a question not easy to determine. The principality of Monaco takes its name from a temple of Hercules Monœcus. The Bourbons derive their name from a place dedicated to the worship of Borvo, a Gaulish deity; while Oisemont recalls the name of Esus, one of the deities of Lucan's Celtic triad. Famars is a corruption of Fanum Martis, Alajou, in the Herault, of Ara Jovis, and Nîmes of the sacred grove called Nemausus. In England the name of Lydney, and as some have thought, of Leicester, London, and the Dee may be connected with the worship of Celtic deities, while Arram, Lund, and Weighton in Yorkshire, and Harrow in Middlesex, were sites of the worship of the heathen English. The Wansdike in Wilts bears the name of Woden, while at the town called Odinse in Denmark there stood, in historical times, a great temple of Odin. India is full of names derived from shrines and temples, among them are Bombay, Seringapatam, Cawnpore, Cape Comorin, and the River Jumna. In other lands Macao, Mexico, and Lima derive their names either from deities or their temples.

In Europe ecclesiastical names are chiefly found among the Celtic races. In Ireland and Scotland we have numerous names beginning with *Kil*, such as Kildare, Kilkenny, or Kilmore, which denote a monastic cell or a church, answering to the Welsh or Breton names in *Llan-*, such as Llangollen or Llanfair, the second part of the name frequently containing the name of the saint to whom the church was dedicated. In England, saint names, such as St. Albans or Peterborough, usually derived from great monasteries, are rare, but they are more frequent in France, as at St. Omer or St. Malo. In the North of England and in the South of Scotland the word *kirk* enters into the composition of names, as Kirkcudbright, Falkirk, and the numerous Kirbys. Names like Holyhead, Halifax, and Penzance have also to be noted. Downpatrick reminds us of the apostle of Ireland; the canton of St. Gallen of one of his Irish followers who evangelised Switzerland; Cape St. Vincent of a hermit who established himself in that desolate eyrie; while, more curious than all, Glasgow has been explained from an affectionate nickname given to St. Kentigern. In the New World we have similar memorials of the Franciscan and Jesuit missions, among the more notable being San Francisco, Sacramento, and St. Louis, while Los Angeles takes its name from a mission dedicated to Santa Maria Reyna de los Angeles.

The calendar frequently dates the discovery of capes and islands. The Virgin Islands were sighted by Columbus during his second voyage on October 21st, the feast of St. Ursula and the eleven thousand virgins. Natal was discovered on Christmas Day, Florida at Easter, while St. Helena, Ascension, Easter Island, Christmas Island, and Mount St. Elias were named from the day of discovery. Maio, one of the Cape Verd islands, was discovered on the 1st of May, and Rio Janeiro on the 1st of January. The stages of the notable voyage, during which the long line of the Brazilian Coast was traced in 1501 by Amerigo Vespucci, are chronicled by a fringe of names still retained by the more notable capes and rivers which he sighted. Thus we find the record of his landfall in Brazil at Cabo de San Roque, which he discovered on St. Roque's Day, August 16th; on August 28th, St. Augustine's Day, he had reached Cabo de San Augustino; on Michaelmas Day, September 29th, he was at the Rio de San Miguel; on the next day, September 30th, St. Jerome's Day, he named the Rio de San Jeronymo. He reached the Rio de San Francisco on St. Francis' Day, October 4th; the Rio das Virgens on the feast of St. Ursula, October 21st; the Rio de Santa Lucia on St. Lucy's Day, December 13th; the Cabo de San Thomé on St. Thomas' Day, December 21st; the Bahia de San Salvador on Christmas Day; the Rio de Janeiro on January 1st; and the Angra dos Reis on January 6th, the festival of the Three Kings.

B

Numerous islands, capes, and bays bear the names of the ships by which they have been discovered, and many reefs and shoals perpetuate in like manner the memory of notable shipwrecks. Columbus set the example by giving to one of the Antilles the name of the Marigalante, the ship in which he sailed on his second voyage. The great Columbia River and British Columbia through which it flows obtained their names, not in honour of Columbus, but from the *Columbia*, a Boston merchant vessel. The names of the *Heemskirk*, the *Arnhem*, the *Zeehaan*, the *Duyfhen*, and the *Geelvink*, in which Tasman and the early Dutch explorers sailed, are duly entered on the map, as well as those of Cook's ships, the *Endeavour*, the *Resolution*, the *Adventure*, and the *Discovery*, together with the *Géographe* and the *Naturaliste*, the ships of his French rivals in Australian discovery. The *Hecla*, the *Griper*, and the *Fury*, the *Erebus* and the *Terror*, the *Dolphin* and the *Union*, the *Herald* and the *Blossom*, in which the great arctic and antarctic explorers made their perilous voyages, are found upon the scene of their exploits. Pitt Island and the Chatham Islands were named, not from those statesmen, but from the ships by which they were discovered, as is the case with the Asia Islands, America Island, Ocean Island, Amsterdam Island, Bounty Island, the Phœnix Islands, Pioneer Island, and many more, not forgetting those named after surveying vessels, such as the *Beagle* and the *Investigator*.

More numerous and more interesting than the names derived from ships are those which commemorate the services of their officers and commanders. Thus it is not a mere barren catalogue of geographical names that we find written upon our ocean charts, but a story of daring and endurance, replete with human interest. The Atlas, if rightly read, forms a sort of *Libro d'Oro*, inscribed with the names of the world's great explorers, recalling the adventurous deeds, the glorious lives and the heroic deaths of the navigators who, in their tiny barques, explored strange coasts and first ventured across unknown oceans. We may thus discover an absorbing biographical interest even in the dry study of geography.

First, perhaps, in order of interest, though not of time, we are reminded how Henry Hudson, who had given his name to a great American river, was cast adrift with his little son in a small skiff by his mutinous and starving crew, and found his grave in the great inland sea whose name forms his imperishable monument. The name of Davis Strait is a no less worthy memorial of a still earlier arctic and antarctic explorer, who, after a long life of strange adventure, was treacherously murdered by Japanese pirates whom he tried to succour.

Coming to Baffin's Bay, we are reminded of another English worthy, who, after exploits hardly less notable, was killed by a chance shot at the siege of Ormuz in the Persian Gulf. Nor must we forget Martin Frobisher, the earliest of our arctic navigators, who, in the tiny *Gabriel*, discovered the Bay which bears his name, and afterwards, in command of the *Triumph*, the largest ship in the British Navy, led the attack on the Spanish Armada. The memory of those Elizabethan merchant princes at whose charges the expeditions of the early arctic explorers were equipped is perpetuated by the names of Lancaster Sound, Smith's Sound, Jones' Sound, Wolstenholm Sound, Sanderson's Hope, and Cape Dudley Diggs, while Boothia Felix and Grinnell Land record the munificence with which their example was followed at the time of the second epoch of arctic discovery, when Parry, Ross, Franklin, M'Clintock, and M'Clure, were leaving their names in regions which Davis, Baffin, and Hudson had failed to reach. Nor have we to search in vain for the name of Raleigh, courtier, adventurer, and martyr, or of Cavendish and Drake, the first Englishmen to follow in the track of Magellan, and circumnavigate the globe. The straits that bear the names of Magellan, Bering, Torres, Juan de Fuca, and Cook, the islands called after Tasman, the most adventurous of Dutch navigators, and after Houtman, Jan Meyen, Fernando Noronha, Fernando Po, Vancouver, Gilbert, and Marshall are all memorable among the biographical records of the map. Neither must we overlook the causes owing to which the great Western Continent acquired the name of Amerigo Vespucci, the Florentine pilot, who first made its existence known to the wondering world. It may be regretted that the name of the Sea of Cortez no longer attaches to the Gulf of California, although we are not altogether without a geographical memorial of the bold adventurer, since Malinche, a conspicuous peak in Mexico, was so named by the Spaniards from the resemblance of the outline to the profile of Malinche, the devoted mistress of Cortez, who rendered him such invaluable services as an interpreter.

Sometimes we discover more than the mere names of the great explorers, and find what we may call biographical survivals, recalling notable incidents, fortunate or unfortunate, in their careers. The map occasionally records their perils and their escapes, their failures and their successes, their hopes and their spring of action. In such names as Point Turnagain, Cape Disappointment, Disaster Inlet, Cape Farewell, Massacre Bay, the Bay of Despair, or Port Famine, which are so numerous on the map, we have miserable records of heart-breaking disaster and baffled enterprise.

Other names are less dismal. In the Antilles the islands of Trinidad, Antigua, and Montserrat recall the religious mysticism, the prayers and vows of Columbus, Cape Gracias-a-Dios tells us of his reliance on the divine protection, and San Domingo of his filial piety. The name of the Pacific Ocean records the tranquil seas over which, by a happy fortune, Magellan sailed in the vessel, which alone, of all his squadron, succeeded in weathering the continual tempests which had beset him in the strait which bears his name, while the name of the Ladrones commemorates the plunder of his starving crew at the islands which were his first landfall after leaving the land of fire, on the unexampled voyage in which, for the first time, the world was circumnavigated.

It was the discovery of the mariner's compass which paved
the way for the great extension of maritime enterprise which
began in the fifteenth century. That the Portuguese led the way
is proved by the Portuguese names in Brazil, and by those which
fringe the coast of Africa from Cape Nun, Cape Verd, and Sierra
Leone to Fernando Po, the Camaroons, Saldanha Bay, and
Natal; while the monumental name of the Cape of Good Hope
speaks of the spirit of undaunted enterprise which made these
discoveries possible, and records the tenacity with which the king
of Portugal, Dom Jão ii., clung to the belief that a sea route to
India would ultimately be found, the fulfilment of this good hope
being witnessed by names in the furthest East, like Ceylon,
the Moluccas, Japan, Macao, the Boca Tigris, and Formosa,
which are either Portuguese, or show by their forms that they
must have reached Europe by Portuguese channels. Next in
succession come the Spaniards, who have filled with Spanish
names such a large portion of the habitable globe; followed by
the Dutch in the Eastern seas, by the French in Canada and
Louisiana, and by the English in America, Australasia, and the
arctic regions.

But though the greater number of what we may call names of
discovery belong to the last four centuries, there are not wanting
records of exploration which carry us back to epochs of much
remoter date. The Phœnicians, who were the fathers of maritime
enterprise, have left, dotted over and even beyond the Mediterranean coasts, a fringe of Semitic names which testify to their
persevering search, first for the oyster which yielded the dye for
the Tyrian purple, and then for tin, a necessary constituent of
bronze, and also for the tunny fish, on which the population of
their great cities so largely subsisted. Samos and Samothrace,
Catania and Syracuse, Cape Boeo and Malta, Port Mahon and
Marseilles, Malaga, Tarragona, Cartagena, Ceuta, Cadiz, Seville,
and Lisbon are all Phœnician names. The Phœnicians were followed by the Greeks, their pupils in the art of navigation, whose
distant colonies are marked by the names of Messina, Palermo,

Cumæ, Naples, Nice, Antibes, and the Balearic Islands, while names like India, the Indus, Java, and Socotra, show by their forms that the knowledge of these Eastern lands first came to Europe through Hellenic channels. Among the numerous memorials of the Arab empire in Spain we note Gibraltar, Trafalgar, Almeria, Alcala, Medina Sidonia, the Guadiana, and the Guadalquiver, while Marsala, Caltanisetta, and Caltagirone testify to their rule in Sicily, and the Forêt des Maures near Fréjus to the footing they obtained in Southern Gaul, which was extended as far as the Mont Cenis, as is proved by St. Jean de Maurienne, the capital of the old county of the Maurienne.

The large number of geographical names derived from those of emperors and kings form what we may call dynastic survivals. Among the names of states included in this class are China, Lorraine, Lodomeria, the Herzgovina, Louisiana, Virginia, Georgia, Carolina, the Philippines, and the Carolines. The names of Alexandria, Scanderoon, and Candahar, of Nicæa, Philadelphia, Eupatoria, Latakieh, Seleucia, and Ptolemais tell us how Greek arms and Greek culture extended into two continents under Alexander and his successors. The name of Provence records the position of the first province acquired by the Romans beyond the Alps. We find the name of Augustus in Autun, Augsburg, and Zaragoza, of his successors at Grenoble, Orleans, Adrianople, and Constantinople, while the records of later European kings, such as Edinburgh, Oswestry, Charleston, Christiania, and Ludwigshaven are too numerous to specify. Dauphiny is an almost unique instance of a name derived from an heraldic bearing.

Records of colonial governors are not uncommon. There are a few of early date, such as Lake Champlain in America, the Marquesas, and the Island of Mahé, but they are most numerous on the map of Australia, where we find the names of most of the successive governors, beginning with Captain Philip, the first governor, and Captain Hunter who succeeded him, followed by Colonel Lachlan Macquarie, General Sir Thomas Brisbane, Sir

Ralph Darling, Sir George Gipps, Sir Charles Fitzroy, Captain
Hindmarsh, Captain Davey, Colonel Sorell, and Colonel Gawler,
with colonial statesmen like Mr. Torrens.   We have the names of
Sir B. D'Urban and Lord C. Somerset at the Cape, and of Lords
Amherst, Dalhousie, and Canning in India.

It is curious to note the way in which the names of English
towns and villages have been indirectly transferred to remote
corners of the earth, not, as in the case of New England towns like
Boston, by repeating in the new country the name of the domicile
of the original settlers, but owing to their having been the source
of territorial surnames or titles borne by statesmen or by naval or
military commanders.   One of the earliest instances is Baltimore
in Maryland, so called, not from the Irish town, but from Lord
Baltimore, an Irish peer, who took his title from the town.   So
Halifax, the capital of Nova Scotia, takes its name from an Earl of
Halifax and not from the town.   The names of New York and
Albany were derived from the territorial titles borne by James ii.
before his accession to the throne.   Through the Earl of Auckland, the Dukes of Wellington and Marlborough, Lord Sydney
and Viscount Melbourne, the New Zealand capitals of Auck-
land, Wellington, and Marlborough, and the Australian capitals
of Sydney and Melbourne derive their names in the same in-
direct manner from English villages in Durham, Somerset, Wilts,
Kent, and Derbyshire.   So the name of Melville, the obscure
Scotch village which gave a title to Henry Dundas, a first Lord
of the Admiralty, has been transferred to a great Arctic Island.
The name of Palmerston, a village near Dublin, and of Bathurst,
Grafton, Rodney, and Kimberley, in England, as well as those of
a few French castles such as Beaufort, Granville, and Albemarle,
have thus been transferred to British colonies.   By far the most
notable case of the kind is that of the insignificant village of
Washington, in Durham, whose name has been transferred to the
federal capital of the United States, to a great North-Western
territory, and to 320 counties, cities, towns, and townships in the
States.   Just half this number, 160, bear the name of Lincoln,

derived indirectly from the English city through the American
President of that name.   The nomenclature of Western States
and Territories bears curious witness to their date of settlement,
and to the popularity of certain Presidents.   Andrew Jackson,
President from 1829 to 1837, comes next to Washington with
313 names, followed by Thomas Jefferson (1801-1809) with 204,
and James Madison (1809-1817) with 224.   Ulysses Grant has had
156 places named after him, James Monroe (1817-1825) following
with 133, and General Harrison with 96.   James Buchanan,
(1857-61) comes last with 11, Fillmore and Tyler rival him,
each with less than 20, Hayes has 22, Pierce 25, Van Buren 36,
Polk 57, and John Adams (1797-1801) has 88.   The constant
repetition in the United States of these Presidential names,
though tiresome and perplexing, is not without significance, but
the same cannot be said of other classes of names which abound
in that land of incongruities, where we find, as Emerson com-
plains in his *English Traits*, that 'the country is whitewashed
all over by unmeaning names, the cast-off clothes of the country
from which its emigrants came.'   Still more unmeaning are the
transferences of ancient names belonging to countries from
which no emigrants could have come, such, for example, as
Troy, Memphis, Utica, Palmyra, Antioch, Syracuse, Babylon,
and Carthage.

Even worse are the odious hybrids, barbarously compounded,
such as Minneapolis, Indianapolis, or the eleven places unhappily
called Jonesville, names even more offensive than those of places
which, as Emerson says, have been 'named at a pinch from a
psalm tune,' or, as in Australia, from the nickname of a prize-
fighter.   Worst of all is the procedure adopted in the new State
of Washington, where the counties were named by shaking the
letters of the Alphabet in a bag and then emptying them, a few
at a time, upon the floor, a process which has yielded such
hideous monstrosities as Wankikum, Klickitat, and Snohomish.
Compared with these we may regard as rational and inoffensive
some of the 'cast-off clothes' of the Old World, when the

emigrants from a European town affectionately gave the name of the old home to their new domicile in the Western wilderness, as is the case with Boston, Ipswich, Worcester, and other New England towns, or when the names of Dutch villages, such as Hoboken and Brooklyn, are repeated by places near New York, a fashion unconsciously imitated from the practice of the Greek colonies of Cumæ, Cyrene, Megara, and Rhodus, which reproduced the name of the parent city.

The names of New Spain, New Granada, New France, New England, and New Jersey set the fashion of such clumsy designations as Nova Scotia, New Caledonia, New Holland, New Zealand, New Britain, New Ireland, and New South Wales, several of which must be laid to the charge of Cook, who, as a rule, was most happy in his nomenclature.

In the Spanish and Portuguese colonies many repetitions of Old World names, apparently meaningless, have arisen from the dedication of churches or convents to localised saints, as in the case of Loretto in Peru from a dedication to our Lady of Loretto, or of Nazareth in Brazil from a dedication to St. Mary of Nazareth, while Belem, also in Brazil, repeats the dedication of a famous convent near Lisbon to St. Mary of Bethlehem. More interesting are the names of two of the Antilles—Antigua, so named by Columbus in fulfilment of a vow which he had made before the altar of Santa Maria La Antigua in a chapel of the cathedral of Seville, and the neighbouring island of Montserrat, so called at the request of his chaplain, Father Boil, who had been a monk in the convent of Montserrat in Catalonia.

At the Cape of Good Hope we have a class of monstrosities, happily few in number, as bad as any in the United States, consisting of manufactured names which have been deliberately and often ignorantly compounded of disjointed fragments of personal names. The fashion was set by the Dutch in the case of Zwellendam, made up out of the name of a Dutch governor and the maiden name of his wife, a bad example which was

followed in the case of Potcherfstrom and Pietermaritzburg, and
of such English names as Harrismith and Ladysmith.   At home
we have a few instances nearly as bad ; Camberley is perhaps the
worst, followed hard by Ben Rhydding and Saltaire.   A similar
offence was committed in 1793 by a decree of the French Convention, which substituted names of Republican complexion for
those which in any way savoured of the old *régime*.   Thus it was
ordained that the historic name of Guise should be replaced by
Réunion-sur-Oise, while Montmorenci, in compliment to Rousseau, was altered to Émile.   These fabrications fortunately failed
to acquire currency, with the exception of the Isle of Bourbon,
which was rechristened Réunion, and of a few street names in
Paris, such as the Place Louis Quinze which was renamed Place
de la Concorde.

Less objectionable are the invented names bestowed on royal
palaces or hunting-seats, such as Sans Souci, Quisisana, Fried-
richslust or Carlsruhe, to which the Hague, Mecklenburg
Strelitz, Bois le Duc, and Richmond may be added.   The
happiest of these modern inventions are Polynesia, Australia,
Australasia, Senegambia, Sebastopol, Pennyslvania, and Philadelphia.   Etruria, now a considerable town, was the name given
by Wedgwood to the place in Staffordshire where he produced
imitations of vases supposed to be Etruscan, but now known
to be Greek.   In America there are many similar names, as
Galena, Silverville, Oil City, and Petrolia.

In the lands of Teutonic settlement or conquest, village names
derived from those of early settlers, such as Ellesmere, Reading,
Malmesbury or Hastings in England, Kissingen or Göttingen in
Germany, and Sévigné or Aubigny in France, probably out-
number those from any other source, with the possible exception of names descriptive either of situation or of natural
features, which abound in every land.   From situation we have
such names as Japan, Piedmont, Algarve, Surrey, and probably Europe and Asia ; from colour, Falkirk and Greenwich,
Dublin, Lichfield, and Helvellyn, Greenland, Cape Verd, Monte-

negro, the Nilgherries, and Mont Blanc; with Turkish names like Ak-su and Kara-dagh, and two of the United States, Vermont and Colorado. From configuration we have Corfu, Spitzbergen, and Skye. Poland, Champagne, and Winchester speak of treeless plains; Batak, Cork, Jarrow, and Culloden of marshes; Coblentz, Condé, Conflans, Aberdeen, and Haltwhistle of the confluences of rivers; Java, Holland, Funchal, Madeira, Madrid, Shrewsbury, Farnham, Auckland, Vernon, and Chatenay of vegetation; while the names of the Azores, the Canaries, the Galapagos, Chili, and the Camaroons are derived from the animal kingdom.

Important towns frequently derive their names from the rivers on which they stand, as, for example, Moscow, Vienna, Schleswig, Amsterdam, Darmstadt, Innspruck, Laybach, Tilsit, Plymouth, Sheffield, Colchester, Lancaster, Doncaster, Exeter, Galashiels, Inverness, Tobolsk, and Omsk. India is the only great country whose name has been taken directly from that of a river, though if Moscovy, the older name of Russia, had been retained, we should have had another notable instance. Portugal is named from the port formed by the estuary of the Douro, and the name of the Argentine Confederation has been not unhappily invented for the state which lies on the banks of the river of the silver—Rio de la Plata. Most of the French departments have been named from rivers, as is the case with several of the United States, as Ohio, Missouri, Arkansas, and Minnesota. Among descriptive names derived from numerals we may count Ceuta, Zweibrücken, Sevenoaks, and Carlow. Near Walenstad, in the Upper Valley of the Rhine, there is a curious series of numeral names, six successive villages bearing the names of Primsch, Gons, formerly Seguns, Tertzen, Quarten, Quinten, and Sewes, which doubtless mark six successive posts or stations, Roman or perhaps Rhætian. In like manner going eastward from Genoa along the Riviera de Levante towards Nervi, we find the villages of Quarto and Quinto, marking the positions of two of the Roman stations. At the fourth mile-

stone on the Roman road from Nîmes to Beaucaire we find
the village of Quart, which in a document of the tenth century
is called *villa Quarto*.   There are few modern names of the
same class.   In the Argentine Province of Cordova, after crossing
the Rio Primero, 'the first river,' and proceeding southwards, we
come successively to Rio Secundo, Rio Tercero, Rio Cuarto, and
Rio Quinto.   Sailing along the Tasmanian coast from east to
west we come to Ninth Island and Tenth Island, which were the
ninth and tenth islands discovered by Flinders in 1798.

English, like German names, are essentially prosaic.   It has
been well remarked that the local names in Ireland and England
accurately reflect the character of the Celtic and Teutonic races.
In the one case the names are fossil poetry, in the other they
are fossil history.   Nothing can be more poetical than many
Irish names, replete with legend and with allusions to the beauty
of Nature.   Carrigcleena is the 'rock of Cleena,' the queen of
the fairies ; Glennawoo means the 'glen of the spectres,' Derry-
evin is the 'beautiful oak grove,' Killykeen the 'pleasant wood,'
Gloragh the 'babbling brook,' and Coolkellure the 'recess of
the warbling birds.'   In English names hardly a trace of imagination, or of any perception of natural beauty, can be discovered ; they record in the most prosaic manner the name of
the earliest settler, or some fact as to the nature or situation of
the place.   We learn, for instance, that Meopham was the home
of Meopa ; that Bentley was a field with long grass stalks ; while
names like Newton, Norton, Middleton, or Sutton occur by
scores in every county.   Hence arises the miserable poverty of
English village nomenclature, the same prosaic names occurring
again and again with wearisome repetition.   There are no less
than one hundred and thirty villages called Newton, seventy-
three called Sutton, sixty-nine called Charlton or Carlton, forty-
nine called Preston ; while Norton, Weston, Barton, Wootton,
and Compton are nearly or quite as common.

To remedy the confusion resulting from so many neighbouring villages bearing identical names they have frequently acquired

distinctive additions, derived in many cases from the name of the tenant *in capite*, ecclesiastical or lay. Thus we have Thorpe Basset, Thorpe Arch, Thorp Mandeville, Bishopsthorpe, Stapelford Abbots, and Melton Mowbray, while Bolton Percy and Wharram Percy both belonged to the great Yorkshire fief of the Percies. But an explanation is required of the curious fact that even in popular parlance the distinctive affixes acquired by many of these villages are derived either from Norman-French or from Latin. Thus we have such names as Stretton-en-le-Field, Sutton-le-Marsh, Barton-le-Street, Barton-le-Clay, Thorpe-le-Soken, Newton-le-Willows, Hutton-le-Hole, Hutton-Ambo, Luttons-Ambo, Newton-Regis, Stratford-sub-Castle, Ashby Magna, Ashby Puerorum, and Ashby-de-la-Zouch. As such affixes frequently appear in the names of city parishes, as St. Martin-le-Grand, St. Mary-le-Strand, or St. Mary-le-Bourne, now Marylebone, it may be conjectured that the Latin titles arose from the necessity of distinguishing parishes of the same name when the parochial lists were called over at Episcopal or Archidiaconal visitations, the Norman-French additions being in like manner due to lists of parishes kept for fiscal or judicial purposes. It may be noted that these descriptive affixes, though later than Domesday, can usually be traced back as far as the thirteenth century.

Such bilingual names are very simple cases of what we may call philological survivals, of which many kinds exist. One class, whose meaning is usually obvious, consists of names with which the definite article has been incorporated. We still speak of The Hague, The Nore, The Chilterns, The Borough, The Wash, and The Curragh, and our grandfathers spoke of The Bath and The Devizes, where we say Bath and Devizes. It is less usual than it was to speak of The Lewis, The Tyrol, The Herzgovina, The Camaroons, The Breisgau, and The Salzkammergut. A Portuguese calls the town at the mouth of the Douro, O Porto, or in the genitive, Cidade do Porto, but more commonly Porto only, while on English maps we find not O Porto but Oporto, without any sign that the first syllable is merely the definite article. A different error is made when we speak of Brazil. Fifty years ago The Brazil was usual, and Southey entitled the most ponderous of his works *A History of the Brazils*, usages both of which are incorrect. The original Portuguese name being Terra do Brazil, the 'land of the brasil-wood,' the genitive, do Brazil, was supposed to imply O Brazil as a nominative, and this was translated as The Brazil, which has now become Brazil. It is to be hoped that we shall not fall into the analogous blunder of shortening Tierra del Fuego into Fuego. The German Feuerland is a translation of the name, and there are signs that Fuegia may ultimately become the English form. In French names the article is common, and has not unfrequently been incorporated; thus the correct form L'Isle has now given place to Lille, in which the consciousness of the article is lost, and the same is the case with the town of Lorient, and the villages of Laborie, Lalande, and Lor, called Hortus in 1184. We commonly speak of the Department of The Lot, without noticing that in so doing we are duplicating the article. In like manner the river which flows past Kilkenny is usually called The Nore, although in the *n* of Nore we have already a fragment of the Celtic article, which has likewise been incorporated in the names of Nenagh, Newry, Nairn, Inverness, and Loch Nell. The old Egyptian article, seen in Thebes, survives also in the names of Philæ and the Fayûm; and we have the Arabic article in the names of Luxor, Algarve, Alcala, Alpuxaras, Almeria, Alcantara, Trafalgar, and the palace which we tautologically style the Alhambra. The Greek article has been incorporated in the names of Navarino and Negropont, and a German preposition, usually followed by the article, forms the first part of numerous names, such as Zermatt, Andermatt, Amsteg, Anspach Anbach, and Amwalde. The Greek name Spalato exhibits an incorporated preposition, common also in Slavonic names, such as Sabor, Zabrod, Zablatt, Potsdam, Pomerania, and Podgoriza.

Not unfrequently, as in the case of Holstein, Hampshire,

Hanbury, or Welwyn, the names have been derived from oblique cases in such a manner as to disguise the true etymology. It is necessary to remember that in early documents local names usually appear not in the nominative but in some oblique case, sometimes the genitive or the accusative, but more often in the locative, which we commonly call the dative. These oblique cases, thus commonly used in speaking of towns, came to be regarded as undeclinable nouns, or were themselves declined as nominatives. Thus the form Canterbury is derived from the dative Cantwarabyrig; if it had been derived from the nominative, the modern form would have been Canterborough, as in the case of Peterborough or Gainsborough. So while Newton represents a nominative, Newington and Newnton owe their forms to the dative. In Clackmannan we have the genitive of Manu, and in Rathlin of Reachra, Erin and Albion also being genitives from *Eriu* and *Albiu*. The place where the Roman road crossed the River Don was called ad Danum, and hence Danum was used as the Roman name of Doncaster. The station at the confluence of the Mosel and the Rhine was called by the Romans Confluentibus, a form which explains the modern name Coblentz. The final *s*, which appears in the name of so many French cities, may also usually be accounted for as the surviving vestige of a grammatical inflexion. In the North of France, as has already been explained, the tribal name in the dative plural usually became the name of the chief city of the tribe. Thus the capital of the Ambiani was called Ambianis, whence Amiens; that of the Remi was Remis, whence Rheims; that of the Meldi, was Meldis, whence Meaux; that of the Bellovaci was Bellovacis, whence Beauvais; that of the Catalauni was Catalaunis, whence Châlons; that of the Cadurci was Cadurcis, whence Cahors; that of the Tricassi was Tricassis, whence Troyes; that of the Treviri was Treviris, whence Trèves.

It is probably from a false analogy that we have affixed a final *s* to the names of southern cities, which, being derived from some other source, do not possess it in French. Thus

Lyon, anciently Lugdunum, we call Lyons, and Marseille, derived from Massilia, we call Marseilles. In like manner the French have added a sibilant to the names of foreign cities, making London into Londres, Dover into Douvres, and Genova into Gènes. Occasionally, as with Bruxelles, Bruges, Malines, and Naples, we have followed the erroneous spelling adopted by the French. In some French names, such as Dijon and Macon, the final *n* is a proof of derivation from an oblique case, and not from the nominatives Dibio and Matisco.

Local dialectic tendencies have had a curious effect in transmuting the same primitive words or syllables. The Celtic possessive suffix -*ac* has, for instance, assumed a variety of forms in different parts of France. Thus Albiniacum, which denotes the 'estate of Albinius,' has become Aubigné in the West, Aubigny in the centre, and Aubignay in the East, while in the South, the full stress falling on the syllable -*ac*, it has been preserved unaltered, and we have Aubignac. In Guienne, Auvergne, and the Lyonais, the suffix takes the forms -*as*, -*at*, and -*a*, while in the Pas de Calais we find -*ecque*.

The effect of dialect is also seen in England. In the North Carlton, Skipton, and Skelton retain the original pronunciation, which in the South has been softened into Charlton, Shipton, and Shelton. The North retains -*burgh*, as in Bamburgh or Edinburgh, in the Danish district it has become -*borough*, as in Gainsborough, Scarborough, and Peterborough, while in the Saxon South we have -*bury*, derived from the dative, as Banbury or Canterbury. But the most remarkable result of dialectic tendencies is seen in the variant forms assumed in different parts of the kingdom by the Anglo-Saxon *ceaster*, a loan word from the Latin *castra*, acquired by the English before their arrival in Britain, and used to denote any Roman town. In the Vespasian Psalter, a Mercian MS., the West Saxon *ceaster* takes the form -*cester*, and accordingly in the old Mercian kingdom we find -*cester* instead of -*chester*, as in the cases of Worcester, Gloucester, Cirencester, Towcester, Bicester, and Leicester. In the Scandinavian districts, especially Cumberland, North Lancashire, Yorkshire, Lincolnshire, Rutland, and Norfolk, *ceaster* becomes *caster*, as in the case of Muncaster, Casterton, Lancaster, Acaster, Tadcaster, Doncaster, Castor, Ancaster, Brancaster, and Caistor. In the Saxon districts such as Wessex, as well as in Durham and the region north and west of the Scandinavian settlement, we find *-chester*. Thus we have Binchester and Chester - le - Street in Durham, Rochester, Outchester, and Hetchester in Northumberland, with Rutchester, Lanchester, Halton-Chesters, Little Chesters, and Great Chesters on the Wall. In South Lancashire and the adjacent counties we have Ribchester, Manchester, Chesterfield, and Chester. In Wessex and other Saxon districts we have Winchester, Silchester, Woodchester, Porchester, Dorchester (two), Chichester, Rochester, Colchester, Grantchester, Godmanchester, Archester, Chesterford, and Chesterton (two). The line between *chester* and *castor* is very sharply marked, Chesterton in Huntingdonshire being opposite Castor in the Danish county of Northampton, separated from it only by the River Nen. As we approach the Welsh border we get a clipped form, not however primitive, as in Ex-eter, Wrox-eter, and Mancetter, to which Gloucester, Worcester, and Bicester, and Cirencester have approximated in pronunciation since the time when the spelling became fixed.

Naturally the first element in these names is often a fragment of the name of the Roman town. London has dropped the suffix and no longer appears as Londonchester, but Venta became Winchester, Glevum became Glou-cester, Vriconium became Wrox-eter, Vinovium became Bin-chester, Portus became Por-chester, Mancunium became Man-chester, Manduessedum became Man-cetter, Epiacum became Eb-chester, and Corinium became Ciren-cester, and in other cases, such as Exeter, Towcester, Alcester, Ilchester, Grantchester, Colchester, Lancaster, Ribchester, Doncaster, and Leicester, the first syllable is derived from the name, usually British, of the river on which the town stood.

C

We find not only these curious dialectic variations in different provinces of the same land, but certain singular national usages or preferences. Thus, as to the name of countries, we differ in England from the practice both of France and Germany, frequently employing the Latin forms of the names, a usage probably originating with our older mapmakers, who, following the pattern of such names as India and Persia, commonly adopted the international Latin forms. Thus while the Germans have Oestreich, Preussen, and Russland, and the French use L'Autriche, La Prusse, and La Russie, we prefer the Latin names, Austria, Prussia, and Russia, and write Bavaria and Bohemia instead of Bayern and Böhmen. We follow the same fashion in the case of Servia, Croatia, Transylvania, Istria, Styria, and Carinthia. Hungary is an Anglicised form, not of Ungarn but of Hungaria, Saxony of Saxonia, and Turkey of Turkeia, while Germany, which has replaced the older English name Allemagne, is an Anglicised form of the Latin name Germania. Australia, Polynesia, and Tasmania have been newly formed on the same principle, and it is to be hoped that Brazilia and Fuegia may yet take their places alongside of Patagonia. Polonia, or our own older form Polayne, would better represent the German name Polen than our irrational modern form Poland, which has been assimilated in a blundering fashion to the Teutonic usage seen in such names as England, Scotland, Ireland, Holland, Lapland, Finland, Courland, Greenland, and Iceland. We call Vienna and Geneva by their Latin names, whereas in the case of Rome, Venice, Syracuse, Florence, Milan, and Naples we use the French names instead of the Latin or Italian forms, which would have been more correct.

Sometimes we use a name which is neither Latin, French, or native, but distinctively Anglican, changing Livorno into Leghorn, and Cape Hoorn into Cape Horn. Occasionally, as in the case of the Cape of Good Hope and the Black Sea, we have boldly translated the foreign names. Perhaps the most curious case is that of Sweden. At the time of the Thirty Years' War, in which many English soldiers of fortune served, we dropped Swedeland, our older and better name, adopting and adapting the German plural form *Schweden*, which, strictly speaking, denotes the Swedish people and not the Swedish land

GLOSSARY

Aachen, in French AIX-LA-CHAPELLE, is a city of Rhenish Prussia, with hot sulphur springs. The Celto-Latin name, *Aquis Granum* or *Aquis Grani*, 'at the waters of the sun,' may be compared with *Aquæ Solis*, the Roman name of Bath, Granos being the name of the Gaulish sun-god. In 972 the Roman name still survived, since we read in a document of that year, *Aquisgrani vulgari vocabulo Ahha*. From the O.H.G. *Ahha* we obtain Aachen, while Aix is from the Latin *Aquis*. To distinguish it from other places named Aix, it was called Aix-la-Chapelle, from the domed basilica, '*quam capella vocant*,' erected by Charlemagne, in which he was interred. (*See* AIX.)

Aargau, one of the Swiss cantons, is the *gau* or 'district' on the River Aar. AARAU, the capital of the canton, is so called from having been built on an *au* or 'waterside meadow' by the Aar. AARBURG, in Canton Aargau, is the 'castle on the Aar.' AARBERG, a town in Canton Bern, stands on a rocky island in the Aar. The Aar River is formed by the junction of two streams, called the Lauter Aar, or 'clear Aar,' and the Finster Aar, or 'dark Aar.' The FINSTER AARHORN, the highest summit in the Bernese Oberland, is not, as is sometimes said, the 'Peak of the Black Eagle,' but the peak from which descends the glacier which is the source of the Finster Aar. Aar is one of a large class of river names, such as the AHR, anciently the Ara, which joins the Rhine near Bonn; the OHR, a tributary of the Elbe; the AIRE in Yorkshire, and many more, whose names are believed to have meant 'river' or 'water' in some primitive form of Aryan speech.

'Abârah, a ford over the Jordan below the Sea of Galilee, bears an Arabic name meaning a 'ferry' or 'crossing.' It is believed to represent BETHABARA, the 'house of the crossing,' where John the Baptist baptized.

Abbeokuta, 'under the stone,' is the chief town of Yoruba. The name refers to a cavern under a mass of porphyry, in which fugitives from Dahomé concealed themselves. This place of refuge at last grew into a permanent settlement, and became a large town. (*See* Yoruba.)

Abbeville, a town on the Somme, called *Abbatis villa* in Latin documents, was in the eighth century a vill belonging to the neighbouring abbey of St. Riquier.

Abbotsford was a fancy name invented by Sir Walter Scott for his house on the Tweed, on the supposition that the abbots of Melrose used here to cross the river.

Aber and **Inver** are common Celtic prefixes, denoting the mouth or confluence of a river. In Ireland we only find Inver, in Wales only Aber. In Argyll, which was occupied by the Irish Scots, there are Invers, as Inveraray, but no Abers. In Inverness, Ross, Aberdeen, and Fife, Invers are more numerous than Abers; in Perth and Forfar they are nearly equal, while Aber prevails in the Lothians and in Dumfries. ABERGAVENNY, in Monmouthshire, stands at the confluence of the River Gaveney with the Usk. ABERYSTWYTH, in Cardiganshire, does not now stand on the River Ystwyth, but on the Rheidol, about a mile north of the Ystwyth, but the coast-line has receded, and the mouth of the Ystwyth has been driven further to the east, and the name of the town must have retreated with the site. ABERCORN, in Linlithgowshire, gives a ducal title to one branch of the Hamiltons. It is on the site of a monastery founded by St. Wilfrid, which is called Aebbercurnig by Bæda. It stands near the confluence (*aber*) of the Midhope beck with a turn called the Cornar, formerly the Cornac, which drains the Cornag moss. ABERGELDIE is at the confluence of the Gelder and the Dee. ABERNETHY is at the mouth of the Nethy. ABERDEEN is at the confluence of the Dee and the Don. ARBROATH, Forfarshire, is a corruption of Aberbrothoc, the 'mouth of the Brothach,' or 'muddy stream,' where William the Lion founded a monastery in 1173.

Abingdon, Berks, the seat of a wealthy abbey, is usually explained as the 'abbot's hill,' but *Æbbandun*, the oldest form of the name, shows that it was the dun or hill of a person named Æbba.

Abraham's Islands, in the Aleutian chain, were discovered in 1741 by Bering on Oct. 29th, which in the Greek Calendar is the festival of the patriarch Abraham.

Abrolhos (or 'wide-awake') **Islands** are dangerous reefs off the Brazilian coast. The name is from the Portuguese *abre olhos*, 'open your eyes,' or 'keep your eyes open,' and is repeated in the ABROLHOS, or HOUTMAN'S ROCKS, which lie off the West Australian coast. ABREOJOS, the Spanish form of this name, has been given to two dangerous atolls north of the Philippines, and to ABREOJOS, on the western coast of the Californian Peninsula, a cape surrounded by dangerous reefs.

Abruzzi, the name of three adjacent provinces in Southern Italy, is derived from *Aprutium*, or *Abrutium*, the seventh century name of the town now called Teramo. The district was called by the Romans *Interamna Prætutiana*, signifying the land of the Prætutii between the rivers. Prætutium, supposed to be the name of the chief town of the Prætutii, became first Aprutium, then Abrutium, and lastly Abruzzo, one of the three provinces called the Abruzzi, while Interamno became Teramne, and then TERAMO. Another *Interamna*, between the Nar and the Velinus, has become TERNI.

Abyssinia, perhaps more correctly Habsesinia, is the Anglicised form of a Portuguese corruption of the Arabic name *Habasha*, which signifies the land inhabited by the Habash or Habish, a word meaning 'mixture' or 'concourse,' applied to the mixed concourse of emigrants from various Arabian tribes who settled in Ethiopia. The adjectival form of the Arabic name was corrupted by the Portuguese into Abassia for the country, and Abexim or Abaxinos for its people. The form Abyssinia for the land of the Abaxinos or Abashinos first appears in *Johnson's Voyage to Abyssinia*, published in 1735. The Abyssinians themselves call their country Ithiopia (Ethiopia).

Acapulco, in Mexico, is said to mean the 'destroyed' or 'conquered' town.

Accra or **Akra**, a British settlement on the Gold Coast, was so called from the native name of the white ant, the district abounding in ant-hills raised by the termites.

Acheen, a state and town in North-West Sumatra, is called Aché by the Malays. Achem, the Portuguese form, was probably derived from the Persian Áchín.

Acre, a town on the Syrian coast, appears in the Book of Judges as *Accho*, 'the inclosed,' referring probably to the circuit or inclosure of the bay. It is now called 'Akka by the Arabs. It received the name of PTOLEMAIS on coming into the possession of Ptolemy Soter. At the time of the Crusades it was held by the knights of St. John, and hence became known as St Jean d'Acre.

Acunha, an island in the South Atlantic, is usually called TRISTAN D'ACUNHA (*q.v.*).

Adalia, in Pamphylia, represents the ancient Attalia, visited by St. Paul (Acts xiv. 25), so called from Attalus Philadelphus, from whom PHILADELPHIA (now Allah Shehr) was also named.

Adam's Peak, the highest mountain in Ceylon, obtained its name from the Mohammedan legend that from hence Adam looked out upon the world when driven from Paradise. His gigantic footprint, five feet long by two wide, is shown in the rock. The legend is, however, older than the Mohammedan conquest, as is shown by the Hindu and Buddhist names, Samanala and Sripada. Samanala means the 'peak of Rama,' from the Singalese *ala*, a 'peak,' and *Saman*, a 'name of Rama,' while Sripada means the 'holy foot,' the Hindus affirming that the imprint is that of the foot of Rama, while the Buddhists hold that it was that of Gautama Buddha. The footprint is called Sivapada by the Siva worshippers, and revered by them as the foot of Siva. The English name is a translation of the Portuguese Pico de Adam. The chain of reefs and islands between Ceylon and India is called Adam's Bridge, from the Mohammedan legend that at low tide Adam crossed it from Ceylon to India.

Add, a river on the west coast of Scotland, is a corruption of the Gaelic name *Fhada* or *Avon fhada*, the 'long river,' a name which Ptolemy, who calls it *Longus*, has manifestly translated.

Adda, a rapid river which joins the Po, formerly the Addua or Adua, is believed to be a Gaulish name.

Adelaide, the capital of South Australia, named in honour of Queen Adelaide, wife of William IV., was so designated by an

GLOSSARY

Act of Parliament passed in 1834. ADE-
LAIDE BAY, in Prince Regent inlet, was
discovered by Ross on August 13th, 1829,
the birthday of the Duchess of Clarence,
afterwards Queen Adelaide. Her name
is also borne by the ADELAIDE RANGE
at the mouth of the Great Fish River, discovered by Ross in August 1834, and by
CAPE ADELAIDE close to the North
Magnetic Pole.

Aden, a British station in Yemen, near
the mouth of the Red Sea, is the crater of
an extinct volcano. It is the *Adane* or
Athana of the ancient geographers, and
is supposed to be the Eden of Ezekiel
xxvii. 23, a name which would mean
'delight' or 'pleasant place.'

Adieu, Cape, in South Australia, was
originally called Cap des Adieux, because
here, in May 1802, the French Expedition
under Baudin took leave of the Australian
coast.

Adirondack Mountains, in the
state of New York, are so called from an
Algonquin tribe, who were derisively nicknamed Adirondack, or 'leaf-eaters,' by
the Iroquois. ALGONQUIN is a corruption of Algomequin, which means 'those
on the other side of the river,' *i.e.* of the
St. Lawrence.

Admiralty Islands, a group north of
New Guinea, discovered by Carteret in
1767, were named after the British Admiralty, by which the expedition had been
despatched. For the same reason Cook
gave the name of ADMIRALTY BAY to
the harbour in Cook Strait where he
anchored in 1770, after having completed
the circumnavigation of New Zealand.
In the Arctic and Antarctic regions, in the
Falkland Islands and elsewhere, this name,
ultimately derived from the Arabic title of
Emir, has been liberally bestowed on various bays and islands.

Adrianople is the English form of
Hadrianopolis, the 'city of Hadrian,' by
whom it was refounded. The modern
Turkish name EDRENE or EDIRNE represents a further corruption of the Greek
name.

Adriatic Sea is so called from the
town of Adria, Hadria, or Hatria, formerly an important port, but now sixteen
miles inland. The name of HATRIA, if
not Etruscan, may have been derived from
the 'black' alluvial soil on which the
town was built.

Adour, a river which flows into the Bay
of Biscay at Bayonne, is the *Aturis* of
Ptolemy, the *Aturus* of Lucan, and the

Atyr of Vibius Sequester. The name is
referred by W. von Humboldt to the
Basque *ura*, 'water,' whence *iturria* or
iturra, a 'source of water.' The RIVER
ADAR in Mayo is probably from the Celtic
eadar (pronounced *adder*), which means
the river 'in the middle.' The ADDER in
Wilts and Berwickshire may be from the
Anglo-Saxon *ædre*, a channel or 'water-
course.'

Advance Bay and ADVANCE BLUFF,
in Arctic America, were named by Kane
from the *Advance*, one of the ships composing the Grinnell Expedition.

Adventure Bay, Tasmania, as well as
ADVENTURE ISLAND, were discovered in
1773 by Captain Furneaux, who commanded the *Adventure*, the second ship
in Cook's second voyage. MOUNT ADVEN-
TURE is a hill in Prince Albert Land, from
which in October 1850 M'Clure, coming
through Bering Strait, sighted Parry
Sound, which had been reached from
Baffin Bay, thus demonstrating the existence of the impassable North-West Passage.

Afghánistán exhibits the Persian suffix
-stan, and means the 'land of the
Afgháns.' Afghán, not Áfghan as often
pronounced, is the general name of the
predominant portion of the congeries of
tribes beyond the North-West frontier of
India.

Africa, according to Suidas, was the
proper name of Carthage. In any case
the name was obtained by the Romans
from the Carthaginians, and originally
denoted only the district round Carthage,
and this district, the first Roman conquest south of the Mediterranean, became
the Roman province of Africa. The name
was gradually extended to the continent
which the Greeks had called Libya, and
the district round Carthage was then distinguished as Africa Propria, just as the
original district of Asia was called Asia
Minor when the name Asia had received
a wider signification. According to one
theory the name Africa denoted the
'greyish' colour of the sand, but more
probably it is derived from the Phœnician
word *Afryqah*, which denoted a 'colony,'
CARTHAGE, the 'new city,' being a colony
of Tyre. Mommsen considers the name
related to that of the Hebrews, who are
the 'emigrants' or 'crossers.' The Arabs
still give the name of *Afryqah* or *Afrikiyah*
to the territory round Tunis, which represents the primitive district of Africa.
LIBYA, the older name of the continent,
is the Greek form of the Semitic *Lehabim*

(or *Lubim* in the Bible), which was the name of the tribe next to Egypt on the east.

Agram, the capital of Croatia, is the Germanised form of the Slavonic name Zagrah, formerly Za-greb, 'behind the trench.'

Agulhas Bank is a great shoal which extends round the southern extremity of Africa, from Saldanha Bay nearly to Natal. It takes its name from the extreme southern point of Africa, south-east of the Cape of Good Hope, called by the Portuguese Cabo das Agulhas, or 'Cape of the Needles,' because here, at the time of the discovery, the needle of the compass showed no deviation, but pointed due north and south.

Ahmádábád in Gujarát, the second city in the Bombay Province, bears the name of Ahmád Sháh, king of Gujarát (1413-1443), by whom the walls were first traced.

Aigle or **Aelen** is a town in Canton Vaud. According to Gatschet the name is a corruption of the Low-Latin *aquale*, equivalent to *aquarium*, a 'water-course' or 'channel.'

Aigues-Mortes, the 'dead waters,' is a town in the Camargue, among the salt marshes and brine lagoons at the mouth of the Rhone, where much bay-salt is made.

Ainos are the short hairy aboriginal race inhabiting the Kurile Islands, Sakhalin, and the Japanese island of Yesso. In the language of the Ainos the word *ainu* means 'men' or 'people.' *Aino*, the Japanese corruption of the name, means 'mongrel' in Japanese, whence the Japanese legend of the canine descent of these people.

Ainsty of York, a wapentake to the west of the city of York, is under the jurisdiction of the Lord Mayor and magistrates of the city. It was formerly a forest, but was disforested in 1208. In Domesday it is called Ainsti or Einesti, in 1208 Aynesti, in 1253 Aynsty, and in 1280 Annesty. The name, which has given rise to much discussion, may be from some well-known *ánstige* or 'path' where the moot was held, or it may be Scandinavian, meaning the 'peculiar' or property of the city ; O.N. *eigen* or *eign*, 'property,' 'possession,' 'patrimony,' that which is one's 'own'; while the last syllable, *sty* or *sti*, may mean an 'enclosure,' a 'place set apart,' from an old word which we have in 'pigsty' (O.N. *sti*, A.S. *stige*).

Aiosoluk (*Aya Soluk*), the village which occupies the site of Ephesus, is believed to be a corruption of the medieval name of St. John (*Hagios Theologos*).

Aisne, a department in the north of France, takes its name from the River Aisne, which is a corruption of the old name *Axona*, which d'Arbois de Jubainville considers to be a pre-Celtic name.

Aix is the name of several French towns with mineral springs. Just as Bath comes from the A.S. *ætBathum*, 'at the baths,' so Aix is from *aquis* or *ad aquas*, 'at the waters.' AIX in Provence, eighteen miles from Marseilles, was the Roman *Aquæ Sextiæ*, so called from the Proconsul Caius Sextius Calvinus, who founded a colony at the hot springs in 123 B.C. AIX-LES-BAINS in Savoy is so called to distinguish it from Aix in Provence. DAX, D'AX, or D'ACQS in the Landes, called Urbs Aquensis by Gregory of Tours, is a corruption of *de aquis*. Aix-la-Chapelle takes its name from a chapel erected by Charlemagne. (*See* Aachen.)

Akabah, the name of the eastern arm of the Red Sea, is derived from a village and castle of the same name at the head of the gulf. It is an Arabic word denoting a 'cliff' or 'slope,' and refers to the steep ascent by which the pilgrim road ascends the hills to the west of the village.

Akyáb in Arracan takes its name from a pagoda containing a relic believed to be a part of Gautama's lower 'jaw,' which gave a name to the pagoda, and then to the adjoining village, which in 1825 was selected as the chief British cantonment in Arracan.

Alabama, one of the United States, is traditionally believed to mean the 'land of rest,' literally 'here we rest.' On the other hand, Hernando de Soto, in his two years' adventurous march with 600 men from Florida to the Mississippi in 1540, met with an Indian tribe called the Alibamu, who lived on the River Alabama which traverses the state. According to Gatschet, the best authority, Alibamu means a 'glade' or 'thicket cleared of trees.' Probably the tribe took its name from the plain, the river from the tribe, and the state from the river.

Alagoas, a Brazilian province, is called so from the town of the same name, which is a corruption of the Portuguese *as lagoas*, 'the lagoons,' two inland lakes near the town.

Alaska, a territory of the United States, is said to mean 'the great country,' from *illapie*, 'earth' or 'land,' and *asco*, 'great.'

Albany is the English form of the Latin Albania, the name given to the kingdom of the Picts when it was inherited by the kings of the Scots, who, in the ninth century, began to be called kings of Alban. Just as Erin is the genitive of Eriu, Alban is the genitive of Albu, so that king of Albu would be a more correct title than king of Alban. BREADALBANE is the breast or upland of Alban. From the Latinised form Albania we get the title borne by James, Duke of York and Albany, before his accession to the throne as James II. ALBANY, the State capital of New York, was founded by the Dutch in 1612-1615, and named Fort Oranien in honour of the Prince of Orange, and when the New Netherlands were conquered by the English in 1664 the place was renamed from the Scotch title of the Duke of York and Albany, which was also given to the RIVER ALBANY, which empties itself into Hudson's Bay. ALBANY, in the Cape Colony, was settled in 1820, and named after the Duke of York and Albany, second son of George III. The meaning of Albu, Alban, or Albania is unknown. The oldest known name of Britain, which occurs in a pseudo-Aristotelian treatise, was Albion, which would be the British pronunciation of the Gaelic Alban. Hence it has been supposed that Albion, originally a name of Southern Britain, gradually retreated into Scotland. Such names as Albium, Alba, and Albici, occur repeatedly in Italy and Southern Gaul, and ALBANIA is the name of the mountainous region east of the Adriatic. If the name is Aryan, it may mean ' white' (Latin *albus*), Britain being called Albion from the white chalk cliffs of Kent, and Albania from its snow-clad mountains. But more probably, as Helbig contends, the word is pre-Aryan, and may have signified hill or highland, which would explain the name of Alba Longa in Italy, as well as the other names. (*See* Alp.) The Albanians of Epirus are called ARNAUTS. The Byzantine writers corrupted the name Albanitæ (the people of Albania) into Arvanitæ, and from this, by a Turkish corruption, we have Arnauts as the modern designation of the Albanians.

Albatross Point, a New Zealand cape, was so named by Cook in 1770, from the multitude of albatrosses. ALBATROSS ISLAND, off Tasmania, was discovered by Flinders and Bass in 1798. To procure fresh provisions, George Bass landed on the island, which appeared white with birds, and returned with a boat-load of albatrosses and seals.

Albemarle Sound, a large inlet in North Carolina, is a name that has a curious history. Albemarle, Aumarle, and Aumâle are corruptions of Aubemare, the name of a border castle on the River Eu (now the Brésle) in Normandy. The castle and its surrounding territory gave the title of Count to Stephen, nephew of William the Conqueror, and under the Plantagenets it became a royal dukedom, which in 1663 was bestowed by Charles II. on General Monk as a reward for his services in bringing about the restoration. The earldom was revived by William III. in favour of Arnold Joust Van-Keppel, one of his Dutch courtiers. While the kings of England, styling themselves kings of France, claimed to bestow this barren honour, the actual lordship and territory of Aumâle came by marriage to the Guises in 1430, and in 1570 the marriage of the heiress of the Guises conveyed it to the Duke of Montpensier, and through him it passed to the Bourbons, and then to the Orleans branch of that family, and finally the family title of Duc d'Aumâle was bestowed on Henry, fourth son of Louis Philippe. The name of this border castle, thus curiously conveyed from Normandy to England, has now been transferred to America and to Africa. In 1663 Charles II. granted the whole territory between Virginia and Florida to eight patentees, among whom were the Duke of Albemarle, Lord Clarendon, and Lord Ashley. In the same year, in honour of the senior proprietor, the River Chowan, at the head of Albemarle Sound, was renamed the ALBEMARLE, the ASHLEY RIVER and the COWPER RIVER receiving their names from Lord Ashley, and the CLARENDON RIVER from Lord Clarendon. In the French form AUMÂLE, the name has passed to Africa, having been given to a town near Algiers in compliment to the Duc d'Aumâle, son of Louis Philippe.

Albert Nyanza, an inland *Nyanza* or ' sea,' forming one of the sources of the Nile, was explored by Sir Samuel Baker in 1864, and named after the Prince Consort, whose name has also been given to the ALBERT RIVER, flowing into the Gulf of Carpentaria, discovered by Stokes in 1841 ; to PRINCE ALBERT LAND, adjoining Victoria Land in the Arctic Archipelago, discovered by M'Clure in 1850 ; to PRINCE ALBERT'S MOUNTAINS, in South Victoria Land, the site of the

South Magnetic Pole ; and to ALBERT, a town in the Cape Colony.

Alcamo, in Sicily, between Palermo and Trapani, is a place with hot springs. The name is a corruption of the Arabic *al-Hammah*, ' the bath.' There are two places in Spain—one in the province of Murcia and the other in that of Granada —with hot springs, which are called ALHAMA.

Alcantara, a town in the Spanish province of Estremadura, preserves the Arabic name, *El-Kantarah*, ' the bridge,' derived from one of the greatest of Roman works, the stupendous bridge thrown over the Tagus for Trajan in 105 A.D. by the architect Caius Julius Lacer. Alcantara was the Norba Cæsarea of the Romans, and afterwards belonged and gave a name to the military order of the knights of Alcantara.

Alcatraz, or BIRD ISLAND, is in the bay ot San Francisco. The original Spanish name was *Isla de los Alcatrazes*, 'island of the Pelicans.'

Alcazar, one of the Arabic names in Spain, means ' the castle.' We have the same word in KASR - EL - KEBIR in Morocco, which means ' the great castle.'

Aldeburgh, as well as ORFORD, in Suffolk, is on the River Alde or Ore.

Alegre, Porto, in Brazil, means in Portuguese the 'cheerful' or 'pleasant' harbour.

Alemtejo, ' beyond the Tagus,' is the name of the Portuguese province south of the Tagus.

Aleppo, a city in Syria, is an Italian corruption of the Arabic name *Haleb*, which is the *Khilibu* of the hieroglyphic inscriptions. In the picture of the battle of Kadesh in the Ramesseum at Thebes we see ' the miserable king of Khilibu' drowned in the river Khal, now the Orontes, and his body held up by the heels.

Alert Reef, in Torres Strait, was discovered in 1817 by the ship *Alert*.

Alessa is an island near Rhodes. The name is a corruption of the Greek *Elaeussa*, the isle of ' olives.'

Aletsch Horn, in the Bernese Oberland, is the ' Avalanche Peak.' The local dialect word *avalenz*, or *alenz*, ' an avalanche,' is derived from the Low Latin *ad-vallare*.

Aleutian Islands, a chain of small islands extending from Kamtschatka to Alaska, were discovered by Bering, the Russian navigator, in 1728, and explored by Krenitzen in 1760 by order of the Empress Catherine. The name is usually referred to a Russian word, *aleut*, a ' bald rock,' but there is no such Russian word. Possibly it may be connected with the Tunugsic *ala*, a ' hill,' but it is more probably a tribe-name.

Alexandria, the name given to at least twelve cities founded by Alexander the Great, is an early instance of the practice, afterwards so common, of cities being named after kings or conquerors. Such a formation had hitherto been confined to the names of deities, and the innovation was a logical consequence of Alexander's assumption of a divine parentage. After the conquest of Egypt, he descended the Canopic arm of the Nile to Racoltis, where Homer had localised the legendary raid by Ulysses upon Egypt, and from here he visited the temple of Amun-Ra (Jupiter Ammon), and there accepted from the priests their recognition of him as the son of the god, the Egyptians holding the divine descent of all their lawful kings. Hitherto only the names of gods had been given to cities by the Greeks, and no effigies, except those of gods, had been placed upon coins, but now, as the son of Amun-Ra, Alexander ventured to place his own head, with the symbols of divinity, on his coins, and also, as a divinity, to found a city bearing his own name. The first and greatest of the cities called Alexandria was consequently founded at Racoltis in 332 B.C. Another, near Aleppo, is now called ISKANDRUN or SCANDEROON, the Turkish corruption of Alexandria. ALEXANDROPOL, Transcaucasia, in the Government of Erivan, ALEXANDRIA, in the Government of Kherson, and ALEXANDROV in the Government of Vladimir, all bear the name of the Czar Alexander I. ALEXANDRA NILE is an inappropriate name given by H. M. Stanley, in honour of Alexandra, Princess of Wales, to the Tengure, a stream which flows into the Victoria Nyanza. ALEXANDRIA, a district in Cape Colony, was named after Queen Alexandrina Victoria. ALESSANDRIA, a fortress in Northern Italy, built about 1170 by the Guelfs against the Ghibelines, was named in honour of Pope Alexander III.

Algarvé is a corruption of the Arabic *El-Gharb*, ' the west ' ; a name applied by the Moors to the whole region west of the Guadiana. It is now confined to the southernmost Province of Portugal.

Algeciras or **Algeziras**, a Spanish town on the Bay of Gibraltar, was the first place in Spain taken by the Moors under Tarik. A small islet formerly called Jezírat-el-khadhra, the 'green island,' which protects the harbour, explains the Arabic name, which means 'the island.' The ancient Mesopotamia, between the rivers Tigris and Euphrates, is now called ALGEZIRA, 'the island.'

Algiers (called in French Alger) was founded by the Moors in 944, and called El-Jezair Beni Mezghanna, 'the islands of the children of Mezghanna,' from a rock in the harbour, now called *Roche sans Nom*, and other rocks on which the lighthouse stands, now joined to the mainland by the mole.

Alicudi, one of the Lipari Islands, is a corruption of the name Ericodes or Ericussa, so called from the heath (*Erica*) growing on it.

Alijos or **Los Alijos,** the 'lighters,' is the Spanish name of a group of rocks off the Californian peninsula.

Aliwal, a district in the Cape Colony, was named from Aliwal on the Sutlej, where Sir Harry Smith, Governor of the Cape, had gained a victory over the Sikhs in 1846.

Allamanna-Gja, 'all men's rift,' in Iceland, is the place where the Allthing or common parliament was held.

Alleghanies are a range of hills in Pennsylvania, from which flows the Alleghany River. The old etymology explains the word as the endless or 'boundless mountains,' but probably both the Alleghany hills and the Alleghewi tribe (who have been identified with the Cherokees) derive their name from the river, the word *oolikhanne* meaning the 'best river' in the dialect of the Delawares.

Allier, a French department, is traversed by the River Allier, anciently the *Elaver*.

Alligator Point, in the Victoria River, North Australia, was so called by Stokes because an alligator was here killed by his crew. The ALLIGATOR RIVER, North Australia, was discovered by King in 1818, and so named from the alligators which abounded in it.

Alma is a Tartar word meaning an 'apple tree.' On the banks of the River Alma in the Crimea the allies gained their first victory in 1854.

Almaden, the name of the great quicksilver mine in Spain, is from the Arabic *El-Ma'aden*, 'the mine.' NEW ALMADEN, a quicksilver mine in California, was named after Almaden in Spain. A fort opposite Lisbon is called ALMADA, gold having formerly been washed from the sands of the Tagus at this point.

Alnwick, Northumberland, is the *wick* or 'village' on the River Alne.

Alp is a widely diffused name which has been the subject of much controversy. The Romans naturally thought the Alps (*Alpes*) were so called because of their snowy summits, the name being connected with the Latin *albus*, 'white.' This explanation, which we find in Festus, has been adopted by Grimm and many other writers. In Switzerland the word *alp* denotes, not the snowy summits, but the mountain pastures. Hence Graff contended that the root is *al*, 'to nourish,' (Latin *al-ere*), and, according to him, the Alps are the high 'pastures.' But the belief now prevails that the name is a Ligurian or Iberian word loaned to the Latins at some period after 218 B.C., and that it meant a 'height.' To the same root we may refer the name of the ALBAN HILLS near Rome, and of ALBA LONGA, whence tradition brought the settlers to pre-Aryan Rome. The Alban Hills do not reach the snow-line, and do not consist of chalk or limestone, but of dark volcanic rock. The name has been referred to an alleged obsolete Celtic word *alp* or *ailp*, 'a hill,' but as the existence of this word is doubtful, and as if it existed it would be isolated in the Celtic languages, we may probably assign it to pre-Aryan Iberian tribes. From this Iberian word we may explain the name of the Albici or 'hill-men,' a tribe of mountaineers near Marseilles, and of two towns called Albium in Liguria, and of ALBENS, anciently Albinnum, in the mountains near Chambéry, as well as other hill-names, such as ALBIS, a range of hills near Zürich, and of ALPNACH, a town on the lake of Lucerne, standing on the Sarner-Aa, formerly the *Alpen-aha* or 'Alp Water,' and of ALBI, anciently Albiga, a town near Toulouse which gave a name to the ALBIGENSES. As the Iberian race preceded the Celts in Britain we may thus explain the name ALBANY (*q.v.*) and of ALBION the oldest name of Britain. When in the fourth century B.C. Pytheas of Marseilles ventured into the northern seas the 'Britannic isles' were known as Albion and Ierne.

Alpta-á, 'swan river,' ALPTA VATN, 'swan lake,' and ALPTANES, 'swan cape,' all in Iceland, are from the O.N. *álpta*, genitive plural of *álpt*, 'a swan.'

Alsey, 'rope island,' one of the Westmanna Islands off Iceland, was so called because men were let down over the cliffs with ropes to collect the eggs of sea fowls (O.N. *ál*, a strap or leather thong).

Altai, a mountain range in Central Asia, rich in the precious metals, is called in Mongolian *Altain ula,* 'mountain of gold,' from *ula,* 'mountain,' and *altain,* genitive of *alta,* 'gold.' Al-tai (for *Al-tagh*) is the Tartaric form of the name. Hence the name Altaic which is applied to languages of the Mongol-Turkic class.

Alta Vela, a solitary rock rising from the sea at the southern extremity of Haiti, is one of the names bestowed by Columbus which still remain upon the map. It was so called because it resembles a ship under full sail.

Althorpe, the name of villages in Northants and Lincolnshire, is from the Danish personal name Ale, as is indicated by the old forms Alethorp and Aletorp. The Northamptonshire village gives the title of Viscount to Earl Spencer, in whose honour the ALTHORPE ISLANDS in Spencer Gulf (*q.v.*) were named.

Alton, Hants, is not the 'old tun,' but, as is proved by the form *Æwel-tun,* which occurs in an early charter, is the *tun* by the *æ-welm* or 'spring of water' from which the celebrated Alton Ales are brewed. The later form Aulton supplies the transition to the modern name.

Altona, near Hamburg, stands on the Altenau, a small stream which divides it from Hamburg. The name is often explained like the English Alton as the 'old town,' or, according to the popular local etymology, as *All-zu-nah,* 'all too near' Hamburg. The ALTENAU is probably named from the *au* or 'meadow' through which it flows, and the first part is probably a personal name, or may mean 'old.'

Altorp, the capital of Canton Uri, is probably the 'old village.'

Alvaredo, a coast town in Mexico, stands on the Rio de Alvaredo, which was discovered by the Spaniard Pedro de Alvaredo.

Amazigh, or 'freemen,' is the name of the Berber nomads of Northern Africa.

Amazon, Amazons, or **Amazonas** is the great South American river whose mouth was discovered in 1500 by Vicente Yañez Pinzon, who called it *Mar Dulce,* the 'freshwater sea.' The central portion of the river has been called the ORELLANA from the adventurous Spaniard Francisco de Orellana who, in 1540, descended from Peru one of its tributaries, the Rio Napo, and finally reached the ocean after a voyage of 4000 miles. The river is usually supposed to have been called the Rio das Amazonas from the female warriors who are said to have opposed Orellana. This etymology was put forward by Garcilasso de la Vega in his *Royal Commentaries of the Incas,* published in 1609. He says, 'the name of the river of the Amazons was given to it because Orellana and his people beheld the women on the banks fighting as valiantly as the men. It is not that there are any Amazons on that river, but that they said there were, by reason of the valour of the women.' As Garcilasso was born in 1540, the year in which Orellana descended the river, and as he cannot have seen or conversed with Orellana, who died in 1549, it is possible that Garcilasso's statement may be only a piece of folk etymology which may have grown up in the sixty-nine years between Orellana's adventurous voyage and the publication of Garcilasso's book. It has been conjectured that the real source of the name is the native term *amassona,* the 'boat destroyer,' used to designate the destructive bore, from 12 to 15 feet in height, which rushes up the estuary at spring tides. This solution is supported by the fact that the Spanish name Rio das Amazonas originally applied only to the lower tidal portion of the river. A similar name is KAIWAKA, the 'boat-eater,' given by the Maoris to a New Zealand river which has dangerous rapids in its course, and in like manner the Eider and perhaps the Humber take their names from their eagers or bores. The native name of the stream is PARANA-AÇU, which means the 'great river.' The Upper Amazon is called the MARAÑON from the edible fruit of the *Anacardium occidentale,* which grows abundantly on its banks. The name Marañon has also given rise to a folk etymology. It is said that when Pinzon in 1500 discovered the mouth of the river he asked the natives the question, *mare an non?* 'is it a sea or not?' an absurd etymology sufficiently disproved by the fact that the part of the river reached by Pinzon is some 1300 miles from the affluent called the Marañon. The Amazons of Greek fable also owe their name to folk etymology. Amazon in Greek would mean 'breastless,' and the Amazons were believed by the Greeks to be a nation of female warriors in Asia Minor, whose right breasts were excised to enable them the better to use the bow. The fable arose from the accounts of the priestesses of the great Asiatic goddess, a lunar deity, whose name is explained from *mazu*, the Tcherkess name of the moon.

Amboise, near Tours, is a corruption of Ambacia, derived from the cognomen Ambactius. The Gaulish *ambactos* meant a client or servant.

America is a name which, almost by accident, came to be adopted for the Western world. As in the case of Europe, Asia, and Africa, the name was at first attached to a portion only of the continent to which it was gradually extended. It has frequently been contended that Columbia, commemorating the discoverer of the New World, would have been a more appropriate name. But without casting any slur on the brilliant achievement of the great Genoese, the name America is not altogether inappropriate, since, although Columbus led the way, a much larger portion of the coast of the continent was discovered by the person whose name it bears. Amerigo Vespucci was a Florentine in the Spanish, and afterwards in the Portuguese service. Considerable doubt rests upon what is called his first voyage, in which it is alleged that in the years 1497-98 he was the actual discoverer of the American mainland. However this may be, his claim to bestow his name on the New World rests on what is called his third voyage, which was undertaken in consequence of the accidental discovery in 1500 of a part of the Brazilian coast by Cabral on a voyage to India (*see* Brazil). Cabral took possession of the country, which he called the island of Vera Cruz, in the name of King Emmanuel of Portugal, and before proceeding on his voyage sent back one of his ships to Lisbon with the news. To explore the new possession, King Emmanuel, in May 1501, despatched an expedition with Amerigo Vespucci as pilot, which returned in September of the following year, during which time the Brazilian coast from Cape St. Roque, five degrees south of the Equator, to the mouth of the Rio de la Plata, in 34° S. latitude, was traced. Thence striking across the South Atlantic, a land now believed to be South Georgia in 54° S. latitude was reached. It was to this great southern continent, whose existence Amerigo had made known, and whose connection with the discoveries of Columbus was not suspected, that the name of America was for nearly half a century exclusively applied. Columbus himself died in the belief that the lands he had found were a part of Asia, and hence they received the names of India Major, 'Greater India,' or Indias

Occidentales, 'the West Indies,' a name which still cleaves to the islands visited by Columbus. But it was plain that the vast southern continent, the coast of which had been traced by Amerigo for 2000 miles, could not belong to India, which was known not to extend south of the Equator, much less could it be supposed to have any connection with North America, discovered by John and Sebastian Cabot in 1497 and 1498, which was called the New Found Land, and supposed to be a Chinese peninsula. The region discovered by Amerigo lying entirely in the Southern Hemisphere was therefore recognised as a country unknown to the ancients, and hence it appears on early maps as Mundus Novus or Novus Orbis. Amerigo's discoveries were first made known in a letter describing his voyage, which he wrote in 1503 to Lorenzo de Medici. This was translated from Italian into Latin, and published in Paris in 1504 with the title *Mundus Novus*, and in two years ran through nineteen editions. Meanwhile a French version of another letter written by Vespucci in 1504 to his school-fellow, Piero Soderini, giving a fuller account of his discoveries, had come into the hands of Martin Waldseemüller, Professor of Geography at the College of Saint-Dié in the Vosges, who in 1507 published a geographical treatise entitled *Cosmographiae Introductio*, in which, after describing Europe, Asia, and Africa, the three parts of the world already known, he goes on to say that a fourth part has now been found by Americus Vespucius, and that he does not see why it should not be called, after its discoverer, the land of Americus, or America. *Quarta orbis pars quem quia Americus invenit, Amerigen quasi Americi terram sive Americam nuncupare licet.* Owing to its convenience, and to its analogy with the names of the other continents, this suggestion rapidly won its way to acceptance, and on the maps of the sixteenth century we are able at once to trace the progress of the conception of a western continent, and the gradual adoption and extension of the name proposed by Waldseemüller. The map of Johann Ruysch, published in 1508, exhibits a vast southern island nearly as large as Africa, which is called Terra Sancti Crucis sive Mundus Novus. This is separated by an ocean, containing the islands of Cuba, Spaniola, and Java, from Greenland, Labrador, and Newfoundland, which are joined to Tibet and India so as to form a great northern Asiatic continent. On the Lenox globe, c. 1510, part of South America appears as a detached southern land, which is called Mundus Novus, to the north of which are three islands : Zipangu (Japan), Isabel (Cuba), and Spaniola (Hayti). Four years pass, and the name of America is adopted for this island south of the Equator. On Boulanger's globe of 1514 the ocean between Europe and Asia has four large islands, namely, Hayti, called Zipangu, because supposed to be Japan ; Cuba ; Java ; and a fourth island, south of Cuba and about the same size, which is called America. About the same date is a map attributed to Leonardo da Vinci, on which the name America appears upon a great Equatorial and South Equatorial island, evidently meant for what we call South America. On a map of 1520 Brazil is called *America vel Brasilia sive Papagalli terra* ; and a map of 1522 has *America provincia* as the name of Brazil. In the next stage America ceases to be represented as a detached island in the Southern Hemisphere. On the Paris globe drawn in 1531 by Oronce Finé (Orontius Finæus), North America is depicted as a peninsula attached to Cathay (China), and connected by an isthmus (Darien) with a great southern continent which bears the name of America. In Sebastian Münster's map of 1540 South America is called Novus Orbis, which is explained by a note as being *insula Atlantica quam vocant Brazil et Americam.* Up to this time the name had not been extended to any part of North America, but in Mercator's map of 1541 this great step was taken, and the word A M E - R I C A is spread out over both the northern and the southern portions of the continent, with the note, ' *a multis hodie Nova India dicta.*' The final acceptance of the name America for the whole continent was due largely to its adoption in the great atlas of Ortellius, which appeared in 1570, but even at that date the name seems to have been unknown to Girava, a Spaniard, who in his *Cosmographia*, published in 1570, observed that some persons called 'India' or the ' New World ' by the name of *India Major*, 'greater India,' in order to distinguish it from *India Oriental*, the ' East Indies,' a term which only came into use after Magellan's voyage. Even in 1608 Acosta, in his *History of the Indies*, prefers the old Spanish designation of the Indies to the newer name America. Amerigo is one of the North Italian names due to Gothic or Lombardic conquest, Amaric, found as early as 744,

being a contracted form of Amalaric, ' strong for labour,' the name of a Visigothic king who died in 531. America, which is thus a Latinised Teutonic name, is not inappropriate for a continent divided between Latin and Teutonic speech. The stars and stripes which appear on the flag of the United States of North America were derived from the armorial bearings of George Washington, three stars with stripes below, which may be seen on the monuments of the Washington family in Great Brington Church, near Northampton.

Amesbury, Wilts, a vast British earthwork containing some forty acres, was called Ambresbyrig (Ambresburh), by the Saxons, and Caer Emrys, ' the city of Emrys,' by the Welsh. It was the fortress and capital of Ambrosius Aurelianus or Aurelius Ambrosius, Dux Britanniarum, a man of Roman family, who, after the departure of the legions in the fifth century, headed the Britons in their resistance to the West Saxon advance.

Amiens, on the Somme, is first known to us by the Celtic name *Samaro-briva*, ' the bridge over the Samara ' or Somme, and afterwards as *Ambianensium civitas*, being the capital of the Belgic tribe of the Ambiani, the modern name Amiens being from the dative plural *Ambianis*. The Ambiani were either the ' numerous ' or the ' wealthy ' people, the stem *ambi* denoting the abundance either of goods or of people.

Ammergau is the district or *gau* of the Ammer, a tributary of the Isar, which was anciently called the Ambra, an old word denoting ' water,' cognate with the Latin *imber*. Another Ammer flows into the Neckar, and the EMMER flows into the Weser.

Ammiraglio, a small stream near Palermo, is so called because crossed by the Ponte dell' Ammiraglio, a bridge built in 1113 by the Sicilian Admiral, George of Antioch.

Amounderness, the ness or peninsula north of the Ribble, was formerly a portion of Yorkshire, taken to form the Duchy of Lancaster. The form Agemundernes, which occurs in Domesday, proves that the name was derived from some Scandinavian chief called Augmundr.

Amoy, a treaty port in the Chinese province of Fokien, is called in the Mandarin dialect Hia-men, which means ' Hall-gate.'

Ampthill, Beds., is probably the ' emmet's or ant's hill,' as is indicated by the Domesday form *Ammetelle*.

Ampurias, in the north-east of Spain, is a corruption of the Greek name *Emporiae* or *Emporium,* the market or trading port.

Amritsar, formerly written Umritsar, a town in the Punjab, is a corruption of *Amrita-saras,* the 'pool of immortality,' so called from a great tank constructed in 1581 by Rám Das, the Guru or Apostle of the Sikhs, who founded the city in 1574.

Amsteg, 'at the climb,' is a village in Canton Uri, where the St. Gothard road leaves the level plain, and the ascent begins.

Amsterdam, formerly Amstelredam, is at the dyke or dam of the River Amstel, which here joins the River Y.

Amsterdam Island, a volcanic cone in the Indian Ocean, midway between Australia and the Cape, bears the name of the ship *Amsterdam,* in which the Dutch navigator, Van Diemen, visited it in 1633. NEW AMSTERDAM, a town in British America, was founded and named by the Dutch.

Amu Daria, the modern name of the Oxus, means the 'Amu river,' from *daria,* a 'river,' and Amu or Amol, a town on its banks.

Amur or **Amoor** is a corruption of the Mongolian name Tamur, which means the 'great river' or 'great water.' It is called Schilkan, 'the river,' by the Buriat tribes; Sagalin-Ula, 'the black river,' by the Manchus, and Che-Shui, 'the black water,' by the Chinese.

Anahuac, the Aztec name of the province in which the city of Mexico is situated, means the 'lake country,' literally 'near or beside the water,' from *atl* 'water,' and *nauac* 'near.' The name was one given by the Aztecs to any region near the sea or a large lake.

Anatolia, the 'Eastern land,' or land of the Rising Sun, is the Greek name by which a Turkish province in Asia Minor is still known.

Ancaster, a village in Lincolnshire, which gave a ducal title to the Bertie family, has been identified with the Roman station of Causennis or Causennæ.

Anchediva, Angedivida, or Anjediva, is a small island on the Malabar coast, in 15° N. lat. The name is a Portuguese corruption of a word meaning in Malayalim the 'five islands,' which is probably an endeavour to make significant an older name of which the meaning has been lost.

Ancona, in Italy, was the Dorian colony of Ankôn, so called from the 'elbow' made by the peninsula on which it stands.

Anchor Island, in the province of Otago, was so named by Cook in 1773, because on its eastern side was his first anchorage in New Zealand waters.

Andalusia, the southern province of Spain, was called by the Moors *Belād-al-Andalus,* the 'land of the Andalus,' Andalus being probably a corruption of the Latin *Vandalos,* 'the Vandals.'

Andaman Islands, inhabited by dwarf savages of a very low type, probably take their name from Hanuman, the monkey who in the Rámayana is commander of the army of monkeys. Handuman being the Malay pronunciation of Hanuman, the islands are called by the Malays Pulo Handuman, the Handuman islands, whence the English name.

Andaw, in Burma, which means the 'sacred molar,' takes its name from a pagoda built in 761 A.D. as a receptacle for a precious relic, a double tooth of Gautama Buddha.

Andermatt in Canton Uri, is a village 'at the meadow' which has been formed by the silting up of the bed of an ancient lake.

Andernach, a town on the Rhine, the Antunnacum of the Antonine Itinerary, and the Anternacha of the Ravenna Geographer, is doubtless from the Celtic personal name Antunnos, with the possessive suffix -*ac.*

Anderson's Island in the Bering Sea, was so called by Cook in 1778 because here William Anderson, the ship's surgeon, died.

Andes, properly 'Cordillêras de los Andes,' the 'chain of the Andes,' is a name of uncertain meaning. Garcilasso de la Vega says that it was derived from the Anti tribe near Cuzco. It has also been referred to a Peruvian word *anta,* 'copper.' Another proposed etymology is from *anta,* a 'tapir,' of which the Portuguese plural would be *antas,* so that the Cordillêras de los Antas would mean the 'mountains of the tapirs.' Possibly the Anti tribe may have had a tapir for their totem, or may have been called the copper-coloured men.

Andover, Hants (A.S. *Andefera*), is on the banks of the Ande or Little Ann, a branch of the Anton. Andover may perhaps be *Ande-ofer,* the shore or 'bank of the Ande,' or the last part of the name may be the Celtic *defer,* which we have in

Dover (*q.v.*). Andover in Massachusetts was so called because the first settlers came in 1643 from Andover in Hants.

Angeles or **Los Angeles,** a town in California, founded in 1781 by Don Felipe de Neve, the Spanish Governor, was called by him *Le Pueblo de Nuestra Señora la Reyna de los Angeles,* 'the town of our Lady the Queen of the Angels.'

Anglesey, often called with needless tautology the Isle of Anglesey, is not, as is often said, 'the isle of the Angles,' but the O.N. *önguls eg,* 'the isle of the strait.' The old Celtic name Mona is preserved in the last syllable of Carnarvon (*q.v.*).

Angola, a West African district, bears the name of Angola, a vassal of the king of Congo, who made Dongo an independent state, calling it Dongo-Angola. Dongo, the real name, was afterwards dropped, and the name of the ruler left as the designation of the territory.

Angora or Enguri, a city in Asia Minor, famed for the wool of its goats, represents the Roman Ancyra.

Angostura, the 'narrow place,' whence the Angostura bitters were obtained, is the Spanish name of a town built where the Orinoco narrows. It has now been officially renamed CIUDAD BOLIVAR after the liberator. (*See* Bolivia.)

Angoulême, the capital of the Charente, is a corruption of Iculisma or Engolisma. Its territory, called the ANGOUMOIS, was the *pagus Engolismensis.*

Anguilla, the 'eel,' is the Spanish name of one of the Antilles; also called Snake Island, from its long and narrow form.

Angus, one of the old Scotch earldoms, now the county of Forfar, is believed to be a Pictish name derived from Oengus, the Pictish king of the men of Fortrenn in the eighth century.

Anhalt or **Anholt,** the town from which the Duchy of Anhalt takes its name, means 'at the wood.' According to the local folk-etymology the name refers to a castle constructed entirely of stone, 'without wood,' which was built by Count Esiko von Ballenstedt.

Anjou, one of the old French provinces, is a corruption of the name of the Gaulish tribe of the Andecavi or Andegavi, which means 'the confederates (*cav-* meaning a 'bond,' while *ande-* is the intensitive particle). Angevin is a corruption of Andecavensis, while ANGERS, the capital, is called Andegavis by Gregory of Tours.

Ann, Cape, north of Cape Cod, was a name placed on John Smith's map of New England by Prince Charles in 1614, doubtless in compliment to his mother, Ann of Denmark, the queen of James I. ANNAPOLIS, the State capital of Maryland, was founded in 1649 under the name of Providence, and in 1708 incorporated and renamed in compliment to Queen Anne, in whose honour ANNAPOLIS in Nova Scotia was named after the Peace of Utrecht, in 1713.

Annam, originally Ngan-nam, means the 'peace of the south,' from *ngan* or *an,* 'peace,' and *nam,* 'the south.'

Annobom, a small island in the Gulf of Guinea, was discovered by the Portuguese at the beginning of the year 1471. In Portuguese New Year's Day is called *Dia de Anno Bom,* or simply *Annobom.*

Anonyma, the 'Nameless Isle,' is one of the Caroline group.

Anspach (or **Ansbach**) in Bavaria, is built on a stream called the Holzbach. Both the town and the river contain the personal name Aunulf, both being corruptions of Aunulf's bach.

Antakieh, in Northern Syria, represents Antioch, the capital of the Greek kings of Syria, one of the sixteen cities which Seleucus Nicator named after his father Antiochus.

Antananarivo or **Tananarivo,** the capital of Madagascar, consists of numerous detached hamlets or groups of houses. The name means 'at the place of a thousand.' The prefix *an* is a preposition meaning 'at,' and gives a localising sense to the word it precedes. The second element, *tana,* means a 'place' or 'town,' as An-tana-malaga, 'at the famous town,' and the third element is *arivo,* a 'thousand,' which we have in Nosi-arivo, the 'thousand isles,' or in the hill called Tsinjo-arivo, 'overlooking a thousand.' Antananarivo was so called either because it consisted of a thousand houses, or, according to the popular belief, because it includes within its circuit a thousand hamlets.

Antibes, a town built on a peninsula between Cannes and Nice, was the Greek Antipolis, which is better preserved in Antiboul, the Provençal form of the name. It was founded by the Greeks of Marseilles, and denotes the 'city opposite' to Nice (Nicæa). The names of Nice and Antibes are interesting as abiding evidences of the Greek occupation of this coast long before the Roman conquest. ANTIPAROS in the Ægean is the island 'opposite Paros.'

Anticosti, an island at the mouth of the St. Lawrence, is a corruption of the native name Natiscotea.

Antigua, one of the West Indian islands, was discovered by Columbus on Nov. 11th, 1493, and named by him after a chapel in the Cathedral of Seville, called Santa Maria la Antigua (Old St. Mary). The *Santa Maria* was the name of the ship in which Columbus sailed. The name was also given by Balboa in 1510 to the town he founded on the River Darien, in fulfilment of a vow, which, in fear of the poisoned arrows of the Indians, he had made before the same miraculous image of Santa Maria la Antigua, to whose altar he dedicated a gift from the gold he had found.

Antilles is the English form of the Spanish name Antilias, which was given to the West Indies soon after their discovery. In the map of Toscanelli, drawn in 1474, which Columbus had with him in his first voyage, we see marked in mid-Atlantic an imaginary island called *Antilia*, west of the Canaries. In this map, the imaginary islands of St. Brandan on the Equator, and of Brazil, some sixty miles west of Ireland, were also marked. In the Portuguese map of Cantino, 1502, the West Indies appear for the first time as *has Antilhas*, the Portuguese form of the Spanish name. The Antilles are now divided into two groups, the Greater Antilles, or Leeward Islands, comprising Cuba, Jamaica, Haiti, and Puerto Rico ; and the Lesser Antilles or Windward Islands, which lie to the south-west.

Antipodes, a small island south-east of New Zealand, discovered in 1800, was so named because it is nearly at the antipodes of London. The antipodes of any place is where a line drawn through the centre of the earth comes out, so that the people would walk feet to feet.

Antwerp, correctly Antwerpen, is usually explained from the Flemish *aen't werpen*, 'at the wharf.' But as early as the eighth century the name was written Andoverpum, and afterwards Andiverpa and Antwerpia, which Förstemann explains as 'opposite the dyke,' *ant* meaning 'opposite' or 'over against,' and the word *warp*, *warf*, or *werf* signifying in Frisian names an *aufwarf* or bank, and hence a place protected from inundation by an embankment. In English to warp still means to make a sea bank.

Anurádapura, the old capital of Ceylon, is the city of Anurádha, the minister of King Vijaya.

Anydros, 'the waterless,' is an island in the Ægean, near Amorgos.

Aosta, a city in Piedmont, which gives its name to the Val d'Aosta, was the Roman colony of Augusta Prætoria, so called because founded for 3000 colonists from the Prætorian guard of Augustus.

Apache, in Colorado and in New Mexico, are places which preserve the name of the fierce tribe of the Apaches, or 'warpeople,' from *apa* 'people,' and *agwa* 'war.'

Apalache Bay in Florida, and the APALACHE RIVER in Georgia, are so called from the Apalache tribe, whose name means 'those beyond the river,' literally the 'other side people.' The APPALACHIAN RANGE was a name given by the French to the Alleghany Mountains.

Apennines is a name now used for the central mountain chain of Italy. The Roman term Mons Appeninus originally denoted the Maritime Alps near Genoa, the Mons Peninus signifying the Dauphiny Alps, more especially the part near the Great St. Bernard. The Romans explained the Mons Peninus or Pennine chain as the Poenine or Punic Mountains, most likely because Hannibal crossed them when he invaded Italy. But the name Mons Peninus doubtless contains the Celtic word *pen*, 'head,' 'summit,' 'mountain,' and the Mons Peninus can hardly be separated from the neighbouring Mons Appeninus, which is probably the same word with a prefixed article or preposition.

Apollinaris, a spring near Neuenahr from which the Apollinaris water is obtained, is named after the neighbouring Apollinariskirche, dedicated to St. Apollinaris.

Appenzell, a Swiss Canton, takes its name from its capital, the town of Appenzell, anciently Abtenzelle, in Latin documents Abbatis cella and Abba cella, the town having been built round a monastic cell or church, founded in 1061 by Nortbert, Abbot of St. Gallen.

Appin, a district in Argyll, was the territory on the mainland which belonged to an abbey on the island of Lismore. The Latinised form Abthania points to the Gaelic *abdhaine*, 'abbey land,' as the source of the name.

Appleby, Westmoreland, is a name of uncertain meaning, but if, as has been supposed, it occupies the site of the Roman station of Aballaba, it is probably a corruption or translation of that name. The neighbouring Appleby in Wigtownshire must be a Norse name, meaning apple (tree) house.

Applecross, in Ross-shire, is an assimilated name, being a corruption of Aporcrosan. Here in 673 a church was built by Maelrubba, and named from a 'little cross' (*crosan*) erected at the 'mouth' (*aber*) of a small stream.

Arabia is a name sometimes derived from the Semitic root *ereb*, the 'west,' to which the name Europe is also referred. But more probably it means the 'wilderness,' since *ereb* also means 'to be waste' or ·barren,' and the name Arabia seems originally to have been confined to the sandy desert between Palestine and Egypt. In like manner, the WADY ARABAH, the dry and barren valley which extends from the Dead Sea to the Gulf of Akabah, doubtless means the 'wilderness.'

Aragon, now a Spanish province, represents the old kingdom of the same name, the nucleus of which was the little realm of Sobrarbe (Sobre Arbe) in the heart of the Pyrenees, where the Goths took refuge from the Moors. In 1035 Sancho II. divided his kingdom, and his son, Ramiro the Bastard, extended his own frontier as far as a tributary of the Ebro called the Aragon, which is now in the extreme north of the province to which it gave a name.

Arakan or **Arracan,** a district in Further India, is a European corruption of the native name Rakhaing, which is believed to be derived from the Sanskrit *Rakshasa*, 'ogres,' a term applied by the Aryans to the indigenous races, and by the early Buddhists to unconverted tribes.

Aral is an inland sea, east of the Caspian. Its eastern coast is fringed with small islands, and hence it obtained the name of Aral Denghis, which means in Kirghis the 'island-sea,' or 'sea of islands,' from the Tartar word *aral*, an 'island.' The Kalmuc name is Aral Noor, which means the same.

Aram, the old name of Upper Syria, means 'the Highlands,' as contrasted with Canaan, 'the Lowlands.' Hence the terms Aramaic and Aramean which are used to denote the languages, people, and script of Northern Syria.

Ararat was originally the name, not of a mountain, but of the country afterwards called Armenia. In the cuneiform inscriptions of Assyria, Urardha is the name given to the district between the Araxes and the mountains south of Lake Van, whose capital was at Van. The name Urardha is explained as Hur-aredh, the 'moon country,' or country of Hur, the moon god. It was only after the Christian era that the name of Ararat was shifted to a mountain far north of the original territory of Urardha, and applied to the snow-clad volcanic peak which is called by the Turks either Aghri-Dagh, 'the painful or steep mountain,' or Ak-Dagh, the 'white mountain.' The Persian name is Kuh-i-Nuh, 'the mountain of Noah.'

Arawak, a South American tribe, bear a totemic name which signifies the 'tigers.' Arrowroot is not, as once believed, connected, but is a corruption of the Brazilian *aru-aru*, 'meal-meal,' *i.e.* the best meal, obtained from the root of an *arum*.

Archangel, a town at the mouth of the Dwina, takes it name from a monastery dedicated to Michael the Archangel, founded in the twelfth century by Archbishop John. The correct name is Archangel'sk, the suffix -*sk* being a Russian formative.

Archipelago, which apparently means the 'chief sea,' occurs in 1268 as a name of the Ægean, It is believed to be a Byzantine corruption of Ægeopelago, the 'Ægean Sea,' to which the name strictly applies. But the Ægean containing many islands, the word Archipelago has come to denote any ocean tract studded with islands. The Ægean is supposed to have been so called from Ægeus, a name given to Poseidon in reference to the motion of the waves.

Arcola, near Verona, the scene of Napoleon's victory in 1796, is the 'little bridge,' from the Low-Latin *arcula*, a diminutive of *arcus*.

Arctic Ocean, which surrounds the North Pole, is so called from the Greek word *arctos*, 'a bear,' the Greek word for the north referring to the constellation of the Great Bear with its seven stars, whence the corresponding Latin word *septentrio*.

Ardennes, a forest in Belgium, is the Arduenna of Cæsar. Fick and Holder refer the name to the stem *ardu*, 'high,' seen in the Latin *ardu-us*, and the old Irish *ardda*, 'heights,' and *arddu*, 'loftier.' The name of the old Warwickshire forest of Arden is preserved in the name of Henley-in-Arden. ARDROS-SAN, in Ayrshire, is the 'spit-hill,' so named from a rocky knoll at the end of a tongue of land, *rossan* being the diminutive of *ross*, 'a promontory.' The prefix, meaning a 'hill' or 'high,' is found in many Scotch and in 600 Irish names, such as ARDRISHAIG, the 'thorny hill,' and several places in Ireland called Ardeen, the 'little hill,' where the suffix is probably the common Celtic diminutive.

Arenas, Punta, 'sandy point,'. is the chief settlement in the Magellan Strait.

Arequipa, till destroyed by the earthquake of 1868, was the second city of Peru. Here the Incas established a station for communication between Cuzco and the coast, and called it *Ari-quepai*, 'Yes, rest here,' whence the name of the city of Arequipa, founded by Pizarro in 1540.

Argentina, 'the silver land,' also called the Argentine Republic, is the usual English designation of the confederation officially styled 'the United Provinces of the Rio de la Plata,' the Latin *argentum* being used to translate or replace the Spanish word *plata*, 'silver.'

Argyle, or **Argyll**, is the part of Scotland of which the Scots or Irish Gaels first took possession. The oldest forms of the name are Arregaithel, Erregaithle, and Errogeil, which have been explained either as Earr-gaidhel, the 'boundary of the Gael,' or as Airer-gaidhel, the 'district of the Gael.' That the first of these is the true explanation is indicated by the old Latin gloss, *Margo Scottorum*, which is used to translate the name.

Arîsh, or, with the article, AL-'ARÎSH, is a village on the coast between Egypt and Palestine, where the Wadi-el-Arîsh, the biblical 'river of Egypt,' a watercourse frequently dry, debouches on the Mediterranean. Arîsh, a corruption of an old Egyptian word meaning the 'boundary,' marks now, as of old, the frontier of Africa and Asia.

Arizona, a territory of the United States, takes its name from an Indian pueblo at the 'little spring' (*ari*, 'small,' and *son*, 'a spring or fountain').

Arjish Dagh, a mountain 13,197 feet in height, is the loftiest summit in Asia Minor. The name is derived from the Greek *Argaion Oros*, the 'white' or 'shining mountain.'

Arkansas, one of the United States, takes its name from the Arkansas River, a tributary of the Mississippi, so called from the Kansa or Kaws tribe of Indians. Father Marquette on his adventurous exploration of the Mississippi in 1673, on arriving at the confluence of the Arkansas River, found four villages of a tribe he calls the *Akansea Sauvages*, who have been identified with what are now called the Ka(n)se, Kaws, or Crow Indians, a Sioux or Dakota tribe, whose name is supposed to mean the 'handsome men.' Arkansas was formerly pronounced Arkánsas, but the State legislature by a 'joint resolution has lately declared that Arkansáw, with the accent on the last syllable, is the right pronunciation, the initial *A* being a locative, means 'at the Kansas.'

Arlberg, a range between the Voralberg and the Tyrol, bears the name of a pass close to Schloss Arlen, built on slopes overgrown with the Arle (*Pinus Montana*).

Arles, a city at the apex of the delta of the Rhone, was anciently *Are-late* or *Are-latum*, which according to Glück and others means 'by the marsh' or 'on the clay.' (Cf. the Welsh *claith*, 'that which is dark or humid.') The dry stony desert called La Crau extends as far as Arles, where the rich fertile soil begins. On the other hand, D'Arbois de Jubainville prefers a derivation from a personal name.

Armagh, an Irish city which gives its name to a county, is not, as is sometimes asserted, a corruption of *Ard-magh*, the 'high field,' but of *Ard-macha*, 'Macha's height,' the name being explained by the legend that Armagh was the burial-place of Macha of the Golden Hair.

Armenia is a name which does not occur before the time of Darius Hystaspes. In the Assyrian inscriptions the country is called either the Land of Nairi, the kingdom of Van, or the kingdom of Urardha, *i.e.* of Ararat. Halévy explains the name Armenia as an Aryan word, Har-minni or Hara-Minya, which means the mountains of Minni, or Mount Minyas (old Persian *ara*, 'a mountain'). The Armenians were a Phrygian people who did not enter the country till after the fall of Nineveh. (*See* Ararat.)

Armoric, the name given to the Celtic speech of Brittany, is derived from Aremorica, a name which originally denoted the coast tribes of Gaul from the Seine to the Loire. In the Middle Ages Armorica became restricted to Brittany. The Aremorici are 'those by the sea,' from the Celtic *mor* (*mori*), 'sea,' and the preposition *are*, which has lost the *p* preserved in the Greek *para*. In Armoric *ar-mor* still means 'on the sea.' (*See* ARLES.)

Arnhem Land in West Australia was so called because discovered in 1623 by the Dutch ships, the *Arnhem* and the *Pera*, equipped by the governor of Amboina. Arnhem Bay and Cape Arnhem were so named by Flinders in 1803, in commemoration of this early voyage of discovery. ARNHEM (Arnheim) in the Netherlands is 'the home of Arn,' a personal name meaning 'eagle.'

Arolsen, the capital of the Principality of Waldeck, is a corruption of the old name *Adalolteshusum*, 'at Adelholt's houses.'

Arran, one of the Western Isles of Scotland, was anciently called Arann, which would be the genitive of Ara. Arann was also the old name of the ARAN ISLANDS in Galway Bay, and ARAN is the name of a mountain in Merionethshire. The meaning of Ara is obscure. It might mean 'ploughed land,' or 'western land,' but most probably 'high land.'

Arrochar in Dumbartonshire is the old *Arachor*, a Gaelic loan word derived from the Latin *aratrum*, corresponding to the Southern carucate or ploughland, the amount of land which could be ploughed in a year by a team of oxen.

Arrowsmith River and Point Arrowsmith in Australia, Mount Arrowsmith in New Zealand, and Arrowsmith Island in the Marshall Group, were named by their discoverers after the cartographer, John Arrowsmith.

Arthur's Seat, more correctly Arthur Seat, the hill overlooking Edinburgh, has been thought to be an English adaptation of the Gaelic *Ard-na-said*, the 'height of the arrows,' a name equivalent to Shooter's Hill. ARTHUR'S SEAT, a mountain in the Australian colony of Victoria, was so named by Lieutenant Murray from its resemblance to the Scotch hill. ARTHUR STRAIT, in the Arctic Archipelago, was named by Belcher in 1853 in compliment to Prince Arthur, now Duke of Connaught.

Artillery Lake, in Arctic America, was so named by Back in 1833 in recognition of assistance received from officers of the Royal Artillery.

Artois, one of the old French provinces, (in medieval times *Adertisus Pagus*,) preserves the Belgic tribal name of its Celtic inhabitants, the Atrebates, a name which means simply the 'inhabitants' or 'owners' of the soil. The name of ARRAS, the capital of Artois (formerly *Nemetocenna* or *Nemetacum*, from the Gaulish *nemeton*, a 'temple,') is a French corruption of the Flemish name Atrecht, in which the name of the Atrebates is more plainly seen than in Artois. From the Belgic tribe we have curiously obtained two English terms, Artesian wells, and Arras for 'tapestry,' as in Beaumont and Fletcher, where one of the characters makes his meals 'in corners, behind Arrases on stairs.'

Arundel in Sussex stands on the River Arun, which, on old maps is called the Tarant. The name Arun may be a mere antiquarian figment to account for the name of Arundel, or possibly through such stages as Tarunt and Arunt the name Tarant may have been corrupted into Arun. Tarant is a corruption of Ptolemy's name Trisantona, a name which Tacitus also gives to the TRENT (*q.v.*).

Ascension, an island in the South Atlantic, was discovered in 1501, by João da Nova, a Portuguese mariner, who named it *Ilha da Concepção* (Conception Island). It was rediscovered on Ascension Day, 1508, and hence called *Ilha da Ascenção*. THE BAHIA DE LA ASCENSION, in Yucatan, was discovered in 1518 by Grijalva, who here celebrated the festival of the Ascension.

Aschaffenburg, in Bavaria, is the castle on the Aschaff, a tributary of the Main.

Ashby Puerorum, in Lincolnshire, was so called because the great tithes were appropriated to the support of the choir boys of Lincoln Cathedral.

Ashstead, a common English village name, usually means the 'place by the ash tree.' ASHSTEAD near Epsom is, however, a corruption of Akestede, 'oak place.' ASTON may be a corruption of Ashton, but is usually the modern form of East-tun.

Asia originally denoted only a portion of what since the time of Orosius has been conveniently termed Asia Minor. By the time of Æschylus and Pindar, and still more by the time of Herodotus, the term Asia had acquired a Continental significance. The name may be either Aryan or Semitic. The prevalent opinion is that Asia is a Phœnician name, being explained as a participial form of the Semitic verb *azu*, in which case Asia would mean the 'east,' literally the 'rising' of the sun, a name paralleled by the Turkish Anadoli, a corruption of the Greek Anatolia, the 'land of the sunrise,' or by the Italian name Levante. Phœnician mariners would naturally call the opposite sides of the Ægean the 'Eastern' and the 'Western' lands, as, if they are Semitic,

GLOSSARY

Europa. The theory which explains the
name as Aryan is based on its earliest
occurrence, which is found in Homer (*Il.*
ii. 461), with whom the Asian plain is
merely the marshy delta of the Cayster,
which afterwards became the site of
Ephesus, the capital and wealthiest city
of the oldest Asia. If Asia was originally
only the territory of Ephesus, the importance of that city would conceivably cause
the name to be gradually extended to the
neighbouring lands, just as the name of
Africa originally denoted merely the plain
of Carthage and Europe the plain of
Thebes. In this case the name Asia
might denote the 'marsh' of which
Homer speaks, and EPHESUS might be
the town 'on the marsh.' It is difficult
to explain as Semitic the parallel name of
ASEA, which denoted a marshy valley in
Arcadia. ASIA ISLANDS, a group in the
North Pacific, east of Gilolo, were discovered in 1805 by the ship *Asia.*

Askhabad, in Central Asia, is a Perso-
Arabic name, meaning the 'place of delight' or the 'abode of love.'

Aspinwall, the western terminus of the
Panama railway, bears the name of one
of the American engineers who designed
the line. The Creoles call the place
Colon, in honour of Columbus. It was
founded in 1710 by the Spaniards under
Nicuesa, who called it Nombre de Dios,
under which name it often appears in the
records of buccaneer adventure.

Assam (Ahom) takes its name from the
Ahom dynasty of Shan princes who conquered the country in the thirteenth century.

Asses' Ears is the descriptive sailors'
name for a rocky island near Japan ; and
also for some rocks in the Straits of
Magellan.

Assiniboia, a Canadian province, is
traversed by the Assiniboine river, so
called from the Assiniboine tribe, who are
commonly known by the translated name
of the Stone Indians, Assini-boine meaning the Stone-Sioux, from *assini*, the Cree
word for a stone, and *bwan* a native name
of the Sioux or Dakotas. From *assini*,
'a stone,' we have also the ASSINI-
PICHIGAKAN or 'stony barrier' on the
Qu'Appelle river.

Assireta, the 'warriors,' form one of the
two divisions of the Kurds.

Assiout or **Siout,** the capital of Upper
Egypt, are French spellings of the Arabic
name *Asyût* or *Siût*, which reproduces
the old Egyptian name *Seut.*

Assouan is a town on the Nile, at the
first cataract, which forms the 'opening'
from Egypt into Nubia. One of the old
Egyptian names, *Sunnu* (in Coptic *Souan*),
signifying the town on the eastern bank
was corrupted by the Greeks to Syene,
whence the mineralogical term *syenite*
for the granitic rocks which cause the
cataract. Neither the Greek nor the Coptic
names being significant in Arabic, the old
name has been transformed into Aswân,
which means 'sad,' 'sorrowful, in Arabic.
Assouan is merely the French way of
spelling Aswân.

Astoria, a town at the mouth of the
Oregon or Columbia river, was named
from John Jacob Astor, a millionaire of
New York who made his fortune in the
fur trade, and sent the ship *Tonquin* in
1811 to found a town on the site of Fort
George, a trading post of the Hudson's
Bay Company.

Astrakhan, a city at the mouth of the
Volga, bears a name usually explained as
Persian, meaning the 'city of the star.'
But Astrakhan or Astorokan is a modern
corruption of the Kalmuk name Aja-
Tarkhan, meaning the city of Haji
Tarkhan, a chief or khan of the Golden
Horde, who, having performed the pil-
grimage to Mecca, had acquired the title
of Haji or 'holy man.'

Asturias, a Spanish province, preserves
the name of the Astures, a Basque people.
The capital of the Astures was the Asturica
Augusta of Pliny, now ASTORGA, a city
in the province of Leon. The Astura,
now the Estola or Ezla, was the name of
the Upper Douro, the Roman Durius
(*q.v.*). These names are usually explained
from the Basque words *asta*, 'a rock,' and
ura, 'water or river.' Asta, now called
MESA DE ASTA, a city near Cadiz, was
probably a fortified rock, or hill fortress,
and we may compare the name of Asta
in Liguria, now ASTI, in Piedmont, which
produces the well-known Vino d'Asti.

Asuncion, the capital of the republic of
Paraguay, was founded by Mendoza in
1535, receiving the name of Nuestra
Señora de la Asuncion, from the festival
of the Assumption of the Virgin Mary.
The names Ascencion and Asuncion must
not be confused. The distinction is seen
in the phrases *Dominus adscendit*, and
Maria adsumpta est. CABO DELLA ASUN-
CION was the name given to the Cape at the
entrance to the Oregon or Columbia River
by Don Bruno de Hecata, who discovered
it in 1775, on August 15th, the festival of
the Assumption. It is also called CAPE

DISAPPOINTMENT, because Vancouver, Cook, and Meares all failed to discover the mouth of the Oregon.

Asurada, or **Ashurada,** an island in the Caspian, signifies the island ' on the other side,' from the Turcoman word *asura,* ' opposite.'

Athabasca, the ' muddy plain,' was originally the Cree name of the delta formed by the Peace River and the Elk River, where they enter the great lake formerly called Lac des Montagnes, which from the delta has now acquired the name of Lake Athabasca. Elk River, a translation of the French - Canadian name Rivière de la Biche, now appears on many maps as the Athabasca River.

Athelney, Somerset, is the A.S. *Æthelinga-íg* or *Ethelinga-íg,* ' the isle of nobles,' *Æthelinga* being the genitive plural of *Ætheling,* a ' noble.'

Athens (*Athenæ*), a name of doubtful etymology, cannot be separated from that of Athené, the tutelary goddess of the city. Athens is either the city of Athené, as the Athenians believed, or Athené may be the goddess of Athens, or both names may be independent formations from the same root. The most recent opinion is that Athené was the goddess of the lightning, her shield representing the thundercloud, and her spear the lightning dart, while her name is from the root *ath,* which we have in *ath-ér,* a ' pike.' If the name of the city is not derived from that of the goddess, the isolated rock of the Acropolis suggests that it may be a locative, meaning ' at the pike' or peak, and the worship of Athené, the spear goddess, may have been localised at a place which bore the same name. Another etymology makes Athens equivalent to Florentia, the city of flowers, or the blooming city, from *anthos* or *athos.* ATTICA is supposed to mean the ' promontory,' from *actia,* a corruption of *acté,* a projecting peninsula. (*See* Athos.)

Athole or **Atholl** is a corruption of Athfotla, Athfodla, or Athhotla, the 'ford of Fodla.' According to the Pictish legend, Fodla was one of the seven sons of Cruithne, the Eponymus of the Cruithnigh, Cruithnich, or Cruithni, the painted or tattooed men (Irish *cruth,* ' colour,' ' form '), whose name was translated as PICTS (*pictı,* or painted men). Fodla, which was also one of the poetical names of Ireland, must be regarded as the Eponymus of a Pictish, and probably non-Aryan tribe.

Athlone is a town on the Shannon, which at one time was here fordable. The old name Athmore, ' the great ford,' was changed to *Ath-Luain-mic-Luighdheach,* ' the ford of Luan, son of Lewy,' a name which has become Athlone, ' the ford of Luan.'

Athos, a mountain in Roumelia, 6778 feet high, at the end of a long peninsula, rises like a watchtower over the Ægean, with numerous monasteries perched on almost inaccessible crags. The name, like that of Athens, is referred to the root *ath,* a spike or peak.

Atlantic, as the name of an ocean, is first mentioned by Herodotus, who tells us that the sea beyond the pillars of Heracles is called the Atlantis ; or, as his words might be rendered, the sea of Atlas. According to Strabo's account, Atlas must have formerly been the name of a conspicuous range, 7200 feet high, which is seen behind Tangier on the left of a person sailing out of the straits, and not of the lofty chain which now bears the name, and is locally called Jebel, the ' mountain,' or Jebel Thalj, the ' snow mountain.' The name of the Atlantic has been derived from a Phœnician word *atel,* signifying the ' darkness' of the west, but it is more probably the sea beyond Mount Atlas, a name which has been plausibly explained from the Berber word *adrar,* a ' mountain,' which we have in the name of one of the loftiest peaks in the chain of the great Atlas, which is called Adrar-n-Iri, ' the mountain of Iri.' Herodotus, or some of his copyists, seems to have turned the name of the Atarantes, the ' mountaineers,' a Libyan people, into Atlantes, a corruption which helps to explain his name of the ' sea called Atlantis.' The significance of the Greek myth of Atlas bearing the heavens on his shoulders is seen by any one approaching Gibraltar at a time when a low canopy of cloud, resting on the mountain which Strabo called the Atlas, extends across the Straits without touching the lower hills on the European side.

Auburn, a communistic settlement in the state of New York, and MOUNT AUBURN, the beautiful cemetery at Boston, Massachusetts, are names doubtless taken from Goldsmith's ' Sweet Auburn, loveliest village of the plain.' The name of the ' deserted village ' in the poem may have been suggested by the deserted village of Auburn near Bridlington, on the Yorkshire coast, whose desertion was caused, not by the encroachments of a grasping landlord, but by the encroachments of the sea, which has washed away the church and all the houses, except a single farm which stands on the very edge of the cliff. Auburn is called in Domesday *Eleburn*, the ' eel-burn.'

Auch, the capital of the Gers, is a corruption of Auscia (Augusta Auscorum), the chief town of the Ausci, an Aquitanian tribe.

Auchterarder, Auchtermuchty, Auchtergaven and similar names are confined to the Pictish part of Scotland ; the prefix *Auchter* being unknown in Wales, or in the Cymric parts of Scotland. It apparently means·an upland field ; *achdar* meaning 'upper' in Gaelic. From *achadh*, a 'field,' we have numerous names, as AUCHINLECK *(achadh-na-leac)*, in Ayrshire, the 'field of the flagstones,' AFFLECK, Aberdeenshire, is a contracted form of the·same name.

Auckland, in the county of Durham, gave a title to William Eden, first Lord Auckland. The AUCKLAND ISLANDS, south of New Zealand, were discovered by Bristow in 1806, and named by him after the first Lord Auckland, who had been a friend of his father. The province of AUCKLAND in New Zealand takes its name from the city of Auckland, in Eden county, which was founded in 1840, and named after George Eden, second Lord Auckland, who had been at the head of the Admiralty, and was at that time Governor - General of India. Auckland appears in the Boldon Book as Alcland, Alclet, Aclet, and Auckland, forms difficult to explain, but which may signify either Elk-land or Oak-land.

Aughrim, or **Aghrim**, in Galway, where James II. was defeated in 1691, is a corruption of *Each-druim*, the ' horse ridge.' Twenty places in Ireland bear this name.

Aurora Island, one of the New Hebrides, was named *Ile Aurore* by Bougainville, because it was discovered at daybreak on May 22nd, 1768.

Austin, the state capital of Texas, was founded in 1830 on the land of Stephen F. Austin of Durham in Connecticut.

Australia. The old geographers believed that a great southern continent must exist in order to balance the land in the Northern Hemisphere, and they named it provisionally *Terra Australis Incognita*, 'the undiscovered southern land.' Between 1605 and 1642 Dutch sailors had discovered a great part of the western coast oɩ Australia, which they called NEW HOLLAND ; but when in 1768 Cook sailed on his first voyage of discovery, the eastern coast, which he named New South Wales, was still unknown, Tasmania, New Guinea, and the western coast of Australia, which were supposed to bɜ portions of the same land, all going by the name of New Holland. The name Australia was first suggested by Flinders in a modest footnote of his *Voyage to Terra Australis*, published in 1814, where he says : ' Had I permitted myself any innovation upon the original term it would have been to convert it into Australia, as being more agreeable to the ear, and an assimilation to the name of the other great portions of the earth.' Australia, ' the southern land,' is·a name which is now adopted because formed on the analogy of the names of the other continents. The largest of the New Hebrides, discovered by Quiros and Torres, was supposed to be a portion of the Terra Australis Incognita, and hence received the name of Tierra Austral del Espiritu Santo, and still appears on our maps as ESPIRITU SANTO.

Austria, the ' eastern realm,' is a geographical term which has been variously applied. In the seventh century, Austrasia or Austria denoted the land of the Eastern Franks, which extended from Frankfort to Aix-la-Chapelle, the west Frankish land being distinguished as Neustria. About 843 we find another Austria and Neustria in Italy, the terms denoting the eastern and western lands of the Lombards. Finally the name migrated to the duchy which formed the kernel of the present Austrian empire, Charlemagne at the close of the tenth century erecting it into a margravate to protect the eastern march of the Empire against the attacks of the Magyars. We now find in Latin documents the name *Orientale regnum*, a translation of the O.H.G. *Ostar-rike*, ' the eastern realm,' where *ostar* is an amplified form of *ost*, from *aust*, ' east.' In modern German, Ostar-rike has become Oest-reich, which in French is softened into Autriche, while in England we use the Latin form Austria, as we do in the case of Bavaria, Bohemia, Galicia, or Moravia. The present Austro-Hungarian monarchy consists of numerous crown lands, mostly matrimonial accretions which have been annexed to the original margravate, now an archduchy. Austro-Hungary consists of (1st) the Archduchy of Austria, with the Bishopric of Salzburg, the Duchy of Styria, the county of

Tyrol, and the kingdoms of Illyria and Dalmatia, to which has been added the kingdom of Bohemia, which includes Galicia and Lodomeria. (2nd) The kingdom of Hungary, which includes the kingdoms of Slavonia and Croatia, and the principality of Transylvania. AUSTRIA SOUND, a strait which divides Franz Joseph Land, was discovered and named in 1873 by Lieut. Payer of the Austrian Arctic Expedition.

Autun, in France, is a corruption of the Celto-Roman name Augustodunum, the hill-fort of Augustus, given by the Romans to the Celtic Bibracte, or 'beaver town.' Augustodunum became successively Agustodunum, Austun, and Autun. The name of Augustus was also given to Augustoritum, 'the ford of Augustus,' now Limoges; Augustobona, 'the town of Augustus,' now Troyes; Augustobriga, the 'fortress of Augustus,' and Augustodurum the 'strong place of Augustus,' now Bayeux. AUGSBURG, in Bavaria, a corruption of Augustburg, was the Roman Augusta Vindelicorum, which was made a colony by the Emperor Augustus 13 B.C. AUGST, in Canton Basel, represents the Roman colony of Augusta Rauracorum, founded by Munatius Plancus in the reign of Augustus, and named in his honour. AUST PASSAGE, on the Severn, is conjectured to have been a Roman ferry called Trajectus Augusta. AGOSTA, in Sicily, a corruption of Augusta, was so named from the Imperial title of the Emperor Frederic II., by whom the town was refounded in 1229. AUGUSTA, the State capital of Georgia, was founded by English colonists in 1735, and named after the capital of England, which was called Augusta by the Romans, and doubtless not without reference to the Princess Augusta of Saxe-Gotha, who was then about to become the bride of Frederick, Prince of Wales.

Auvergne, a corruption of *Arvernia*, a mountainous district in Central France, preserves the name of its former inhabitants the Arverni, a Celtic name of uncertain meaning but usually supposed to signify the 'highlanders.'

Ava, or **Awa,** formerly the capital of Burma, is the Malay form of the Burmese name *Eng-wa* or *Ang-wa*, which means the 'lake mouth,' the city having been built at the entrance into the Irawadi of a lagoon. (Burmese *eng*, a 'tank' or 'pool,' and *wa*, 'entrance'.)

Avallon, in the department of the Yonne, is the Celtic *Aballo*, an 'orchard.'

Avignon, the Roman Avennio, is from the Gentile name Avennius.

Avoid Bay and **Point Avoid,** South Australia, were so called by Flinders in 1802, because of dangerous rocks.

Avranches, in the Department of La Manche, is called on Merovingian coins *Abrenctas*, which is a corruption of *Abrincatuis*, the dative case of the tribal name Abrincatui, which means, according to Holder, the 'leaders.' (Cf. the Cornish *hebrenciat*, 'dux'.)

Aylesbury, Bucks, is called in the Chronicle *Æglesburg*, *Ægelesburg*, and *Æglesbyrig*, probably from a proper name which we have also in AYLESFORD and AYLESTHORPE, Kent (A.S. *Æglesford* and *Æglesthrep*), and in AYLESWORTH, Northants (A.S. *Ægleswurth*). Aylesthorpe is one of the few thorpes which are found beyond the boundaries of the Danelagh. It is probably a Jutish name. The foregoing names are referred by Dr. Guest to the British *eglws*, a 'church,' but this is improbable.

Ayrshire, a Scotch county, comprises the older districts of Carrick, Kyle, and Cunninghame. It takes its name from Ayr (formerly spelt Are and Air) the county town, which stands at the mouth of the River Ayr. As there is a Point of Ayr in Cheshire, and another in the Isle of Man, which are both indubitably Scandinavian names from the O.N. *eyrr*, a beach or spit of shingle, the Scotch town may be from the same source, whence we have Ireland in Shetland and Irland in Orkney, both of which mean 'beach island.' It is however possible that the town may take its name from the river, possibly a Celtic name meaning slow or gentle.

Azerbaijan, the name of a province in Persia, testifies to the ancient cult of the fire-worshippers. (*azer*, 'fire,' and *baijan*, 'keeper'.)

Azores is the English spelling of the Portuguese name *Os Açores*, so called from 'the hawks' (Falco milvus) by which they were frequented (Portuguese *açor* a 'hawk,' plural *açores*) at the time of the discovery. Gonçalo Velho discovered SANTA MARIA on August 15th, 1432 and S. MIGUEL on May 8th, naming them from the calendar saints. TERCEIRA, as the name implies, was 'the third' island to be discovered. It was originally named Ilha de Jesu Christo, from the day of discovery, 21st March 1450. Graciosa, San Jorge, and Fayal were found between

1450 and 1453, and Pico nine years later. FAYAL, 'beech-tree' island, was at first called *Ilha dos Framengos*.

Azov, Sea of, the modern name of the Palus Maeotis, is from the town of Azov or Asof, a modern Tatar or Mongolian name, probably meaning the 'moist or wet place,' given in the thirteenth or fourteenth century to the city of Tana, at the mouth of the Tanais, now the Don.

Aztecs is an English plural form, substituted for the Aztec plural substantive *Azteca*. Ac.rding to the Aztec legend the name was derived from Aztlan, a northern region from which they migrated. Morgan explains Aztlan as the 'place of cranes,' Father Duran as the 'place of whiteness,' Dr. Brinton as the 'place by the salt water.' A group of ancient earthworks in Wisconsin has been fancifully named AZTLAN or AZTALAN, on the theory that the Aztecs were the primitive mound builders.

Azucar, Pan de, 'the sugar-loaf,' is the Spanish name of various conical hills in South America and elsewhere.

Babel Islands, in Bass Strait, were so named by Flinders in 1798, on account of the discordant screams of the immense flocks of sea-fowl which inhabited them. BABYLON, the modern Hillah, is the Greek form of Bab-ilu (Babel), which was a Semitic translation of the Accadian name Ca-dimirra, the 'gate of God.'

Bab-el-Mandeb, at the entrance of the Red Sea, is often called the Strait of Bab-el-Mandeb, a mere pleonasm, as the Arabic *bab* means a 'gate' or 'strait.' The name is explained as the 'gate of sorrow,' or, more literally, the 'gate of tears' or 'wailing,' being beset with several small islands, which make the passage dangerous. But Bab-el-Mandeb is probably an assimilated form due to folk-etymology, the name also appearing as Bab-el-Mandel, which is believed to be a corruption of Bab-el-Menheli, 'the small passage,' as distinguished from the broader passage to the east, called BAB-ISKANDER, 'Alexander's Strait,' from a tradition that Alexander's fleet passed through it.

Bacalhaos, Isla de, the island of stockfish or dried cod, was the name given in the early Portuguese maps to Newfoundland, off the east coast of which is a small island still called BACALHAO ISLAND.

Back Land, in Arctic America, was discovered by Captain George Back in 1831. BACK POINT, BACK'S BAY, BACK'S INLET, BACK'S RIVER, and CAPE GEORGE BACK, all in the Arctic regions, also bear his name.

Backhouse Point, near the mouth of the Great Fish River, discovered in 1834, and BACKHOUSE RIVER, a tributary of the Mackenzie River, discovered in 1826, were named after John Backhouse, Under Secretary for Foreign Affairs.

Badajos on the Guadiana, a frontier fortress of Spain, stormed by Wellington in 1812, is the Bathalyosh of Abulfeda, probably a corruption of the Paxanguita (*Pax Augusta*) of Strabo.

Baden, 'at the baths,' is the dative plural of the O.H.G. *bad*, a 'bath.' The name is borne by a watering-place near Vienna, by another in the Swiss Canton of Aargau, and by a third in the Breisgau. The last, which was the *Aurelia Aquensis* of the Romans, has given a name to the Grand Duchy of Baden, of which it was formerly the capital; hence the town itself is now distinguished by the name of BADEN-BADEN, *i.e.* 'Baden town in Baden Duchy,' to distinguish it from the other towns called Baden. See *Wiesbaden, Carlsbad,* and *Bath*.

Badenoch, Inverness-shire, is probably the Gaelic *badenach*, a 'bushy place.'

Baffin Bay was first explored in 1616 by William Baffin, one of the most adventurous of England's seamen. BAFFIN'S LAND and BAFFIN ISLAND also bear his name. In 1609 Baffin sailed with Hall to Greenland. In 1612 he went as Hall's pilot in an expedition fitted out by four merchant-princes, Sir Thomas Smith, Sir James Lancaster, Sir William Cockayne, and Mr. Bell. In 1613, and again in 1614, he sailed to Spitzbergen. In 1615 he was pilot to Bylot in an attempt to discover the North-West Passage. In 1616 he went as pilot of the *Discovery* in an expedition which discovered the 'London Coast' of Greenland, named in honour of the London merchants, Sir Thomas Smith, Sir Francis Jones, Sir Dudley Digges, and Sir John Wolstenholm, by whom the expedition was despatched. After his patrons a headland was named CAPE DUDLEY DIGGES, and a deep bay was called WOLSTENHOLM SOUND. He was stopped by the ice at the entrance of a strait which he called SMITH SOUND, and sighted two openings which he named JONES SOUND and LANCASTER SOUND. In WHALE SOUND he saw several whales. In 1621 he sailed to the East Indies, and joined in the siege by the East India Company of a Portuguese fort near Ormuz, in the Persian Gulf. Baffin went ashore with his instruments to determine the height and distance of the castle wall, in order to find the range, ' but, as he was about the same, he received a shot from the castle into his belly, wherewith he gave three leaps, and died immediately.' Baffin, Davis, and Hudson, the most intrepid of our early navigators, were all cut off in their prime by tragic deaths.

Baghdád was built in 763 A.D. by the Caliph Mansúr on the west bank of the Tigris, and officially styled Madínat-as-Salám, the 'city of welfare,' but in practice the older name of Baghdád has remained in use. It would mean in Persian the 'garden of justice' or redress, but according to a local tradition, it was the 'garden of Dad,' a hermit who was believed to have inhabited a cell on the site of the city. The name is probably much older, and of Iranian origin, meaning, according to Spiegel, the 'gift of God' (*dad*, 'gift,' and *baga* or *bagh*, 'god'). From Baldac, the Italian corruption of the name, we have the word *baldacchini*, for the silk and gold brocades used for the canopies of Italian dignitaries, and hence the word *baldacchino* for a canopy.

Bahamas, or **Lucayas**, are a group of islands extending south-east from Florida for 600 miles. One of them, probably Watling Island, was the first landfall of Columbus, who called the group *Las Princesas*, probably because they were the 'first' islands he discovered. The name Lucayas is a corruption of the Spanish name Los Cayos, 'the keys,' 'cays,' or reefs, which was given by early Spanish mariners. The meaning of the name Bahama is doubtful, but is most probably derived from a small group, still called Bimani, opposite Cape Florida, of which the Spaniards in Haiti heard tidings, and from the resemblance of the name identified it with a place in Asia called Palombe by Mandeville, where he asserted there was a miraculous fountain of youth, of which he had himself drunk. Palombe was an imaginary name, Mandeville having cribbed his account of the place and its fountain from a spurious letter purporting to have been written by Prester John. It was in search of Bimani that Juan Ponce de Leon discovered the Great Bahama in 1513, and rediscovered and named Florida. In Herrera's map of 1601 Bahama is an island placed next to Bimani.

Bahia, till 1763 the capital of Brazil, means the 'bay' in Spanish and Portuguese. It stands on the Reconcavo, commonly called the Gulf of Bahia, an extensive inland sea, 100 miles in circumference, discovered by Amerigo Vespucci on Nov. 1st, 1501, All Saints Day, and therefore named *Bahia de Todos os Santos*. The name has been attributed to Christovão Jaques in 1503, but that is impossible, as it appears on the Cantino map, which was made in 1502. In 1549, Thomé de Souza, the Portuguese Governor, landed in the bay, and founded a city which he called Cidade do Salvador, 'the city of the Saviour.' The official style became Cidade do San Salvador da Bahia de Todos os Santos, 'the city of the Holy Saviour in All Saints Bay,' which has been abbreviated in common usage into Bahia, 'the bay.'

Bahr-el-Yûsef, or **Bahr-Yûsef**, 'the river of Joseph,' is a gigantic canal which takes in from the Nile near Assiout, and after watering thousands of acres west of the Nile, finally enters the Fayûm. Its origin is lost in antiquity, but, as the name shows, it is traditionally ascribed to Joseph.

Baikal, a large lake in Eastern Siberia, is the Mongol or Yakut *bai-kul*, the 'abundant lake,' so called because it abounds with the *omul*, a species of salmon.

Baillie's River, a tributary of the Great Fish River, was discovered by Captain Back in 1834, and named after George Baillie, Agent-General for the Crown Colonies; whose name is also borne by BAILLIE'S ISLANDS, near Cape Bathurst, discovered by Franklin in 1826.

Baily Islands, off the coast of Japan, were discovered by Captain Beechey in 1827, and named in honour of Francis Baily, President of the Royal Astronomical Society.

Bakewell, Derbyshire, is *Badecan-wylle* in the Saxon Chronicle (in Florence *Badecan-welle*), meaning the 'well of Badeca.'

Bakhchisserai, the capital of the Tartar Khans of the Crimea, is a Turkic name meaning 'palace garden,' or garden of the *Khan serai*, the 'palace of the Khan.'

Balaclava, a port in the Crimea, is a corruption of the Genoese name, *bella chiava*, 'the beautiful quay.'

Balearic Islands, a Spanish group, retain their old Greek name. The inhabitants, being skilful slingers, and employed as such in the Carthaginian and Roman armies, were called Baleares, the 'slingers,' by Greek writers. Possibly the name is an assimilated form derived from some lost Phœnician name of the same class as BAALBEC, of which Heliopolis, the 'city of the sun,' was a sort of Greek translation.

Balkan is the range of mountains which divides the BALKAN PENINSULA from the Danube valley. The word *balkan* denotes in Turkish a 'wooded height' or high ridge.

Balkash, the Mongolian name of an inland sea in Central Asia, means the 'Great Lake.' The Kirghiz call it *Ak-Dengis*, the 'white sea,' or simply *Dengis*, 'the sea.' Chinese writers call it *Si-Hai*, the 'western sea.'

Balkh, a city in Bokhara on the Oxus, is, according to Vámbéry, the Turkic *balik* or *balikh* (Mongolian *baluk*), a 'city.' It is probably an assimilated form of the old name Bactra, the capital of Bactria or Bactriana, the Bachtaris of Darius, and the Bachdhi of the Zend Avesta.

Ballaigue, the name of a village near the falls of the Doubs, is a corruption of *Bellæ aquæ.*

Balleny Islands, an Antarctic group on the meridian of New Caledonia, bear the name of the captain of an English whaler who discovered them in 1839.

Bally, the Anglicised form of *baile*, is the commonest element in the names of Irish townlands, in 6400 of which it is found. It now means a townland, village, or town, but its original meaning was simply a 'place,' usually a place fenced round. (Cf. the Latin *vallum*, Low-Latin *ballivum*.) BALTIMORE (*q.v.*) is the 'town of the great house.' BALBRIGAN is the 'town of Brecan.' BALRATH is the 'town of the fort.' Followed by the article and a masculine noun in the genitive, we have *Ballin-*, as in BALLINCURRIG from *Baile-an-churraigh*, the 'town of the marsh,' and when followed by the article and a feminine noun in the genitive, we have *Ballina-* as in BALLINAHINCH, from *Baile-na-hinch*, the 'town of the island.' BALLEEN, the 'little town,' is a diminutive. Baile is also common in the Gaelic parts of Scotland, as BALLACHULISH (Gaelic *Baile-na-caolish*), the 'town on the strait'; BALLANTRAE, the 'town on the strand'; BALLATER, the 'town on the slope'; and BALQUHIDDER, the 'town at the back of the country.' In the Isle of Man *baile* becomes *balla*, as BALLASPICK, the 'bishop's farm,' from *aspick* the Manx

corruption of *episcopus.* Bally being such a common prefix, forms of different origin are occasionally assimilated, more especially *bella*, the Anglicised form of *bel-atha*, the 'entrance to a ford.' Thus BALLINA in Tipperary and in Mayo is a corruption of Bel-an-atha. BALLYSHANNON, in Donegal, at a ford over the Erne, has nothing to do with the Shannon, the old name was *Bel-atha-Seanigh*, the 'entrance of Shannagh's ford.' So in Scotland *Balloch-*, a common prefix, is usually from *bealach*, a 'pass.'

Balm, a word of Celtic origin meaning a precipice, overhanging rock, or cave (old French *balme*, a 'cave,' Low-Latin *balma*), occurs in many names in Switzerland and France, such as the BALMENHORN, one of the peaks of Monte Rosa ; BAULMES, in Canton Vaud ; BEAUME near Besançon ; and the COL DE BALME, on the route between Martigny and Chamounix, where the rock in one place completely overhangs the road.

Baltic Sea (called in German *Ost See* or 'East Sea') is a name which can be traced back to Adam of Bremen in the eleventh century. Pliny mentions a large island called *Baltia*, probably either Zealand or Fünen, which are separated from each other and from Jutland by two channels called respectively the GREAT BELT and the LITTLE BELT, names derived from the O.N. *belti*, a 'girdle' or 'belt,' a word used in Norse poetry to denote the sea, as being the girdle which surrounds islands or the earth. But it is probable that the Baltic took its name, not from the Belts but from the island of Baltia, a name explained from the Lithuanian *baltas*, 'white,' in reference to the chalk cliffs which border the islands. BALTA, called in the Orkney Saga *Baltey*, is a small island off Unst in the Shetlands, and gives a name to BALTA SOUND. Balta may be from the O.N. *belti*, assimilated to the Gaelic *balt*, a 'border' or 'belt' (Latin *balteus*).

Baltimore, Maryland, one of the most important cities in the United States, was laid out in 1729 and named after Lord Baltimore, who founded the colony of Maryland. Sir Charles Calvert, the first Lord Baltimore, obtained in 1620 a grant of land in Newfoundland from James I. A large territory, north of Virginia, was granted in 1632 to his son, George Calvert, who died in the same year. His son, Cecilius Calvert, the second Lord Baltimore, became a Romanist, and removed the colony from Newfoundland to

Maryland. Sir Charles Calvert, who had obtained a grant of land in Ireland, took his title from a town in county Cork called Baltimore, or Balintimore, in Irish *baile-an-tighe-mhoir*, the 'town of the great house,' the great house being the castle of the O'Driscoll family, the ruins of which crown a rock near the town.

Bamberg, in Franconia, is shown by the ninth century form *Babinberg* to be a patronymic from the personal name Bab. BOBENHEIM, near Worms, and BABEN-HAUSEN, near Bielefeld, are from the same source.

Bamburgh, or **Bamborough**, on the coast of Northumberland, stands on a mass of basaltic rock frowning over the sea and approachable only by steps cut in the precipice. The name appears as *Bebban-burh* and *Bebba-burh* in the Saxon Chronicle. It was the fortress and capital of Ida, the Flame-bearer, and is said by Baeda to bear the name of a Queen Bebba or Bebbe, probably not the Queen of Ida, but, as we are told by Nennius, the Queen of Ædilfrid, the grandson of Ida,

Ban, or **Man**, which means 'village,' occurs frequently in the Shan States. BAN-NONG, for instance, is the 'village at the lake.'

Banat is a Slavonic word meaning 'lordship,' and is applied to a district ruled by a Ban or military governor. Thus the Ban of Croatia is the title of the Austrian governor of that country. The district usually known as the Banat is the TEMES-WAR BANAT, a lordship in Hungary, of which the town of Temeswar is the capital.

Banbury, Oxon., was the A.S. *Beran-burh*, the 'Bear's Fortress,' *beran* being the genitive singular of *bera*, a 'bear,' which was a common personal name.

Banda Oriental, officially styled BANDA ORIENTAL DEL URUGUAY, 'the eastern bank of the Uruguay,' is the local name of the Republic of the Uruguay, which includes so much of the Argentine Confederation as lies east of the Uruguay. The inhabitants call themselves *los Orientales*, 'the Easterns.'

Banderas, Rio de, the 'river of flags,' on the eastern coast of Mexico, was so called because, when discovered by Juan de Grijalva in 1518, the natives waved white flags at the ends of spears, in token of amity.

Banff, the county town of Banffshire, is called in the thirteenth century *Bamphe* and *Banffe*. According to an Irish legend

Banba was a queen of the Tuatha de Danann, who came from Scotland. Hence Mr. Whitley Stokes conjectures that Banff (*banbh*) is a Pictish name cognate with Banba, an old name of Ireland. The Irish *banb* (Welsh *banw*) means a pig.

Bangor, County Down, is a corrupted form of the common Irish name BANAGHER (*Beannchar*), a derivative of *Beann* (Ben), a 'hill,' with a cumulative suffix, thus meaning a 'group of hills.' From the word *beann*, a gable, horn, peak, or pointed hill, we have numerous mountain names in Scotland such as BEN NEVIS, BEN LOMOND, or BENLEDI. In Ireland the word usually denotes smaller elevations, as BANAGHER, or the TWELVE PINS (Twelve Bens) in Connemara.

Bangor, in Wales, was the name of a great monastery, meaning either the 'white choir,' or possibly the 'high circle.'

Banias, at the source of the Jordan, is a corruption of the Greek name Panias, the grotto of Pan. In the New Testament it is called CÆSAREA PHILIPPI, Philip the Tetrarch having built a town near the temple erected here by his father, Herod the Great, in honour of Augustus Cæsar.

Banks Land, one of the largest islands in the Polar Archipelago, was discovered by Parry in 1819, and named after Sir Joseph Banks, who had accompanied Captain Cook as naturalist in his first voyage, and was afterwards for forty years President of the Royal Society, in which capacity he took a leading part in inducing the Government to undertake voyages of exploration. Naturally such services were recognised by explorers in many parts of the world. Captain Cook (1770-78) named after him CAPE BANKS in Australia, POINT BANKS at the entrance of Cook's River, Alaska, and BANKS ISLAND in New Zealand, afterwards found to be a peninsula. BANKS PENINSULA, in Coronation Gulf, was discovered and named by Franklin in 1821; BANKS STRAIT, north of BANKS LAND, by M'Clure in 1851; BANKS BAY in Lancaster Sound, by John Ross in 1818; BANKS ISLANDS, in the New Hebrides, by Bligh in 1784; and BANKS GROUP, in Spencer Gulf, by Flinders in 1802.

Baños de Inca, 'the baths of the Inca,' near Caxamarca in Peru, is a place where the unfortunate Atahuallpa, the last of the Incas, used to pass a portion of the year,

Bantry Bay takes its name from Bantry, a town in County Cork. The old Irish name was *Beann-traighe*, the tribe or 'race of Beann,' the son of Connor, king of Ulster.

Bantu (Ba-ntu or Aba-ntu), a name which, like so many tribe-names, means 'the men' or 'the people,' is a general appellation of the great South African race, of which the Zulus and the Caffres are prominent representatives. The Bantu languages are characterised by prefixes. Thus U-GANDA is the country of Ganda, Mu-ganda is a native of Ganda; Baganda or Wa-ganda, the plural of Mu-ganda, means the people of Ganda; and Ki-ganda is the language of Ganda. The syllable Ba-, Aba-, Ama-, Ma-, or Wa- is a plural pronominal prefix, meaning 'those of.' Thus the BA-KALAHARI, 'those of Kalahari,' are a Bechuana tribe inhabiting the Kalahari desert; the BA-KWIRI are the 'jungle people,' or 'those of the jungle,' from *kwiri*, 'jungle'; the BA-TLAPI are the 'fish people'; and the BA-KATLAARE are the 'ape people.' The BA-TAUANA, or 'people of the little lion,' a Bechuana tribe, were followers of Tauene, 'the little lion,' who settled near Ngami, south-west of Bechuanaland. The BA-QUAINA, one of the most powerful of the Bechuana tribes, are the children or people of the *quaina* or crocodile. It has been thought that Bechuana may be a corruption of Ba-quaina, but more probably the Be-chuanas, who have given their name to BECHUANALAND, are 'those who are alike' or equal, from the Bantu word *chuana*, 'alike,' 'similar,' or 'equal.' Their language is called Se-chuana, which means 'the same speech,' or speech of those who are alike. The Wa-jiji are the people of U-jiji, and the Wa-nyamwezi of U-nyamwezi, the 'country of the moon.' We have dialectic forms of the same prefix in the tribe-names of the Ama-tonga, the Ama-Swazi, the Ma-tebele, the Ma-shona, the Ma-kua, the Ma-kolokni, the Ba-suto, the Ba-tau, the Ba-puli, the Ba-rolong, the Ba-meri, the Wa-zinga, the Wa-nyoro, the Wa-songora, the Wa-nyankori. (p.292).

Barbadoes, one of the British West Indian islands, is believed to have obtained its Spanish name of Barbados from the *barbados*, or 'bearded' fig-trees, whose pendulous branches, terminating in bunches of fibres resembling beards, descend and root themselves in the earth. BARBUDA, another West Indian island, is believed to mean the island of the 'bearded' men.

Barbary is the 'land of the Berbers,' a name believed to be a reduplicated form derived from *ber*, 'men.' It is doubtful whether the name is related to the word barbarian, which we have borrowed from the Greek, or to *Afer*, from which the name of Africa has been derived.

Barcelona, in Spain, anciently *Barcino*, was founded, according to the Roman tradition, by Hamilcar Barca, about 237 B.C. The cognomen Barca, which corresponds to the Hebrew Barak, means 'the lightning.'

Bareilly (Bareli), in the North-West Provinces, was founded in the sixteenth century by Barel Deo.

Barents Sea, between Spitzbergen and Novaya Zemlya, bears the name of Willem Barents or Barentz, a Dutch mariner who, endeavouring to find a north-east passage to China, discovered in 1594 the whole western coast of Novaya Zemlya, and two years later discovered the north-west coast of Spitzbergen. After wintering on the north-east coast of Novaya Zemlya, the ship was abandoned, the crew escaped in boats, and Barents died in the midst of the sea he had discovered. BARENTS LAND, eastern wing of Novaya Zemlya, and BARENTS ISLANDS, an outlying group, were also discovered by him.

Bari, a town in the south of Italy, anciently *Barium*, is believed to be a Messapian name. The Messapians were Illyrians, who had crossed the Adriatic, and their speech is now represented by the Albanian, in which language Bari may be explained as the 'meadow.' The name is repeated at ANTIVARI, a place on the Illyrian shore of the Adriatic.

Baring Island, BARING LAND, BARING STRAIT, and BARING BAY, in the Arctic Archipelago, were named after Sir Francis Baring, who, at the time of their discovery (1850-52), was First Lord of the Admiralty.

Barker, Mount, in South Australia, was so named by Captain Sturt after a friend who was killed by the natives in Encounter Bay (*q.v.*).

Barkly West, Cape Colony, formerly called Griqualand West, was annexed to the Cape Colony by Sir Henry Barkly.

Bar-le-Duc, BAR-SUR-SEINE, BAR-SUR-AUBE, BAR-SUR-CORRÈGE are ultimately from the Celtic *bar*, an enclosure, whence come the Low-Latin *barrum*, a fortress, and the doublets *barra* or *barræ*, an intrenchment, and ultimately our words *barrier* and *barrack*. In Gaelic, *barr* means a hill-top, whence some 500 Scotch names, such as BARGLASS, the 'green top,' or LOCHINVAR, 'lake of the hill.' In Ireland we have BARMONA, the 'top of the bog,' and BARRAVORE, the 'great top.'

Barmouth, a watering-place on the Welsh coast, is a curious English corruption of the older name *Aber-maw*, the town at 'the mouth of the Maw or Mawddach.'

Barnabas, Cape, in Alaska, was discovered by Cook in his third voyage on June 11th, St. Barnabas Day.

Barnard Castle, on the Tees, in the county of Durham, is a town which has gathered round a castle built by Barnard Baliol, grandfather of John Baliol, competitor with Bruce for the Scottish crown. Barnard Castle was afterwards one of the strongholds of the Nevilles of Raby, one of whom erected NEVILLE'S CROSS, in commemoration of the battle of 1346 in which the Scots were defeated and King David was taken prisoner. In like manner MALCOLM'S CROSS, near Alnwick, marks the spot where Malcolm, King of Scots, was slain in ambush.

Barnevelt's Islands, off Cape Hoorn, were discovered in 1616 by Le Maire, and named after the Dutch statesman Jan van Barnevelt, Grand Pensionary of Holland, who was beheaded in 1619.

Barnstaple, in Devon, is locally called Barum, which may be either the A.S. *bearwum*, dative-plural of *bearu*, a 'swine pasture,' or *barum*, dative-plural of *bær*, 'bare, open,' as in the phrase *on barum sondum*, 'on bare sands.' The word staple in Barnstaple signifies a market.

Barra, the name of one of the Hebrides, is supposed to be derived from the Scandinavian *bara-ey*, the 'isle of the wave' or the 'isle of the ocean,' a name which, from its exposed situation, would be appropriate. But as the parish was formerly called Kilbarr, it has been conjectured that it may have been the Isle of St. Bar, or St. Finbar, a friend of St. Columba, to whom the cathedral of the diocese of Caithness was dedicated, and to whom the name of DUNBAR has also been referred.

Barrackpore is commonly known to the sepoys as Achánock or Chának, and the local tradition affirms, probably with truth, that Job Charnock or Channock, the founder of Calcutta, built a bungalow here in 1689, round which a bazaar arose,

before the site of Calcutta had been determined on. Troops were stationed here in 1772, and the place received its name from the barracks. According to Schlagintweit, the name means the 'city of victory.'

Barrier Reef was the name given by Cook in 1770 to the belt of coral reefs and islands extending for many miles along the coast of Queensland. The BARRIER ISLANDS, also named by Cook, protect the entrance to the Hauraki Gulf in New Zealand.

Barrow Strait, the continuation of Lancaster Sound, was discovered by Parry in 1819-20, and named after Sir John Barrow, who in his office of Secretary to the Admiralty was 'the great promoter of Arctic research.' His name is also borne by CAPE BARROW in Victoria Land, discovered by James Ross in 1841; by CAPE BARROW in Grinnell Land, discovered by Kane in 1853; by CAPE BARROW in Coronation Gulf, discovered by Franklin in 1821; by CAPE BARROW in the Gulf of Carpentaria, discovered by Flinders in 1803; by MOUNT BARROW near the mouth of the Great Fish River, discovered by Back in 1834; by MOUNT BARROW, between the Coppermine and the Mackenzie, discovered by Richardson in 1826; by BARROW BAY in the Parry Islands, discovered by Belcher in 1852; by BARROW BAY in Corea, discovered by Basil Hall in 1816; by BARROW ISLAND, discovered by Beechey in 1826; by BARROW'S ISLAND off the north-west coast of Australia, discovered by King in 1818; and by BARROW RIVER, which enters the Fox Channel, discovered by Parry in 1822.

Barrule is the name of two conspicuous mountains in the Isle of Man, called respectively North and South Barrule. The Norse name VÖRD-FJALL, 'Beacon fell' became Varfl, then Varrul, and finally Barrule under the influence of a popular etymology which explained the name as meaning in Manx the 'top of an apple.'

Barter Island, near the mouth of the Mackenzie River, was so called because the Eskimos bartered certain objects with Franklin's men in 1826.

Barton, the name of some forty-five places, mostly insignificant, is not to be confounded with Burton. It is the A.S. *bere-tún*, literally a 'barley-yard,' a word used for a grange or outlying inclosed threshing-floor, often the *prædium dominicum* or demesne farm of the lord, which still survives in the dialect word *barton,* denoting the outlying yards or buildings of a manor. Of nearly the same signification is the A.S. *bere-wíc,* literally a 'barley village,' to which we may assign most of the nine places named BERWICK and the four named BARWICK, usually called *Berewic* in Domesday. BERWICK-ON-TWEED being in A.S. *Beor-wíc,* must signify the 'village on a hill.' From *bere,* 'barley,' we have the A.S. *bere-cærn, berern, beren, bearn* or *bern,* a 'barn,' genitive *bernes,* literally the 'place for the crop,' whence probably BARNES in Surrey, and BARNACK in Northants, A.S. *Bernake,* 'at the Barn oak,' and BARNWELL, Northants, A.S. *Bernewelle,* 'at the barn well.' In Domesday BARNBROUGH, Yorks, is called *Berneburg,* and BARNSLEY, Yorks, is *Berneslai,* apparently from personal names.

Basel (in French BÂLE, formerly BASLE) is a city on the Rhine which gives its name to one of the Swiss cantons. It is usually affirmed that the name was derived from a *basilica,* a conjecture not supported by the oldest forms, *Basilia,* used by Ammianus Marcellinus (A.D. 374), *Bazela* by the Ravenna geographer, and *Civitas Basiliensium* in the Notitia. More probably, as Zeuss suggests, the town may have been founded by Basilus, who served in Gaul under Julius Cæsar.

Bashee Islands, a group in the North Pacific, were so named by Dampier in 1687 from a beverage called *bashee* by the natives, which they obtained from the juice of the sugar-cane.

Basilicata, an Italian province, was the basilicate or domain ruled by a *basilico* of the Byzantine Emperor, as the province of the CAPITANATA was by a *capitano,* and the EXARCHATE OF RAVENNA by an Exarch.

Bass Strait, which divides Tasmania from Australia, bears the name of George Bass, assistant-surgeon of the *Reliance,* in which ship he sailed with Flinders in 1798-99 round Tasmania, already discovered by Tasman, thus proving that it was an island. In an open whale-boat, with a crew of six men, Bass explored 600 miles of unknown sea-coast, and penetrated into Bass Strait. Lieutenant Matthew Flinders, who commanded the expedition, generously refrained from giving his own name to this important strait, on the ground that Bass had been the first to enter it in the whale-boat. At Sydney Flinders and Bass had previously equipped the *Tom Thumb,* a boat 8 feet

long, and with a boy as crew, had sailed from Port Jackson to explore the coast, discovering GEORGE'S RIVER, which falls into Botany Bay. BASS POINT, in New South Wales, was also discovered by George Bass; and BASS RIVER, in Victoria, was named after him by its discoverer, Captain Stokes.

Bassorah, Bussorah, or **Basra,** a frontier town of Turkey, near the head of the Persian Gulf, founded by Omar in 636 A.D., may be equivalent to the Biblical Bozra, the 'fortress,' or an Arabic name meaning the 'margin' or 'frontier.'

Batak in Bulgaria bears a Turkish name meaning 'the marsh.'

Batavia, the Dutch capital of Java, occupying the site of Jakatra, the old Javanese capital, was founded in 1619 by the Dutch General, John Petersen Coen, and named from the Batavi, a tribe mentioned by Tacitus as living on the Lower Rhine. Zeuss explains the name from the Teutonic stem *bat,* 'good,' which yields our comparative and superlative *better* and *best.* Thus *bat-au* would be the 'good land.' PASSAU, anciently *Patavium,* at the confluence of the Inn and the Danube was the station of the ninth Batavian Cohort, whence the name.

Bath, a city in Somerset, is renowned for its hot springs, which the Romans called *Aquæ Solis,* 'the waters of the sun.' In a charter of 676 it is mentioned as a place *quæ vocatur Hat-Bathu,* 'the hot baths.' In other charters we have *æt Bathum,* 'at the baths,' and *æt Hátum Bathum,* 'at the hot baths,' where *Bathu* is the nom. pl. and *Bathum* the dat. pl., as in the German BADEN. Caer Badon is an impossible Welsh name invented by antiquaries out of the A S. Bathum for the prehistoric earthwork on the hill above the city. In the last century the article was retained, the town being called The Bath, and not Bath as now.

Bathurst Island, one of the larger islands of the Arctic Archipelago, was discovered by Parry in 1819, and named after Henry Bathurst, third Earl Bathurst, the Secretary of State for the Colonies from 1812 to 1827, whose territorial name was probably derived from Bathurst, a wood in Sussex. His long tenure of office caused his name to be given to BATHURST BAY, discovered in 1818 by John Ross; CAPE BATHURST, discovered in 1826 by Dr. Richardson; and BATHURST INLET, discovered in 1821 by Franklin, all in Arctic America; as well as to BATHURST

ISLAND, Tasmania, discovered in 1838 by Stokes; BATHURST ISLAND, off the north coast of Australia, discovered in 1818 by King; BATHURST, New South Wales, so named in 1815; BATHURST, in Western Africa, at the mouth of the Gambia; and BATHURST, in BATHURST BAY, New Brunswick.

Bâton Rouge, a town on the Lower Mississippi, in Louisiana, is usually said to have taken its name from a pole, painted red, on the shore of the Mississippi, marking the boundary between two native tribes, but according to the local tradition it was from a large red cypress stem, free from branches, and resembling a giant's staff, which marked the frontier between the French settlers and the territory of the red men.

Battersea, in Surrey, belonged to St. Peter's Abbey, Westminster, and is usually supposed to be ' St. Peter's,' or ' island.' But in a spurious or doctored deed of gift by which in 693 A.D. it purported to be conveyed to St. Peter's by Agelric, Bishop of Dorchester, it already bears the name of *Batrices-ég*, where the A.S. name *Beadoríc* is confused with Patrick, whence the Domesday name *Patricesey*, ' Patrick's island.' We may compare the name of PETERSHAM, near Richmond in Surrey, called *Piteriches-ham* in an early charter, which is from the A.S. name *Peohtríc*, and of Bury St. Edmunds, formerly *Beadriches-worth* or *Beaderices-weorth*, ' Beadoric's estate.'

Battle, a town in Sussex, takes its name from Battel Abbey, erected by William the Conqueror on the hill where the so-called Battle of Hastings was fought, the high altar marking the position of Harold's standard. BATTLEFIELD, a parish in Salop, is the place where the Battle of Shrewsbury was fought in 1403.

Batum, a Russian port on the Black Sea, was the Greek *Bathys Limen*, the ' deep harbour.'

Bautzen, in Saxony, is a corruption of *Budissin*, a Slavonic name probably derived from the proper name Budise.

Bavaria is the Latinised name we use for the kingdom called Bayern or Baiern in German. About 500 A.D. the Marcomanni, a Teutonic frontier tribe, migrated hither from Bohemia, the *Baias* of the Ravenna geographer, who calls its inhabitants *Baiuvarii*. They must have called themselves Baiawaras or Baiwaras, from the name of their former home. We next hear of them as *Bawarii* or *Bavarii*, and of their land as *Baiuvaria* or *Bavaria*, which means the land of the men of Bohemia (*q.v.*).

Bayeux, in Normandy (Calvados), is believed to represent *Augustoduron*, the ' fortress of Augustus,' the chief town of the Bodiocasses of Pliny, who are identified with the Baiocasses of the Notitia. The name Baiocassis for the town is used by Ausonius; later forms are Baiocas, Baiex, and Baieux. The territory of the tribe is represented by the old diocese of Bessin (Saxones Baiocassini). The tribe-name is supposed to mean either 'great conquerors' or the 'fair-haired.'

Bayonne, at the mouth of the Adour, is a Basque name meaning the ' good haven,' from the Basque *ona*, 'good,' and the loan word *baia*, a ' haven.'

Bazas, a city in the Gironde, was the *Civitas Vasatas* of the Antonine Itinerary. The territory of the *Vasates* of Ptolemy corresponds to the modern diocese of Bazas.

Beagle Island and **Beagle Channel** were discovered by Admiral Fitzroy in the *Beagle*, during his survey of Patagonia, 1828-34. BEAGLE BAY, BEAGLE VALLEY, BEAGLE BANK, and BEAGLE'S REEF were discovered by Captain Stokes while surveying the Australian coast in the *Beagle*, 1838-39.

Bear Island, in Bathurst Inlet, was so named by Franklin in 1821, because when the provisions were nearly exhausted a bear was here found and killed. GREAT BEAR LAKE is a misleading translation of *Lac du Grand Ours*, the name given by the French trappers to one of the largest lakes in the Hudson Bay territories.

Béarn, one of the old French provinces, takes its name from a Roman town called *Beneharnum* in the Antonine Itinerary, which is supposed to be derived from the tribe-name of the Benarni.

Beaufort, the ' fine fort,' in Anjou, came in 1276 into the possession of John of Gaunt, from whom the name and title of Beaufort passed to his descendants. BEAUFORT and SOMERSET in the Cape Colony, were named at the time when Lord C. Somerset, son of the Duke of Beaufort, was Governor of the Cape. BEAUFORT ISLAND, BEAUFORT BAY, POINT BEAUFORT, and MOUNT BEAUFORT, in the Arctic Archipelago, were named after Admiral Sir Francis Beaufort, Hydrographer to the Admiralty.

Beauly Firth in Scotland, takes its name from a priory founded in the thirteenth century, and well called by the French monks *beau lieu*, the 'beautiful place,' which in Latin documents becomes *prioratus de bello loco.*

Beauvais (Oise) is a corruption of the tribe-name of the Bellovaci, the dative plural Bellovacis becoming Biauvais and then Beauvais.

Bedfordshire takes its name from the county town of Bedford, in A.S. documents successively called *Bedicanford, Bedcanford, Beadcanford, Bedanford,* and *Bedeford. Bedican* is the genitive of the A.S. personal name *Bedica.*

Bedouin is the French form of the Arabic *bedewiyyin,* the accusative of *bedewiyun,* which is the plural of *badiah* or *bedew,* which means 'one inhabiting a desert.' Bedouins is a meaningless double plural. Bedewin, the proper English form, is nearer to the Arabic than the objectionable French term Bedouin.

Bedretto, Val, in Canton Tessino, is a corruption of Betuleto, from *betuletum,* 'a birch wood.'

Beechey Island, in the Arctic Archipelago, was so named by Parry in 1819 after the lieutenant of his ship the *Hecla,* afterwards known as Sir William Beechey, in whose honour CAPE BEECHEY, POINT BEECHEY, and LAKE BEECHEY were subsequently named by Kane, Back, and Franklin.

Behar (Bahár), a province in Bengal, takes its name from the old city of BIHÁR, so called from having been the site of a *vihára* or Buddhist monastery, probably one of those founded in this district by Asoka, who became a convert to Buddhism about 257 B.C.

Behring Strait, more correctly BERING STRAIT, which divides Asia from America, was so named by Cook in honour of Vitus Bering or Behring, a Dane in the Russian service, who in 1728 was the first to traverse the strait which has received his name. Although Bering coasted through the strait on the Asiatic side, he did not sight the American shore, or even suspect its existence, though it was not more than 36 miles distant. BERING'S BAY in Alaska was so named by Cook in 1778. BERING'S SEA lies between the Aleutian Islands and Bering Strait. BERING'S ISLAND, the most westerly of the Aleutian chain, is a desolate rock on which Bering was wrecked, and on which he died in 1741, at the age of 60, of scurvy and ague. He spelt his name Bering, but Behring, an incorrect German form, is frequently employed.

Beira, a Portuguese station at the mouth of the Pungeve River in south-east Africa, is a descriptive name, meaning a 'spit of sand' in Portuguese.

Beja, a town in Portugal, is believed to be the *Pacca Julia* of the Ravenna Geographer, and Ptolemy's *Pax Julia.*

Belcher Channel, leading out of Jones' Sound, was discovered by Captain Edward Belcher in 1852-53. BELCHER ISLAND, one of the Gambier Group, and POINT BELCHER, in the Arctic Ocean, also bear his name.

Belem, more correctly NOSSA SENORA DE BELEM, is a city at the mouth of the River Para in Brazil, founded in 1616 by Francisco Caldeira. Belem is the Portuguese corruption of Bethlehem, the Brazilian name being derived from a convent near Lisbon, dedicated to St. Mary of Bethlehem. BELEM is the name of the suburb of Lisbon which surrounds this convent. The convent of St. Mary of Bethlehem in London having been appropriated for the reception of lunatics, has given us the word *bedlam,* the English analogue of the Portuguese *belem.* BEIT LAHM in Palestine preserves the old name of Beth-lehem, the 'place of bread,' from the Semitic *beth,* 'house' or 'place,' whence numerous names, such as Bethel, now BEITIN, which means the 'place of God'; Bethany, the 'place of dates,' now EL-'AZARIYEH, a corruption of Lazarieh, so called because it was the residence of Lazarus; Bethshan, now BEISAN, the 'house of rest'; Beth-horon, the 'place of caves'; and Bethsaida, the 'place of fish.'

Belfast, in Ulster, is a corruption of the Irish *Bel-feirsde,* the 'ford of the sandbank.'

Belgium, the name applied by Julius Cæsar to a portion of the territory of the Belgæ, a Celtic people, was revived to designate the kingdom separated from Holland in 1831. The meaning of the name of the Belgæ is disputed. It is not connected, as has been supposed, with that of the Irish *Fir-bolg,* but may mean the 'fighters,' or more probably it was a nickname descriptive of corpulence, from **bhelgo,* 'the swollen' (root *belg,* 'to swell'), connected with the Old Irish *bolc,* a pouch or bag, and the English verb to bulge.

Belgrade, the capital of Servia, is the 'white fortress.'

Belize, the capital of British Honduras, is a name usually explained from the French *balise,* a 'beacon,' but as the town is built on a stream called, in the

Treaty of 1783, the River Wallis or Belize, it is more probably a corruption of the name of a Scotch adventurer, Wallace or Wallis, who, in 1610, endeavoured to establish himself in Honduras. The older Spanish name of the town, Valize or Balize, would be the Spanish way of writing Wallis.

Belle Isle, the 'fair isle,' is a small island discovered and named in 1525 by Jacques Cartier, who proved Newfoundland to be an island by sailing through the narrow Strait of Belle Isle, dividing Newfoundland from Labrador, which took its name from the island. Two other islands, one near St. John's, Newfoundland, and one in Brittany, are also called Belle Isle. BELVOIR CASTLE, as he name implies, commands a beautiful view. The French name is due, as in other cases, to a religious house founded, soon after the Conquest, by a Norman knight. ISOLA BELLA, the Italian equivalent of the French Belle Isle, is the name of an arid rock in the Lago Maggiore, which was transformed into a beautiful garden in 1670. A larger island is called ISOLA MADRE, the 'mother island' of the group.

Bellowan, in Cornwall, exhibits the Cornish prefix *bel-*, which has been adduced as a proof of Phœnician occupancy, being supposed to refer to Baal. It is, however, merely the Cornish *bel*, 'a mine.' Cornwall is called *Belerion* by Posidonius, probably in reference to its tin mines.

Belton, in Lincolnshire, Rutland, and Suffolk, and Bilton in Yorkshire, are probably from the O.N. *býli*, an 'abode,' which becomes *böl* or *bel*, a 'farmhouse,' in Danish. Thus NEBEL in Denmark was formerly *Nyböl*, the 'new farmhouse.'

Beluchistan is a Persian term signifying the place or land of the Beluchs.

Belur-Tagh, or **Balar-Tagh**, a lofty range in Turkistan, is a name meaning the 'white mountain,' from the Uigur *bollur* or *bellur*, 'crystal,' and hence 'white.' (Arabic *billar*, 'cut glass,' *see* p. 316).

Benáres, locally called Banáras, is a corruption of the Sanskrit name *Váránasi*. The popular etymology explains the name from the two rivers the Varana (now the Barna) and the Asi. It has also been conjectured that the name means 'having the best water,' the sacred water from Benáres being sent in bottles to all parts of India.

Bencoolen or **Benkulen**, a town and province on the west coast of Sumatra, which belonged to England from 1685 to 1826, when it was ceded to Holland in exchange for Malacca. The name is a corruption of the Malay *Bang-Kulon* or *Bangkaülu*, 'the west coast.'

Bendameer is a popular name for the River Kur, anciently the Araxes. Properly speaking it is the name not of the river but of a dam across it, which was constructed in 965 A.D. by a Persian prince, and hence called *Band-i-Amir*, the 'Prince's Dam.' The Persian word *band* (Sanskrit *bandh*), often spelt *bund*, is used to signify any artificial dam, dyke, or causeway.

Bender, a town in Bessarabia, is a Perso-Turkic name primarily meaning a 'harbour,' and hence a 'market.' BENDER-EREKLI, on the Black Sea, represents the port of the Greek city of Heraclea. The word occurs in the names of several coast towns on the Persian Gulf.

Bendigo, a town in the Australian colony of Victoria, famous for its rich gold diggings, originally Bandicote Creek, came to be called Bendigo from the nickname of William Thompson, a celebrated Nottingham pugilist. He was one of three boys born at a birth who were nicknamed Shadrach, Meshach, and Abednego. William Thompson's first challenge in *Bell's Life* in 1835 was signed 'Abednego of Nottingham.' The name of the place was afterwards officially changed to Sandhurst, but it has now returned to Bendigo.

Benevento, a port in Italy, was the Roman *Beneventum*, 'good entrance.' We are told by Pliny that the older name was Maleventum (supposed to have been a corruption of Maluentum, 'rich in apples'), which, being considered to be an inauspicious name, was changed to Beneventum.

Bengál, an Indian province, is the English form of Bangála, the native name of a city near Chittagong, now washed away by the Brahmaputra. According to the Indian legend, Bangála, a corruption of *Bangálaya*, was the 'home of Banga,' a prince who appears in the Mahábhárata, and to whose portion it fell. Banga is probably only the eponymus of Bangála.

Benguela, in Western Africa, means 'defence' in the Buneda language. It has also been explained as a corruption of *bayuella*, 'highland.'

Beni Hasan, 170 miles above Cairo, is the village of 'the children of Hasan.' The Arabic tribal prefix Beni is common.

Berbice, the capital of British Guiana, was founded in 1796 at the mouth of a river of the same name.

Beren Eylant, or 'Bear Island,' midway between Spitzbergen and the North Cape, was discovered in 1596 by Barentz, in an attempt to make the passage to China by way of the North Pole. The name originated from a chase after a polar bear, which was killed by the sailors after a combat of two hours. In 1603 it was rediscovered by Cherry, an English whaling captain, and hence it is sometimes called CHERRY ISLE.

Berens Isles, in Coronation Gulf, were discovered by Franklin in 1821, and named after the Governor of the Hudson's Bay Company.

Beresina, an affluent of the Dnieper, may be regarded as the northern portion of that river. The breaking of the bridge over the Beresina in November 1812 was the cause of the overwhelming disaster to the French army in the retreat from Moscow. Beresina is a corruption of *Borysthenes,* the name applied by the Greeks to the DNIEPER, which again is a corruption of the Scythian name *Danapris,* of which Borysthenes is believed to be a sort of Greek translation. It is curious that the Greek name should have adhered to the northern course of the river, and the Scythian name to its lower portion.

Berg, a common element in German names, is usually from the O.H.G. *berg,* a 'hill.' There are 359 names in Germany which are proved by the old forms to be from this stem, which is liable to be mixed with the stem *burg* (O.H.G. *burug*), 'a castle' or fortified place, to which 223 German names are known to belong. There are 38 places called simply Berg or Bergen, such as BERG on the Lower Rhine ; BERGEN OP ZOOM in Holland, on the River Zoom : and BERGEN in Norway, formerly Bergenhuus, so called from the seven peaks which surround it.

Berkeley, in Gloucestershire, appears in A.S. charters as *Bercled,* 'the birch field.'

Berkhampstead, Great and **Little,** Herts. The first syllable of this name is usually supposed to be the A.S. *beorc,* 'a birch tree,' but the form *Beorh-hamstede,* which is found in an A.S. charter, shows that it is the 'homestead on the hill.'

Berkshire is called *Bearuc-scir, Bearroc-scir,* and *Barruc-scir* in the A.S. Chronicle, *Bearruc-scir* or *Bearwuc-scir* by Asser, and *Bearruc-scyr* or *Baroc-scir* in A.S. charters. The meaning of the name is doubtful. Brompton, who was abbot of Jervaulx in the thirteenth century, tells us that Baroc-scir was so called from a certain polled oak (bare oak) in Windsor Forest, at which the shire-mote assembled, an etymology repeated in the next century by Higden in his Polychronicon : *Barocshira quae sic denominata à quadam nuda quercu in Foresta de Windesora* ; and Asser, who wrote in the ninth century, tells us that the name is from a forest (Windsor Forest) called *Berroc,* in which box-trees grew. In this case *bearwuc* might be a diminutive from the A.S. *bearu,* a 'grove.' Ettmüller takes *bearuc* as equivalent to *bearovic,* 'vicus saltosus,' an impossible etymology, as well as that from A.S. *beorc,* a 'birch-tree,' or from the A.S. *bearug,* which means a 'barrow-pig' or porker, so called because fed on the mast and acorns in a *bearu,* 'a wood, wooded hill, or barrow.' Professor Rhys offers a conjectural derivation from the tribe-name of the pre-Saxon inhabitants, the Bibroci, or 'beavers' who have left their name in the Hundred of BRAY.

Berlin, the capital of Prussia, is a name the meaning of which has been much discussed, but with small definite result. Celtic, Slavonic, and Teutonic etymologies have been proposed, in addition to the popular but impossible derivation from the name of the Margrave Albert the Bear, which has been supported by the fact that a bear appears in the city arms. The Celtic etymologies, 'small linn' or lake, and that proposed by Mahn, 'heath' or 'bush,' may be rejected, as well as the Teutonic etymology from *brühl,* a 'marsh.' The name is probably Wendish, either from *berle,* 'uncultivated ground,' or, as Krebs thinks, from *barlin,* a 'shelter' or 'place of refuge,' or, according to Klöden, an 'enclosure' or 'field,' while Vilovski suggests *brljina,* a 'pool,' which conforms to the local conditions.

Bermudas, or **Somers Islands,** in the North Atlantic, were discovered, it is believed, by Amerigo Vespucci in 1498, probably on St. Bernard's Day, August 20th, whence the early name of the Archipelago of San Bernardo. They owe their name of Bermudas to Juan Bermudez, who, on a voyage from Spain to Cuba with a cargo of hogs in 1522 or 1527, was shipwrecked on an island of the group. To the wreck of Admiral Sir George Somers in 1609 we owe the name Somers Islands, which by popular etymology has been corrupted into the Summer Islands. This shipwreck probably suggested Shakespeare's play of *The Tempest*, in which he names ' the still vexed Bermoothes.' *The Tempest* appeared in 1610, a few months after the publication of Jourdan's account of the wreck of Sir George Somers' ship, the *Sea Venture*, in a tempest off ' the Bermudas, otherwise called the Ile of Divels.' ST. GEORGE'S, which was the seat of government till it was removed to Hamilton, is the place where Sir George died in 1612.

Bern (in French BERNE) is a Swiss canton which takes its name from its chief town, which grew up round a castle built in 1191 by Duke Berchtold v. of Zähringen. The name Berne appears in 1224 on a seal of the town. Not improbably Berchtold gave the place the name of Berne in memory of Dietrich of Berne (Verona), a favourite hero of Alamannic poetry. Another theory as to the meaning of the name refers it to the Romansch word *brena*, ' bush ' or ' forest,' which is believed to be the source of the names BERNEGG and BERNBODEN. According to the local legend, the town was named from a bear, the first animal killed in a hunting expedition in an oak forest on the site of the town. Hence a bear rampant on a gold field has been taken as the heraldic shield of the city, and a tame bear is always kept in a cave, like the wolf at Rome.

Berncastel, on the Mosel, is proved by the old form Berencastel, which dates from 1036, to be from a personal name (O.H.G. *bero*, a ' bear ').

Bernoulli, Cape, in South Australia, was named by Baudin in 1802 in honour of Bernoulli the mathematician.

Berri or **Berry**, one of the old French provinces, is a corruption of the tribe-name of the Bituriges, a name meaning, according to d'Arbois de Jubainville, ' always kings.' Zeuss explains the name as *semper dominantes*, ' ever ruling,' or as the powerful or wide rulers. The city of BOURGES, in the department of the Cher, also a corruption of Bituriges, was the old capital of Berri.

Berwick-on-Tweed appears in the oldest documents as *Beorwic*, and in the twelfth century as *Berewic*. The first form points to *beorh-wic*, ' hill village,' an appropriate etymology, and the second to *bere-wic*, a term frequently used in Domesday to denote a ' barton,' ' grange,' or ' barn.' The form Abevicum, which is found in Latin documents, points to Aber-wick as an early conjectural etymo-

logy, just as BERRIEW in Wales, at the mouth of the River Rhiw, is a corruption of Aber-Rhiw, and BARMOUTH of Aber-Maw.

Besançon, in Franche Comté, the capital of the Doubs department, represents Vesontio or Visontion, the chief town of the Sequani. It is called Besantio by Ammianus Marcellinus, and in the time of Charlemagne became Bissancion, a corruption of *Besontionem*.

Bessarabia is a Russian province on the Danube. The district was occupied in the seventh century by a Slavonic or Turkic tribe called the Bessi, and there seems to have been a Wallachian dynasty called Bessaraba, from whom the principality is said to have been named.

Bessemer is an iron smelting town in Alabama, of 40,000 inhabitants. In 1887 the site was overrun by primeval forest. It has been appropriately named from the inventor of the modern process for making steel. Two other iron-making towns, one in Michigan, founded in 1884, the other in Virginia, founded in 1890, also bear the name of Bessemer.

Beverley, in Yorkshire, is a perplexing name. It appears in the Chronicle as *Beoferlic*, and later as Beverlith, Beverlea, Beverlac, and Beforlac. The A.S. names might be explained as the beavers' field, pool, or stream. (A.S. *led*, a ' field,' *lacu* a ' pool,' *lagu* a ' stream '; cf. O.N. *læki*, a ' brook '), but the uncertainty of the early forms lends probability to the theory which identifies Beverley with the Roman *Petuaria*, whose British name may have been *Pedwarllech*, denoting the ' four stones ' which marked the boundaries of the settlement ; and *Pedwarllech*, by folk-etymology, might have become Beoferlea or Beforlac, ' the beaver's field or pool.' (cf. p. 374.)

Bewcastle, Cumberland, is so called from the castle erected soon after the conquest by Bueth, lord of Gilsland.

Bex is a town in Canton Vaud. The Roman name Botiacum, which we find as late as 574, is replaced in 600 A.D. by *Bacus Villa*, a Romansch formation from the German *bach*, a ' brook,' signifying the ' village on the brook,' now called the Arvençon. Later forms are Villa Bejo and Bexium.

Beyrout, more correctly BEIRUT, a town on the Syrian coast, called Berotha in the time of Rameses II., is the Phœnician *beroth*, ' the wells,' or rather the ' cisterns,' the plural of *beer*, ' a well,' which we have in BEERSHEBA.

Bhamo, a town in Burma, is a corruption of the Shan name *Manmaw*, ‘pottery village.’

Bhartpur, or **Bhurtpore,** a native state in Rajputana, takes its name from the chief town, Bhartpur, a corruption of Bharat-pur, ‘the town of Bhárata,’ brother of Rama, one of the ancient legendary kings of India.

Bhaulpur, or **Bháwalpur,** in the Punjab, is the capital of a feudatory state of the same name, is the ‘town of Baháwal,’ a Khan of the Dáúdputras.

Bheels (Bhíls), a pre-Aryan Indian people, are named from their weapon, the *billa* or ‘bow.’

Bhutan, or **Bhotan,** an independent state in the Himalayas, is properly *Bhotant.* ‘the end of Thibet,’ from *Bhot*, the local name of Thibet and *anta*, ‘end.’

Bibury, Gloucestershire, is *Beage's burh*, as we learn from a charter executed between 721 and 743 by which the place was bestowed on the Church at Worcester after the death of a certain Comes Leppa and of his daughter Beage. On the margin of the charter there is a later note in which the place is identified as *Beaganbyrig*, showing that it had been possessed by the daughter long enough to acquire her name.

Bicester, near Oxford, formerly *Burenceaster* and then *Burnacester*, has been supposed to be the chester of Bishop Biren, but was more probably named from the small River Bure on which it stands.

Bièvre, near Laon, probably the *Bibrax* of Cæsar, is from the Gaulish *bebros*, ‘a beaver.’ From the same source we have Bibracte, the Gaulish name of the place called by the Romans Augustodunum, now AUTUN.

Bigorre, in the Pyrenees, bears the tribe-name of the *Bigerriones* of Cæsar, who are the *Begerri* of Pliny. Their chief city was *Turba*, now TARBES.

Biscay, Bay of, takes its name from the Spanish Province of BISCÂYA or VISCÂYA, which means the land of the Basques or Vasks. The Roman writers called them Vascones, whence we obtain the medieval names GASCONS and GASCONY (*q.v.*). The name BASQUE or VASK is believed to be the Basque word *vasok*, ‘man.’ This is to be preferred to W. von Humboldt’s derivation from the Basque *basoa*, ‘forest,’ whence *baso-coa*, ‘belonging to the forest.’ The Basques now call themselves Euscaldunac, the ‘speakers,’

whence the technical term Euscarian for the language of the Basques.

Bismarck, a small town in the Prussian Altmark, called *Biscopesmark* (Bishop’s march) in 1209, claims the honour of giving a patronymic to the great German Chancellor. CAPE BISMARCK, a grim headland on the eastern coast of Greenland, was discovered in 1869 by Captain Koldewey in the ship *Germania.* This was the furthest point reached on this coast till 1892, when the United States Expedition, under Lieut. Peary, followed the coast northwards as far as lat. 81° 37′ N. Here on Independence Day, July 4th, a large bay was discovered, to which the name of INDEPENDENCE BAY has been given.

Bissagos Islands, near Sierra Leone, bear the name of Bissague, who was the native chief when the islands were discovered by the Portuguese.

Bister, in Shetland names, is a corruption of the Norse *Bu-stadr*, a ‘dwelling-place,’ the first element being the *-by* in Kirby and Derby, and the second the *-ster* in Leinster and Ulster. We have in the Shetlands such names as KIRKABISTER, ‘the dwelling by the church’; KELDABISTER, ‘the dwelling by the well’; and SYMBISTER, ‘the dwelling with a view.’

Blackall, a town in Queensland, bears the name of Colonel Blackall, the governor of the colony from 1868 to 1870.

Blackfeet, a North American tribe, form the westernmost branch of the great Algonkin race. Blackfoot is a translation of the almost unpronounceable native name *Cuskoetch-waw-thessetuck.*

Black Forest, the English translation of the German name SCHWARZWALD, refers to the dark pines which cover the hills.

Black Sea, a translation of *Mauri Thalassa*, the modern Greek name, may refer to its storms, contrasted with the cloudless skies of the *Aspri Thalassa* (Mar Bianco or White Sea), as the eastern part of the Mediterranean was called. The old Greek name Axine, the ‘inhospitable’ sea, being of evil omen, is believed to have been changed to Euxine, or ‘hospitable,’ when the coasts became surrounded by Greek colonies.

Blackwater is the name of a river in County Cork, and of another in Ulster. Both of them are still called in Irish Avonmore or Owenmore, the ‘great river.’ The Blackwater is frequently called by early Anglo-Irish writers the ‘Broadwater,’ a sort of translation of Avonmore.

Blair-Atholl is 'the field of Athol.' The Gaelic word *blair* or *blár*, which is common in Scotch names, means a plain or field, and in the later Ossianic poetry usually denotes a field of battle. BLARNEY, near Cork, which contains the blarney.stone, is a diminutive of *blár* (Irish *Blárna*, the 'little field'). From the Scotch surname Blair (which is equivalent to the English surname Field) we have PORT BLAIR, the chief settlement in the Andaman Islands, which were first surveyed in 1789 by Lieutenant Blair of the Indian Navy.

Blantyre, a settlement of the Presbyterian missionaries in the Shire Highlands, was named after Livingstone's birthplace, Blantyre in Lanark.

Blenheim Palace, near Oxford, was built by Parliament for the Duke of Marlborough, and named in commemoration of the decisive battle fought on August 13th, 1704, at the village of Blindheim Höchstadt. The capital of the New Zealand province of Marlborough has received the appropriate name of BLENHEIM.

Blida, in Algeria, is a diminutive, from the Arabic *belad*, 'a place' or 'town.'

Block Island, near the mouth of the Connecticut River, bears the name of Adrian Block, a Dutch sailor who in 1614, when his ship had been burnt at Manhattan Island, the future site of New York, built a sixteen-ton yacht, of timber cut in the island, in which he sailed through Long Island Sound, and after discovering Block Island, finally reached Massachusetts Bay.

Bloemfontein, or JAN BLOMS FONTEIN, the capital of the Orange Free State, bears the name of the first Boer settler.

Bloody Falls, the lowest cataract on the Coppermine River, was so named by Hearne in 1770 on account of a massacre of the Eskimos by the Chippewyan Indians who accompanied him. BLOODY BAY, in Egmont Island, was so called because of a native attack on the crew of Captain Carteret's cutter in 1767.

Bludin, in European Turkey, is a corruption of the Roman name *Plotinopolis*, so called in honour of Plotina, wife of Trajan.

Boavista, one of the Cape Verd Islands, was the 'good sight' seen by three caravels which, sailing from Lisbon to Senegambia in 1486, were driven out to sea by a tempest, and on the third day of the storm sighted land, which the sailors appropriately called Boavista.

Bocca Tigris is the name applied to the estuary of the Canton River. It appears to be an inaccurate reproduction of the Portuguese *Boca do Tigre*, which is a translation of the Chinese name Hu-Mén, 'Tiger Gate.' The famous BOGUE FORTS are the defences of the Boca or 'mouth' of the Canton River, Bogue being an English corruption of *Boca*.

Boden See, the German name of the lake which the French call Lac de Constance, is derived from *Bodoma*, now BODMAN, a castle of the Carolingian Emperors, built in a hollow between two hills at the northwest end of the lake. Near Bodman is a place called the Bodenwald. The name Bodoma is probably from the O.H.G. *bodam* (German *boden*, English *bottom*), which is used in Switzerland to denote a flat plain or meadow bottom. The lake was called Lacus Podamicus as early as 890, and in 905 we have *ad lacum Bodinse.* Its older name was Lacus Brigantinus, from the Celtic tribe of the Brigantes or 'highlanders,' who have left their name in the town of BREGENTZ (*q.v.*), the *Bregantium* of the Romans.

Bodo means 'peaceful.' Hence H. M. Stanley gave the name of FORT BODO to the station which he constructed in 1888 near the Albert Nyanza.

Boëo, Capo, the extreme western point of Sicily, preserves a mutilated fragment of the Roman name Lilybæum (now Marsala, *q.v.*) which was derived from the Phœnician *Lilybe*, the 'station' of the Carthaginian fleet.

Bœotia, the chief plain in Greece, is the 'land of cattle,' a name which may have given rise to the legend that Europa was discovered by Cadmus in Bœotia under the form of a cow.

Bogotá, or **Santa Fé De Bogotá,** the federal capital of the United States of Columbia, bears the name of Bagotta, a native chief who in 1538 was here encountered and vanquished by the Spaniards under Gonzalez Ximenes de Quesada, who called the place Santa Fé from his own birthplace.

Bohemia is the Latinised name of the Austrian crown-land which the Germans now call Böhmen, a corruption of Bö-heim, the name officially used till the close of the eighteenth century. It is called *Boihaemum* or *Boihemum* the 'home of the Boii,' by Tacitus and Ptolemy, the inhabitants being called *Bohemi* or

Boemanni. Our form Bohemia is comparatively recent, Fynes Moryson in 1617 calling it Bohmerland. The name is derived from the Boii, the 'terrible' ones, a Celtic tribe who were driven out of Italy by the Romans in the second century B.C. In the first century A.D. the 'home of the Boii' was occupied by the Marcomanni, a Teutonic tribe. At the beginning of the sixth century the Marcomanni, then called Bohemi, moved into BAVARIA (*q.v.*) to which they gave a name derived from their residence in the old 'home of the Boii,' and Bohemia was occupied by the Slavonic Czechs, but still retains the name of its pre-Teutonic conquerors.

Boileau, Cape, in Tasman's Land, West Australia, was named in 1803 by Baudin after the French poet Boileau (1636-1705).

Bois le Duc, in Brabant, is the French translation of the Flemish name 's Hertogenbosch, 'the Duke's wood,' so called because it was a hunting seat of the Dukes of Brabant.

Bojador, a prominent cape in Western Africa, first rounded by Gil Eannes in 1433, was appropriately named Cabo Bojador, the 'cape that juts out' (Portuguese *bojar,* 'to jut out').

Bokhara, the capital of the Khanate of the same name, means 'town of learning,' literally the 'treasury of science.' It is regarded as the centre of Mahommedan erudition, and possesses numerous mosques and colleges. The inhabitants are called by the Uzbeks, who are the ruling race, either *Sarts,* which applies to settled traders, or *Tajiks,* who are the aborigines.

Bolivia, one of the South American republics, formerly called Alto-Peru, 'Upper Peru,' was renamed in honour of the dictator, Simon Bolivar, who, after a struggle lasting for fourteen years, from 1811 to 1825, freed Peru from the Spanish yoke. In honour of the 'Liberator,' one of the states of Columbia and one of the states of Venezuela are called Bolivar.

Bolsena, in Central Italy, preserves the ancient Etruscan name Volsenio.

Bolton is a large manufacturing town near Manchester. The name is common in the North of England. In Yorkshire alone there are eight places so called, all of which appear in Domesday as *Bodeltone* or *Bodeltune,* which denotes a *tún* or 'enclosure' containing a 'house or dwelling,' generally of timber (A.S. *bótl*). So NEW-BOTTLE, the 'new building,' is from *botle,*

dat. sing. of *botl.* In Germany, *büttel,* a 'dwelling,' is a common suffix, as in WOLFENBÜTTEL. In Old Saxon it takes the form *-budil.*

Boma, or **Embomma,** is a trading post 65 miles from the mouth of the Congo. The word *boma* means a 'palisade,' and the name is applied to any village or collection of huts so fortified.

Bombay. The conjectural etymology from the Portuguese *bom-bahia,* the 'good bay,' is impossible, because while *bahia* is feminine, *bom* is masculine, and hence the Portuguese name would have been *Boa-bahia.* The oldest forms of the name, *Maimbi, Maimbai, Mombaim,* and *Bombaim,* are derived from a great temple dedicated to Devi, wife of Siva, who was worshipped by the name of *Maht-má,* the 'great mother,' a title which became *Maimbái* or *Mumbai* in the Maratha dialect.

Bombay Hook, New York, is an English adaptation of the Dutch name *Boompties Hoeck,* 'tree-point.'

Bon, Cape, at the north-eastern corner of Tunis, is apparently a Spanish name meaning the 'good cape.' The Arabic name is *Ras Adar.*

Bona, in Algeria, is from an oblique case of *Hippo,* 'the walled town,' on whose site it stands.

Bonavista Bay, Newfoundland, takes its name from CAPE BONAVISTA, one of the eastern capes of Newfoundland, where John Cabot, the discoverer of North America, is said to have made his landfall on June 24th, 1497, but as June 24th is St. John's Day, it has been urged that St. John's, further to the south-east, was his real landfall, and that the name Bonavista marks the landfall of Corte Real.

Bonchurch, in the Isle of Wight, is an abbreviated name of the same class as Boston (*q.v.*). The patron saint being St. Boniface, Bonchurch is an obvious corruption of Boniface-Church.

Bonifacio, Strait of, separating Corsica and Sardinia, is so called from the Corsican fort of San Bonifacio, which guards the passage.

Bonn, a city on the Rhine, preserves the name of a Roman castrum on the site, which is called Bonna by Tacitus. The word *bona* is believed to be Celtic, probably meaning a 'town,' as it enters into the composition of such names as Colobona or Equabona. VIENNA was anciently Vindo-bona, which was afterwards changed to Julio-bona. LILLEBONNE, near the mouth of the Seine, is a corruption of Julio-bona, which in medieval times became Illebona, from which Lillebonne was formed by prefixing the article. RAAB, in Hungary, on the River Raab, is a corruption of the Roman name Arrabona, the 'town on the Arra.' The Roman name of TROYES was Augusto-bona, afterwards Augusta Trecorum; while BOLOGNA, in Cisalpine Gaul, and BOULOGNE (*q.v.*) are both corruptions of Bononia. In the Saxon Chronicle Boulogne is called Bune or Bunne. In French charters of the ninth and tenth centuries *bonnarium* or *bunnoarium* frequently occurs in the sense of an enclosed place, and according to Valesius, *bonna, lingua Gallica, limitem ac terminum significat.* Holder derives the word from the Celtic **bau-nos,* 'built,' and compares the Welsh *bon,* a 'foundation,' and the Irish *bun-ait,* a 'dwelling' or 'habitation,' where the suffix *-ait* means a 'place. (*See* Ratisbon.)

Booby Island, in Torres Strait, was so named from the immense number of boobies, *Pelicanus sula,* frequenting it.

Boothia Felix, in Arctic America, is a large peninsula in which the North Magnetic Pole is situated. It was named after Sir Felix Booth, a wealthy and public-spirited London distiller, who provided funds for the expedition of John and James Ross (1829-1833), which led to its discovery. BOOTHIA GULF, FELIX HARBOUR, POINT BOOTH, BOOTHIA ISTHMUS, BOOTH ISLANDS, and BOOTH SOUND were also named after him, and BROWN ISLAND and ELIZABETH HARBOUR after his sisters, Mrs. Brown and Miss Elizabeth Booth.

Bordeaux, a chief town of the Bituriges, was the Roman Burdigala. It is the capital of the district formerly called the BORDELAIS, which is an obvious corruption of Pagus Burdigalensis. The name Bordeaux cannot be so easily explained, as it cannot be derived directly from Burdigala, but may have originated in the medieval name Burdegalis. In Low Latin *bordigala* signifies a 'fish tank,' and we learn from Ausonius that a small stream formed a tidal pool or dock. The popular punning etymology makes it the town on the 'brink of the water,' *au bord des eaux.*

Borneo is a Portuguese corruption of *Bruné, Bruni, Brunai, Burni,* or *Burné,* originally the Malay name of the largest city in the north-western part of the island, which became the capital of the Sultanate

now called Brunei, a name extended to denote the whole island.

Bornholm, an island in the Baltic, is called *Burgendaland* in the A.S. translation of Orosius. In 1245 the name becomes *Burgunder Holm,* the 'island of the Burgundians,' of which Bornholm is a corruption.

Bornu is a district in the Soudan, east of Lake Tchad. After the deluge, according to a local legend, the ends of the rainbow rested on the mountains of Bornu, and the name is popularly held to mean 'the land (*bar*) of Noah.'

Bosnia takes its name from the River Bosna, a tributary of the Save. The capital, BOSNA SERAI, is the 'palace on the Bosna.'

Bosphorus would mean 'ox-ford' (*Bosporos*) in Greek. According to the Greek myth, Io, in the form of a heifer, swam across the strait from Asia to Europe. It is possible that the name may have originated from the myth, but it is more probable that it is an assimilated Greek form of some earlier barbarian name.

Boston, Massachusetts, was a Puritan settlement, founded in 1630. The settlers landed first at Charlestown on the River Charles, and then crossed to a place which they called Trimountain, now TREMONT, from three hills, now called Windmill Hill, Beacon Hill, and Fort Hill. On September 17th, 1630, a court was held at which it was determined that the settlement should be called Boston, doubtless because three of the leading settlers, Johnson, Hough, and Leverett came from Boston in Lincolnshire.

Boston, Lincolnshire, formerly *Icanho,* is a corruption of *Botolph's tun,* so called from the great monastery dedicated to St. Botolph, who, in the seventh century, was one of the apostles of the East Angles.

Bosworth, Leicestershire, A.S. *Bosuurth* and *Bosuirth,* denotes a *worth* or 'small estate' on which stood a *boose* (A.S. *bos*), a dialect word meaning a 'cow-stall' or 'ox-stall.' It cannot be the 'estate of Bosa,' as it has been usually explained, as that would have been *Bosanworth* in A.S., like BOSHAM, Sussex (A.S. *Bosanham*). BOSCOMB, Wilts, A.S., *Botescumb,* is also from a proper name.

Botany Bay was discovered by Cook in 1770, and so named because 400 new plants were found by Banks and Solander, the naturalists of the expedition, during a stay of less than three weeks.

Bothnia, Gulf of, takes its name from Botten, a district partly in Sweden and partly in Finland, at the head of the Gulf. The Swedish word *botten* (O.N. *botn*, German *boden*, English *bottom*) denotes the end of anything, especially the head of a bay. Bothnia is the Latinised form, first used by Olaus Magnus in his book *De Gentibus Septentrionalibus*.

Botocudos, a name derived from the Portuguese *botoque*, a 'stopper' or 'bottle cork,' was given to the natives of the Brazilian coast on account of their practice of distending the lower lip by the insertion of bones or wooden plugs. Their neighbours the GUARANIS are the 'brave' men.

Botzen, a town in the Tyrol, represents the Roman *Pons Drusi*. The old forms Pozen, Poszen, Pauzana, Bauzan, and Bozan, suggest the possibility that Botzen may be a corruption of *ad pontem*.

Bougainville Island and **Bougainville Strait,** in the Salomon Group, were discovered by Mendaña in 1567, and rediscovered in 1768 by Bougainville, the first Frenchman who circumnavigated the globe (1766-69). CAPE BOUGAINVILLE, in Tasman's Land, also commemorates his name.

Boulogne, the Itius Portus of Cæsar, was called *Bononia* by the Emperor Constantine, possibly from *Bononia*, now BOLOGNA, in Italy. In the ninth century Bononia became Bolonia. (*See* Bonn.)

Boune County and **Bouneville,** Missouri, were named from Daniel Boone, one of the pioneer trappers and backwoodsmen of the West, who went from Kentucky to Missouri in 1794, when Missouri was a Spanish province.

Bounty Islands, a New Zealand group, were discovered in 1788 by Bligh in the ship *Bounty*. CAPE BOUNTY in Melville Island was so named by Parry in 1819 because his officers and crew were here enabled to claim the bounty of £5000 voted by Parliament to those who should first reach 110° west longitude. BOUNTIFUL ISLAND, one of the Wellesley group in the Gulf of Carpentaria, was so named by Flinders in 1802, because of an abundant supply of turtle obtained by his men, who had been long without fresh provisions.

Bourbon, the chief town of the Bourbonnais, possesses hot springs, which were dedicated by the Gauls to their healing Deity, the sun-god Bormo or Borvo, identified with Apollo by the Romans, who called the place *Aquæ Borvonis*. A castle on a rock above the town gave a name to the Bourbon dynasty, from whom the ISLE DE BOURBON, now usually called Réunion, and other places have been named. Several other places in France with hot springs are called BOURBON or BOURBONNE.

Bourges, the capital of the old French province of Berry (*q.v.*) was the chief city of the Bituriges. The Roman name was Avaricum, but in Gregory of Tours we find the name *Biturigas*, of which Bourges is a corruption.

Bowen, Port, in Queensland, was discovered by Flinders in 1802, and named after James Bowen, one of the commissioners of the navy. His name is also borne by CAPE BOWEN in Baffin's Bay, by PORT BOWEN in Regent's Inlet, and by BOWEN STRAIT on the north shore of Australia. The BOWEN DOWNS and the town of BOWEN in Queensland were named after Sir George Bowen, first Governor of Queensland, and grandnephew of James Bowen.

Bowery is one of the few surviving Dutch names in New York, having been the *bouwerie* or 'farm' of the Dutch Governor Stuyvesant.

Boyne, a river in Ireland, is called by Ptolemy, *Buvinda*, 'the white cow,' a name which must contain some mythological reference. According to Professor Rhys, Buvinda was a river goddess, who, in Irish mythology, was the wife of the sea-god Nodens or Nuada. We may compare the common Irish name INISBOFIN, which means the 'island of the white cow.'

Brabant, a province in Flanders, is called Bracbantum in a document of the eighth century. It means the 'ploughed district' or 'arable land' from *bracha*, land newly 'broken' up for tillage, and *bant* a district or gau.

Brahmaputra, or less correctly Burrampooter, is a mythological name meaning the 'offspring of Brahma,' given by the Hindoos to the largest affluent of the Ganges. In Upper Assam it is called LOHIT, 'the red' river ; in Tibet, SANPU, or TSANGBO-CHU, 'the pure water,' from *tsangbo*, ' pure.'

Brancaster, in Norfolk, and BRAMPTON, also in Norfolk, a place which abounds in Roman remains, are rival sites claiming to represent the Roman station of Brannodunum. BRAMPTON in Cumberland has been supposed to be the Roman Bremenium.

Brandenburg, a Prussian province, derives its name from a castle built on an island in the Havel. The bishopric dates from 945. The name was afterwards extended to the town, and then to the mark, which subsequently became a Margravate and Electorate. The name Brandenburg, which means the 'forest fortress,' is a corruption of the Slavonic *Brennibor,* from *bor,* 'wood' or 'forest,' and *brenny,* a 'shelter,' 'protection,' or 'strong place.'

Bras d'or, the 'arm of gold,' is an arm of the sea which divides the island of Cape Breton, in Nova Scotia, into two peninsulas.

Bravo, Rio, the 'fierce river,' dividing Texas from Mexico, is also called Rio Grande del Norte.

Bray, a town in Wicklow, called Bree in old records, received its name from Brayhead, which rises 793 feet above the sea. The name is from the Old Irish *bri* or *brigh* (Gaulish *briga*), a 'hill.'

Brazil was discovered accidentally in 1500 by Pedro Alvarez de Cabral, who, sailing from Lisbon for India with twelve ships, was driven from his course, and reached the Brazilian coast on Easter Eve, at a place he called Pascoal. Bad weather arising, he took refuge in a neighbouring harbour which he named PORTO SEGURO, where on May 1st, the festival of the Invention of the Cross, mass was celebrated under a tree at the top of which a large wooden cross was fixed, and the country, which was supposed to be one of the Antilles, received the name of Ilha da Vera Cruz. Three years later Vespucci discovered that it was not an island, and the name was changed to Terra da Santa Cruz. If Columbus had not sailed in 1492, America would thus have been discovered eight years later. Before Cabral's voyage, the name Brazil is found on maps attached to an imaginary island in the Atlantic to the west of Ireland. We learn from William of Worcester that in 1480 John Jay of Bristol despatched two ships to search for the island of Brazil. There is no proof that the name was transferred to the land discovered by Cabral ; all we know is that as early as 1532 the country became known as the Terra do Brazil, a valuable red dye called *brazil,* from the Portuguese *braza,* 'live coal,' being obtained from the wood of the *Cæsalpina brasiliensis,* or brazil-wood tree, which the Spaniards had previously procured from Haiti. The origin of the name being forgotten, out of Terra do Brazil, 'land of the Brazil,' a nominative O

Brazil was constructed, and this became in English the Brazil, the Brazils, and finally Brazil, which strictly means the dyewood and not the country. The German name Brazilien is not open to this objection ; a corresponding correct English form would be Brazilia, or Brazil Land.

Breadalbane is the *bragat* or 'breast' of Alban—as DRUMALBAN is the *drum* or 'back' of Alban. BRAEMAR, the *braigh* or 'upper part' of Mar, preserves the name of the great Earldom of Mar, to which CROMAR also belonged. At the time of the rising of 1715 Braemar was still the castle of the Earls of Mar.

Brecon or **Brecknock** are English forms of the Welsh name *Brycheiniog,* derived, according to the tradition, from the name of Brychan, a Welsh prince.

Bregaglia, Val, north of the Lake of Como, is usually said to be a corruption of the Latin Prægallia, so called because it lay in front of Gallia Cisalpina. But the old form Vallis Bergallia, which occurs in 1036, points to the Italian *berbicaglia,* from the Low-Latin *berbicaria,* a 'sheepfold,' as the source of the name.

Breisgau, or **The Breisgau,** a district in Baden, was called in the eighth century Brisagowe, which means the 'district of the breach,' either because it was liable to be flooded by a breach in the Rhine embankment, or because the river here 'breaks' into several channels.

Bremen, anciently *Bremun* or *Bremon,* is the dative plural of *bram* or *bräm* (English *brim*), which means 'wave, flood, sea.' Bremen means, therefore, 'at the waves,' or 'by the sea-shore.' BREMERHAVEN, the new 'harbour of Bremen,' was founded in 1830 on the Lower Weser.

Brentford, Middlesex, is the ford over the River Brent, which here joins the Thames. The A.S. name was Bregentford, Brægentford, Bregantford, or Bragentford, and as there was here a ford over the Thames it is possible that, as in other cases, a River Brent may have been invented to explain the name Brentford. Brigant, as a British name, would mean the hill-country.

Brent Knoll, in Somerset, rising above the villages of EAST BRENT and SOUTH BRENT, is the 'steep knoll' (A.S. *brant,* 'steep'). But BRENTWOOD, Essex, is probably the 'burnt wood,' and not the 'steep wood.'

Brescia, the chief town of the Cenomani, a Celtic tribe, was the *Brixia* of Livy. Old Celtic *brix,* a 'hill.'

Breslau, the capital of Silesia, is called *Wrozlawa* in 1018. The city arms are those of Wratislaw, king of Bohemia, by whom, according to the local legend or tradition, the town was founded.

Briançon, in the Hautes-Alpes, is a corruption of the old name *Brigantium*, which was the chief town of the Brigiani or ' hillmen' (Gaulish *briga*, ' a hill'). BRIENZ, in Canton Bern, which gives a name to the Brienzer See or Lake of Brienz, takes its name from the tribe of the Brigantii or 'hill-men.' BREGENZ, on the Lake of Constance, formerly *Brigantium* or *Brigantia*, is also supposed to be named from the Brigantii, from whom the lake was called Lacus Brigantinus. An old name of Bregenz was *super Brigam*, which must refer to a bridge over the Rhine which here enters the lake. Names from the Gaulish *briga*, Irish *brigh*, ' a hill' (which is cognate with the German *berg*), are liable to be mixed with names from the Teutonic *brig*, a ' bridge.'

Briare, a town in the Loiret, is a corruption of the Celto-Roman name *Brivodurum*, the 'fortress at the bridge.' BRIOUDE in the Haute Loire, was *Brivate*, signifying a place where there was a bridge, and BRIOUDE in the Nièvre, formerly *Brives*, must be explained in the same way.

Bridgenorth, a town in Salop, is called in A.S. *Bricg*, *Brycg*, *Brig*, *Cwatbricg*, and *Cwatbrycg*. We are told in the Chronicle that Æthelfred built a fortress *æt Bricge*, ' at the bridge.' The form Cwatbrycg contains the Welsh word *coed*, ' a wood or forest,' which helps to explain the later name Bridgenorth, which is believed to be a corruption of Bricg-Morfe, *i.e.* the bridge across the Severn leading to the great Morfe forest, called *Silva Moerhab* or *Moreb* in an early charter.

Bridgewater, in Somerset, is a curious corruption of the old name *Burgh Walter*, so called because it was a castle of Walter of Douay, who obtained the manor from William the Conqueror. It gave a title to the Egertons. CAPE BRIDGEWATER, BRIDGEWATER BAY, and the town of BRIDGEWATER, all in Australia, are believed to have been named after the eighth Earl of Bridgewater, to whom we owe the Bridgewater treatises.

Brieg, a town in Silesia, on the Oder, takes its name from the Polish word *brzeg*, ' shore,' as is indicated by the translated name *Civitas Altæ Ripæ*, used in old Latin documents. The town of BRIEG or BRIG, in Canton Valais, was so called from the bridge over the Saline torrent. In 1291 we have *ad locum Brigæ*, in 1331 *via super Brigam*. The German *brücke*, a bridge, is pronounced *brig* in the Upper Valais.

Briggs His Mathematics, an island in Hudson's Bay, was so named by Fox in 1631 from Henry Briggs, a mathematician, who promoted Fox's expedition, and wrote a treatise on the north-west passage.

Brighton is a corruption of the A.S. name *Brihthelmestan*, which means the ' stone of Brihthelm.' There was a South Saxon bishop of that name. The word *stan* may mean a stone house or castle, a boundary stone, or a stone marking a place for a religious or popular assembly. It has been conjectured that Brihthelm's stone may have been set up on the Old Steyne to which it gave a name. But this is doubtful, as the greater part of the old village was swept away by the sea in 1599.

Brindisi is a corruption of the name Brundisum or Brundusium, the Latin form of the Greek name *Brentision*, which is explained from the Messapian word *brention*, a ' stag's head,' the configuration of the harbour with its branching gulfs resembling the antlers of a stag.

Brisbane, the capital of Queensland, is so called because built on the River Brisbane, which was discovered by Lieutenant Oxley in 1823, and named after General Sir Thomas Brisbane, then Governor of New South Wales.

Bristenstock, a conspicuous mountain in Canton Uri, is named from the hamlet of Bristen at its base.

Bristol is first mentioned in the Chronicle, A.D. 1087, as *Bricgstow*. Later forms are Brycg-stow, Bricstow, Brigestou, Bristou, and Bristow, signifying the ' place at the bridge' over the Avon, and answering to the Roman *Trajectus ad Abonam*. The old spelling favours the foregoing derivation from the A.S. *bricg*, ' a bridge,' excluding another which has been proposed from the breach (A.S. *brice*) at the gorge of the Avon near Clifton. Before the rise of Liverpool Bristol was the most important English port after London, and hence the gulf by which it was approached acquired the name of the BRISTOL CHANNEL. Bristol gave a peerage title to the Harvey family, and hence Cook named CAPE BRISTOL and BRISTOL BAY after Admiral Augustus Harvey, the third Earl of the Harvey line. After an earl of an older creation BRISTOL ISLAND in Hudson's Bay was named by Captain James in 1631.

Britain, officially styled GREAT BRITAIN to distinguish it from Brittany, is a name of obscure origin. The oldest form of the name is the Pretanic Island of Greek writers, followed by the Roman name of Britanni for the people, and Britannia for the country. The chief conjectures as to the meaning of the name may be briefly noted. It must have been either a native name, or one used by foreign merchants. If the Greeks obtained it from Phœnician traders, the only etymology which has been suggested is one from the Phœnician *baratanak*, the 'land of tin.' If from Basque sailors, the name Bretani may be compared with Aquetani, Lusitani, Mauretani, Oretani, and similar tribe-names, which contain the Basque plural locative suffix *-etan*, denoting 'inhabitants,' literally 'those who are in' the place denoted by the first part of the name, which in this case might be a Celtic word. Another hypothesis derives the name from the Welsh *brethyn*, 'cloth,' making the Britons the 'clothed men' as distinguished from the naked savages of the north. None of these etymologies have found much support among scholars. The most recent hypothesis, advocated by d'Arbois de Jubainville, Stokes, and Rhys, makes the name equivalent to Cruithnech, 'tatooed' or 'painted' men, the Irish name of the Picts. Since an Irish *c* corresponds to a Welsh *p* or *b*, the Irish *cruth* is the Welsh *pryd*, just as *cen* becomes *pen*, and *mac* becomes *map*; hence *Cruitnech* would answer to the Gaulish Pretanicos, whence the Pretanic island of Pytheas, and the Ynys Prydain of the Welsh writers, which may have been confused with a name from a different source, perhaps non-Aryan, whence the Roman name Britannia.

Brittany, in French BRETAGNE, was originally called Armorica, a Celtic name meaning the land 'by the sea.' In the fifth century the Cymri, flying from the Saxon invaders of Britain, took refuge in Armorica, which in the sixth century begins to be called Britannia Minor, or Britannia Cismarina, as distinguished from Britannia Major or Great Britain. In the thirteenth century Britannia became Breteigne, and Bretaigne in the sixteenth. The Cornouaille of Brittany corresponds to the Cornwall of Britain ; the people of Brittany, like the people of Wales, calling themselves Cymri. CAPE BRETON is an island belonging to the province of Nova Scotia, which as early as 1504 was frequented by cod-fishers from Brittany. NEW BRITAIN was discovered in 1616 by the Dutch navigators Le Maire and Schouten, and was again visited by Tasman in 1642, but was supposed to be a part of New Guinea. Dampier, in 1700, sailing through the strait which bears his name, proved that it was a distinct island, and called it New Britain. Carteret, in 1767, sailed through the channel called after him, and bestowed the name of NEW IRELAND on the northern portion of the land which had hitherto been known as New Britain.

Brixton, a suburb of London, is called *Brixistan* in Domesday, which must mean ' Brihtsige's stone.' BRIXTON DEVERILL, in Wilts, is also from a proper name, if, as is probably the case, it is to be identified with the *Ecgbrightesstan* (Egbert's stone) of the Saxon Chronicle. There are other places of the same name in Devon and the Isle of Wight.

Broadstairs, in the Isle of Thanet, gathered round a chapel saluted by all passing vessels, dedicated to Our Lady of Bradstow, which means a 'broad place,' perhaps referring to the breadth of the chalk cliff, as seen from the sea.

Brodick, a town in the Isle of Arran, stands on Brodick Bay, a corruption of Brathwik or Bradewik, the 'broad bay.'

Brooklyn, now a suburb of New York, is, like Hoboken and the town of Utrecht, one of the Dutch names transferred from Holland. Brooklyn is an English form of the Dutch Breukelen, a village between Amsterdam and Utrecht. It means either the broken ground (Dutch *breuk*, a 'breaking') or the marshy land (Dutch *broek*, 'a marsh ').

Broussa, or **Brusa,** in Asia Minor, the capital of the Bithynian kings, and afterwards of the Ottoman Turks, is said to have been founded by Prusias, king of Bithynia.

Brown's Strait, POINT BROWN, and MOUNT BROWN, in Australia, as well as CAPE BROWN and BROWN'S CHANNEL, in the Arctic Archipelago, were named after the botanist, Robert Brown, who accompanied Flinders in his voyage. BROWN ISLAND, Boothia Felix, was named by Ross after Mrs. Brown, a sister of Sir Felix Booth.

Bruges, in Flanders (Flemish Brügge), is called *Brugae* as early as 678. In the Saxon Chronicle it appears as Bryge and Brycg, 'the bridge.' The name is said to be derived from the bridge called the Brugstock, which was frequented as a market.

Brunn and **Brunnen,** common German place-names, are from the O.H.G. *brunno,* a 'well' or 'fountain.' BRUNNEN, on the Lake of Lucerne, was the meeting-place of the men of the Forest Cantons. BRÜNN, in Moravia, is from the Slavonic *brno,* a 'ford.'

Brunswick, 'Bruno's village,' called in German Braunschweig (formerly Bruneswic), was founded by Bruno, Duke of Saxony, about 861 A.D. The town gave its name to the surrounding Duchy and to the House of Brunswick, which afterwards became electors and kings of Hanover. NEW BRUNSWICK, one of the English colonies in North America, was named in honour of the reigning family of England in 1784, when the colony was separated from Nova Scotia. BRUNSWICK BAY, in Western Australia, was named by Captain King in 1820, 'in honour of the illustrious House of Brunswick.'

Brussels, in French Bruxelles, anciently *Broxola, Bruxelle,* and *Brosella,* derives its name, according to the local tradition, from the 'bridge,' which as early as the sixth century led to the 'cell' of St. Gery, on an island of the Senne, a tributary of the Scheldt. The etymology may, however, be the same as that of BRUCHSAL, near Carlsruhe, called in the tenth century Brochsale, and afterwards Bruchsala, Brusala, and Brusele, which probably means the 'house on the marsh,' from O.H.G. *bruoch,* a 'marsh,' and *seli,* a 'house.'

Buccaneer Archipelago, on the north coast of Australia, was so named by King in memory of Dampier's voyage along this coast.

Buchan, a district in Aberdeenshire, formed one of the seven Pictish kingdoms or earldoms. Buchan is the genitive singular of the old name, the meaning of which is unknown. It is doubtless a Pictish word.

Bucharest, the capital of Roumania, is locally called Bucuresci, the 'pleasant' or 'beautiful' city, from *bucurie,* 'pleasure,' 'joy,' or *boukoure,* 'beautiful,' a loan word from the Albanian, believed to be ultimately of Turkish origin. A local legend refers the name to Hilarius, a Roman Governor.

Buckingham, the county town of BUCKINGHAMSHIRE, is called *Buccingaham* in the Saxon Chronicle. This name is usually said to mean the *-ham* of the men of the beech forest (A.S. *bôc,* 'a beech'). But in this case the A.S. name would have been *Bôcingaham,* and therefore, the name of Buckingham must be referred to the family or clan of the Buccings, who took their name from an ancestor, called Bucca, the Buck, or whose totem was a buck. (A.S. *bucca* or *buc,* 'a he-goat.') The Bucinobantes, an Allemannic tribe, may have been the people of the land of beeches (O.H.G. *buocha,* 'a beech'). (*See* Brabant.)

Buckland Island and the BUCKLAND CHAIN in the Arctic regions, as well as MOUNT BUCKLAND in Fuegia, were named after the geologist, William Buckland, Dean of Westminster. BUCKLAND, the name of twenty English villages, usually signifies book-land, that is, land given by charter out of the Folkland to individuals or to monasteries.

Buckrose, a parliamentary division of the East Riding, takes its name from the ancient Wapentake of *Buc-cros,* so called from the moot-place, which must have been a cross whose locality is indicated by BUCKTON, a lost township in the parish of Settrington, where a field still goes by the name of Buckton Holms.

Buda or **Buda-Pesth,** called OFEN in German, is the capital of Hungary. It consists of two towns, Buda on the right bank of the Danube, and Pesth on the left. The German name Ofen is a translation of the Slavonic word Pesth, which means an oven or grotto, and may refer to the remains of the Roman Thermæ erected over the hot sulphur springs. Buda may be a Magyar translation of Pesth, or from the Slavonic word *buda,* which means 'huts,' or, as has been conjectured, it may refer to Buda the brother of Attila.

Budaun, a town and district in Rohilkhand, was so called, according to the tradition, from Budh, an Ahar prince who founded the town about 905 A.D.

Buenos Ayres, the capital of the Argentine Republic, was founded in 1535 by Don Jorge de Mendoza, and received its name on account of the 'fine weather' which prevailed at the time.

Buffalo, in Western New York, now one of the largest cities in the Union, was founded in 1801, when the region was still frequented by the bison or North American buffalo. The city of Buffalo is at the western corner of Lake Erie, where the vast herds of buffaloes would easily pass the chain of lakes in their annual migration.

Buitenzorg, the mountain retreat of the Governor of Java, is a Dutch translation of SANS SOUCI (*buiten*, 'without,' and *zorg*, 'care.'

Bukovina, an Austrian crown-land in Galicia, means 'beech land' or beech forest, from the Slavonic *bukve*, 'a beech-tree.'

Bulgaria takes its name from the Bulgars, a Turkic tribe which migrated from Great Bulgaria on the Volga, on whose banks, not far from Kazan, their capital of Bulgar or Bolgari was situated. In 487 they settled in a Slavonic district on the Lower Danube, to which they gave their name. The old theory which derives the name of the Bulgars from the name of the Volga is now given up, though the comparatively modern name Volga (called Bulga by Greek writers) may possibly be from that of the Bulgars. (*See* Volga.) Marco Polo calls the Volga by the name Tigris or Tigeri. Burgari or Wurgari, which are early forms of the name of the Bulgars, are analogous to those of the Onoguri, Uturguri, and Kutriguri. Vámbéry explains the name as 'rebels,' deriving it from the Turkic *bulga-mak*, 'to revolt.'

Bundelcund, or in the modern spelling BUNDELKHAND, is an Indian territory which was conquered in the fourteenth century by a Rajput tribe called the Bundelas.

Bungay is the 'good ford,' *bon-gué*, over the Waveney. The castle erected by Hugh Bigod to command the ford accounts for the existence of this Norman name in Suffolk.

Bunker Islands, on the east coast of Australia, bear the name of the captain of the whaler *Albion*.

Burdekin, Australia, was so named by Leichhardt after a merchant at Sydney.

Burdwan (Bardwán) is a town in Bengal which gives a name to a district containing valuable coal-pits. It owes its name to a temple of Vishnu, being a corruption of the Sanskrit *Varddhamána*, the 'fortunate,' an epithet of Vishnu.

Burghhead, a promontory in Elgin between the Findhorn and the Spey, was the site of a *borg* or castle built in the ninth century by Sigurd, the Norwegian Earl of Orkney, on the southern border of his conquests in Moray. BURRA, one of the Shetlands, is the 'castle-isle,' deriving its name from a *borg* or castle, the remains of which can still be traced. The name Borgar fiord, 'castle frith,' occurs in 1299. BURRAY, formerly Borgar, one of the Orkneys, is a similar name. In like manner BORROWDALE in Cumberland is believed to owe its name to a Scandinavian *borg* or castle which stood on a rock now called CASTLE CRAG.

Burgos, one of the few Teutonic names in Spain, and the capital of the former province of Old Castile, is said to have been founded in 884 by a German knight serving against the Moors. In its houses, streets, and Gothic cathedral, it exhibits the style of the Gotho-Castilian period. The German *burg* occurs in at least 200 German names, dating from the first century onwards, as Salzburg, Regensburg, Magdeburg, and Freiburg. The Scandinavian form is *borg*, as in Flemsborg, Svenborg, and Viborg in Denmark. In Gothic we have *baurgs*, a 'town.' The A.S. form *burh* gives *burgh*, *borough*, and *bury*, the last being from *byrig*, the dative sing. of *burh*.

Burgundy, anciently Burgundia, a district in Gaul, settled in 413 by the Burgundians, a Teutonic people called Burgundiones by Pliny, Jerome, and Orosius, and Burgundii by Ammianus Marcellinus. According to Grimm and Zeuss the name means 'burghers,' the dwellers in burghs or strong places. The two Burgundian realms are to be distinguished: the old Burgundian kingdom, whose capital was originally at Arles, which comprised the Rhone valley and Savoy, with the Netherlands and the western cantons of Switzerland, and came to an end in the eleventh century, and the Burgundian duchy, a fief of the French kings, whose capital was at Dijon, which forms the district still known as Burgundy.

Burma, or **Burmah,** is a corruption of *Mranma* or *Mianma*, the national name of the Burmese, which, unless speaking emphatically, they generally pronounce Bam-ma or Byamma. Mran or Mian, the original name of the Burmese, is identical with the Chinese form Mien, used by Marco Polo, -*ma* being an honorific affix. According to Lassen it means 'those who are strong,' and was probably a title of the warrior caste.

Burnett River, Queensland, was named after a Government surveyor.

GLOSSARY 79

Burton, the name of some sixty English villages and towns, is usually from the A.S. *búr-tún,* which denoted a *tún* or farmyard containing a *búr* or 'bower,' the word *búr* meaning a 'storehouse' in O.N., and in A.S. a 'chamber,' 'sleeping place,' or building of some kind. But when, as in the case of BURTON-ON-TRENT and BURTON in Warwickshire, the early form is Burh-tún, it signifies a protected *tún,* the difference between a *burh* and a *tún* being that the *tún* was the farmstead of the peasant surrounded by a hedge, while the *burh* was the dwelling of a more powerful man, protected by a ditch with a bank of earth or sods ; a Burh-tún would therefore be a tún subsequently protected by a bank, or, if protected by a wall, the name would be WALTON, A.S. *Weal-tún.* When, as in the case of BURTON CONSTABLE or BURTON DALE, the Domesday form is Bertun or Bortun, it may be suspected that the primitive name was Beorh-tún, the 'hill-tun.'

Bury, or St. Edmundsbury, or more commonly **Bury St. Edmunds,** is called in the Saxon Chronicle *Eadmundesburh.* In 870, Edmund, the king of the East Saxons, was slain by the Danes, and a great abbey rose over his shrine.

Bushire, a sea-port on the Persian Gulf, is a corruption of *abu-shahr,* the 'father of towns.'

Bushnan Island and **Bushnan Cove,** in the Arctic Archipelago, were named from John Bushnan, a midshipman in the *Hecla.*

Bustard Bay, on the eastern coast of Australia, was so named by Captain Cook from a large bustard, which was caught in a trap, and which furnished, as he tells us, an excellent dinner.

Bute, one of the Hebrides, is probably the *Ebuda* of Ptolemy, which, owing to a misreading in a MS. has given rise to the ghost-name of the Hebrides (*q.v.*). The meaning of the name is uncertain.

Byam Martin Island, Byam Martin Channel, and Byam Martin's Mountains, all in the Arctic regions, were so named by Parry, Beechey, and Ross (1810-1826) after Sir Thomas Byam Martin, comptroller of the Navy.

Byron's Island, in the South Pacific, and CAPE BYRON, New South Wales, were named after Commodore Byron, grandfather of the poet.

Cabes, Gulf of, Tunis, takes its name from the town of CABES or Khabs, anciently Tacape.

Caceres, the capital of the Spanish province of the same name in Estremadura, is a corruption of *Castra Caecilia,* the Roman name.

Cadér Idris, the seat or 'chair of Idris,' is the name of a mountain in Merioneth, which from the north bears some resemblance to a chair. Idris, according to the Welsh myth, was a giant, and it was believed that if a man spent a night on the mountain where Idris had his seat he would, when he descended in the morning, be either a madman or a bard.

Cadiz, which has kept its unbroken position as a great city longer than any other in Europe, longer even than Marseille, preserves nearly unchanged the Roman name of Gades, though the Greek form Gadeira approaches nearer to the Phœnician name Gadir or Gaddir, the 'enclosure' or 'walled place.' The wall was probably carried across the sandy isthmus to protect the city, which stood, like the modern Cadiz, at the western extremity of the spit, which is about six miles in length. We have the same Semitic name in GADARA and GEDOR in Palestine, while AGHADER on the coast of Morocco retains the form Agadir, which we have on the Phœnician coins of Cadiz, where the first letter merely represents the prosthetic article.

Caen, the capital of the Calvados, is a name of obscure meaning. Old forms are *Cadon, Cathum, Kadum, Cathim, Cahem, Cahen, and Caem.* The name has been supposed to be from the French *cade,* a kind of juniper, *caden* meaning a place surrounded by a hedge of juniper, or it may be Teutonic, involving a personal name. The medieval Latin form *Cadomus* would point to a Celtic *Catumagos,* the 'battle-field.'

Caerleon, Monmouthshire, was the Roman *Isca Silurum,* so called because it stood on the Usk (Isca), in the territory of the Silures. Here the second Augustan legion was stationed, whence the Welsh name Caer-leon, the 'city of the legion.' The British word *Caer,* a 'stone fort,' and hence a 'walled city,' was commonly applied to Roman sites, thus corresponding to the A.S. *ceaster* (chester). It is often contracted to *Car,* as in CARLISLE or CARNARVON. CAERWENT was the Roman *Venta Silurum.* There is a Roman camp at CAER-MOTE in Cumberland, while at CAERSWS, CAERWYS, and

CAERGWRLE, places in Wales, Roman remains have been found. In Salop there are two hills called CAER CARADOC, crowned by British earth-works, and CAER BADON is the invented name of the great earth-work overhanging Bath. CAER-VORAN in Northumberland is *Caer Vawr*, the 'great castle.' CARSTAIRS, in Lanarkshire, is probably the *caer* or fort of a man named Terras. CAREW (pronounced Carey), on Milford Haven, is a corruption of the Welsh *caerau*, the plural of *caer*, and means 'the forts.' In CARDINHAM near Bodmin, the suffix is not the English -*ham*, the name being a corruption of *Caer-dinam*, the *Caer* or 'fort of Dinam.' In Ireland *caer* is found in the form *cathair*, pronounced *caher*, which usually denotes a stone fort, though the word is glossed *civitas*. There are more than thirty Irish townlands so called, the best known being CAHER in Tipperary. There are also more than five hundred townlands or towns whose names begin with Caher or Cahir, thus CAHERGAL (Cathair-geal), the 'white fort,' is the name of eleven places.

Caffres. (*See* KÁFIRISTÁN.)

Cagliari, Sardinia, is a corruption of the ancient name *Caralis* or *Calaris.*

Cahors, in the Department of the Lot, was anciently *Civitas Cadurcorun*, 'the city of the Cadurci.' Cahors is a corruption of Cadurcis, the dative plural of the tribe-name.

Cairns, a town in Queensland, bears the name of Sir William Cairns, a brother of Lord Cairns, formerly Governor of Queensland.

Cairo, in French LE CAIRE, is a corruption of the Arabic *El Kâhira*, 'the victorious,' so called because *Kâhir* (Mars), the planet of victory, was visible on the night when the city was founded. El Kâhira is, however, a mere epithet or nickname, the natives calling the city EL MISR, or EL MASR, from Mizraim, the Semitic name of Egypt, sometimes adding the honorific epithet *Masr-el-Kâhira.*

Caithness is the northernmost county of Scotland. From the old name Caith the Norwegians formed the name *Kata-nes*, Latinised *Cathanesia*, and spelt in the Book of Deir, *Cat-nes*, meaning the ness or promontory of Caith, which is supposed to be the same word as Keith, found in several local names in the Pictish region, such as KEITH in Banff and Elgin, DALKEITH near Edinburgh, INCH-KEITH in the Firth of Forth, as well as PEN-CAITH-LAND, KEITH-HUMBIE, and

KEITH WATER on the Upper Tyne. In the legendary history of the Picts, Cait is a son of Cruithne, the eponymus of the Cruithneach or Picts. Hence Cait or Keith may be regarded as the eponymus of one of the Pictish tribes, and, as a Gaelic *k* corresponds to a Welsh *p*, Keith is probably the same name as the Welsh Peith (Pict), a probability supported by the fact that the sea north of Caithness is called the PENTLAND FRITH (*q.v.*) a corruption of Pict-land Frith.

Calatayud, the birthplace of Martial, and after Zaragoza the chief city in Aragon, is the Arabic *Kala't-Ayûb*, the castle of the Wali Ayûb (Job), the nephew of the Moorish chief Musa (Moses), who became the Fourth Emir of Spain. CALATRAVA is the 'castle of Rabah,' but CALAHORRA, on the Ebro, is a corruption of the classical name *Calagurris.* With the prefixed article we get the form ALCALA, as in Alcala-real, the 'royal castle,' or Alcala-de-Henares, the castle on the River Henares, which is the Arabic *an-Nahr*, 'the river' (p. 160). The word *kala't* is also found in such Sicilian names as CALATAFIMI and CALATABLANCA, which have Italian suffixes, but CALATA-BELLOTTA is *Kala't-el-Belut*, 'oaktree castle,'and CALTANISETTA is from *Kala't-el-Nisa*, the 'castle of the women' or the 'ladies' castle.'

Calais has been derived from the Caletes, a tribe-name which may more probably be recognised in the PAYS DE CAUX, near the mouth of the Seine, the district where we should place the Caletes, who were probably the 'men of the inlet' or estuary of the Seine. The name of Calais may be either from the Celtic *caolas* or *caolish*, a 'strait' (Old Celtic *koilos*, 'narrow'), which we have in the KYLES OF BUTE, and in BALLA-CHULISH, the 'village of the strait,' or from the word *cale* or *cala*, an 'inlet' or 'harbour,' which we find in *Portus Cale*, the old name of Oporto, whence the name of Portugal (*q.v.*).

Calaveras, a county in California, takes its name from the Punta Calaveras, a Spanish name meaning the Cape of the cattle skulls.

Calcutta, called *Kalkatta* in the Ain-i-Akbari, has been supposed to be a corruption of the Indian name *Kált-Káta*, the 'dwelling' or 'sacred place' of Káli, the wife of Siva. At Kálíghat, on the Ganges near Calcutta, there is a temple of Káli, erected because of the legend that one of her fingers fell here when her body was cut to pieces. CALICUT (*Kolikódu*), on the Malabar coast, whence we obtain the word *calico*, was the first place in India visited by European ships, Covilham landing about 1486, and Vasco de Gama arriving in 1498. It is supposed to be the Indian *Kolikotta*, the 'cock fort, or possibly *Kalikot*, the 'fortress of Káli,' a goddess whose name is found in KALIGANJ, 'Kali's market,' KALIMATH, 'Kali's temple,' KALINADI, 'Kali's river,' and KALIPANI, 'Kali's water.'

Caldas, or **Las Caldas,** the 'hot baths,' is the name of towns in Spain, Portugal, and Brazil.

Caledonia, the land inhabited by the Caledonii, was probably the great central forest of Scotland which stretched from Inveraray to Inverness. The name probably means a 'forest,' the root of Caledonia answering to the German *holt*, which we have in Holstein. As *called* means 'thistles' in Gaelic, Caledonia was supposed to mean the land of thistles, and hence the thistle has been adopted as the national emblem. The usual etymology, which makes Caledon the 'dun of the Gael' must be rejected. NEW CALE-DONIA, discovered by Cook in 1774, was the name given to a large island near the New Hebrides, which marches with the neighbouring islands of New Ireland and New Britain. CALEDON, in the Cape Colony, was named in compliment to Lord Caledon, an Indian official.

Calf of Man is a small island south of the Isle of Man. The Norsemen called a smaller island lying off a larger one its calf. So when a fragment breaks off from an iceberg it is said to calve.

California bears a name which the Franciscan monks attributed to Cortez, and explained as meaning *calida fornax*, the 'hot furnace.' It has also been supposed to be a corruption of the native name of a small inlet at the south-east end of California, discovered by Ximenes in 1533, named Santa Cruz by Cortez, and now called Puerto de la Paz. But Dr. Hale's investigations have made it probable that the name was taken from a Spanish romance, *Las Sergas de Esplandian*, a continuation of *Amadis de Gaula*, published by Montalvo in 1510, in which the writer describes an imaginary island abounding in gold and precious stones, for which he invented the name of California. As applied to the peninsula the name first appears in Preciado's diary of Ulloa's voyage. On the map which Dr. Dee gave to Queen Elizabeth in 1580, the name of Cape California is given to

the extreme southern point of the peninsula. In 1579 Sir Francis Drake took possession of Upper California in the name of Queen Elizabeth, calling it New Albion. The GULF OF CALIFORNIA formerly bore the name of Mar de Cortez, from its discoverer. No more appropriate name than the Gulf of Cortez could be found, and it is a pity that such a memorial of the daring Captain should have lost its place upon the map.

Calvados, a department in the North of France, received its name at the time of the French Revolution from the Calvados reef, a dangerous ledge of rocks stretching for fifteen miles along the coast, on which, according to the local legend, one of the ships of the Armada, said to be the *San Salvador*, was wrecked in 1588.

Cambay, Gulf of, in Gujarát, takes its name from the town of CAMBAY or Khambhat, formerly *Kumbáyat*, from *Khumbavati*, 'the city of the pillar,' so called because of the pool of Mahádeva, worshipped here under the form of the pillar god. Marco Polo uses the forms *Cambaet* or *Cambeth*, which are less incorrect than the Anglicised name *Cambay*. In the time of the Portuguese it was a wealthy and populous city, of sufficient importance to give the European name to the gulf on which it stands. (*See* p. 312.)

Cambodia or **Camboja,** a country in further India, possibly a European corruption of the Annamese name *Cao-mer*, is believed by Yule to be a Sanskrit name transferred from North-Western India to Indo-China.

Cambrai (Nord) is a corruption of the old name *Cameracum*, which, according to d'Arbois de Jubainville, is from the personal name Camarus, a preferable etymology to that which makes it a place appertaining to a *camera* or demesne house.

Cambus, in Stirlingshire and in Tyrone, is the Gaelic *camus*, which means a 'bay,' or the 'bend' of a river, whence CAMBUS-NETHAN, the 'bend of the River Nethan,' CAMBUSLANG, CAMBUSBARRON, CAM-BUSKENNETH, and other names.

Cambridge is usually supposed to mean the bridge over the River Cam, the real name of which is the Granta. In the A.S. Chronicle it is called *Grantabrycg*, *Grantebrycg*, and *Grantanbrycg*, and in early charters Cambridgeshire is called *Grantebrigiæ comitatus*, *Grantecestriæ comitatus* and *Grantebrigeshire*, which must in some way have become corrupted into *Cantebruggescr*, which first appears in a charter of 1142. The name of the Granta is retained by GRANTCHESTER, a village two miles above Cambridge, which, as the name implies, must have been a Roman station. Cambridge castle, which stands near the bridge which must have replaced an older ford, is believed to be the site of another Roman station, as is indicated by the adjacent suburb of CHESTERTON, the 'tun by the Chester.' This second station, from which we may perhaps derive the name of Cambridge, has been identified with considerable probability with the *Camboritum* of the Fifth Itinerary. Camboritum would represent an ancient British name *Camboriton* or *Cambo-rhed*, the 'crooked,' or 'skew ford,' a name paralleled by the Derbyshire name of CROMFORD, the 'bent or crooked ford.' Cambo-rhed would normally become Cambret, and when the ford was replaced by a bridge, by popular etymology Cambret would become Cambrycg, easily confused with, and ultimately replacing, the name Grantebrycg, a change which dates from the time of Henry II. In the same way the A.S. *Hreódford*, 'reed ford,' in Hampshire, became REDBRIDGE after the bridge was built. As early as the time of Milton the River Granta had come to be called the CAM, doubtless in order to account for the name of Cambridge, just as the river EDEN in Kent acquired its present name in order to explain the name of EDENBRIDGE. The Celtic word *cam*, which means 'crooked,' could not have been used to designate a river whose course is so remarkably straight, not to say that Celtic speech had disappeared long before the twelfth century, when Cambridge acquired its present name.

Cambridge, near Boston in Massachusetts, is the seat of the Harvard University, founded in 1636, and endowed by the munificent bequest of John Harvard, a graduate of Emmanuel College, Cambridge. The place was originally called Newtown, which was changed to Cambridge in honour of John Harvard's university. CAMBRIDGE GULF, on the northern coast of Australia, was named by King in 1819 in honour of the first Duke of Cambridge.

Camden Town, a suburb of London, was built on part of the Prebendal Manor of Cantelows, the lessee of which was the Marquis of Camden, who took his title from Camden Place in Kent, which had been the residence of the great antiquary William Camden. CAMDEN BAY, in Australia and in Arctic America, were named in honour of Lord Camden. CAMPDEN, in Gloucestershire, which gives a title to Viscount Campden, probably means the 'crooked valley.'

Camelford, Cornwall, is the A.S. *Gafolford*, the ford where tribute was paid (A.S. *gafol*, 'tribute'). GUILDFORD (*q.v.*) may be a similar name.

Cameroons, properly Camaraons, the European name of the greatest mountain mass in Western Africa, is called by the natives *Mongo-ma-loba*, the 'throne of thunder.' Curiously enough the European name of this great mountain means 'shrimps,' the Portuguese having given the name of RIO DOS CAMARÂOS (Camaraons), the 'river of shrimps,' to the Diba, a stream south of the mountain, which subsequently took its name from the river.

Campbell Island, an isolated volcanic isle south of New Zealand, was discovered in 1810 by the whaler *Perseverance*, owned by the Messrs. Campbell of Sydney. CAMPBELTOWN, in Cantire, bears the family name of the Duke of Argyll, head of the Clan Campbell, a name which, though Latinised as *de bello campo*, is a Gaelic nickname, *cam beul*, 'crooked mouth.'

Campeachy, a town in Yucatan, which has given a name to the BAY OF CAMPEACHY, is a corruption of *Quimpech*, the native name of the district.

Canaan is a biblical name given to some twenty places in the U.S.A. The word, which means the 'lowlands,' originally designated the narrow strip of coast between the Lebanon and the sea, where the great Phœnician cities lay, afterwards being extended much further to the south.

Canada, called *La Nouvelle France* by the French settlers, is probably the native word *Kanata*, which means a collection of huts or wigwams. Cuoq, in his Iroquois Lexicon, defines the word *Kanata* as meaning 'ville, village, bourg, bourgade, camp, groupe de tentes.' The CAÑADA RIVER, in the State of Mississippi, is a tributary of the Arkansas River. It flows through a deep gorge, and the name is explained by the Spanish *cañada*, 'a ravine.' The gorge of the St. Lawrence below the Falls of Niagara has suggested a similar etymology for Canada, but this is inadmissible, Canada being a French and not a Spanish colony.

Canara, properly KARNADA, a coast district in Western India, probably means the 'Black Country,' from its black cotton soil. The CARNATIC (*Karnátik*), a district on the Eastern Coast, is believed to have the same signification, the Sanskrit *Karnátaka* being the adjectival form of *Karnáta*, of which Canara is a Portuguese corruption.

Canary Islands, a group in the North Atlantic, were identified by the Spaniards with the *Fortunatæ Insulæ* of Pliny (vi. 202, *seq.*), one of which, according to Ptolemy and Juba (quoted by Pliny), was called Canaria, from the *multitudine canum ingentis magnitudinis.* The Spaniards in 1492 found a breed of large dogs, now extinct, on the largest island of the group, which they called Gran Canaria. On his second voyage, Columbus took with him some of these dogs to fight the natives of Haiti and Cuba. The Cuban bloodhound probably continues the race. A finch with a patch of yellow on the wing coverts, brought from the island of Grand Canary, was called the canary bird, the colour which the bird developed under domestication being afterwards called canary.

Candahar. (*See* KANDAHAR.)

Candia is a mere ghost-name, improperly used by Western geographers for the island of Crete. The error arose from the city of MEGALO-CASTRON having been called Candia by the Venetians. The usual etymology is from the Arabic *khandak*, signifying the 'moat' or 'trench,' which the Saracens were supposed to have constructed round their fortified camp when they conquered Crete in the ninth century. This explanation cannot, however, be supported, Candia being merely the neo-Hellenic word *kandia*, used by Greek sailors to denote the narrow navigable 'channel' through the mud-locked harbour. Even for the town the name Candia is never used in the island, the local designation being 'Castron.' To call Crete by the name of Candia is an error of the same kind as if England were to be called the Nore.

Candlemas Isles are a Pacific group discovered by Captain Cook on Candlemas Day (Feb. 2nd), 1775. From the same festival comes the name BAJIOS DE CANDELARIA, given by Mendana in 1567 to a reef in the Salomon Islands, which is now usually called EL RONCADOR, 'the snorer,' from the noise made by the breakers on the rocks.

Candover, the name of three contiguous parishes in Hampshire, is probably Celtic, perhaps *can dwfr*, the 'white water,' or *cam-dwfr*, the 'crooked water.' The River Itchin rises in the parish of Chilton

Candover (A.S. *Can-defer* òr *Cendefer*). There is a Candover in Teviotdale, and CONDOVER is the name of a hundred and a parish in Shropshire.

Candy. (*See* KANDY.)

Canne, in Apulia, preserves the old name *Cannae*, the 'reeds' or 'canes.' CANNES on the Riviera, and several places in South America called CANETE or CANETA are so called because overgrown with reeds or 'canes.'

Canonbie, Dumfriesshire, takes its name from a priory of Austin Canons, founded in 1165.

Canosa, the castle in the Parmese Apennines, where Hildebrand kept the Emperor Henry waiting in the snow, was probably so named from the hoary limestone cliff on which it stands, or perhaps from the ashy paleness of its walls.

Cantal, a French department, takes its name from the volcanic mass of the Cantal, which is perhaps connected with *cantalon*, a Gaulish word occurring in inscriptions, which appears to mean a 'tower.'

Canterbury was the *burh* of the *Cantware* or men of Kent. We are told in the Saxon Chronicle that in 675 *Cantwaraburh* was burnt. The oblique case *Cantwarabyrig*, from which comes the modern form Canterbury, is seen in such entries as *to Cantwarabyrig* (A.D. 655), or *innan Cantwarabyrig* (A.D. 689). Kent is called *Cantwararice*, 'the realm of the men of Kent,' where *wara* is gen. pl. of *ware*, the same word which we have in burghers (A.S. *burhware*), Bavarians (*Baio-varii*), or in the German *land-wehr*. It means primarily defenders, warders, or guardians, and then inhabitants. The men of the Isle of Wight were called *Wihtware*, just as the men of Kent were called *Cantware*. (*See* KENT.)

Canton is the European name of the city called by the Chinese either *Kwang-chou-Fu* or *Sang-Ching*. It is the capital of the province of Kwang-tung or Quang-tung, of which Canton is a Portuguese corruption. QUANG-TUNG is the 'wide east,' *tung* meaning the 'east,' and *quang*, 'extent' or 'width.' The province to the west of Quang-tung is called QUANG-SI (Kwang-si), 'the wide west.'

Cape Town and the **Cape Colony,** of which it is the capital, take their names from the CAPE OF GOOD HOPE, discovered in 1487 by Bartolomeo Diaz, despatched in July or August, 1486, by King John II. of Portugal, with two vessels of fifty tons each, in order to find a sea route to India.

Diaz reached the mouth of the Congo and erected a pillar north of Wallfisch Bay. At CAPE VOLTAS he found the coast 'trended' eastward to St. Helena Bay. Battling with tempests for thirteen days he doubled, without knowing it, the southern extremity of Africa, reaching the mouth of the great Fish River and landing in Algoa Bay, which he called Angra dos Vaqueiros, 'bay of the cowherds.' On his return he sighted the Cape of Good Hope, which he called in memory of the tempests he had braved, *Cabo de todos los Tormientos*, 'Cape of all the storms,' or more shortly, *Cabo Tormentoso*, 'the stormy cape.' In the 'good hope' that the sea route to India had at last been found, King John changed this appropriate but ill-omened name to *Cabo de Bôa Esperança*, of which the English name Cape of Good Hope is a translation. The Cape was not again visited for ten years after it had been thus discovered. Diaz commanded one of the ships in Cabral's expedition by which Brazil was accidentally discovered, and in crossing the South Atlantic from Brazil to the Cape he was lost in the fearful storm of May 23rd, 1500. There is also a CAPE OF GOOD HOPE which appears on many English maps as the northernmost point of New Guinea. The name properly belongs to another cape on Schouten's Island further to the east, which in 1616 was called Caep van Goede Hoop by Le Maire and Schouten, in the good hope they entertained of speedily rejoining their fellow-countrymen. Tasman and Dampier erroneously transferred this name to the northern point of New Guinea, and Columbus also gave the name of Cabo de Buena Esperanza to the furthest point he reached on the south-western shore of Cuba in his second voyage, because, finding the coast here trending to the south, he felt assured that Cuba was a part of the Asiatic Continent, and therefore believed himself to be nearer China than Diaz was at the other Cape of Good Hope discovered seven years before.

Cape Verd was discovered in 1445 by Diniz Dias, who had been a page of King John I. of Portugal, and was named *Cabo Verde*, the 'green cape,' because it was covered with palms, thus upsetting the old belief derived from Aristotle, and entertained by Ptolemy, Edrisi, and Roger Bacon, that the tropics were to be so burnt up by the heat of the sun as to be uninhabitable deserts. The CAPE VERD ISLANDS were called by the Portuguese discoverers *Ilhas do Cabo Verde*, because they lay opposite the Cabo Verde.

Cappadocia, according to Herodotus, is a Persian name. In old Persian *Hvaspadakhim* would mean 'the land of good horses.'

Caprera, a small island near Elba, the retreat of Garibaldi. CABRERA, one of the Balearic islands, the ISOLA DI CAPRI, in the Bay of Naples, and two of the Azores called ILHAS DAS CABRAS, are names signifying 'islands of goats.'

Capricorn, Cape, in Queensland, was so named by Cook in 1770 because it lies precisely on the Tropic of Capricorn.

Capua, in Italy, called *Campanus* by Livy and Cicero, and *Campana Urbs* by Virgil, was the chief town of Campania, the great 'plain,' now called CAMPAGNA FELICE. Its coins bear the legend *Cappan* and *Campano*.

Carabela, a rocky two-peaked island in the West Indies, near St. Thomas, was so called because at a distance it resembled the Spanish ship called a caravel.

Caracas, or SANTIAGO DE CARACAS, the capital of Venezuela, was founded in 1567, and named from a warlike native tribe.

Cardiff, according to a local legend, was the *Caer* or fortress of Didius (Aulus Didius), a legend supported by *Caerddydd*, the Welsh form of the name. It has also been explained as the *Caer* or fortress on the River Taff.

Cardigan, the county town of Cardiganshire, is properly the name of the county, and not of the town, which the Welsh call Aber-Teivi, because it lies at the 'mouth of the Teivi.' The old name *Keredigion*, of which Cardigan is a corruption, was derived, according to the Welsh tradition, from Keredig or Caredig, son of Cunedda, a prince who conquered the district in the sixth century.

Caribee, or WINDWARD ISLANDS, in the West Indies, were so called because at the time of the Spanish discovery they were inhabited by the Caribs, a native word meaning the 'fighters,' which was given by the more peaceful islanders to the fierce invaders from the South American coast. Columbus seems to have misheard the native term *Cariba* as *Caniba*, and this served to confirm his belief that he had discovered the islands on the eastern coast of China, supposing they were subjects of the Great Khan (*i.e.* Genghis Khan) of Pekin, whom it was his object to convert, and to whom he carried letters of introduction. On December 11th he makes this curious entry in his log, 'Caniba must mean subjects of the Chan, who must reside in the neighbourhood.' The imaginary name Caniba was then transferred to the man-eating savages of South America, and the word cannibal, originally a corruption of *carib*, was derived from *canis*, 'a dog,' and supposed to have been given *propter rabiem caninam anthropophagorum gentis.*

Carinthia and CARNIOLA are the Latinised forms of the German names KÄRNTHEN and KRAIN. They are believed to denote the land of the Carni, a tribe whose name probably meant 'the mountaineers.'

Carisbrooke, in the Isle of Wight, is first mentioned in the Chronicle, where we read '*Her Cerdic and Cynric genamon* (took) *Wihte ealond, and ofslogon* (slew) *feala* (many) *men on Wihtgarœsbyrg.*' The forms *Wihtgarabyrig* and *Gwihtgaraburhg* are also found. In a later MS. of the Chronicle we have *Wihtgaresburh,* from which the form Carisbrooke was obtained by dropping the first syllable. The Chronicle also informs us that *of Iotan* (the Jutes) *comon Cantware and Wihtware,* which suggests the theory that *Wihtgaraburh* was the *burh* of the men of Wight, just as *Cantwaraburh* (Canterbury) was the *burh* of the men of Kent. But in the Chronicle Wihtgar is the nephew of Cerdic and Cynric, although Cynric was the son of Cerdic, which looks as if Wihtgar was an eponymic name invented to explain Wihtgaresburh, just as Port is an eponymus invented to explain the name of Portsmouth (the *Portus Magnus* of the Romans), where he is said to have landed. The difficulty lies in the change, at such an early date, of *Wihtwara* to *Wihtgara.* Professor Earle suggests that the original name of Carisbrooke was *Wiht-caer,* the 'city of Wight,' and that there was an assimilation of this Celtic name and the Teutonic *Wiht-ware,* the 'men of Wight,' out of which Wihtgar and Wihtgaraburh were evolved. (*See* CANTERBURY.) Possibly the change may have been due to a surviving British element in the population, Welsh regularly changing *w* to *gw,* the Latin loan words *vinum, ventus,* and *virgo* becoming in Welsh *gwin, gwynt,* and *gwraig.*

Carlisle, owing to its position in the British kingdom of Strathclyde, has preserved a purely Celtic name. It is the *Luguvallum* or *Luguvallium* of the An-

tonine Itinerary, the *Lugubalum* and the *Luguvalio ad Vallum* of the Ravenna geographer, and Bæda's *Lugubalia,* which was corrupted into Lluel, Simeon of Durham speaking of 'Lugubalia, which is called Luel.' With the British prefix *caer,* a 'city,' this became *Caer-luel.* In the ninth century we find the Anglo-Saxon equivalent *Lul-chester,* but in the tenth we again find the British form *Caer-luel,* which degenerated into *Carliol,* and finally became CARLISLE. Carlisle was at one extremity of the *vallum* of Hadrian, which extended from Wallsend to Carlisle. *Lugu-vallum* signifies the 'wall-tower,' that is the tower or fort at the end of the *vallum.* The Celtic *lugus* of Mela, and the Cornish *lug,* meaning a tower, is seen in the name Lugdunum, 'tower-hill,' now LYONS (*q.v.*).

Carlow, an Irish county, takes its name from the county town of Carlow, on the River Barrow, which, according to the tradition, here formed four lakes. The old name was *Cetherloch* (pronounced Caher lough), which means the 'quadruple lake.'

Carlsruhe, properly Karlsruhe, 'Charles' rest,' the capital of the Grand Duchy of Baden, was originally a hunting seat, built in 1715 by Karl Willhelm, Margrave of Baden, on a spot where he had rested in the shade. KARLSBAD, or Kaiserkarlsbad, is a mineral bath in Bohemia, with hot saline springs, which are said to have been accidentally discovered by the Emperor Karl IV. during a hunting excursion.

Carlstad and **Carlskrona,** two towns in Sweden, capitals of the provinces to which they give their names, were both founded by Charles IX. of Sweden. CARLSTAD in Croatia, and CARLOWITZ on the Danube are named from German emperors, and CARLSHAMMA, a Swedish port, is 'Charles' enclosure.'

Carmarthen, the county town of Carmarthenshire, is believed to be the Roman *Maridunum,* the fort or 'dun by the sea.' This name was contracted to *Marthen,* and with the prefix *caer,* 'fortress' or 'city,' became Caer-marthen. Another Maridunum in Devon has become SEATON, a translated name.

Carmel, a cape and mountain in Syria, now called RAS-EL-KIRMEL, or JEBEL KIRMEL, is believed to have been named from an altar to Karm-el the 'vineyard god.' It was a venerated sanctuary in the time of Thothmes III.

Carnarvon, or **Caernarvon**, the county town of Carnarvonshire, was the town which gathered round Edward's castle, and became the capital of the land of Arfon. The Welsh name is *Caer-yn-Arfon*, ' the city of Arfon,' Ar-fon (with the regular letter change of *m* to *f*) meaning the land over against Mon, Mon being the island of Mona, now called Anglesey. Gray's line, ' on Arvon's dreary shore they lie,' preserves the memory of the land of Arfon, now a Parliamentary district, as well as the true meaning of Carn-arvon. Carnarvon took the place of the neighbouring Roman station of *Segontium*, now called CAER SEIONT, a name probably invented by the antiquarians.

Carolina. In 1629 Sir Robert Heath obtained from Charles I. a grant of the territory south of Virginia, on which he bestowed the name of Carolina in gratitude to his royal master. No settlement was made under this patent, of which nothing remained but the bare name. In 1663 the patent was revoked by Charles II., and a new grant made to eight patentees, among whom were Lords Albemarle, Clarendon, and Ashley, who renamed the territory after Charles II. In 1665 the patent was recast, and in 1667 a body of colonists landed, under the command of Captain William Sayle. In 1729 Carolina was divided into two colonies, North Carolina and South Carolina. The name Carolina had, however, been already given to a part of the territory included in the grant of Charles II. In 1562 Admiral Coligny obtained permission to plant a colony of Huguenots on the coast of Florida, and the colonists erected a fort on an island in the St. John's river in the north of Florida, which they called *Arx Carolina*, after Charles IX. of France, the surrounding territory being called Florida Française. The Spanish name was Tierra de Ayllon, from Vasquez Ayllon who had visited the coast forty years before. Carolina was the name given in 1686 by Lazeano to an island in the North Pacific in honour of Charles II. of Spain. The name was subsequently extended to the neighbouring group which go by the name of the CAROLINE ISLANDS.

Carpathians, the range of mountains north of Hungary, is a name derived from *Krapat* or *Karpa*, the local name of the main chain, which is explained by the Slavonic root *chrb*, signifying a ' ridge ' or ' range of hills,' whence also the word *Chrawat*, or Croat, a ' highlander, and CROATIA, the ' land of the Croats.'

Carpentaria is the name of the great gulf on the northern coast of Australia. In 1623 Jan Cartensz gave the name of Carpentier to a small river near Cape Duyfhen, in honour of Pieter Carpentier, at that time President of the Dutch East India Company. After the second voyage of Abel Tasman in 1644 the great Australian Gulf which he explored begins to appear on the maps as the Gulf of Carpentaria. It had, however, been discovered before the voyage of Cartensz, the Dutch ship *Duyfhen* having in 1606 sailed along the coast from Cape York as far as CAPE KEER WEER (Cape Turnagain). The ship had missed Torres Strait, and it was supposed that the lands discovered were a part of New Guinea, but the *Duyfhen* had in reality been the first to discover Australia, as well as to penetrate into the Gulf of Carpentaria.

Carrick-on-Suir, a town in Tipperary, is the Anglicised form of the old Irish name *Carraig-na-Siuire*, ' the rock of the Suir,' so called from a large rock in the bed of the river. CARRICKFERGUS, in County Antrim, is so called from a rock where Fergus, an Irish king, was drowned. Carrick-on-Shannon is a corrupted name, derived from a *carra* or ' weir ' on the Shannon. More than 600 Irish names contain the word *carrick* or *carrig*, a ' rock,' which also appears as *creag, craig, crag*, or *creg*. CARRICK, an old Scotch earldom, now included in Ayrshire, is from the same source, referring possibly to a big boulder on the march of Ayrshire and Galloway, now known as the Taxing Stone.

Carrow is found in more than 700 names of Irish townlands. It is a corruption of *ceathramhadh*, a ' quarter,' from *cethair*, ' four.' The old townlands were frequently divided into quarters, distinguished by their shape or position. CARROWBEG, the ' little quarter,' is common, while LE-CARROW, the 'half quarter,' and CARROW-KEEL, the ' narrow quarter,' each occur more than sixty times.

Carson City, the state capital of Nevada, was named from Kit Carson, a famous western hunter, who guided Fremont's exploring expedition across the mountains in 1842.

Cartagena, or CARTHAGENA, in Spain, was founded about 243 B.C., by Hasdrubal. To distinguish it from *Carthago Vetus*, on the site of Tarragona, it was called by the Romans ' New Carthage,' *Carthago Nova*, whence the Arabic form *Kartajina*, of which Cartagena is the Spanish corruption. CARTAGENA, on the north coast of South America, was founded in 1533 by Pedro de Heredia, and named after Cartagena in Spain. There is also a CARTAGO in Costa Rica, and another near Bogotá. Cartagena means New-Newtown, the African Carthage being a Tyrian colony planted on the site of the Sidonian colony of Byrsa (*Bozra*, the 'city'), and called *Keretchadeschat*, the 'New town,' whence the Greek name Karthada and the Roman name Carthago.

Carteret's Island, one of the Salomon group; CARTERET'S HARBOUR in New Ireland; and CARTERET POINT in Egmont Island were discovered and named in 1767 by Captain Philip Carteret.

Cartier River, an affluent of the St. Lawrence, bears the name of the discoverer, Jacques Cartier, who, in 1535, sailed up the St. Lawrence as far as the site of Montreal.

Casco Bay, in Maine, U.S.A., signifies 'Heron Bay,' from the native word *casco*, a 'heron.'

Cashel in Tipperary, the capital of the kings of Munster, is from the old Irish *caiseal*, which denotes a circular stone fort. The word is derived from, or cognate with, the Latin *castellum*. No less than fifty Irish townlands are called Cashel, and in fifty more it forms the first element in the name. The Irish *caislen*, a 'castle,' is a corruption of *castellum*. *Caislen-riabhach*, the 'grey castle,' a town in Roscommon, gave to the surrounding barony the well-known name which has been Anglicised as CASTLEREAGH, and *Caislen-an-Bharraigh*, 'Barry's castle,' has now become CASTLEBAR in Mayo.

Cashmere (KASHMIR) is the European form of the Sanskrit *Kasmíra*, probably the *Kaspeiria* of Ptolemy, since the native legend explains the name as *Kâsyapa-mar*, the 'dwelling of *Kâsyapa*,' a personage who, in Hindu mythology, opens the cleft through which the Jhelum drains the valley.

Caspian, the European name of the great inland sea of Asia, was so called by the Greeks from the Caspii, a tribe who, in the time of Herodotus, dwelt on its western shore, probably in the district of JASP, which is supposed to preserve their name.

Cassel, which crowns an isolated hill near Lille, is believed to be the Roman *Castellum Morinorum*. CASSEL, the capital of the former electorate of HESSE-CASSEL, was probably also a Roman

castellum. The name appears as *Chasselle* in 913 and *Casella* in 1008. BERNCASTEL, written *Berincastel* in the eleventh century, evidently contains a personal name.

Castel-Sarrasin (Tarn et Garonne), on the River Azine, is not a Saracenic castle, but merely a corruption of *Castel-sur-Azine*. So PONTRESINA in the Graubünden, formerly *Ponte Saraceno*, may be explained from the Rhætian word *serras*, a 'barrier.'

Castellamare (Castel-a-mare), a town on the Bay of Naples, surrounds the 'castle on the sea,' built by Frederic II.

Castile is the English form of the Spanish name CASTILLA, so called from the line of castles érected against the Moors on the frontier of the kingdom of Leon in the ninth and following centuries. Old Castile and New Castile mark the successive stages of the conquest.

Castleton, in Derbyshire, is the town near Peak Castle, which was erected by William Peverel, a natural son of William the Conqueror. CASTLETON in Cleveland is the town near the Castle of de Brus (Bruce). CASTLETOWN, the capital of Isle of Man, is the English translation of the Manx name *Bally Cashtel*. It surrounds Castle Rushin, long the residence of the kings of Man.

Castro, the chief town in the Isle of Chilóe, was founded in 1566 by Lope Garcia de Castro.

Castro Giovanni, in Sicily, occupies the site of Enna, a natural fortress called by the Romans *Castrum Ennæ*, a name which was assimilated by the Arabs as *Kasr-Janni*, and this, after the erection of a castle by Frederick II. of Aragon, became *Castro Janni*, and finally by folk-etymology, CASTRO GIOVANNI, which apparently would signify 'John's Castle.' The modern Greek names of KASTRO, a town in Lemnos, and of KASTRO, a town in Imbros, refer to castles erected by the Turks.

Catalonia, in Spanish CATALUÑA, is a name the meaning of which is unknown. It was occupied by the Alans, and about 470 A.D. by the West Goths, whence the conjecture that the name might be a corruption of *Gothalania*, or *Gotholunia*.

Catania, a town in Sicily, at the foot of Etna, anciently *Katana*, is believed to be from the Phœnician *Kothon*, 'small,' meaning either the little town, or more probably the little harbour, as compared with the great harbours of the neighbouring settlements of Syracuse and Messina. The variant form Catina, which has been referred to the Italic word *catinus* (Sicilian *cetinon*), a 'dish' or 'bowl,' is probably only an assimilated form of the Phœnician name.

Catastrophe, Cape, at the western entrance of Spencer Gulf, South Australia, was so called by Flinders, because, on February 2nd, 1802, his cutter was upset with a loss of eight men.

Catawba River, South Carolina, is named from the Catawba, a Dakota tribe, once the most powerful people in South Carolina, but now reduced to some hundred and twenty souls.

Caterick, in Yorkshire, preserves the name of the Roman station of Cataractonium.

Catmere or CATMORE, in Berks, is the A.S. *Catmere.* There is no mere, the land being high, hence the name is probably a corruption of the British *Coedmawr*, the 'great wood.' To the O.N. *katz*, a 'boat,' we may refer such names as CATFOSS, the 'boat foss' or brook; or CATWICK, Domesday *Catinwic*, the 'boat bay,' both in Yorkshire. KETTWIG, near Dusseldorf, was formerly *Katwik*, the 'boat bay.'

Cato's Bank, off the Great Australian Barrier reef, was discovered in 1803 by the ship *Cato.*

Catoche, Cape, at the north-east corner of Yucatan, was discovered by Hernandez de Cordoba on March 1st, 1517. Bernal Diaz tells us that the cazique welcomed the Spaniards with the words *Con escotoch, Con escotoch,* 'Come in to my house'; and hence the Spaniards took Catoche for the name of the village, now transferred to the Cape. According to recent researches *conex cotoch* would mean in the Maya language 'come into our town.'

Cattaro, in Dalmatia, is the *Cattarus* of Procopius, and probably the *Dekadaron* of the Ravenna geographer.

Caucasus was anciently *Graucasus,* explained by Pliny as a Scythian name meaning *nive candidus,* an etymology partly supported by scholars, who think that the first element is *grau* or *crau,* a 'rock' or mountain, the second meaning 'white.'

Cavalli Islands, on the N.W. coast of New Zealand, were so named by Cook in 1769 because he obtained from the natives some fish which they called *cavalles.*

Cavan, a town occupying a remarkable hollow, gives its name to an Irish county. It is explained by the Gaelic *cabhan,* a 'cavity,' whence also the Scotch names of COWAN and CAVEN.

Cawthorne in the West Riding, and CAWTHORNE CAMPS in the North Riding of Yorkshire, were probably named from some leafless or 'callow thorn,' an etymology supported by the Domesday form *Caltorn.*

Cawnpore (KÁNHPUR), in India, means the 'city of Kánha,' according to the tradition from a Zemindar named Kánha, but more probably from Kánha (Krishna) the 'beloved one,' whence we have CANNANORE, in Malabar, which is the English form of *Kahnúr* or *Kahnanúr,* the 'town of Kánha.'

Caxamarca, a town high up on the Andes in Peru, is a corruption of *Kassamarca,* the place or town of frost, the word *marca* meaning a 'stockade' in Quichua.

Caxoeira or CACHOIRA, the 'waterfall,' is a not uncommon name in Brazil.

Cayenne, at the mouth of the river of the same name, is the capital of French Guiana. It is probably a variant form of Guiana, as is indicated by the old form *Cainana.*

Cayo, plural **Cayos,** a Spanish word of Celtic origin cognate with the English *quay,* is used in the West Indies and elsewhere to denote coral reefs or sandbanks. It often Englished as Cay or Key, as GUN CAY, FLAMINGO CAY, KEY WEST, the GRAND CAYS, and the town of LAS CAYES in Haiti.

Cefalu (Greek *Cephalœdium*), on the northern coast of Sicily, is a conspicuous 'skull-shaped' limestone boss on whose summit stood the Greek city, and at whose base is a noble Norman cathedral built by King Roger. CEPHALONIA, the largest of the Ionian Islands, preserves the old Greek name *Kephala, Kephallonia,* or *Kephallenia,* which is a sort of translation of the older Phœnician name *Samos,* the 'lofty.' KEPHALO, the 'head,' is the Neo-Greek name given to headlands in Imbros and elsewhere.

Celébes, one of the Sunda Islands, was called by the Portuguese *Ilhas dos Celébes e dos Macaçares,* from the native names of two tribes which inhabited it. From the Macaçares comes the name of the town and peninsula of MACASSAR (*q.v.*).

Celts, or **Kelts,** is a name which, owing to a curious misapprehension, has become attached to the Irish and Welsh, as well as to the ancient Gauls and Britons. The people called Celtæ by classical writers were probably of Basque race, some of whom, in Central Gaul, acquired the language of the Belgæ. Hence the term Celtic was wrongly applied to the Belgic speech, and the races speaking languages of the same family were called Celts. There is no evidence that the word Celtæ was used by ancient writers to denote any of the so-called 'Celtic' races of our islands.

Cette, a French Mediterranean port, anciently *Sition, Setius,* or *Seta,* becoming *Ceta* in 1250, is probably a Greek name referring to the export of corn.

Ceuta is a town on the coast of Morocco, nearly opposite Gibraltar. The Roman name *Septem Fratres,* the 'seven brothers,' was derived from the seven conspicuous hills which rise above the town. The Maghrebi name *Sebta,* 'the seven,' is a dialectic corruption of the Arabic *Sebat* which translates the Roman name.

Cévennes, a range of mountains in the south of France, called *Cevenna* or *Cebenna* by Cæsar, and *Kemmenon Oros* by Strabo, is a name explained by Glück and others from the Celtic *cefn,* a 'ridge,' but Helbig assigns reasons for referring it to a pre-Aryan word, meaning a hill or mountain, which survives as the word *Cima,* which we have in the CIMA DE JAZI and other Swiss peaks, as well as in CIMIEZ, near Nice, and in the mountains of Viterbo, north of Rome, anciently called the Ciminian Forest. (*See* CIMIEZ.)

Ceylon is a corruption of the Sanskrit name *Sinhala,* 'the dwelling of lions'; the followers of Vijaga, who, according to Indian history or legend, conquered the island in 543 B.C., calling themselves 'the lions.' Lunka (Sanskrit *Lanka*), 'the island,' is, however, the oldest name in the literature of Buddhism and Brahminism. The name *Siele diba* in Cosmas Indicus, and the *Serendib* of the Arabian geographers, are corruptions of the Sanskrit *Sinhaladvipa,* or Sinhala Island. The Malays, wishing to make the name significant in their own language, derived it from *sila* or *sela,* a 'precious stone,' and called it *Pulo Selan,* the 'isle of gems,' which was translated by the Arabs as *Jaziràt-ul-Yakut,* 'the isle of rubies.' Marco Polo, seemingly deriving his knowledge from Javanese sources, calls it *Seilan,* whence the Portuguese forms *Cilan* and *Ceilaon,* from the last of which the English form Ceylon has been obtained.

Chablais, a district in Savoy, south of the Lake of Geneva, is usually said to be a corruption of a Low-Latin name, *Pagus Caputlacensis,* a translation of the Celtic name *Pennelocos,* 'the head of the loch,' which we have in the Antonine Itinerary. But the medieval form *Chablasium* points, as Gatschet contends, rather to the French *chablis,* Old French *chaable,* Low-Latin *cadabalum,* meaning fallen trees, or a place where the wind has levelled the trees on the mountain slopes. This is supported by the village-names of CHABLIE and CHABLOZ in Canton Vaud.

Chadileuvu, a Patagonian river, is from *chadi,* 'salt,' and *leuvu,* a 'river,' whence the LIULEUVU or 'white river,' and the RUGILEUVU or 'reedy river.'

Chaleur Bay, New Brunswick, was called by Jacques Cartier in 1534, *Baye des Chaleurs,* 'warm bay,' in contrast to the cold he had experienced on the eastern coast of Newfoundland.

Challock, in Kent, has been identified with a place called in a charter *æt Cealflocan,* which would mean an enclosure (*loca*) for calves. SHIPLAKE, Oxon, may possibly be from *sceap-loca,* a 'sheep-fold.'

Châlons-sur-Marne was the Roman *Durocatalaunum,* 'the stronghold of the Catalauni.' The name Châlons is from *Catalaunis,* the dative plural of the tribe-name. CHALON-SUR-SAÔNE is a corruption of *Cabillonum,* supposed to signify a place where horses were bred, but referred by d'Arbois de Jubainville to the personal name Cabillo.

Chalmers, the Port of Dunedin, New Zealand, bears the name of Dr. Thomas Chalmers, a leader of the Disruption.

Chambéry, the capital of the Dukes of Savoy, on the River Leysse, is a corruption of the Celto-Latin name *Camperiacium,* usually supposed to mean the place at the bend (*cam*) of the water (*bior*), but is more probably from a personal name.

Champagne, one of the old provinces of France, owing to the chalky soil, was free from forest, and hence obtained its name which signifies the 'open country' or 'plain.' Down to the sixth century it was known by the Latin name *Campania,* which in the thirteenth had become *Champangnie.* In the CAMPAGNA of Rome the Italian form of the same word is used to designate the broad plain, formerly called *Latium,* whose inhabitants were called LATINS. (*See* CAPUA.)

Champion Bay, in Western Australia, was first visited by the schooner *Champion* in 1838.

Chamounix or CHAMOUNI, in Savoy, is a corruption of *Campus Munitus* or *Champ Muni*, the 'defenced field,' a name given by the Benedictine monks to the site of their priory. In 1287 we have a mention of *Richardus, prioratus Campi muniti*, and in 1290 it is called *la terre de Chamonix*.

Champlain, Lake, between the States of Vermont and New York, was discovered in 1608 by Samuel de Champlain, the great French explorer, who also discovered the Lakes of Huron and Ontario, and founded the city of Quebec. The CHAMPLAIN RIVER, and CHAMPLAIN, a city in the province of Quebec, also bear his name.

Chaos Islands, a group near Port Elizabeth in South Africa, bear a Portuguese name, *Ilhas Châos*, the 'flat islands.'

Charleroi is a town in Belgium, of which the citadel was built in 1666 by Charles II., king of Spain, when the name was changed from Charnoy to Charleroi. ST. CHARLES, in Missouri, where a Spanish fort was established in 1769, was so called from the name-saint of Charles III., king of Spain.

Charleston is the capital of South Carolina. In 1670 a town was built on Albemarle Point to which Lord Shaftesbury gave the name of *Charles Town* in compliment to Charles II., from whom the patentees had obtained the grant of Carolina. In 1680 the settlement was removed to Oyster Point, on the Ashley and Cowper Rivers, and was then for a time called *New Charleston*.

Charlestown, in Massachusetts, was founded in 1629 on the River Charles by fifty colonists from Salem. The RIVER CHARLES was one of the names placed on Captain John Smith's map of New England by Prince Charles, afterwards Charles I.

Charlton Island, in Hudson Bay, was so named by Captain James in 1632 in compliment to Prince Charles, afterwards Charles II.

Charlottenburg, near Berlin, is so called from a schloss built in 1696 for the Electress Sophia Charlotte, wife of Frederick I. In QUEEN CHARLOTTE SOUND, Cook's Strait, Cook landed, and formally took possession of New Zealand in the name of George III., naming the place after Queen Charlotte of England,

Her name is also borne by CAPE CHARLOTTE, POINT CHARLOTTE, QUEEN CHARLOTTE'S FORELAND, and QUEEN CHARLOTTE'S ISLAND.

Charmouth and CHARMINSTER, in Dorset, stand on the River Char. The Domesday names *Cernemude* and *Cerminstre* show that the name of the CHAR was identical with that of the CHURN, called *Cirn-ea* (Cirn-water) by the Saxons, whence the names of CIRENCESTER and of the village of CERNEY.

Charters Towers, Queensland, a place with basaltic hills resembling towers, bears the name of an officer of the colonial police.

Chartres (Eure et Loir), the Merovingian *Carnotas*, was a town of the *Carnutes* of Cæsar. The surrounding territory, now called PAYS CHARTRAIN, was the *Pagus Carnutensis*, which becomes *Pagus Carnotenus* in Gregory of Tours.

Chartreuse, anciently *Catorissium*, a wild valley in Dauphiny, was the place selected by St. Bruno in 1086 for his hermitage, which ultimately became the mother-house of the great Carthusian Order to which it gave a name, as well as to numerous Carthusian monasteries, which are called CERTOSA in Italian, CARTUJA in Spanish, CARTHAUSE in German, and CHARTERHOUSE in English. In like manner the Cluniac Order takes its name from CLUGNY, the Cistercian from the forest of CITEAUX (*Cistercium*), and the Premonstratensian from PRÉ MONTRÉ.

Châteauroux (Indre), in Latin documents *Castrum Rodolphi,* 'Rudolph's Castle,' took its name from a castle built in the tenth century by Raoul, prince of Déols. CHÂTEAU-GONTIER (Mayenne) is named from a castle built in 1037 by Gunther, the steward of the Counts of Anjou. CHÂTEAU-BRIANT (Loire Inférieure) is so called from a castle built in 1015 by Briant, Count of Penthièvre. CHÂTEAU-THIERRY (Aisne) is named from a castle said to have been built by Charles Martel for Thierry IV. CHÂTELHERAULT was *Castellum Eraldi*; CHÂTELARD was *Castellum arduum*; CHÂTEAUFORT was *Castrum Forte,* and CHÂTILLON was *Castellulum*.

Chatham, Kent, is in A.S. *Cethaema mearc*. Since CHETWOOD in Bucks is the A.S. *Cetwudu*, where *cet* is apparently the Welsh *coed*, a 'wood,' and CATMERE, Berks, is probably a corruption of *Coedmawr*, the 'great wood,' Chatham may perhaps be explained from the same source. (*See* CAEN.) CHATHAM ISLANDS, a group east of New Zealand, were discovered in 1791 by Lieutenant Broughton in the brig *Chatham.*

Chaudière Falls, above Ottawa, are so called from the French Canadian *chaudière,* a 'boiling kettle.' They give their name to an expansion of the Ottawa River which is called LAC DE LA CHAUDIÈRE.

Chautauqua is a town and county in New York, on LAKE CHAUTAUQUA, a name signifying a place where fish are caught.

Cheam, in Surrey (called *Ceigham* or *Cegham* in a charter of 727, and *Cheham* in one of 933), is possibly from a personal name, but more probably from *caege,* an 'enclosure' or 'warren'—*clausula, quod Angli dicunt caege,* denoting the royal hunting enclosure in which the palace of Nonsuch was afterwards built. KEYSOE or CAYSHO, in Bedfordshire, is a related name. In 793, Offa, king of the Mercians, gave to the Abbey of St. Albans land at *Caegesho* or *Caegsho,* now Keysoe.

Chelmsford, the county town of Essex, is at the ford over the River Chelmer.

Chelsea, Middlesex, was formerly supposed to be the *Ceóles-íg,* 'ship isle' or 'ship shore,' of the Chronicle (A.D. 1006), which is now identified with CHOLSEY near Wallingford, in Berks, and not with Chelsea.

Cheltenham stands on a brook called the Chelt. The form *æt Celtanhomme,* which we have in a charter, points to a nominative *Celtanhom,* the *hom* or 'enclosure' by the River Celte (genitive *Celtan*).

Cherbourg, traditionally explained as *Cæsaris burgus,* which occurs in a charter of 1234 (*Caroburgus* in 1252), is probably a Teutonic name, equivalent to our Yorkshire SCARBOROUGH, the 'burg on the scar,' or cliff.

Chertsey, Surrey, appears as *Cerotes íg,* 'Cerot's isle,' in a seventh century charter. The later forms, *Ceortesig, Certeseye,* and *Cherteseye,* give the transition to the modern name.

Chesapeake Bay, which bisects Maryland, is an Indian name usually said to mean ' mother of waters' or 'great water place,' from the number of rivers that are poured into its bosom; but is probably from the Abenaki *Kche-seippog,* meaning 'great salt water.' At the time of the settlement of Virginia a tribe called Chesapians or Chesapeake Indians, lived on the banks of the Elizabeth River.

Chesham, Bucks, may take its name from the River Chess, which rises in a large pool in the middle of the town. CASHIOBURY, in Herts, near the junction of the Chess with the Colne, was the *burh* of the Hundred of *Cashio,* referred by Camden to the name of the Cassii, a British tribe who were ruled by Cassivelaunus, but possibly to be explained from the name of the Chess.

Chester, the county town of CHESHIRE (Chestershire), was the *Deva* of the Romans, so called from standing on the Dee, the 'divine river' of the Britons. Being the station of a Roman legion it acquired the name of *Civitas Legionum,* the 'city of the legions.' This became the British *Caerleon,* from the Welsh *Caer,* a 'city,' and *leon,* a corruption of *legione,* an indeclinable substantive, formed, as in other cases, from the ablative of *legio.* While CAERLEON on the Usk, which was the Roman *Isca Silurum,* has retained its British name, Caerleon on the Dee, the 'city called legione,' became in A.S. *Lega-Ceaster* or *Lege-ceaster,* the 'legion chester,' and finally Chester, the prefix being dropped. CHESTERTON, near Cambridge, CHESTERFORD, between Cambridgeshire and Essex, and CHESTERFIELD, in Derbyshire, are names which record the sites of Roman stations.

Cheviots, a range of hills on the Scotch border, take their name from a massive broad-topped hill called the Cheviot, 2767 feet high, which forms the loftiest summit in the range. The name, like that of Chevy Chace, is doubtless from the Welsh *cefn,* a 'ridge,' literally the 'back,' which we have in the name of the CHEVIN, a hill near Otley in Yorkshire, and of another near Belper in Derbyshire, and perhaps in that of the CEVENNES (*q.v.*).

Cheyenne, the name of towns in Kansas, Nebraska, and Wyoming, is derived from the Shyenne or Cheyenne tribe, who dwelt on the Shyenne River. Their name, according to Boyd, means 'those who speak a different language.' They are a branch of the Crees, who call themselves *Né-a-ya-og,* 'those who speak the same tongue.' The Assiniboines call them *Shi-é-ya,* and the Dakotas call them *Shi-é-ala,* words of nearly the same meaning as *Né-a-ya-og.*

Chiapas, the southern province of Mexico, is a corruption of *Teochiapanecos,* the name of the tribe who held the district in the time of Cortez.

Chicago, in Michigan, stands at the mouth of the Chicago River, which rises in a boggy district of 'evil savour,' either because frequented by 'skunks' (*cikak*, plural *cikakong*), or because overgrown with garlic or 'skunk cabbage' (*shikagou*, a 'leek').

Chichakoff, a cape at the southern extremity of the Japanese Island of Kiusu, bears the name of a Russian Admiral.

Chichester, in A.S. *Cissan-ceaster*, *Cissa-ceaster*, and *Cisse-ceaster*, forms which support the tradition preserved in the Saxon Chronicle that the Roman city of Regnum became the fortress of the Saxon chieftain Cissa, son of Ælle, who, we are told, landed in 477 at *Cymenes-ora*, now KEYNOR on the Bill of Selsea, with his three sons Cymen, Wlencing, and Cissa. Wlencing being clearly the eponymus of LANCING in Sussex, makes it probable that Cymen and perhaps Cissa are also mythical names.

Chickahominy, a river in Virginia, is said by Boyd to mean the 'turkey lick.'

Chiemsee, a large lake in Bavaria, is usually said to mean the 'pine lake' (O.H.G. *kien* or *chien*, a 'pine tree'), but the oldest form of the name, *Chiminc-see*, points to a derivation from the village of CHIEMING, which must be from the personal name *Chimo*.

Chili or CHILE, a South American republic, was called by the natives *Chili mapu*, 'Chili land,' probably from the Peruvian word *chili*, 'cold,' which, according to Garcilasso de la Vega, was merely the name of the valley in which Santiago is situated. The popular etymology derives the name from *Chile-Chile*, the cry of a bird common in the country. CHILOE, a large island in the southern part of Chili, is the native name *Chil-hue*, which means a 'district of Chili.'

Chillon, a castle at the eastern end of the Lake of Geneva, called *Chilon* in 1224, was named from the stratified flagstone rock on which it stands. In the local patois paving stones are called *chillond* or *chillon*, strictly a slab of stone or ledge of rock.

Chimborazo, a volcano in Peru, 20,498 feet in height, takes its name, according to Humboldt, from the *Chimus*, a tribe near Lima who were conquered by the Incas.

China was first known to Europeans as *Serice*, and the people as *Sinæ*, names which come to us from Ptolemy (*c.* 150).

Serica must be the land of the Seres or 'silk people,' from the Chinese *ser*, silk. Sinæ must be from the name China, transmitted to the Greeks through a Semitic channel. The Periplus, A.D. 80-89, has the form *Thin*, Cosmas Indicus, *c.* 545 A.D., has *Tzinitza* and *Tzinistan*, and the Nestorian inscription of Singanfu, 781 A.D., mentions the 'King of Tzinia,' and 'Adam, Bishop of Tzinesthan' (*i.e.* Chinistan), a Persian form. Colonel Yule thinks the origin of the name is from Jih-nan, an old name of Tongking, which was the only port open to foreign trade at the beginning of our era. Professor Terrien de la Couperie thinks that it was from Tsen (Mandarin, Tien), the old name of Yunnan, through which lay the trade route to the West. The more usual opinion is that the name was derived from the great Tchin or Thing dynasty. This is supported by the name Cathay, by which the country was known to Marco Polo, which is from the Khitai or Kitai dynasty, the Mongolian name of the Liao race which ruled China from 1125 to 1207. China is still spoken of in Central Asia as the country of the Kitai, a name which became Cathay in European ears. China is a Malay form which we obtained through the Portuguese, and the Malays seem to have obtained it from the Japanese. It is noteworthy that not only our name for China, but for Ceylon (Seilan), Siam (Siyam), Paigu, Barma, Ava, and Kamboja are all Malay forms. The Chinese call their country *Chung-Kwok*, the 'middle kingdom,' or *Tien-chew*, the 'celestial dynasty.' The name of China has been curiously transferred to Canada, LA CHINE being now the name of a village near Montreal, and of the adjacent rapids on the St. Lawrence, which come from the name La Chine, given to the house built by La Salle on his feudal domain of St. Sulpice, either seriously by himself, or derisively by his neighbours, in allusion to his project of reaching China by descending the Mississippi, which he thought emptied itself into the China sea.

Chippenham, in Wilts, stands at a bend of the Avon which almost surrounds it. In the Chronicle we have *tó Cippan-hamme* and *tó Cyppanhamme*, which shows that the suffix is *-hám*, 'an enclosure,' and not *-hám*, a 'home.' The first element is usually explained from *cypa*, a 'merchant,' but is probably the genitive of the personal name *Cippa*.

Chiusi, in Central Italy, is a corruption of *Clusium*, the Roman name of the

Etruscan city of *Camars*, of which, according to the legend, Lars Porsenna was king.

Chontales, a district in Nicaragua, was so called from the tribe of the Chontals, an Aztec name meaning 'strangers.'

Christchurch, the capital of the New Zealand province of Canterbury, was so called because Christchurch is the official name of Canterbury Cathedral. CHRIST-CHURCH, a town in Hampshire, is so called from a priory built by Ralph Flambard, Bishop of Durham, and dedicated to the Saviour. MONTE CHRISTO, a small island near Elba, takes its name from a convent with the same dedication.

Christiania, the capital of Norway, was founded in 1624 by Christian IV., from whom are also named CHRISTIANSUND, at the head of a *sund* or inlet in Norway, and CHRISTIANSTAD in Sweden. From kings of the same name we have also the Danish settlements of CHRISTIANSBORG on the Gold Coast, CHRISTIANSHAAB in Greenland, and CHRISTIANSTED, the capital of St. Croix, one of the Danish West Indian Islands. CHRISTMAS SOUND, Tierra del Fuego, CHRISTMAS HARBOUR, Kerguelen's Land, and CHRISTMAS ISLAND, Polynesia, mark the places where Cook spent Christmas in the years 1774, 1776, and 1777.

Chunárgarh is a famous rock-fort on the Ganges above Benares, apparently meaning 'plane-tree fort.' But the name is believed by Dr. Burnell to be a corruption of *Charanagiri*, 'foot-hill,' a name probably given from the resemblance of the rock seen in longitudinal profile to a human foot.

Chur, or **Coire,** the capital of the Swiss Canton of the Graubünden or Grisons, was the *Curia Rætorum*, the Rhætian court of justice. The name occurs in documents of the fourth century, but is doubtless much older. CHUR is the German and English corruption of *Curia*, which takes the form COIRA in Italian, and COIRE in French, while in Romansch we have the local forms Quoira, Quera, and Cuera. The Latin word *curia*, which was used to denote the residence of a Roman procurator, is derived from the Curia at Rome, built, according to the tradition, by Curius Hostilius. The modern French *cour* and *court*, as in COURCELLES, AGINCOURT, or GRANDCOURT, are from *curtis*, a corruption of *cohors*.

Churfirsten, a range of mountains in Canton St. Gallen, are not, as is usually

supposed, named from the seven Electors (Kurfürsten) but from the dialect word *firsten*, denoting the 'summits' which once formed the linguistic boundary to the north of the Rhætian district of Chur.

Churchill River, which enters Hudson Bay at FORT CHURCHILL, is a name which first appears in 1688, and was probably bestowed in compliment to the Duke of Marlborough, then Lord Churchill, the Governor of the Hudson's Bay Company.

Cimbric Chersonese is a name sometimes applied to Jutland, from the ancient inhabitants the Cimbri, whose name, according to Grimm, is a Teutonic word meaning 'the fighters.'

Cimiez, a hill-town near Nice, is, according to Helbig, from the Ligurian or pre-Aryan word *cima*, meaning a 'hill.' Hence the name of the Ciminian forest, clothing the hills north of the Tiber, and probably of the Kemmenon Oros, now the Cévennes (*q.v.*).

Cincinnati, in Ohio, was originally called Fort Washington. The name was changed because General St. Clair, the officer in command, had been decorated with the short-lived military Order of Cincinnatus, bestowed on soldiers of the revolutionary army who, like the Roman Cincinnatus, had left their wives and farms to serve their country.

Circassia is the land of the Circassians, a Genoese corruption of the Turkish name *Tcherkess*, which means 'brigands,' literally 'those who cut off the road,' from *tcher*, a 'road,' and *kes-mek*, 'to cut off.'

Circeo, or **Circello,** an Italian cape between Naples and Ostia, is the *Circeii* of the Romans. Here one of the Homeric legends of Ulysses was localised, and a temple was built to Circe. In like manner the Romans located the Isle of the Sirens at Cape Misenum, and the Isle of Æolus in the Lipari Islands. Caieta, the nurse of Æneas, is an eponymic name invented by Virgil from the place now known as fortress of GAËTA (*q.v.*).

Cirencester, in Gloucestershire, is the A.S. *Ciren-ceaster*, *Cirne-ceaster*, or *Cyren-ceaster*, the chester on the River Churn. The Roman name *Corinium* also contains the old name of the Churn. CERNEY, A.S. *Cernéa*, is a village on the Churn, a few miles south of Cirencester.

Ciudad Rodrigo, the 'city of Roderick,' a border fortress of Spain, stormed by Wellington with great loss in January 1812, was founded by Count Rodrigo Gonzalez Giron in 1150.

Cività Vecchia, the port of Rome, was the *Portus Trajani*, which in 828 was destroyed by the Saracens. In 854 the inhabitants returned to the site of what then began to be called the 'ancient city.'

Clackmannan, a Scotch county, takes its name from the village of Clackmannan, 'the stone of Manu,' a sacred stone which still remains. The word *clach*, which in the form *cloch* is common in Irish names (*see* CLOGHER), means 'stone' in Gaelic, and *mannan* is the genitive of *manu*, a name borne by Mona, now Anglesey, by the Isle of Man, and by a district on the Forth. The name of the district of *Manu* is also preserved by SLA-MANNAN MOOR in the county of Linlithgow, which is from *Sliab-mannan*, 'the mountain of Manu.'

Clanmaurice, a barony in Kerry, is named from the *clann* or descendants of Maurice Fitzgerald. Two baronies, in the counties of Tipperary and Limerick, called CLANWILLIAM, take their names from the descendants of William Burke. CLANDEBOY, in County Down, which gives the title of Baron to Lord Dufferin, is also a tribal name, being a corruption of *Clann-Aedha-buidhe*, the 'descendants of Hugh the yellow,' who was slain in 1283.

Clare, an Irish county, takes its name from the village of Clare, so called from a plank bridge (Irish *clàr*, a 'board') which crossed the stream. CLARE, a town in Suffolk, arose round the vast castle of Gilbert de Clare, the last Earl of Gloucester and Hereford, who died in 1313. Elizabeth, his sister, who founded CLARE COLLEGE, Cambridge, married William de Burgh, Earl of Ulster, carrying the lordship of Clare into that family. Her granddaughter, Elizabeth de Burgh, married Lionel Plantagenet, who inherited the Suffolk barony in right of his wife, whereupon his father, Edward III., created him *Dux Clarensis*, erecting the 'town, castle, and honour of Clare' into a duchy. From the Dux Clarensis we have the royal dukedom of CLARENCE and the Clarenceux King-at-Arms. In compliment to William, Duke of Clarence, afterwards William IV., CAPE CLARENCE, PORT CLARENCE, the CLARENCE RIVER, and the CLARENCE ISLANDS, all in Arctic America, were named in the years 1818-1829. CLAREMONT, Esher, once belonged to Lord Clare.

Clarens, a village on the Lake of Geneva, is a corruption of *glareanus* (*locus*), the 'gravelly' place, so called because built on gravel.

Clarke's Island, near Plymouth, Massachusetts, bears the name of the master's mate of the *Mayflower*. CLARKE'S FORK, a branch of the Yellowstone River, was reached by Lewis and Clarke when they crossed the Continent to the Pacific. CAPE CLARK, on the east coast of Greenland, was named by Scoresby after his brother-in-law John Clark.

Clee Hills, Salop, often called the Clees, are mentioned in a charter as *Les Clives*, 'the cliffs,' which is probably an adaptation of an older name. Near the foot of the Clees stands the town of CLEOBURY MORTIMER, in Domesday *Claiberie*, which must mean *Clebury*, 'Clee town.'

Clermont, in Auvergne, was the Roman *Augustonemetum.* The Merovingian castle on the hill was called *Castrum de Claro Monte*, of which Clermont is the modern form. So *Clara vallis*, the mother convent of the Cistercian order, became CLAIRVAUX, the daughter houses of Rievaulx and Jorvaulx, in the Yorkshire valleys of the Rye and the Ure, being designated as *Rie-vallis* and *Yore-vallis.* LAC SAINT CLAIR, between Lake Huron and Lake Erie, was discovered and named by La Salle, in August 1679, probably from St. Clare of Assisi, whose festival is on August 12. CLERMONT, a town in Queensland, bears the name of Lord Clermont, a friend of the Governor.

Cliffe, or **Cliffe-at-Hoo,** in Kent, has been identified as the place where the Council of Cloveshó was held. Hoo, spelt *Hógh* in the seventh century, and afterward *Hó*, denotes the 'hough,' or heel of land which projects between the Thames and the Medway.

Clogher, an Episcopal See in Tyrone, means the 'stony place.' A local legend derives the name from the Irish *cloch-oir*, the 'stone of gold,' a gilt idol of the heathen Irish, said to have been preserved in the church till recent times. CLOGHER is the name of sixty townlands in Ireland. CLOGHAN, CLACKAN, or CLACHAN, the 'stones,' is a common village name, sometimes denoting stepping-stones, also the stones in a churchyard, or the stones of which the houses were built. CLADDAGH, in Ireland and in the Isle of Man, and CLADICH in Islay, are Gaelic names signifying a stony shore or shingly beach.

Cloyne, an ancient Episcopal See in County Cork, was formerly called *Cluain Uamha*, the 'meadow of the cave,' the cathedral having been founded by Colman on the meadow near a cave which had probably been the dwelling of a hermit. CLONMEL, the county town of Tipperary, is a corruption of *Cluain-meala*, a name older than the town, since it refers to a meadow abounding with nests of wild bees. CLONFERT, in Galway, is a corruption of *Cluainferta*, the 'meadow of the grave,' on which St. Brendan built a monastery in 533. Similarly CLONTURK is the 'meadow of the boar,' CLONBOY is the 'yellow meadow,' and CLONBANE the 'white meadow.' There are places in Scotland called CLONE and CLUNY, the 'meadow.' CLONCURRY, in Kildare, is the Old Irish *Cluain-Conaire*, the 'meadow of Conary,' a personage unknown to history or tradition. CLONCURRY, a town in Queensland, was so named by Mr. Lawless, a squatter, after Lord Cloncurry, the head of his family.

Clyde, the great Scotch river, is called *Clota* by Tacitus. Professor Rhys thinks the name may be that of a Celtic river goddess. But the name cannot be connected with the Welsh river name CLWYD, which is supposed to mean 'warm.'

Coati, an island in the Peruvian Lake Titicaca, is a corruption of *Coya-ta*, the 'place of the Coya,' or 'spouse,' from a temple of the moon-goddess Quilla, who being the sister and wife of Inti, the sun-god, was called Coya-Inti, the spouse of Inti, *coya* being the name given to the sister and wife of the reigning Inca.

Coblenz, at the confluence of the Rhine and the Mosel, where a post was established by Drusus about 9 B.C., is called *Confluentes* by Suetonius, afterwards *Confluentibus*, and finally *Castrum Confluentis* by Gregory of Tours. COBLENZ, or KOBLENZ, in Canton Aargau, at the confluence of the Aar and the Rhine, also a Roman station, was probably called Confluentes. The usual French corruption of the word is CONFLANS. There are places of this name at the confluence of the Seine and the Marne, of the Seine and the Oise, and of the Orne and the Yron ; and a CONFOLENS in the Charente at the confluence of the Vienne and the Goire.

Coburg, in the principality of Saxe-Coburg-Gotha, appears in a document of the eleventh century as KOBURG, perhaps the 'cow castle' (O.H.G. *Ko*, 'a cow '). COBURG BAY in Lancaster Sound, and the COBURG PENINSULA in North Australia were so named in 1818 in compliment to Prince Leopold of Saxe-Coburg, who married Princess Charlotte of England in 1817.

Cocha means a lake in Quichua. Hence the hybrid name of Caballo Cocha, the 'horse lake,' in Peru.

Cochin, a native state on the Malabar coast, takes its name from the town of COCHIN (*Kochchi-banda*), the 'small fort.' Here Vasco da Gama died in 1524, and Xavier preached in 1530. COCHIN, on the delta of the Mekong River, was called by the Portuguese COCHIN-CHINA, a misleading name, in order to distinguish it from Cochin on the Malabar coast. The name is derived from *kochi*, a 'marsh.'

Cockburn Island, one of the South Shetlands, was named in 1843 after Admiral Sir George Cockburn, one of the Lords of the Admiralty, whose name is borne by many places in the Australian and the Arctic Regions, among them CAPE COCKBURN, POINT COCKBURN, COCKBURN BAY, and the COCKBURN GROUP.

Cod, Cape, in Massachusetts, is the oldest English name in New England. It was discovered in 1602 by Bartholomew Gosnold, who landed on the headland, and named it from the abundance of cod-fish.

Cognac, in the twelfth century called *Coignac*, is supposed to be a corruption of *Coniacum*, 'the place in the corner,' from the Celtic *kon* (French *coin*), cognate with the Latin *cuneus*, a 'wedge.'

Coimbra, in Portugal, was the Roman *Conembrica*.

Colchester, Essex, on the Colne, was the Roman *Colonia Camalodunum*, the Welsh *Caer Collun*, and the A.S. *Colenceaster* and *Colne-ceaster*. The coincidence is puzzling, but the name signifies probably the chester on one of the many rivers called the Colne (A.S. *Coln*) or 'stony' river. It is possible, however, that the Essex Colne may be the river of the Colonia, but the River Colne in Gloucestershire is *Cunuglan* or *Cunuglæ* in A.S. Geoffrey of Monmouth's King Coel is not an historical or mythological personage, but merely the eponymus of Colchester.

Coleraine, in Londonderry, takes its name from a piece of land covered with ferns, and hence called *Cuil-rathain*, 'fern corner,' which was given to St. Patrick on which to build a church, round which the town grew up.

Colesberg, a division in the Cape Colony, was named in 1839 after Sir Lowry Cole, then Governor of the Cape.

Coll, one of the Hebrides, is named from the Gaelic *coll*, a 'hazel.'

Colmar, in Elsass, was called *Columbaria* in 865. The medieval Latin form *Collis Martis*, 'Mars Hill,' is merely an attempt to explain the name.

Cologne is' the French form which we irrationally use of the German name KÖLN. It occupies the site of the *Oppidum Ubiorum*, where in 51 A.D. a Roman colony was planted by the Emperor Claudius, and named *Colonia Agrippina*, because it was the birthplace of his wife Agrippina, the daughter of Germanicus. In the sixteenth century we called German and Italian towns by their right names, but owing to the general use of French, and ignorance of German and Italian, we have now unfortunately adopted such French forms as Cologne for Köln, Mayence for Mainz, Trèves for Trier, Liège for Lüttich, Malines for Mecheln, Louvain for Leuven, Aix la Chapelle for Aachen, Ratisbon for Regensburg, Alsace for Elsass, Nice for Nizza, Venice for Venezia, Rome for Roma, and Naples for Napoli.

Colonna, Cape, more correctly Kabo Kolonnais, is the modern name of Cape Sunium in Attica. It acquired the name from thirteen columns of white marble, belonging to a temple of Athené, which stand on the highest point, forming a prominent landmark for sailors.

Colon, or **Aspinwall,** a town on the isthmus of Panama, bears the Spanish form of the name of the Genoese discoverer of the New World, Christoforo Columbo, who, when naturalised as a Spanish subject, called himself Colon. Columbus is the Latinised form of the Italian name Columbo, which is believed to have been derived through the Irish monks in Northern Italy from St. Columba, the 'dove,' whence COLONSAY, the 'Isle of St. Columba,' in the Hebrides. In memory of Christopher Columbus many American names have been bestowed. In 1790 the name of COLUMBIA was given to the federal district in the United States which contains the city of Washington, the federal capital. COLUMBIA is also the name of the State capital of South Carolina, and of more than sixty places in the United States. The State capital of Ohio, and some thirty other places in the United States are called COLUMBUS. The UNITED STATES OF COLUMBIA in South America were federated under this name in 1820, and the Spanish province of Nueva Granada, in Central America, was renamed COLOMBIA in 1811. The COLUMBIA or OREGON RIVER, the entrance of which had been missed by Captain Cook and by Vancouver, was discovered in 1787 by the Boston merchant ship *Columbia* of 200 tons, and the sloop *Washington* of 90 tons. On the second voyage of the *Columbia* in 1792, the commander, Captain Robert Gray, ascended the river as far as GRAY'S BAY, and named the great stream after his vessel. The colony of BRITISH COLUMBIA was named in 1858, not from Columbus but from the river.

Colorado, one of the United States, takes its Spanish name from a great river ultimately falling into the Gulf of California, which was called Colorado, the 'red' or 'coloured' river, from the red mud held suspended in the water. The RED RIVER, which forms the northern boundary of Texas, is a translation of its former Spanish name Rio Colorado. There is a third RIO COLORADO in the Argentine Republic.

Columbo, the capital of Ceylon, is the Singalese *Kolûmbu, Kolômbo, Korûmbo,* or *Corumbu* which is said to mean a 'haven' or harbour.

Como, a city in Northern Italy which gives a name to the LAGO DI COMO, was the Roman *Comum,* a name probably Gaulish. The English *combe,* a loan word from the Welsh *cwm,* a 'hollow' or 'valley' is the source of numerous English names. We have places called COMPTON in Worcestershire, Berks, Somerset, Sussex, and Gloucestershire, all called *Cumtun* in A.S. charters, while COMPTON in Dorset and Surrey are spelt *Cumbtun* and *Comptun.* From the same source we have many French village names, such as LA COMBE, COMBES, COMBAS, and COMBET. (*See* pp. 359, 375.)

Comorin, the Cape at the southern extremity of India, is so called from a temple, which still exists, of Kumárí, the 'virgin,' one of the names of the goddess Durgá, the wife of Siva. The temple must be very old, Cape Comorin being the *Kamaria Akron* of Ptolemy, and Marco Polo mentions a country which he calls *Comari.*

Comoro is the largest of the COMORES, or COMORO ISLANDS, west of Madagascar. Comoro is a Portuguese corruption of the Arabic *Komaïr,* 'little moons,' or little moon islands.

Compiègne (Oise) is the *Compendium* of the Antonine Itinerary, so called because it lay on the direct or short road between Beauvais and Soissons.

Conception Bay, in Newfoundland, is the English translation of the Portuguese name, *Bahia da Concepção,* given by Corte Real in 1501. PUERTO DE LA CONCEPCION, in Haiti, was the name given by Columbus to a bay discovered by him on December 7th, 1492, the eve of the feast of the Conception of the Virgin Mary. Columbus also called one of the Bahamas (probably Rum Kay) *Isla de S. Maria de la Concepcion*. CONCEPCION is a town on the River Uruguay; and CIUDAD DE LA CONCEPCION is the name of a seaport in Chili, founded by Pedro de Valdivia, 1550-1558.

Concord, the State capital of New Hampshire, was so designated in commemoration of the amicable settlement of a dispute as to the State and county to which it belonged. The Indian name was *Penacook*, and in 1733 it had been incorporated as a town of ESSEX COUNTY, Massachusetts, under the name of Rumford, many of the early settlers in Essex County coming from Essex in England.

Condamine, a town in Queensland, bears the name of the secretary to Sir Robert Darling, Governor of New South Wales.

Condé, the title of an illustrious branch of the Bourbons, is derived from the town of Condé in the Nord, which, with many similar names, is derived from a Celtic word *condate*, denoting the confluence of two streams. CONDÉ, called *Condatum* in 870, and afterward *Condat*, stands at the confluence of the Haine and the Scheldt. CONDÉ-SUR-NOIREAU, in Normandy, is at the confluence of the Noireau and the Drouance. COSNE, in the Nièvre, called *Condaté* in the Antonine Itinerary, is at the junction of a small stream with the Loire, and CANDES is at the junction of the Vienne and the Loire. CANNSTADT, near Stuttgard, formerly Candistat, is at the junction of the Canbach and the Neckar. CUMBER, COMBER, COMMER, and COMERAGH, in Ireland, and CUMMERTREES and CUMBERNAULD, in Scotland, are from the Gaelic *comar*, a 'confluence.'

Conejera, 'coney island,' one of the Balearic group, is from the Spanish *conejo*, a 'rabbit.'

Cong is an Irish name meaning a narrow strait or a river between two lakes. At CONG ABBEY, in Mayo, which stands on the river connecting Lough Mask with Lough Carrib, the last native king of Ireland, Roderick O'Connor, passed his last days.

Congo is the European name of the great river of Central Africa, which is called the ZAIRE (*q.v.*) by the natives. The word Congo, which means 'mountains,' is a mere ghost name, due to a curious blunder. In 1484 the Portuguese navigator, Diego Cão (Diego Cam), accompanied by the geographer, Martin Behaim, reached the mouth of a great river, where he erected a Padrão (Padran) (*q.v.*) or stone-pillar, bearing the Portuguese arms, and the name of a saint. Hence the river was at first called Rio do Padrão. The Portuguese were informed by the natives that the country near the mouth of the river was subject to a great monarch whom they called *Mwani Congo*, or 'Lord of Congo,' who lived at a place called Ambasse Congo. From this Congo kingdom the river which traversed it acquired the name of the Congo River. In the Mandingo language *Kong* means mountains, and the coast-range in Guinea goes by the name of the KONG MOUNTAINS (*q.v.*). In 1876-77 the river was descended by H. M. Stanley who called it the LIVINGSTONE, a barbarous name which has deservedly fallen into disuse. If any change is made, the native name of the Zaire should be restored.

Connaught is a corruption of the old name *Con-nacht*. Irish legend divided Ireland into two halves, *Leth-Chuinn* or Conn's half, and *Leth-Moga* or Mog's half, which have dwindled to Connaught and Munster, Conn's half becoming Connacht, which may be rendered 'Conn's people' or Conn's descendants. The word *-nacht* may be recognised in the tribal name of the *Nagnatæ* of Ptolemy.

Connecticut, one of the New England states, is named from its chief river, discovered by the Dutchman Adrian Block in 1614, and called by the natives *Quonektacut*, *Quonehtacut*, or *Qunnitukut*, which means the 'long river,' literally the 'river without end,' from the Cherokee *Koon* or *Ko*, 'river,' which we have in the rivers KEN-NEBUSH and KEN-NEBEC, both in Maine.

Connemara, a corruption of the Old Irish name *Conmaicne-mara*, is a tribal name which has become territorial. Conmaic-ne are the descendants (*ne*, 'progeny') of Conmac, and *mara* is the genitive of *muir*, the 'sea.' Connemara is therefore the land of the 'O'Conmacs of the sea.'

Constantia, a district in the Cape Colony, was so named in 1686 after the wife of the Dutch Governor, Simon van der Stell. Here the celebrated Cape Vintage, called Constantia, was grown.

Constantine, a town in Algeria, was so called because having been destroyed in 311 A.D. it was rebuilt two years afterwards by order of the Emperor Constantine. CONSTANTINOPLE is the Anglicised form of Constantinopolis, the 'city of Constantine,' the name given by Constantine to Byzantium when he made it the Eastern capital of the Empire. STAMBOUL, or ISTAMBUL, 'at the city,' is the modern Greek name, and may be compared to our own usage when we say of a visit to London that we are going 'to town.' On some Turkish coins, the name Istambul has been corrupted to Islambul or 'much Islam.' In Chinese πόλιν became *Fulin*.

Constanz, in French CONSTANCE, is a town which has given a name to the LAKE of CONSTANCE, as we call the BODEN SEE (*q.v.*). Local tradition assigns the foundation of the town to Constantius Chlorus, the father of Constantine, but it may well be a complimentary name of the same class as Florentia, Placentia, or Valentia. The same Constantius is also said to have founded COUTANCES, the *Castra Constantia* or *Civitas Constantia* of the Romans. It is the capital of the CÔTANTIN or *Pagus Constantinus*. KUSTENDJI, in Bulgaria, at the termination of Trajan's wall, is a corruption of *Constantia* or *Constantiana*.

Conway Castle guards the passage of the River Conway, beneath it nestles the town of Conway, believed to be the *Conovium* of the Antonine Itinerary. Whether the name of the Conway is connected with that of the Solway or the Medway is doubtful.

Cook's Strait is the most important of the names which preserve the memory of James Cook, the greatest of English explorers, to whom we owe innumerable names, so well chosen and appropriate that most of them still keep their places on the map. On August 26th, 1768, Cook sailed in the *Endeavour* on his first voyage in order to observe the transit of Venus at Otaheite (Tahiti) on June 3rd, 1769. He then set sail for New Zealand, and explored the eastern coast of Australia, and after being wrecked on June 10th, 1770, reached England in June 1771. On July 13th, 1772, he sailed on his second voyage in the *Resolution*, with the *Adventure*, commanded by Captain Furneaux, and explored the Antarctic Seas, New Zealand, the New Hebrides, and New Georgia, and returned by Cape Horn to England, which he reached on July 30th, 1775. On his third voyage in the *Resolution*, with the *Discovery* commanded by Captain Charles Clerke, he sailed on July 12th, 1776, and after exploring Kerguelen Land, New Zealand, the Friendly Islands, Alaska, and Bering's

Straits, he returned to Owyhee (Hawaii), where he was killed by the natives on February 14th, 1779. The ships reached England in October 1779. COOK'S STRAIT, which separates the two larger islands of New Zealand, was missed by Tasman in 1642-1643, and first discovered by Cook in 1770. COOK'S RIVER (or COOK'S INLET), in Alaska, was the most northern point reached by Cook while exploring the western coast of America in his third voyage, 1776-1780. As Cook had proposed no name, Lord Sandwich, the First Lord of the Admiralty, gave it the name of the discoverer, for whose untimely death the country was then mourning. MOUNT COOK, the highest summit in New Zealand, 12,349 feet high, was so named in 1862 by Julius Haast, in honour of the first explorer of the islands. The native name AO-RANGI, meaning 'Scud-peak,' refers to the cloud banners constantly gathering over the summit. The usual translation, 'sky piercer,' is wrong. COOK'S ISLANDS, in the South Pacific, also called the Harvey Group, were discovered by Cook in 1777. COOK TOWN, Queensland, commemorates the place where Cook careened his ships.

Copenhagen, in Danish KJÖBENHAVN, the capital of Denmark, is first mentioned in 1027 by the name Höfn, 'the haven,' and in 1043 it was still a mere fishing village. Owing to its position it became a great resort for merchants, and to distinguish it from other havens was called *Kaupmanna höfn* or *Kjobmannshavn*, names translated by Saxo Grammaticus in the twelfth century as *Portus Mercatorum*, the 'haven of the merchants.' In Latin documents it is usually called *Hafnia*, 'the haven.' Similar names are NORRKÖPING, the 'north market,' and SODERKÖPING, the 'south market.'

Coppermine River, flowing into the Arctic Ocean, was explored by Samuel Hearne in 1771, and so named because he believed (wrongly as it now appears) that the tribe called the Copper Indians procured copper from mines in the COPPER MOUNTAINS, near its mouth. Hearne, by descending the Coppermine, was the first Englishman to reach the shores of the Arctic Ocean.

Copiapo, a city in Chili, takes its name from the River Copiapo on which it stands.

Copts, the name given to the adherents of the old Egyptian or Coptic Church, was unknown in Western Europe before 1600. It is the Arabic *qubt*, a collective term for the native Egyptians, derived from the Coptic *guptios*, which is the Greek Ægyptios, an Egyptian, and has taken the form Copt from a supposed connection with a town called Koptos by the Greeks (Hieroglyphic *Qebt*), now Koft, where the Copts are numerous, and which is an emporium for merchandise coming from the Red Sea. (*See* EGYPT.)

Cordova, in Andalusia, represents the Roman *Corduba*, supposed to be a Phœnician name. Bochart explains it from the Syriac *coteb*, an 'oil press.' Condé, with more reason, prefers *carta-tuba*, the great or 'important city.' Cordova was at one time the capital of the Moorish empire, and hence we obtained the word *cordwainer* for a worker in Cordovan leather, which we should now call Morocco. The name of CORDOVA was transferred to an Argentine province and city founded in 1573, and also to a town in Mexico.

Corea is the European form of the Japanese *Kooraï* (Chinese *Kaoli*), a name which properly denotes only a small part of the peninsula.

Corfe Castle, in Dorset, commands a defile called in the Chronicle, *Corfes geat*. The names of Ramsgate, Margate, and Reigate also exhibit this word *geat*, 'a defile or pass.'

Corfu, one of the Ionian Islands, is named from the town of Corfu, which is the Italian form of the Neo-Hellenic name *Korphoi* (Turkish *Korfus*), anciently *Corcyra*. The ancient Acropolis did not occupy the site of the modern citadel, which stands on an isolated rock whose summit is split into two peaks, which the medieval Greeks called *Koryphô* or *Koryphi*, 'the summits,' a name which has now become Corfu, and has been extended to denote the whole island. There is no etymological connection between Corfu and the old Illyrian name Corcyra.

Corinth is the English name of the place called anciently *Qorinthos*, *Korinthos*, or *Corinthus*, and in modern Greek GORTHO. The name is supposed to have been descriptive of the helm-shaped rock, 1770 feet in height, called Acrocorinthus, on which the Acropolis was built. The town gives a name to the ISTHMUS and GULF of CORINTH, as well as to the 'currants,' small dried grapes thence exported, which were called *raisins de Corinthe*.

Cork, an Irish county, takes its name from its chief city, which is called *Corcach*, 'the marsh,' by those who speak Irish, In the sixth century St. Finbar founded, on the edge of the great morass at the mouth of the River Lee, a monastery round which the city grew. It was long known as *Corcach-mor-Mumhain*, 'the great marsh of Munster.' This became *Corcach Mor*, and then *Corcach*, which has been Anglicised as Cork.

Cornwall is a tribal name, which, as in other cases, has become territorial. In A.S. we have *Cornwealas*, a nom. plural, which means 'Cornishmen'; the dative plural *on Cornwealum* signifying 'in Cornwall.' Our modern form Cornwall cannot be obtained either from *Cornweal*, which means a Cornishman, or from the nom. plural *Cornwealas*, which, since *Wealas* gives Wales, would have given Cornwales, but it is doubtless from the gen. plural *Cornweala*, the form Cornwall being thus an abbreviation of *Cornweala-land*, the 'land of the Cornwelsh.' The syllable *corn* is usually said to have been a Welsh word meaning a horn or promontory, equivalent to the Latin *cornu*, but Cernyw, the Welsh name of Cornwall, which is as old as the tenth century, rather points to the Cornish word *kernow*, the plural of *carn*, a 'rocky hill,' which we have in PORTHKERNOW, in Cornwall. This is supported by the Greek and late Latin forms *Kornaouioi* and *Cornubia*. CORNOUAILLES, the old name of Lower Brittany, was Latinised as *Cornu-Galliæ*, the horn of Gaul, but is probably from the Breton *Kerneo* (Cernyw) or Cornwall, whence the Bretons had come. NORTH CORNWALL, a district lying north of Belcher's Channel, was so named by Belcher in 1852, from the ducal title of the Prince of Wales. For the same reason Cook, in 1770, gave the name of CAPE CORNWALL to one of the capes in PRINCE OF WALES ISLAND, in Torres Strait.

Cornwallis Island, in the Arctic Archipelago, was so named by Parry after Admiral Sir William Cornwallis, his 'first naval friend and patron.'

Coromandel Coast, the name given to the coast of the Carnatic, is a Portuguese corruption of *Chôra-mandala*, the *mandala* or 'realm' of Chôra, the Tamil title of a dynasty which reigned in Tanjore. The town of COROMANDEL, from which the name of the Coromandel Coast was formerly derived, is a corruption of *Kareimanal*, the 'sandy coast.' The two names have been assimilated.

Coronation Gulf, at the mouth of the Back River, was discovered by Franklin on July 19th, 1821, the Coronation day of George IV. CAPE CORONATION, in New

Caledonia, and CORONATION ISLANDS, on the Australian Coast, were discovered on September 22nd, the Coronation day of George III.

Corrientes, a city at the confluence of the Paraná and the Paraguay, called officially *La Ciudad de Siete Corrientes*, the 'city of the seven currents,' takes its name from seven channels formed by islands in the river. CAPE CORRENTES, inaccurately called Corrientes, on the African Coast, north of Natal, was so named by the Portuguese on account of the dangerous currents setting against the rocks.

Corryvreckan is the Sound between Jura and Scarba. The Gaelic *coire*, Anglicised as Corrie or Corry, means a cauldron, and appears frequently in the names of deep round hollows in the mountains, such as CORRIE in the Isle of Arran. It also denotes the swirling pool under a water-fall, and hence was used to denote a whirlpool in the sea. In a whirlpool between Antrim and Rathlin Island, Brecan, son of Nial of the nine hostages, was lost with fifty ships. Hence the whirlpool was called Corryvreckan, or 'Brecan's cauldron.' The name was subsequently transferred by the monks of Iona to the whirlpool between Jura and Scarba, and the legend having been forgotten, the name has been explained as the 'boiling cauldron,' from the Gaelic *bruich*, 'to boil.'

Corsica, in French LA CORSE, was the Greek *Kurnos*, and the Roman *Corsica*. It is explained by Bochart as a Phœnician word, meaning the 'wooded' or 'forest' island, a very appropriate name.

Corunna, in Spanish La Coruña, was formerly called La Cruña, which became *the Groyne* in the mouths of English sailors. All these forms are corruptions of the old name *Caronium*.

Cossack, more correctly written Kazak, has given a name to a part of the valley of the Don which is called the country of the Don Cossacks. The Kazaks were at first those whom we term Kirghiz, the Kirghiz calling themselves Kazaks. The word was used to mean a gazelle separated from the herd, hence a vagabond or wanderer, then nomads or horsemen, and, in a secondary sense, 'robbers.'

Cosseir, a place on the Red Sea, is an Arabic name meaning the 'little castle,' or perhaps the 'breach' which forms the harbour.

Costa Rica, the 'rich coast,' a Central American republic, was originally named the *Costa del oro*, or 'gold coast,' by Columbus on his third voyage in 1502.

Cotopaxi (in Spanish Cotopaji), in the Andes near Quito, is the loftiest volcano in the world, 19,613 feet in height. Its snow-clad cone, standing out in bold relief against the sky, bears a descriptive name signifying the 'shining pile,' the word *ccoto* meaning in Quichua a 'heap' or 'pile,' and *pasca*, 'brilliance, splendour, brightness.'

Cotswolds, a range of hills in Gloucestershire, is apparently a hybrid name from the Celtic *coed*, 'wood' or 'forest,' and the A.S. *weald*, M.E. *wold*, which was used in the sense of waste or uninclosed ground. (*See* CATMERE.)

Cottian Alps, the western part of the main chain, commemorates the Segusian chief Cottius, who became an ally of Rome in the reign of Augustus, and constructed a road for the Romans. The triumphal arch, erected by Cottius in honour of Augustus, still stands in SUSA, anciently *Segusio*, the capital of Cottius.

Cottonwood is a common name given to North American rivers, valleys, and islands, from a species of poplar, *Populus monilifera*, called the Cottonwood.

Coudres, Isle aux, in the Gulf of St. Lawrence, was so named by Cartier in 1535. It is also known by the translated name FILBERT ISLAND. COUDRAY, COUDRET, LE COUDRÉ, and the like, are common French village names, corruptions of *Coryletum*, a 'hazel grove.'

Council Grove, a flourishing city in Kansas, was formerly a meeting-place of the Indian tribes.

Council Bluff, on the Missouri River, was so called by the American explorers, Lewis and Clarke, because they landed here to hold a council with the Otoes.

Coventry, in Warwickshire, is usually supposed to mean the 'convent town' (Welsh *tre*, a town), from a Benedictine priory founded in 1043 by Earl Leofric and his wife the Lady Godiva (*a monachorum conventu sic dictum putant quidam*). But the A.S. form *Cofantreó* or *Cofentreó* proves that the name must mean the cave-tree (A.S. *cofa*, genitive *cofan*, a cove, cave, chamber, or bed, and *treó*, a tree), either a large hollow tree or a tree near a cave. So RUNCORN in Cheshire is called *Rumcofa*, the 'roomy cave' or 'cove,' in the Chronicle; and COVENEY, in Cambridgeshire, is A.S. *Coveneia*. (*See* p. 359.)

Cozumel, or Cocumel, an island off the coast of Yucatan, was discovered by

Juan de Grijalva, on May 3rd, 1518, the feast of the Invention of the Cross, and called by him, from the day of the discovery, SANTA CRUZ. Coçumel is a corruption of the native name *Acusamil*, which means 'swallow island.'

Cracow, the capital of Galicia, and a former capital of Poland, is the English form of the Polish name Krakov, said to have been founded about 700 A.D. by the Polish Prince, Krak I. (Krakus), who is doubtless a mere eponymus.

Cradock, a district in the Cape Colony, bears the name of the Governor, Sir J. Cradock, afterwards Lord Howden.

Cray, a village in Kent, on the River Cray, is in A.S. *Cregsetanahaga*, the 'enclosure of the settlers on the Cray.' The neighbouring village of CRAYFORD is in A.S. *Crecganford*, the 'ford over the Cray.'

Cremorne, a barony in county Monaghan, is a corruption of the old name *Crioch-Mughdhorn*, 'the country,' *crioch*, of the people called the *Mughdhorna*, who claimed to be descended from Mughdhorn, the son of Colla Meann. In the twelfth century a tribe of the MacMahons emigrated from Cremorne and settled in County Down in a place to which they gave their tribe-name of Mughdhorna, and which is now the barony of MOURNE, whence the name of the MOURNE MOUNTAINS. From a Lord Cremorne the Cremorne Gardens in Chelsea were named.

Cressage, Salop, was an early preaching station, being called in Domesday *Cristesache*, evidently meaning 'Christ's oak.'

Crew, a common Irish name, is a corruption of *Craebh*, a 'wide-spreading tree,' under which games or religious rites were celebrated. Hence also CREWE, CRAVIE, CORRIECRAVIE, and other names in Scotland.

Cricklade, Wilts, is the A.S. *Creccageléd* and *Crecca-léd*. In A.S. *crecca* is a 'creek,' and *léd* or *geléd* means a 'way' or 'course,' and also a 'lode' or watercourse. The name Cricklade therefore denotes either a 'road over the creek,' or the lodes or passages dug to facilitate the entrance of a small stream or creek into the Thames.

Crimea, in Russian *Krym*, the modern name of the Tauric Chersonese, is derived from the village of *Stari-Krym* (in Tartar *Eski-Krim*), or 'Old Krym,' a heap of ruins probably representing the Greek city of *Krēmnoi*, 'the crags.'

Croatia is the country of the Croats (Slavonic *chrawat*), the men of the hills or mountaineers. (*See* CARPATHIANS.) From the Croats or Chrawats we get the word *cravat*.

Croker River, CROKER ISLAND, and CAPE CROKER, in the Arctic and Australian regions, were named after John Wilson Croker, secretary to the Admiralty, in whose honour John Ross, in 1818, laid down on the chart a lofty range of mountains extending across the entrance to Lancaster Sound, which he named the Croker Mountains. In the following year the *Hecla* and *Griper*, under Parry, sailed right across this imaginary chain of hills, thus giving occasion to the epigram:

'Old Sindbad tells us he a whale had seen
So like the land, it seemed an island green;
But Ross has told the converse of this tale,
The land *he* saw, was—very like a whale.'

Crooked Lake or **Lac de la Croix**, north-west of Lake Superior, was so named from its shape. There is also a CROOKED LAKE in Assiniboia.

Cross Sound, on the north-west coast of America, was discovered by Cook on May 3rd, 1778, the day of the Invention of the Cross. The ISLE À LA CROSS, in Winnipeg, is where the Indians assembled to play the game of La Cross.

Croydon, Surrey, is spelt *Crogden* in a charter of 871. In a twelfth century copy of the same charter it becomes *Croindun*, whence the transition to Croydon is easy. The A.S. *crog* (or *croc*) means a 'bottle' or pitcher. Hence Crog-den might denote a bottle-shaped den or valley in the chalk hills. This is preferable to the usual etymology from A.S. *croh-dun*, the 'hill of meadow saffron.'

Croyland or **Crowland**, in Lincolnshire, is in A.S. Crouland, Cruland, Crowland, Cruwland, or Croyland de S. Guthlaco, a name explained by the pseudo-Ingulf as *cruda et canosa terra*. The name appears as Croland in William of Malmesbury, Cruiland in Roger of Hoveden, and as Croyland from the thirteenth to the eighteenth century. It has been doubtfully explained from the A.S. *cráwe*, a 'crow' (*cráw* in composition), or from *croh*, 'meadow saffron,' from which we have CROWLE in Worcestershire, which is *Croh-léd* in a Saxon charter.

Crozier Island, CROZIER CREEK, POINT CROZIER, and CAPE CROZIER, all in the Arctic regions, were named after Captain Crozier, who commanded one of Franklin's ships.

Crozet Islands, south-east of the Cape of Good Hope, were discovered in 1772 by the French Captain Crozet.

Cuba, the largest island of the West Indies, was discovered by Columbus in 1492, on his first voyage. He sighted the island on October 27 or 28, and records in his log-book that the land can only be Zipangu (*i.e.* Japan). He landed at Puerto de las Nuevitas, where he observed the natives smoking certain herbs rolled up in dry leaves like cartridges, which they called *tabocos.* Here he heard of a town four days' march inland which was called Cuba, to visit which he despatched Luis de Torres, a baptised Jew, who knew Hebrew, Chaldee, and a little Arabic, in order to interview the Emperor of Japan, who, he hoped, might be able to understand Don Luis. A neighbouring cape Columbus named Cabo de Cuba (now Punta de Mulas), and from this cape it is believed that the name of Cuba was extended to the whole island. The word CUBA seems to have been a general term meaning 'district,' since we learn from Las Casas that the district was called *Cuba nacan,* the 'central province,' from *cuba,* a 'territory' or 'province,' and *nacan,* 'middle.' Columbus called the island Juana in honour of Don Juan, son of Ferdinand and Isabella, and heir to the Spanish throne, it was afterwards called Fernandina, after King Ferdinand, and subsequently Santiago, from the patron saint of Spain.

Culloden, in Inverness-shire, is from the Gaelic *cùl,* 'behind,' and *lòdan,* the diminutive of *lòd,* 'a pool' or 'swamp.' The preposition *cùl* is common in Gaelic topography, as CULROSS, 'behind the promontory,' or CULBEN, 'behind the hill.' The second element is seen in CUMLODEN and LODDAMORE, the 'great swamp.'

Cumberland, an English county, is a small part of the district which in the Saxon Chronicle appears as *Cumbraland,* 'the land of the Cymry,' as the Welsh called themselves, the name meaning 'compatriots' or 'fellow - countrymen,' *Combrog* meaning the 'united people,' just as Allo-broges means the 'other men' or foreigners. After the Northumbrians had taken Chester, the two divided lands of the Cymry were called indifferently Cambria and Cumbria. The latter, which is the more correct form, was gradually specialised to denote the land of the Stræcled Wealas, or Welsh of Strathclyde; Cumbria, or Cumbraland, denoting the kingdom which stretched as far as the Clyde. In 1132, when the northern part of the Cumbrian kingdom was annexed to the

Scottish crown, the name retreated southwards to the modern county of Cumberland, just as Northumberland retreated northwards from the Humber. As late as the reign of Edward III. Ranulf Higden speaks of Caerlielleshire cum Cumberland. CUMBERLAND SOUND, a large gulf on the western side of Davis' Strait, was explored by Davis in 1585, and named after his friend George Clifford, Earl of Cumberland. CUMBERLAND RIVER, in Kentucky, a tributary of the Ohio, was discovered in 1747 by Dr. Walker of Virginia, the first white man who penetrated into Kentucky, and named by him after the victor of Culloden. The CUMBERLAND ISLANDS, off the coast of Queensland, were discovered by Cook in 1770, and named after the Duke of Cumberland. CAPE CUMBERLAND, in Kerguelen Land, and CUMBERLAND BAY, in South Georgia, were also discovered and named by Cook. CUMBERLAND STRAIT, on the north coast of Australia, was discovered by Flinders in 1803 in the ship *Cumberland.*

Cumnor or **Cumner,** in Berks, immortalised by Scott, belonged to the neighbouring Abbey of Abingdon. The A.S. name *Cumen-ora,* from *cumena,* the genitive plural of *cuma,* a guest or stranger, literally a 'comer,' shows that it was the landing where visitors descending the Thames, either to Abingdon or Oxford, would land, thereby cutting off a great bend in the river.

Curaçao or **Curaçoa,** variously spelt by Dampier, Qurisao, Curasao, and Corrisao, an island off the coast of Venezuela, is said to have been so called from a gallinaceous bird which inhabited it called the *curassow* by the natives. But *Curasaote,* the oldest form of name, points rather to a Guarani word which means 'the great plantation.'

Curragh, an Irish word meaning a 'bog,' is a common Irish name, the best known being the CURRAGH OF KILDARE. The great bog in the north of the Isle of Man is also called the CURRAGH.

Curtis' Isles, in Bass Strait, and PORT CURTIS, in Queensland, were named after Admiral Sir Roger Curtis.

Cuttack, the capital of Orissa, was one of the five ancient fortresses of *Odra-desa* (Orissa). The name is a corruption of *Kataka,* a Sanskrit word meaning 'army' or 'camp,' and hence 'fortress' or 'royal city.'

Cuvier, Cape, West Australia, was so named by Baudin in 1800 in honour of the great French naturalist.

Cuzco, in Peru, the capital of the empire of the Incas, is a native term meaning the 'navel' of the realm, so called from its central and dominating position.

Cyclades, a group of islands in the Ægean, which as Callimachus says lie 'encircling' Delos, and forming as it were a belt of dangers ; and so distinguished from the Sporades or 'scattered' islands.

Cyprus, which gave a name to copper (*æs cyprium*), is believed to be a Phœnician name meaning the island of the tree, called *chopher* in Hebrew, which was probably a kind of pine.

Dacca (Dháka), the 'concealed,' is a city in Bengal which grew up, according to the legend, round a temple built on the spot where about 400 A.D. an image of Durga, wife of Siva, was found concealed. The legend probably arose to account for a name derived from the *dhák* tree (*Butea frondosa*).

Daghestan, in the Caucasus, is a Turko-Persian name meaning the 'mountainous country.'

Dahomey is a West African town and kingdom. According to the native tradition, Da, a chief who ruled in the seventeenth century, having been killed by a rival, the body was ripped up, and a new capital was built on the spot where it was buried, whence the name *Da-omi*, which means literally 'the belly of Da.'

Dakota, one of the United States, takes its name from a confederation of seven tribes calling themselves *Dahcota*, which signifies 'friends,' 'allies,' or 'confederates,' who occupied the watershed of the Upper Mississippi and the Missouri, finally retreating into the territory which forms the present State of Dakota. The Dahcotas were called by their enemies *Nadowe-ssi-wag,* an Algonkin term which signifies 'the snake-like ones,' 'the enemies,' and a portion of this opprobrious name, *ssi-wag* or *siwug,* was corrupted by the French into Sioux. The term Sioux or Sioan is now used as a linguistic term, Dahcota being reserved in a narrower sense as an ethnic designation.

Dalai Noor, a Mongolian lake, means the great or 'sea-like lake' (*dalai,* 'sea,' and *noor,* 'lake').

Dalmatia, an Austrian crown-land, takes its name from its former capital, *Delminium* or *Dalmium,* an Illyrian name believed to signify a 'sheep pasture.'

Dalrymple, a Tasmanian port, was so named in 1798 after Alexander Dalrymple, hydrographer to the navy. Cape Dalrymple in Sagalin Island also bears his name.

Damascus, the Greek form of the Semitic name *Dammeseq* or *Darmeseq,* means, according to Gesenius, the 'place of industry. It is now called *Dimeshk-ash-Shám,* abbreviated in common parlance to Ash Shám or Shám, 'the left,' *i.e.* Syria.

Damietta, the third largest town in Egypt, is the Italian form of the native name *Damiat* or *Damyat,* a corruption of the Old Egypto-Greek name *Tamiathis,* the first element of which is probably the Egyptian *Tema,* a 'city,' which we have also in Damanhûr, between Cairo and Alexandria, in old Egyptian *Tema-en-Hor,* the 'city of Horus.'

Dampier Strait, at the western end of New Guinea, bears the name of William Dampier, who sailed through it in 1700. The Dampier Archipelago, off the Australian coast, was discovered by Dampier in 1699. Dampier Land, and the Buccaneer Archipelago, on the northern coast of Australia, were also named in honour of the bold buccaneer.

Dampière, or Dompière, a name borne by eight places in France, is derived from the patron saint, *Dominus Petrus,* equivalent to St. Pierre. In like manner the nine places called Dammartin or Dommartin (*Dominus Martinus*) are from dedications to St. Martin, Domleger from St. Leger (*Dominus Leodegarius*), and Domrémi, the birthplace of Joan of Arc, from *Dominus Remigius.* Dominus, abbreviated to Domnus, and afterwards to Dom, was an honorific title given in Merovingian times to ecclesiastical dignitaries, especially to bishops and abbots, such as St. Martin or St. Remigius.

Danby's Island, in James' Bay, was discovered by Thomas James in 1631, and named after the Earl of Danby.

Danebrog, the name of the Danish flag, was given by Captain Graah in 1829 to a cape on the east coast of Greenland, the most northerly point which had then been reached.

Danger River, West Africa, is a curious sailor's assimilation of the Portuguese name *Rio d'Angra,* the 'river of the bay,' so called because it falls into the Bight of Biafra. Point Danger, near the boundary between New South Wales and Queensland, was so called by Cook in 1770 because of the dangerous shoals around it. Danger Island is the name of several coral atolls in the Pacific. (*See* Mount Warning.)

Dantzig, more correctly DANZIG, a Baltic port, is usually supposed to be a corruption of *Dansk-vik*, the Danes' town, from a Danish settlement made in the time of Waldemar II. More probably, as suggested by the Slavonic name *Gyddanizc* or *Gdansk*, the name is a corruption of *Godanske*, the town 'of the Goths,' *ske* being the common derivative suffix in Slavonic.

Danube, the English name of the great river which the Germans call the DONAU, is derived from the Roman name *Danubius* or *Danuvius*. Zeuss and Glück reject any connection with the Scythian *don*, which we have in the names of the Rivers DON and DONETZ, and explain the name as Celtic, signifying the river with the strong current, the first element being the Celtic word *dan*, 'strong,' and the second being a formative suffix. From the Celtic name *Dan-u-vios*, the Teutonic invaders, when they reached the river, obtained the form which we have in the Nibelungenlied, *Tuon-owe* or *Tuon-awa*, which would signify the 'thundering water,' and from *Tuonawa* came the modern form DONAU. The Greek name *Ister* or *Istros* only applied to the lower course of the river, and it is probable that the name of Istria gave rise to the curious belief that the Danube by one of its mouths discharged itself into the Adriatic. DONAU-WÖRTH, in Bavaria, takes its name from an island (O.H.G. *warid*) in the Danube, while the reputed source of the river is a spring in the Castleyard at DONAU-ESCHINGEN.

Dardanelles, the modern name of the Hellespont, is derived from two Turkish forts guarding the passage, called by the Italians Dardanelli, a name derived from the old Greek city of Dardanus in the Troad.

Darfur or DARFOOR, in Central Africa, is the 'land of the Fur or Foor.' It consists of four circuits or provinces, DAR DALI being the Eastern, DAR UMA the Southern, DAR DIMA the South-Western, and DAR-EL-GHARB the Western Province.

Dariâ, (*Darya*) is a Persian word meaning 'sea,' 'river.' The modern name of the OXUS of the Greeks, the Gihon of the Arabs, is AMU or AMU-DARIÂ; the Jaxartes is called the SYR-DARIÂ, or 'yellow river,' while the YAMAN-DARIÂ is the 'bad river.'

Darien, a city founded by Balboa in 1510, has given a name to the Gulf and Isthmus of Darien. Balboa's town, which he called *Santa Maria del Darien*, was built on the River Tarena, a native name of which

Darien is a corruption. The Tarena, a small stream, has been commonly identified with the Atrato, which the earliest Spanish settlers called the Rio Grande, or Rio S. Juan. It was Vasco Nunez Balboa, and not, as Keats says, 'stout Cortez,' who in 1513, 'with eagle eyes,' stared at the Pacific, and all his men 'Looked at each other with a wild surmise, Silent upon a peak in Darien.' In 1695 the projector, William Paterson, founded his bubble Darien Company, and three years later sent 12,000 Scotch emigrants to perish in New Edinburgh and New St. Andrews, founded in the territory which they called New Caledonia.

Darjeeling (DÁRJÍLING), a hill station in Sikkim, bears the name of a neighbouring monastery whose popular Tibetan spelling is *Dorje-glin*, the 'land of the Dorje,' *i.e* of the 'adamant' or 'thunderbolt,' the ritual sceptre of the Lamas. The correct spelling is probably *Dár-rgyas-glin*, which would mean 'island of contemplation,' from *dar-gias*, 'wide extension' or 'extensive view,' and hence metaphorically 'contemplation,' and *glin*, 'land' or 'island.'

Darling, one of the largest rivers in Australia, called the Callewatta by the natives, was discovered by Stuart and Hume, and named in compliment to General Sir Ralph Darling, then Governor of New South Wales (1825-31), and not, as sometimes supposed, from Sir Charles Darling, who forty years later was Governor of Victoria. The DARLING DOWNS in Queensland, and the DARLING RANGE in West Australia also bear the name of Sir Ralph Darling.

Darmstadt, capital of Hesse-Darmstadt, is a town which stands on a small stream bearing the descriptive name of DARM, the 'gut.' But, from the eighth to the eleventh century, the town was called Darmundestadt, and hence it is supposed that the name of the stream is comparatively modern, and derived as in other cases from the town, which would be from the personal name Taramund or Daramund.

Dartmouth, Devon (A.S. *Dærenta-mutha*), is at the mouth of the DART, formerly the Darent, which rises in the wild upland district called DARTMOOR. DARTFORD in Kent, a corruption of *Darentford*, is the ford on the river which still keeps the name of Darent, on which stands the village of DARENTH (A.S. *Derant-tun* and *Dærenton*). The Southern name Darent or Dart is doubtless the same as that which appears as DERWENT in Yorkshire, Derbyshire, Cumberland, and Durham, the Kentish Darent being called *Derguuint* by Nennius. The etymology is unknown. The old explanation from the Celtic *dwfr* (afterwards *dwr*), 'water,' and *gwent*, open country or plain, is now abandoned. Professor Rhys suggests the Welsh *Derwennydd*, from *derw*, 'an oak.' DARTMOUTH, in Massachusetts, is believed to have been so called from a fancied resemblance to Dartmouth in Devon. DARTMOUTH in Nova Scotia, and DARTMOUTH in Prince Edward's Island, seem to have been named in honour of Lord Dartmouth.

Darwin Islet, one of the Danger Islets, South Shetland, MOUNT DARWIN in New Zealand, and PORT DARWIN in Arnhem's Land, Australia, bear the name of the naturalist Charles Darwin.

Dasht means a 'plain' in Persian :— thus MAN-DASHT means the 'mid-plain.' The chief river of Beluchistan is called the DASHT, an abbreviation of *Khor-i-Dasht*, the 'river of the plain.'

Dauphiny, in French DAUPHINÉ, one of the old French Provinces, was so called from the dolphin assumed by the Counts of the Viennois in the twelfth century as a symbol of the mildness of their rule. In 1349 the county was sold to Charles of Valois, but with the condition that the heir to the French crown should bear the arms and assume the style of Dauphin of the Viennois. In compliment to the Dauphin sundry capes, bays, and islands, have been named. Among them FORT DAUPHIN, at the southern extremity of Madagascar, founded by the French in 1644, destroyed in 1672, and reconstructed in 1768 ; whence *Île Dauphin*, a French name for Madagascar. The Dolphin, Greek *Delphis*, was so called from its cleft tail, and DELPHI, in like manner, was named from the cleft chasm over which the temple stood, and hence, from the resemblance of the name, the dolphin became the emblem of the Delphian Apollo.

Davey, a Tasmanian river, flows into PORT DAVEY, which was discovered by Captain Kelly in 1815 and named after Colonel Davey, the Governor of Tasmania. DAVY ISLAND and MOUNT DAVY, both in Arctic America, were named in compliment to Sir Humphry Davy, President of the Royal Society.

Davis Strait, which divides Labrador from Greenland, bears the name of John Davis, our first great Arctic explorer, who was born in Devonshire in 1550. In 1584 Queen Elizabeth gave a charter to Sir

Walter Raleigh, Adrian Gilbert, and John Davis, for the discovery of a North-West passage to China. Master William Sanderson, a wealthy merchant, who had married Raleigh's niece, found the greater portion of the funds, and on June 7th, 1585, Davis sailed with the *Sunshine* of 50 tons, and the *Moonshine*, a pinnace of 35 tons. He reached the eastern coast of Greenland, probably near Cape Discord, naming it the LAND of DESOLATION. He anchored near Goathaab, calling it GILBERT SOUND, after his friend and playmate at Dartmouth, and thence struck across Davis Strait to a point which he named CAPE WALSINGHAM, anchoring in EXETER SOUND close to a lofty cliff which he called MOUNT RALEIGH. The point of land at the north of Exeter Sound he named CAPE DYER. He then explored Cumberland Gulf, naming the point at the entrance the CAPE OF GOD'S MERCY, and thence sailed homeward. On his second voyage, in 1586, he reached the southern extremity of Greenland, but finding it impossible to land on account of the pack-ice which extended for many leagues from the shore, he called it CAPE FAREWELL, and sailed north. He laid down the coast of Greenland from Cape Farewell to SANDERSON'S HOPE (*q.v.*), and then crossed the Strait, discovering the entrance to Hudson Strait, and finally examining the whole coast of Labrador, thus preparing the way for Baffin and Hudson. He afterwards explored the Straits of Magellan, discovering the Falkland Islands, and also took part in Houtman's expedition to Achen, and went with Lancaster as pilot of the *Red Dragon*. He commanded a tender against the Spanish Armada, acting as pilot to the Lord High Admiral, and served in the brilliant attack on Cadiz. His last expedition was in the *Tiger*, which was boarded by the crew of a Japanese junk in the Straits of Malacca, Davis being killed in repulsing the attack. He needs no tombstone, as he has written his name conspicuously upon the map of the world.

Davos Thal, in Canton Graubünden, is a valley which turns round and runs back to the north from the Albula. Hence its name, from the Romansch *davos*, 'behind,' or 'at the back,' thus explaining the shelter from winds which causes so many invalids to resort to the chief village in the valley called AM PLATZ IM DAVOS THAL, usually shortened to DAVOS PLATZ.

Dazio Grande, a village on the Italian side of the St. Gothard Pass, is the place where the 'great toll' for the repair of the road used to be taken.

Dead Sea is probably so called because it contains no fish. DEAD BIRD RIVER, near Nain in Labrador, is the memorial of a hunting expedition in which, though nothing was killed, a dead bird was found near the camp. The MOUNTAIN OF THE DEAD on the Colorado River was so called because the Indians believed it to be inhabited by the spirits of the departed. On DEADMAN'S ISLAND, in the Great Slave Lake, there lay for many years the unburied bones of the victims of a massacre of the Dogribs by the Beaver tribe.

Dease River flowing into DEASE BAY, on the Great Bear Lake, bears the name of Peter Warrens Dease, an officer in the service of the Hudson's Bay Company.

Deccan, properly spelt DEKHAN, means 'the South Country,' from *dakkhina*, a Prakrit form of the Sanskrit *Dakshina*, 'the right hand,' the south being to the right hand at sunrise.

Dee, the chief river in North Wales, was called by the Welsh *Dubr-Duiu*, or *Dufr-dwy*, the 'water of the goddess,' in Latin form *Deva*, equivalent to the 'divine' river. The same meaning probably attaches to the names of other rivers called the Dee.

Delagoa Bay, in South Africa, discovered by Vasco de Gama in 1498 is a curiously jumbled version of the Portuguese name *Bahia de Lagoa*, the 'Bay of the lagoon' or swamp.

Delaware, one of the United States, originally a Swedish colony, takes its name from DELAWARE BAY, so called by Sir Robert Carr, when he took the colony from the Dutch in 1644, in memory of Lord Delaware, who, having been appointed in 1609 Captain-General and Governor of the English colonies to be planted in Virginia, is believed to have anchored the following year in Chesapeake Bay. In 1617, on his second or third voyage, he died at St. Michael, one of the Azores, on his way out, poisoned, it was believed, by the Spaniards.

Delft, a town in Holland, stands on the canal joining the Rhine and the Maas. The name dates from the eleventh century, and denotes the place beside a *delf*, which means a 'ditch,' or canal,' from *delfan* to 'delve.' Here the delft pottery ware was made.

Delgado, a cape south of Zanzibar, was called by the Portuguese *Cabo Delgado*, 'the slender cape' (Portuguese *delicado,* 'delicate,' *delgado,* 'thin, slender').

Delhi or DEHLI was the capital of the Moghul emperors. *Delli*, the old Hindu form, dates from the first century A.D., Dehli being a later Moslem form. According to the popular etymology the city was named from a Rájáh Dilu, of the Mayura dynasty which succeeded the Gautama line of princes. Other etymologies explain it as the 'threshold,' or the 'quicksand' (Sanskrit *dahal*), but the derivation now generally accepted is from an old Hindi word *dil*, an 'eminence.'

Deli, an Ægean island, is steep and rocky, forming a conspicuous landmark for sailors coming from the neighbouring seas. Hence the old name DELOS, the 'conspicuous.'

Delly, Mount, a high mountain on the Malabar coast, is a corruption of the Portuguese name *Monte d'Eli*, which is derived from the Malayálam *Eli Mala*, 'high mountain.' The name is sometimes applied to an adjoining city and state.

Demavend, the great volcanic peak which towers over Teheran, is a corruption of *Div-band*, the 'dwelling of the 'Divs' or Genii.

Denbigh, the county town of DENBIGH-SHIRE, means in Welsh the 'cliff.' It is the same name as TENBY (*q.v.*).

Denison Range, in South Australia, and PORT DENISON, in Queensland, bear the name of Sir William Denison, Governor of New South Wales (1854-60).

Denmark is called *Dan-mörk* in the Sagas. In Old Norse *mörk* means a 'forest,' and, as forests commonly formed the boundaries of tribes, we obtain such words as *mearc* in A.S. and *marca* in O.H.G. meaning a 'march land' or 'boundary.' But *marca* in Old Saxon means a district, and in Modern Danish *mark* means a 'field,' 'plain,' or 'open country.' Hence Denmark probably means the 'forest of the Danes,' a name parallel to that of Holstein (*q.v.*) which also was densely wooded. The Anglo-Saxons would doubtless understand *Dene-mearc* or *Dænmarc*, their own form of the name, as the Danish frontier. The ALTMARK, the NEUMARK, and the BRAN-DENBURG MARK in Germany were the successive frontiers or marches against the Slaves, while FINMARK, a name of Scandinavian provenance, might mean the plain of the Finns. In England the kingdom of Mercia, and the Welsh and Scotch marches were border-lands.

Dent du Midi, DENT DE MORCLES, and DENT BLANCHE are the French names of Swiss mountains like rocky teeth, which are usually designated in German as *horns*, as the ROTHHORN, SCHWARZHORN, WEISSHORN, SILBERHORN, or MITTAGHORN, named from their colour or position. The DENT DE MORCLES is so called from the village of MORCLES at its foot. MORCLES is a diminutive of Morge, which is from O. H.G. *muorag*, a 'marshy moor.'

Denver City, the commercial capital of the State of Colorado, was founded in 1858 and named from James W. Denver, Governor of Kansas, to which the territory then belonged.

Deptford, between Surrey and Kent, formerly *Depeford*, is the 'Deep Ford' over the Ravensbourne where it joins the Thames.

Derbent, DERBEND, or DARBAND, literally a 'gate' or 'pass closer,' a Persian term for mountain passes, is frequently applied to forts or towns at the entrance to defiles. There are several places of the name in Persia, notably one representing the *Pylæ Albaniæ* where the Caucasus approaches the shore of the Caspian so closely that the road has to pass through the two gates of the town. There is another, a Perso-Turkish name, in Macedonia, and a third at the gorge where the Indus issues from the Himalayas.

Derby, the county town of Derbyshire, appears in the Saxon Chronicle as *Deoraby*, a name usually explained as the 'village of wild beasts' (A.S. *déora*, gen. plural of *déor*, a 'wild beast,' our 'deer'). But such a signification is difficult to understand, and *Deora-by* might with equal propriety be explained as the 'village of Deirians' or inhabitants of the adjacent *Deora mǽth*, the 'province of the Deirians,' or possibly from the River Derwent on which it stands, an explanation supported by the fact that on the same river there are two places called Darley, while *Dorventania* is used in Latin documents for Derbyshire. But names in -*by* have so commonly a personal name as their first element, that it is not improbable that Derby was so called from an early Scandinavian settler. The older name of Derby was *Northworthig*, which would have become Norworth in modern English. We may compare DEERHURST and DERHAM in Gloucestershire, which are *Deorhyrst* and *Deorham* in A.S., but DEREHAM in Norfolk and DARLASTON in Staffordshire are both derived from personal names, as is shown by the A.S. forms *Derhâm* and *Déorlâfestún*.

Derry or LONDONDERRY was originally *Daire-Calgaich*, the 'oakwood of Calgach' (cf. the Calgacus of Tacitus). It was afterwards called *Derry-Columkille*, because St. Columba here erected a cell or monastery in 546, and the name was finally changed to Londonderry when James I. gave it by charter to a company of London merchants.

Derwent River, in Tasmania, was so named (probably with reference to the English Derwent) by Captain Hayes in 1794. In the previous year the French Admiral d'Entrecasteaux had discovered it, and given it the name of *Rivière du Nord*.

Deserters is a corruption by English sailors of the Portuguese name *as Desertas* given to three 'desert' islands east of Madeira. LAS DESIERTAS is the Spanish name of some small uninhabited isles in the Canary group. DESERT is a name for the hermitages of Irish anchorites. (*See* DYSART.)

Desire River, in Patagonia, is so called because it flows into PORT DESIRE, which was so named in 1586 by Thomas Cavendish, the circumnavigator, from his ship the *Desire*. CABO DESEADO, the 'desired' cape, now usually called CAPE PILLAR, guards the western entrance of the Straits of Magellan, whose sailors, we are told, wept for joy when, on November 27th, 1520, they sighted the open sea, and found they had come to the end of the long dreary passage through the straits.

Desolation Land was the appropriate name given by Sir John Narborough in 1670 to a part of the western coast of Tierra del Fuego. Cook, again visiting this coast in 1774, gave the names CAPE DESOLATION and DESOLATE BAY to two places in this region, which he describes as the most desolate and barren he had ever seen, 'entirely composed of rocky mountains, without the least appearance of vegetation. These mountains terminate in horrible precipices, whose craggy summits spire up to a vast height, so that hardly anything in nature can appear with a more barren and savage aspect.' DESOLATION ISLAND, on the west coast of Greenland, near the head of Baffin's Bay, was so called in 1852 by Belcher. At the southern extremity of Greenland we find the names DESOLATION LAND and CAPE DESOLATION, which were given by JOHN DAVIS in 1585 and 1587.

Despair, Bay of, on the south coast of Newfoundland, is a pathetic name given by Hoare and his band of colonists, who were here nearly starved to death.

Detention Harbour, in Coronation Gulf, is the place where Franklin was detained by ice in 1821. In DETENTION COVE, New Zealand, Cook was detained by calms.

Detmold, capital of the principality of Lippe-Detmold, is a corruption of the old name *Theot-malli,* a 'folk-moot,' from O.H.G. *mahal,* 'a place of assembly or of justice,' and *diot,* 'people or tribe.'

Detroit is a city in Michigan on the 'narrow' passage between Lake Erie and Lake St. Clair, called by the French colonists DETROIT RIVER, which is believed to be a translation of the native name.

Devenish, an island near Enniskillen, is a corruption of *Daimh-inis,* the 'island of the oxen.'

Deventer, on the Rhine, anciently *Davontria,* contains the name of Davo, a friend of St. Lebuin.

Devil's Bridge, which spans a gorge of the Reuss in Canton Uri, is a translation of the German name Teufel's Brücke. So a lofty arch spanning the Ebro, and possibly of Carthaginian construction, is called the PUENTE DEL DIABLO (Devil's Bridge), the peasantry believing that it could have been built by no human hands. The DIABLERETS, near the upper end of the Lake of Geneva, are a range of torn peaks, from which disastrous falls of rock have frequently descended. Cook gave the name of the DEVIL'S BASIN to a desolate land-locked bay in Tierra del Fuego, mostly, even at midsummer, shut out from the sun by precipitous cliffs. In England such names as the DEVIL'S DYKE, the DEVIL'S PUNCHBOWL, or the DEVIL'S ARROWS, testify to the popular tendency to ascribe to diabolic agency various natural or artificial objects for the origin of which it is difficult to account.

Devizes, in Wilts, is one of the few names in England which are neither British, Roman, English, or French, but Latin without being Roman. As late as Clarendon's time it was called The Devizes, and the present local name is The Vize. The name *Divisæ,* of which Devizes is a corruption, does not occur before the foundation of the castle of Bishop Roger of Salisbury, in the reign of Henry I., but may have been given at an earlier time to the march or frontier forest which

divided the Saxon conquerors from the Welsh, who long retained the wooded valley of the Bristol Avon. In twelfth century documents the word is used to denote the boundary of an estate or of a jurisdiction, which may be its meaning in the present case.

Devonshire is a corruption of the A.S. *Defena-scir,* the shire of the Defenas or Devonians, *Defena* being a genitive plural. DEVON is a corruption of the dative plural *Defenum* or *Defnum.* The Defenas or Defnas are the Damnonii or Dumnonii of classical writers, a name explained by Professor Rhys from the Celtic *dumno-s,* which we have in Dumnorix, which may mean the 'king of the people,' in which case the *Dumnonii* would be 'the people' or 'tribe.' On the other hand it has been urged that Dumnonia may be a dialectic equivalent of *Dufneint* or *Dyfneint,* the Welsh name of Devonshire in the time of Nennius, which would signify the 'land of the deeps,' either the land of the deep valleys or of the deep seas. NORTH DEVON, in the Polar Archipelago, was so named from his native county by Lieutenant Liddon, who commanded the *Griper* in Parry's expedition of 1819-20. DEVONPORT, a suburb of Plymouth, is a modern name meaning the 'port of Devon.'

De Vries Strait, between the two Kurile Islands of Iturup and Urup, bears the name of the discoverer, a Dutch seaman despatched by Van Diemen in 1643 on a voyage of exploration.

De Witt's Land, North Australia, was discovered in 1628 by the Dutch ship *Vianen* which is believed to have been commanded by William de Witt. The DE WITT ISLANDS, Tasmania, discovered by Tasman in 1642, are commonly said to have been named by him after John de Witt, Grand Pensionary of Holland. But as De Witt was only seventeen at this time, and his less celebrated brother Cornelius was only nineteen, this can hardly be correct. Either the name must be of later date, or, more probably, Tasman may have named them after William de Witt, his predecessor in Australian discovery.

Dhawalagiri, one of the loftiest peaks in the Himalayas, 26,836 feet in height, is the 'white mountain' (Sanscrit *dhavala,* 'white,' and *giri,* 'a mountain.')

Diamantina is the modern name of a town in the diamond district of Brazil, formerly called TEJUCO, 'dirt' town. The DIAMANTINA RIVER, Queensland, has no reference to diamonds, but repeats the

Christian name of Lady Bowen, wife of the first Governor.

Diarbekr, an important town on the Upper Tigris, derived its name from the 'camp,' *diyar*, of Bekr, an Arab tribe. So DERA ISMAEL KHAN in the Punjab is the 'abode' or 'tent' (*dera*) pitched by Ismael Khan, which ultimately grew into a city.

Diedenhofen in Lorraine, called THION-VILLE in French, is a corruption of *Thio-denhofen*, Latinised as *Theodonis villa*, from a personal name cognate with the Gothic *thiuda*, 'people.'

Diego Ramires, a group of rocky islands off Cape Hoorn, were so named by Bartolomeo Garcia de Nodal, in 1619, after a cosmographer who accompanied his expedition.

Dieppe, in Normandy, derives its Scandinavian name from 'the deep' (*diep*), or the 'deep water' (*diupa*) of the River Arques on which it stands.

Dijon, the former capital of the duchy of Burgundy, is from an oblique case of *Dibio*, believed to be a Celtic name referring to its position at the confluence of the two streams the Ouche and the Suzon.

Dingle, in Kerry, is a corruption of the old Irish name *Daingean* 'strong,' denoting a stronghold or fort.

Direction Islands, CAPE DIRECTION, and DIRECTION BANK, are so called because they give the direction to ships steering respectively for the Straits of Magellan, for an opening in the Australian Barrier reef, and for the harbour of Bombay.

Dirk Hartog's Island, Australia, was discovered in 1616 by Dirk Hartog of Amsterdam in the *Eendragt* (*q.v.*) outward bound from Holland to the Dutch East Indies, which sailed along the western coast of Australia from S. lat. 23° to 26½°. A record of this strange voyage, scratched with a knife on a tin plate, was found in Sharks Bay in 1697, and again in 1801.

Disappointment Bay, on the west coast of Patagonia, was so called by Fitzroy in 1830, on account of the disappointment of his expectation that it would lead out of FITZROY PASSAGE. CAPE DISAPPOINTMENT, in South Georgia, was so called by Cook in 1775, because, on rounding it, he found that the land he had supposed might be a part of the great Antarctic continent, proved to be only an island. The ISLANDS OF DISAPPOINT-MENT, a group in the Low Archipelago, discovered by Byron in 1765, were so called because after two days' search no

fresh provisions for his sick men were found.

Disaster Inlet, in the Gulf of Carpentaria, was so called by Stokes in 1841 on account of the bursting of a fowling-piece, on which he had relied to procure food. On his third voyage Columbus gave the name of RIO DE DESASTRE to a river on the Mosquito coast of Central America (now called the Bluefields River) because of the disastrous wreck of one of his ships in September 1502.

Discovery Bay, South Australia, forms an interesting record of early Australian exploration. It was here that Major Mitchell, descending the Glenelg in his overland journey from the Murray River, reached the coast, and found the boat *Discovery* awaiting him.

Disentis in the Graubünden is a corruption of *Desertina*, the desert place in which Sigbert, the companion of Columbanus, founded the monastery around which the town subsequently grew up. (*See* DYSART.)

Dislocation Harbour, in Tierra del Fuego, is an ill-chosen name bestowed by Fitzroy in 1829 because one of his officers here got his shoulder out of joint.

Dismal Swamp is the appropriate name of the great cedar swamp near Norfolk in Virginia.

Dispersion, Mount, on the Darling River, New South Wales, was so called by Mitchell because a threatening band of natives dispersed when a few shots were fired at them.

Dniepr or DNIEPER, a great Russian river, retains the old Scythic name *Dana-pris*, of which the later Greek name *Borysthenes* is believed to be a rough translation. (*See* BERESINA.) In like manner the DNIESTR or DNIESTER retains the Scythic name *Danaster*, whose later name *Tyras* is preserved in its Turkic name the TURLA. In *Dan-apris* and *Dan-aster* we may recognise the Scythic word *dan*, a 'river,' the Danapris being the 'northern' or 'upper' river and the Danaster the 'southern' or 'lower' river.

Doab is a Persian term signifying the district between 'two rivers.' In Upper India it denotes especially the tract between the Ganges and the Jumna. The districts between the rivers of the Punjab are all called Doabs, with a distinctive prefix, the Richna Doab, for instance, lying between the Chenab and the Ravi.

Dobrudja or DOBRUTCHA (Bulgarian *Dobritch*), a district on the Black Sea, south of the Delta of the Danube, means the good district or pasturage. The Old Slavonic *dobru*, 'good,' common in Slavonic names, is a loan word adopted by the Turks from the Bulgarians. Mr. Freeman, in his *Historical Geography*, asserts that it was so called because it was part of the possessions of the despot Dobroditus, *c.* 1357, but more probably the despot took his name from the territory.

Dodabetta, the highest peak of the Nilgherries, is the 'great mountain,' from the Dravidian *doda*, 'great,' and *betta*, 'mountain.'

Dog River, an affluent of the Slave River, was so called because the banks were inhabited by the 'Dog Rib' tribe, a translation of the native name, *Thlingcha-Dinneh*. The Dog Ribs are also called SLAVE INDIANS, a translation of the name given them by their enemies the Crees. (*See* SLAVE RIVER, p. 260.)

Dogger Bank, a trawling station in the North Sea, was so called because frequented by the Dutch fishing smacks called 'doggers.'

Dollart, a bay at the mouth of the Ems, formed by a great storm in 1277, is from the Frisian word *dollerd* or *dullert*, a 'depression' or 'hollow.'

Dolores, the name of sundry places in Spain and the Spanish colonies, is derived from Franciscan missions commemorating the sorrows of St. Francis, or from churches dedicated to our Lady of Sorrows. The oldest building in California is the church of the *Mission de los Dolores de San Francisco*, established by Father Serro at San Francisco in 1776. The RIO DOLORES in Colorado also takes its name from a Franciscan Mission.

Dolphin and Union Strait, in Arctic America, was discovered and traversed by Dr. Richardson in two small boats, the *Dolphin* and the *Union*, during Franklin's expedition, 1825-26. DOLPHIN ISLAND, West Australia, was discovered by the barque *Dolphin*.

Dominica, 'Sunday Island,' one of the Lesser Antilles, was the first land discovered by Columbus on his second voyage. He sighted it on Sunday, November 3rd, 1493. HISPANIOLA, the Spanish part of HAITI, is also called SAN DOMINGO, from the town of that name founded in 1496 by Bartolomé Colon, the brother of Columbus. According to Las Casas it was so called because the first stone was laid on a Sunday, but Don Fernando Colon asserts, with greater probability, that it was named in honour of the patron saint of Domenico Colon, the father of the two brothers. The differentiated form DOMINICA is sometimes used to designate the whole island of Haiti.

Don, the name of a river flowing into the Sea of Asov, must have meant 'river' or 'water' in Sarmatian, and still bears that signification in Ossetic. Thus a stream in the Caucasus, which flows over black rocks is called by the Ossetes SAW-DORGINY-DON, the 'black-stone water.' The DONETZ, and perhaps the DANUBE, the DNIEPER (*q.v.*), and the DNIESTER may contain the same root. The Don was the *Tanais* of the Greeks.

Donaghmore, the 'great church,' is the name of fourteen Irish parishes. The first part of the word is a corruption of the Irish *domhnach*, an early loan word from the Latin *dominica*, meaning, like the English word church, the Lord's house, or possibly a church consecrated on a Sunday, *dies dominica*. DONNYBROOK, near Dublin, famous for its fair, is a corruption of *Domhnach-Broc*, the Church of St. Broc.

Doncaster, Yorkshire, in A.S. *Donaceaster* or *Done-ceaster*, the chester on the River Don, is the place called *ad Danum*, or *Danum*, in the Antonine Itinerary. The name is probably from the Celtic word *dānu*, 'strong.' There is also a RIVER DON in Aberdeenshire.

Donegal, an Irish county, takes its name from the town of DONEGAL, anciently *Dun-na-nGall*, 'the fort of the strangers' or Danes. The old Danish fortress, which stood at the ford over the Esk, was burnt by the Irish in 1159.

Dongola, a district in Nubia, is named from its inhabitants the *Dankla* (singular *Dongolavi*).

Dorchester, in Oxfordshire, where Cynegils and Cwichelm were baptised by Berinus, became the seat of the bishopric afterwards removed to Lincoln. In A.S. it is *Dorces-ceaster*, *Dorcan-ceaster*, *Dorcaceaster*, *Dorce-ceaster*, or *Dorceaster*, the meaning of which is not obvious, but is probably from an older Celtic name, apparently unconnected with the name of DORCHESTER, the county town of Dorset (*q.v.*), which has been transferred to DORCHESTER in Massachusetts, which was founded in 1630 at a place whose native name was Mattapan. The colony was projected by John White, the Puritan Rector of Dorchester in Dorset, and was carried out by merchants of Dorchester in order to obtain supplies for their vessels fishing near Cape Cod.

Dornford, the older name of CHESTERTON in Hunts, was the A.S. *Dormanceaster* or *Dorm-ceaster*, called in the Antonine Itinerary *Durobrivæ*, 'the fortress bridge,' showing that a ford had replaced a Roman bridge over the Nen.

Dorpat, in Livonia, is a corruption of the Lettish name *Tehrpat*, Latinised as *Tarpatum*.

Dorset, a corruption of the A.S. *Dornsæte,* afterwards *Dor-sæte,* is a name of the same class as Somerset. It must mean the settlers near Dorchester, which is called in A.S. *Dornwaran-ceaster, Dornwara-cester, Dornware-ceaster, Dornea-cester,* or *Dornceaster,* names evidently derived from *Durnovaria,* the Roman name, which doubtless designated not the modern town, but the huge British fortress, now called Maiden Castle, which crowns the summit of a hill a mile or so south of Dorchester, to which it bears much the same relation as Old Sarum does to Salisbury. The Anglo-Saxons would understand Dorn-wara-ceaster as meaning the chester of the inhabitants of Dorn. (*See* CANTERBURY). The meaning of Durnovaria is obscure. In Celtic *dur* means a strong place, and *-varia* means a 'descent,' so that Dur-no-varia might be the 'fortress of the descent,' Maiden Castle standing on the summit of a steep descent leading to Weymouth. It has also been suggested that the name may be from the Celtic *dwr,* 'water.' Ptolemy calls the people of Dorset the *Dour-o-triges,* (Cornish *trige,* 'to inhabit,') and Asser tells us that in the British tongue Dorset was called *Durn-gueis, i.e.* the Durn country (Welsh *gwys,* 'country').

Dortmund, in Westphalia, is not, as might be supposed at the mouth of the Dort, but is a corruption of *Throtmanni,* which we find in the tenth century. *Throtmanni,* which is from a personal name, became successively *Trutmonnia, Drutmunne,* and *Trutmonde,* from which the transition to Dortmund is easy.

Doubs, a French Department, takes its name from the River Doubs, anciently the *Dubis,* probably a Celtic name meaning the 'black water.'

Doubtful Bay, in Tasmanland, was so called by Stokes because he was doubtful whether it was a bay or an estuary. DOUBTFUL ISLAND, in the Paumotu group, was so named by Cook because he was doubtful whether it had not been previously discovered and named by Bougainville.

Douglas, which means the 'black brook' (Gaelic *dubh-glaise*), is the name of several small streams, and hence of places on their banks; among them DOUGLAS, a town in the Isle of Man, and DOUGLAS, a village in Lanarkshire, which gave a patronymic to the great Douglas family. CAPE DOUGLAS, Cook's River, was so named by Cook after Dr. Douglas, Canon of Windsor. PORT DOUGLAS, Queensland, bears the name of Mr. John Douglas, a Prime Minister of Queensland.

Douro is the Portuguese name of the river called DUERO in Spanish, and *Durius* by the Romans. It is usually explained as a Celtic name from *dur,* 'strong,' or *dwr,* 'water,' but as the existence of Celtic names in Spain is doubtful it may not improbably be from the Basque *Astura,* 'rocky river,' which was the old name of the IZLA, its chief affluent. But the DORIA in Piedmont, and the DORDOGNE, formerly the *Duranius,* which gives a name to a French Department, are probably Celtic.

Dover, Kent, is the Roman *Dubris,* probably a locative form. In the Saxon Chronicle the name appears as *Dofere* and *Dofre,* and in the dative as *æt Doferan* and *Dobrum,* the inhabitants being called *Doferware.* The name was probably Belgic, from the Celtic *dubr,* 'water' (Irish *dobhar,* Welsh *dwr* (*dwfr*), Manx *duobar*), and may have denoted primarily the little stream which enters Dover harbour. We have the same word in *Cam-dubr,* the 'crooked water,' in the Liber Landavensis, also in Pliny's *Vernodubrum,* 'aldertree water,' in Gaul, while the TAUBER, an affluent of the Main, is called the *Dubra* by the Ravenna geographer. DOVERCOURT, near Harwich, is *Dovor-cort* in a charter, and DOVERDALE, in Worcestershire, is A.S. *Doferdael* and *Doverdel.* We have WENDOVER in Bucks (A.S. *Wændofra*), MITCHELDEVER or Micheldever, A.S. *Myceldefer* (mycel, 'great'), as well as Andover (*q.v.*) and Candover (*q.v.*).

Down, an Irish county, takes its name from DOWNPATRICK, the county town, so called from a large entrenched *dun* near the cathedral, originally called *Dunkeltar,* the fort of Keltar of the battles. The name of Keltar was ultimately dropped and that of St. Patrick substituted from his connection with the place. Down is an English corruption of the Celtic *dun,* a strong place or hill-fort.

Dragon's Mouth and SERPENT'S MOUTH are the English translations of the Spanish names *Boca del Drago* and *Boca della Sierpe*, given by Columbus in 1498 on his third voyage, to the two outlets of the Gulf of Paria, because of the dangerous surge caused by the furious currents from the mouths of the Orinoco.

Drakenstein, in the Cape Colony, was so named in 1675 in honour of the Baron van Rheede, Lord of Drakenstein in Geldern.

Drake's Harbour, now usually called SIR FRANCIS DRAKE'S BAY, is a name which has been given by the Californians to a bay at the entrance of the Golden Gate, near San Francisco, in order to commemorate the visit of Sir Francis Drake to the Californian coast in July 1579, during his circumnavigation of the globe. The older name PUERTO DE LOS REYES, bore witness to the prior discovery by the Spaniards in 1542, on January 6th, the Festival of the Three Kings, which we call the Epiphany.

Drave or DRAU, a tributary of the Danube, is the *Dravus* or *Draus* of the Romans. The name is distinctively neither Celtic, Slavonic, or Teutonic, but of the primitive Aryan type, and has been referred by Bopp to the Sanskrit *dravas,* 'that which flows.' To the same stem we may refer the name of the TRAVE in Holstein, formerly the *Travena,* and possibly of the TRAUN, formerly the *Druna* or *Truna.* TRAVEMÜNDE is the town 'at the mouth of the Trave.'

Dreary, Mount, is one of two mountains in the York Peninsula, Queensland, which, in 1820, were appropriately named MOUNT DREARY and MOUNT HORRID by King.

Drenthe, a province in the Netherlands between the Zuyder Zee and the Dollart, is a corruption of the old name *Thrianta,* which Grimm explains as equivalent to *Thri-banta,* denoting the union of 'three districts.' (*See* BRABANT.) So the district of TWENTHE in the Netherlands retains the name of the *Tubantes* of Tacitus, who were the people of 'two districts.'

Dresden, the capital of the kingdom of Saxony, is locally called *Dräsen.* The second *d* is intrusive, as is shown by the older form *Dresen,* which would mean 'at the ferry,' from the Slavonic *trasi,* a 'ferry.' Buttmann derives the name from the Wendish *drezdzany,* a 'haven' or 'wharf.'

Dreux, in the Department of the Eure et Loire, is a corruption of the Low-Latin name *Drocæ,* a name which appears in the Antonine Itinerary as *Durocasses,* apparently a tribe name.

Drogheda is a corruption of *Droichead-atha,* 'the bridge at the ford,' so called from a bridge built at the ford where the northern road crossed the Boyne. The Gaelic *drochaid,* Old Irish *droichet,* a 'bridge,' is also the source of the name DROCH HEAD in Wigtownshire.

Droitwich, in Worcestershire, has brine springs rising in the centre of the town. It was the *Salinæ* of the Romans, and is called *Saltwich* in a charter of 880. The name Droitwich signifies the *wych* or 'salt-house' where the droits or dues on salt were paid.

Dromedary, Cape, on the coast of New South Wales, was so called by Cook in 1770 from its shape.

Drummond, a common name in certain parts of Ireland and Scotland, is a corruption of the Gaelic *dromainn,* 'a ridge,' derived from, and probably a diminutive of, the Gaelic *druim,* 'the back,' hence a 'ridge,' a word cognate with the Latin *dorsum.* The DRUMMOND HILLS, at the source of the Spey, as well as LOCH DROMA and ACHADRUM, may preserve the name of Drum-Alban, the *Dorsum Britanniæ* of Latin writers, erroneously called the Grampians (*q.v.*). DRUM is found as the initial syllable in about 2400 Irish names, and is often disguised, as in AUGHRIM, a corruption of *Each-dhruim,* 'horse ridge,' or LEITRIM for *Liath-dhruim,* 'the grey ridge.' It is also common in Scotland, as in TYNDRUM, CAIRN-DRUM, and DROMORE, the 'great ridge.'

Druses, properly *ed-Derûz,* a people in the Lebanon, are so called from the prophet Ismael Darazi or el Derzi, the founder of their religion.

Dsungaria, in Central Asia, is the territory of the *Soongarr,* 'those to the left,' a nomad Mongol tribe, so called because they are on the left hand, that is to the north, of the other nomads.

Dublin, anciently *Duibh-linn* (dubh-linn), the 'black pool,' is properly the name of that part of the Liffey where the city was built. Compare BLACKPOOL in Lancashire. The older name was *Ath-Cliath,* the 'ford of hurdles.' DUPPLIN CASTLE, in Perthshire, is a variant form of the name Dublin.

Dubuque City, in Iowa, takes its name from Julien Dubuque, a French-Canadian trader who obtained permission to work the lead mines where the city of Dubuque now stands.

Ducato, Cape, at the South-West extremity of LEUCADIA (Santa Maura), is an Italian corruption, with a prefixed article, of the ancient name *Leucatas,* so called from the dazzling cliff of white marble, which rises 2000 feet above the sea.

Dudley, in Worcestershire, according to a baseless tradition preserved by Camden, took its name from Dodo, a Saxon prince, but is merely the *leah* or 'field' of some unknown person bearing the name of Dudda. DUDLEY DIGGES, a cape at the head of Baffin's Bay, was so named by Baffin, in 1616, after his patron Sir Dudley Digges, a contemporary writer and politician, whose name is also borne by CAPE DIGGES at the entrance to Hudson's Bay, a cape discovered and named by Hudson in 1610.

Duff Islands, in the Santa Cruz Group, bear the name of the missionary ship *Duff,* which visited them in 1797.

Dufferin, a barony in County Down, which gives the title of Marquis to the Blackwoods, was anciently *Dubh-thrian,* the 'black third,' a name referring to an old tripartite division of territory. TREAN-LAUR, a similar name, is the 'middle third.'

Dulcigno, a coast town in Albania, is a corruption, with a prefixed article, of the Roman *Olcinium,* a name better preserved in the Turkish form OLKIN or OLGUN.

Dumdum, a military cantonment near Calcutta, is doubtless from the Hindustani *damdama,* 'a mound,' hence an elevated battery.

Dunbar, in Haddingtonshire, may be either the 'fort on the height' (Gaelic *barr*) or the hill of St. Barr or Finbar, an Irish Saint. The Gaelic and Irish *dun,* a hill-fort or strong place, is the Welsh *din,* and the Gaulish *dunon,* Latinised as *dunum,* which we have in AUTUN and other French names. It seems to have obscure relations with the common Anglo-Saxon suffix *-don* in English names, and also with the A.S. *tún* (whence our word *town*) and the German *zaun.* It is a very common prefix in Irish and Scotch names, as DUNDRUM, County Down, the 'fort on the ridge.' It is often followed by a personal name as DUNDONALD, 'Dunall's fort,' DUNCANNAN, 'Conan's fort,' or Dungannon, in Tyrone, a corruption of *Dun-Geanainn,* the 'fort of Geanan.' DUNDALK, originally the name of a great neighbouring earthwork, is a corruption of *Dun-Dealgan,* the 'fort of Delga,'

one of the chieftains of Irish legend. DUNROBIN is supposed to be the 'fort of Robin,' or Robert, Earl of Sutherland. DONERAILE, County Cork, anciently *Dun-air-aill,* is the 'fort on the cliff.' DUNMYAT, a peak of the Ochils, which overlooks Stirling, is believed by Professor Rhys to be the *dun* or hill-fort of the tribe of the Meatæ. DUNKELD, called the Gate of the Highlands, is usually explained as the fort of the Calidones, whose southern outpost it was. But the Gaelic name *Dun-celden* or *Dun-calden* points, as Mr. Stokes has shown, to the 'fort of the woods' or the 'forest fort' as the true meaning, *caillen* being the genitive plural of *caill,* a wood or forest. DUNDEE, at the mouth of the Tay, has been supposed to be a corruption of *Dun-Tatha,* the 'fort on the Tay,' but this derives no support from the early forms of the name; *Dunde,* a twelfth century form, being apparently *dùn Dé,* the 'hill of God.' The prefix *dun-* sometimes takes the form *dum,* as in Dumfries and Dumbarton. DUMFRIES, anciently *Dun-fres,* is probably the 'fort of the Frisians,' while DUMBARTON, originally called Alclud (Al-clyde), the 'rock on the Clyde,' having in the sixth century been taken by the Welsh prince Rhydderch Hael who made it his capital, was called by the Gaels Dun-brettan or Dun-breatan, the 'fort of the Britons' or Welsh of Strath-Clyde. The name became *Dumbriton* in the seventeenth century, and finally Dumbarton.

Duncan Island, an isolated isle in the Pacific, N.W. of the Galapagos, bears the name of the Captain of a merchant ship by whom it was discovered in 1787.

Dundas in Linlithgow is the Gaelic *dun-deas,* the 'southern fort,' hence the territorial surname Dundas, the source of many colonial names mainly due to Henry Dundas, Viscount Melville, First Lord of the Admiralty, whose name is borne by DUNDAS STRAIT between MELVILLE ISLAND and the North Australian coast, by FORT DUNDAS on Melville Island, where an attempt was made in 1829 to establish a convict settlement, as well as by MOUNT DUNDAS, and POINT DUNDAS, in the Gulf of Carpentaria, discovered in 1803, and by DUNDAS POINT in the Arctic MELVILLE ISLAND, discovered in 1820.

Dunedin, a Gaelic equivalent of Edinburgh (*q.v.*), was the name given to the capital of the New Zealand province of Otago, in which about 1847 a settlement was made by an association formed by the Free Church of Scotland, under whose auspices a number of emigrants, conducted by a Captain Cargill, were landed at a place they named PORT CHALMERS. A neighbouring river was called the CLUTHA, which was supposed to be the ancient name of the Clyde, one of their towns receiving the absurd name of INVERCARGILL.

Dungeness or DENGENESS, in Kent, is the dangerous shingle point which forms the extremity of Romney Marsh, formerly called Denge Marsh. In the Saxon Chronicle Dungeness is called simply *Næs*, the 'Ness' or nose; the meaning of the distinguishing prefix, which is of later origin, is unknown. Dungeness might signify the ness at the extremity of the Denge Marsh, a name possibly derived from an old French word denoting 'a feudal toll;' the sea wall protecting the marsh being maintained by the 'Lords of the Marsh,' who levy scot-payments on the district, and have the benefit of all fines, writs, and forfeitures. But the Marsh may have been named from the Ness, in which case the name might refer to the waves 'beating' on the point, or to the 'noise' of the sea rolling the large shingle of which the Ness is composed.

Dunkirk (French DUNKERQUE) takes its name from a church founded in the seventh century by St. Eloi, on the sandhills or *dunes* on the Flemish coast. DUNSTABLE, Bedfordshire (A.S. *Dunestapel*), is the *staple* or market on the chalk downs.

Durazzo, a Turkish port on the Adriatic, is a corruption of the old Greek name *Dyrrhachion*.

Durban, properly D'URBAN, the capital of Natal, was founded in 1834 by Captain Gardiner, and named after Sir Benjamin D'Urban, Governor of the Cape Colony.

Durham, capital of the County Palatine of the same name, stands on a precipitous hill, 80 feet high, almost encircled by a bend of the River Wear. Here, in 995, the monks of Lindisfarne, bearing the body of St. Cuthbert, took refuge from the Danes. They called it *Dunholm*, the *holm* or river island forming a *dun* or hill-fort. Dunholm was softened on Norman lips to *Duresme*, whence by assimilative folk etymology came the English form Durham.

Durness, in Sutherland, is probably the Norse name *Dyrnaes*, 'Stag Cape.'

Dusky Bay, New Zealand, was discovered by Cook in the dusk of the evening of March 13th, 1770. He put out to sea without anchoring, because he found he could not land before it grew dark.

Düsseldorf, at the confluence of the Rhine and the River Düssel, was, till the thirteenth century, merely a village, as its name implies.

Dutch,, the English form of *Deutsche*, the national name of the German race, is from the O.H.G. *diot* (Gothic *thiuda*), 'people' or 'tribe,' whence the *Teutoni* of Cæsar and the *Teutones* of Strabo. Deutsche, 'the people,' is used in opposition to Walsche (Welsh), 'the foreigners' or 'strangers,' a name which the Germans give to the Italians and Walloons, while we confine it to the Celts of WALES and CORNWALL (*q.v.*). An etymology recently advanced by Mr. Bradley derives Teutones from a primitive Teutonic *theuth-o* (Gothic *thiuths*), 'good.' As late as the time of Charles I. we used the name Dutchland (German *Deutschland*) for Germany, and in the United States Dutchman still means a German. In England it is now restricted to the people of the Netherlands, properly the Low Dutch.

Duxbury, near Plymouth, Massachusetts, was occupied about 1630, and named after Duxbury in Lancashire, the birthplace of Miles Standish, the puritan hero.

Duyfhen Point, in the Gulf of Carpentaria, commemorates the visit of the Dutch yacht *Duyfhen*, despatched in 1606 from Bantam. (*See* CARPENTARIA.) This was in fact the earliest discovery of the Australian continent, though at the time it was supposed that these coasts were part of New Guinea.

Dwina is the name of two large Russian rivers. One, which flows into the Arctic Ocean, bears a name derived from the old Scythic word *don*, 'water' or 'river.' The other, which falls into the Baltic at Riga, is of recent origin, being a Russian corruption of the German name *Düna*, given, it is believed, to the river by Bremen sailors because of the dunes or sandhills at its mouth.

Dyer, a Cape on the western side of Davis Strait, was named in 1585 by Davis after his friend Sir Edward Dyer, afterwards Chancellor of the Order of the Garter.

Dysart, a populous town on the coast of Fife, has grown up near the cave inhabited by St. Serf. The Scotch and Irish hermits often lived in separate cells in some solitary place. Hence *diseart* or *desert*, from the Latin *desertum*, became the Celtic name of a hermitage. DESERT-MARTIN in Derry was the hermitage of St. Martin; DESERT-SERGES, in County

Cork, of St. Sergius ; ISERTKEERAN of St. Ciaran. ISERTKELLY, a corruption of Disertkelly, is ' Kelly's retreat. We have also DYSERTH in North Wales, DYZARD in Cornwall, and DYSERTMORE, ' the great hermitage,' in Kilkenny. (*See* DISENTIS.)

Eagle Island and LIZARD ISLAND are two adjacent islets on the Queensland coast. On the first Cook found an eagle's nest, on the other he saw only lizards.

Earn is a Perthshire river flowing from LOCH EARN through STRATHEARN. The oldest form of the name is *Eirenn*, which Professor Rhys explains as *Erann*, the genitive plural of *Erna*, the Ivernians or Irish.

Eastbourne, in Sussex, is called *Burne*, the ' brook,' in the Chronicle. The prefix is a later addition which may have served to distinguish the stream from another burn further west, now called the Cuckmere River.

East Cape, the extreme eastern point of Asia, was discovered and named by Cook in 1778.

Easter Island lies in the South Pacific, midway between Peru and New Zealand. It was discovered in 1686 by Edward Davis, and hence Cook proposed to call it Davis Land. Its present name is due to the rediscovery by the Dutchman Roggeween on Easter Monday, 1722. Fitzroy spent the Easter of 1830 in a Patagonian bay which he called EASTER BAY. GOOD FRIDAY HARBOUR, in the EASTER ISLANDS, West Australia, was discovered by Stokes on Good Friday, April 17th, 1840.

Ebchester, in Durham, represents the Roman *Ep-eiacum*.

Ebro, a river in Spain, was the *Iberus* of the ancients. The Greeks acquired their earliest knowledge of Spain from their colonies near the mouth of the Ebro, and the names Iberia and Iberians are probably derived from the name of the River Iber-us, south of which the Iberia of the Romans began. The name has been explained from the Basque *ibarra*, ' a valley,' and has also been compared with that of the Eure, anciently the *Ebur-a*, and of the Yorkshire Ure, formerly, it is supposed, the *Ebura* or *Ebora*. (*See* YORK.)

Eclipse Islands, off King George's Sound, West Australia, derive their name from a lunar eclipse here observed by King on October 2nd, 1819. Ross was at ECLIPSE HARBOUR, Boothia Felix, during the lunar eclipse of September 12th, 1829.

Ecuador, a South American State, is officially styled LA REPUBLICA DEL ECUADOR; Quito, the capital, lying almost precisely upon the Equator.

Edam, in North Holland, best known for its cheeses, takes its name from the dam or embankment of the small River Ee. or Ey, now called the Die.

Eddington, Wilts, apparently a patronymic, occurs in the Chronicle in the dative form *to Ethandune*, where *éthan* is the dat. def. of *éthe*, ' desert, desolate, or waste.' Eddington therefore means the ' desolate dun ' or hill.

Eddystone, a rock and lighthouse in the English Channel off Plymouth, doubtless obtained its name from the dangerous eddy round the rock. Byron in 1765, Cook in 1777, and Shortland in 1788 gave the same name for the same reason to dangerous rocks in the Falkland Islands, off Tasmania, and in the Salomon Group.

Edelsland, Western Australia, was discovered in 1619 by Jans Van Edel, a Dutch seaman.

Eden, a river in Cumberland, is not, as has been supposed, from the A.S. *Ed-dene*, the ' river valley,' but must be identified with the *Ituna* of Ptolemy, a pre-Teutonic name, seemingly a river - name cognate with the Welsh Ythan or Ithon. More than a hundred names in Ireland, and many in Scotland contain the word *eden*, which is usually from the Gaelic *eadann*, the forehead, hence the brow of a hill. EDENDERRY, for instance, is the ' oakwood brow.'

Edenbridge, in Kent, is named from a bridge which crosses a river now called the EDEN. But since it appears from the Textus Roffensis that Edenbridge is a corruption of Eadhelm's Bridge, it would seem that the name of the River Eden is merely an inference from the name of Edenbridge, and there is reason to believe that the original name of the river was Avon, since, in a charter of 814, there is a mention of a river called the Avene, which is apparently to be identified with the Eden.

Edge's Land, Spitzbergen, was discovered in 1616 by Thomas Edge, captain of a whaler.

Edinburgh, formerly *Edwines burg*, means ostensibly the fortress of Eadwine, the Northumbrian king, who was converted by Paulinus. He extended the Anglian dominion as far as the Forth, and may probably have erected a frontier fortress on the commanding rock on which Edinburgh Castle stands. But in the Pictish

Chronicle Edinburgh is called *oppidum Eden*, translated as *Dunedin*, and in the annals of Tighernac (A.D. 638) it appears as *Etin*. These forms point to an older Pictish name, of which Edinburgh may possibly be an assimilated form.

Edmonton, Middlesex, is in Domesday Adelmetone, pointing to an A.S. *Éadhelmingtún*, from the proper name *Éadhelm*.

Eendragt, is a small river in Holland. In 1616 the Dutch ship *Eendragt*, named perhaps from the river, and commanded by Dirk Hartog (*q.v.*), discovered Eendragt Land, West Australia. EENDRAGT BAY, in the Australian Island of Hoorn (or Horn), off Cape York, bears the name of the same ship.

Egede's Minde, a Danish settlement in Greenland, was founded in 1759 by Captain Egede, and named in mind (*minde*, 'remembrance') of his father Hans Egede, the first Greenland missionary, a Norwegian pastor who came to Greenland, and by his self-sacrifice and zeal civilised and converted many of the Eskimos.

Eger, a town in Bohemia, is on the river Eger, formerly the Agara.

Egmont Island, one of the Low Islands in the South Pacific, was discovered by Wallis in 1767, and named after the Earl of Egmont, First Lord of the Admiralty, whose name is also borne by MOUNT EGMONT and CAPE EGMONT, in New Zealand, discovered by Cook in 1770, and by PORT EGMONT, in the Falklands, discovered by Byron in 1765.

Egypt is the Greek and not the native name of the country which on the monuments is called *Kem* (*Ham*), 'the black,' probably from the dark alluvial soil. The Semitic name was *Mizraim*, a dual form denoting Upper and Lower Egypt, the two kingdoms symbolised by the double crown of the Egyptian kings. *Mazor*, the singular form, usually denotes the Delta. The meaning of the Greek name *Ægyptos* has been much disputed. It has been explained as the 'land' (*aia*) of the vulture (*guptos*), or rather of the sacred kite of Horus, which is the most conspicuous animal in the country. Another etymology derives it from the Copts (*q.v.*) or from the town of Koptos, the seat of the earliest dynasties, where the caravan route from the Red Sea reached the Nile, and hence the place that would first become known to strangers from the East. The latest conjecture explains the name as a Greek misconception of the sacred name of Memphis, *Het-ka-Ptah*, the

'house of the Genius of Ptah' or *Ha-ka-Ptah*, 'the city of the Genius of Ptah.'

Eider or EYDER, a large river of Germany, was called *Egidora* in the eighth century. *Oegisdyr*, the Scandinavian translation of an older Frisian name, shows the meaning to be the 'sea door' or 'sea entrance,' which aptly describes the great estuary to which, and not to the river, the name was originally given. Ægir was an old Scandinavian sea-god, and in A.S. and Old Frisian the River Eider was called by the translated name *Fifel-dor*, the word *fifel* meaning in A.S. a 'giant' or 'sea monster.' (*See* HUMBER.) EIDER ISLAND, in Smith's Sound, was so called by Kane in 1854 from the multitude of eider ducks.

Einsiedeln, a well-known place of pilgrimage in Canton Schwyz, appears in the eleventh century as *Einsidelin*, Latinised as *Solitarium* and *Locus Hermitarum*. The great Benedictine Abbey, founded in the tenth century, was built near to the cell of St. Meinrad (Meginrad), who lived as a Hermit (*einsiedler*) in the forest, and was killed by two robbers in 861.

Ekaterinburg, in the Ural, was one of the 216 towns founded by the Empress Catherine II. of Russia. Others are EKATERINODAR, 'Catherine's gift'; (1790); EKATERINOGRAD, 'Catherine's city' (1777); and EKATERINOSLAV, 'Catherine's glory' (1784).

Elba represents the old name *Ilva*, which was probably, as Mommsen has pointed out, a Ligurian name, the *Ilvates* being one of the Ligurian tribes. Ilva may therefore be a dialectical form of *Alba*, *Alb*, or *Alp* (*q.v.*), a Ligurian word, believed to mean a 'mountain.' Elba is notably a mountain isle.

Elbe River, the *Albis* of Tacitus and Strabo, has been variously interpreted as a Celtic name, meaning the 'white water,' the 'great water,' or the mountain river'; but is regarded as Teutonic by the best authorities, such as Pott and Förstemann. *Elf* means 'river' in Anglo-Saxon, Old Norse, and Swedish. In Sweden *Elf* or *Elv* is the usual word for a river, and in O.N. all the great rivers are called *Elver*. Other river names of this class in Germany are the ELBER, the ALF, and the ALB.

Elburuz, the highest summit in the Caucasus, bears an old Persian name which means 'the shining mountain.'

Elephanta, an island six miles from Bombay, is locally called Gharipuri, the 'place of caves.' The Portuguese name

Elephanta is derived from the colossal figure of an elephant carved on the rock, guarding the entrance to a magnificent cave-temple, which dates from the eighth century. ELEPHANTINE, the Greek name of the island of Philæ at the first cataract of the Nile, was so called because it was the mart to which the Nubians brought their ivory for sale.

Eleuthera, one of the Bahamas, was granted in 1646 to Captain Sayle, who gave it the Greek name of Eleuthera, meaning the 'free' isle or the isle of free thought, in the hope, he says, that it would prove a place 'where every one might enjoy his own opinion on religion without control or question.'

Elgin, a Scotch shire which takes its name from the town of Elgin, represents the lowland part of the old Earldom of Moray. The name Elgin is an oblique case of *Elga,* an old poetical name of Ireland, which, according to Mr. Stokes, probably means 'noble.'

Elias is a common mountain name in the Levant, Elijah being in the East the mountain saint, because of the altar he built on Carmel. Several peaks in Syria are called MAR ELIAS (Saint Elijah) from churches or convents dedicated to him which have been built on their summits, among them the convent of MAR ELIAS on Carmel, the mother house of the Carmelite order. Mountains in Eubœa, Paros, Scio, Melos, Santa Maura, and the Morea also bear the name of HAGIOS ELIAS. Indirectly we owe to the Russians the name of MOUNT ST. ELIAS, the loftiest summit in North America, 14,970 feet in height, on the border line between Alaska and the Canadian Dominion. Bering in 1741 gave the name of St. Elias to a cape which he reached on July 20th, the feast of St. Elias, and Cook in 1778 erroneously transferred the name to the snow-clad mountain behind the cape.

Elizabeth Island, off the coast of Massachusetts, was discovered by Gosnold in 1602, and named after the English Queen. ELIZABETH ISLAND, in Magellan's Straits, which is said to have been discovered by Sir John Narborough, on his Patagonian voyage in 1670, had been named by Drake in 1578, who took possession of it in the name of Queen Elizabeth. ELIZABETH COUNTY, New York, was named after the daughter of James I., who married the Elector Palatine (the 'winter king') and became the mother of Prince Rupert. CAPE ELIZABETH, Massachusetts, was one of the names placed by Prince Charles, in 1614, on John Smith's map of New England, doubtless in compliment to his sister, afterwards Electress Palatine. CAPE ELIZABETH, at the entrance of Cook's River, Alaska, was so called by Cook, because discovered on May 21st, 1778, the birthday of the Princess Elizabeth, afterwards Landgravine of Hesse Homburg. CAPE ELIZABETH, at the north end of Sagalin Island, was so named by Krusenstern, in 1805, in honour of the Empress Elizabeth of Russia. PORT ELIZABETH, in Cape Colony, bears the name of Elizabeth, the wife of General Donkin.

Elk Mountains, ELK RIVER, ELK CREEK, ELK ISLAND, ELK LICK, ELKHORN, ELKHART, and other North American names refer either to the Moose, (*Cervus original*) or to the Wapiti (*Cervus Canadiensis*) which are locally called the Elk. That the true Elk (*Cervus alces*) was found in some parts of Europe is proved by the ancient forms of such names as ELLWANGEN in Würtemberg (called *Elehenwang,* 'elk field,' in the eighth century), ALTDORF, also in Würtemberg (formerly *Alahdorf*), or ELBACH in Bavaria.

Ellenbogen, 'the elbow,' is a not uncommon name in Germany for places which stand at the elbow either of a river or of a boundary.

Ellore (ELÚR), in the Madras Presidency, is from *El-úru,* the 'ruling city' (*elu,* 'ruling,' and *uru,* 'a town').

Elmet was a British kingdom conquered in the seventh century by Eadwine of Northumbria. The name is preserved by the West Riding villages of Sherburn-in-Elmet and Barwick-in-Elmet. (*See* LEEDS.)

Elmina, a British settlement on the Gold Coast, is the oldest European station in Africa. The name, which means 'the mine,' was given by the Portuguese discoverers.

Elphin is an episcopal city in Ireland. The original church was built by St. Patrick near a spring over which stood a large stone called *ail-finn,* the 'rock of the clear spring.'

Elsass is the German name of the land called ALSACE by the French. In the eighth century we have *Alisatia,* and in the ninth *Elisatia,* which are Latinised forms of the O.H.G. *alisazo,* probably meaning the 'other seat' of the Alemanni beyond the Rhine, or possibly the seat by the River Ill, formerly called the Ell, which runs parallel to the Rhine. In

England the form would have been Elset, as in Somerset and Dorset.

Elton, the name of a large salt lake in the Lower Volga steppe, is a corrupt Russian form of the Kalmuc *Altan Noor,* the 'golden lake,' which probably refers to the red glow on the surrounding cliffs at sunset.

Ely, an episcopal city in Cambridgeshire, should have been called Elyborough or Elybury, the A.S. name being *Eligburh.* Bæda's statement that Ely contained 600 hides, shows that ELY, in A.S. *Élíg,* 'the isle of eels,' must have formerly denoted not the town but the district now tautologically known as the 'ISLE OF ELY,' famous for the excellence and abundance of its eels, in which rents were formerly paid.

Embrun, a town on the Durance, in the Hautes Alpes, is the EBURODUNUM of the Romans.

Emden-am-Dollart, in East Friesland, anciently *Emedun,* takes its name from the RIVER EMS, anciently the *Amicia* or *Amisius,* at the mouth of which it stands. EMS in Nassau, stands on another River Ems, called *Emisa* in the eighth century, a river name probably cognate with the Latin *amnis* and the Sanskrit *ambhas,* 'water.' There is a RIVER EMME in Berkshire.

Emilia is a modern name given to an Italian province constituted out of the former Duchies of Parma and Modena, and of the Romagna, a part of the Papal States. It is a revival of the Roman name *Æmilia,* given to the district traversed by the *Via Æmilia,* commenced by M. Æmilius Lepidus.

Encounter Bay, South Australia, was the spot where in 1802 Flinders encountered the rival French exploring expedition under Baudin. At POINT ENCOUNTER, in Arctic America, Richardson encountered a party of Eskimos, and at EN-COUNTER COVE, in De Witt's Land, King, in 1819, encountered some hostile natives.

Endeavour River, Queensland, bears the name of Cook's ship the *Endeavour,* which on June 10th, 1770, struck on a reef, and after being got off was hauled ashore for repairs in a bay at the mouth of a river which he called the Endeavour River.

Enderby Land, South of the Cape of Good Hope, possibly a portion of the Antarctic Continent, was discovered in 1599 by the Dutch Captain Dirk Gherritsz, who was driven out of his course by a storm, and was rediscovered in 1831 by the *Tula,* a whaler owned by Messrs. Enderby of London, from whom ENDERBY ISLAND, one of the Auckland Group, was named, and also, it is believed, ENDERBY ISLAND, on the north coast of Australia, discovered by King in 1818.

Enfield, Middlesex, is *Enefelda* in Domesday, apparently a mutilated form of an A.S. *Enedfeld,* the 'duck field.' ENMORE, in Somerset, is *Animere* in Domesday, which may represent an A.S. *Enedmere,* the 'duck pond.'

Engadin, the upper valley of the Inn, is believed to be a corruption of the Romansch *en cò d'Oen,* of which a form found in Latin documents, *in capite Oeni,* 'at the head of the Inn,' would be a translation. Another old form is *Vallis Oenigadina,* which gives the transition to the modern Italian name Engadina. In like manner SAMADEN, in the Upper Engadin, is a corruption of the Romansch name *Summo d'Oen,* 'at the top of the Inn.'

Engelberg, a town in Canton Unterwalden, has gathered round a great Benedictine monastery of the same name. According to the legend the angel choir was heard singing as the founder died, and the monastery received from Pope Calixtus II. in 1124 the name of *Mons Angelorum,* of which Engelberg is the translation. The original name may have been *Anger-berg,* 'meadow hill,' out of which the legend was evolved.

England is a corruption of *Englaland,* the 'land of the Angles' (Latin *Anglorum terra*), from *Engla,* gen. plural of *Engle.* In Bæda's time, *c.* 731, it excluded Wessex, Sussex, and Essex, which were the lands of the Saxons, as well as Norfolk and Suffolk, which we now call East Anglia. The old England extended along the eastern coast from Lincolnshire northward as far as the Frith of Forth. Egbert, an Anglian prince who succeeded to the Saxon throne, extended the name of England to include the whole of his dominions. The Engle or Angles, who gave their name to England, originally inhabited Anglen (A.S. *Engel*) in Sleswick, and are identified with the *Anglii* of Tacitus and the *Angili* of Procopius. They were probably the same people as the *Angrivarii,* who are called *Anglevarii* in the Notitia. Zeuss and Förstemann make them the 'dwellers on the meadows,' from the O.H.G. *angar,* a 'mead' or 'pasture.' NEW ENGLAND is the name given to the north eastern portion of the United States. The coast from Cape

Cod in Massachusetts to the Penobscob River in Maine was explored by Captain John Smith in 1614, and at his suggestion his patron, Prince Charles, afterwards Charles I., gave the name of New England to this region, which had hitherto been known as North Virginia. Smith's ' Description of New England,' which appeared in 1616, gave currency to the name. In 1643 a confederation styled the United Colonies of New England, consisting of the four colonies of Massachusetts, Plymouth, Connecticut, and Newhaven, was formed for defence against the Indians, and survived till 1684.

English Company Islands, on the north coast of Australia, were discovered by Flinders in 1803, and named in compliment to the East India Company, which had promoted his expedition. The islands composing the group were named WIGRAM, COTTON, INGLIS, BOSANQUET, and ASTELL, from prominent directors of the Company.

Ennet - thur, in Switzerland, is the district ' beyond the Thur,' from the Swiss dialect - word *ennet,* ' beyond,' ' on the other side of.' So ENNED-À is the district ' beyond the Aa,' and ENNET-LINTH, that ' beyond the Linth.'

Enniskillen, the county town of Fermanagh, built on an island in Lough Erne, is a corruption of *Inis-Cethlenn,* the ' Island of Cethlenn.' According to the legend she was the wife of Balor, an Irish kinglet, and fought at the second battle of Moyturey.

Enterprise, Fort, on Winter Lake, was the name given by Franklin to the block house where he passed the winter of 1820-21 in preparation for his descent of the Coppermine.

Entrecasteaux Channel, at the south-east corner of Tasmania, usually called STORM BAY PASSAGE by the colonists, was first traversed in 1792 by the French Admiral D'Entrecasteaux. RECHERCHE BAY at the entrance of the channel, and ESPERANCE ISLAND near its termination, were named after his two ships, *La Recherche* and *L'Espérance.* The same names occur in the south-west corner of Australia, which was visited by the expedition; POINT D'ENTRECASTEAUX bearing the name of the Admiral; the RECHERCHE ARCHIPELAGO and ESPERANCE BAY the names of his ships.

Entre Rios, in the Argentine Confederation, lies ' between the Rivers' Paraná and Paraguay. ENTRE DOURO E MINHO is a Portuguese province ' between the Douro and Minho.'

Entry Isle is the name given by Cook to an island at the western entrance to Cook's Straits, New Zealand. An island at the entrance to Dusky Bay he called ENTRY ISLAND. Flinders named the island at the entrance to Port Bowen ENTRANCE ISLAND, and Stokes gave the same name to an island at the entrance to the Victoria River, and to another at the entrance to Roger's Strait.

Epirots are the people of Epirus, the ' mainland,' a name given to the western coast of Greece by the inhabitants of the adjacent islands, but now confined to the part of Albania opposite Corfu. Similar names are the TERRA FIRMA, given to part of the South American coast, and the SPANISH MAIN, *i.e.* the Spanish mainland, as distinguished from Cuba and the isles.

Epsom, in Surrey, is a corruption of the A.S. *Ebesham,* the ' home of Ebe.' As in the case of the adjoining village of CHEAM (A.S. *Cegham*) the suffix *-ham* has been obscured.

Ercal is a Salopian name appearing in HIGH ERCAL, CHILDE ERCAL, and ERCAL WOOD near the Wrekin. In Welsh *argel* means a ' retreat,' and in Irish *aireagal* is a ' hermit's cell.' ERRIGAL, in Derry, was formerly *Aireagal Adhamnan,* the ' cell of Adamnan.'

Erebus, Mount, an active volcano, 12,400 feet high, in South Victoria, and the adjacent MOUNT TERROR, an extinct volcano, 10,900 feet in height, are nearer to the South Pole than any other land hitherto sighted. They were discovered in 1841 by James Ross, and were named after his two ships, the *Erebus* and *Terror,* from which we have other Antarctic names, as EREBUS BANK and TERROR COVE.

Erfurt, in Thuringia, called *Erpesfurt* in the eighth century, is from a personal name meaning ' brown.'

Erie, one of the four great lakes of North America, bears the name of the Erie or ' cat' tribe of the Iroquois nation, which inhabited its banks when it was first discovered. In 1650 we find the lake called ' *Erie, ou du Chat.*'

Erith, Kent, in A.S. *Earhýth,* is a doubtful name, possibly meaning the ' seawharf' (A.S. *ear,* ' the sea,' or the ' mudwharf'; O.N. *aurr*). Cf. CLAYHITHE, near Cambridge, and CHALK in Kent (A.S. *cealc-hýth*).

Erivan, a city in Armenia, gives its name

to the Lake of Erivan. In Persian the city is called *Rewan*, from the name of its founder.

Erlangen, in Germany, anciently *Erlangun*, is a patronymic derived from the personal name Erlo.

Ermitaños, the ' Hermits,' a group north of New Guinea, were so named by Maurelle in 1781. A neighbouring group is called the ANCHORITES.

Erzerûm or ERZEROUM, is the capital of Armenia. When the neighbouring town of Arzek was taken by the Seljuk Turks in 1043, the inhabitants fled to the fortress of Carana, which acquired the name of *Arzek-el-Rum*, ' Roman Arzek' (afterwards Erzerum), to distinguish it from the old Arzek, which became a Turkish city. The district round Erzerûm was the last fragment of the Eastern Empire which held out against the Turks, and hence it acquired the Turkish name *Arzi-rum* meaning the 'lands of the Romans,' from *arazi*, 'lands,' the plural of *arz*, an Arabic loan-word which means 'land.' The names of the town and the pashalik were naturally assimilated.

Erzgebirge, the ' ore mountains,' a range dividing Bohemia from Saxony, were so called from a vein of silver ore discovered in 1163.

Escape Point, in King's Sound, North Australia, commemorates Stokes' escape from an alligator, or, from the alligator's point of view, the alligator's escape from Stokes. ESCAPE CHANNEL, also in King's Sound, commemorates King's escape from shipwreck through a change of wind. In ESCAPE RIVER, North Australia, King's ship nearly grounded. On ESCAPE CLIFFS, in Clarence Strait, an apprehended attack by the natives was averted by the performance of a dance by two of his officers. On ESCAPE ISLAND, in the Ellice group, the American ship *Rebecca* narrowly escaped shipwreck. In ESCAPE RAPID, on the Coppermine River, Franklin's canoes nearly foundered.

Eschscholtz, one of the Marshall Islands, is named after a Dorpat naturalist who accompanied the Kotzebue expedition in 1825, and after whom a gaudy genus of Californian flowers has also been named.

Escorial, commonly but incorrectly called the Escurial, is a gigantic convent and palace near Madrid built by Philip II. in the form of a gridiron, and called by him *San Lorenzo el Real*, having been dedicated to San Lorenzo in pursuance of a vow made by Philip after his victory over the French at St. Quentin on August 10th, 1557, the festival of St. Laurence. The official name is *El real Monasterio de San Lorenzo del Escorial*. During the construction the workmen were sheltered in a neighbouring village, EL ESCORIAL, so called from the scoriæ of some abandoned iron works. CINDERFORD, in the Forest of Dean, is an analogous name. (*See* TUILERIES.)

Esdud is a village in Palestine which occupies the site of *Ashdod*, one of the five cities of the Philistines, believed to be a Semitic name meaning 'the strong' place.

Eskimos is the Danish, and ESQUIMAUX the French-Canadian corruption of the name given by the red men to the Arctic race who call themselves *Innuit*, the 'people.' The name Eskimo, an Algonquin word, seems to have originated in Labrador, being afterwards extended to the tribes in Greenland and on the Polar Sea. The Ojibwa form *Askimeg* or *Ayeskimeou* is allied to the Abenaki name *Eskimantsic*, *Eskimatsic* or *Eski-Mantic*, all meaning, in various dialects, ' eaters of raw' fish or flesh.

Espirito Santo is a coast province of Brazil, where Vasco Fernandes Continho, invoking the ' Holy Spirit,' established a Portuguese colony in 1548.

Essen, where Krupp's great iron works are situated, is not from the German word *eisen*, 'iron,' as is shown by the unexplained ninth century form *astenidum*.

Essex, in A.S. *Eást-Seaxe* and *Eást-Seaxan*, or in the dative plural *Eást-Seaxum*, is a tribal name originally denoting the East Saxon people, and afterwards transferred to their territory.

Essington, Port, in North Australia, was so named by King, in 1818, in memory of Admiral Sir William Essington.

Esthonia, in German ESTHLAND or EST-LAND, is the land of the Esths, a Finnic people who are probably the *Aestui* of Tacitus. They call their land *Wiroma*, the 'frontier country,' and themselves *Rahwas*, the 'people,' and they are called by the Russians TCHUDS or 'foreigners.'

Estremadura is the name of two provinces on the Tagus, one Spanish, the other Portuguese. It is alleged that the old Estremadura lay on the Douro (*extremum ad Durium* or *extrema Durii*), and that the name has retreated southward from the Douro, as Northumberland has retreated northwards from the Humber. The name is usually explained as *Extrema-*

ora, the extreme or last conquest from the Moors made by Alfonso IX. in 1228, A.D.

Etaples, one of the names on the Saxon shore in the North of France, compares with such English names as Dunstaple or Barnstaple, where *staple* signifies a market held at a place marked by a post.

Ethiopia is the land of the *Aethiopes* or ' burnt faces,' a name given by the Greeks to the black races of Africa, who have since been called by the corresponding names MOORS and NEGROES. Very possibly the name may be an accommodation or translation of some older Egyptian word now unknown.

Etna, the great Sicilian volcano, is explained by Benfey as a Greek name, *aitna*, from the root *aith*, to burn or smoke. Very possibly this may be an adaptation of an older name derived from the Phœnician *attuna*, 'the furnace.' After the Arab conquest it was called *Gibel Uttamat*, 'the mountain of fire.' The modern Sicilian name MONGIBELLO is a combination of the Italian and Arabic words for a mountain.

Eton, Bucks, is the *tún* by the water (*ed*). EATON (A.S. *Eátún*), the more usual form of the name, is found in Berks, Oxon, Staffordshire, and Cheshire.

Etruria, in Staffordshire, was a name bestowed by Wedgwood on the place where he endeavoured to imitate the forms and patterns of the Greek vases which were then supposed to be Etruscan because they had frequently been found in Etruscan tombs.

Eu, whence the royal castle of CHÂTEAU D'EU in the Seine Inférieure, is derived from the Low-Latin *Augia* (German *au*), which signifies a meadow or low marshy place.

Eugenio, Cabo San, appears on the maps as the name of a prominent cape on the eastern coast of the Californian Peninsula. The name has arisen out of a curious blunder of the map makers. The cape was discovered by Ulloa in 1539-40. North of the cape the land trends due east for seventy miles, which led him to suppose that the peninsula was an island, and that he had found a channel leading into the northern part of the Gulf of California. Hence he named the cape which had misled him *Punta de Engaño*, the 'Point of Deception,' or 'Cape Mistake.' This name led to a more serious delusion, for the chartographers, misreading the *n* for a *u*, manufactured the name Cape St. Eugenio, which still remains on our maps.

A CAPE ENGAÑO in Haiti, and another in the Philippines have preserved the Spanish name uncorrupted.

Eupatoria, a town in the Crimea where the Allies landed in 1854, derives its name from Mithridates Eupator, who founded it.

Euphrates is a name which has a long history. The pre-Semitic Accadian name was *Pura*, the 'water,' or *Pura-nunu*, the 'great water.' The Semitic Babylonians by the addition of the feminine suffix *-t* made this into *Purat,* *Burat*, or *Puratu*, which the Aryan Persians converted into *Hufrat*, which occurs in an inscription of Darius Hystaspes, the prefix having probably been added to make the name significant in Persian, as the 'good abounding,' or 'very broad' river. Euphrates is merely a Greek adaptation of the Persian name *Hufrat* or *Ufrâtu*. The later Persian form, *Phrat* or *Frâta*, has again been converted by the Arabs into *Farat*, the 'sweet water,' so as to make the name significant in Arabic. The upper course of the Euphrates is still called the FRAT.

Europe is a name which the Greeks explained by the myth of Europa, a royal maiden who was carried off from Phœnicia to the West by Zeus, who took the form of a bull. She was followed by her brother Cadmus, who found her, in the form of a cow, lying down on the site of Thebes in Bœotia. The myth may be explained from Semitic sources. Cadmus is the man of the East, while the name of Europa is derived by Oppert from *ereb*, a Semitic word meaning the 'dark,' 'the land of sunset,' 'the west,' and also 'exchange' or 'barter.' The Phœnicians called their trading settlement in the West by this name, and the Greeks, to make the name significant in Greek, made it into Europé, 'the broad-faced' plain of Thebes. The original Phœnician myth may have related to Istar (Astarte) the moon or the evening star, accompanying Taurus, the leader of the zodiacal constellations, on his westward journey.

Evening Island, north-east of Gilolo, was discovered in 1767 by Carteret at sunset. It is also called LORD NORTH ISLAND, having been revisited in 1782 by a ship of that name.

Everest, Mount, a Himalayan peak, 29,002 feet above the sea level, is believed to be the highest mountain in the world. It would have been better to have selected one of the native names, *Deva Dunghi*, *Gaurisankar*, or *Chengopami*, instead of giving it the name of a Colonel Everest of the Indian Survey. The second in height of the Himalayan peaks is one between Gilghit and the Karakoram Pass, officially designated on the Indian maps as K$_2$, which Mr. Conway has proposed to call the WATCH TOWER, while the Royal Geographical Society has adopted the name MOUNT GODWIN AUSTEN, in honour of an officer of the Indian Survey who was the first to visit and describe the Mustagh peaks and glaciers.

Evesham, in Worcestershire, is a name of which, owing to the preservation of early charters, we have a fairly complete record. In the earliest charters it appears as *et Homme*, 'at the enclosure,' which was corrupted into *Ethom*, and distinguished as *Cronuch-hom*, or in the dative *Cronuch-homme*, a form which suggests that the enclosure was formed by a bend of the river frequented by cranes. The hamlet in this bend then became known as *Eofesham* (in the genitive *Eofeshammes*) probably from the name of its owner, the usual etymology, the 'ham by the eaves' or margin of the river being rendered improbable by the oldest forms. Near this hamlet the great monastery was built around which the town of Evesham arose.

Evian, in Savoy, is famous for its mineral baths, whence the old name *Aquianum*, which has normally become Evian.

Evolena, a Swiss valley, is explained by Gatschet as the valley of the 'gentle stream,' *ivoue lena* being the dialectic equivalent of *aqua lenis*.

Evora, in Portugal, was the Roman *Ebora*, probably a Phœnician name, meaning the 'ford' or 'passage.'

Evreux, the capital of the Department of the Eure, was the chief town of a Belgic tribe called the *Eburovices*, whose name, meaning the dwellers on the Ebura or Eure, was softened into EVREUX.

Ewell, Surrey, called *Æwille* in an early charter, and *Euuelle* in a charter of 983, signifies a place by a spring, literally 'a welling up.' (*See* ALTON.)

Exeter, the county town of Devon, is called in the Chronicle *Exanceaster*, the 'chester of the Exe,' *Exan* being the genitive of *Exa*, the Saxon form of *Isca*, the Brito-Roman form of Exe. The later A.S. form *Exaceaster*, and *Excester* used by Roger of Hoveden, give the transition to the modern name. The Roman name of Exeter was *Isca Damnoniorum*, just as CAERLEON on the Usk was *Isca Silurum*.

The present castle of Exeter represents the earthwork called by the Welsh *Caer Isc*, the 'fortress on the Isc,' Caerleon being the 'fortress of the legion.' This river name Isca, which has become Exe, Usk, and Axe, is believed to be an old form of the Welsh *wysg*, a 'stream,' or of the Gaelic *uisge*, which means 'water.'

Exmouth, Devon, at the mouth of the River Exe, is the A.S. *Exanmutha*. AXMOUTH, at the mouth of the Axe, is also *Examuth* in A.S., and AXMINSTER, also on the Axe, is the A.S. *Exanmynster* and *Axemynster*, showing that Axe is only a variant form of Exe. Exmouth gave a title to Admiral Pellew, who commanded the English fleet at the bombardment of Algiers, in memory of which achievement EXMOUTH GULF in Australia, and EXMOUTH ISLAND in the Arctic Archipelago received their names.

Eyria, a great peninsula in South Australia, takes its name from the explorer E. J. Eyre, afterwards Governor of Jamaica, by whom LAKE EYRE, north of Lake Torrens, was discovered.

Fain, Val da, in the Engadine, means 'Hay Valley,' from the Romansch *fain*, Latin *fœnum*.

Fairweather, Mount, in Alaska, 14,750 feet in height, was so named by Cook in 1778, because a spell of fine weather began on May 3rd, the day he sighted it. The neighbouring cape is called CAPE FAIRWEATHER.

Falkirk, Stirlingshire, locally pronounced Fawkirk, is the English equivalent of the Gaelic name *Eaglais breac*, the 'speckled church' (A.S. *fáh*, 'of various colours'). In a Latin charter, the name is translated as *Varia Capella*.

Falkland, a town in Fife, gave a title to Lord Falkland, which has been transferred to the FALKLAND ISLANDS in the South Atlantic. Amerigo Vespucci is believed to have sighted them on his third voyage in the year 1502, but did not name them. John Davis, the Arctic navigator, rediscovered them in 1592, and for a time they were known as Davis' Land. In 1594, they were again visited by Richard Hawkins, who, combining his own name with that of the Virgin Queen, gave them the name of Hawkins' Maidenland. In 1690, Strong landed and named the strait between the two larger islands the Falkland Channel, after his patron Lord Falkland. The name was then extended to the two islands, and in 1764 Byron took possession of the entire group as the Falkland

Islands, in behalf of George III. Rightly they should be called the Davis Islands, as was proposed by Burney.

False Point, in Orissa, is so called because vessels proceeding up the Bay of Bengal are liable to mistake it for Point Palmyras, a degree further north. FALSE BAY, in the Cape Colony, was so called because of a delusion as to the anchorage it afforded.

Famagusta, in Cyprus, is the Venetian corruption of the ancient name, which appears in the Assyrian inscriptions as *Amtichadasti*, 'the new fortress,' and in Ptolemy as *Ammokhostos*. It is the *Amathus* of Strabo and other writers, a name corrupted by the Turks to *Ma'usa*.

Famars (Nord) is believed to occupy the site of a temple of Mars. It was called *Fanum Martis* in 861, and we have *Pagus Fanomartensis* in 671.

Famine, Port, in Magellan Strait, is where Cavendish in 1592 inhumanly landed all the sick of his ship the *Leicester*, and left them to perish. Five years before he had given the name of PORT FAMINE to the Spanish settlement of San Felipe, where in 1587 he found, and then left to their fate, eighteen survivors of the four hundred and thirty people sent out by Philip II. under Pedro Sarmiento. In 1590 John Chudleigh took away the sole survivor, the rest having perished by hunger and cold, or by the attacks of the natives. (*See* p. 250.)

Fans are West African cannibals, who inhabit what is called the Fan country. If the name is tribal it may be derived from the *fa*, a large knife carried by the natives, but it is more probably territorial, and derived from the native word *fana*, which means 'jungle.'

Fanning, a Polynesian island, was discovered in 1798 by Edward Fanning, captain of the American ship *Betsy*.

Fano, in Italy, a town on the Adriatic, is the Roman *Fanum Fortunæ*, so called from a temple to Fortune, doubtless erected to commemorate some victory.

Faraglioni is the name of seven precipitous 'rocks' off the Sicilian coast between Messina and Catania, and also of three rocks on the south of the island of Capri. LOS FARALLONES, the Spanish form of the word, is the name of seven 'rocks' which lie at the entrance of the bay of San Francisco.

Farewell, Cape, is the southern point of Greenland. In 1586 John Davis, on his second voyage, sighted the Cape, but the pack ice making it impossible to land, he called it Cape Farewell, and sailed northward up Davis Strait. Unlike some other names given by early voyagers the name has retained its place on the map, probably because it is the point where whalers on their homeward voyage take their farewell of Greenland. CAPE FAREWELL was also the name given by Cook to the point where, in 1770, he took leave of New Zealand on his return to England. FAREWELL ISLAND, the northernmost of the Fiji group, was so named by Wilson in 1797, because here, taking leave of the dangerous Coral Islands, the navigation of the open sea began.

Faröe Islands is the incorrect English name of a group of twenty-two small islands in the North Atlantic, which were discovered and occupied by the Norwegians in 861. The name is Norse, and the correct form would be Färöer (O.N. *Fær-eyjar*, 'sheep islands'), or else Fär or Fair Islands (O.N. *fær*, 'sheep') and not Faröe Islands, which means strictly 'Sheep Island Islands.' There is a *Färö* off the Swedish coast, and one of the Shetlands is called FAIR ISLE and one of the Orkneys FARAY, all of which mean 'sheep island.' FAIRFIELD, the mountain nearest to Helvellyn, is the 'sheep fell.'

Far Out Head, better FARRID HEAD, near Cape Wrath, is believed to be the *Vervedrum* of Ptolemy, of which the modern name would be a popular corruption.

Farukhnagar, in the Punjab, was founded in 1713 in the reign of the Mughal Emperor Farrukh-siyyar, after whom it was named by the governor of the country, a Beluch chief, Dalel Khán, better known by his title of Faugdár Khán. FARUKH-ÁBÁD, in the N.W.P., founded by Nawáb Muhammed Khán about 1714, was named after the same Emperor.

Faulhorn, a mountain in the Bernese Oberland, is composed of dirty and crumbling schist.

Fayal is a Portuguese word signifying a 'place where beeches grow,' from *faya* (Latin *fagus*), a 'beech tree.' The name was given to one of the Azores at the time of the discovery, because the island was overgrown with the *Myrica Faya*, a shrub resembling the beech. The word *fagetum*, a 'beech grove,' has been a fertile source of village names, such as FAY, FAGET, FAYET, and FÉE in France, and FAIDO, FAIDA, and FAI in Italy (p. 334).

Fayûm or FAYYÛM is an Egyptian province, containing the great lake called

Moeris by the Greeks, which was supplied by the overflow from the inundation of the Nile. Fayûm is the Arabic form of the Coptic *Piom* or *Phiom*, in old Egyptian *Pa-iuma*, 'the water,' *pa* being the definite article, which we have in Potiphar, Philæ, and other names. The Greek name MOERIS is a corruption of the Egyptian *ma-ur*, the 'great water' or inundation.

Fear, Cape, in North Carolina, is also spelt Cape Fair on old maps. Here the fleet of seven ships, sent out by Raleigh in 1585, under the command of Sir Richard Grenville, to establish a colony in Virginia, narrowly escaped shipwreck 'on a beach called the Cape of Feare.'

Fearn Island, sometimes called HUNTER ISLAND, east of New Caledonia, was discovered in 1793 by Captain Fearn of the ship *Hunter*.

Feldkirch and FELDKIRCHEN are not uncommon village names in Germany, denoting a church originally standing in a *feld* or open plain.

Felix, Cape, the northern point of King William's Land, was so named in 1830 by James Ross after Sir Felix Booth. (*See* BOOTHIA FELIX.)

Fermoy, a district in County Cork, which gives a title to an Irish peer, is a tribal name which has become territorial, being a corruption of *Feara-muighe*, 'the men of the plain.' FERMANAGH, an Irish county, is also, according to Irish tradition, a tribal name, having been peopled by the *Fir-Monach*, the 'men of Monach,' who fled from Leinster to the shores of Lough Erne.

Fernando Noronha, correctly Fernão de Noronha, a lonely island in the South Atlantic, off the Brazilian coast, was bestowed in 1504 by the king of Portugal on Fernão (Fernando) de Noronha, the commander of the ship which brought to Lisbon the news of its discovery in August 1503. In early voyages round the Cape it formed the objective where supplies were obtained.

Fernando Po, correctly FERNÃO DO POO, an island in the Gulf of Guinea, bears the name of its discoverer, a Portuguese, who named it *Ilha Formosa*, 'beautiful island.' The new name had come into use by the middle of the sixteenth century, less than a hundred years after its discovery by Fernão do Poo, who, in 1474, was the second to cross the Equator, which three years earlier had been passed by João de Santarem and Pedro de Escobar.

Ferns, an episcopal see in County Wexford, is a corruption of the old name *Fearna*, the 'alders.' FERNEY and FERNAGH in Ireland, FEARN and FERNAN in Scotland, were also places producing alders. VERNON in Normandy is from the same Celtic word (Welsh *gwern*, an 'alder'). VERNEX, near Vevay, is a corruption of *verniacum*, a place planted with alders. FERNEY, Voltaire's retreat near Geneva, is properly *Frenex* (*fraxinetum*), an 'ash grove.' (*See* p. 334.)

Ferro, meaning ostensibly the 'iron' island, is one of the Canaries, from which longitude is reckoned in many German maps. Ptolemy drew his prime meridian through the most westerly of the Canaries; believing that here the world began. Mercator drew his first meridian through Corvo in the Azores, because in his time the needle had there no declination. The Pope drew the line dividing the world into two hemispheres, Spanish and Portuguese, through Santiago, one of the Cape Verd islands. In 1634 a royal commission at Paris fixed on the westernmost point of the island of Ferro, with the object of making Paris in exactly 20° East longitude, but this now proves to be 23′ 09″ too much. Hence the so-called meridian of Ferro does not actually pass through the island. The meridian of Greenwich is now increasingly adopted because the best charts have been made by English surveyors. It is believed that the name Ferro, in Spanish Hierro, is an adaptation from *hero* or *herro*, a Guanche word meaning 'wells' or 'cisterns.'

Fetterangus preserves the name of the old Scotch earldom of Angus, now called Forfarshire. The word Fetter, which is common in Scotch names, such as FETTERCAIRN or FETTERNEAR, means a 'croft,' a 'bit of land,' or a field. It frequently becomes *for*, as in FORFAR, the 'cold land,' FORDYCE, the 'south land,' FORDUN, the 'land near the fort,' or FORTEVIOT, called in the Pictish chronicle *Fothuirtabaicht*, the 'land of the abbey.' FORRES is the Gaelic *Foreas*, the 'land by the waterfall,' and FORTINGALL is the 'land of the stranger.' (*See* FINGALL.)

Feurs (Loire) is derived from the Roman name *Forum Segusianorum*.

Fezzan, anciently *Phazania*, a district in Tripoli, is a corruption of the old tribe-name of the Phazanii. FEZ, in Morocco, is probably an Arabic name meaning 'fertile' or 'beautiful.' According to a local legend, the name is due to a hatchet, *fas*, having been found by the workmen when they were digging the foundations of the city walls.

Fichtelgebirge, the ' Pine Mountains,' in Bavaria, are so called from the pine forests which clothe them.

Fife, anciently *Fibh,* 'the forest.' one of the seven Pictish provinces, formerly comprehended the greater portion of the territory between the Forth and the Tay. The county town is CUPAR-FIFE, and FIFENESS is the ness or nose at its Eastern extremity. According to the Irish Nennius, Fibh was a son of Cruithne, the eponymus of the Cruithni or Picts. The old earldom was called Fibh with Fothreve, a name preserved in that of the Deanery of Fothri.

Fiji Islands are a South Pacific group, discovered on February 6th, 1643, by Tasman, who named them *Prinz Willem's Eylanden,* in honour of William of Nassau. The native name is *Viti,* the form Fiji being the Tonga pronunciation of Viti, which was learnt by the Wesleyan missionaries in the Friendly islands from the native teachers sent from Tonga. The two largest islands in the group are VANUA LEVU, the ' great land,' and VITI LEVU, ' great Viti.'

Filey, on the Yorkshire coast, is called *Fivelac* in Domesday, a name which is supposed to refer to the ' five pools ' made by a small stream which descends the cliff in the gorge near the church. Cf. p. 374.

Fingall, a district North of Dublin, was anciently *Fine-gall,* the ' tribe ' or territory of the Galls, or Danish ' strangers.' FINGAL'S CAVE, a basaltic grotto in Staffa, was, according to the legend, a temple built by the Ossianic hero Fingal, ' the white stranger.'

Finisterre, the modern name of the extreme North-Western Department of France, is equivalent to our own ' Land's End.' The same name has been bestowed on a cape at the North-Western extremity of Spain. The Spanish FINISTERA appears on the Catalan Map of 1275.

Finland is the land of the Finns or Suomi, who call themselves *Suoma-laiset,* the ' people of the fens ' (Finnish *Suoma,* a ' marsh '). The name Fenni, which we have in Tacitus, is believed to be an early Teutonic translation of the native name. Finnland is the German, and Finland the Swedish spelling, which has been adopted in England. Both are translations of the Finnish name *Suomen-maa,* ' fenland.'

Finsteraarhorn. (*See* AARGAU.)

Fish River, or GREAT FISH RIVER, flowing into the Arctic Ocean, explored by George Back in 1834, translates the formidable native name *Thlew-ee-chohdesseth.* Another GREAT FISH RIVER in South Africa translates the Dutch name *Groote Vischrivier,* which was given by the Boers to the Rio Infante, so called by Bartolomeu Diaz in compliment to João Infante, the captain of his second ship. FISCHA, a river in Lower Austria, was called *Fisc-aha,* ' fish water,' in 798.

Fitton Bay and POINT FITTON, both in Arctic America, bear the name of Dr. Fitton, President of the Geological Society.

Fitzroy River, in the Australian colony of Victoria, was named in 1836 after Sir Charles Fitzroy, then Governor of New South Wales. FITZROY ISLAND, Queensland, FITZROY DOWNS and FITZROY RIVER in North Australia, were named after Admiral Robert Fitzroy, commander of the surveying ship the *Beagle,* and afterwards Governor of New Zealand.

Fiume, a town in Croatia, 40 miles from Trieste, stands at the mouth of the REKA, a Slavonic word meaning ' river,' of which Fiume, formerly *S. Vitus ad Flumen,* is the Italian equivalent. The Latin *flumen,* which becomes *fiume* in Italian, becomes *flim* in Romansch, whence the name of FLIMS in the Graubünden.

Flamborough Head, in the East Riding, is a lofty chalk promontory, with a huge prehistoric ditch or rampart, called the Danes' Dyke, making it into a *burh* or stronghold. The Domesday forms Flaneburg and Flaneburc, and Flaynburg in a charter of King Stephen, dispose of the old etymology Flame-burh, or ' beacon-burh,' from a flame or beacon fire to warn mariners. This theory is untenable on other grounds, as also is the suggestion that the name may refer to ' flemings ' or refugees. The true etymology is the A.S. *flán,* genitive *fláne,* an ' arrow ' or ' dart,' which would hence be used to denote an obelisk, or needle rock, an etymology explained by the conspicuous needles of chalk called the HIGH STACKS (stakes) which stand out in the sea at the extremity of Flamborough Head.

Flanders, called in French *Flandre,* in German *Flandern,* and in Dutch *Vlaendern,* is a name of unknown etymology, but possibly related to the Latin *planum,* the ' flat ' country. We have *Flamingi* as early as the ninth century, and afterwards *Flandri* and *Flandrenses,* with *Flandria* and *Flandra* for Flanders. The

Flemings, as Richthofen explains, are probably the 'fugitives,' but it is doubtful whether there is any etymological connection between Flamingi and Flandria.

Flattery, Cape, on the coast of North Queensland, was so named by Cook in 1770 because he had flattered himself that 'here he should find a passage out of the labyrinth of coral reefs in which he was entangled. Cook also gave the name of CAPE FLATTERY to a promontory in Washington Territory, U.S.A., at the South side of Fuca Strait, opposite Vancouver's Island, because of an opening 'which flattered us with the hopes of finding an harbour,' hopes doomed to disappointment.

Flinders Island, in Bass Strait, bears the name of Captain Matthew Flinders, who in conjunction with George Bass surveyed a large part of the South Australian coast between the years 1795 and 1803. In 1795 Flinders served as a midshipman in the *Reliance*, which took Captain William Hunter to New South Wales. In command of the *Investigator*, with John Franklin as midshipman, he sailed from Spithead in July 1801. Returning home in the *Porpoise*, he was wrecked, and obtained a passage in the *Cumberland*, which, in ignorance of the renewal of the war between France and England, touched at the Mauritius for water in 1803. He was made prisoner by the French Governor and detained on the island for more than six years. MOUNT FLINDERS, FLINDERS BAY, FLINDERS GROUP, FLINDERS ISLE, FLINDERS RANGE, FLINDERS RIVER, and FLINDERS REEF also commemorate 'the adventures and sufferings of the intrepid Flinders, and his discoveries on the shores of the great continent, his imprisonment on his way home and cruel treatment by the French Governor of Mauritius.'

Flintshire, North Wales, takes its name from the town of FLINT on the estuary of the Dee. In old documents we have *Castellum apud Fluentum*, which somewhat later becomes *apud le Flynt*, 'on the flow' or tideway. The name of Flint affords a good example of the old guesswork style of etymology, since we are gravely informed that it is so called because it abounds in flints.

Florence is the French form we have adopted for the city whose Italian name, formerly *Fiorenza*, is now FIRENZE. In one MS. of Florus the Roman name is *Florentia*, in another it is *Fluentia*. If the latter is the true reading, which on

various grounds is improbable, Florence would be named from the confluence of the Arno and the Mugnone. In the other case it might be the 'flourishing city,' a name of the same class as Valentia and Faventia, or meaning, as the Romans seem to have thought, the city of flowers.

Flores, in Portuguese ILHA DAS FLORES, the 'isle of flowers,' the most beautiful island of the Azores, is now well known from the opening lines of Tennyson's *Revenge*, 'At Flores In the Azores, Sir Richard Grenville lay.' One of the smaller Sunda Islands is called FLORIS or FLORES, which is also a name believed to be due to the Portuguese.

Floriana, a colony in the Galapagos Islands belonging to Ecuador, was so named in 1832 in honour of General Flores.

Florida, one of the United States, bears a name given by Juan Ponce de Leon, who, in search of the fountain of youth, landed near St. Augustine in 1513, on March 27th, Easter Day, which is called in Spanish *Pascua Florida* or *Pascua de Flores*. Ponce de Leon was not, however, the discoverer of Florida, as the coast-line appears on the Cantino map of 1502—a strong argument that it was circumnavigated in 1498 by Pinzon and Solis, with Amerigo Vespucci as pilot. LA FLORIDA, one of the Salomon Islands, was discovered by Mendaña at Easter (Pascua Florida) in 1567.

Foggy Island, on the N.W. coast of America, was passed by Cook during a thick fog. Bering had discovered it in 1741, and for the same reason had called it *Tummanoi-Ostrov*, which means 'Foggy Island' in Russian.

Foix, the capital of the Ariège, which gave a title to a well-known line of Counts, is a corruption of the Roman name *Fuxum*.

Folkestone, in Kent, is Folcanstan in an early charter, and Folcestan or Folcstane in the Saxon Chronicle. It seems, like Brighton (*q.v.*), to contain a personal name, meaning the stone or stone-house of Folca (Fulk), genitive Folcan, but is usually explained as the 'stone of the people' (A.S. *folc*, genitive *folces*).

Fonseca Bay, on the western coast of Central America, was discovered in 1523 by Andres Niño, pilot of Gil Gonçales, who named it after his patron Don Juan Rodriguez Fonseca, Bishop of Badajos, Cordova, and Palencia, the powerful President of the Council of the Indies.

Fontainebleau, a hunting-seat built in 998 by Louis the Pious, is called *Fons*

Bleaudi in early documents. FONTE-VRAULT or FONTEVRAUD (*Fons Ebraldi, or ad fontem Evraldi*), is the name of the great abbey founded in 1099 by Robert of Arbrissel, which contains the historic effigies of Henry II., Richard I., and their wives Eleonora and Isabella. FONTENAY on the Yonne, where Lothair was defeated in 841, is *Fontanetum*, the 'place of springs,' and FONTENOY in Belgium, where the English were defeated by Marshal Saxe, is one of many names from the same source. WELLS in Somerset is called *Fontanetum* in Latin documents. From the A.S. *funta* we have several English names, such as Chalfont, Fovant, Havant, Fonthill, and Fontmell, which are explained elsewhere. (*See* p. 386.)

Forchheim, in Bavaria, formerly *Foraheim*, is the 'home in the firs.' A similar name is VOORHOUT, near Leyden, which is a corruption of *Foranholt*, 'the firwood.'

Forest Gate, in Essex, now a suburb of London, takes its name from an old five-barred gate where the road from London to Romford entered Wanstead Flats, an outlying portion of Hainault Forest.

Forli, in the Emilia, is a corruption of *Forum Livii*, supposed to have been founded about 207 B.C. by the Consul M. Livius Salinator. FORLIMPOPOLI, in the same district, is the Roman *Forum Popilii*, doubtless named from the founder. FORCALQUIER, in France, is a corruption of *Forum Calcarium*. FORO APPIO, on the Appian way, between Rome and Naples, represents the *Appii Forum* of Acts xxviii.

Formentera, one of the Balearic Islands, is so called because it produces much 'corn,' locally called *forment* (French *froment*, Latin *frumentum*). The Greeks called it *Ophiusa*, 'snake island,' and the Romans by the translated name *Colubraria*, because snakes were found here and not in the adjacent island of IVIZA, the 'Isle of Pines.'

Formiculi, in the Lipari Islands, LE FORMICHE off the West Coast of Sicily, and AS FORMIGAS in the Azores are clusters of small rocks, resembling swarms of ants.

Formosa, or ILHA FORMOSA, the 'beautiful island,' was the appropriate name given by the Portuguese to the large island East of China. The Chinese designate it by the name of the chief harbour on the western coast, *Tai-wan*, which means the 'terraced beach.' ANGRA FORMOSA, 'beautiful bay,' is the Portuguese name of a bay on the Zanzibar coast.

Forth, one of the chief rivers in Scotland, empties itself into the estuary called the FIRTH or FRITH OF FORTH. Forth, if not ultimately Celtic, would be the Anglian and Firth the Middle English form of the O.N. word *fjörthr*, which signified an 'estuary' or 'long inlet' of the sea. In Scotland we have the FIRTH OF TAY, the MORAY FIRTH, and the DORNOCH FIRTH. In Ireland we find the Anglicised form *ford*, as in Strangford, Carlingford, and Wexford; but the barony of FORTH in Wexford and Carlow, anciently *Fotharta*, derives its name from Ohy Finn Fothart, to whom it belonged. The suffix *-forth* in many Yorkshire names, such as AMPLEFORTH, DISHFORTH, STAINFORTH, GARFORTH, GATEFORTH, and RUFFORTH, is a dialectic corruption, which hardly appears before the Tudor period, of an earlier *ford*.

Fortrenn was the old name of the district between the Forth and the Tay, especially of Menteith and Stratherne, whose inhabitants still go by the name of the 'Men of Fortrenn.' Fortrenn possibly preserves the name of the tribe of the *Vecturiones*, probably a copyist's error for *Verturiones*, 'the powerful,' who are mentioned by Ammianus Marcellinus as one of the nations of North Britain.

Foss, a stream which joins the Ouse at York, thereby adding greatly to the military value of the position, is believed by Canon Raine, the historian of York, to have been a natural drain for surface-water, which was deepened by the Romans to protect the city, and so called *fossa*, the 'ditch.' Foss, near Pitlochry, is from the O.N. *fors*, a waterfall.

Fostat, a suburb of Cairo founded by Amru in 642, was so called because when Amr-ibn-el-Asi invaded Egypt in 638 it was the place where his tent was pitched (Arabic *fostat*, 'a tent.') Fustian was first made at Fostat. (*See* CAIRO.)

Fox Channel, north of Hudson Strait, was discovered by Luke Fox, who, dropping his name of Luke, called himself North West Fox, and sailed in 1631 to follow up Hudson's discoveries. He reached a point in 66° 47′ N. lat. which he called FOX HIS FARTHEST, which still remains the UltimaThule in the ice-blocked inlet to which Parry gave the name of FOX'S CHANNEL, East of which lies Fox LAND. He gave the islands at the entrance to Fox Channel the names of his patrons, Digges, Salisbury, Nottingham, Mansell, and Southampton.

France (German *Frankreich*) and FRAN-CONIA (German *Franken*) are names derived from the great confederation of Teutonic tribes who called themselves Franks, which probably means 'freemen,' or possibly those armed with a light javelin called *framea*, believed to be a copyist's error for *franca*. Francia, the Latinised form from which we get the name France, signified originally the *Terra Francorum*, or 'land of the Franci,' while Franken, from which the Latinised form Franconia has been constructed, is the dative plural of the name of the Ripuarian Franks who settled on the Main. In 488 Hlodowig (Clovis), chief of the Salian Franks, founded in Northern Gaul the kingdom which has developed into France. Europeans in the Levant are called FRANKS, owing to the fact that the leading crusaders and the first King of Jerusalem were Frenchmen. The ISLE DE FRANCE, the French province which included Paris, originally denoted merely the island in the Seine on which Paris was built, and which is still called La Cité. In early Latin documents it is called *Insula*, 'the Isle.'

Franche Comté, one of the old provinces of France, was called the 'Free county,' because its Counts claimed to be exempt from doing homage to the Emperor.

Frankfurt-am-Main is the 'ford of the Franks.' A legend relates that when Charlemagne was retreating from the Saxons, he and his army of Franks were shown the way across the river by a doe. According to a variant form of the legend, it was Hlodowig, King of the Franks, to whom, when marching against the Alamanni, the doe indicated the ford. Authentic history begins in the pages of Eginhard, who tells us that Charlemagne spent the winter of 793-4 in the *Villa Franconofurt*, Latinised as *Francorum vadum*, the O.H.G. *francono* being a genitive plural equivalent to *Francorum*. FRANKFURT-AN-DER-ODER is the ford of the Frank merchants who settled there in the thirteenth century.

Franklin Bay, between the mouths of the Mackenzie and the Coppermine in Arctic America, was discovered and named by Dr. Richardson, July 22nd, 1826, during Franklin's third Arctic expedition. The name of either Sir John or Lady Franklin is found in about twenty places on the map. The FRANKLIN ISLES in the St. Francis Group, South Australia, are a memorial of his early service as a midshipman in the *Investigator* under Flinders in 1802. Returning from this voyage, he was

wrecked in the *Porpoise* on an Australian reef. His first Arctic voyage was to Spitzbergen in 1818. In 1819-21 he descended the Coppermine to the Arctic Ocean. In 1825-26 he descended the Mackenzie, wintering at FORT FRANKLIN on the Great Bear Lake. POINT FRANKLIN, in King William's Land, was the furthest point reached by James Ross in 1830. LAKE FRANKLIN, discovered by Back in 1834, is the last of the chain of lakes on the Great Fish River. In 1836 he was made Governor of Tasmania, and in 1842 FRANKLIN CHANNEL in Bass Strait was named after him by Stokes. In 1845 he sailed in the *Erebus* and *Terror*, and, having practically discovered the North-West Passage, died on June 11th, 1847. The ships were abandoned in 1848. SIR JOHN FRANKLIN ISLAND was the northernmost point seen by Kane in 1853-55. (*See* p. 274.)

Franz-Josef Land, a Polar tract divided by AUSTRIA SOUND, discovered in 1873-4 by the Tegethoff Austro-Hungarian expedition under Captain Weyprecht and Lieutenant Payer, was named after the Austrian Emperor, in whose honour the FRANZ-JOSEF GLACIER in New Zealand was also named in 1865 by the Austrian geologist Julius Haast.

Frascati, near Rome, was so called from a Roman villa overgrown with underwood (*frasche*).

Frauenfeld, the chief town in Canton Thurgau, originally *Unserer Lieben Frauen Feld*, 'our dear Lady's field,' arose in the eleventh century on land belonging to the Abbey of Reichenau, which was dedicated to 'Our Lady.'

Frazer River, the great artery of British Columbia, bears the name of Simon Frazer, an agent of the Hudson Bay Company, the first European who crossed the Rocky Mountains (1806-8) from Lake Athabasca, founding the trading post called FORT FRAZER on FRAZER LAKE.

Frederik Hendrik's Bay, and CAPE FREDERIK HENDRIK, on the eastern coast of Tasmania, are believed to bear the name of one of Tasman's crew, who here in 1642 took refuge from a storm.

Frederiksborg, in Seeland, was founded by Christian IV. of Denmark, and named in 1609 after Frederik, the infant Crown Prince. FREDERIKSHAAB, 'Frederik's Hope,' in Greenland, was founded in 1742 by Jacob Leverin, a Danish merchant, and doubtless named after the

Crown Prince of Denmark, afterwards King Frederik V.

Freemantle, a town in West Australia, bears the name of Captain Freemantle, an officer sent in 1829 as a pioneer to take charge of the settlement on its first foundation.

Freetown, the capital of the English colony of Sierra Leone, was so called because here the negroes taken from the slave-ships were landed, liberated, and declared free.

Freewill Islands, a small group north of New Guinea, were so called by Carteret in 1767 from a native who volunteered to go with the ship, and hence was nicknamed Joseph Freewill by the sailors.

Freiburg (in French FRIBOURG), a city which gives its name to a Swiss canton, was a 'free town' built in 1177 on his own estates by Berchtold IV., Count of Zähringen, to which he granted a charter giving the same liberties as had been granted in 1120 by his uncle Berchtold III. to the sister city of FREIBURG IM BREISGAU. These privileges, confirmed in 1178 by the Emperor Frederick I. (Barbarossa) were to be similar to those possessed by Cologne. FRIBURGO NOVO, in Brazil, was founded in 1820 by colonists from Freiburg in Switzerland. VRYBURG, the capital of British Bechuanaland, was founded in 1882 by Mr. Barend Fourie, a Dutch Boer, who called it *Vrijburg*, the 'free town,' a name now Anglicised as Vryburg.

Fréjus, a town in the Dép. of the Var, with numerous Roman remains, was founded by Julius Cæsar, and called *Forum Julii*, of which the modern name is a corruption.

Fremont's Peak, in the Rocky Mountains, 13,570 feet in height, bears the name of Lieut. John C. Fremont, an officer in the United States service, by whom it was ascended in 1842 during his exploration of this region.

French Frigate Island, in the Sandwich group, is the place where the frigate of La Perouse narrowly escaped shipwreck in 1786.

Freycinet Estuary and **Cape Freycinet,** both in Western Australia, commemorate the services of the brothers Louis and Henri Freycinet, who accompanied the French expedition which surveyed portions of the Australian coast in 1801-3. (*See* GÉOGRAPHE.)

Friedrichshafen (Frederick's harbour), on the Lake of Constance, was founded in 1810 by Friedrich, King of Würtemberg.

Friendly Islands, a Pacific group, discovered by Tasman in 1643, were so named by Cook, who visited them in 1774, on account of the friendly behaviour of the natives. The group is now usually called by the native name, Tonga Islands.

Friesland, formerly FRISIA, FRESIA, or FRISONIA, now called VRIESLAND by the Dutch, and FRIESEN by the Germans, is the land of the Frisians, the *Frisii* of Tacitus. The meaning of the name is uncertain, as the length of the vowel is unknown. According to Zeuss and Grimm the name may be derived from the Old Frisian word *frise*, which means 'frizzled,' 'curled,' or 'matted' hair, but not, as formerly maintained, from the Gothic *freis*, 'free,' since the *s* is not radical.

Frio, Cabo, in Brazil, is the 'cold cape.' SERRO DO FRIO, the 'cold range,' is a desolate and sterile region in Brazil. PUERTO FRIO, the 'cold harbour,' in Magellan's Strait (also called BAHIA NEVADA, 'snowy bay'), was so called because at the time of Loaysa's expedition in 1526 many of the natives perished by cold. In 1741 Middleton gave the name of CAPE FRIGID to the northern point of Southampton Land in FROZEN STRAIT (*q.v.*).

Frisches Haff, 'fresh [water] bay,' in the Baltic, is so called because the Vistula makes the water almost fresh.

Friuli, in Venetia, is a corruption of the Roman name *Forum Julii*.

Frobisher's Strait, now called FROBISHER BAY, is an inlet, 250 miles long, discovered in 1576 by Martin Frobisher, one of the most daring of English navigators, and the first to conceive the idea of a North-West passage to China. On June 7th, 1576, he sailed from Blackwall with thirty-five men in two tiny boats, the *Gabriel* and the *Michael*, of about 20 tons each, and a 10-ton pinnace, in search of a N.-W. passage. The pinnace was lost, and the *Michael* deserted and returned home. Frobisher, in the *Gabriel*, pushed on undaunted, sighting a headland near Cape Farewell, which he called QUEEN ELIZABETH'S FORELAND, and crossed the sea afterwards known as Davis Strait, imagining that the land on one side was America, and on the other the continent of Asia. He then sailed up the inlet, which he called Frobisher Strait, as far as BUTCHER'S ISLAND, where five of his men were captured by the Eskimos. In a third expedition he penetrated up Hudson's Strait as far as Frobisher Bay. For his

I

services against the Spanish Armada he was knighted in 1588, and died of a wound received in 1594 at the siege of Crozan, near Brest.

Frome is a town in Somerset, on the river Frome. In a charter of 701 we read : *monasterium positum juxta fluvium qui vocatur From.* The name of the river, called *Fraw* by Asser, may be explained from the Welsh *ffraw*, 'brisk,' or 'lively,' corresponding to the A.S. *frum*, which means rapid or vigorous. As the minster on the Axe has become Axminster, so Frome by analogy should have been Frominster.

Froward, Cape, or CAPE FORWARD, midway in the Straits of Magellan, was the appropriate name given to the most southerly point of the American continent by Thomas Cavendish in 1587. This dangerous point is difficult to double on account of the intricacy of the channel.

Frozen Strait, a channel leading into Hudson's Bay, north of Southampton Island, was so called by Middleton in 1741 because he found it blocked by ice. In 1821 Parry found it open.

Fuca Strait, correctly JUAN DE FUCA STRAIT, south of Vancouver Island, and leading to the mouth of the Frazer river, was discovered by Juan de Fuca in 1592.

Fuegia, 'fire-land,' is a recent English formation from the Spanish name TIERRA DEL FUEGO, the 'land of the fire.' In November 1520, Magellan, passing through the straits which bear his name, gave this name to the land on his left, from a fire kindled by the natives which at night was seen burning on the shores. The BAY OF FIRES in the N. E. corner of Tasmania, was so called by Furneaux in 1773 because of the uninterrupted row of fires which he observed as he sailed past. CAPE BLAZE, in North Australia, was so called because a large fire was burning on it when it was discovered by Captain King in 1819. A volcano in Guatemala, 12,500 feet high, is called VOLCAN DE FUEGO, the 'Volcano of Fire,' in contradistinction to the loftier neighbouring VOLCAN DE AGUA, which emits water and mud. FOGO, one of the volcanic group of the Cape Verd Islands, was in continuous eruption from 1680 to 1713. The Spaniards called it Fuego, answering to the Portuguese name Fogo, which means 'fire' (Latin *focus*, 'hearth').

Fuenterrabia, on the Spanish frontier near Biarritz, exhibits a curious instance of popular etymology. It was conjecturally explained as the 'fountain of the Arabs,' giving rise to the legend of Charlemagne's defeat by the Moors, referred to by Milton in the lines, 'Where Charlemagne and all his peerage fell, By Fontarabia.' The name is a corruption of the Basque *Ondarrabia*, 'two sandbanks,' which was corrupted first to *Unda rapida*, then to *fons rapidus*, and finally to Fontarabia.

Fuglo, 'bird island,' is the name given to several Scandinavian islets. FITFUL HEAD, in the mainland of Shetland, is a curious English adaptation of the Scandinavian name *Fitfugla höfdhi*, the 'sea-fowl cape' (O.N. *fitfugl*, a 'webfooted bird ').

Fuji-Yama or **Fusi-Yama**, the beautiful volcano whose cone appears so often in Japanese drawings, is the 'great mountain,' just as the snowclad peak called SIRO-YAMA is the 'white mountain.' In Japanese poetry Fuji-Yama is often called FUJI-SAN, the 'lady Fuji,' *san* being the usual honorific appellation of a woman.

Fukien, or FOKIEN, one of the wealthiest provinces in China, is the 'fortunate settlement.'

Fulah, or FULA, is the Mandingo name of a dominant race spread across the Soudan from Darfur to the Senegal, and called Fula, 'red,' or perhaps 'yellow,' from the light brown colour of their skins. FULBE (*be*, 'people') means the 'red men.'

Fulda, a city in Hesse-Nassau, rose round a monastery founded by S. Boniface on the river Fulda, which was called in the eighth century *Fuldaha*, probably meaning, according to Grimm and Förstemann, 'land river.'

Funchal is the chief town in Madeira. In Portuguese *funcho* means 'fennel,' and *funchal* a 'bed of fennel,' which still grows abundantly on the hills round Funchal.

Funcheon, in County Cork, is the 'ash tree' river, from the Irish *fuinnsean*, an ash. At UNSHOG, Armagh, the initial consonant of this word has fallen out. It may be noted that names from the ash are much less common in Ireland than in England, Germany, or France, where *fraxinetum*, an ash-grove, has yielded numerous village names like FRAISSENET, FRESNEY, and FRENEY. (*See* p. 334.)

Furca is a pass between Cantons Uri and Valais. For such passes the usual Swiss form is *Furyge*, which signifies a 'fork,' used to denote a notch forming a pass over a mountain chain.

Furneaux Group, in Bass Strait, and FURNEAUX ISLAND, in the Low Archipelago, commemorate the services of Captain Tobias Furneaux, who commanded the *Adventure*, one of the two ships which took part in Cook's second expedition (1772-74).

Fürth, a town in Bavaria, is at the 'ford' over the river Regnitz. There are several places in Germany called FÜRTH, FURT, FURTH, and the like, which were anciently *Furti* or *Furden*, 'the ford,' or 'at the ford.'

Fury and Hecla Strait, discovered by Parry in 1822 on his second voyage, bears the names of his two ships the *Fury* and the *Hecla*. On his third voyage the *Fury* was forced ashore by the ice in Prince Regent's Inlet, and abandoned in August 1825 at a place which bears the name of FURY BEACH. FURY COVE, in Patagonia, sheltered King and Fitzroy, in 1830, from the fury of a storm.

Füssen, a town in Bavaria, is a corruption of the name of *ad Fauces*, given to a Benedictine monastery, built in 746, at the gorge of the Lech.

Gaeta, an Italian fortress on a cape of the same name, with numerous caves formerly inhabited by troglodytes, bears a name of Greek origin, meaning 'the place of caves.'

Gainsborough, Lincolnshire, is often said to have been the *burh* of the Gainas, but *Gegnesburh* and *Genesburuh*, the forms in the Chronicle, point to a personal name. GAINSTHORPE, also in Lincolnshire, is a Danish name; it is the thorpe of Gamel, 'the old,' as is shown by *Gamelstorp*, the Domesday spelling.

Galápagos Islands, in Spanish *Islas de los Galápagos*, 'the turtle islands,' are a Pacific group belonging to Ecuador. The word *galápago* (whence *calipash* and *calipee*) denotes in Spanish a giant-tortoise or turtle, of which five species inhabit the group. Dampier notes that nowhere else did he find turtles so abundant. In the Gulf of California there is also a small island called ISLA DE LOS GALAPAGOS.

Galashiels, in Selkirkshire, signifies the huts or shielings (O.N. *skali*) on the Gala river.

Galatia, in Asia Minor, was settled by a tribe of Galli or Gauls from GALLIA, a name now believed to have nothing to do with Gael or Gaidhel, being derived from *gal*, 'passion, violence,' and hence 'valour,' the Galli meaning the 'warriors' or 'valiant men.'

Galena, a town in the centre of the lead-mining district of Illinois, was so named from an ore of lead called *galena*.

Galera Point, Trinidad, is the English form of the Spanish name *Punta de la Galera*, given to it by Columbus on his third voyage (1498), from the resemblance of the cape to a galley in full sail.

Galicia, the North-West province of Spain, is the Roman *Calæcia*, the land of the *Gallaici* or *Calaici*, the tribe near Oporto, anciently *Portus Cale*, whence the name of Portugal was derived (*q.v.*).

Galicia, an Austrian crownland, is the Latinised form of the German name *Galizien*, which again is a Teutonised form, given when the district passed under Austrian rule, to the Slavonic Halicz, the place 'of salt,' the name of a town and district in the salt-producing region of the Carpathians.

Galilee, or Galilee of the Gentiles, means the 'circuit' or district of the Gentiles, so called by the Hebrews because largely inhabited by Sidonians. In the Old Testament there are several *Geliloths*, a word usually translated 'borders' or 'coasts' in the English Bible. The name GALILEE has been given to an island in Lake Michigan.

Galla is the name of a numerous people to the south of Abyssinia who speak an Hamitic language. They call themselves ORMA or OROMO, the 'men.' According to Bruce, Galla means 'herdsmen'; accord to D'Abbadie, it is a term used to denote the young warriors when ready for the fight.

Galle, or, with a needless French addition, Point de Galle, is the name of a rocky cape in Ceylon, derived from the Singalese *galla*, a 'rock,' seen in Tang-gale and other names in Ceylon. The Portuguese erroneously connected the name with their own word *gallo*, a cock, as is shown by their having given the town a cock for a crest or armorial bearing.

Gallipoli, a town on the Dardanelles, is called *Gelibolu* by the Turks. The name Gallipoli, which also occurs in Southern Italy, is an Italian corruption of the Greek *Kallipolis*, 'beautiful city.'

Galloway is a territorial term used to designate the counties of Kirkcudbright and Wigtown. Galloway is an Anglicised form of the Latin *Galwethia* or *Galwetha*, which was derived from *Galwyddel*, the name used by the Welsh of Strathclyde as the equivalent of the older Gaelic name of *Gallghaidhel*, given to the Gaelic allies of the Norwegian vikings. Gallghaidhel is a compound formed from *gall*, 'a foreigner,' and *gaidhel*, the national name of the Gaels. Hence Galloway denotes the land of a Gaelic race who were under the rule of the Galls, or Norwegian foreigners.

Galtres Forest, a large and formerly turbulent district north of York, which was ruled with great severity, may owe its name to the frequent executions of malefactors (A.S. *galg-treów*, a 'gallows-tree' or 'gibbet').

Galveston, a town in Texas, is a name believed to refer to the Conde de Galves, Viceroy of New Spain.

Gambia, properly GAMBRA, a river in Senegambia, is the Portuguese corruption of *Gambre*, the native name. (*See* Senegambia.)

Gambier's Isles, at the entrance to Spencer Gulf, South Australia, were so named by Flinders in 1802 in compliment to Admiral Lord Gambier, whose name is also borne by the GAMBIER GROUP of coral islets in the Dangerous Archipelago, discovered in 1797 by the missionary ship *Duff.*

Ganges was the Greek transformation of the name of the great Indian river. Handed on to the Romans and then to the Portuguese, it has been generally adopted throughout Europe as the equivalent of the Indian name *Ganga*, which signifies a 'stream' or 'flowing water' (Sanskrit *gam*, to go). The word is found in other Indian river names—for instance, in the RAMGANGA and the KALIGANGA.

Ganjám, the northernmost district in the Madras province, takes its name from the port of GANJÁM (*Ganj-i-ám*), which means the 'granary of the world.'

Gannet Island, on the western coast of New Zealand, so called by Cook because frequented by great numbers of gannets.

Gap, a French town near Grenoble, is the *Vapincum* or *Civitas Vapincensium* of the Antonine Itinerary or the Notitia, *v*, as in other cases, becoming *g*. The GAPENÇAIS, or district round Gap, was the *Pagus Vapincensis.*

Garabed, the 'Forerunner,' is the Armenian name of places with convents or churches dedicated to St. John the Baptist. Such places are also called SURP GARABED, *Surp* meaning saint, as in Surp Elias for St. Elijah.

Gard, a French department, is traversed by the river GARD or GARDON, the Roman *Vardo*. The so-called PONT DE

GARD is not a bridge, but an aqueduct, built by the Romans to supply Nîmes with water.

Garda, Lago di, one of the Italian lakes, takes its name from the castle of Garda.

Garhwál, the 'district of the forts,' in the N.-W. Provinces of India, was ruled five centuries ago by fifty-two petty chiefs, each possessing his fort (*garh*).

Garonne, the Roman *Garumna* or *Garunna*, is supposed to be a Celtic name meaning the 'rough' or perhaps the 'grassy' river. From *Garunda*, the fifth-century form of the name, we obtain the name of the GIRONDE, at the mouth of the Garonne.

Garry, a river in Perthshire, which flows from Loch Garry through Glengarry, is believed to be the rough river (*garw* or *garb*, 'rough'). LAKE GARRY, on the Great Fish River in Arctic America, was so named by Back in 1834 after Nicholas Garry, Deputy Chairman of the Hudson Bay Company, whose name was also given in 1825 by Parry to CAPE GARRY in Prince Regent's Inlet, by Franklin in 1825 to GARRY ISLAND in the delta of the Mackenzie River, and by James Ross to GARRY RIVER in Boothia Felix.

Gascony, the French GASCOIGNE, and the Low-Latin *Vasconia*, is the land of the Vasks or Basques. (*See* BISCAY.)

Gateshead, Durham, (A.S. *Gátesheved*, as appears from the forms in Bæda and the Boldon Book) is a doubtful name, probably referring to a 'goat's head,' set on a pole as a tribal emblem.

Gawler, a town in South Australia, as well as the GAWLER RANGES and PORT GAWLER, were named after Colonel Gawler, a Governor of the colony.

Geelvink Channel, West Australia, was first traversed in 1697 by the Dutchman Vlaming, in the ship *Geelvink.* In 1705 the same ship discovered GEELVINK BAY, on the north coast of New Guinea.

Geitholl, in Iceland, is 'goat hill,' as GEITA, also in Iceland, is the 'goat river.' GOWRIE, in Scotland, a name familiar from the song called the 'Lass o' Gowrie,' signifies, like GOREY and GOWREE in Ireland, the 'place of goats.'

Geneva (French *Genève*, German *Genf*), the *Genava* of Cæsar, is explained by Glück and De Jubainville as an equivalent of the Latin *Ostia*. The Celtic *genava*, Welsh *genau*, 'mouth,' is a derivative from *genus*, Welsh *gen*, a 'jaw,' like *ostia* from *os*. At Geneva the island of Rousseau makes, as it were, two openings or 'mouths' through which the lake vomits the Rhone. There is probably only a dialectic difference between the name of Geneva and of GENOA, which is the English form of the Italian *Genova*. The Germans prefer the Roman form *Genua*. The harbour of Genoa is remarkably jawlike in its form.

Géographe Bay and GÉOGRAPHE CHANNEL, in Western Australia, are English forms of the names *Baie du Géographe* and *Détroit du Géographe*, given by Baudin in 1801 from the corvette *Géographe*, one of his two ships. From his other ship, the *Naturaliste*, and from his enterprising officers, Henri and Louis Freycinet, he named CAPE NATURALISTE, the N.-E. corner of Tasmania, and the FREYCINET PENINSULA in Tasmania, which is divided from Schouten Island by Géographe Channel. FREYCINET HARBOUR and NATURALISTE CHANNEL are also records of Baudin's explorations in 1801 and 1802.

George Town, the port of entry for Washington and the district of Columbia, lies on the Potomac, two and a half miles from Washington. It was founded by the colonial Government of Maryland in 1751, and named in honour of George II. GEORGETOWN, in British Guiana, the modern name of the Dutch settlement *Stabrock*, was adopted in 1814 when Guiana was annexed during the reign of George III. There is also a GEORGE-TOWN in Ascension Island, in Prince Edward's Island, in the province of Ontario, and several in the U.S.A. CAPE GEORGE in Kerguelen's Land and CAPE GEORGE in South Georgia were so named by Cook in 1775 and 1776 in honour of George III. LAKE GEORGE, in the State of New York, was discovered by William Johnson in 1755, and named after George II. KING GEORGE'S ISLANDS, a group in the Low Archipelago, discovered by Byron in 1765, and KING GEORGE'S PLAINS in Tasmania, discovered by Hayes in 1793, were named after George III. PORT GEORGE THE FOURTH, in West Australia, was so named by King in 1821, and KING GEORGE THE THIRD'S SOUND, in Nuytsland, N.-W. America, by Vancouver in 1791. GEORGINA, a river in Queensland, was so named in compliment to Sir George Bowen, the Governor. GEORGE'S RIVER, Botany Bay, was discovered by George Bass and Flinders in the *Tom Thumb*, a boat eight feet long.

Georgia, one of the United States, was a colony separated from Carolina in 1732 by George II., whose name it bears. It

was bestowed on General James Oglethorpe, M.P., to be 'a colony for the poor and helpless,' and 'an asylum for insolvent debtors and persons fleeing from religious persecution.' SOUTH GEORGIA, in the South Atlantic, is believed to have been discovered by Vespucci on April 7th, 1502, in his wonderful third voyage, and was rediscovered in 1775 by Cook, who named it after George III. GEORGIA, a Russian province in the Caucasus, is probably a Western accommodation of the Persian name Gürdschistan, the 'land of the Gürdschi,' or 'dwellers on the River Kur.'

Germany is the English form of the Latin *Germania*, the land of the *Germani*, a name by which the Gauls designated their Eastern neighbours. The word has been supposed to mean either 'the neighbours,' or the 'shouters' from their fierce war cries. But according to the investigations of Zeuss, the Germani who gave their name to Germany were not Germans at all, the name *Germani*, meaning 'hillmen' or 'mountaineers,' having originally been given by the Belgæ, who were Celts, to the Celtic people of the Ardennes. It may be noted that the Celtiberians called the Oretani, a hill people, by the same name Germani, as we learn from Pliny, *Oretani qui et Germani cognominantur*. We have also the notice of a place *quæ dicitur Germana, vel ad montem*, where *ad montem* seems to be intended as a translation of *Germana*. The Aryan stem *gara* or *gari* means a 'mountain' (Sanskrit *giri*, Zend *gari*, Old Slavonic *gora*, a 'hill.' In Lithuanian *gira* means wood or forest). GERMAN and GERMANY are terms specially of English use, the Germans calling themselves *Deutsche*, 'the people,' and their country DEUTSCHLAND. The German tribes nearest to Gaul called themselves the 'all-men,' a term Latinised as *Allemanni*. Hence the name Allemagne and Allemands for Germany and Germans in French, Alemania and Alemanes in Spanish, Allemanha and Allemanos in Portuguese, and in Italian Allemagna and Alemanni, or more commonly Tedeschi, corrupted from Theodiscans, an earlier form of Deutsche. Our English usage is comparatively recent, the term Germans beginning to supplant the older names Almains and Dutchmen in the reign of Henry VIII., though as early as 1337 the term *Germenie* is used by Robert of Brunne.

Gerona, a town in Catalonia, preserves the old name *Gerunda*.

Ghauts, in the new spelling GHÁTS, is

the name given to the coast range of Western India. The word *ghât* means a 'pass through a mountain,' also the 'landing-stairs' from a river.

Ghent is the English name of the Belgian city which in Flemish is called GEND, in German GENT, in French GAND, and in medieval records GANDA, GANDAVUM, and GANTUM. The etymology is doubtful, possibly from the obscure local word *gant*, a 'stone,' or 'rock,' or 'bank.'

Ghuzzeh is the modern form of Gaza, a 'fortress' of the Philistines. The fabric called *gauze* (O.F. *gaze*) was so called because brought from Gaza.

Gibraltar is a corruption of *Gibel-al-Tarik*, the Arabic name which commemorates its capture in 771, and the subsequent erection of a fort by the one-eyed Berber chief Tarik-ibn-Zayad.

Giessen, in Hesse, at the confluence of the Lahn and the Wieseth, is called in 1197 *burc zë din giezzen*, 'the town at the streams.' So the GIESBACH, in Canton Bern, is a 'beck' which 'pours' or streams down a mountain side into the Lake of Brienz.

Gigantes, Campo de, in Bogotá, abounds in skeletons of the mastodon, which being supposed to be huge human bones, the place came to be called the 'plain of the giants.'

Gilbert's Point, Massachusetts, was named by Gosnold after his second officer, Bartholomew Gilbert (1602). GILBERT ISLE, Fuegia, and GILBERT'S ISLES, New Zealand, were discovered by Cook, 1773-74, and named after Joseph Gilbert, master of one of his vessels, the *Resolution*. The GILBERT ISLANDS, in the North Pacific, and the MARSHALL ISLANDS, an adjoining group, were discovered in 1788 by Gilbert and Marshall, the commanders of two merchant vessels, the *Charlotte* and the *Scarborough*, on a voyage from Port Jackson to Canton. GILBERT'S SOUND, in Greenland, the site of Godhaab (*q.v.*) was named after an Elizabethan worthy, Sir Humphry Gilbert, half-brother of Raleigh, who in 1576 published a book on the possibility of the discovery of a north-west passage to China, and after taking possession of Newfoundland and Virginia in the name of Queen Elizabeth, perished in a storm off Cape Breton in his little barque the *Squirrel* (1583).

Gillis Land or GILES LAND, N.E. of Spitzbergen, in 81° N. Lat., was discovered in 1707 by Cornelius Gillis, and rediscovered in 1864 by the Swedes.

Gilolo, correctly JILOLO, is the name given on European maps to the largest of the Moluccas. The native name is *Halmahéra*, which means the 'mainland.' Gilolo was merely the name of a certain bay on the western coast, where European ships were accustomed to anchor in order to procure the bags in which the cargoes of cloves were to be packed for exportation. Hence the name of the place first visited, the objective of the voyage, came to be extended to the whole island.

Gippsland, a district in the Australian colony of Victoria, and GIPPS ISLAND, New Britain, were named after Sir George Gipps, Governor of New South Wales from 1838 to 1846.

Girgenti, a city on the Sicilian coast, is the Italian form of *Agrigentum*, the Roman corruption of the Greek name *Acragas*, which originally denoted the stream which flows in a deep ravine outside the walls of the Greek colony.

Glamorgan is a corruption of *Gwlad-Morgan*, the country (*gwlad*) ruled in the tenth century by the Welsh prince Morgan, a personal name from the Old British *morcant*, 'sea-bright.' (Welsh *mor*, 'sea,' and *cant*, cognate with the Latin *candidus*.)

Glarus, the capital of a Swiss Canton of the same name, is usually said to be a corruption of Hilarius. In the fifth century Fridolin, an Irish monk, built a church on the site of the present town, which he dedicated to St. Hilarius of Poitiers, his patron saint, who is locally called St. Glaris. The valley of the Linth which constitutes the present Canton belonged to the Abbey of Seckingen on the Rhine, also founded by Fridolin and dedicated to St. Hilary. The name Glarus first occurs in 1343, the earlier forms being *Glarona* and *Clarona*, probably from the Romansch *glarauns*, 'gravelly (Latin *glarea*, 'gravel.') Glarona would designate a place on a bed of gravel. (*See* CLARENS.) The older name has probably been assimilated by reason of the dedication of the church.

Glasgow, the second city in the British Isles, was called *Glas-gu* in 1301. Numerous etymologies have been proposed, such as *clais-dhu*, the 'black ravine,' *glaise-dhu*, 'the black brook,' or *glas-coed*, the 'grey wood,' but the most probable is that given by Professor Rhys, who holds that the name is from one of the Gaelic pet-names of St. Kentigern, or St. 'Mungo,' around whose cell the place grew up. The British name Kentigern would be pronounced

Cunotigernos, in the first letters of which the Gaels discovered their own word for a hound. Hence they affectionately called him either Munchu, the 'dear dog,' which became Mungo, or Deschu, the 'southern hound,' or from his white hair, Glaschu, the 'grey hound,' by which last name his cell came to be known. LINLITHGOW (*q.v.*) is a name of similar origin. GLASGOW ISLAND is in the Bay of Islands, New Zealand, and under its lea the brig *Glasgow* rode out a severe storm.

Glastonbury, an early seat of British Christianity, occupies a former site of Druidical worship. It stands on the ISLE OF AVALON (in Latin *Avallonia*, Welsh *avall*, 'an apple-tree'), which is translated *Insula Pomorum.* The A.S. name *Glæstina-burh* (in Latin *Glastonia*) is believed by Professor Rhys to be a corruption of the British word *glasten*, an 'oak' (Cornish *glastenen*), the Druids cultivating both the oak and the apple as foster parents of their sacred plant the mistletoe. Glastena-burh was assimilated by the Saxons to their gentile form Glestinga-burh or Glæsting-burh, which being supposed by a false etymology to mean the 'shining' or 'glassy town' was mistranslated by the Welsh at no very early date as Ynys-Widrin, the 'island of glass.'

Glatz, in Silesia, is a corruption of the Czech name *Kladsko,* which occurs in 1010, and denotes a place built or palisaded with 'trunks of trees.'

Glenelg, in Inverness-shire, a name of doubtful meaning, gave a title to Lord Glenelg, Secretary for the Colonies (1836-37), after whom GLENELG, a town in South Australia, and two Australian rivers were named.

Gloucester was the Roman *Glevum,* called *Glebon* by the Ravena Geographer, a name representing a British *Glevon,* whence the A.S. name *Gledwan-ceaster,* and the later forms *Gledw-ceaster, Glôwe-ceaster,* and *Glêu-cester.* It is called *Cair Gloui* by Nennius. The British *Glevon* would be the neuter of *glevos,* whence the modern Welsh *gloew,* 'bright, clear,' a name descriptive either of the British town, or of the river on which it stood. To the royal dukedom of Gloucester many names are due, such as CAPE GLOUCESTER and GLOUCESTER ISLAND in Queensland, and CAPE GLOUCESTER in Fuegia, which were named by Cook in 1770 and 1774, and GLOUCESTER ISLAND in the Low Archipelago, discovered by Wallis in 1767. CAPE GLOUCESTER, in New Britain, was discovered by Dampier in 1680.

Gmünden, in Lower Austria, is the place 'at the mouth' of the Traun. GMÜND, in Würtemberg, is also at the junction of two streams.

Goa, properly GOWA, in Marathi *Goven,* the capital of the Portuguese possessions in India, is supposed to be a corruption of an older name *Goe* or *Goe moat,* meaning the 'fruitful land.'

Goatfell, the highest summit in the Isle of Arran, is a hybrid name, the Gaelic *Gaoth-Beinn,* 'mountain of the winds,' having exchanged its Celtic suffix for the Scandinavian *fell,* a 'mountain.'

Gobi is a Mongolian word meaning a 'desert.' Hence the name Gobi Desert which appears on many English maps is a pleonasm. The Chinese call the Gobi either *Han-hai,* the 'dry sea,' or *Sha-mo,* the 'sea of sand.' The name GOBI SHAMO, found on some maps, is a combination of the Mongolian and Chinese names, attributable to ignorance of the meaning of the words.

Godalming, Surrey, is a patronymic or clan name. The A.S. form *Godelmingum* is a dative plural, meaning 'at the Godelmings,' or settlement of the descendants of Godhelm.

Godesberg, a town on the Rhine, near Bonn, appears in 947 as *Wodanesberg,* 'Woden's hill.'

Godhaab, on the inlet called Gilbert Sound by Davis, the earliest Danish settlement in Greenland, was so named by Hans Egede, the first missionary to the Eskimos, to express the 'good hope' he entertained of civilising and converting them. (*See* EGEDE.)

Godmanchester, in Hunts, called *Godmundcestre* in Domesday, is a chester which became the dwelling-place of an Englishman called Godmund. It was probably the Roman *Durolipons.*

God's Providence, Harbour of, in Hudson's Bay, is an inlet where, in 1631, Captain James took refuge from the ice which threatened to destroy his ship. Hudson, in 1610, sought shelter from a storm behind the ISLES OF GOD'S MERCY in Hudson's Strait. The CAPE OF GOD'S MERCY in Davis Strait and the HARBOUR OF GOD'S MERCY in Magellan Strait were so named by John Davis in 1585 and 1593.

Gold Coast, a part of the Guinea coast, was so called because of the gold obtained from alluvial washings. In order to work the suspected gold mines the Portuguese in 1482 built the castle of *S. Jorge de la Mina* now called ELMINA, 'the mine.'

Golden Horn, Constantinople, is a translation of *Chryso-Keras*, a laudatory Greek name denoting the excellence of the harbour. A similar name is that of the GOLDEN GATE given in 1578 by Sir Francis Drake to the entrance into the Bay of San Francisco.

Golden Valley, in the counties of Brecon and Monmouth, is traversed by the River Dore, a Celtic name meaning the 'water.' The name of Golden Valley is probably due to some monk acquainted with the French word *doré*, 'golden,' who perverted the old name *Vallis Doræ*, the 'valley of the Dore,' into *vallis deaurata*, afterwards Englished as the golden valley.

Goletta, the 'throat' or 'gorge,' the port of Tunis, is the Italian translation of the descriptive Arabic name.

Goodmanham, Yorkshire, the site of the heathen temple destroyed by Coifi, is in A.S. *Godmundingaham*, the 'home of the Godmundings or descendants of Godmund,' *Godmundinga* being a genitive plural.

Goole, in Yorkshire, stands at a marshy place believed to have been the former confluence of the Don and the Ouse. In this district the M.L. *gulla* (O.F. *goule*, 'throat') is used in documents to denote a 'drain' or gulley. GOUL, GOWEL, GOWL, ADDERGOUL, and EDARGOULE in Ireland, places which all stand on the forks of rivers, are from the Irish *gabhal*, a 'fork.' LOCH GOIL in Scotland forks off from Loch Long. From the cognate German word *gabel* we have such German names as GABELBACH and GABELHOF. (*See* GOULBURN.)

Goose Island, in CHRISTMAS SOUND, Fuegia, is the place where, in 1774, Cook's crews procured seventy-six geese for their Christmas dinner.

Görlitz, the second city in Silesia, was formerly called *Drebenau*. It was burnt in 1131, and when rebuilt received the name of the 'burnt town,' in Slavonic *Zgorzelice*, of which Görlitz is a corruption.

Göschenen, in Canton Uri, is probably from the dialect word *geschi*, a small house,' plural *geschini*.

Gotha, a town which gives its name to Saxe-Coburg-Gotha, was called *Goth-aha* in 770.

Gothland, the name of a province in the South of Sweden, is the Swedish GÖTA-LAND, meaning the 'land of the Götar,' (O.N. *Gautar*, A.S. *Géatas*), *göta* being an old genitive plural. GOTLAND or GUTLAND, an island in the Baltic, is

on the other hand the 'land of the Goths.' GOTHENBURG, in Sweden, the German form of the Swedish name GÖTA-BORG, stands on the GÖTA ELF, the 'river of the Götar.'

Göttingen, a German University town, appears in the ninth century as *Guddingun*, the dative plural of a patronymic.

Goulburn Islands, on the north coast of Australia, were so named by King in 1818 after Henry Goulburn, the Under Colonial Secretary, afterwards Chancellor of the Exchequer, from whom were also named the town of GOULBURN in New South Wales, GOULBURN RIVER, a tributary of the Murray, and the Arctic GOULBURN ISLANDS. Goulburn is a territorial surname from GOULBURN in Cheshire. (*See* GOOLE.)

Govat's Leap is the name of a deep gorge in the mountains of New South Wales, named, but not leapt by Govat, a land surveyor.

Governor's Straits is a translation of the Portuguese name *Estreito do Gobernador*, applied to the Straits of Singapore because, in 1615, the galleon of the Governor, Dom João da Silva, grounded on the reef at the point of the Strait.

Gower is a peninsula in South Wales. In the Arthurian legend 'Goire, whence nobody returns,' is the land of the dead. The name Goire or Gwyr probably signified the land of the sunset, and the mythical land of Goire seems to have been localised in the peninsula which to the people of Glamorgan would be the sunset land.

Goyaz, a province in Brazil, was the territory of the Goya, a native tribe. The chief town, GOYAZ, properly CIDADE DE GOYAZ, founded in 1739, takes its name from the province.

Gozo, one of the Maltese Islands, is a corruption of the old name *Gaulos*, afterwards *Gaudos*.

Graaft-Reynett, a town in the Cape Colony, which gives its name to a district, was founded in 1786 by the Dutch Governor, Van der Graaft, whose wife's maiden name was Reynett.

Gracias-a-Dios, 'thanks be to God,' was the name given by Columbus to the Eastern Cape of Honduras, which he reached on September 12th, 1502, after battling for forty days with contrary winds and currents.

Graciosa, the name given by the Portuguese to one of the Azores, and by the Spaniards to one of the Canaries, means the 'gracious' or 'pleasant' island.

Grafenort, 'the count's place,' in Canton Unterwalden, was granted in 1210 by Count Rudolf von Habsburg to the monks of Engelberg.

Grafton (A.S. *Gráftún*), a common English village name, is from the A.S. *gráf*, a 'grove.' CAPE GRAFTON, in Queensland, was so named by Cook in honour of the Prime Minister, the third Duke of Grafton. The DUKE OF GRAFTON'S ISLE was so named by Dampier in 1687 after the first Duke of Grafton. GRAVESEND, in Kent, called *Gravesham* in Domesday, is probably from the A.S. *græf* (gen. *græfes*), a 'ditch.'

Graham's Land, an antarctic region discovered (1830-32) by the whaling captain Biscoe, was named in honour of Sir James Graham, first Lord of the Admiralty. GRAHAM'S TOWN in the Cape Colony was founded in 1812, and named after General Graham, Lord Lynedoch, one of Wellington's Peninsular officers, who died in 1814.

Grain Coast, on the Gulf of Guinea, was so called because of the export of cardamons or grains of Paradise, and not of cereals as is sometimes asserted. On the other hand the ILHA DOS GRANOS, 'grain island,' near Gilolo in the Moluccas, was so named by the Portuguese Menezes in 1527 on account of the stores of corn he procured from the natives.

Grampians, the modern name of Drumalban, the backbone of Scotland, which extends from Ben Nevis to Ben Lomond, is one of the ghost names of geography. It arose from a mistaken reading of a passage in Tacitus (Agricola, c. 29), in which he describes the victory of Agricola over Galgacus and the Caledonians, who were posted on a small hill whose name reads in all the best MSS. as *Mons Graupius*. In one bad MS., *Graupius* is corruptly written *Grampius*. Hector Boece was the first to apply the misread name to the central ridge of Scotland, and the audacious forgery which goes by the name of Richard of Cirencester brought the name Grampius into fashion.

Grampound, a small Cornish borough disfranchised in 1824, takes its name from a bridge over the Fal, the *grand pont* represented on the corporation seal.

Granáda, the last of the Moorish kingdoms in Spain, bears the name of its capital which the Arab historians tell us was called *Garnatha*, the 'pomegranate,' because the city is built on four hills which are divided somewhat like the divisions of a pomegranate. The Iberian name *Illiberis*, the 'new town,' is preserved by the

SIERRA DE ELVIRA, the range of mountains above Granáda. NEW GRANÁDA, a South American republic, was called by the Spaniards *Nuevo Reyno de Granáda*, from the resemblance of the scenery in the Cordillera to that of the Sierra Nevada in the old Kingdom of Granáda. The city of NUEVA GRANÁDA was founded in 1522 by Francisco Fernandez de Cordova. GRANÁDA, one of the Antilles, was discovered by Columbus in 1498, and doubtless named after the Spanish city which had then been newly captured from the Moors.

Grandson, a town in Canton Vaud, on the Lake of Neufchâtel, where in 1476 the Swiss defeated Charles the Bold of Burgundy with great slaughter, is called in Latin documents *Grangia Isonis*, the barn or 'grange of Iso.' LA GRANGE is a common name in France and Switzerland. From the Spanish form of the word we have LA GRANJA, near Segovia, a palace built by Philip V. which has been called the Spanish Versailles.

Grantchester (A.S. *Granta-ceaster*), a village near Cambridge, is the chester on the River Granta, erroneously called the Cam (*q.v.*).

Gratz, GRÄTZ, or GRAZ, the capital of Styria, is called in Servian *Gradats* or *Gratsa*, the 'fortress.'

Graubünden is the German name of a Swiss Canton, called in Romansch GRISCHUN, and in French LES GRISONS. It was formed from the union of three leagues, of which the earliest was the Gotteshausbund, formed under the protection of the Bishop of Chur. The Zehngerichtenbund, or League of the Ten Jurisdictions, was organised at Davos in 1436. The Oberbund, formed at Trons in 1424, was nicknamed the Grauebund (in Romansch *Ligia Grigia*), either from the grey coats of the delegates, or more probably from the grey banner which indicated their neutrality between the white and black banners of two powerful lords, Count Hugo and Count Heinrich of Werdenberg. In 1471 the representatives of the three leagues united under the name of the Ligia Grigia, or 'grey league,' and are henceforth known as 'i Signori Grigioni' or 'les Grisons.'

Grave Creek, a tributary of the Ohio, is so called from a great prehistoric gravemound.

Gravelines, in French Flanders, is the French form of the Flemish name *Gravelinghe*, formerly *Graveninghe* (for *Graveninghen*), the 'home of the Counts' of Flanders.

Great Bear Lake is properly Great-bear Lake, being a translation of *Lac du Grand Ours*, a name doubtless due to some unusually large bear having been killed by the French Canadian hunters.

Greece, Latin *Graecia*, was the land of the Graeci, the Epirot tribe who first became known to the Romans, who extended the name to the whole peninsula. The people of the land which had thus accidentally acquired the name of Greece did not call themselves Greeks but Hellenes, signifying originally the people of Hellas, a small town in Thessaly which gave its name to the surrounding district.

Greenland was the name given by Eric the Red in 983 to the sheltered nook where he founded his colony from Iceland, thinking that 'much people will go thither if the land has a pleasant name.' The name was not altogether unsuitable, as the place chosen by Eric for the settlement which he named Greenland is the pleasantest spot in the country, a smooth grassy plain at the head of Igaliko fiord, near the modern Julianshaab, where the ruins of seventeen houses may still be seen. The name was afterwards inappropriately extended to the whole ice-clad country.

Greenwich, Kent, is the A.S. *Grenewíc*, signifying either the 'green village' or more probably the 'green bay' or 'reach' on the Thames. GREEN BAY, an arm of Lake Michigan, is so called from the colour of the water, and GREEN RIVER is a common name in the U.S.A. In Irish and Scotch names the prefix *green-* is commonly derived from the Gaelic *grian*, the 'sun,' or from *grianan* (pronounced greenan), 'a sunny place.' In Ireland forty-five places are called GREENAN and the like, among them the fort of cyclopean masonry called GREENAN ELY, which was the palace of the O'Neill kings. ELY here means a stone fort or house. GREENOGE is the diminutive of Greenan. In Scotland, from the same source, we have GREENOCK on the Clyde and several places called GREENAN, which may have merely denoted a 'sunny place' for drying peats, or perhaps clothes.

Gregory, Cape, in Oregon, was discovered by Cook on St. Gregory's Day, March 12th, 1778. LAKE GREGORY in South Australia bears the name of the Australian explorers, the brothers Gregory.

Grenoble, in Dauphiné, now the capital of the Isère, is a corruption of *Gratianopolis*, the city of the Emperor Gratian, by whom it was rebuilt and fortified.

Greta, a river near Keswick, is a Scandi-navian name, meaning the rock (grit) river. The ROTHA is the 'red river,' the BRATHAY, the 'swift river,' and the CALDEW, the 'cold river.'

Greytown, in Central America, was named after Sir Charles Grey, Governor of Jamaica. GREYTOWN and the GREY GLACIER, in New Zealand, bear the name of Sir George Grey, Governor of New Zealand. CAPE GREY, in the Gulf of Carpentaria, was so named by Flinders, in 1803, after General Grey, commander of the forces at the Cape of Good Hope. The DE GREY RIVER, in West Australia, was so named by Frank Gregory in 1861, after Earl De Grey, now Marquis of Ripon.

Gries, a pass over the main chain of the Alps, derives its name from its glacial gravel. (O.H.G. *grioz*, N.H.G. *gries*, 'gravel, grit.') There is a GRISCHBACH or 'gravel beck' near Saanen in Canton Bern.

Grijalva, Rio de, in Mexico, was discovered by Juan de Grijalva on June 7th, 1518.

Grim, Cape, a black precipitous foreland, at the north-west corner of Tasmania, was named by Flinders in 1798, 'from its appearance.'

Grimsel, a pass in Canton Uri, takes its name from a gloomy lake near the Hospice, formerly called the Grimisol, the 'enclosed tarn.' (M.H.G. *krimmen*, 'to cramp or confine,' and *sol*, a 'tarn or small lake.')

Grindelwald, Canton Bern, is the *wald* or 'forest,' divided from the *Haslithal* by a *grindel* or 'rail-fence.'

Grinnell Land and GRINNELL ISLAND, in Arctic America, were discovered by Dr. Kane in 1850 and 1853, in the course of the two Franklin search expeditions equipped by the munificence of Mr. Grinnell of New York.

Griqualand, in the Cape Colony, was inhabited by the Griquas, a race of half breeds between Boers and Hottentots, who were so named from one of their leaders. GRIQUATOWN was a missionary station among the Griquas, founded in 1801.

Groningen, a town in Friesland, which gives a name to the Dutch province of which it is the capital, is a patronymic or gentile name.

Gross-glockner, 'the great bell,' a mountain in the Tyrol, is so called from its shape. The German *glocke*, a 'bell,' is the same word as our *clock*, properly a timepiece which strikes the hours on a bell.

Groote Eylandt is the 'great island' in the Gulf of Carpentaria. The name which first appears on the Dutch maps in the seventeenth century was probably given by Tasman.

Grütli, a meadow famous from its association with the Tell legend, overlooks the Bay of Uri. It is the Swiss form of *Grütlein*, a diminutive of *grüt* or *ge-rüti*, denoting a place where a forest has been 'grubbed' or rooted out.

Guachos or GAUCHOS dwell on the banks of the Rio de la Plata, whose native name is *Parana-guaçu*, the 'great water.'

Guadalquiver, the great River of Andalusia, bears a pure Arabic name, *Wad-al-Kebir*, 'the great river.' The Arabic *wadi* meant primarily a ravine, hence a river course. The Anas of the Romans is now the GUADIANA, which thus preserves, with an Arabic prefix, the prehistoric name bestowed by the Iberian race. The GUADALAVIAR, the chief river in Valencia, is *Wad-al-abiadh*, 'the white river.' GUADALAJARA, a Spanish province, takes its name from its capital, so called from the River Guadalajara, a corruption of the Arabic *Wad-al-hajarah*, 'the river of stones.' GUADALAJARA, in Mexico, was founded in 1531 by Nuñez de Guzman, who named it after his Spanish birthplace. The GUADALIMAR is *Wad-al-hamra*, the 'red river,' and similarly the GUADALERTIN is the 'muddy river,' the GUADARAMA the 'sandy river,' the GUADALETE the 'small river,' the GUADALCAZAR the 'river of the palace,' the GUADALBANAR is the 'river of the battle-field,' and the GUADAIRA the 'river of the mills.'

Guadalupe, one of the French Antilles, was discovered by Columbus on November 4th, 1493, in the course of his second voyage. He called it *Santa Maria de Guadalupe* after the famous sanctuary of Nuestra Señora de Guadalupe in Estremadura, because he had promised the monks to name one of his discoveries after their convent, which takes its name from the River Guadalupe on which it stands.

Guardafui or GARDAFUI, CAPE, the name of the Eastern horn of Africa, is usually said to be a corruption from the Portuguese *Cabo de Guarda fu*, which may be rendered 'Cape Gardez vous,' originating in the belief that navigation was dangerous, because the compass was deflected by a neighbouring magnetic mountain. This, however, is a mere folketymology, which has transformed the spelling of the name, really a corruption of the Arabic *Jard-Hafún*, in Egyptian Arabic *Gard-Hafún*. The word *gard* or *jard* denotes a wide tract of land without herbage, and *Hafún* was the name of the adjacent district ; hence we have the *Cabo de Gardafun* or *Cabo d' Orfui* of the old maps, now corrupted into Cape Guardafui.

Guatemala, one of the Central American republics, takes its name from its old capital, *Guatemala l'Antigua*, a Spanish formation from the native name *Quauhtemallan*, which, according to Gomara, signified 'the rotten tree.' Other etymologies have been proposed.

Guayaquil, correctly SANTIAGO DE GUAYAQUIL, the chief seaport of the republic of Ecuador, was founded on St. James' Day, July 25th, 1531, at the mouth of the Guayaquil River. GUAYCURU, 'the fast runners,' is the native name of a Brazilian tribe.

Gudbrandsdal, in Norway, now much frequented by tourists, bears the name of Gudbrand, a chief who lived in the time of Halfdan the Black, the father of Harold Fairhair.

Guiana, more correctly Guayana, is a district in South America, now divided between the French, Dutch, and British. The term was formerly of more extensive application, extending from the River Amazons to the Orinoco. The name may have been derived from the Guainia River, a little south of the Orinoco, or from a tribe north of the Orinoco, who called themselves Guaya, 'the esteemed people' or Guaya-na, 'we, the esteemed.' The suffix *-gua* in South America, Cuba, and Honduras, is a Carib or Guarani word meaning a 'bay,' as in PARANA-GUA.

Guienne was one of the old French Provinces. The Roman name Aquitania, which is found as late as the tenth century, became Aquitaine, and then L'Aguienne, and finally La Guyenne, from which arose the English form Guienne. In the name of the Aquitani, the inhabitants of Aquitania, we have the Basque plural locative suffix *-itan* or *-etan*, signifying 'those that are in,' found in Iberian tribe-names, such as the Oretani, Lusitani, Mauretani, and many more.

Guildford, the county town of Surrey, in A.S. *Gildford*, *Gyldeford*, or *Guldeford*, is called in Domesday *Gilda ad vadum*. The word *gild* in A.S. means a 'fraternity' or 'guild,' and also a 'payment' or 'tribute.' The ford at Guildford may have belonged to some fraternity, but more probably, as in the case of CAMEL-

FORD (*q.v.*), was a ford at which a payment of some kind was made. The old form of the name does not support the etymology 'dry ford' (A.S. *gelde*, 'siccus').

Guinea, the name of an immense district in Western Africa extending from Senegambia to the south of the River Congo, is the English spelling of the Portuguese name *Guiné*, a fifteenth century corruption of the Negro name Ginnie, Genna, or Juinie, a town on the Niger, and the capital of a Negro kingdom, which in 1481 was called Ghenea or Ginea. Our *guineas* were coined from alluvial gold brought by the African company in 1663 from that part of Guinea called the Gold Coast. The *guinea fowl* came from the same region. NEW GUINEA was so named from the resemblance of the Papuan Negritoes to the Negroes of Guinea.

Gujarát, GUJRÁT, or GUZERÁT, a peninsula in Western India, was the *raj* or kingdom of the great Hindu clan called Gújar, spread over the whole of Northern India, who have left their name not only in Gujarát but also in GUJRAT and GÚJRÁN-WÁLÁ in the Punjab.

Gulf Stream is the name of the great current which issues from the Gulf of Mexico conveying its heated waters into the North Atlantic.

Gumesh Tepe, a town on the Caspian, means 'silver hill.' GUMESH KHANI, the 'silver town,' near Trebizond, was so called from the neighbouring silver mines.

Gun Island, one of Houtman's Abrolhos, was so named by Stokes, in 1840, because he found on it a bronze four-pounder, a relic of the Dutch ship *Zeewyk*, wrecked in 1727.

Gunnbjörn's Rocks, between Iceland and Greenland, were discovered by the Norseman Gunbjörn in 876.

Gwalior (GWÁLÍÁR), the famous rock fortress of Sindhia, is so called from a shrine dedicated to the hermit *Gwáli* or *Gwáli-pa*, whence it received the name of *Gwáli-awár*, contracted to Gwálíár.

Gweedore, in Donegal, anciently *Gaeth-Dóir*, 'Dóir inlet,' is an historic spot commemorating the spot where, in 619, Dóir, son of Hugh Allan, king of Ireland, was slain.

Habets Oe, 'the Island of Hope,' on the Greenland coast, is the appropriate name given by Hans Egede, the first missionary to the Eskimos, to the place where he began his forlorn enterprise.

Hague, properly THE HAGUE, in Dutch den *Haag*, formerly '*s Gravenhage*, 'the count's enclosure,' was originally a hunting seat of the Counts of Holland. The place is first mentioned in a document of Count Floris II., dated in 1097, and in the time of William II. (1234-1256) it became the residence of the Counts. The palace was built about 1250. HAGE, near Norden, was a hunting seat of the Counts of East Friesland. The word denotes a place surrounded with a fence for inclosing game, and answers to LA HAYE in France and Belgium, and to warren or park in England. HANAU, in Hesse, anciently *Hagenowa*, is 'the inclosed meadow.'

Hai-nan, 'south of the sea,' is the Chinese name of the large island south of the Sea of China. TONG-HAI is the 'eastern sea,' NAN-HAI, the 'south sea,' and TA-HAI is the 'great sea' or lake. SHANG-HAI is the town near or 'above the sea.'

Hainault or HAINAUT is the French name of the Belgian province which is called *Henegouw* in Flemish, and *Hennegau* in German, names signifying the *gau* or district on the River Haisne, Haine, or Henne, called *Hagna* in the tenth century. The oldest forms of the name Hainault are *Hagnauvum territorium* and *Hainau pagus*, both dating from the seventh century.

Haiti or HAYTI, is one of the native names of the great island discovered by Columbus in 1492, on his first voyage. From the resemblance of the northern coast to the mountainous region of Castile he named it *Isla Española*, Latinised as HISPANIOLA, which means not the island of 'little Spain' as is usually supposed, but the 'Spanish island.' Espafiola is the feminine of Espafiol, 'Spanish,' hence Española stands for *Española isla* or *tierra*. Haiti (properly Haïti) means 'roughe, sharpe, or craggie.' Other native names were *Quizquica*, the 'great land' and *Cibao*, the 'stony' land, which has been retained for the central range of mountains, still called SIERRA DE CIBAO. HISPANIOLA is the name of the whole island, now divided into the two negro republics of Haiti and Dominica. Since 1790 the name of Haiti has been revived for the Western or French portion of the island, while the Eastern or Spanish part is called San Domingo or Dominica from the capital San Domingo (*q.v.*), founded, in 1490, by the brother of Columbus.

Hakluyt Headland, the north-west cape of Spitzbergen, discovered by Baffin in 1614, was probably sighted by Hudson in 1607. HAKLUYT ISLAND, in Whale Sound, at the head of Baffin Bay, the northernmost point reached by Baffin in 1616, also commemorates the services of Richard Hakluyt, the Elizabethan geographer (1553-1616).

Halifax, in Yorkshire, is not mentioned in Domesday, the name being first found in a twelfth century deed, by which the Church was given by William de Warren to the Priory at Lewes. According to a local legend reported by Camden, the name refers to a tress of 'holy hair,' belonging to a virgin, who having been murdered by a wicked clerk, was found suspended from a tree. The conjecture that the name refers to a picture of the head of St. John the Baptist, and means 'holy face' is untenable. HALIFAX, the capital of Nova Scotia, was founded in 1749 under the patronage of George Montagu, third Earl of Halifax, the President of the Board of Foreign Plantations. One of the best harbours in Queensland is HALIFAX BAY, so named by Cook in 1770, perhaps from its resemblance to Halifax Bay in Nova Scotia, which he had surveyed in his early life. On the other hand the fact that Cook named the next bay after Lord Rockingham may suggest that Halifax Bay was named after Lord Halifax.

Halikeld is a wapentake in the N. Riding. The moot, as the name implies, was held at a 'Holy Spring,' of great reputed sanctity.

Halle, in Prussian Saxony, called *Halla* in 806, was formerly believed to be a Celtic name derived from the deposits of salt (Celtic *hal*), which have been worked from very early times. It stands on the SAALE, or 'salt' river. The names of HALLSTADT, HALLEIN (formerly *Salina*), and REICHENHALL, were also adduced to prove that their salt-works dated from the Celtic period. This, however, is now doubted, and it is thought that *halla*, meaning a 'salt-house,' may be explained from Teutonic sources.

Hamadân, in North-West Persia, is the *Ecbatana* of Greek writers, and the *Hagmatana* or 'treasure-house' of the cuneiform inscriptions. There were other places of the same name, which may have been used to designate royal cities.

Hamat or HAMA, on the Orontes, preserves the ancient name of *Hamath* (Hebrew *khamath*), the 'hot bath.'

Hamburg, anciently called *Hammaburg* and *Hammanburch*, the 'forest fortress,' took its name from a blockhouse built by Charlemagne in 808 or 811 on the Slavonic march, in a woodland which long went by the name of the *Hamme*, between the Bill, the Elbe, and the Alster. The Old Saxons gave the name of *hamme* to any extensive woodland. In Friesland, according to Koolmann, *hamme* is a common designation for meadows, pasturages, or chases. The word originally denoted a pasture inclosed or 'hemmed' in by a ditch or hedge. We have also HAMME in Belgium, and HAMAR, a province in Norway, is the district of the 'hams.' HAMBURGER HAFEN, in Spitzbergen, was so called because frequented in the seventeenth century by Hamburg whaling ships. HAMBURGH, a town on the Savannah River, South Carolina, opposite Augusta, was founded by a German merchant and named after the German city.

Hameln, a town in Hannover, stands on the River Hamel.

Hammerfest, in Norway, is the most northern town in Europe. The word *fest* means a 'haven,' or place where ships are made fast, and the O.N. *hamarr*, Swedish *hammare*, means a steep crag. The Shetland dialect word *hamar* denotes land covered with boulders, which describes the places in the Shetlands which go locally by the name of HAMMARS.

Hampshire, a contraction of Hamptonshire, takes its name from the county town of Hampton, now called Southampton (*q.v.*) to distinguish it from Northampton.

Hampton is the name of twenty-two places in England, and forms the suffix in many more. The usual explanation of Hampton as the 'home tun' is not supported by the forms in the older charters. HAMPTON MAISY in Gloucestershire, HAMPTON GUY in Oxon, and HAMPTON in Warwickshire, and perhaps SOUTHAMPTON, appear in early charters as *Heántúne* or *æt Heántúne*, which must be explained from *heán*, the dative singular masculine of *heáh*, high. The subsequent change of *n* to *m* and the intrusion of the euphonic *p* present no difficulty, *tentation* having become temptation, while Compton appears in Domesday as *Cumtuna*. HAMPTON in Worcestershire is from another source, being called in a charter of 757 *Huntenatún*, the 'tun of the hunters,' *huntena* being the genitive plural of *hunta*, a hunter. Where -*hampton* is a suffix it may be a corruption of *heántúne*, as in the case of WOLVERHAMPTON, called *Wulfrune Hantune* in a charter of 996, but it is usually an assimilated form from some other source. Thus

WALKHAMPTON in Devon is a corruption of Wallcombton, from the River Wallcomb on which it stands, while CULLAMPTON or COLLOMPTON, and OAKHAMPTON, also in Devon, are on the rivers Colomb and Oakment. In an A.S. charter BISHAMPTON in Worcestershire is *Biscopesdun*, the 'bishop's hill.' BEDHAMPTON, Hants, in A.S. *Beaddingtun*, and BRICKLEHAMPTON, Worcestershire, in A.S. *Brihtulfingtun*, are both plainly corruptions from personal names. CARHAMPTON, Somerset, is in A.S. *Carentún*. In Domesday ALHAMPTON, Somerset, appears as *Alentona*, STUBHAMPTON, Dorset, as *Stibemetune*, and LECKHAMPTON, Gloucestershire, as *Lechantun*. BROCKHAMPTON in Dorset may serve as the type of another class of names. The A.S. name was *Buchǽmatún*, which seems to have denoted a tun or farmyard belonging to the people of Bucham. In the same way we may explain the names of POLHAMPTON, Hants, A.S. *Polhǽmatún*, and of DITCHAMPTON, Wilts, A.S. *Dichǽmatún*. WICH-HAMPTON, Dorset, is called *Wichemetune* in Domesday. (*See* p. 172.)

Hanglip, Cape, False Bay, near Capetown, is a Dutch name derived from an almost overhanging precipice called the Hanglip, or 'Hanging lip.'

Hanover, the English form of the German name HANNOVER (called *Hanovere* in the eleventh century) means the 'high shore,' the town having been originally confined to the cliff, some twenty feet high, on the right bank of the River Leine. The name was afterwards extended to the whole town, then to the Electorate, and lastly to the Kingdom. NEW HANOVER, an island west of New Ireland, was discovered and named by Carteret, in 1767, in compliment to the House of Hanover.

Haparanda, a town on the Gulf of Bothnia, is from *Haaparanta*, the 'aspen shore.'

Happy Island, one of the Smith or CORNWALLIS group in Micronesia, was discovered and named in 1807 by Captain Johnstone of the ship *Cornwallis.*

Hapsburg or HABSBURG, in Canton Aargau, the stamm-schloss of the Austrian dynasty, appears in an eleventh century document as *Habechisburc*, 'hawk's castle.' According to the well-known legend, Radbot, an ancestor of Rudolf of Hapsburg, while hunting in the Aargau lost his favourite hawk, and found it sitting on the ridge of the Wülpelsberg. He was so delighted with the view from the spot that he chose the site for the erection of a castle, which he called Habichtsburg.

Harfleur, formerly Herosflot, Harofluet, and Hareflet, contains, like BARFLEUR, HONFLEUR, and other names in Normandy, the Norse suffix *-fljot* (English *fleet*), a 'navigable channel' or river mouth.

Harlem or HAARLEM in Holland, called *Haralem* in a ninth century document, is a name of doubtful meaning. In Old Saxon we have *lemo*, 'clay' or 'mud,' and *hara* 'an estuary,' and the dialect-word *har* or *haar* denotes a rising ground or small eminence. HARLEM, now a suburb of New York, stands on the Harlem River, a tidal channel. With Brooklyn and Hoboken it is one of the few names surviving from the time of the Dutch occupancy.

Harlinger Land, in East Friesland, takes its name from the small River Harle.

Harmony, near Pittsburg, and NEW HARMONY, in Indiana, were settlements founded by the Communist disciples of Georg Rapp.

Harris, in the Outer Hebrides, is the hilly part of Lewis. It was formerly called *Harige*, a descriptive Norse name identical with that of HARRAY, one of the Orkneys, meaning 'high island.'

Harrisburg, the State capital of Pennsylvania, bears the name of John Harris, a quaker, who settled on the site in 1726. In 1753 his son established a ferry over the Susquehanna, the town being founded and named in 1785. In like manner James Harrod settled in 1774 at a place in Kentucky which is now called HARRODSBURGH.

Harrogate, a noted watering-place in Yorkshire, formerly called *Heywraygate*, is not mentioned in any early records, probably owing to its insignificance. Before the sixteenth century it consisted only of a few scattered dwellings near the 'gate' in Knaresborough Forest on the road from Knaresborough to Heywray, now Haverah Park.

Harrow on the Hill is called *Hearge*, *Hearges*, *Hargas*, *Hergas*, and *Hǽreghes* in A.S. charters, and in Domesday *Herghes*. These are oblique cases of the A.S. *hearh* or *hearg* (gen. *hearges*; dat. *hearge*; nom. plural *heargas*) which denotes a heathen idol, a temple, or sacred grove. The word *Hearh* would normally give Harrow in modern English, just as *mearh* gives marrow. From the same source we have HARROWDEN in Bedfordshire (in Domesday *Herghetone* and *Herghtone*), as well as Arras, Arram, Erghum, and other names, as is proved by the old forms. HARROWBY, in Lincolnshire, is, however, from a personal name, the Domesday form *Herigerebi* showing that it was the *-by* of Heregar. HARROWBY BAY in Arctic America was so named in 1826 by Richardson in compliment to the Earl of Harrowby.

Hartford, the State capital of Connecticut, was settled in 1635 by emigrants from Massachusetts and called Newtown. In 1637 it was renamed Hartford after Hartford (? Hertford) in England.

Hartlepool, a town in Durham of recent and rapid growth, was the pool or haven of the mother parish of HART, distant about four miles, and once a place of some importance, which is supposed to be named from the neighbouring Hart-forest (deer forest). In a charter of 1201 Hartlepool is called Harterpol, and in Bishop Hatfield's survey this becomes *Hertpol* and *Hertilpole*, where Roger de Fultorp holds of the Bishop a tenement called le Herynghows. In an Inquisition of 1279, Peter de Brus holds of the Bishop of Durham the fee of *Herternes*, now HARTNESS, a district which includes Hart and Hartlepool.

Harvard, Mount, one of the highest peaks of the Rocky Mountains, was measured and named in 1869 by Prof. Whitney and a party of students from Harvard University, which was founded in 1636 by the General Court of Massachusetts. In 1638 the Rev. John Harvard bequeathed his library and half his estate to the college, which was thenceforth called by his name.

Harwich, in Essex, is usually explained as the 'army place,' from the A.S. *here* an 'army,' an etymology supported by the A.S. name *Herewic*. But as Harwich stands on the Orwell, whose old name was the Arwe, Harwich, it has been thought, may be a corruption of Arwe-wic, the 'place on the Orwell.' ARROW, a parish in Warwickshire, on the River Arrow, probably localises the people called the *Arosetna*.

Harz or HARTZ MOUNTAINS, in German HARZGEBIRGE, were called in the eighth century *Hart* (Old Saxon *hard*, O.H.G. *hart*, 'wood' or 'forest'). The present spelling, Harz, is supposed to be due to a folk etymology which has made the name into Harzwald, the 'forest of resin' (*harz*). The HARDT, a wooded range of hills near Carlsruhe, is the 'wood.'

Hastings, in Sussex, called *Hæstingaceaster* in King Alfred's Laws, and *Hæstingas* or *Hestingas* in the Saxon Chronicle, is plainly a clan name. The oldest form of the name discredits the legend that the name was derived from the Viking Hastings who ravaged Sussex in 893. There is also a HASTINGS in Northants, and a HASTING and a HASTINGLEIGH in Kent.

Hatteras, Cape, in North Carolina, formerly called *Cape Haterask*, is believed to be from a native tribe name.

Hauenstein, a well-known pass over a precipitous line of cliff in the Jura, is so called from a road made in 1160 between Basel and Lucerne, and named *Gehowenstein*, the 'hewn rock.'

Haurân, a volcanic district east of the Jordan, is the land of 'caves.'

Havre, the 'haven' at the mouth of the Seine, was before 1516 merely a fishing village, with a chapel dedicated to *Notre Dame de Grâce*, whence the official name LE HAVRE DE GRÂCE. The French *havre*, an harbour, is descended from the O.F. *havle*, originally *hable*, which is derived from the Low-Latin *habulum*, a word of Teutonic origin related to the English *haven*.

Hawaii, formerly called OWHYHEE, where Cook was killed, is the largest of the Hawaiian group, named by Cook the SANDWICH ISLANDS (*q.v.*) in honour of Lord Sandwich.

Hawick in Roxburghshire and HAUGHTON in Northumberland are so called from standing on a *haugh*, which signifies a flat piece of ground surrounded wholly or in part by a river, as is the case with HUMS-HAUGH on the Tyne, or BRAINSHAUGH and PEPPERHAUGH, both on the Coquet. The word *haugh* must not be confounded with *heugh*, which denotes an inland bluff, as KEYHEUGH on the Coquet, or RATCHEUGH near Alnwick. Both *haugh* and *heugh* are characteristic Northumbrian forms. The Northumbrian *haugh* is the A.S. *healh*, which has become *halgh* in Lancashire, and elsewhere *-hale*, *-hall*, or *-all*, while *heugh* is A.S. *hôgh* or *hôh*, now usually Hoo or Hu. (*See* HUTTON.)

Hawke's Bay, a province of New Zealand, surrounds a large bay, discovered by Cook in 1769, and named after Sir Edward Hawke, then First Lord of the Admiralty, from whom CAPE HAWKE in New South Wales was also named by Cook in 1770. CAPE HAWKS, in the North Polar Sea, was named by Kane after Francis Hawks, an American writer.

Hay, Cape, at the mouth of the Great Fish River, was so named by George Back in compliment to an under Colonial Secretary whose name is also borne by POINT HAY in Melville Sound, discovered by Franklin in 1821, and by CAPE HAY in Melville Island, discovered by Parry in 1819. CAPE HAYES, in Grinnell Land, was discovered by Dr. Hayes in 1854.

Headfort, in Meath, which gives a title to an Irish Marquess, is the translation of the Irish name KELLS (*q.v.*), a corruption of *Ken-lis*, which means head or chief fort.

Heard Island, in the Antarctic Ocean, was discovered in 1853 by an American Captain whose name it bears.

Hearne Point, Melville Island, and CAPE HEARNE, near the mouth of the Coppermine River, bear the name of Samuel Hearne, an agent of the Hudson's Bay Company, who, descending the Coppermine in 1769-72, was the first European to reach the Arctic Ocean. In 1821 Franklin commemorated this memorable exploit by giving the name of Cape Hearne to the most conspicuous of the headlands at the mouth of the Coppermine.

Hebrides, the modern name of the Western Islands of Scotland, is doubtless a mistake for *Hebudes*, the form Hebrides arising from the letter *u* being wrongly read as *ri* in one of the MSS. of Pliny (*H.N.* iv. 16, § 103) where the correct reading should be *Haebudes* and not *Haebrides*. This reading is confirmed by the notice in Solinus, *Hebudes insulæ quinque numero*, and by the fact that they are called *Ebudæ* by Ptolemy. If BUTE was the ancient *Ebuda*, the Ebudes may have derived their name from it. The NEW HEBRIDES, a Melanesian group, were so named by Cook in 1774 from the resemblance of their torn and rocky summits to those of the Scotch islands. Torres, who visited the largest island of the group at Whitsuntide, 1606, believed it to be a part of the great Antarctic continent, and named it, from the date, *Tierra Austral de Espiritu Santo*.

Hebron, one of the most certain sites in Palestine, where Abraham the Hebrew purchased a tomb, and hence wrongly supposed to contain the name of Heber, the eponymus of the Hebrews, probably denotes a 'confederacy' of Hittites and Amorites who jointly occupied it.

Hecla, more correctly HEKLA, is a conspicuous volcano in Iceland, whose white frock of snow, surmounted by a hood of darker smoke, caused it to be called *Heklufjall* (Hekla-fell) by the Norsemen, the O.N. word *hekla* denoting a hooded frock of knitted wool of divers colours.

Hecla and Griper Bay, in Winter Harbour, Melville Island, was so named by Parry in his first voyage with the *Hecla* and *Griper* (1819-20). In his second voyage with the *Fury* and *Hecla* (1821-23), he discovered and named the FURY AND HECLA STRAIT (*q.v.*). In his third voyage with the *Fury* and *Hecla* (1824-25) the *Fury* was lost on FURY BEACH. HECLA COVE, in Spitzbergen, where Parry anchored in 1827, commemorates his attempt on his fourth voyage to reach the North Pole in the *Hecla*.

Heemskerk, Mount, and MOUNT ZEEHAAN, were the first points of land in Tasmania sighted by any European. Discovered by Tasman on November 24th, 1642, they were appropriately named by Flinders in 1798 after Tasman's two ships, the *Heemskerk* and the *Zeehaan*.

Heidelberg, in Baden, is a name of uncertain etymology. It has been conjectured to mean 'bilberry hill' (German *heidelbeere* 'bilberries').

Heilbronn, in Würtemberg, was called in the ninth century *Heiligbrunno*, 'holy well' or 'holy spring.' According to the local legend, Charlemagne, wearied with the chase, drank from this spring, to which he gave the name. Till 1857 the spring of holy water was to be seen issuing from under the high altar of the Church of St. Kilian, founded in 1019.

Heiligenblut, in Carinthia, is so called from the possession of a bottle brought from Palestine, and reputed to contain a few drops of the 'holy blood.' The Cistercian Abbey at HEILIGENKREUZ in Baden possessed a reputed fragment of the Cross, brought in 1182 from the Holy Land. (*See* WALTHAM HOLY CROSS.)

Heima-ey, 'home island,' the largest of the Westmanna Islands, Iceland, is so called because it is the only inhabited island in the group. Another is called HELLIREY, 'cave island,' from two caverns in which the sheep and cattle take shelter at night.

Helder or THE HELDER, is the north cape of Holland, opposite the island of Texel. The word *helder* or *heller*, literally the 'holder,' or 'that which holds on,' is used in Holland to denote the land, usually overflowed at spring-tides, which lies outside the dikes which protect the *polder*, or land inside the dikes, *polder* and *helder* being the technical terms for protected and unprotected lands.

Helensburgh, Dumbartonshire, a watering-place on the Gareloch, feued in 1776, and made a burgh of barony in 1802, was named from Helen, wife of Sir James Colquhoun, the superior of the soil.

Heligoland (German HELGOLAND), an island in the North Sea, may have been so called from the personal name Helgo, but as in the eleventh century the name is written *Halagland,* it is more probably the 'holy land' (O.H.G. *heilag,* 'holy'). Here St. Willibrord preached, and here were the temples of the god Fosete, whence the ninth century name *Fosetis land.* The green grass, the red sandstone cliffs, and the white sand at their foot explain the saw of the islanders, expressed in a Platt-Deutsch dialect approaching English—

'Grön is dat land,
Rood is de kant,
Witt is de sand,
Dat is de flogg vun't Hillige land.'

Hellville, a town on Nossi-bé, a French island near Madagascar, bears the name of a M. Hell, formerly Governor of Réunion.

Helsingfors, in Finland, near a waterfall (*fors*) on the River Wanda, is the chief city of the district of Helsinge, which was colonised in the sixteenth century by Swedes from Helsingland. From the tribal name of the Helsings, we have HELSINGLAND and HELSINGBORG in Sweden, and HELSINGOR (*ör,* a 'sandspit') in Denmark.

Helvellyn, a conspicuous summit between Thirlmere and Ulleswater, is the 'yellow mountain,' doubtless so called from its gorse-covered slopes. The first syllable is supposed to be the British word for a 'rock,' which we have in the old name of Dumbarton, *Al-cluid* the 'Clyde-rock.' We have the suffix *-velen,* 'yellow,' in RIVELYN by Ennerdale Lake, and in RHIWVELEN in Wales, which mean the 'yellow slope.'

Hen and Chickens, so named by Cook in 1769, are a swarm of rocks off Bream Head, New Zealand. A group of small islands in Lake Erie bears the same name.

Henrietta Maria, a cape at the entrance of James Bay, at the southern end of Hudson's Bay, was so called by Thomas James in 1631 in honour of the Queen of Charles I. who had named his ship of 70 tons the *Maria.*

Henry's Foreland, in Hudson's Strait, was so named by Hudson in 1610, in compliment to Henry, Prince of Wales. The colonists sent out by the Virginia Company in 1607 called the two capes at the entrance to Chesapeake Bay CAPE HENRY and CAPE CHARLES, after the two sons of James I.

Henzada, in Burmese *Hansa-ta,* is a large city in Pegu. The name means literally 'the lamentation of the Goose' (*hansa,* a 'goose,' and *ta,* 'lamentation'). An eponymic legend explains the name by a story about the death of a goose, a bird represented on the standard of Pegu.

Hepburn Island, in Coronation Gulf, commemorates the heroism of John Hepburn, an English sailor who greatly distinguished himself in Franklin's disastrous land expedition in 1819-21, and to whose pluck, skill, and hardihood, the preservation of the lives of the party was largely due.

Herald Island and HERALD SHOAL, north-west of Bering Strait, were discovered in 1849 by Captain Kellett in the *Herald,* one of the vessels employed in the search for Franklin.

Herat stands on the HERI RUD, *Rud* meaning 'river' in Persian, as in SEFID RUD, the 'white river' or SHAH RUD, the 'king's river.' In the great inscription of Darius we have *Hariwa,* and in the Vendidad *Haroyu,* words doubtless cognate with the Sanskrit *Sarayu,* a 'river.' Herat was the capital of Ariana, but the resemblance of the names is probably fortuitous.

Hérault, a French department, is so called from the River Hérault, the *Araris* of Pliny and the *Rauraris* of Strabo.

Herbert Bay in ADMIRALTY INLET, South Shetlands, was named by James Ross in 1843, after Sidney Herbert, then Secretary to the Admiralty.

Herberton, Queensland, was named after Sir Robert Herbert, the Colonial Secretary.

Hereford, the county town of Herefordshire, is in A.S. *Herefordtún* and *Hereford,* which would mean the 'ford of the army' (A.S. *here,* an 'army'). The Welsh name was *Henfford,* the 'old road.' One of these names must be a corruption or assimilation of the other. A similar name is HERFORD, near Minden, anciently *Herifurd.* HERISTAL, near the Lippe, marks the place which Charlemagne in 782 made the winter quarters of his army, calling it *Heristallum,* 'army place,' possibly also with a sort of punning reference to the ancestral home of his race, the founder of the Carling house being Pippin of Heristal.

Hermanas, correctly LAS DOS HER-MANAS, 'the two sisters,' are two islands in the North Pacific, which were discovered and named by the Spaniard Villalobos in 1543.

Hermite Island, south of Tierra del Fuego, properly L'HEREMITE EYLANDT, bears the name of Admiral Jacques L'Heremite who, in 1624, with a Dutch fleet anchored here for a time.

Hermon, the 'lofty' hill, a conspicuous mountain in Palestine, was an ancient site of hill worship. On the slope and summit are the remains of numerous temples.

Herrnhut in Saxony, the first settlement of the Moravian brethren, hence called Hcrrnhuter, was founded under the 'Lord's protection.' To their missions we owe numerous biblical names scattered over the map, such as Nain and Hebron in Labrador, and in the West Indies Nazareth and Bethany in Jamaica, Mount Tabor in Barbadoes, Bethel in St. Kitts, Lebanon in Antigua, Emmaus and Bethany in St. Jan.

Herschel Island, discovered by Franklin in 1826 ; CAPE HERSCHEL, discovered by Parry in 1819, and MOUNT HERSCHEL in South Victoria, discovered by James Ross in 1841, bear the name of Sir William Herschel, the astronomer.

Hersfeld, in Hesse-Nassau, is from a personal name, as appears from the ancient form *Heriulfis-felt.*

Hertford, the county town of Hertfordshire, appears in a charter of 673 A.D. as *Heorut-ford,* and afterwards as *Heorotford, Heortford, Hartford,* and *Hertford,* a name which, like those of other places in England called Hartford or Hartforth would mean the 'hart's ford' (A.S. *heorot* or *heort,* a 'stag or hart'). There is no sufficient reason for connecting it with the Welsh *Rhyd,* a 'ford.'

Hervey Group, also called COOK'S ISLANDS, in the South Pacific, were discovered by Cook in 1773, and named after Captain Augustus John Hervey, a Lord of the Admiralty, who afterwards became Earl of Bristol, and whose wife was the famous or infamous Duchess of Kingston. Captain Hervey's name was also given to HERVEY BAY, Queensland, discovered by Cook in 1770.

Herzegovina, properly THE HERZE-GOVINA, is a Bosnian district erected into a duchy in 1440 by Frederick IV. The Slavonic subjects of Stephen Cosaccia, the first duke, borrowed his German title Herzog, and styled him Herzega, whence the Slavo-Teutonic name Herzegovina, the 'duchy.' 's HERTOGENBOSCH, a town in Brabant, usually called by the French name BOIS-LE-DUC (*q.v.*), was founded in 1184 by Gottfried, Duke of Brabant.

Hesse, an old German Landgravate on the Main and Rhine, afterwards divided into several principalities, was originally a tribal name. According to Grimm and Zeuss the Chatti, Catti, or Hatti were so called from their headcovering or 'hat.' The form Chatti was used till the third century. In 720 it becomes Hessi and Hessii, followed by Hassia, Hessia and Hessen for the country.

Hestmandö, 'horseman island,' lying off Norway in the Arctic circle, is a lofty rock, 1000 feet in height, which resembles a horseman clad in a cloak.

Hexham, a great monastery in Northumberland, once the See of a bishop, is called *Hagustaldensis Ecclesia* by Bæda, and in the Saxon Chronicle *Hagustaldes eá* and *Hagustaldes ham.* The Hagustaldes eá on which the monastery stood is now the HEXTOLD BURN. In A.S. *hægsteald* or *hægosteald* means a celibate or unmarried person. Hence the form *Hagustaldesham,* of which Hexham is a corruption, if not from a proper name, would denote the home of a celibate. As in other cases the monastery may have arisen around the earlier cell of an anchorite.

Hex Valley, near Capetown, is traversed by the HEX or 'witch' river, so called by the Boers, because it flows through a hidden cleft.

Hibbs, Point, in Tasmania, was named by Flinders in 1798 after the master of his ship.

Hibernia Shoal and ASHMORE SHOAL, between Australia and the Sunda Islands, were discovered by the *Hibernia,* commanded by Samuel Ashmore.

Hicks, Point, was the first land in Australia discovered by Cook, April 18th, 1769. It was named after Lieutenant Hicks, by whom it was sighted, and who died of consumption just before reaching England. His name was also given to HICKS BAY, New Zealand, discovered in 1770.

Hildesheim, in Hanover, near the battlefield where Arminius defeated Varus (A.D. 9), is usually explained from the O.H.G. *hilti,* 'battle,' but the ninth century form *Hildinisheim* shows that it is from a personal name belonging to the same stem.

Himálaya, the 'abode of snow,' is from the Sanskrit *hima*, 'snow,' a word cognate with the Latin *hiems*, and *álaya*, 'abode, dwelling.' The HIMAPRASTHA is the 'snowy head,' and the classical names IMAUS and HAEMUS are cognate words.

Hindmarsh, a river, town, and county in South Australia; a lake in Victoria; and a town in New South Wales, were all named after Captain Hindmarsh, the first Governor at Adelaide.

Hindu-Kush is the Persian name of the western continuation of the Himalaya, known to the ancients as the *Caucasus Indicus.* Humboldt thinks that Hindukush is a corruption of *Hindu-kuh* 'Indian mountain.' Ibn Batuta records the legend that one of the higher passes in the chain was called *Hindu-Kush,* 'the slayer of Hindus,' because Indian slaves carried across to Balkh often perished of cold.

Hindustan is a Persian term signifying the country or place of the Hindus or Indians, HINDU being the Persian form of the Sanskrit *Sindhu,* a dweller on the Indus, which means the river. The names Hindustan, Sindh, and India are parallel forms, respectively Persian, Sanskrit, and Greek. (*See* INDIA.)

Hispaniola is the Latin form of *Isla Española,* the 'Spanish isle,' the name given by Columbus to the island now divided into the republics of HAITI and ST. DOMINGO. (*See* HAITI.)

Hissarlik, the mound in the Troad excavated by Schliemann, is from the Turco-Arabic word *Hissar,* a 'castle.'

Hiva, 'island,' is a word frequently found in the Marquesas, as NUKA-HIVA, FATU-HIVA, and HIVA-CA.

Hoang-Ho, in China, is the 'yellow river,' which borders HO-NAN, the province 'south of the river,' and flows into the HOANG-HAI, or 'yellow sea,' so called because discoloured by the yellow mud brought down by the Hoang-Ho.

Hobart, or HOBART TOWN, the capital of Tasmania, founded in 1804, was named after Lord Hobart, then Secretary of State for the Colonies.

Hoboken, in New Jersey, opposite New York, is often said to be a native name meaning 'the smoked pipe,' marking the spot where the first colonists smoked the pipe of peace with the Indian chiefs. It is, however, a reminiscence of the Dutch village of Hoboken, three miles from Antwerp.

Hobson, Mount, the highest point in Great Barrier Island, New Zealand, bears the name of Captain Hobson, the first Governor of New Zealand.

Hohenlinden, a battle-field in Bavaria, is a corruption of *Hol-lenden,* 'at the hollow lime-tree.' HOHENSTAUFEN, the stamm-schloss of the Hohenstaufen dynasty, is the 'high rock' (O.H.G. *stauf,* 'a rock').

Holderness is a division of the East Riding between the Wolds and the sea. The chalk wolds are treeless, but the coast district, which is covered with glacial drift, was a forest called *Deira-wudu, Dyra-wudu,* or *Dera-wudu,* the 'forest of Deira,' which denoted the land between the Humber and the Tees. Bæda calls Beverley Minster the '*monasterium quod vocatur in Derwuda, id est in silva Derorum,*' and in the Saxon Chronicle, A.D. 685, it is called the 'mynstre on Derawudu.' The ness or promontory of Holderness is an obscure name; the suggested etymologies from *hol,* 'hollow' or 'flat,' and from *holt,* 'wood' or 'forest,' not being supported by the Domesday form *Heldrenesse* (*see* HELDER), or by the O.N. *Hellornes.*

Holland is usually supposed to be the low or hollow land, nearly equivalent to the modern name Netherlands. But the earliest form of the name, which occurs in 866, is *Holtland,* the 'woodland,' denoting the forest region round Dordrecht which belonged to the Counts of Friesland. The name was afterwards extended to the neighbouring lands, and then corrupted into Holland, a form which occurs in 1021, 1083, and 1097. NEW HOLLAND, the name by which Australia was long known, was given by Abel Tasman in 1644, in commemoration of the part taken in its discovery from 1606 to 1644 by himself and other Dutch seamen.

Holland, or PARTS of HOLLAND, is the name of the southern division of Lincolnshire. The old name, *Hoiland,* is an indication that the etymology is not, as usually asserted, from the A.S. *hol,* 'hollow,' but from *hóh,* 'heel,' a word which denotes a piece of land which juts out, in this case denoting that part of the county which runs out as a peninsula at HOLBEACH. HOLLAND, in Orkney, is the sloping and (O.N. *hallr,* 'sloping').

Höllenthal, the 'valley of hell,' a gloomy gorge in the Black Forest, leads to a smiling plain which goes by the name HIMMELREICH, 'heaven.'

Holstein is a name that has undergone curious assimilation through folk-etymology. In the tenth century the people were called *Holt-sati*, the 'settlers in the forest,' a name of the same class as our own Somerset and Dorset. Holstein is a corruption of the dative plural *Holtsatin*, whence the successive forms *Holsten, Holsteen*, and *Holstein*. HOLSTENBORG, a Danish colony in Greenland, was named after a Graf von Holstein, who was president of the Danish Missionary Society.

Holyhead, Anglesea, is the rough English equivalent of the Welsh name *Pen-Caer-Gybi*, 'the hill of the fort of St. Cybi.' HOLYWOOD, in Dumfriesshire, is the 'holy wood of St. Congal,' a sort of translation of the Celtic name *Darcon-gall*, 'Congall's oakgrove.' HOLYROOD, the royal palace at Edinburgh, includes the Abbey of the 'Holy rood' or cross, whence the name of the palace was derived. HOLY ISLAND is a name given to Lindisfarne, an island off the coast of Northumberland, because of the monastery founded in 635 by Oswald King of Northumbria, which became the see of St. Cuthbert, afterwards removed to Durham. HOLYWELL, in Flintshire, renowned for miraculous cures, is so called from the 'holy well' of St. Winifred, which, according to the legend, gushed up at the spot where her head fell when she was decapitated.

Homburg, a corruption of *Hohenburg*, the 'high burg,' is the name of several towns in Germany, corresponding to the English Hanbury. There are also several places called HOMBERG, a corruption of *Hohenberg*, 'high hill.' HOCHHEIM, on the Main, anciently *Hohheim*, from which we obtain the designation of Hock for the Rhine wines, means 'high home.'

Home's Islands and CAPE HOME in Arctic America, and HOME'S GROUP in Queensland bear the name of Sir Everard Home.

Honden Eylandt, 'dogs' island,' in the Low Archipelago, was discovered in 1616 by the Dutch mariners, Le Maire and Schouten, and so named because they found it inhabited by three half-starved Spanish dogs.

Honduras, a British possession in Central America, takes its name from the Rio Hondo, which forms the boundary between Yucatan and British Honduras. In the Argentine province of Santiago there is another RIO HONDO, which means 'deep river' in Spanish.

Hong Kong, an island in British possession near Canton, is an English corruption of the Chinese name *Heang Kiang*, 'sweet water,' or 'fragrant-waterway,' which originally denoted not the island, but the channel separating it from the mainland, whose water is sweetened by the fresh water brought down by the Canton river. The change from *Heang Kiang* to Hong Kong is probably due to assonance with the name of the Kong-hong, or company of Chinese merchants through whom the East India Company conducted their trade.

Hood's Island, in the Marquesas, was named by Cook, in 1774, after the midshipman who first descried it. HOOD'S ISLANDS, a group in the Low Archipelago, and POINT HOOD, in West Australia, were named after Lord Hood. HOOD'S RIVER, which flows into Coronation Gulf, bears the name of the unfortunate officer, ROBERT HOOD, who, on Franklin's return from the descent of the Coppermine River in 1821 was murdered by Michel, the Iroquois hunter.

Hooper's Inlet, in Fury and Hecla Strait, bears the name of the purser of the *Fury.*

Hoorn, a town on a 'horn' or spit of land in the Zuyder Zee, was the birthplace of Schouten, the discoverer of CAPE HOORN, usually called Cape Horn (*q.v.*).

Hope, Cape, in Rowe's Welcome, north of Hudson's Bay, was so called by Middleton in 1741-42 because of the hope that beyond it lay the north-west passage. Finding the supposed strait was merely an inlet, he called it REPULSE BAY. In Australia we find HOPE ISLANDS, discovered by Cook; HOPE INLET, HOPE REACH, and HOPELESS REACH, discovered by Stokes; MOUNT HOPELESS discovered by Mitchell, and HOPE SPRING discovered by Stuart; in Vancouver Island we have HOPE BAY, discovered by Cook; and in Patagonia HOPE PROMONTORY and MOUNT HOPE, discovered by Fitzroy; and in Spitzbergen HOPE ISLAND, discovered by a whaler in 1613, all of which express the hopes, mostly vain, of various explorers. CAPE HOPE, and HOPE'S BAY, in the Arctic Archipelago, were named after Sir W. J. Hope; and HOPE'S ISLANDS, Australia, after Sir G. Hope. HOPE ISLAND, Micronesia, was discovered by the ship *Hope* in 1807. (*See* CAPE OF GOOD HOPE.)

Hopedale, in Labrador, is the English

translation of HOFFENTHAL, a missionary station established by the Moravian brothers.

Hoppner's Strait, HOPPNER'S INLET, CAPE HOPPNER, and HOPPNER'S RIVER, all in Arctic America, bear the name of one of Parry's officers, Lieut. H. P. Hoppner.

Horn, Cape, correctly CAPE HOORN, or KAAP VAN HOORN, is the most southern point in America. It was first rounded on January 29th, 1616, by the Dutch seamen Jacob Le Maire and Willem Schouten, who after passing through the STRAIT OF LE MAIRE named the cape in honour of Schouten's birthplace, the town of Hoorn in Holland (q.v.), where his ship had been fitted out, and which was the home of most of his sailors. FALSE CAPE HOORN is the southern extremity of Tierra del Fuego, whereas the true Cape Hoorn is on HOORN ISLAND, a little further south. Passing round Cape Hoorn into the Pacific, they gave the name HOORNISCHE EILANDEN to two islands north-east of the Fijis, which are now erroneously marked on most English maps as the Horne and not the Hoorn Islands.

Horncastle, a town in Lincolnshire, derives its name from a castle built on a horn or spit of land, at the junction of the rivers Bane and Waring. Before the erection of the castle the place was called *Hornan,* 'at the horn.' HORN POINT, north of Bass Strait, was named from its two hornlike spits of land. THE HORNLI, a range of hills near Zürich, is named from a peak called the Hornli, a diminutive of Horn, a name given to several of the higher Swiss peaks, as the Schreckhorn, or the Wetterhorn. HORN SOUND in Greenland was so called by Baffin in 1616, on account of his having obtained by barter from the Eskimos some horns of the narwhal, which he believed to be veritable horns of the unicorn.

Horsburgh, Cape, at the entrance to Lancaster Sound, was named by Ross in 1818 in compliment to the hydrographer of the East India Company.

Horsham, Sussex, is shown by the A.S. form *Horsham* to be simply the 'horse-enclosure.' If, as asserted, it had been the home of Horsa, the leader of the Jutes, the A.S. form would have been Horsanham. HORSLEY, a common name, is the 'horse pasture,' and ROSSBACH in Germany, anciently *Hrosbach,* is from the O.H.G. *hros,* a 'horse.'

Horton River, discovered in 1826, enters the Arctic Ocean between the Cop-

permine and the Mackenzie Rivers. It bears the name of Wilmot Horton, Under Secretary for the Colonies.

Hospenthal, in Canton Uri, is the 'valley of the Hospice,' erected in the thirteenth century to shelter travellers about to cross the St. Gotthard Pass.

Hotham Inlet, discovered by Beachey in 1826, and CAPE HOTHAM discovered by Parry in 1819, both in the Arctic Ocean, bear the name of Sir Henry Hotham, a Lord of the Admiralty.

Hottentot is a derisive name given by the Boers to a South African race who call themselves either *Khoi-Khoim,* 'men of men,' *Ama-Khoim,* 'real men,' or *Gui-Khoim,* 'first of men.' Hot-en-tot is said by Dupper and Hahn to be a Dutch slang term meaning a 'stutterer,' probably given to the Hottentots because of the 'clicks' which characterise their speech.

Hounslow, Middlesex, was called in A.S. *Hundes-hláw,* the 'hounds-barrow.' It may have been the burial-place of a favourite dog.

Houston, at one time the capital of Texas, bears the name of General Samuel Houston, who defeated the Mexicans in the battle of San Jacinto, and who was afterwards President, and then Governor of Texas. He doubtless took his territorial surname from HOUSTON, 'Hugh's town,' in Renfrewshire, which was granted to Hugo de Padvinan in the reign of Malcolm IV.

Houtman's Abrolhos, a rocky group off the West Australian coast, were discovered in 1619 by the Dutch seaman Jans van Edel, and named after his comrade Frederik Houtman. Frederik Houtman and his brother Cornelius, a drunken rascal afterwards murdered by the Malays at Acheen, had in 1598 sailed with John Davis in the twin ships the *Leeuw* (lion), and the *Leeuwin* (lioness).

Howe's Foreland, Kerguelen Land, discovered by Cook in 1776; CAPE HOWE, at the south-east corner of Australia, discovered by Cook in 1770; LORD HOWE ISLAND, between Australia and New Zealand, discovered by Lieut. Ball in 1788; LORD HOWE'S group, north of the Salomons, discovered by the Dutch in 1616, rediscovered and named by Hunter in 1791; HOWE'S ISLAND, in the Low Archipelago, discovered by Carteret in 1767; and HOWE'S ISLE, one of the Society Islands, discovered by Wallis in 1767, are names showing the repute of the naval exploits of Admiral Lord Howe (1725-1799).

Hoy, a lofty island in the Orkneys, is the O.N. *Há-ey*, 'the high island.'

Hudson's Bay, the American Mediterranean, is both the tomb and the monument of the daring seaman who discovered it. In 1607 Henry Hudson, with ten men and a boy, sailed in the *Hopewell*, a ship of 80 tons, for Spitzbergen, sighting and naming HAKLUYT HEAD, and reaching a higher latitude than was subsequently attained for 166 years. In 1609, in the service of the Dutch East India Company, he discovered the HUDSON RIVER, and ascended it for 150 miles as far as the site of Albany, and landed on Manhattan Island, afterwards the site of New York. On April 10th, 1610, he set sail in the *Discoverie*, a ship of 55 tons, fitted out by Sir Thomas Smith, and penetrating through HUDSON STRAIT, the entrance to which had been reached by Sebastian Cabot in 1517, he discovered the great inland sea which bears his name, and wintered at the southern extremity. In June 1611, his crew mutinied, fearing the provisions would run short, and on midsummer day, he, his son, and seven of the crew, were put into the shallop with one fowling piece, some powder and shot, and a little meal, and were cast adrift in the middle of the bay. A month later, on July 25th, the five chief mutineers met the fate they so well deserved, being killed in a skirmish by the Eskimos. The HUDSON RIVER, which now so worthily bears his name, was at first called the Mauritius River by the Dutch colonists, in honour of Prince Maurice of Orange.

Huesca, a city in Aragon, which gives its name to a province, is the *Osca* of Cæsar.

Húglí, or in the old spelling the HOOGLY RIVER, an arm of the Ganges on which Calcutta stands, derives its name from the town of HUGLI on its right bank, so named, it is believed, from the gigantic jungle reed, *Typha elephanta*, called *hugla* in Bengáli.

Hulan, HURUN, or KULUN NOOR, the 'holy lake,' is a large lake in Mongolia, which is also called DALAI, the 'sea.'

Hull, correctly KINGSTON-UPON-HULL, is the third port in England. The name Hull denotes properly a small stream which flows into the Humber. In 1280 'the port of the river of Hull' is mentioned, and there was a hamlet at its mouth called Wyke-upon-Hull. By a charter of Edward I., the rising port obtained certain privileges as a free borough, and the name Wyke-upon-Hull was

changed to Kyngeston-super-Hull (Kingston-upon-Hull) which has been gradually shortened into Hull, a name which denotes strictly the river and not the town.

Humber, the sea-like estuary which receives so many streams, is called *Abus* by Ptolemy. Hence the name Humber is most likely not Celtic but Teutonic. The A.S. forms are *Humbre* and *Humbra*, the root being probably the O.N. *húm*, 'the sea,' so called from its dusky colour. From *húm* comes the name of the sea giant Hymer, of Norse Mythologic poetry, who owned an ocean cauldron a mile in depth (*Corpus poet. Boreale*, i. 220), and became the King Humber of later eponymic legend. The estuary may well have been supposed to be Hymir's cauldron. The tidal bore, locally called the Eager, that rushes up the Humber to the Trent, is supposed to be the O.N. mythologic giant Ægir (A.S. *Eagor*, the 'sea'), whence the name of the EIDER, formerly *Ægis-dyrr*, 'Oceani ostia.'

Humboldt Glacier, in Greenland, the chief source of the larger icebergs which reach the Atlantic, was discovered by Kane, in 1853, and named after Baron Alexander von Humboldt, in whose honour sundry lakes, rivers, capes, bays, and mountains have also been named.

Hume's Creek, a tributary of the Darling River, was so called by Mitchell because he found cut on the bark of a tree the name of Hamilton Hume, an earlier explorer.

Hungary (German UNGARN) is the English form of the Latinised name *Hungaria* for *Hungavaria*, 'the land inhabited by the Huns,' who first occupied it about 380 A.D. In 453 the territory fell into the hands of the Ostrogoths and the Gepidae, who were followed by the Longobards, 526-548, by the Avars in 568, and finally in 889 by the Magyars, a Finnic race.

Hunter's Isles, north-west of Tasmania, discovered by Flinders in 1798 ; HUNTER'S ISLANDS, north of the Salomons, discovered by Mortlock in 1796 ; PORT HUNTER, sometimes called Coal River, New South Wales, discovered by Shortland in 1797 ; and POINT HUNTER, in New Zealand, all bear the name of Admiral Hunter, the second governor of New South Wales. HUNTER ISLAND, New Caledonia, sometimes called Fearn Island (*q.v.*), was discovered in 1793 by the ship *Hunter*. HUNTERS' LAKE, between the Coppermine and Yellow Knife Rivers, was so named by Franklin in 1820 because the native hunters brought

in a seasonable supply of reindeer meat.
HUNTER'S RIVER, De Witt's Land, was
so named by King in 1820, after his
comrade James Hunter.

Huntingdon, the county town of Huntingdonshire, contains a genitive *huntan,*
which has been assimilated to the common
gentile or patronymic form, as appears
from the A.S. name *Huntandún,* afterwards *Huntendun,* and in Domesday
Huntedune. Huntandun may be from
the personal name Hunta, or it may be
the 'hunter's hill' (A.S. *hunta,* a 'hunter'). From *huntena,* gen. pl. of *hunta,*
a 'hunter,' we have HUNTINGTON in
Salop, called *Hantenetune* in Domesday.
HUNTINGDON, in Pennsylvania, was so
named in 1777 in honour of Selina,
Countess of Huntingdon.

Huon River, flowing into ENTRECASTEAUX CHANNEL, in Tasmania, bears the
name of Captain Huon Kermadec, who
commanded the *Espérance* in the expedition of Admiral d'Entrecasteaux.

Hurd Island, HURD CHANNEL, CAPE
HURD, in Arctic America ; PORT HURD
and MOUNT HURD, in Australia ; and
HURD ISLE, in the Gilbert Group, bear
the name of Captain Thomas Hurd,
hydrographer to the Admiralty.

Huron, one of the great North American
Lakes, takes its name from a tribe now
located in Kansas, who in the seventeenth
century occupied the peninsula between
Lakes Huron, Erie, and Ontario. Huron
was a nickname, of French origin, given
to the tribe called by the English *Wyandot,* a corruption of *Wendat,* 'people of
one speech,' from *wenda,* 'speech,' and
at, the root of *skat,* 'one.' In the French
patois of the colonists, the Wendats were
called *Hurons,* or 'shockheads,' from the
lines of bristly hair resembling the crest
of a wild boar, which adorned their halfshaven crowns. According to Littré the
French *hure* means *tête hérissée et en
désordre.* The French nickname of the
tribe was applied to the great fresh-water
sea round which they dwelt, and has superseded the proper name of the tribe and of
the lake.

Hutton, a common Northern village
name, is from the A.S. *hóh, hógh,* or *hó,*
a *Hoo,* or point of land shaped like a
'heel' or 'hough' stretching out into a
plain or into the sea.

Huzara, the name of certain wild hill
tribes in Afghanistan, is from the Persian
hazár, a 'thousand.' The Mongolian
regiments of Jingiz Khan and his successors were called *hazáras,* and the

Huzaras of Afghanistan, whose facial type
is strikingly Mongolian, are believed to be
descendants of some of these predatory
bands which settled there.

Hvita, in Iceland, means the 'white river.'

Hythe, in Kent, is called in the Saxon
Chronicle *Hýth,* which means a haven,
port, wharf, or any place where ships or
boats can land. There is another Hythe
on Southampton water, but *hythe* appears
more usually in composition, as in GREENHITHE, Kent, or CLAYHITHE near Cambridge, and often in an abraded form as
in Erith, Lambeth, Maidenhead, Redriff,
or Stepney.

Ibargoïtia, one of the Caroline Islands,
bears the name of a Spanish Captain who
visited it in 1799.

Ibera or IVIRA, the 'clear water,' is a
large lagoon in the Argentine province of
Corrientes (Guarani *ivi,* 'water,' and *ira,*
'clear').

Iceland was called *Snœland,* the 'land of
snow,' by the Viking Naddodd who discovered it in 868. On account of the icefloes which then beset the northern coast,
Flóki, who followed him, called it *Island,*
of which Iceland is the English translation. IJSKOEK, 'ice cape,' was the name
given by Barents in 1594 to the north cape
of Novaya Zemlya, which he found surrounded with ice. IJSHAVEN, 'ice haven,'
in Barents Land, was reached by Barents
in 1596, and so called because on August
26th the ship became hopelessly frozen in,
and on June 14th, 1597, was abandoned by
the crew in their two boats. ICY CAPE,
Alaska, in the Arctic Ocean, was the
furthest point reached by Cook on his
third voyage. On August 18th, 1778, he
was compelled to return, finding that the
sea was closed by ice.

Idaho, one of the United States which
possesses immense mineral wealth, bears
the appropriate native name *E-dah-hoe,*
the 'jewel mountains,' or 'gem of the
mountains.'

Ikurangi, 'reaching to heaven' (Maori,
rangi, 'heaven'), is a lofty volcano in New
Zealand.

Ilanz or GLION, in Canton Graubünden,
is built at the junction with the Rhine of
a small stream of the same name, which
is from the Romansch *ils ogns* or *ils ons,*
'the alders.'

Ilchester, in Somerset, formerly *Ivelchester,* the chester on the River Ivel, was
the *Ischalis* of the Romans. (*See* YEOVIL.)

Ilfracombe, Devon, formerly *Alfreds-combe, Ilfridcombe,* or *Ilfarcombe,* is the combe or valley of some person named Elfrec or Alfred.

Ilheos or **Os Ilheos,** 'the islands,' more correctly **Porto dos Ilheos,** the 'port of the islands,' is a Brazilian coast town, so called from four islands which protect the harbour. Here in 1540 a town was built under the protection of St. George, and called **San Jorge dos Ilheos.**

Ili, a Mongolian word meaning 'bright' or 'glistening,' is the name of a river which enters Lake Balkash.

Ilkley, near Leeds, is believed to occupy the site of the Roman station of *Olicana,* of which there may be an assimilated reminiscence in the modern name, which appears in Domesday as *Ileclive* and *Illeclive,* the 'bad cliff,' the Danish form *il* being the equivalent of the A.S. *evil.* In Iceland there is a place called **Illa-klif,** a 'nasty bit of cliff.'

Illimani, in Peru, is the 'snow mountain' (Quichua *illi,* 'snow ').

Illinois, one of the United States, admitted in 1818, is traversed by the Illinois River, on whose banks dwelt a tribe known ever since Marquet and Joliet reached their territory in 1673 as Illinois, a French corruption of the native name Illini, or Iliniwok, 'the men.'

Illyria, an Austrian crownland on the Adriatic, continues the classical name *Illyris* or *Illyricum regnum.* The meaning is unknown, the old Illyrian language having perished.

Ilocos, the name of several districts in the Philippines, is from the Tagala word *iloc,* a 'river.'

Imperial, Ciudad, a city in Chili, was founded between 1550 and 1558 by Pedro de Valdivia, and named in honour of the Emperor Charles v., king of Spain.

Impérieuse Shoal, on the north-west coast of Australia, was discovered by H.M.S *Impérieuse* in 1800.

Inchcolm, in Fife, takes its name from a monastery called in a charter by the translated name *Insula Sancti Columbæ.* In Scotch names *inch* is the usual modern form of the Gaelic *innis,* an 'island,' as **Inchkeith** in the Firth of Forth, **Inchinnan,** the 'isle of St. Adamnan,' or **Inchaddon,** the 'isle of St. Aidan.' In Ireland *innis* often appears as *ennis* or *inish,* as in **Enniskeen** and **Iniskeen,** the 'beautiful island.' In Wales the form *ynys* is usually retained, as **Ynysddu** or **Ynysowen.**

Indefatigable Strait, a passage through the Great Barrier Reef of Australia, was discovered in 1815 by the *Indefatigable,* an English ship.

India is a Greek form derived from *Hindu,* the Persian equivalent of the Sanskrit *Sindhu,* a 'river,' or 'sea,' used specially to denote the **Indus,** the chief river of the land in which the Aryan invaders of India first established themselves. The name **Indus** shows in like manner that our knowledge of the river came through the Greeks from the Persians. The name **Scindh** for the lower valley of the Indus, comes to us directly from India, while the names **Hindu** and **Hindustan** (*q.v.*) came from the Persians without Greek intervention. The name of the **West Indies** reminds us that Columbus imagined that the lands he had discovered were a part of India, while **Indian Isle,** New Zealand, and **Indian Bay** in Australia, are a curious proof that Cook regarded as Indians the dark-skinned natives of New Zealand and Australia.

Indiana, one of the United States, admitted in 1816, is a name which marks the progress of European settlement in the lands of the 'Red Indians,' the territory called Indiana having been purchased by the Union in 1795 from the native chiefs. It is one of the curiosities of nomenclature that the name of one of the United States should have to be explained by the Greek corruption of the Persian form of a Sanskrit word m aning a river. That this should be the case is ultimately due to the curious misconception of Columbus, who believed that the lands he had discovered were the Indies. In his letters he calls the natives Indians, and in this he was followed by all Spanish writers. The name Indian only gradually spread to the natives of North America. Early English writers call them the 'savages,' and it was not till the beginning of the seventeenth century, when it was recognise l that the English and Spanish colonies formed parts of the same continent, that the term Indian begins to be used for the natives of North America, who were also called **Americans,** as in the well-known line of Wesley's hymn, 'The dark Americans convert.' **Indianapolis,** the state capital of Indiana, is a barbarous hybrid compound of Sanskrit and Greek, manufactured in 1821 by the State legislature of Indiana.

Indispensable Strait, in the Salomon Islands, was first traversed in 1794 by the ship *Indispensable,* which also discovered the INDISPENSABLE REEF in the Coralline Sea, a perplexing name if its origin were not known.

Ingermanland, a district near St. Petersburg, was inhabited by the Finnic people called Ingerern. It is said to have formed the morning gift of Ingirgerd, a Swedish princess married in 1049 to King Jaroslaw.

Ingleborough, in the West Riding, was doubtless a border fortress of the Angles, overlooking on the west the unconquered kingdom of the Strath-Clyde Welsh. INGLEFIELD or ENGLEFIELD, in Berkshire, called in the Chronicle *Englafeld*, the 'plain of the Angles,' is a token of Anglian conquest in the Saxon domain of Wessex.

Inman River and INMAN HARBOUR, in Arctic America, and CAPE INMAN, in Fuegia, bear the name of Professor Inman, of the Royal Naval College at Portsmouth.

Innspruck, or INNSBRUCK, the capital of the Tyrol, is at the 'bridge over the Inn,' anciently called the *Aenus* or *Oenus*, a form preserved in OEN, the modern Romansch name of the river. (*See* ENGADINE.) According to Glück, the name was **Ainos*, from the Aryan root *i* or *ai*, 'to go,' seen in the Latin *i-re.*

Inscription, Point, in the Gulf of Carpentaria, was so called by Stokes in 1841 because he found inscribed on a tree the name of Flinders' ship, the *Investigator*, which must have been carved forty years before. In the same way, the CAP DE L'INSCRIPTION, on Dirk Hartog's Island, West Australia, was so called because in 1801 Captain Hamelin of *Le Naturaliste* found a tin plate, bearing records of the visit of Dirk Hartog's ship, the *Eendraght* (*q.v.*), in 1616, and of the *Geelvinck* (*q.v.*), in 1697.

Institut, Iles de L', a group of Australian islands, so named by Baudin in 1801, in recognition of the share taken by the French Institute in procuring the despatch of his expedition. The individual islands were named after the members of the Institute, a few of which, VOLTAIRE, CASSINI, and LACÉPÈDE still retain their places on the map.

Intercourse Islands, on the northwest coast of Australia, were so named by King in 1818, because the natives held friendly intercourse with his crew.

Interlaken, in Canton Bern, is a corruption of *Inter Lacus*, the Low-Latin name of a convent founded in 1130 between the lakes of Thun and Brienz. It is a sort of translation of UNTERSEEN, the name still borne by a neighbouring village.

Inverness, a Scotch county, takes its name from the county town of Inverness, 'at the mouth of the Ness.' (*See* NESS.) INVERARAY, the county town of Argyle, is at the 'mouth of the Aray' which drains Loch Awe. INVERURIE, a town in Aberdeenshire, is at the confluence of the Ury with the Don, and INVERNETHY is at the confluence of the Nethy with the Earn. The Scotch and Irish prefix *Inver-* is derived from the Gaelic *inbhir*, which denotes the mouth of a river. Inver sometimes becomes *Inner* in Scotland, and *Enner* in Ireland, as INNERPEFFRAY, INNERLEITHEN, or ENNEREILLY. Inver does not occur in Wales, where it is replaced by *Aber* (*q.v.*), which also prevails in the Brythonic parts of Scotland. INVERCARGILL, in New Zealand, is an absurd compound constructed out of the name of a Captain Cargill. (*See* DUNEDIN.)

Investigator Group, South Australia, was discovered in 1802 by Flinders, in the sloop *Investigator*. INVESTIGATOR ROAD, in the Gulf of Carpentaria, bears the name of the same vessel. INVESTIGATOR SOUND, in Arctic America, was so called after M'Clure's ship, the *Investigator*.

Iona is an island in the Hebrides where St. Columba established his first monastery. It is supposed that Iona is a ghost-name arising out of the misreading of *Iona* for *Ioua* (*Iova*), an adjectival form used by Adamnan. The island was also called *Hii*, *Ia*, and *I* (probably variants of *Iou*), which, though not found in modern Gaelic, is supposed to mean 'island,' Iona being also called ICOLMKIL (*I-cholum-cille*), usually translated the 'island of Columba's cell.'

Ionian Islands, off the western coast of Greece, were so called because situated in the *Mare Ionium*. Ionians, the oldest name of the Greeks, is the same word which appears as Javan, the son of Japheth, in the ethnographic table in Genesis, and as *Yavâna* in the Indian inscriptions of Asoka. Dodanim, the name of the Dorian tribes in Genesis, is an error for Rodanim, the men of Rhodes, due to the close resemblance of the letters *r* and *d* in the Hebrew alphabets.

Iowa, one of the United States, admitted in 1845, was so named from the Iowa River which traverses it. The Iowa River took its name from Iowa town, an Indian settlement on its banks, able to furnish 300 warriors of the tribe of the *Iowas* or *Otos*, called *Ayauways* by Lewis and Clarke. Iowa is a Dakota nickname said to mean the 'drowsy' or 'sleepy' ones. Kiowa (or Iowa), literally, 'this is the place,' is a term used for a camping spot. The French plural formation was *Ayavois*.

Iphigenia Rocks, in the Moluccas, were discovered in 1788 by Captain Douglas, in the ship *Iphigenia*.

Ipswich, Suffolk, A.S. *Gypeswic*, is at the junction of the River Gipping with the Orwell. Ipswich, in Massachusetts, the oldest settlement of the East Anglian Puritans, and the early rival of Boston, and Ipswich, the second town in Queensland, repeat the name of the Suffolk town.

Irawaddy (IRAWÁDI), the great Burmese River, is a corruption of *Airawati*, 'the water container,' or 'water possessor,' a name also given in the Indian mythology to Indra's elephant.

Ireland (A.S. *Íraland, Ýraland*, or *Irland*) was the Roman *Hibernia*, the Greek *Ierne*, and the Celtic *Erin*, which is from an oblique case of a nominative *Eriu* (gen. *erenn*, acc. *erinn*), Ireland being from *eire*, a later form of the nominative *eriu*. Professor Rhys supposes that *Eriu* may represent an older nominative **Iverjo*, the genitive of which would give the *Iuverna* of Juvenal, whence the Roman *Hibernia* and *Ivernii*, while the Greek *Ierne* has lost the *v*. The usual explanation of the name is from the Celtic *iar*, 'back,' 'behind,' and hence 'to the west,' while Professor Windisch thinks an initial *p* has disappeared, and that the name is cognate with the Greek *piōn*, the name referring to the fat, rich soil. More probably the name is pre-Celtic, perhaps Iberic. It has been conjectured that a pre-Aryan race, called Iverni, Ierni, or Erni, may have given their name to Ireland, as well as to LOCH ERNE in Ulster and to the RIVER EARN (*q.v.*) formerly the *Eirenn*, in Scotland.

Ireland's Eye, an island near Howth, is a translation of the old name *Innis Erenn*, 'the isle of Erin.' NEW IRELAND, in the South Pacific, so named by Cook, is separated from NEW BRITAIN by a strait to which he gave the name of ST. GEORGE'S CHANNEL.

Irharhar, a valley in the Algerian Sahara, is a Berber name meaning 'the River.'

Irkutsk, the capital of Eastern Siberia, was founded in 1661 on the River Irkut.

Iroquois, a County in Illinois, takes its name from the Iroquois River, which perpetuates the name of the great Iroquois nation. Most writers have adopted the explanation of Charlevoix, who considers the name to be a French adaptation from *hiro*, 'I have spoken,' the phrase with which the Iroquois close their speeches. But this is impossible, since the name Iroquois was known to Champlain before the French had come in contact with the Iroquois. Hewitt believes the word is Algonkin, from the Mohegan *irinako*, with the French suffix *-ois*, meaning 'those who are true snakes.' The word *irin* or *ilin* is common to most Algonkin tongues, and is found in the name of the *Linapi* or *Lenape* tribe (Delawares), the 'real men,' from *api*, 'men.' Hale, on the other hand, suggests, with greater probability, that Iroquois is from the verbal form *ierokua*, 'they who smoke,' *rokwa* being the theme of the noun *garokwa* or *karokwa*, a 'pipe.'

Isabela was a town founded by Columbus in 1493 on the northern coast of Haiti, but subsequently abandoned on account of its unhealthy site, the name being however retained by CAPE ISABELA, the northernmost point of the island. In honour of the Spanish Queen, Columbus, in 1492, had given the name Isabela to the fourth island he discovered, believed to be Crooked Island, one of the Bahamas.

Ischl, in the Austrian Salzkammergut, stands on a river of the same name.

Iseo, Lago d', one of the North Italian lakes, takes its name from Iseo, a small town on its eastern shore.

Isis, a name given to the Upper Thames, seems, like that of the Cam, to be merely a ghost-name evolved by conjectural ingenuity. The Thame being a tributary of the Thames, it was supposed that the Latin form *Tham-isis* must signify the united stream of the Thame and of an imaginary river Isis, which, however, is as old as the fourteenth century, since Higden speaks of Dorchester as *inter collapsus Thamæ et Ysæ sitam*.

Islands, Bay of, in New Zealand, was so named by Cook in 1769, from the numerous islands which shelter it. In 1778, Cook gave the same name to a bay in Alaska, which had been discovered by the Spaniards in 1775, and named by them *Bahia de los Remedios*, 'Reparation Bay.' In 1775, Cook called a bay in South Georgia the BAY of ISLES. ISLAND BAY, in New Zealand, contains a rocky island, as does ISLAND LAKE on the Saskatchewan.

Ismailia, the half-way station on the Suez Canal, was so named by de Lesseps in honour of the Khedive Ismail Pacha.

Isnik, near Brusa in Asia Minor, is the Turkish corruption of *Nicœa*, the capital of Bithynia, and the seat of the council which framed the Nicene Creed. The city was built by Lysimachus, and named after his wife Nicœa, a daughter of Antipater.

Ispahán, or ISFAHÁN, in Persia, is a corruption of the old name, the *Aspadana* of Ptolemy, which was either *açpadhane*, the 'horse enclosure,' or derived from the family name of the race of Feridun, the Athvîyan of romance, who in Pehlevi were called Aspiyân, 'horse lovers.' The local etymology explains the name of Isfahán as *Nisf-Jahan*, the 'half of the world.'

Isquawistequaannak-Kaastaki, 'where the women's skulls lie,' is the Cree name of an affluent of the Qu'appelle River, so called because the skulls of two squaws, killed by the Mandans, lay there a long time unburied.

Istria, an Austrian crownland, preserves the old name which may have suggested the curious belief of the Greek geographers that a branch of the Ister (Danube) here flowed into the sea.

Italy originally denoted the extreme southern portion of Calabria, merely the heel of the boot. In the fifth century B.C. the name was extended as far as Metapontum ; in the fourth it included Magna Græcia ; in the first century B.C. the Rubicon was the *finis Italiæ*, and the name was finally extended as far as the Alps. The oldest numismatic form is *Viteliu*, and the Sabine denarii (B.C. 90) have *Vitelu* for Italia. The name is believed to mean the 'land of cattle' (Latin *vitulus*, a 'calf').

Itamaraca, 'the sounding stone,' is the native name of an island near Pernambuco, probably derived from a bell, belonging either to a chapel or a wreck. ITA, a 'stone,' is a common component of Brazilian names. Thus ITAHAEM means the 'speaking stone,' from the echo from a cliff, ITACOATIARA is the 'coloured stone,' ITÁMIRINTIBA is the river of the 'round pebbles,' while ITACOLUMI, the 'stone with a son,' is a common name for the higher of two peaks of unequal size.

Ithaca, or THIAKI, one of the Ionian Islands, was probably a trading station of the Phœnicians ; the oldest form *Ityca*

being apparently to be identified with the Phœnician name UTICA.

Iviça, or IVIZA, more correctly IBIZA, is one of the Balearic islands. On Phœnician coins the group is called *Ibusim* or *Ibrusim*, which means the 'Islands of Pines,' while *Pityusœ*, the Greek translation of the Phœnician name, was used for the whole group, the older Phœnician name still adhering to Ibiza.

Ivory Coast, Guinea, is a name recalling the traffic in ivory which was commenced by the Portuguese in 1447.

Ivrea, in Piedmont, stands on the site of the Celto-Roman *Eporedia*, the 'horse course,' or place for training horses (Welsh *rhed*, a 'course').

Iztaccihuatl, or IXTACCIHUATL, the 'woman in white' (Aztec *iztac*, 'white,' and *cihuatl*, 'a woman '), is a snow-clad mountain in Mexico, near Popocateptl, 15,705 feet in height. The base of the mountain being invisible at a distance or in the dusk, the snow-clad ridge which forms the summit looks like the ghost of a white-robed woman lying on her back and floating in the air.

Jackson, the State capital of Mississippi, and more than 250 cities, counties, and townships, in the U.S.A. are named after General Andrew Jackson, the seventh president of the United States. PORT JACKSON, New South Wales, on whose shores the city of Sydney stands, was discovered by Cook on May 6th, 1770, and named after one of the secretaries to the Admiralty. JACKSON'S BAY, New Zealand, was named after an early settler, who owned a whaling establishment. JACKSON'S INLET, in Arctic America, was named by Parry in 1819 after Captain Samuel Jackson, R.N.

Jaen, a Spanish city, takes its name from the River Jaen on which it stands.

Jaffa or YAFA, in Palestine, was the ancient *Joppa* (Hebrew *Yapho*), a name which Gesenius thinks meant 'the beautiful,' while Movers explains it as 'the hill' or 'rising ground ' (Hebrew *nophe*).

Jahaz-garh, a fort east of Delhi, was built by George Thomas, an English sailor, who established himself in 1798 as Raja of Hansi, and built a fort, which from his own name he called *George-garh*. This became Jahaz-garh, 'ship fort,' the name George being perverted in popular parlance into *jahaz*, 'the ship,' in recollection of the Raja's origin.

Jaisalmer, capital of the Rajput State of

the same name, was founded by Ráwal Jaisal in 1156.

Jalapa or XALAPA in Mexico, whence the drug called *jalap*, is the Aztec *xalapan*, the 'sand beside the water,' from *xalli*, 'sand,' *atl*, 'water,' and *pan*, 'upon.'

Jam, a frontier district of Persia, perpetuates the name of a local poet. From his tomb comes the name of its chief town Jam, an abbreviation of *Tarbat-i-Sheikh-Jami*, 'the tomb of the Sheikh Jami.'

Jamaica was called by Columbus in 1494 *Santiago*, from St. James, the patron saint of Spain. As in other cases this has been replaced by the native name, *Xamayca*, *Xaimaca*, or *Yamaca*, which means 'abounding in springs,' from the numerous streams descending from the mountains.

James and Mary is the name of a well-known sandbank in the Hugli River below Calcutta, which has been fatal to many ships. The name was formerly explained by ingenious etymologists as an English corruption of the Hindi *jalmari*, ' dead water,' but recent research has discovered that a vessel called the ' Royal James and Mary' (*i.e.* James II. and Mary of Modena) was wrecked on this b ink on September 24th, 1694.

Jamestown, Virginia, was founded on May 13th, 1607, on the banks of the James River, under a charter granted to the Virginia Company by James I., whose name is also borne by JAMESTOWN, Barbado-s, founded in 1625. In JAMES' BAY, the great southern gulf of Hudson's Bay, Captain Thomas James in the *Maria* of Bristol, a seventy ton ship, was driven ashore, and wintered in 1631-1632.

Janeiro, Rio de, in Brazil, now usually called RIO (*q.v.*), was discovered by Amerigo Vespucci on the 1st January 1501.

Janina or YANINA, in Albania, is the 'town of St. John.' It is called *Ioannina* by Anna Comnena.

Jan Mayen Island, a stupendous and inaccessible volcanic cone, midway between Iceland and Spitzbergen, was discovered by Henry Hudson in 1607 on his return from the attempt to reach China by way of the North Pole, and called by him *Hudson's Tutches*. It now bears the name of Jan Mayen, a Dutch sailor, who rediscovered it in 1611, and called it by the name of his ship the *Esk*.

Japan is the English form of the Portuguese *Japão*, which is a corruption of the Chinese *Zhi-pan-kwe* (*Jih-pan-kwe* or *Je-puen kwe*), the 'kingdom of the sunrise,' literally the 'sun origin kingdom.'

In Marco Polo's travels the Chinese name is more correctly represented by *Zipan-gu*, *Cipango, Chipan-gu*, and *Jipan-ku*. The name NIPPON or NIPHON (*q.v.*), used by the Japanese for the largest island, is believed to be a variation of the same name.

Jardinillos are a group of cays on the south coast of Cuba in the BAIA DE LOS JARDINES. These names have been transferred from the group now called CAYOS DE LAS DOCE LEGUAS, 150 miles further east, which Columbus discovered on his third voyage, and named *Jardines de la Reyna*, 'the Gardens of the Queen.'

Jaroslav, a town on the Volga, bears the name of its founder.

Jarrow-on-Tyne, the site of Bæda's monastery, is called by Simeon of Durham *aet Gyrvum*, 'at the fens.' YARM, on the Tees, is a dialectical form of the same word, the oldest form (temp. Edward I.) being *Jarom*, and then *Yarom*. Peterborough, we are told by Bæda, was in the *Regio Gyrwiorum*, and in the ninth century the men of the fens were called the *North Gyrwa* and *South Gyrwa*.

Jassy, the capital of Moldavia, is believed to bear the name of a Dacian people who are called *Jassi* in a Roman inscription.

Jativa, or XATIVA, in the Spanish province of Valencia, is the *Sætabis* of Pliny.

Java is a name which exhibits the old *y* sound of the English *j*, and hence, with our modern pronunciation, ought to be written Yava. In the Ramáyana it is called *Yava dvipa*, the 'island of *yava*,' a word which means 'grain,' probably rice or millet. In an inscription of 762 A.D. the island is said to be ' excessively rich in grain and other seeds.' The name appears in Ptolemy as *Iabadiou nesos* (*Java-diu*), which he explains as meaning the 'isle of barley.' The Javanese call the island *Siti-Yawa*, 'the land of Yawa.'

Jazzi, Cima di, is one of the peaks of Monte Rosa. The Italian *cima* is believed to be an old Ligurian word meaning 'mountain' (*see* CIMIEZ), and *jaz* is a local dialect word denoting a small Alpine meadow.

Jedburgh, the county town of Roxburgh-shire, is an assimilated name, being a corruption of *Jedworth* or *Gedworth*, the *worth* or estate on the River Jed, a tributary of the Tweed.

Jefferson City, the State capital of Missouri (and 203 counties, townships, and rivers, chiefly in Arkansas, Indiana, Iowa, Missouri, Ohio, and Pennsylvania), are named after Thomas Jefferson, third President of the United States, 1801-1809.

Jelum (JHÍLAM), the most westerly of the five rivers of the Punjab, is so called from the city of Jhílam on its banks. Its real name is the BEHUT (BEHAT), a corruption of the old Sanskrit name *Vitastá*, the source of the Greek name *Bidaspes* or *Hydaspes*, as well as of Behat.

Jena, a German University, near which, in 1806, was fought the battle in which Prussia was brought under the heel of France, is believed to be a Slavonic name, meaning a 'clearing' in the forest.

Jensen's Nunatak is a peak in the interior of Greenland, ascended in 1878 by Captain Jensen, a Dane. *Nunatak* is the Eskimo name for peaks standing out from the inland ice-sheet.

Jersey, one of the Channel Islands, is usually explained as a corruption of *Cæsarea*, a very doubtful etymology. JERSEY CITY, opposite New York, is so called from being within the limits of the State of NEW JERSEY, so named in 1665 by Sir George Carteret, who had been Governor of the Isle of Jersey.

Jerusalem is the 'city of peace.' The earliest mention of the name is on one of the cuneiform tablets from Tel-el-Amarna, written in the reign of Khuenaten, on which it is called *U-ru-sa-lim*, the 'city of Salim,' the god of peace. The word *uru*, 'city,' is the Assyrian *âlu*, Accadian *eri*. On this tablet it is called the city of the god Marruv, 'the lord,' whence the name of MOUNT MORIAH. Marruv or Salim is identified with the Babylonian god Uras, whose name became Ares among the Greeks. On one of these tablets, Ebed-tob, the priest-king of Jerusalem, a successor of Melchizedek, says that he had been appointed to his office by the oracle of the god Salim, whose temple stood on Mount Moriah.

João da Nova was an early Portuguese navigator, who gave his name to the ILHA DE JOÃO DA NOVA, in the Mozambique Channel.

Johannes, Ilha de, the great island in the delta of the Amazon River (known also by its native name *Marajó*), was named in honour of John IV., king of Portugal.

Joliet, a town in Illinois, commemorates the French explorer who in 1673 was the first to penetrate into this region.

Jones' Sound, at the head of Baffin's Bay, was discovered by Baffin in 1616, and named after Alderman Sir Francis Jones, one of the four London merchants who equipped the *Discovery* for Baffin's fifth and most important voyage. (*See* BAFFIN.)

Jordan River, the chief affluent of the Great Salt Lake in Utah, was so named by the Mormons after the great affluent of the Dead Sea, the Great Salt Lake of the Eastern Land of Promise. JORDAN means the 'rusher' or 'descender,' an appropriate name, as it descends 610 feet in its short course from the Sea of Galilee. It is now called by the Arabs either *Sheriat-el-Kebir*, the river of 'the great ford,' or 'great watering place,' or simply *Esh Sheriah*, the river of 'the ford.' In 1606 the Spaniards gave the name JORDAN to a river near Vera Cruz, and it has also been given to a river in Nova Scotia. JORDAN, HEBRON, and NAIN are among the Biblical names given by the Moravian brethren to their missionary stations in Labrador.

Jorge Grego, a Brazilian island near San Paulo, bears the name of an early Portuguese settler.

Jotun-fjeldene, apparently a pseudo-antique name invented for the loftiest range in Norway, would mean 'giant mountains.'

Juan de Fuca, the strait which separates Vancouver Island from the territory of the United States, was discovered in 1592 by a Spaniard, whose name it bears.

Juan Fernandez, an island in the South Pacific, off the coast of Chili, bears the name of its discoverer, a Spanish pilot, who, in 1563, fell in with it on a voyage from Lima to Chili, and stocked it with goats and pigs. It is also called MAS-A-TIERRA, 'more to land,' in contradistinction to another island, twenty miles further west, which is called MAS-AFUERA, 'more out.' The island of Juan Fernandez was for four years and four months the residence of Alexander Selkirk ('I am monarch of all I survey'), son of a Fifeshire shoemaker, who, having been summoned before the kirk-session for disorderly behaviour in church, ran away to sea. In October 1704 he had a dispute with Captain Stradling of the ship *Cinque Ports*, and at his own request was put ashore on the uninhabited island, from which he was taken off in 1709. His adventures are supposed to have suggested to De Foe the tale of *Robinson Crusoe*.

Jouare in the Seine et Marne, and ALAJOU in the Hérault, are believed to be corruptions of *Ara Jovis.*

Jug, a large tributary of the Dwina, is the Finnic *jögi* or *joki*, 'river,' of which we have a fragment in the name of the Pinega and other Russian rivers. (*See* LADOGA.)

Juggernaut (JAGGANÁTHA or JAGGÁ-NÁTHPUR) is a popular name given to Puri, the 'city,' on the Orissa coast, which contains a temple of Jagganátha, the 'Lord of the world' (*jagat*, 'the world,' and *nátha*, 'lord'), a title of Vishnu.

Jülich (French JULIERS), in Rhenish Prussia, is called *Juliacus* by Ammianus Marcellinus (fourth century). There is no reason for believing, as usually affirmed, that it was founded by Julius Cæsar. More probably it was the estate or *fundus* of some obscure Julius, who had assumed the name of the Julian gens. There are in France twenty - seven village names which may be thus explained, such as JUILLAC, JUILLÉ, JUILLEY, JULLIÉ, and JULLY.

Jumna, the *Jomanes* of Pliny, an Indian river which joins the Ganges at Allahabad, is the English form of the Indian *Jamuna* or *Yamuna*. In the Hindu mythology Yamuna was the daughter of Surya, 'the sun,' and the sister of Yama.

Junagarh, or JHUNAGARH, the capital of Káthiáwár in Gujarát, means, according to the popular etymology, the 'old fort,' but is believed to be an interesting memorial of the Greek dominion in India, the old name *Yavana-garh* meaning the fortress (*garh*) of the Greeks; *yavana* being the Indian corruption of Ionian, the name by which the Greeks were known in India.

Jungfrau, the 'virgin,' is a peak in the Bernese Alps, clad in a robe of spotless snow.

Junquera, a Spanish city near Gerona, was the Roman *Campus Juncarius*, the 'plain of rushes.' From the Low - Latin *Juncariæ* we have some fourteen French village names, such as JONQUIÈRES (Vaucluse), JONCHAIRE, and JONCHERY.

Jura, a limestone range in Western Switzerland, the *Mons Jura* of Cæsar, is believed to be a name of Celtic origin, meaning 'forest.' In Western Switzerland medieval records constantly employ the word *joria, jura*, or *dzoura* to denote woodlands, and this has become *Joux* in modern French, as in PRÉ DE JOUX, while in the local patois of Western Switzerland the words *jour, jeur, jure*, and *joux* signify 'forest.' It is possibly the same word as the Gaelic *doire*, an 'oak wood,' from which we have DERRY and many other names. JURA, one of the Hebrides, is called *Doirad Eilinn* in the Annals of Ulster. The Gaels seem to have taken it to mean the 'island of oaks,' and the Norsemen as 'deer-island.'

Jutland, the name of the Cimbric Chersonese, is 'the land of the Jutes' (*Iótas* or *Iútas*), the *Juti* of Latin writers.

Kabul, or CABUL, the capital of Afghanistan, is, according to Spiegel, a Persian name, meaning a 'warehouse,' or place for the deposit of merchandise.

Kabylia, in Algeria, is the district inhabited by the KABYLES, an Arabic name meaning the 'tribes' or 'confederates.'

Kadem means a 'foot' in Arabic. According to the Moslem legend the village of AL-KADEM, south of Damascus, was so called because here Mohammed halted without entering the city.

Kades, a mound on the Orontes, preserves the name of the Hittite capital of *Kadesh*, 'the sanctuary.' The battle of Kadesh is repeatedly depicted on the monuments of Rameses II., and is the subject of the poem of Pentaur, the great Egyptian Epic. Other sacred places, such as Kadesh Naphtali, the holy place of that great tribe, bear the same name. 'AIN QADIS, the one large and fertile oasis in the desert of the Wandering, with a plentiful perennial spring, represents *Kadesh Barnea*, where the Israelites halted for thirty-eight years of their wanderings in the wilderness. The modern Arabic name of Jerusalem is *El Kuds*, 'the holy.'

Káfiristán, in Central Asia, the 'land of the Infidels,' is a Perso-Arabic name given by the Iranian Moslems to the district inhabited by the pagan tribes of the Hindu Kush, who are also called SIAH-POSH or 'black-robed' Kafirs. The word Caffre is the Arabic *Káfir* (plural *kofra*), 'infidel' or 'unbeliever' in Islam, a name which skirts the zone of Moslem conquest, much as the word WELSH or 'foreigners' encircles the region of Teutonic occupancy. The name Kafir was applied to the Papuas of New Guinea, who were sold for slaves in the Philippine Islands. CAFFRARIA or KAFFRARIA in the Cape Colony, is the 'land of the Kafirs' or unbelievers, a name given by the Swaheli Moslems to the neighbouring Bantu races.

Kaisariyeh, between Acre and Jaffa, preserves the name of the Roman capital of Palestine, built by Herod the Great, who called it *Cæsarea* in honour of Augustus Cæsar. Another KAISARÍYEH, in Asia Minor, represents *Cæsarea*, the name given to the capital of Cappadocia by Tiberius Cæsar when he made it a Roman province. From the German

Kaiser (Cæsar) we have many names, such as KAISERSWERTH, the 'Kaiser's Island,' formerly *Warida*, the 'island'; KAISERBERG, in Elsass, the 'emperor's hill'; or KAISERSLAUTERN, in Bavaria, so called from an imperial palace on the River Lauter.

Kalgan, the frontier emporium between China and Asiatic Russia, is a Tartar word meaning the 'gate.'

Kali-hari, a great South African desert, is believed to bear a name identical in meaning with that of the KARRI-KARRI desert further to the south-east, signifying 'painful' or 'tormenting.' The GREAT KARROO, an arid plateau, baked hard in the dry season, is from the Hottentot word *karroo*, 'hard.'

Kalmuck Steppe, north of the Caucasus, is the plain inhabited by the Kalmaks, a tribe of Mongolian nomads, who, according to their tradition, 'remained behind' when Jingiz Khan marched westward (Tatar *khâlmak*, 'to stay behind ').

Kalopotamo, a stream near Trebizond, preserves its old Greek appellation of the 'beautiful river.' KALOSCOPI, the 'fair view,' is the modern Greek name of the hill on which Elis stood.

Kaltbad, the 'cold bath' on the Rigi, obtains its name from a spring whose temperature is 41° Fahrenheit.

Kama, a great affluent of the Volga, and KEMI, a large river in Finland, are Finnic names meaning the 'river' (Wotiak, *kam*; Koibal, *kem*; Suomi, *kemi*), whence also the name of the KUMA, which drains the Northern flank of the Caucasus. The Nogai Tartars call it the Kuman, pronounced Kubin by the Abassians, whence the corrupt Russian form, KUBAN.

Kamtchatka was originally the name not of the whole peninsula, now so called, but only of the central valley, and of the river which flows through it. The Kamtchadals call themselves ITALME, which means the 'inhabitants.' The names *Kamtcha-tka* and *Kamtcha-dal* are supposed to be from *kamsha*, a 'man' (*homo*). According to a tradition *Kamtchat-ka* and *Kamtchad-al* are names of Cossack origin, derived from the name of *Kontshat*, a native chief.

Kanakas, 'the men,' is a name given to natives of the Sandwich Islands.

Kandahar, or CANDAHAR, the largest city in Afghanistan, is supposed to have been one of the military colonies called Alexandria, which were founded by Alexander the Great, the Eastern form of whose name is *Scandar* or *Iskandar*. Colonel Yule, however, thinks it was most probably a name transferred from the Indian people who were called *Gandhara*.

Kandy (KÁNDÍ), formerly spelt CANDY, became the capital of Ceylon in 1592. The name is believed to be a Portuguese corruption of a native word meaning the 'hill' or the 'hills.' The inhabitants call it *Mahá-nuvera*, the 'great city,' or simply *Nura*, the 'town.'

Kane's Sea, north of Smith's Sound, was discovered by Dr. Kane, an American explorer.

Kangaroo Island, off the coast of South Australia, was so named by Flinders in 1802 on account of a seasonable supply of Kangaroo meat obtained by his crew, 'after four months' deprivation from almost any fresh provisions.' The WALLABY ISLANDS, were so named by Stokes from a small species of Kangaroo, called *Wallaby* by the natives, which he found there in great numbers.

Kansas, one of the United States, admitted in 1858, is watered by the Kansas or Kaws River, which like the Arkansas River (*q.v.*) bears the name of the Akansea, Ka(n)se, or Kaws tribe, a branch of the Sioux. KANSAS CITY stands at the junction of the Kansas River and the Missouri.

Karapiti, a crater in New Zealand, means 'round shaped' in Maori.

Kara Sea, south of Novaya Zemlya, is so called from the small river KARA, which here divides Europe from Asia (Samoyedic *kar*, the 'east ').

Karl XII. Island, north-east of Spitzbergen, was discovered in 1861 by Nordenskiöld's Swedish expedition, and named after 'the madman of the north.'

Kasan, the old Tartar capital on the Volga, is a Tartar name signifying a 'hollow,' literally a 'kettle.'

Kasimoff, a Russian town on the Oka, bears the name of Kasim, a Tartar prince to whom it was given about 1452 by Basil the Dark.

Kater Isle and CAPE KATER, in Baffin's Bay, are among the names given in recognition of Captain Henry Kater's improvements in scientific instruments, especially the pendulum and the compass.

Káthiáwár, a district in Gujarát, is the 'country of the Káthi,' the people of Kach (Cutch) by whom it was overrun in the thirteenth and fourteenth centuries.

The RUNN OF CUTCH is the designation of the sandflats and salt wastes, often covered by high tides, which extend between the peninsula of Cutch and the mainland. Runn (Ran) is a corruption of the Sanskrit *irina*, a 'salt swamp' or 'desert.'

Káthmándú (*Káshthamandapa*), the capital of Nepal, takes its name, which signifies a 'wooden edifice,' from a building near the palace erected in 1598 to accommodate religious mendicants.

Kattegat, between Sweden and Denmark, mistranslated *Trou de Chat* in French, is the 'ship-passage' (*kati*, a 'boat' or 'ship,' and *gata*, a 'gate' or 'passage').

Katunga, formerly the capital of Yoruba in Western Africa, signifies the 'wall' or 'building.'

Kaumayet, 'the shining,' is the Eskimo name of a mountain range in Labrador.

Kavah-Upas, the 'poisonous crater,' a volcano in Java, is so called from its sulphurous fumes.

Káveri or **Cauvery** (Tamil *Kávira*), a large river in Southern India, is possibly from the Dravidian *kavi*, 'red ochre,' and *eri*, a 'river' or 'sheet of water,' the river in flood assuming a reddish hue. It is more probably the Tamil *ka-viri*, 'grove developer' (*ka*, a 'grove'), the river being fringed by forest.

Kaye's Island, off the north-west coast of America, was named by Cook in 1778 in compliment to Dr. Kaye, afterwards Bishop of Lincoln.

Kazbec, one of the loftiest peaks in the Caucasus, 16,532 feet in height, takes its name from a village of the same name at its foot. It is called *Mquinwari*, the 'ice mountain,' by the Georgians, and *Ursschoek*, the 'white mountain,' by the Ossetes.

Keats, Port, in Western Australia, and POINT KEATS, in Arctic America, were named after Admiral Sir R. G. Keats.

K'edela, the 'wall,' is the Georgian name of a precipitous snow mountain in the Caucasus.

Keeling Islands, a group in the Indian Ocean, 600 miles south of Sumatra, were discovered in 1609 by William Keeling on his way home from the Moluccas.

Kelát, KHELAT, or KALAT, the capital of Belúchistan, which gives a name to the state of Kelát, is an Arabic word meaning a 'castle' or 'fort.' The terminal *t* is only pronounced when the word is the first part of a compound name, as in CALAT-AYUD (*q.v.*). Kelát must therefore mean 'Castle of Nasir Khan,' the last part of the name having been dropped. KELÁT-I-NADIRI, the 'fort of Nadir Shah,' is a natural fortress in the North of Persia, 60 miles in circuit, and defended by a parapet of naked vertical rock, 700 to 1000 feet in height, where Nadir Shah deposited the spoils of India and the treasures of the Great Moghul. We have the same word in many Spanish and Sicilian names, such as ALCALA and CALTANISETTA, and also in GALATA, a suburb of Constantinople, and in KALEDAGH, 'castle hill,' and KALEDERESSI, 'castle valley,' in Asia Minor. GELÄA, in Kabylia, is a natural fortress surrounded by ravines and scarped precipices.

Kelephina, the 'murderous,' is the modern Greek name of a river near Sparta, by whose sudden floods cattle are often drowned.

Kells, in Meath, is a corruption of *Kenlis*, of which Headfort, the English translation, gives a title to an Irish marquisate.

Kelso, Roxburghshire, was called in the twelfth century *Calkou*, the 'chalk hill,' a calcareous hill near the town being still called the Chalk Heugh.

Kempland, south of Kerguelen Land, bears the name of the captain of a whaling vessel who discovered it in 1833. CAPE KEMPE in Fuegia was named after one of Fitzroy's officers.

Kempten, in Bavaria, is the Roman *Campodunum*. Another KEMPTEN, near Bingen, was called in the eighth century *Chamunder Marca*, plainly a tribal name.

Kendal, properly KIRKBY IN KENDAL, stands in the dale of the River Kent or Ken, but KENDAL in Yorkshire is *Cheldal* in Domesday, meaning the dale with a spring or well (*kelda*).

Kendall Islands and CAPE KENDALL in Arctic America, bear the name of an officer in Franklin's second expedition.

Kendeng, a common name in Java, signifies a 'mountain range.' KARANG, a mountain in Java, means 'rock' in Malay.

Kenilworth, in Warwickshire, is called in a charter *Cinildewyrth*, which would mean the 'estate of Cynehild,' a female name. It is said to have been a manor of Cenwulf, king of the Mercians, but this seems to be merely an etymological guess.

Kennedy Channel, the northern continuation of Smith's Sound, was discovered by Kane in 1853, and named after

J. P. Kennedy, one of his predecessors in Arctic exploration. KENNEDY ISLAND, LAKE KENNEDY, KENNEDY RANGE, and KENNEDY RIVER, bear the name of E. B. Kennedy, an Australian explorer. KENNEDY RIVER, LAKE KENNEDY, and KENNEDY RANGE in Vancouver's Island, bear the name of a Governor of the colony.

Kenn's Reef, between New Guinea and Australia, was discovered in 1827 by Alexander Kenn, in the merchant ship *William Shand.*

Kenobin, a convent in the Lebanon in which the Maronite patriarch resides, is a corruption of the Greek *Coenobion.*

Kensington, Middlesex, (Domesday, *Chenesitun*) is probably from the proper name *Cynesige.*

Kent is a name the meaning of which has been much discussed, but without any very definite result. The Roman name was *Cantium*, and the British name, as we are told by the Welsh writers, was *Chent* or *Ceint*. According to Owen Pughe *caint* was a Welsh word meaning a plain, field, or open country, which would well describe the woodless wolds of the chalk downs, as distinguished from the great forest of Anderida, now known as the Weald of Kent. The Romans may easily have made Caint into Cantium. On the other hand, Ptolemy apparently employs the name *Kantion* for the North Foreland ; hence it has been supposed that the Cymric name was a misunderstood form of a Gaelic *Ceann-tir*, the 'head of the land.' Professor Rhys, with more reason, explains *Cant-ium* from the Welsh *cant*, a 'rim' or 'margin.' According to another theory Cantium became known to the Romans through the Teutonic tribes at the mouth of the Scheldt, in whose Frisian speech *Kant* meant a 'cliff' (*See* HELIGOLAND), and Mr. Wedgewood compares the name with the Danish *Kant*, which means the 'sea-coast.' Mr. Stokes suggests an explanation from the British *cant*, 'bright,' a word cognate with the Latin *candidus*, and in like manner Esser explains the name as referring to the 'white' chalk cliffs of the South Foreland. NORTH KENT, DUKE OF KENT'S BAY, DUCHESS OF KENT'S RANGE, and PRINCE EDWARD'S CAPE, all in Arctic America, were named in honour of the parents of Queen Victoria. KENT'S GROUP in Bass Strait, was named by Flinders in 1798 after his friend Captain William Kent,

and CAPE JAMES KENT, in Kane's Sea, was named by Kane after a friend.

Kentish Town, a London suburb, was so called from the prebendal manor of Cantlers or Kantelowes, on which it was built. (*See* CAMDEN TOWN.)

Kentucky, one of the United States, admitted in 1792, bears an Iroquois name, *Kahenta-ke* 'where plains are,' *-ke* being the locative suffix, and *Kahenta* being contracted to *Kenta*, which we have in Quinté Canada. This is better than the old explanation ' bloody ground,' from tribal conflicts.

Keppel's Isle, one of the Friendly Islands, discovered by Wallis in 1767, KEPPEL'S ISLAND, one of the Queen Charlotte Group, KEPPEL'S ISLANDS and KEPPEL'S BAY in Queensland, discovered by Cook in 1770, were all named in honour of Admiral Lord Keppel.

Kerak, 'the fortress,' a stronghold of the Crusaders near the Dead Sea, was the castle of Renaud of Chatillon, slain by Saladin. It occupied the site of the Biblical Kir-Moab, the 'fortress of Moab.' The name Kerak (Syriac *karkâ*, a 'fortress') is as old as the time of the Maccabees. Being the chief place in the land of Moab, it gives names to the Wady and the district of Kerak. In Asiatic Turkey, 140 miles north of Bagdad, we have a similar name, KERKUK, a corruption of *Karkâ d' Beth Slok*, 'the fortress of the house of Seleucia.'

Kerguelen Land, an Antarctic Island, was discovered by the French navigator Kerguelen in 1772. Till proved by Cook to be an island it was supposed to be a part of the hypothetical Antarctic continent.

Kermadec Islands, north of New Zealand, were discovered in 1793 by d'Entrecasteaux, and named after one of his officers.

Kern River and KERN LAKE, in California, were named in 1846 after one of Fremont's companions, killed in 1853 by the Utah Indians.

Kerry, an Irish county, is, like Dorset or Essex, a tribal rather than a territorial name. The old form was *Ciar-raidhe*, the tribe or 'race of Ciar,' who, according to Irish tradition, was a son of Fergus, king of Ulster.

Kersers, a village in Freiburg, is a corruption of the Latin name *Ad Carceres.*

Kertch, Straits of, connecting the Black Sea and the Sea of Azov, are so called from the town of Kertch (Russian

L

K'rtcheff), which is probably a corruption of the descriptive Genoese name *Cerchio*, ' the circle ' or ' round.'

Késmark, in Hungary, originally one of the Saxon settlements, is believed to be a corruption of the German *Käsemarkt,* ' cheese market.' In medieval Latin documents it appears by the translated name *Forum Caseorum.*

Kesteven is one of the ridings or ' parts ' of Lincolnshire. It includes the steep limestone range locally called ' The Cliff.' The A.S. name *Ceostefne* is unexplained, but the Domesday form, *Chetsteven*, supports a conjecture of Mr. Bradley that the first element in the name may be the Celtic *coed*, a ' wood,' the district having been densely wooded before the Norman Conquest, in which case *steven* might mean ' dense' (Welsh *ystyfnig*, ' stubborn ').

Key West, one of the Florida Keys, a low coral island, is a curious English assimilation of the Spanish name *Cayo Hueso*, ' bone reef,' so called because of a quantity of bones, supposed to be those of the aborigines, found there by the Spaniards. From the Spanish *cayo*, a ' shoal ' or ' reef,' we have RUM CAY, SALT CAY, SAND CAY, and the other numerous Cays or Keys in the West Indies, as well as the Pacific Islands called KÉ or KI. (*See* CAYO.)

Khalkha, or CHALCHA, which means ' the frontier,' is the Mongolian name of the district contiguous to the great Wall of China.

Khartum, in Nubia, at the confluence of the Blue and the White Nile, was founded in 1823 by Mohammed Ali on a spit of land called from its shape *Ras el-Khartum*, ' the cape (*ras*) of the elephant's trunk ' (*khartum*).

Kherson, or CHERSON, a town near the mouth of the Dnieper, was founded in 1778, and so named because it was erroneously supposed that the site was that of the old Greek city of *Chersonesus Heracleotica*, founded by the Dorians of Heraclea in the Tauric Chersonesus.

Khiva, a town of Central Asia in an oasis in the desert, was formerly called *Khaivak*, a name explained by Vambéry from the Turkic word *khavak*, ' dry,' applied to the steppe by which it is approached.

Khorásan, or KHORÁSSAN, the 'land of the sun,' now the north-east province of Persia, was so called because it formed the eastern quarter of the four parts into which the Sassanian monarchy was divided.

Khotan, a town in Eastern Turkestan, is believed to be a corruption of *Ku-stana,* a ' nipple,' or ' teat,' an Aryan name referring to the shape of the hill on which it stands.

Khyber (KHÁIBAR), a pass through the Khaibar hills, leads from Peshawar to Cabul. The hills and the pass are so called from the village of Haibar or Khaibar.

Kiachta, the frontier town on the trade route between Russia and China, stands on the River Kiachta, a name derived from the Mongolian word for a grass (*Triticum repens*), which affords excellent fodder for the transport animals.

Kiang-nan, a Chinese province, means ' south of the river ' (*kiang*). So KIANG-PEH is the province ' north of the river,' and KIANG-SI that ' west of the river.' The name of the province of KIANG-SU means ' abundance of rivers,' inasmuch as it is watered by the two great rivers, the HOANG-HO or ' yellow river,' and the YANG-TSI, the ' son of the ocean,' also called YANG-TSI-KIANG, whose lower course goes by the name of TA-KIANG, or ' great river,' being the largest river in China. The western arm of the Canton River is called SI-KIANG, ' west river,' the northern arm is the PE-KIANG, ' north river,' and the eastern arm is the TONG-KIANG, ' east river,' all joining the TA-KIANG or ' great river,' which forms the main stream. The TSIN-KIANG is the ' clear river,' the KIN-KIANG is the ' golden river,' and the HOANG-KIANG in Tonquin is the ' yellow river.'

Kicking-Horse Pass, which crosses the Rocky Mountains in Lat. 51° N., is so called from the KICKING-HORSE RIVER, in crossing which the geologist Hector received a kick in the chest which laid him up for several days.

Kidderminster, Worcestershire (A.S. *Chider-minster*), was the minster built by Earl Cynebert on the brow or cliff above the Stour. It is commonly alleged, but without due authority, that there was a British word *chedder*, meaning a ' cliff,' which we have in the name of the CHEDDER HILLS, Somerset, whence the name of Chedder cheese.

Kidnappers, Cape, at the southern extremity of Hawke's Bay, New Zealand, was so called by Cook, in 1769, because a boy who had been brought from the Society Islands was kidnapped by the Maoris, who, however, were so frightened by the discharge of a gun, that the boy managed to escape by swimming.

Kiel, 'the bay,' in the province of Schleswig Holstein, is the great arsenal of the German fleet (Dutch *kiel*, a 'bay,' Norwegian *kil*, a 'small bay,' O.N. *kill*, a 'channel').

Kieng-Kei, the 'district of the Court,' the chief province of Corea, contains the capital SEOUL, KIENG, or KIENG-KEI-TAO, which is the permanent residence of the Court. (*See* PEKING.)

Kiglapait, the 'great saw teeth,' is the Eskimo name of a serrated mountain range in Labrador. KIKKERTARSOAK, 'great island,' is the Eskimo name of an island on the Greenland coast.

Kil or **Kel** means 'people' or 'tribe' in Berber, as in KIL-TAMAR, the 'people of Tamar,' KEL-OWI, the 'people of Owi,' KEL-ULLI, the 'goat-herds' or 'people of the goats.'

Kildare, an Irish county, takes its name from the county town Kildare, a corruption of *Cill-dara*, the 'cell of the oak,' under whose boughs, according to the legend, St. Brigit constructed her cell. KILKENNY, another Irish county, takes its name from the town of Kilkenny, the 'church of St. Cainnech' (517-598), abbot of Aghabo, Queen's County. KILLARNEY, in Kerry, is a corruption of *Cill-earneadh*, the 'church of the sloes.' KILLALOE is *Cill-dalua*, the 'church of St. Lua' or Dalua. KILBRIDE is the name of thirty-five Irish parishes, from churches dedicated to St. Brigit, and KILMUREY of fifty dedicated to St. Mary. KILMAINHAM, the site of a large prison near Dublin, is the 'church of St. Maighnenn,' who was abbot in the seventh century. The name has acquired by assimilation the English ending -*ham*. We have a curious corruption in CLOSEBURN, Dumfriesshire, which appears in 1200 as *Kylosbern*, the 'cell of St. Osbern,' and in KILLAMARSH, Derbyshire, which is 'Cynewold's marsh.' Nor can KILBURN, *Middlesex*, be the 'stream by the cell,' as the Benedictine nunnery founded in the reign of Henry I. was at first called *Cuneburn*, or *Keneburn*, which only became Kilburn in the thirteenth century. Though there are some 2700 Irish names with the prefix *kil-*, which means either 'church' or 'monastic cell,' yet since the Latin *cella* does not seem to have become an English loan word before the thirteenth century, we must distrust the tradition that the cell of Robert de Alneto, which in 1138 was converted into a Cistercian Abbey, gave a name to KILBURN in Yorkshire, which probably means 'the cold burn.'

Kilima is a common East African mountain name, which we have in KILIMA-NJARO or KILIMA-NDJARO, a mountain 22,000 feet high, Ndjaro being the name of a demon believed to bring cold. The Wa-kilima or Wa-kirima tribe are 'the mountaineers.' (*See* QUILIMANI.)

Killersoak, 'the great wound' or 'hurt,' an island off the coast of Labrador, was, according to tradition, the scene of a bloody struggle between the Eskimos and the Red Men.

Kim-Bandi, 'the land of pots,' is a clayey district in Benguela to which neighbouring tribes resort for pottery.

Kimberley, in South Africa, was named after Lord Kimberley, Colonial Secretary.

Kimbolton, Hunts, called *Kynebauton* in 1276, is probably the *tún* of Cynebald. It stands on a river now called the Kym, a name seemingly an antiquarian fiction evolved out of Kimbolton. CHILBOLTON, in Hants, also apparently a southern occurrence of the northern form *bolton*, is *Ceolbaldington* in a charter, evidently from a personal name.

Kinchinjanja, one of the loftiest summits of the Himalaya, 28,156 feet in height, is a Tibetan name meaning 'the five treasuries of the lofty snow,' so called from the five great snowfields which surround the peak.

Kinderton, near Middlewich in Cheshire, is a corruption of the Celtic name *Condate*, a word meaning a 'confluence,' of which various places in France called CONDÉ (*q.v.*) are obvious corruptions. We learn from the Antonine Itinerary that the Roman station of *Condate* was twenty miles from *Deva* (Chester), and eighteen from *Mancunium* (Manchester). At Kinderton there is a Roman camp; it is twenty miles from Chester and nineteen from Manchester, and is at the confluence of the Dane and the Weaver. But CONGLETON, frequently identified with *Condate*, is thirty-one miles from Manchester, and the Domesday form *Cogletone* suggests that Congleton may have been a *tun* surrounded by a fence built of 'coggles' or pebbles, the *n* being intrusive and merely euphonic.

King's County and QUEEN'S COUNTY formed the territory of the O'Mores, the O'Connors, and the O'Carrolls, which was forfeited in Elizabeth's reign. The western district was constituted into a shire in 1557, and called King's County by Queen Mary, in honour of her husband King Philip, the assize town being called

PHILIPSTOWN, the eastern district, with Maryborough for its county town, being named Queen's County (*q.v.*).

Kings, The Three, three small islands at the northern extremity of New Zealand, were discovered by Tasman on January 6th, 1643, the festival of the three kings, which we call the Epiphany.

Kingston is the name of twenty-two places in England, and KINGTON of nine, several of which appear in charters as *Cyningestún*, *Cingestún*, *Cyngtún*, or *Kingtún*, all denoting royal manors. KINGSTON-ON-THAMES was a royal demesne, where seven kings, from Edwin in 901 to Ethelred in 978 were crowned. It is usually asserted that the name is Kings-stone, referring to the ancient coronation stone, still preserved in the centre of the town, but this is disproved by the A.S. name *Cyninges tún*. KINGSTON, at the outlet of Lake Ontario, was so named in honour of George II. when Canada was taken by the English. It was previously called Fort Frontenac, from the Comte de Frontenac who had improved its defences. KINGSTON, the capital of Jamaica, was founded after the destruction of Port Royal by an earthquake in 1692, and was named in compliment to William III. KINGSTON, New York, settled in 1665, was named in compliment to Charles II. The capital of the island of St. Vincent also bears the name of KINGSTOWN. KINGSTOWN, the mail packet station for Dublin, was formerly called Dunleary, but was renamed Kingstown in compliment to George IV. when he embarked here for England after his visit to Ireland in 1821. KINGSGATE, in the Isle of Thanet, was a name given to commemorate the spot where Charles II. landed on his return from exile. KINGSCLERE, Hants, was a residence of the kings of Wessex, the suffix -*clere*. which we have in BURGHCLERE, HIGHCLERE, and a few other names, signifying, it is supposed, a palace. KINGSBURY, close to Houghton Regis, is supposed to mark the site of the palace built by Henry I. near Dunstable.

King Sound and KING'S COVE, North Australia, CAPE KING in the South Shetlands, and POINT KING, near the mouth of the Mackenzie River, bear the name of Captain P. P. King, who surveyed the Australian coasts between 1818 and 1822. KING ISLAND, at the mouth of the Great Fish River, bears the name of Richard King, who took part in Back's expedition. KING'S ISLAND, in Bass Strait, and KING'S ISLAND, New Caledonia, bear the name of Philip Gidley King, Governor of New South Wales, 1800-1806. KING'S ISLAND in the Bering Sea, discovered in 1778, bears the name of James King, one of Cook's officers.

Kintbury, Berks, (A.S. *Cynetan byrig*) as well as KENNET in Wilts, take their names from the River Kennet (A.S. *Cynete*) on which they stand.

Kintyre or CANTIRE, the great peninsula in Argyll, is from the Gaelic *ceann-tir*, the 'head of the land.' In Scotch and Irish names *ceann* (nom.) or *cinn* (dat.), 'a head,' corresponding to the Welsh *pen*, is a common element. KINCARDINE, near the head of the Firth of Forth, is the Gaelic *cinn gairdein*, 'head of the arm' or inlet of the sea. KINTAIL, which stands at the head of Loch Duich, a sea loch, has the same signification, being from the Gaelic *ceann-t-saile*, the 'head of the brine' or salt water, and KINSALE, in County Cork, means the same. KENMARE, in Kerry, is *ceann-mara*, the 'head of the sea.' It is the highest point in a long sea loch to which the tide reaches. KINLOCH, the 'head of the loch,' is the name of several places at the upper end of Scotch lochs, as KINLOCH RANNOCH and KINLOCH ARD, at the heads of Loch Rannoch and Loch Ard. KENMORE is *ceann-mòr*, the 'great head'; KINNAIRD is the 'head of the height'; KINGUSSIE, the 'head of the firwood'; KINROSS, which gives its name to a Scotch county, is the 'head of the wood,' and KANTURK, in County Cork, was anciently *ceann-tuirc*, the 'boar's head.'

Kirghiz Steppe, in Central Asia, is inhabited by the Kirghiz Hordes. The Kirghiz are the 'Steppe rangers,' from *kir*, 'desert,' and *ghiz*, 'rangers.' Horde is the English corruption of *ordu* or *urdu*, a 'camp.' The Kara Kirghiz Horde are so named from the colour of their tents (*kara*, 'black'). The Middle Horde call themselves Kasaks, the 'riders' or horsemen, a name which the Russians have adopted in the form Cossack. The Kirghiz folk-etymology explains their name by a legend about forty girls and a dog (*kyrk*, 'forty' and *kyz*, a 'maiden'). Another legend, given by Radlof, is that the tents of one horde were forty (*kyrk*), and those of the other horde were a hundred (*is*), *Kyrk-is* thus meaning 140.

Kirk's Range, west of the River Shire, was so named by Livingstone in 1863, after Dr. Kirk, afterwards Sir John Kirk, the resident at Zanzibar.

Kirkwall, the chief town in the Orkneys,

possessing a cathedral built by Earl Ragn-vald, is a corruption of the Scandinavian name *Kirkjuvagr*, afterwards Kirkvaw, 'church bay.' KIRBY, 'church village,' a common name in the Danish districts, usually has a distinguishing suffix. Thus KIRBY MOORSIDE stands beside the York-shire Moors; KIRBY UNDERDALE is in the Hundledale or dale of the Hundle beck; KIRBY GRINDALYTHE is in the green dale district (A.S. *læth*, a lathe or district, O.N. *leith*, a levy); KIRKBY WHARFE stands on the Wharfe; KIRBY WISK on the Wisk, and KIRBY LONSDALE in the dale of the Lune. (*See* KENDAL.)

Kishm is the Arabic name of an island at the mouth of the Persian Gulf, so called from its chief town, Kishm, which means 'beautiful.' In Persian it is called JEZE-RAT-AT-TAWILAH, 'long island.'

Kisliar, 'the girls,' a town on the Kisliar, one of the mouths of the River Terek, which falls into the Caspian, was so called, according to the local tradition, because superfluous girls were formerly drowned in the stream.

Kissingen, the celebrated Bavarian baths, is an assimilated German form of the ninth century Slavonic name *Chizzicha*, descriptive of the 'bitter bubbling' water of the chief spring.

Kistna, an Indian river, is probably not named from the god Krisna, as sometimes asserted, but is rather the 'black' river, so called from the dark alluvial soil through which it flows.

Kitchi-Natchi, the 'great spit,' is the Ojibwy name of the great promontory which stretches far into Lake Winnipeg.

Kittiks-ungoit, the 'small islands,' is the Eskimo name of a Greenland group.

Kiusiu, the 'nine districts,' the southern-most of the Japanese islands, is so called from the number of the provinces into which it is divided.

Klagenfurt, the capital of Carinthia, is probably the ford over the River Chlagen (now called the Glan), and not, as some-times asserted, a corruption of *Claudii Forum*.

Klapmuts, the 'riding cap,' a mountain in the Cape Colony, so called from its shape, has given its name to an adjacent town.

Klausen, KLAUSE or KLAUS, the 'clo-sure,' is a common name for Alpine defiles, where the mountains close upon the road. KLAUSENBURG, the capital of Transylvania, received its name in 1178 from the Saxon colonists, probably from

a desire to render significant the Magyar name *Kolozsvar*, 'the fortress of Kolozs,' which is still the name of the county in which it is situated.

Klaver, 'clover,' a town in the Cape Colony, and KLAVER VLEY, 'clover valley,' are so called from the luxuriant herbage.

Kleb, the 'heart,' a volcanic cone in the Hauran, is so called from its shape.

Kling, the name given to the Dravidian settlers in the Malay Peninsula, is from Kelinga or Telinga, the Malay pronuncia-tion of Telugu.

Klingen, a 'ravine,' is not uncommon in Swiss names, such as KLINGENBERG, KLINGENBACH or KLINGAU. KLINGEN-ZELL, in Canton Thurgau, derives its name from the cell or monastery of Maria Hilf, founded by John Walter of Hohen-klingen, who, attacked by a wild boar when hunting, made a vow to found a chapel to the Virgin in gratitude for his preservation.

Klipfontein and KLIPBERG, in the Cape Colony, are from the Dutch *klip*, a 'cliff.'

Klosterthal, in the Vorarlberg, means the 'convent dale.'

Knee Lake is the name of three knee-shaped lakes in the Canadian dominion.

Knocker's Bay, Port Essington, North Australia, was so called because a hafted stone axe was found there by the dis-coverers in 1818.

Knuckle Point, New Zealand, was so named by Cook in 1769 from its shape.

Koft, a town on the Nile below Thebes, represents the old *Koptos*, where the monu-ments of the earliest dynasties have been found. (*See* COPT.)

Kola, a town on the River Kola, gives its name to the Peninsula of Kola, north of the White Sea.

Kong, which means 'mountains,' is the Mandingo name of the coast range in Guinea. (*See* CONGO.)

Konieh, near Smyrna, represents the old name *Iconium*.

Königsberg, the 'King's hill,' in East Prussia, was so called from the castle the Bohemian King Otakar Premysel built in 1255, and called Królewicz, a Slavonic name of which Königsberg is the German translation. KÖNIGSFELDEN, the 'King's plain,' a town in Baden, grew up round a monastery built by Agnes, Queen of Hungary, on the spot where her father, King Albrecht of Habsburg, son of the

Emperor Rudolf III., was stabbed by John of Swabia in 1308. The high altar marks the spot where he expired in the arms of a poor beggar-woman. Such names as KÖNIGS-STUHL, KÖNIGSHOFEN, etc., are common in Germany. From the Swedish *kong*, 'king,' we have sundry Scandinavian names such as KONGSBERG, KONGSDAL, or KONGSTRUP.

Koriaks, a tribe to the North of Kamtchatka, are the 'reindeer people,' *kora* or *chora* meaning a 'reindeer' in the Koriak language.

Kosciuszko, Mount, in New South Wales, one of the summits of the Australian Alps (6500 feet high), was so called by Count Strzelecki because its form resembled the tumulus raised at Cracow over the grave of the great Polish patriot.

Kotelnoi Ostrov, 'Kettle island,' the largest of the New Siberia Islands, was discovered in 1773 by the Russian merchant Lächow. The name is supposed to have been transferred from the island of the same name near St. Petersburg on which the fortress of Cronstadt stands.

Kotzebue Sound is a large gulf north of Bering Strait which Cook passed without noticing it. It was discovered in 1816 by the Russian Lieutenant von Kotzebue, who informs us that at the unanimous request of his shipmates he consented to bestow upon it his own name.

Krenitzin Islands, a group in the Aleutian chain, were discovered by a Russian Captain, whose name they bear.

Kremlin, the citadel of Moscow, means the 'fortress.'

Kreuzlingen, in Canton Thurgau, is so called from a monastery which prided itself on the possession of a fragment of the true Cross. KREUZLI, the 'little cross,' a pass between Canton Uri and the Graubünden, takes its name from a small iron cross at the summit.

Kromme Rivier, the 'crooked river,' in the Cape Colony, is so called from its tortuous course. There is a river of the same name at Utrecht.

Krusenstern (or Ailu), an island in Marshall's Archipelago, was discovered by Kotzebue in 1816, and bears the name of Admiral Krusenstern, the first Russian who circumnavigated the world (1803-6). His name has also been given to two Arctic Capes, to an island in Bering Straits, and to an island in the Dangerous Archipelago, also known by the native name Tikehau.

Kufstein, in the Tyrol, appears in the tenth century as *Chuofstein,* a name explained by the 'bowl-shaped rock' on which the castle dominating the pass was built.

Kuka, or KUKAWA, near Lake Tsad, is the capital of the kingdom of Bornu. It received its name from a monkey breadtree (*Adansonia digitata*), locally called *kuka,* which attracted the attention of the settlers as being a rare tree in this district.

Kulja, locally pronounced Gulja, is a large town in Chinese Tartary on the River Ili. The word *gulja* means an 'elk' or 'mountain goat.' It is also called Ili Balik and Ili Khoto, names signifying the 'town on the Ili.'

Kultuk means a 'gulf' in Russian. The north-east bay of the Caspian is called MERTVY KULTUK, the 'Dead Gulf,' because of the stillness of the water. Other bays on the Caspian are called GOLYI KULTUK, 'naked gulf,' and BOGATYI KULTUK, 'rich gulf.'

Kuntersweg is a district in the Tyrol, through which, in 1314, Heinrich Kunter, a burgher of Botzen, made a road.

Kunupeli is a marshy coast district in Elis, infested by the *Culex cunupi,* a minute midge.

Kur, a river flowing into the Caspian, whence the name of the GEORGIANS (*q.v.*) is the Cyrus of Pliny.

Kurdistan is the country of the Kurds, the 'braves' or valiant men. At the dawn of history they were called *Gutu,* 'warriors,' of which *Gardu* or *Kardu* was the Assyrian translation, whence the Greek name *Karduchi.* In Armenian *kordu,* and in Persian *gurd,* means 'valiant.' In Georgian *kurd* means a 'robber,' and in Turkish *kurt* means a 'wolf.'

Kurile Islands, a chain stretching from Japan to Kamtchatka, bear the name of the inhabitants, who call themselves *Kurili,* the 'men' or the 'people.'

Kurisches Haff, on the Baltic, is the Courland Haven or gulf.

Kusnetsk, the 'smithy,' is a Siberian mining town on the River Tom, founded in 1618.

Kustendji, or CONSTANTINO, is a port on the Black Sea near the mouth of the Danube. Both names are corruptions of the old name *Constantia,* given in honour of the sister of the Emperor Constantinus to the city of Flavia Nea, founded by Titus.

Küstrin, a fortress on the Oder, is surrounded by a sedgy marsh, which explains the Slavonic name *Koztrzyn,* 'reed basket.'

Kutab Minar, at Delhi, often called the 'polestar minaret,' was named from a Saint, Kutb-ud-Dín, the 'pole of the faith.'

Kutch, or CUTCH, a province in India (in the new spelling Kachch), is explained by Yule as the 'marshy' and by Hunter as the 'sea-coast land.' There are salt marshes on the coast. The Gulf or Run of Cutch takes its name from the province.

Kutusoff, Cape, on the Japanese Island of Yesso, and KUTUSOFF (or Button) ISLAND in the Marshall group, bear the name of a Russian Admiral.

Kyles of Bute are the 'Straits' which divide Bute from the Mainland. Kyle is the Gaelic *caol*, a 'strait.' So the Sound of Mull is *Caol Muileach* in Gaelic, the Sound of Isla is *Caol Isla*. EDDRACHILIS is the place 'between the Straits,' and BALLACHULISH is the 'town on the strait.'

Kyuk Phyu, the 'white stones,' is the name of a large Burmese coast town, so called from the white pebbles of which the beach is composed.

Laach, near Andernach, appears in an eighth century document as *Lacha*, a word meaning 'lake' (unrelated to the Latin *lacus*) whence the Benedictine Abbey founded in 1093 was called *Abbatia Lacensis*, the 'Abbey by the Lake,' now called the LAACHER SEE, a remarkable circular lake which fills the crater of one of the extinct volcanoes of the Eifel.

Labrador bears a name which is believed to testify to the early maritime enterprise of the Portuguese. On a Portuguese chart of 1504 it is called *Terra de Corte Real*, and on another chart of 1508 it appears as *Terra Corterealis*. Gaspar de Cortereal was a Portuguese navigator who visited the coast in 1500 or 1501, and Pasqualigo, the Venetian ambassador at Lisbon, relates that Cortereal, sailing along the coast, captured and brought back with him to Lisbon fifty-seven natives who, it was thought, would prove excellent labourers (*lavradores*). Hence the country seems to have acquired the name of *Terra de Lavradores*, the 'land of the labourers.' According to another explanation Bradore Bay, formerly called Labrador Bay, acquired that name from the visit of a Basque whaler called the *Labrador*, the name of the Bay being subsequently extended to the whole coast.

Labuan, a British settlement in Borneo, is a corruption of the Malay name *Pulo Labuhan*, 'anchorage island' (*pulo*, 'island,' and *labuh*, 'to anchor.'

Laccadives, a corruption of *lakshadvipa*, 'the hundred thousand (*lakh*) islands,' is the name of a group of coral islets off the Malabar coast. The name was probably intended to include the myriad Maldives as well. In Malay and Javanese *lakh* means 10,000.

Lachlan River, a tributary of the Murray, discovered in 1815, bears the name of Colonel Lachlan Macquarie, who was at that time Governor of New South Wales.

Ladoga, the largest sheet of fresh water in Europe, is very shallow, with marshy banks. The name is doubtless Finnic, *laddo* meaning a 'marsh' in Lapp, and *-ga* being the common suffix denoting 'water,' as in the names ONEGA and PINEGA. The name has also been explained as the 'duck lake.'

Ladrones, or MARIANAS, a Pacific group of islands, were the first land reached by Magellan and his starving crew when he crossed the Pacific on his circumnavigation of the world in 1521. He called them *Islas de los Ladrones*, 'Islands of the Robbers,' because the natives were such pertinacious thieves. Las Marianas, the official designation, was given in 1668 in honour of Maria Anna of Austria, mother of Charles II. of Spain.

Lagrange Bay, LACÉPÈDE BAY, and LACÉPÈDE ISLAND, in Australia, were named by Baudin in 1801-3 after two eminent Frenchmen, the mathematician and the naturalist.

Laguna, a Brazilian coast town, takes its name from a lagoon by which it stands.

Lahn, a river in Nassau, was called in the eighth century *Logan-aha*, 'lye water' or 'laundry river,' the colour of the stream resembling water in which clothes had been washed. LAUGARVATN, 'bath lake,' and LAUGARDALR, 'bath dale,' are places in Iceland with hot springs (O.N. *lauga*, 'to wash').

Lahol, in Tibet, means the 'southern region' as distinguished from the northern LADAK.

Lahore (LAHÓR), the capital of the Punjab, is probably a corruption of *Lohâwar* or *Lohâwarana*. Indian legend ascribes the foundation of the city to Loh, who in the Rámáyana is a son of Ráma and Sítá. The legend is supposed to have arisen from a corruption of an earlier name, conjecturally *Lavana-pur*, the 'city of Lavana,' the 'salt' district west of the Jhelum.

Laibach, or LAYBACH, in Carinthia, stands at the confluence of the Laibach and the Save.

Lambert Island, in Arctic America, and POINT LAMBERT, North Australia, bear the name of A. B. Lambert, vice-president of the Linnean Society.

Lambeth, Surrey (A.S. *Lambhȳth* or *Lambehȳth*), was probably a wharf or landing-place for lambs (A.S. *lamb*, a 'lamb'), or possibly from a personal name. The old etymology from *lam*, 'loam, clay,' is precluded by the A.S. form of the name. LAMBEY, near Dublin, is the 'lamb island,' so called because in the spring lambs were sent there to graze.

Lammas Island, North Australia, was discovered on Lammas Day, August 1st, 1821. MOUNT LAMMAS, in Gualcamar, one of the Salomon Group, was first sighted on Lammas Day, 1788.

Lampedusa, an island west of Malta, has preserved the old Greek name *Lopadussa,* the 'oyster bank.'

Lamsaki, a town opposite Gallipoli, on the Asiatic shore of the Dardanelles, retains the Greek name *Lampsacus,* which means 'the passage.'

Lanark, a town which gives a name to a Scotch county, was formerly *Lanerch,* which has been explained from the Cymric *llanerch,* which signifies either an enclosure in a wood, or a glade, or open space in a forest.

Lancashire, a corruption of Lancaster-shire, as Cheshire is of Chestershire, was formed into a County Palatine for the Earl of Lancaster out of Blackburnshire, Salfordshire, Amounderness, and Furness. LANCASTER, the county town (A.S. *Lunceaster*), is the chester on the Lune, formerly the *Alauna,* whence the name *Ad Alaunam,* as the Roman station at Lancaster was called.

Lancaster Sound, the main channel leading from Baffin Bay into the Polar Archipelago, was discovered by Baffin in 1616, and named after his patron, Sir James Lancaster, the first Englishman who sailed round the Cape to the East Indies (1591-1594), and who in 1600 commanded the first expedition despatched to India by the East India Company, of which he was one of the directors.

Lance, or LA LANCE, on the Lake of Neufchâtel, is called in Latin documents *Monasterium de Lancea,* because it possessed a reputed fragment of the Holy Lance as a relic.

Lanchester, County Durham, is called *Langchestre,* the 'long chester,' in the Boldon Book, which is, however, of too late a date to be decisive as to the etymology, which may be from the Roman name, either *Clanoventum* or possibly *Longovicum.*

Landes is a French department containing the vast heath called LES LANDES, a name formerly supposed to be a German loan word, but it is now believed that there was a genuine Gaulish word *landa,* denoting 'untilled land.'

Landfall Island, at the western end of the Straits of Magellan, was the first land sighted by Cook, in 1774, on his return from New Zealand round Cape Horn.

Landquart is a Swiss river, whose older names, *Langarum* (1219) and *Languuar,* point to *longum aquarium,* the 'long watercourse,' as a probable etymology.

Land's End, Cornwall, has replaced the Celtic name *Pen - with.* In the Chronicle it is called *Penwith-steort,* the Saxons adding to the Cornish name their own word *steort,* a 'tail,' whence the name of START POINT in Devon, and of the bird called the red-start or 'red-tail.'

Langenes, the 'long ness,' a spit on the north-west coast of Novaya Zemlya, was discovered and named by Barents in 1594. LANGE KLOOF, the 'long ravine,' and LANGE FONTEIN, the 'long brook,' are Dutch names in the Cape Colony. LANGÖ, Denmark, is the 'long island.'

Langres, in the Haute Marne, in Old French *Langoinne,* derives its name from the tribe of the Lingones, whose chief town it was.

Languard, Piz, in the Graubünden, is so called from the vast panorama it commands.

Languedoc, the fourteenth century name of one of the old provinces of France, was the region of the 'tongue of Oc' as distinguished from that of the Langue d'oïl, or 'tongue of Oïl,' in the North. A line drawn from La Rochelle to Grenoble represents approximately the boundaries of the two dialects. The Langue d'oc originally extended to the Ebro, embracing the Catalan district. In Southern Gaul the sign of affirmation was *hoc,* which became *oc*; in Northern Gaul it was *hoc illud,* which became *oïl,* and then *oui*; in Italy it was *sic,* which became *si.* Hence Dante calls Italian *la lingua di si.*

Lamlash in Arran, formerly called *Molas,*

is a corruption of *Lann - Molais*, the 'church of St. Molios' or Molaise.

Lanzarote, formerly *Lancilote*, one of the Canaries, bears the name of Lancilote (Lancelot) Malocello, a Genoese knight in the Portuguese service, who built a castle on it about 1344. In some old maps it is called *Maloxelo*.

Laon, in the Aisne, is, like Lyons (*q.v.*), a corruption of the Celto-Latin name *Lugdunum*, believed to mean the 'tower on the hill,' an etymology favoured by the situation of the city, which is perched on an almost impregnable rock. The name *Lugdunum* became *Laudunum* in the tenth century, and *Loun* in the thirteenth.

Laos is the Portuguese plural form of *Lao*, the native name of the people on the Lower Mekong, who are called Shans by the Burmese.

Lapland is the land of the Lapps, who were called by the Finns *Lapp-alaiset*, 'people of the frontier,' literally 'people of the end of the land.' The Lapps call their country *Same*, and themselves *Same-lads*, which means 'people of the marshes' or tundras. Similar names are SAMOYED, (*q.v.*) and *Suomi-laiset*, the name by which the Finns call themselves.

Larcom, Mount, in Queensland, was named by Flinders in 1802 in compliment to Captain Larcom, R.N.

Larne, a town in Ulster, formerly *Latharna* or *Laharna*, was in the district assigned to Lathair, son of Hugony the Great.

La Salle, a city in Illinois, was so called in memory of La Salle, the intrepid French explorer who discovered the Mississippi River.

Latakia or LADAKIYEH, a Syrian seaport whence the Latakia tobacco was exported, was one of the five cities built by Seleucus Nicator, and named after his mother Laodicea. The *Laodicea* of the Bible is now represented by the desolate ruins in Asia Minor called LADÎK.

Latitude Bay, Tierra del Fuego, is a foolish name, commemorating an observation for latitude here obtained by Fitzroy in 1829.

Lauenburg, a duchy in Holstein, takes its name from the town and castle of Lauenburg, a corruption of *Labenburg*, 'the castle on the Labe,' which was the Slavonic name of the Elbe, on which it stands.

Laufen, 'at the rapids,' is the name of a castle and village below the falls of the Rhine at Schaffhausen, and also of a place near the falls of the Traun. LAUFENBURG, the 'castle at the rapids,' is a town at the rapids midway between Basel and Schaffhausen.

Laughlan Islands, a group lying between New Guinea and the Salomons, were discovered in 1812 by the ship *Mary*, commanded by the seaman whose name they bear.

Launceston, in Cornwall, is a corruption of *Lan - Stephen - dun*, the 'hill by St. Stephen's Church,' an adjacent monastery being dedicated to St. Stephen. The name has been transferred to the town of LAUNCESTON in the Tasmanian county of Cornwall.

Lausanne, anciently *Lausodunum*, *Lausonium*, or *Losene*, called *Lausanna* in the Peutinger Tables, and *Vicus Lausonii* in the Antonine Itinerary, was a Celtic *dun* or hill fort on the Laus or Lauso, a small river now called the Flon.

Lausitz or LUSATIA, a district in Prussia and Saxony, is a Slavonic name meaning the 'Marshland,' from *luzice*, the diminutive of *luz* or *luh*, a 'marsh,' which is the source of numerous names in Eastern Europe.

Laut signifies in Malay the 'sea' or 'ocean.' Hence the names of two islands on the coast of Borneo called PULO LAUT or 'sea island,' and of a coast district in the south of Borneo called TANAK-LAUT or 'sea land.' The sea south of Java is called by the Javanese LAUT-KIDUL, the 'south sea.'

Lauterbrunnen, a village in the Bernese Oberland, takes its name from the 'clear springs' which issue from the limestone cliffs. To the O.H.G. *hlutar*, 'pure' or 'clear,' we may also refer the LAUTERBACH and the RIVER LAUTER, anciently *Hlutraha* or 'clear river.' But LAUTERSHEIM as Worms is shown by the old form *Liutersheim* to be from the personal name Liuter (Luther) which also appears in LUTTERHAUSEN, LÜDERSTEDT, LIGGERSDORF, and other names in Germany.

Lavizzara, Val, in Canton Ticino, takes its name from the *laveggi* or cooking pots made out of a serpentine rock found in the upper part of the valley.

Lawford's Islands, in Coronation Gulf, at the mouth of the Coppermine River, were so named by Franklin, in 1821, after Captain John Lawford, R.N., the seaman under whom he first served in the *Polyphemus* at the battle of Copenhagen in 1800.

Leamington, near Warwick, on the River Leam, called Leamington Priors to distinguish it from Leamington Hastings, also on the Leam, may be the tun of the Leamings, or people of the Leam ; but more probably the syllable *ing* may have, as it occasionally has, the force of a possessive, or it may be a mere assimilation, as in the case of ITCHINGTON, on the Itchen, a tributary of the Leam. Similar questions arise in the case of ERMINGTON on the Devonshire Erme, of TYNINGHAM on the Tyne, and LEAVINGTON on the Yorkshire Leven.

Leatherhead, in Surrey, is a name which, like Maidenhead, has been curiously assimilated to make it significant in modern English. In King Ælfred's will he bequeathes to his son Eadward his land, *æt Leodrithan*, where *rithan* is plainly the dative of *rithe*, a 'rivulet' or 'stream of running water.' As the first part of the name cannot well be *lád*, a 'water-course' or 'lode,' or *lióht*, 'quick,' 'bright,' 'shining,' it must be referred to *leód*, 'people,' 'country,' 'district.'

Leavenworth, a city in Kansas, laid out in 1854, is two miles below Fort Leavenworth, a frontier post established in 1827 by Colonel Henry Leavenworth.

Lebanon, the 'white' mountain, from the Semitic root *laban*, 'to be white,' was probably so named from its cliffs of white chalk and limestone, rather than from its snows. It is now locally called *Jebel Libnan.*

Lebda, in Tripoli, preserves the name of the Roman *Leptis Magna*, and LEMTA in Tunis that of the *Leptis Parva*. Leptis was a Carthaginian name meaning a 'station for ships.'

Lecompton, the State capital of Kansas, was named from Samuel D. Lecompte, who was the Supreme Territorial Judge of Kansas before its reception as a State.

Ledbury, Herefordshire, called *Leideberge* in Domesday, takes its name from the River Leden on which it stands.

Leeds, in Yorkshire, represents the British kingdom called *Loidis* by Bæda, which with the neighbouring kingdom of Elmet (*q.v.*) held out against the Angles, after York had become the capital of Deira, and Chester had fallen before Æthelfrith. It was probably subdued by Eadwine in the seventh century. There was another kingdom of *Loidis* which is believed to be LOTHIAN (*q.v.*).

Leek, a town in Staffordshire, is supposed to be from the Welsh *llech* or *lech*, a 'flat stone,' whence the name of AUCHINLECK, in Ayrshire, which means the 'field of the stone,' and of HARLECH, Merionethshire, supposed to be *Hardd-lech*, 'the fair rock.' Leake in Lincolnshire is probably from M.E. *leche*, a 'swampy pool.' The river name LECH may mean the 'stony' river, or may be from the Celtic root *lek*, 'to bend.' LECHLADE, in Gloucestershire, is at the *lád* or 'passage' of the River Leech or Leck into the Thames. There is a river Leck in Belgium, and the LECHFELD in Bavaria is the district traversed by the River Lech.

Leeuwin Land and CAPE LEEUWIN, West Australia, bear the name of the Dutch ship *Leeuwin*, the lioness, by which they were discovered in 1622. LEEUWENBOSCH and LEEUWEN RIVIER, in the Cape Colony, were so called from the lions which infested them.

Leghorn is an English sailors' corruption of LIVORNO, the *Portus Liburnus* of the Romans.

Leicester, erroneously supposed to be *Legionis castra*, was the Roman station of *Ratæ* or *Ratiscorium*. The A.S. name was *Legra-ceaster* or *Ligora-ceaster*, while Nennius has *Kair-Lirion*, and Domesday *Ledeceaster*, names which must be explained as the chester on the River Ligera, Ligra, Lear, or Leire, now called the Soar. A village called Leire, on the Upper Soar, still preserves the old name of the river. Llyr was the Celtic water-god, whose name has been embodied in Shakespeare's play of *King Lear*. Geoffrey of Monmouth says that Llyr (King Lear) was buried at Caer Lyr, or Leicester.

Leichhardt's Range and LEICHHARDT'S RIVER bear the name of Dr. Leichhardt, the intrepid but ill-fated Australian explorer.

Leinster, like Ulster and Munster, exhibits the Danish suffix *-stadr*, a 'place' or 'district.' The Irish name of the province was Laighen, Leinster being a corruption of Laighen-stadr, which in the sixteenth century had become Laynster. In Irish the word *laighen* denotes a peculiar kind of broad-pointed spear, which, according to a venerable legend, was the weapon used by the foreign mercenaries of an early king of Leinster, who settled in the district which was hence called Laighen.

Leipzig, Saxony, is a German corruption of the Slavonic name *Lipsk* or *Lipzk*, which means a 'linden wood.' The word *lipa*, a 'lime tree,' is the source of many names in Eastern Europe, such as LEIPE, LEIBNITZ, LIPNITZ, and LIPTEN.

GLOSSARY

Leith, the port of Edinburgh, appears in a twelfth century document as *Inverlet.* The name Leith is therefore an abbreviated form of Inverleith, the place 'at the mouth of the Leith,' a stream which has now acquired from the town to which it had originally given a name its present appellation of the WATER OF LEITH.

Leitrim, the name of an Irish county and of many Irish townlands, is a corruption of *Liath-dhruim,* the 'grey ridge.'

Leixlip, a village at the falls of the Liffey, in Kildare, is one of the few local names in Ireland testifying to the dominion of the Danes, being a corruption of the O.N. *Lax-hlaup,* 'salmon leap.' The apparently similar name of ABBEY LEIX in Queen's County affords a good example of the danger of etymological speculation based merely on the modern form of a name. It is not Scandinavian, but Celtic, LEIX being in this case the modern form of the tribal name *Laeighis,* which denoted the territory acquired by Lughaidh, an Ulster chief. LAXWEIR on the Shannon, near the Danish settlement at Limerick, is, however, a genuine Norse name meaning a 'salmon weir.' There are several streams in the Hebrides and the Isle of Man called LAXAY and LAXEY, which, like the LAXA in Iceland, mean 'salmon river.' LAX VOE, in Shetland, is the 'salmon bay,' while LOCH LAXFORD, in Sutherland, is a reduplicated name, *ford* being the O.N. *fjördr,* a 'firth' or loch.

Le Maire, a strait between Tierra del Fuego and Staaten Island, was discovered in 1616 by Jakob Le Maire, a Dutch seaman.

Lemberg, LEMBURG, or LÖWENBURG, in Latin documents *Leopolis,* is the capital of the Austrian crownland of Galicia. It was founded about 1259 by the Ruthenian prince Daniel for his son Leo, whose name it bears. A similar name is that of LEONBERG, a town in Würtemberg, founded in 1248 by the Graf von Calw. By an almost unique inversion of the usual relations between heraldry and geographical onomatology, the name was derived from the founder's crest, a lion on a hill.

Leominster, pronounced Lempster, is a town in Herefordshire which arose round a monastery founded about 658 by Merwald, king of the Mercians, on the River Lug. The name has been thought to be a corruption of Lugminster, from the river on which it stands. This will not explain the name of another LEOMINSTER in Sussex, where was a priory of Bene-

dictine nuns. *Leofminstre,* the early form of both names, suggests the A.S. *leof,* 'beloved' or 'dear,' as the probable explanation. The *Lulling mynster* mentioned in King Ælfred's will is believed to be Lullington in Sussex.

Leon, a city in Spain, the capital of the medieval kingdom and the modern province of the same name, was fortified by Trajan. It is the *Legiōn* of Ptolemy, a name explained by its having been the station of the Seventh Legion, *Legio Septima Gemina.* The name has been transferred to two cities in Central America. CAER-LEON (*q.v.*) is a name of similar origin.

Leones, a Patagonian harbour, properly *Puerto de Leones y Lobos,* the 'port of Sea Lions and Seals,' was so named by Alcazora in 1535. In 1520 Magellan named an island in the straits which bear his name, ISLA DE LOS LEONES on account of the number of sea lions (*Platyrhynchus Leoninus,* a large maned seal) seen upon the rocks. MONTE LEONE, on the eastern side of the Simplon Pass, is believed to be named from its resemblance to a lion when viewed from a certain point on the Italian side of the pass.

Leopoldville, the station at Stanley Pool on the Congo, bears the name of Leopold II., king of the Belgians. PORT LEOPOLD and PRINCE LEOPOLD ISLE, at the entrance of Prince Regent's Inlet, discovered by Parry in 1819, and CAPE LEOPOLD, at the entrance of COBURG BAY, discovered by Ross in 1818, bear the name Prince Leopold of Saxe-Coburg, son-in-law of the Prince Regent, and afterwards Leopold I., king of the Belgians. LAKE LEOPOLD, in Central Africa, was so named by Joseph Thomson in honour of Prince Leopold, Duke of Albany.

Lepanto, a Greek port, where a Turkish fleet was defeated in 1571 by the Spanish, Papal, and Venetian forces under the command of Don John of Austria, gives its name to the GULF OF LEPANTO (or Gulf of Corinth), at the entrance to which it stands. Lepanto is an Italian corruption of the Neo-Hellenic *Epakto* or *Epaktos,* which represents the old Greek name Naupactus, the 'ship station.' According to the eponymic Greek legend, the Heracleidæ here built the ships in which they crossed over to the Peloponnesus.

Lerida, a Spanish city, which gives its name to a province, was the Roman *Ilerda,* believed to be an Iberian word meaning 'town.'

Lerwick, the chief town in the Shetlands, is a Scandinavian name, from the O.N. *leir*, 'clay,' and *vik*, a bay. The bottom of Lerwick Harbour still consists of clay, mud, and sand. There is also a LERVIK in Norway.

Lesghi, the name of one of the races in the Caucasus, means the 'men' or 'people.'

Lesina or LUSSIN, the 'cobbler's awl,' a long and narrow Istrian island, derives its Italian name from its shape.

Lett, an Australian stream, derived from the last syllable of rivulet, is one of the silly names which were given by Mitchell.

Leucadia, one of the Ionian Islands, formerly *Leucas*, was so called from the white cliffs which fringe its western shore. The island is also called SANTA MAURA, from a fort erected to command the northern entrance to the channel. CAPO DI LEUCA is the southern point of Calabria. Here on the site of the old Greek town of Leuca, the 'white,' stands the ancient church of *Santa Maria di Leuca*, also called *Madonna di Finisterra*, who is believed to help sailors in peril.

Leuk, in Canton Valais, at the foot of the gorge through which the Gemmi Pass descends, is called *Leuca* in 1153, explained by Gatschet as a dialectical form of the O.H.G. *luog*, 'a cleft or chasm.'

Levant, the region of the 'sunrise,' is an Italian name given to the lands in the Eastern Mediterranean. So the Eastern Riviera is called RIVIERA DE LEVANTE.

Leventina, a name given to a part of the valley of the Ticino, is derived from the tribe of the *Lepontii*, by whom it was inhabited, whence also the modern name of the LEPONTINE ALPS.

Lew-Chew, LOO-CHOO, or LIU-KIU Islands, lying between Japan and Formosa, are called by the Japanese *Riu Kiu*, which is believed to be a corruption of the Chinese name *Lung khieu*, 'the horned dragon.'

Lewes, Sussex, was anciently called *Læwe* and *Læwes*, probably a corruption of the A.S. *Hlaewas*, 'mounds, tumuli,' and not, as usually said, of *Læswe*, 'the pastures,' a name which appears repeatedly in Salop and Cheshire as LEASOW or LEASOWES.

Lewis, or The Lewis, locally called THE LEWS, forms together with Harris the largest island in the Outer Hebrides. The name is probably from the Gaelic *leoghas*, 'marshy land.' In a Gaelic tract on the wars of the Gaidhil it is called *Lodhusa* and *Leodus*, Scandinavian forms which

may have beeen influencd by the Gaelic *lód*, a 'pool,' or by a supposed connection with the neighbouring clan Leod or Mac Leod. In the Norse Sagas we have *Liódhús, Leodhus,* and *Lyodhuus,* an assimilated name apparently denoting a 'house' of some kind, but of what kind is not so clear. The local word *lod* means a bund'e of fishing lines, and in O.N. *lod* means crop or produce, and *lióð*, a lay or song. Hence it has been supposed that the Norse name referred to a 'grange,' or a storehouse for fishing gear, or to a house for popular assembly for speech or song. HARRIS (*q.v.*), the lofty southern end of the island, is in striking contrast with Lewis, the 'marshy land,' at the northern end.

Lewis and Clarke' Pass, over the Rocky Mountains, bears the name of two American explorers, Captain Meriwether Lewis, afterwards Governor of Louisiana, and Captain William Clarke, both of them Virginians, who in 1803-1805 were sent by Jefferson to ascend the Missouri and reach the Pacific. They were among the first Europeans to cross the continent north of Mexico. Two tributaries of the Columbia River, CLARKE FORK and LEWIS FORK, with the town of LEWISTON, also commemorate their names.

Lewisham in Kent, called *Liofshema*, *Leofshéma*, or *Leofsnhéma mearc*, 'the mark of the men of Leofsham,' is from a personal name. (*See* p. 142.)

Lexington has become a favourite name in the United States, being given to more than twenty places, of which the most important is Lexington in Kentucky, which occupies the site of a camp fire, assembled round which a party of hunters first heard the tidings of the battle fought on April 19th, 1775, at Lexington, in Massachusetts.

Leyden or LEIDEN, in Holland, has for centuries been identified with the Roman *Lugdunum Batavorum*, a name which appears on the title-pages of books printed at Leyden. This identification is however very doubtful, the tenth century name *Leithon* making it probable that Leyden is a dative form, meaning 'at the lode' or watercourse.

Lhasa or L'ASSA, the capital of Thibet, is the residence of the Dalai Lama, who receives divine honours as the incarnation of the Deity, whence the name Lhasa, which means 'God's ground' or the 'divine land,' from *lha*, 'god,' and *sa*, 'land' or 'ground.'

Liakov, one of the New Siberia Islands, near the mouth of the Lena, bears the name of a Russian merchant who discovered it in 1770.

Libau in Courland, was called *Lywa* in the thirteenth century, probably from the Finnic *liwa*, 'sand,' the town standing on sand dunes by the sea.

Liberia, the 'land of the free,' now a Negro republic in Western Africa, was a settlement founded by American philanthropists in 1822 for liberated slaves.

Liberty is a common town name in the United States. The oldest is LIBERTY HILL in South Carolina, the station of the American force which compelled the British troops to evacuate the town of Augusta in Georgia.

Lichfield, an Episcopal see in Staffordshire, is usually explained as the 'field of corpses,' from the A.S. *líc*, a corpse, an etymology which has given rise to the legend of the massacre of a thousand Christians during the Diocletian persecution. But for this legend there is no historical evidence, and the etymology is grammatically impossible, as the older forms of the name are *Licidfeld* and *Licitfeld* in Bæda, *Licetfeld* and *Liccedfeld* in the A.S. Chronicle, *Licetfeld* and *Liccidfeld* in A.S. charters. The clue to the etymology, as Mr. Bradley has pointed out, is given by Nennius, who, writing in the ninth century, enumerates *Cair Luitcoit* as one of the ancient cities of Britain. The Welsh forms are Kaer Loidcoit, Caer Ludcoth, Caer Lwydgoet, and Llwyt Koet. St. Chad, we are told, was born at Llwydgoet. In the Antonine Itinerary we have *Etocetum*, and in the Ravenna Geographer *Lectocetum*, corrupt forms which point to an Old Welsh *Letocetum*, which in Middle Welsh would give the *Luitcoit* of Nennius, and in Modern Welsh would be *Llwyd-goed*, the 'grey wood.' Hence we may explain Lichfield as the 'plain of the grey wood.'

Liddon Island and LIDDON GULF, in Arctic America, bear the name of Matthew Liddon, one of Parry's officers.

Lidsey, Sussex, is the A.S. *Lydes íg*, 'ship isle,' apparently from *lides*, genitive of *lid*, a 'ship.'

Liechtenstein, a sovereign and independent principality on the Upper Rhine, between Switzerland and the Vorarlberg, was constituted in 1719 out of the Lordships of Vaduz and Schellenberg. The name is derived from the princely Austrian house of Liechtenstein, to which it was assigned. Its capital, the town of VADUZ (Romansch *Val-dultsch*, the sweet valley'), is often wrongly called Liechtenstein, which properly is the name of the State.

Liége is the French name of the Belgian city called LÜTTICH in German, LUIK in Flemish, and *Leodium* or *Legia* in Latin documents. The old forms *Laudovicum* and *Luticha* are referred to *liud*, 'people.' But the French name Liége, which goes back to the old form *Legia*, may have been derived from the brook Légie which flows through the town.

Lifford in Donegal, which gives a title to an Irish peer, is a corruption of *Leith bhearr*, a name which has been assimilated to the Danish names in 'ford.' The intrusive *d* has crept in since the sixteenth century, when the spelling was Liffer.

Lighthouse Hill, a rock in Bass Strait, 910 feet high, was so called by Stokes because of an imaginary lighthouse for which he thought it might prove useful.

Liguanea Island and CAPE WILES, in South Australia, were so named by Flinders in 1802, in compliment to a friend named Wiles, residing at Liguanea in Jamaica.

Lille, in French Flanders, founded in the tenth century on a river island, is called *Insula* in early Latin documents, and in the thirteenth century *L'Isle*, 'the island.' The Flemish name RIJSSEL, for *ter Ijsel*, 'the island,' retains a fragment of the Flemish article.

Lima, the capital of Peru, was founded by Francisco Pizarro on January 18th, 1535, and called *Ciudad de los Reyes*, the 'city of the kings,' probably because the site was chosen on January 6th, the Festival of the Epiphany, or possibly in honour of Charles V., and his mother, Dona Juana. The modern name, Lima, is a corruption of *Rimac*, the Quichua name of the plain on which it stands. The plain took its name from a temple called *Rimac-Tampu*, the 'house of Rimac,' now corrupted to *Limatambo*, the ruins of which may still be seen a little south of the city. The god was called Rimac, ' he who speaks,' from a hollow idol in which a priest concealed himself and gave oracles to the worshippers.

Limburg, on the Lahn, was anciently *Lindburg* and *Lintburd*, which would signify 'linden castle' (O.H.G. *linda*, a 'lime tree'), or the dragon castle (*lint*, a 'dragon'). LIMBOURG, or LIMBURG, in Belgium, has given its name to a province now divided between Belgium and Holland.

Limerick is a corruption of the Old Irish name *Luimneach*, which commemorates the 'bare' or 'barren' site, on which the now prosperous city is built.

Limmen Bight, a large bay in the Gulf of Carpentaria, is a translation of the early Dutch name *Limmen's Bogt*, supposed to have been given by Tasman on his second voyage in 1644, from the *Limmen*, one of his ships.

Limno, or LIMNI, also, with the prefixed Greek preposition and article, called STALIMENE, is an island in the Ægean, anciently *Lemnos*, which is believed to be a Phœnician name meaning 'white,' from the colour of the cliffs.

Limoges, the capital of the district called the LIMOSIN, preserves the name of the Gaulish tribe of the *Limovices* or *Lemovices*, explained by Glück as the 'dwellers among the elms.' Their capital was the Roman Augustoritum, 'the ford of Augustus,' a name superseded in the seventh century by Lemovecas, which became Lemovigas in the eighth century and Lemoges in the fourteenth, the *pagus Limovicensis* becoming the Limosin.

Linares, a town in Mexico, was founded in 1716, during the Viceroyalty of the Duke of Linares, who took his title from Linares, a town near Jaen.

Lincoln was the Roman *Lindum*, which is probably from *lindon*, the prehistoric form of the Welsh *llyn*, but often supposed to be the British name *Llyn-dun*, the 'dun' or 'hill fort' at the pool. Lincoln is usually explained as a corruption of *Lindum Colonia*, supposed to have been the name of the Roman colony on the hill where the minster now stands. But there is no evidence except that of the Ravenna Geographer to show that Lindum was a *colonia*. The modern name may be traced to the *Lindocolina* of Bæda, and the *Lindkylne* and *Lincolle* of the Saxon Chronicle. LINCOLN is the name of no less than 160 places in the United States, which were named after Abraham Lincoln, President from 1860 to 1865. PORT LINCOLN, in Spencer Gulf, South Australia, was named by Flinders in 1802 after his native county.

Lindau, on the Lake of Constance, anciently *Lindaugia*, is from O.H.G. *linda*, 'a lime tree.' There also is a LINDAU in Canton Zürich.

Lindsey, or Parts of Lindsey, one of the Ridings of Lincolnshire, is the A.S. *Lindes-īg*, also *Lindessi*, *Lindesse*, or *Lindesie*, meaning apparently the 'Isle of Lindum' (Lincoln) which it includes. It is called an island in the same sense as the Isle of Ely or Isle of Axholm, being

nearly surrounded by the waters and marshes of the Trent and the Witham.

Line Island, in the Ohio River, was so called because the line dividing the States of Ohio and Pennsylvania here intersects the river.

Linlithgow, which gives a name to a Scotch county, is the place at the linn or pool of Liath-chu, probably a personal name or nickname meaning the 'grey dog.' (*See* GLASGOW.)

Linz, a town on the Danube, is believed to represent the Roman station *Lentium* or *Lentia*.

Lions, Gulf of, is often wrongly called the Gulf of Lyons or Golfe de Lyon, from a supposed connection with the city on the Rhone. The name which occurs as *Mare Leonis* in the fourteenth century, and afterwards as *Leonis Sinus*, is doubtless to be attributed to the roaring waves raised by the mistral blowing down the valley of the Rhone.

Lipari Islands, north of Sicily, are so called from Lipari, the largest island, which preserves the ancient name of *Lipara*, the 'rich island.'

Lippe-Detmold, a German principality, takes its name from its capital, the town of Detmold (*q.v.*), which stands on the River Lippe. LIPPSTADT, the former residence of the princes of Lippe, is on an island in the Lippe. LIPPE-SCHAUMBURG is so named from the Stamm-Schloss of its princes, which is called *Scouwen-burg*, the 'watch-tower,' in an eleventh century document.

Lisân, or *El-Lisân*, 'the tongue,' is the Arabic name of the great tongue of land which projects into the Dead Sea.

Lisbon, in Portuguese LISBOA, is derived from an oblique case of the old name *Olisipo*, supposed to contain the Phœnician word *hippo*, a 'fortress' or 'walled town,' which we have in Hippo, the Herodian fortress at Jerusalem, and in Hippo, a Sidonian colony near Carthage, which became the see of St. Augustine. The modern name BONA is, like Lisbon, from an oblique case of Hippo. The form Lisbon may have been influenced by *Oshbûna*, *Lashbûna*, or *Lixbona*, the Arabic corruptions of Olisippo, which was also written *Ulissipo*, by reason of a legend referring its origin to the wanderings of Ulysses.

Lisiansky, correctly LISIANSKOY, an isolated Pacific Island, north-west of the Sandwich Group, was discovered in 1805 by Captain Lisianskoy.

Lisieux, in Normandy, the *Noviomagus* of Cæsar, was the capital of the Lexovii. The twelfth century forms, *Liseuis* and *Lisieues*, point to the dative plural *Lexoviis* as the source of the modern form.

Lismore, a cathedral town in County Waterford, derives its name from a monastery founded in 633 by St. Carthagh, which he called *Liass-mor (Atrium Magnum)*, the 'great enclosure.' The 'Book of the Dean of Lismore' was written at LISMORE, the 'great enclosure' surrounding a Columban monastery on one of the islands in Argyll, which became the seat of the Bishop of Argyll. LESMAHAGOW, in Lanarkshire, was the 'enclosure of St. Machute,' being called *Ecclesia Machuti* in a Latin document of the twelfth century. The prefix *Lis-*, which occurs in 1400 Irish names, usually denotes a secular fort and not a monastic enclosure, as in the case of LISDUFF, the 'black fort'; LISBANE, the 'white fort'; LISBOY, the 'yellow fort'; LISLEA, the 'grey fort'; LISSARD, the 'high fort'; or LISTOWEL, which signifies 'Tuathal's fort.'

Lissa, an island in the Adriatic, off which Captain Hoste gained a victory over the French in 1812, and the Austrians over the Italians in 1866, would mean the 'bald' island in Slavonic, but is an assimilated form of the Syracusan name *Issa*, which must not be confounded with *Lissos* on the Albanian coast, now called ALESSIO in Italian and LESH in Albanian.

Liu-Malal, the 'white enclosure,' and LIU-LEUVU, the 'white river,' are Patagonian names.

Lively Shoal, off the north coast of West Australia, became known from the wreck of the whaler *Lively*.

Liverpool, according to the local tradition, was so called from a pool frequented by the liver or lever, a waterfowl represented in the arms of the city. No very early form of the name has been preserved. It appears at the close of the twelfth century as *Liverpul*. An earlier form is *Litherpul*, which might mean the 'stagnant pool.' Among the conjectural etymologies proposed is the Cymric Llyrpool, the 'sea pool,' Llyr (Shakespeare's King Lear) being the old Celtic sea-god.

Livingstonia, a missionary settlement on Lake Nyassa, and the LIVINGSTONE FALLS on the Congo, bear the name of David Livingstone, the missionary explorer.

Livonia, or LIVLAND is a Russian province inhabited by the Liefs, a Finnic people.

Lizard, a Cornish promontory, is a Celtic name meaning the enclosure or fort on the height. LIZARD ISLAND, Queensland, when discovered by Cook in 1770 was inhabited only by large lizards. LIZARD ISLAND, Tasmanland, was so named by Stokes in 1838 for a similar reason.

Llangadwaladr in Anglesea is believed to be the place where Cadwaladr, grandson of Cadvan, the leader of the Welsh in their struggle with the Angles of Northumbria, was buried in 664. LLANTHONY, in Monmouthshire, is not, as might be supposed, the Church of St. Anthony, but a corruption of *Llan-dewinant-honddu*, the 'Church of St. David in the valley of the Honddu.' Llan, which forms the prefix in the names of so many Welsh parishes, is now believed to be the same word as the Teutonic *land (see* LANDES), though it was formerly supposed to be from the Latin *planum*, denoting originally a level spot of ground, hence a churchyard, and finally a church. We may compare the Spanish word LLANOS, used to denote the great plains or steppes on the Orinoco. In Texas there is a plateau called LLANO ESTACADO, the 'staked plain,' or field of battle. The Spanish *llano* is indubitably from the Latin *planum* (Italian *piano*), the change from *pl* to *ll* in Spanish being seen in *llorar*, to weep, from *plorare*, *llegar* from *plicare*, *lleno* from *plenus*, and *llaga*, a wound, from *plaga*. Hence a plain in California, where many of the early settlers were wounded in a conflict with the natives, is called LAS LLAGAS, 'the wounds.'

Loanda, or LUANDA, is an island off the coast of Angola, on which stands the town of S. Paulo de Luanda, the capital of Angola. Luanda is a native word meaning 'tribute,' which was applied to this coast, because here the negroes fished for the shells (*zimbos*), in which the annual tax was paid to the King of Congo.

Lobos Islands, off the Peruvian coast, well known from their vast deposits of guano, derive their name from the Spanish word *lobo* (Latin *lupus*), 'a wolf,' which was applied to the sea-wolf, a large seal which frequented this group, as well as CAPE LOBOS, in Peru. One of the sights of San Francisco is to watch the seals basking on the rocks at POINT LOBOS, formerly called *Punta de los Lobos*, at the entrance of the harbour. CAMERA DE

LOBOS, Madeira, is a cave formerly frequented by seals.

LOCARNO, a town on the Lago Maggiore, appears in 807 as (villa) *Leocardi*, the personal name Liutgard becoming Leocarda in Italian.

LOCHABER, a district in Inverness, takes its name from a loch now called LOCH LOCHABER, formerly *Lochabor*, the 'Loch at the river mouth.' LOCH LONG is believed to be the 'Loch of the ships' (Gaelic *long*, 'a ship'). LOCH BUIE in Mull is the 'yellow loch,' and LOCHINVAR is *Lochan-a-bharra*, the 'lake of the height.'

LODÈVE, a town in the Hérault, called *Loteva* in the Peutinger Tables, represents the tribal name of the *Lutevani*.

LODOMERIA, a Polish principality, is the realm of Vladimir, a Polish prince who governed it in the twelfth century.

LOGAN, a river in Australia, bears the name of a Captain Logan who was killed by the natives.

LOIRE, called in 1080 *Legrum*, is derived by Brachet from *Lig'rim*, the accusative of *Liger* or *Ligeris*, the Roman name of the river, which may be connected with that of the *Ligures*, who inhabited the coast district called Liguria, names probably from a pre-Aryan or Aryan root meaning water. We may compare the name of *Llyr* (King Lear), the old Celtic water-god.

LOMA, PUNTA DELLA, in California, is 'the hill cape' (Spanish *loma*, a 'hillock').

LOMBARDY, anciently *Langobardia*, is the land settled by the Langobardi or Lombards. Isidore of Seville and Paulus Diaconus tell us that the Langobardi were named from their long beards (*bart*, 'beard'). Grimm prefers this explanation to another from *parta*, the name of a weapon preserved in the words *hal-bert* and *part-izan*, which would make the name analogous to that of the Saxons, from *seax*, a short sword, and that of the Franks from *franca*, a kind of javelin. Some doubt is thrown on both these etymologies by the early forms *Bardi* for Langobardi, and *Bardungawi* for the *gau* or district on the left bank of the Elbe where they are placed by Velleius who accompanied Tiberius. In this region the dialect word *börde* or *bord* still signifies a fertile plain by the side of a river. A district near Magdeburg is still called the Lange Börde, and lower down near Lüneburg, we find the local names Bardengau and Bardewik.

LOMOND is a corruption of *leoman*, the old form of the Gaelic *leamhan*, pronounced *leven*, the plural of *leam*, a 'wych elm.' LOCH LOMOND, the *Leamanonius Lacus* of Ptolemy, and BEN LOMOND, the mountain at its head, retain the older form, while the RIVER LEVEN, which drains Loch Lomond, and STRATH LEVEN, through which the Leven flows, exhibit the newer form of the word. We have the same two forms in Fife, LOCH LEVEN, drained by the River Leven, being overlooked by the LOMOND HILLS. From the Fifeshire Leven we have the name LESLIE, a corruption of *Lis-Leven*, the enclosure or 'fort by the Leven'; while LENNOX, the old name of the district which corresponds to Dumbartonshire, is a corruption of the Gaelic *Levenach*, the 'district of the River Leven.' The RIVER LEAM, from which LEAMINGTON takes its name, may possibly be explained as an allied Cymric name.

LODI on the Adda, the scene of Napoleon's victory in 1796, is derived from the Roman name *Laus Pompeia*, the site of which is occupied by the village of LODI VECCHIO, five miles from the modern city of Lodi to which the name was transferred. LODI is from *laudi* the dative of *laus*.

LONDON is a name of uncertain etymology. It was known to the Romans as *Londinium*, and to the Saxons as *Lunden ceaster, Lundenwíc, Lundentun, Lundenburh, Lundena, Lundone, Lundun, Lundonia*, and *Lundenia*. The name is usually compared with that of *Lindum* (*See* LINCOLN), as meaning the 'dun by the llyn,' or pool; the dun being the hill on which St. Paul's stands, surrounded by the great tidal pool which covered the south bank of the Thames, and ran up the valleys of the Fleet and the Lea. The first vowel being a difficulty, it has been alleged that the Welsh *lynn* answers to the Cornish *lo*, which, however, is not the case. The name is doubtless Celtic, but the Welsh names Cair Lundain and Kaer Lundene, which we find in the Mabinogion and in Nennius, do not help us, as they were evidently derived from the Anglo-Saxon name. It is different with Geoffrey of Monmouth's *Cair Lud* (*Caer Lûd*), or 'city of Lûd,' which may preserve an important tradition, or may be one of his numerous inventions, suggested by the name of Ludgate, which might mean a 'postern gate' in Anglo-Saxon. But since Ludgate Hill leads directly to St. Paul's it is possible that the site of the cathedral may have been occupied by a temple of Llûdd, the Celtic war - god, otherwise known as Lodens, Nodens, or Nuada. The remains of one of his temples have been found at LYDNEY, (*q.v.*), the 'isle of Lodens,' on the Severn. He is also called King of the Lothians (*Lodonesia*). Whether *Lludd - dun* or *Luddon* could have become *Lun-dun* is a difficult question, but since the Domesday *Lodenesburg* has become Londesborough, and the *Pettalandfjörth* is now the PENT-LAND FIRTH, it is possible that *Loden-dun* or *Lud-dun* may have become Lundun or London. It has also been proposed to derive the name from a possible personal name **Londinos*. Some other untenable conjectures may be briefly noticed ; one deriving the name from the Gaelic word for a ship which we have in Loch Long, or from the Celtic *lom*, 'bare,' or from *clon* (*cluain*) which signifies land surrounded on one side by bog and on the other by water, which is common in such Irish names as Clontarf or Clonboy, and finally it has been proposed to explain the name as *Luna-dun*, on the supposition that the site of St. Paul's was occupied by a temple of Diana. The name London has been transferred to LONDON in Canada, and to LONDON in the Cape Colony. Davis gave the name of the LONDON COAST to the western shores of Greenland, in honour of the London merchants who had equipped his expedition. LONDONDERRY was long known as Derry (*q.v.*), the 'place of oaks,' but when in 1613 it was granted by James I. to the Irish Society of London, it was incorporated under the name of London-Derry. The town of LONDONDERRY, in New Hampshire, was settled in 1719 by 120 Presbyterian families from the North of Ireland. LONDRES DE CATAMARCA, an Argentine town in the province of Catamarca, and the district of Nueva Inglaterra, was founded by order of Philip of Spain, at the time of his marriage in London with Queen Mary of England.

Longford, the Anglicised form of the Irish *Longphort*, 'a fortress,' 'stone fort,' or 'castle,' is the name of twenty places in Ireland, one of which gives a name to an Irish county.

Lookers-on was the name given by Cook in 1770 to a part of the coast in the New Zealand province of Marlborough, where the natives gazed 'with a look of vacant astonishment' at his approach. The name has now been transferred to the coast range, which bears the name of the LOOKER-ON MOUNTAINS.

Look-out Head, Bass Strait, was as-cended by Flinders in order to take observations. MOUNT LOOK-OUT, on the Murray, was so called by Mitchell for a similar reason. Cook gave the name of POINT LOOK-OUT to two Australian capes seen by him from the mast-head, where he had stationed himself in order to discover a practicable passage through the maze of coral reefs around him.

Loon Lake in New Brunswick, and LOON HEAD on the Greenland coast, were named from the abundance of the water fowl called loons. LOMSBAY in Novaya Zemlya was so named for a similar reason by Barents in 1594, *lom* being the Dutch equivalent of *loon*.

Lopatka, the southern cape of Kamtchatka, which means a 'shoulder-blade' or 'shovel,' was so called by the Russians from its shape.

Lorca, a city in Spain, the *Eliocroca* of the Antonine Itinerary, and probably the *Ilorci* of Pliny, was called *Lorka* by the Arabs, whence the modern name.

Lorch, a town on the Rhine, was called in the third century *Lauriacum*, a Celto-Latin form derived from a personal name.

Loreto, near Ancona, is the place where according to the legend the Holy House of Joseph and Mary at Nazareth, carried by angels through the air, was deposited in a laurel grove, *lauretum*. It is officially called *Sacellum gloriosæ Virginis in Laureto*, whence the name Loreto, which has been transferred to LORETO in Lower California, and to NUESTRA SEÑORA DE LORETO in Peru, founded by the Jesuits in 1710.

Lorn, a district in the north-west of Argyll, bordering the Firth of Lorn, gives a second title to the Duke of Argyll. The modern spelling Lorne is wrong. It was the territory of the *Cinel Loarn*, or 'race of Loarn,' one of the three branches of the Dalriad Scots ; Loarn Mor, the 'great fox,' being one of the three brothers who in the fifth century are said to have led the colony of the Scots from Ireland to Argyll.

Lorraine is the French equivalent of the German name LOTHRINGEN. By the treaty of Verdun in 843 Burgundy and Provence were allotted to the Emperor Lothar I., son of Louis the Pious and grandson of Charlemagne. On the re-division of the Carlovingian Empire in 855, this great dominion, which has now dwindled to the modern province of Lorraine, fell to his son King Lothar II. in whose reign (855-968) it became known as the *Regnum Lothari* or *Lotharingia*, whence LOTHRINGEN, which signifies the land of the Lotharingi, as the subjects of Lothar were called, while either *Lotharingia* or *Lothari regnum* might become *Lot-règne* and then LORRAINE in French.

Los Angeles, in California, was founded in 1781 under the name *Pueblo de la Reina de los Angeles,* the 'town of the Queen of the Angels.'

Lot, a French department, was named from the River Lot, anciently the *Oltis,* which by prefixing the article became *L'Olt,* and finally Lot.

Lothian (Lodonia) was the name of the English district north of the Tweed, which now forms three Scotch counties. Skene holds it was the *Regio Loidis* of Bæda (654). It is called *Lothene* in the Saxon Chronicle, *Laodonia* in an early charter, and *Lethead* in Gaelic. The name is supposed to be Celtic, the old name *Lodonesia* being derivable from Lodens, Nodens, Llûd, or Nuada (King Lud), the Celtic war-god, who was said to have been king of Lodonesia. (*See* LONDON and LEEDS).

Louisiana, one of the United States, comprises a very small part of the vast region to which the name was first given. In 1681 La Salle left Lake Michigan, and after establishing a fort, which he called ST. LOUIS, on the Illinois River, descended the Mississippi to the Gulf of Mexico. On April 9th, 1682 he took formal possession of his discoveries in name of Louis XIV., in whose honour he gave the name of Louisiana to a great territory in the valley of the Mississippi, which by a secret treaty was transferred to Spain in 1762 ; it was ceded back to France in 1800, and purchased by the United States from Napoleon in 1803. The old territory of Louisiana now constitutes the states or territories of Louisiana, Arkansas, Missouri, Iowa, Nebraska, Idaho, Dakota, Montana, and parts of Minnesota, Wyoming, Colorado, and Kansas. ST. LOUIS, near the junction of the Mississippi and the Missouri, was founded as a trading station by Pierre Liguste la Clède in February 1764, the year in which France surrendered her possessions in this region. The settlers urged La Clède to give it his own name, but he insisted on calling it after Louis IX., the name-saint of Louis XV. (*See* ST. LOUIS.) LOUIS LE GRAND was the name given by Beauchesne in 1699 to one of the Fuegian islands, in honour of Louis XIV. LOUISBOURG, the French capital of Cape Breton, bears the name of Louis XV. who is said to have spent two millions sterling on its fortifica-

tions. LOUISVILLE, in Kentucky, is a large city on the Ohio. The name was bestowed in 1780 by the Virginian legislature as a compliment to Louis XVI., who was then assisting the Americans in their struggle for independence. ST. LOUIS, the capital of the French settlement of Senegambia, was founded in 1662 ; the name of ST. LOUIS has also been given to a town in Réunion, to a lake in Canada, to a river in Minnesota, and to one of the French West Indian Islands. The LOUISIADE ARCHIPELAGO, east of New Guinea, was discovered by Torres in 1606. In honour of Louis XV., Bougainville in 1769 gave the name of *Golfe de la Louisiade* to a supposed bay, called Louisiade Archipelago when in 1793 it was proved by d'Entrecasteau to be a group of islands, and not, as had been thought, an indentation in the coast of New Guinea.

Lourenzo Marquez, a district stretching from Delagoa Bay to the Limpopo, was so called from a trading station for ivory established by Lourenço Marquez, a Portuguese trader.

Lourmel, a town in Oran, bears the name of a French General who took part in the conquest of Algeria.

Louth, an Irish town which gives its name to the county of LOUTH, is a corruption of *Lugh-magh,* the 'field of Lugh.' LOUTH in Lincolnshire is on the River Lud, anciently the *Ludd.*

Louvain is the French, LÖWEN the German, and LOVEN or LEUVEN the Flemish name of a Belgian city called *Lovanium* in the seventh century.

Lowell, a manufacturing town on the Merrimack, in Massachusetts, was named after Francis C. Lowell of Boston. The native name, PATUCKET, which means 'at the falls,' occurs repeatedly in the States. There is a river called the PAWTUCKET in Rhode Island, and the PAWTUXUNT flows into Chesapeake Bay.

Loyalty Islands is the name of a Pacific group missed by Cook, and only discovered in 1794 by the ship *Walpole.* The name first appears on a map of 1799, but why it was bestowed is not known.

Lübeck bears the name of its founder, Liuby, a Slavonic prince. Old Lübeck was destroyed in 1139, and rebuilt on the present site in 1143.

Lucerne is the French form of the German name LUZERN. According to an old etymology, which dates from 695 A.D., a certain watch-tower served as a lighthouse, *lucerna,* for vessels navigating the

lake. In 844 mention is made of the *Monasterium Lucernense*, and in 1227 of a *Prior de Lucerna*. In some old documents the name is written *Luceria*, which might mean 'fishers' huts.' Possibly these names may be adaptations of an older Celtic name *lug-cern*. (*See* LYONS.) From the town the VIERWALDSTÄTTER SEE, or ' Lake of the four forest Cantons,' is often called the LAKE OF LUCERNE.

Lucknow (LÁKHNAO), the capital of Oudh, may be a corruption of *Lakshma-nauti*, the 'fortunate' or 'lucky.' Local legend refers its foundation to the mythical Lahshmana, who in the Rámáyana is the brother of Ráma, and son of Dasartha, Maharaja of Oudh.

Lucky Bay, West Australia, commemorates the good luck by which, at a critical moment, Flinders found a sheltered anchorage.

Ludwigsburg, a town in Würtemberg, was originally a hunting seat built in 1704 by Duke Eberhard Ludwig. LUDWIGS-LUST, in Mecklenburg-Schwerin, was a hunting seat erected by Duke Christian Ludwig II. in 1756. LUDWIGHAFEN, on the Lake of Constance, bears the name of Ludwig, Grand Duke of Baden, by whom it was founded in 1826. LUDWIGHAFEN, a free port on the Rhine, opposite Mannheim, was completed in 1843 by Ludwig, king of Bavaria, who also constructed the LUDWIG CANAL, which forms a communication between the German Ocean and the Black Sea, by uniting the Main, a tributary of the Rhine, with the Altmühl, a tributary of the Danube. LUDWIGHÖHE, one of the peaks of Monte Rosa, was first ascended by the Austrian Baron Ludwig in 1822.

Lugo, a town in the Spanish province of Galicia, represents the Roman *Lucus Augusti*, the ' grove of Augustus.'

Lukmanier is an Alpine pass leading from Medels in the Graubünden to Canton Ticino. The name was derived from the church at Medels, which is called in Latin documents *Santa Maria in luco magno*, ' St. Mary in the great wood.'

Luncheon Cove, Dusky Bay, New Zealand, is where Cook and Forster lunched on crabs, on April 13th, 1773.

Lund, which means ' a wood' or ' sacred grove,' is a common element in Scandinavian names, as LUND in Sweden, Denmark, and Yorkshire. LUNDY ISLAND in the Bristol Channel is so called because of the puffins (O.N. *lundi*, a puffin), by which it is frequented.

Lüneburg, a town in Prussia, anciently *Liuniburg*, is from the stem *hliun*, formed from the O.H.G. *hleo* (A.S. *hlaw*, now *law* or *low*), ' a hill.' LUNÉVILLE on the Meurthe, referred by the local legend to an ancient cult of Luna, the moon-goddess, is probably from the same root.

Lurgan is an Old Irish word meaning the ' shin' which is applied topographically to denote a long low ridge. There are thirty places in Ireland called Lurgan, and sixty more in which it forms part of the name.

Luton, in Bedfordshire, is the '*tún* on the River Lea,' as is shown by the name appearing as *Lygetún* in Offa's charter to St. Albans. In 1148 Henry of Huntingdon has *in finibus Luitoniæ*, which gives the transition to the modern name. LEYTON in Essex is also, like Luton, a tun on the Lea. Cuthbert went from Bedford to Aylesbury through *Lygeanbyrig*, the 'burh on the Lea,' which is most probably to be identified with LODBURN in Bucks. Lygean-burh is usually identified with Leighton Buzzard in Bedfordshire, but Leighton stands on the Ouse and not on the Lea, as does LENBURY, in Bucks, which has also been supposed to be the *Lygeanbyrig* or *Lygeanburh* of the Chronicle.

Luxemburg is a corruption of *Luzilunburch*, afterwards *Lutzelburg*, ' the little castle ' (O.H.G. *luzil*, 'little'). The name was extended from the castle to the town, and from the town to the Grand Dutchy of which it is the capital. By a folk-etymology the name was Latinised as *Lucis burgum*, the ' city of light,' and curiously enough the great discovery of the polarisation of light was made by viewing through Iceland spar the reflection of the sun's rays from the windows of the Luxembourg Palace at Paris.

Luxor, one of the villages on the site of the Egyptian Thebes, is a European corruption of the Arabic el-Aksor, ' the palaces,' an old plural of *Kasr*, p. 42. The modern plural is *el-Kasur*.

Luzon, or LUÇON, the largest of the Philippines, obtained its name from Lozon, a conspicuous promontory at the entrance to the bay of Manila, so named by the natives because its shape resembles that of the wooden trough or mortar, locally called *lasung* or *losong*, used for pounding rice. The name, denoting at first merely the district near Manila, was gradually extended to the whole island.

Lydney, or LIDNEY, a Gloucestershire village on the Severn, is notable for the remains of a British temple in which have been found inscriptions to the Celtic war-god, who became the King Lud of tradition, and from whom Ludgate and possibly London (Lud-dun or Ludendun) may be named. He is called Nodens, the Latin form of the Gaelic Nuada, in Welsh Nûdd and Llûdd.

Lyell Range, and MOUNT LYELL, in Australia, bear the name of Sir Charles Lyell the geologist. The Arctic LYALL BLUFF, and the Antarctic LYALL ISLETS, commemorate the services of Dr. David Lyall, who accompanied the expeditions of Captains Belcher and James Ross.

Lymne near Hythe in Kent is the *Portus Lemanis* of the Itineraries. Lemanis is a locative-plural meaning at the pools or lagoons. From the same source LAKE LEMAN, the classical name of the Lake of Geneva, is derived.

Lynn Regis or KING'S LYNN, Norfolk, was formerly Lynn Episcopi, or Bishop's Lynn, the name having been changed when at the Reformation the town passed into the hands of Henry VIII. The name is Celtic, denoting the 'pool' on the Ouse which formed the port. (*See* LINCOLN.) LYNN in Massachusetts, near Boston, was founded in 1627 and named after Lynn Regis, the home of its first pastor.

Lyon Inlet, in Fox Channel, bears the name of Captain G. F. Lyon, who commanded the *Hecla* in Parry's second voyage (1821).

Lyons, in French LYON, at the confluence of the Rhone and the Saône, is a corruption of the Celto-Roman name *Lugdunum* or *Lug-u-dunum*. The meaning of the Celtic name Lugu-dun is doubtful. The older etymologies make it either the 'dun on the marsh' or the 'raven fort.' Professor Rhys, following d'Arbois de Jubainville, considers that it is the dun or fortress of the god Lugus (Irish *Lug*), the Celtic solar hero. It is explained by Guest as 'Tower Hill' from a supposed Celtic word *lug*, a 'tower,' a meaning which Camden inferred from Mela's *Turris Augusta* being called *Lugo-Augusti* in the Antonine Itinerary. So Carlisle (*q.v.*), anciently *Luguballium*, would signify the tower or fort at the end of the Roman wall. (*See* LAON.) The GULF OF LIONS (*q.v.*) is not named from the city.

Lyra's Island, Corea, bears the name of the *Lyra*, Captain Basil Hall's ship. LYRA SHOAL, New Ireland, was discovered in 1826 by Captain Rennett in the ship *Lyra*.

Lyskamm, a ridge forming part of Monte Rosa, stands above the LYSTHAL or VAL LESA, which is drained by the River Lys or Lesa.

Lyttleton, Port, in New Zealand, founded in 1851, bears the name of Lord Lyttleton, the President of the association under whose auspices the province of Canterbury was colonised.

Maas, anciently the *Mosa*, is the Dutch name of the river called MAES in Flemish, and MEUSE in French. The meaning is unknown. Zeuss thinks the name is Celtic, while Ferguson suggests a Teutonic etymology, either the 'winding' or the 'marshy' river.

Maatsuyker Islands, Tasmania, were named by Tasman after a member of the Council of the Dutch East India Company in Batavia. They are also called De Witt Islands (*q.v.*), which is probably a later name.

Macadam is an absurd name given by Stokes to a range of Australian hills composed of a pudding-stone conglomerate, which reminded him of the macadamised roads invented by John Macadam.

Macao, a settlement near the mouth of the Canton River, occupied by the Portuguese since 1557, was built on the site of a temple of the goddess Ama, the so-called queen of heaven, a patroness of seamen. The Chinese name *Ama-ngao,* which means 'Ama Bay,' became successively *Amagoa, Amacao* (the usual form in old documents), and finally Macao. The Chinese now call it NGAO-MAN, the 'gate of the bay' (*ngao*, a bay or inlet, and *man*, a gate).

Macassar, the Dutch capital of Celébes, whence the name of the STRAITS OF MACASSAR, is a corruption of *Mangkasara* (in Portuguese *Macaçares*), the name of the paramount native tribe in the island.

M'Clintock Channel, in the Arctic Archipelago, bears the name of Captain M'Clintock, who, in 1859, discovered the fate of Sir John Franklin.

M'Clure Strait, CAPE M'CLURE, and M'CLURE BAY, bear the name of the officer to whom is due the final discovery of the North-West Passage, which had, however, practically been found by Sir John Franklin's ill-fated expedition, though none of his party survived to report the discovery that had been made.

M'Culloch Island and CAPE M'CULLOCH, in Arctic America, commemorate the services of the medical officer and geologist who accompanied the first expedition of John Ross.

M'Diarmid's Island was named after the medical officer in the second voyage of John Ross.

M'Gary Island, in Kane's Sea, bears the name of Kane's second officer.

M'Kay River, Queensland, bears the name of the first settler on its banks. M'KAY'S PEAK, on the Great Fish River, was called after a Highlander in Back's expedition, who volunteered to ascend it.

Mackenzie River, flowing into the Arctic Ocean, was discovered and descended in 1789 by Alexander Mackenzie, the first European who reached the Arctic Ocean. Till Franklin in 1825 gave it its present name it was known as the Great River. In 1793 Mackenzie crossed the continent, and reached the Pacific near the Strait of Fuca at MACKENZIE'S OUTLET. MACKENZIE ISLANDS, in the Caroline Group, bear the name of Captain MAC-KENZIE, commander of the *James Scot*, who discovered them in 1823 on a voyage from Acapulco to Calcutta.

Mackinaw, a corruption of *Michilli-mackinack*, 'the great tortoise,' is an island in the strait between Lakes Michigan and Huron, which resembles a tortoise asleep on the water.

Mâcon, a town in Burgundy, formerly *Mascon*, is from an oblique case of *Matisco*, a town of the Ædui.

Macquarie Island, seven hundred miles south-west of New Zealand, is named after General Lachlan Macquarie, Governor of New South Wales from 1809 to 1821. From him are also named MAC-QUARIE RIVER, MACQUARIE STRAIT, LACHLAN RIVER, PORT MACQUARIE, and the MACQUARIE MOUNTAINS, all in Australia, as well as MACQUARIE HARBOUR and the MACQUARIE RIVER in Tasmania. Governor Macquarie had a craze for naming places, bestowing many during his visit to Tasmania in 1810. To him we may probably attribute the numerous Scotch names in the colony, such as BOTHWELL and BEN LOMOND, and the Rivers CLYDE, LEVEN, ESK, FORTH, and GORDON, if not those of the TAMAR, SHANNON, OUSE, and CAM. Two small outlying islands north of Macquarie Island, discovered in 1811, are called the JUDGE and HIS CLERK, and two similar islands, south of Macquarie Island, are called the BISHOP and HIS CLERK. The MACDONNELL RANGES in Australia bear the name of Sir R. G. Macdonnell, a Governor of South Australia.

Madagascar is a name which, owing to a curious misconception, has been transferred, in European maps, from a place on the mainland to the great African island. It is only within recent years that the Hovas have adopted from the missionaries the name *Madagaskara* as the designation of their island. It was possibly the *Menruthias* of the Greek geographers, and was certainly known to the medieval Arabs, probably as *Komr* or *Komara*, the 'moon' island. The first European who visited it was Fernão Soares, a Portuguese captain who sighted the East Coast on February 1st, 1506, the eve of St. Lawrence (Archbishop of Canterbury), the West Coast being discovered by João Gomez d'Abreu on August 10th in the same year, the feast of St. Lawrence the martyr, hence it was named *Ilha de San Lourenzo*, and was long known as *St. Laurens*. The name Madagascar is due to Marco Polo, who at the end of the thirteenth century described, seemingly from the hearsay reports of Arab or Malay sailors, a large island, which is called in various MSS. of his travels *Magastar, Mandeschar, Mandesgascar, Madagastar, Madeigascat,* and *Madeigascar*. He says the country abounded in lions, leopards, elephants, and giraffes, and that the people are Moslems, who eat camels, a description excluding Madagascar, where there were neither lions, giraffes, elephants, or Moslems, but manifestly referring to some part of the mainland of Africa, probably to Magadascar or Magadoza (now called Magadoxo), a town and State in the southern part of the Somali peninsula, called *Macdasur* in Fra Mauro's map (1459) and *Makdaschau* by Ibn-Batuta, who describes the people as eating camels. In 1492 Martin Behaim, endeavouring to represent on his globe Marco Polo's account of Magadoza on the mainland, depicted it as a large island which he calls Madeigascar, the name found in one MS. of Marco Polo's travels, placing it some 1400 miles north of 'Zanguebar,' and not 400 miles south of it like the real island. The false Madagascar also appears in 1546 in the map of Honterius, but has disappeared in that of Peter Apian in 1551, of Mercator in 1569, and of Ortelius in 1570. In 1591 Captain Lancaster calls this island which he visited ST. LAWRENCE or MADAGAS-CAR. The word Malagasy or Malagasi is now used to designate the people and language of Madagascar, with which it seems to have no linguistic connection. The old Swahili, a language which was spoken on the coast from the Straits of Bab-el-Mandeb nearly as far as Zanzibar, was called *Ki-n-gozi*, 'the speech of the men,' and their country was called *U-n-gozi*, 'the land of the men,' *n-gozi* or *m-gozi* meaning 'men,' the *n* or *m* being a plural affix. Malagasi would therefore mean in Swahili the 'Mala men.' What Mala means is doubtful. Malagasi is essentially a Malay language, having no affinities with any African tongue, and hence Malagasi might mean the 'Malay men.'

Maderaner Thal, in Canton Uri, is so called from an Italian named Maderano, who worked a mine at the entrance to the val'ey.

Madeira is the chief island of the Madeira Group in the North Atlantic. From the Medicean map of 1351 it appears that the Italian mariners in the fourteenth century called it *Isola do Legname*, 'the wooded island,' of which the Portuguese name *Ilha da Madeira*, 'island of timber,' is a translation. The RIO DA MADEIRA, one of the great tributaries of the Amazons, is a descriptive name referring to the vast tropical forest through which it flows. The Spanish and Portuguese word *madeira* or *madera* is the Latin *materia* (whence our words *matter, materials,* and *immaterial*), originally timber for building, and afterwards wood or forest. (*See* MADRID.)

Madison, the State capital of Wisconsin, and two hundred and twenty-three counties, towns, and townships, chiefly in Ohio, Indiana, Iowa, Pennsylvania, and Missouri, bear the name of James Madison, fourth President of the United States (1809-1817).

Madras is usually explained as if from the conjectural name *Madrisa-patam*, 'the city of the college' (Arabic *Madrissa*, a college or university). But the oldest known form of the name is *Mandraj*, apparently from *Mandra-raj*, the 'realm of Mandra,' a name of the god Yama. An older Tamil name was *Chinna-patnam*, the 'little town.'

Madrid was made the capital of Spain in 1560 by Philip II. The name is usually explained from the Arabic *madarat*, a 'town.' But the early form *Mazerit* or *Magerit*, given in the Chronicle of Sampiro, points to *materita*, a 'small wood' or 'copse,' a diminutive of *materia*, as the true etymology. (*See* MADEIRA.)

Maelson, an island near Novaya Zemlya,

was discovered by the Dutch in 1594 and named after Franz Maelson, a member of the Dutch Council.

Maelström, correctly MALSTRÖM, a whirlpool south of the Lofoden Islands is the 'grinding stream' (Norwegian, *male*, 'to grind').

Maentwrog, in Merioneth, is the 'Stone of Twrog.' The OLD MAN of Coniston, the OLD MAN in Cornwall, the OLD MAN of Hoy in the Orkneys and the DEADMAN or DODMAN, a Cornish headland, are supposed to be from *maen*, 'a rock.'

Magdala, the 'tower,' a hill fortress in Abyssinia, gives a title to Lord Napier of Magdala, by whom it was stormed in 1868. Another MAGDALA, a town of Galilee, is best known as the birthplace of Mary Magdalene or Mary of Magdala, whence MADALENA, one of the Marquesas, discovered by Mendana on July 21st, 1595, the eve of her festival, and MAGDALENA, the largest affluent of the Orinoco, which gives its name to a State in the South American republic of Columbia.

Magdeburg, in Prussian Saxony, called in Latin documents *Parthenopolis*, the 'maiden's town,' obtained its name according to the local tradition, because the Empress Eadgyth (Edith) received it as a dowry on her marriage with the Emperor Otho (936-973). This tradition is disposed of by the fact that the name is much older, appearing in 805 as *Magathaburg* (O.H.G. *magad*, 'a maid'). The 'maiden' from whom the town was named was a heathen idol, destroyed by Charlemagne. We are told it was an image of Venus, by which the chronicler doubtless meant Holda.

Magellan's Strait, between Fuegia and Patagonia, was discovered by a Portuguese in the Spanish service, who is called Fernão de Magelhães in Portuguese, Fernando de Magellanes in Spanish, and in English books Ferdinand Magellan, a name which should not be pronounced Magéllan but Magellán, with the accent on the last syllable. With a squadron of five ships equipped by the Emperor Charles V. he sailed from Seville in 1519. Arriving at Port St. Julian in Patagonia, a mutiny broke out among the captains, which was suppressed with great but necessary vigour. On October 21st, the festival of the eleven thousand virgins, Magellan discovered the entrance to the strait which now bears his name, calling it *Estrecho de las Virgines*, a name still preserved by CAPE VIRGINS at its northern entrance. On

November 1st, All Saints Day, he began the passage of the actual strait, which he named from the day *Estrecho de Todos los Santos.* Other names have been proposed, but by common consent the name of the discoverer has been justly preferred. He was thirty-seven days working through the strait, and on November 28th, 1520, he reached the much 'desired Cape,' CABO DESEADO, and passed out into the open ocean to the West, ignorant of its identity with the 'South Sea,' discovered seven years before by Balboa. For more than three months he sailed over it without a storm, and hence he called it MAR PACIFICO, the 'peaceful sea.' After touching at the Ladrones (*q.v.*) he reached the Philippines, where, on April 26th, 1521, he was killed in a skirmish with the natives. One only of the ships, the *Victoria,* in command of her pilot, with eighteen survivors on board, reached Seville on September 8th, 1522, after an absence of nearly three years, thus accomplishing, for the first time, the circumnavigation of the globe.

Maggiore, Lago, in Italy, the 'larger lake,' is fed by the RIVER MAGGIA, probably a back-formation from Maggiore.

Magnetic Isle, Queensland was so called by Cook, in 1770, on account of a local deviation of the compass. A similar reason explains the names of MAGNETIC ISLE, Newfoundland, MAGNETIC CAPE, in Corea, and MOUNT MAGNET in West Australia.

Mahé, the largest of the Seychelles, whence the group is sometimes called the MAHÉ ARCHIPELAGO, was so named by Picault, in 1742, in honour of Mahé de Labourdonnaye, Governor of the French possessions in India.

Mahon, or PORT MAHON, the capital of Minorca, was founded c. 702 B.C. by Magôn, a Carthaginian general, the father of Hanno, and grandfather of Hamilcar, whence the Roman name *Portus Magonis.* In 1708 Port Mahon was taken by the English under General James Stanhope, afterwards created Earl Stanhope and Viscount Mahon ; the name of the Carthaginian General being thus curiously retained in the title of an English peer who lived twenty-four centuries later.

Mahrattas were the people of the *Mahrath* (Sanskrit *Mahârâshtra*), the 'great raj' or kingdom of Central India.

Maidenhead is a town in Berkshire, on the Thames. According to the local legend the name arose from the veneration paid to the head of a martyred British virgin. This legend finds expression in the corporation seal, which bears a maiden's head. Maidenhead is however a corruption of *Maidenhythe,* apparently signifying the 'maiden's wharf,' a meaning so improbable that it has been conjectured to be either *mædu-hythe,* the 'wharf by the meadow,' or *midde-hythe,* the 'landing-place' mid-way between Marlow and Windsor. Another etymology is the 'timber wharf,' from the A.S. *mæd,* which, according to a conjecture of Professor Leo, meant a tree-trunk. Before 1297 a timber bridge had been built over the Thames, and the Crown granted to the town the right to have a tree every year from Windsor Forest to keep the bridge in repair, the name *Mædena-hythe,* denoting the wharf where these tree-trunks were landed, thus replacing the older name Aylinton or Elington.

Maidstone, the county town of Kent, takes its name from the Medway, on which it stands, as appears from the A.S. name *Medwæges-tún,* 'Medway tun,' which became *Medwæston,* and finally Maidstone.

Maimatchin, which means 'market town' in Chinese, stands on the frontier of China opposite to the Russian station of Kiakhta or Kiachta (*q.v.*), where goods are exchanged. The word *chin,* 'a walled town,' is a common element in Chinese names, as in CHIN-KIANG, the 'town on the river,' one of the treaty-ports.

Main, a river joining the Rhine opposite Maintz, was the *Roman Moenus* (Gaulish *Moinos*), a name derived from the root *moi,* seen in *me-are* to 'move' or 'go.' The name MAINTZ has taken its present form owing to a very natural popular etymology deriving it from the name of the River Main. The French form, MAYENCE, is less corrupt, and points to the Roman name *Mogontiacum,* afterwards *Moguntia,* possibly derived either from an hypothetical tribe-name Moguntii, or from a personal name Mogontios, 'the mighty,' but most probably from a deity commemorated in an inscription found in Wales, *Deo Mogonti,* who has been identified with Belenos, the god of light. CASTEL, a suburb of Maintz, represents the *Castellum Drusi* built by Drusus, B.C. 13.

Maine, an old French province, was the territory of the Cenomani. The chief town, LE MANS, occupies the site of the place called *Cenomani* in the Notitia. The form Maine is derived from *Cenomania,* and Le Mans from the dative plural *Cenomanis*, just as Rheims and Amiens are from the dative plurals Remis and Ambianis. According to Glück the Celtic name means a place or district. (*See* MAN.)

Maine, one of the New England States, doubtless repeats the name of the French province. In some old Portuguese maps it appears as Terra de Bacalhaos, 'the land of stock fish' or dried cod. In 1603 Henry IV. of France granted it by charter to De Monts, a French gentleman, who, though there is no evidence of the fact, may have given it the name of Maine. In 1622 the territory was granted by James I. to Gorges and Mason, who proposed, with the approbation of the Council, to call it the Province of Maine, possibly in compliment to Henrietta Maria, who was married to Charles I. in 1625, and whose dowry was charged on the revenues of the French Province of Maine. It has also been conjectured that the name originated with the cod fishers, who called it the mainland as distinguished from the neighbouring islands.

Majo, one of the Cape Verd islands, which means 'May' in Portuguese, was discovered by the Portuguese on May 1st, 1462.

Majorca, in Spanish MALLORCA, the larger of the two great Balearic islands, is the Roman *Balearica Major*; MINORCA, in Spanish MENORCA, the lesser island, being *Balearica Minor*. In the seventh century Isidore of Seville has *Majorica* and *Minorica*. The Arabs made the name into *Mayurkàh*, whence the name Majorca, a form introduced on English maps at a time when *j* was pronounced as *y*. The correct Spanish spelling is Mallorca, *ll* being pronounced as *ly*. From a manufactory at Ynca, in Mallorca, came the Majolica ware. Dante mentions the pottery from the island of Maiolica.

Majunga, correctly MOJANGA, the chief port on the north-west coast of Madagascar, was a settlement of Swahili Arabs, who called it *Mji-angaia*, the 'town of flowers,' from the flowering shrubs on the shore.

Makololo are a South African people. Chibitano, a Bantu conqueror, formed an army of men of different races and origins, who were hence called the *kololo* or 'mixed people,' which, with the prenominal prefix usual in Bantu tribe names, became *Ma-kololo*. (*See* BANTU and WASU-KUMA.) MANICALAND, in like manner, is the land of the Nica people or *Ma-Nica*, and MASHONALAND that of the Shona people or *Ma-Shona*. Mashonaland has been exploited by the British Chartered Company of South Africa, who have named their principal stations FORT VICTORIA, FORT CHARTER, and FORT SALISBURY after the Prime Minister under whom the charter was granted by Queen Victoria.

Mekong, or MECHONG, the great river of Cambodia, is believed to mean the 'head of the waters.'

Makronisi, the 'long island,' lying off the coast of Attica, was anciently called *Makris*, a name also applied to Euboea.

Malabar, in Southern India, is called in the eleventh century Tanjore inscription, *Malai-nadu*, 'the mountain country.' MALAYALAM, now the name of the language spoken on the Malabar Coast, is a corruption of *Malaya-lan*, which means the 'mountain region,' *malaya* being the Sanskritic form of *malai*, the Dravidian word for a 'mountain.' (*See* MALAY.) MALABAR is believed to be an Arabic formation, as it first appears in the geography of Edrisi (c. 1150, A.D.), while Ibn Batuta has *Mulai-bar*. The suffix *-bar* is probably the Arabic *barr*, a 'continent' (whence the Persian loan-word *bár*), which appears in ZANZIBAR, the 'country of the blacks,' in Hindubar, the Arab name of India, and in the Nicobar Islands, or, as Lassen thinks, it may be a corruption of the Sanskrit *vara*, a 'region,' as in MAR-WAR or DHAR-WAR. MALABAR HILL, a favourite site for villas on Bombay Island, is believed to have acquired its name from the fact that the ships of the Malabar pirates, who haunted this coast, used to lie behind it.

Malabrigo Road, an open roadstead on the Peruvian Coast, means 'bad shelter.' The Spaniards gave the same name to an open roadstead near the mouth of the Oregon, and a group of islands in the North Pacific, east of the Bonin Islands, discovered by Villalobos in 1542, are called the MALABRIGOS.

Malacca (*Málaka*), a town which has given its name to the Straits of Malacca, was founded, it is said, in 1253 by a king of Singapore, and was doubtless so named on account of the abundance of the *malaka* tree, *Phyllanthus emblica*. From the town the name spread to the Malay peninsula and then to the straits which separate the peninsula from Sumatra. The natives believe the name is from *maha-lanka*, the 'great island' or peninsula, an obvious folk-etymology.

Malaga, in Spain, anciently *Malaca*, is believed to be from a Phœnician word *malah*, which means 'salt,' perhaps because it was a station where the tunny fish were salted for export.

Malakoff, a hill whose capture decided the fate of Sebastopol, bears the name of a Russian sailor who established a tavern on the hill. It gave the title of duke to Marshal Pelissier. (*See* PIMLICO.)

Malay Peninsula is a modern European name for one of the chief regions inhabited by the Malays, so called by the Indians because they inhabited the *Maléala* or 'highlands' on the Western Coast of Sumatra. They call themselves *Orang Malayu*, 'Malay men' or 'mountain men.' We have the Tamil word *málai*, 'mountains,' in the name MALABAR (*q.v.*), and of MALWA, a South Indian district, which signifies the 'mountainous country,' as well as in the PACHA-MÁLAI or 'green mountains,' and the ANA-MÁLAI or 'elephant mountains,' both in Southern India. MALAY ROAD, North Australia, was so named by Flinders in 1803 because he here encountered six Malay praus from Macassar. In MALAY BAY, North Australia, King, in 1818, found some Malay vessels at anchor.

Maldives are a cluster of coral islets in the Indian Ocean. The usual etymology 'the thousand isles,' from *mal*, a 'thousand,' and *diva*, 'an island,' is probably erroneous. There is some reason for supposing that the correct form is *Malaya diva*, the Malay or Mala-bar Islands. The oldest form is simply *Divas*, 'the islands.' Another old form is *Mahal-dib* or *Dhibat-al-Mahal*, 'the islands of Mahal,' the largest of the group being *Mahal*, now called MALI. The islands being arranged in a chain, like a necklace, it has also been suggested that the name may be from the Sanskrit *mala*, 'a chaplet' or 'row.'

Maldon in Essex, and MALTON in Yorkshire have both been erroneously identified with the Roman *Camalodunum*, the *dun* or hill of Camalos, a British deity. Maldon is called Mældun in the Chronicle, and is supposed to have acquired its name from a cross erected on the hill (A.S. *mæl*, a mark, sign, or cross). MALTON, called Maltun in Domesday, is apparently from the A.S. *mal*, which means a 'place of assembly,' and also 'rent, toll, or tribute,' either from some local tenure, or from a toll which may have been taken at the ancient bridge which here connects the North and East Ridings. MALDEN or MALDON, a Pacific Island,

west of the Marquesas, discovered in 1825, bears the name of an officer of Byron's ship the *Blonde*.

Malines, the French name of the city called MECHLIN or MECHLEN in Flemish, was in the eighth century a group of cabins surrounding the monastery of St. Rombaul. The name is explained from the O.H.G *mahal*, a 'place of assembly' or 'place of justice.'

Mallow, in County Cork, is called in Irish *Moyalla*, a corruption of *Magh-Ealla*, the 'plain of the River Ealla,' now the Allow. The Irish *magh* frequently becomes *moy*, as in FERMOY, the land of the 'men of the plain.' MOYNE is from the diminutive *maighin*, the 'little plain.' A common derivative of *magh* is *maghera* (*machaire*) which we have in MAGHERA-MORE, the 'great plain,' MAGHERALOUGH, the 'plain of the lake,' and MAGHERA-BOY, the 'yellow plain.' In Welsh *magh* becomes *ma*, as in MALLWYD in Merioneth and Denbighshire, which is *ma-llwyd*, the 'grey plain.'

Malmesbury, in Wilts, is the place where Mailduf, an Irish monk, dwelt as a hermit. About 642, with the assistance of St. Ealdhelm (Aldhelm), the nephew of King Ina, a monastery and a stately church were erected on the site of Mailduf's cell. The name Malmesbury seems to have arisen from a confusion between the names of the two founders, Maildulf and Ealdhelm, the early forms *Maildulfesburh*, *Mœldubesberg*, and *Maldubesburg* coming from the name of Maildulf, and *Ealdelmesbyrig* from Ealdhelm. *Maldumesburuh* and *Mealdumsbyrig*, which are found in a charter of 675, exhibit a combined form from which the name Malmesbury arose. MALMESBURY in the Cape Colony was named from Lord Malmesbury, Secretary for Foreign Affairs.

Malmö, in Sweden, means 'sand island,' from *malm*, 'sand,' a common element in Swedish names.

Malpais, 'bad land,' is a name given in Mexico and the Canaries to barren lava fields. MALPAS on the Welsh border takes its name from a Norman castle, erected to command the 'bad pass' or road. MAUPAS (Aisne) is a similar name

Malta, a corruption of the old name *Melita*, has been supposed to mean the island of 'honey.' But, as Bochart and Gesenius maintain, the name is probably Phœnician, meaning the 'refuge,' either for fugitives, or on account of its excellent harbours, for ships.

Malvasia, in the Morea, whence Malmsey wine was exported, is the Italian *Napoli de Malvasia*, a corruption of the Greek name *Monembasia*, the place with a 'single approach' or entrance.

Man is an island in St. George's Channel. The Welsh name was *Manau*, and the Irish *Manann*, both of which are genitive forms. We have the first in the name of the MENAI STRAITS, *i.e.* the Straits of Manu, or Anglesea, and the second in CLACKMANNAN (*q.v.*). The nominative *manu* (Cæsar's Mona) became *Maun* or *Mön* among the Scandinavians. Glück and Zeuss refer the name to the Cymric word *man*, a 'place' or district,' which we have in MAINE. THE ISLE OF MAN, in St. George's Channel, between New Britain and New Ireland, was discovered by Carteret in 1767, and named from its position.

Manaos, a town at the confluence of the Rio Negro and the Amazon, bears the name of the Manaos, a native tribe.

Mancha is a Spanish word meaning 'ground covered with weeds.' LA MANCHA, a district in the South of Castile, is best known from the title given to his hero by Cervantes.

Manchester, is believed to represent the Roman *Mancunium* or *Manutium*. The variant reading *Mamucium* is supported by the *Mameceaster* of the Chronicle. Baxter's conjecture, made in 1719, that Mancunium represents a Cymric word *Man-cenion*, the 'place of skins' (*i.e.* tents), has been adopted by several subsequent writers. Another etymology has been proposed from *maen*, a 'stone,' which we have in Maen-twrog (*q.v.*) and other names. Most probably *man* is a Celtic word meaning a 'place.' MANCETTER or MANCHESTER in Warwickshire, represents the Roman *Manduessedum*.

Manchuria is the European name of the region inhabited by the Manchus, a Tungusic tribe, who furnished the dynasty which has ruled China for the last three centuries. According to Prof. Douglas *Manchu* means 'pure,' a name chosen by the founder as a suitable designation for his family. The MANTZU, a wild race on the Upper Kiang, bear a Chinese name meaning, according to Colonel Yule, 'sons of the barbarians.'

Mandalay or MANDALÉ, the capital of Burma, was founded in 1860. The usual etymology is from the Pali *mandala*, a 'flat plain,' but, according to Colonel Yule, the name was that of an isolated conical hill, rising high above the alluvial plain of the Irawadi, and crowned by a gilt Pagoda. The name of the hill represents, he thinks, that of the sacred mountain called *Mandara*, which in the Hindu mythology served the gods as a churning-staff at the churning of the sea.

Mandan, a place in Dakota, preserves the name of the Mandan tribe, who called themselves *Mi-ah-ta-nes*, the 'people on the bank,' *i.e.* of the River Missouri.

Mandingo, a powerful people in Western Africa, are the inhabitants (*ngo*) of Mandin, one of the districts they occupy.

Manfredonia is a town in Southern Italy, built in 1265 by Manfred, king of Naples. It gives a name to the GULF OF MANFREDONIA.

Manga, which means in Maori the 'branch of a river,' is a common prefix in New Zealand names, such as MANGWHARA and MANGARERA.

Manhattan, the island on which New York is built, was formerly called the Manhattans, or the Manhudoes, probably from the Indian tribe which occupied it. Boyd explains it as *munohan*, 'the island.' There is a story that it was called *Mana-hacteneid*, 'the place of drunkenness, Henry Hudson in 1609 having taken some chiefs into his cabin and made them drunk.

Manila, the capital of the Philippines, was founded in 1571 by Legaspi on the site of a native village of the same name, which is derived from a shrub called *nila*, the prefix being the Tagala verb substantive; Manila thus meaning ' Nila is,' or ' here is Nila.'

Manipur is a native State between Burma and Assam. About 150 years ago the Manipuris, a Naga tribe, having accepted Hinduism, called their country Manipur, because in the Mahábhárata the hero Arjan is said to have travelled eastward to a mythical locality called Manipur, and to have married a Manipuri princess.

Manisa, in Asia Minor, is the Galatian name *Magnesia* (whence the words magnet and magnetism), supposed to contain the Gaulish word *magh*, a 'plain.'

Manitoba, the central province of the Canadian Dominion, formerly called the Red River Settlement, takes its name from Lake Manitoba, whose islands were believed by the natives to be the habitation of the Manito or great spirit. In the Algonquin language, *manito, manitu*, or *manitou* means a spirit, a ghost, or anything supernatural. The last syllable of Manito-ba is a fragment of the Cree word *waban*, a 'strait.' The MANITU ISLANDS in Lake Michigan, the MANITOULIN ISLANDS in Lake Huron, and LAKE MANITU on the White Sand River were also supposed to be the abodes of spirits. A town in Wisconsin is called MANITOWOC.

Mannheim, a city on the Rhine, was called in 764 *Manninheim*, evidently from a personal name.

Manning Strait, in the Salomon Group, was first traversed in 1792 by Captain Manning in the ship *Pitt*.

Mansfield, Notts, is a corruption of *Maunsfeld*, the field on a small stream called the Maun.

Mansura, or MANSOORAH, a town on the Damietta branch of the Nile, is the Arabic *mansura*, 'victorious.' MANSOURA, in Algeria, is the same name in the French spelling.

Mantua, in Northern Italy, was an Etruscan town, probably named from *Mantu*, one of the Etruscan deities.

Manukau is the name of the western harbour of Auckland, New Zealand. It is so called from the *Leptospermum scoparia*, called *manuka* in Maori, which grows abundantly on the rocks.

Manzanares, in Spain, means the 'apple orchards' (Spanish *manzanar*, an orchard,' from *manzana*, an 'apple tree'). From the same source comes LAS MANZANAS, a mission station in the Patagonian Cordillera, where the Jesuits planted many apple trees, which now grow wild.

Maoris is the duplicate plural formation by which we designate the New Zealand aborigines, who call themselves *Tangata Maori*, 'the native men,' or simply *Maori*, 'natives.'

Mapledurwell in Hants, MAPLEDURHAM in Oxon, and MAPPOWDER in Dorset are from the A.S. *mapulder*, a 'maple tree.'

Maracaybo, a town in Venezuela, has given a name to the Lake and Gulf of Maracaybo. The name is said to be that of a Cacique, encountered here by Alonzo de Hojeda in 1499.

Marañon, the name of the Upper Amazon, is believed to be from the native name of the edible fruit of the *Anacardium occidentale*, which grows abundantly on its banks. Marañon is a Spanish form which would become Maranhon (Maranhão) in Portuguese, the name which, possibly through some confusion, was given to one of the mouths of the Amazon, and then

extended to the largest island of the Delta, and finally to the adjacent province of Maranhão. The names may, however, be independent, *maranha* meaning in Portuguese a 'tangled skein,' and thus denoting the network of streams in the Delta of the Amazon. On the island of MARANHÃO the French built a fort which they called St. Louis. In 1615 the Portuguese took the place, which is now called SAN LUIS DO MARANHÃO.

Marathona in Attica retains the old Phœnician name *Marathon*, 'abounding in fennel,' though the name may have been transferred from *Marathus*, a city in Phœnicia.

Marazion, in Cornwall, is often said to be a Phœnician name, a wild theory supported by the name Market-Jew, by which it is also known. But Market-Jew and Marazion are doubtless the Cornish names *Marchasow* and *Marchasion*, two forms of the plural of *Marchaz*, 'the market.'

March Harbour, in Fuegia, was entered by Captain Fitzroy on March 1st, 1830.

Marengo, a battlefield near Alessandria, in Piedmont, is one of the patronymic Lombard names in Northern Italy.

Margarita, an island off the coast of Venezuela, was discovered on August 13th, 1498 by Columbus, who called it Isla Margarita, the 'pearl island,' imagining that pearls, which he had recently obtained by barter from the natives, would here be found.

Margate, in Kent, is a corruption of *Meregate*, either meaning the gate or gap leading to the sea, or the passage by which a small stream, locally called a 'mere,' flowed into the sea.

Mariazell, in Styria, is a place of pilgrimage possessing a miracle-working picture of the Virgin Mary. MARIASTEIN is a Benedictine Abbey in Canton Solothurn, standing on the edge of a precipice over which, according to the legend, a child fell, but was miraculously saved by the aid of the Virgin. MARIENBURG, near Dantzig, called in Polish MALBORG, takes its name from a castle built by the Teutonic knights in 1276, and dedicated to the Virgin, which formed for a hundred and fifty years the residence of the Grand Masters of the Teutonic order. SANTA MARIA, one of the Azores, was discovered by Cabral on the Feast of the Assumption of the Virgin, August 15th, 1432. SANTA MARIA DA SERRA is a shoal off the Arabian Coast, on which the Governor of the Indies, Alfonso d'Albuquerque, grounded in his ship the *Santa Maria da Serra*. MARIE GALANTE, one of the French Antilles discovered by Columbus on his second voyage, 1493, received from him the name of his ship, the *Marigalante*. MARIETTA, the oldest town in Ohio, was founded in 1788 by General Putnam, and named in honour of Marie Antoinette. MARIA ISLAND, on the East Coast of Tasmania, was so named by Tasman in 1642, after Maria Van Diemen, daughter of the Governor of the Dutch East Indies, after whom MARIA BAY in Amsterdam Island, one of the Friendly Islands, was also named by Tasman in 1643. CAPE MARIA VAN DIEMEN, the north-western point of New Zealand, and an island in the Gulf of Carpentaria are also believed to bear the name of the same lady. MARIANAS (or Ladrones), a Pacific group, were named in 1668, in honour of Maria Anna of Austria, wife of Philip IV. of Spain. Magellan, who discovered them, wished the name to be *Islas de las Velas Latinas*, because the native boats were rigged with lateen sails, but his sailors cho-e to call them *Islas de los Ladrones*, the 'thieves' islands,' because of the thievish propensities of the natives. MARIANNA, a Brazilian town, was so named in 1745 in honour of the Arch-duchess Marianna of Austria, wife of John IV. of Portugal. . MARIEN CANAL, connecting the Volga with the Lake of Onega, was constructed by Peter the Great, and bears the name of his mother, Maria Feodorowna. MARIENSK, a Russian town, founded in 1853, on the Lower Amoor, was named after Mary of Hesse Darm-stadt, wife of the Czarevich.

Mark is a Teutonic word meaning a frontier. The ALTMARK was the 'old march' or military frontier erected by the Emperor Henry I. against the Wends. The names of the MITTELMARK, the UKERMARK, and the NEUMARK exhibit the successive extensions of the Teutonic frontier. (*See* DENMARK.)

Marlborough, Wilts, gave to the victor of Blenheim the ducal title from which the province of MARLBOROUGH in New Zealand has been named. Marl-borough appears in the Saxon Chronicle as *Mærle-beorh*, apparent from *mærlic*, 'noble,' 'glorious' or 'lofty,' and *beorh*, a 'hill.' MARWELL, Gloucestershire, called *Mærwil* in a charter, is the 'boundary well.'

Marmora, an island so called from its quarries of white marble, has given a name to the SEA OF MARMORA, between the Bosphorus and the Dardanelles.

Marne is the modern name of the river known to the Romans as the *Matrona*, a name referred to the Celtic goddess Matrona, the matron or mother. But our use of the term Father Thames, or Macaulay's line, 'Oh Father Tiber, to whom the Romans pray,' may suggest a simpler reason for designating a river by a name meaning the mother. Other con-jectural etymologies are given by Ferguson.

Maronites, a Christian people in the Lebanon, ultimately derive their name from the monastery of Mâr Mârôn (St. Maron), where the founder of the sect, hence called John of Mârôn, had studied.

Màroparàsy, 'many fleas,' is a frequent and appropriate village name in Mada-gascar.

Marpori, a mountain in Tibet, is so called from its 'red' rocks. MARPO LUNGBA, also in Tibet, is the 'red river.'

Marquesas, 'the Marquis Islands,' a South Pacific group, sometimes called the MENDAÑA ARCHIPELAGO (*q.v.*), were dis-covered in 1595 by Alvaro Mendaña, and named by him *Marquesas de Mendoza* in honour of his uncle the Marqués de Men-doza, Viceroy of Peru, who had despatched the expedition. In 1791 Captain Ingra-ham of the American ship *Hope* called them the *Washington Islands*, and in the same year Captain Marchand of the French ship *Le Solide* called them *Les Isles de la Révolution*. Vancouver named them *Hengist Islands* after Lieutenant Hengist who had visited them in 1792, but the historical name given by the first discoverer has fortunately survived all endeavours to replace it.

Marquette is a name given to a city in Michigan and other places in the United States in order to commemorate the ex-plorations of Father Marquette, a Jesuit who came to Canada in 1666, and died in 1675. After establishing a mission at the foot of Lake Superior in 1673 he coasted along Lake Michigan in company with Joliet, and by way of the Wisconsin River reached the Mississippi, which he descended as far as the mouth of the Arkansas River, discovering on his route the mouths of the Missouri and the Ohio.

Marsala, in Sicily, is the Arabic name of Lilybæum, which is preserved in a frag-mentary form by CAPE BOËO (*q.v.*). The Arabs called the harbour *Marsa Ali*, the 'port of Ali,' which became Marsala in Italian. MERS-EL-KEBIR, ' the great port,' in Oran, is the Arabic translation of the *Portus Magnus* of Pliny.

Marseilles, the English form of the French name MARSEILLE, preserves with little change the old name Massilia. The *r* is derived from the corrupt Middle Latin form Marsilia. The etymology is doubtful. The name has been supposed to be Phœnician, but may more probably be Ligurian or Numidian, the Massyli being the most powerful of the Numidian tribes.

Marsh Island, in the Gambier Group, was named by Beechey in 1826 after his purser, George Marsh.

Marshall Archipelago or MARSHALL ISLANDS, a North Pacific group, was discovered in 1529 by Saavedra, and called by him *Buenos Jardines,* the 'good gardens.' In 1788 two English merchant vessels, the *Scarborough* and the *Charlotte,* commanded by Marshall and Gilbert, fell in with them, on a voyage from New South Wales to China. Hence the northern group has acquired the name of the MARSHALL ARCHIPELAGO, and the southern group that of the GILBERT ARCHIPELAGO, which includes a belt of islets called the SCARBOROUGH RANGE. In the Marshall Archipelago the Eastern Belt is called the RADACK CHAIN, and the Western Belt the RALICK CHAIN, which are the native designations. The MARSHALL ISLANDS, a small North Pacific group, north-east of the Ladrones, not to be confounded with the preceding group, which is conveniently distinguished as the Marshall Archipelago, were also discovered in 1788 by Captain Marshall of the ship *Scarborough.* On some maps they erroneously appear as *Los Jardines,* a name which properly belonged to the Marshall Archipelago.

Martaban, Gulf of, takes its name from Martaban, a decayed Burmese town whose trade, formerly of great importance, has been transferred to Moulmein. Martabané was a Portuguese corruption of the Malay name *Maritanan.*

Martha's Vineyard, an island off the coast of Massachusetts, is said by Stith to have been so named by Bartholomew Gosnold in 1602 from the abundance of wild vines, but according to Benson the name is probably due to the Dutch skipper Adrian Block, who passed it in 1614 on a voyage from New York to Cape Cod, and called it, after a Dutch seaman, Martin Wyngaard's Island, a name subsequently corrupted into Martha's Vineyard.

Martigny, in Canton Valais, is usually said to bear the name of St. Martin, one of the apostles of the Valais, but the form *Martigniacum,* found as early as 1210, shows that it was merely the estate or property of some person bearing the common name of Martinus.

Martin Garcia, an island in the Rio de de la Plata, bears the name of Martin Garcia, the steersman of Juan Diaz de Solis who discovered it. Near this island de Solis and eight of his comrades were killed by the natives.

Martinique, one of the French Antilles, was discovered by Columbus on June 15th, 1502. The modern French name Martinique may be a corruption of *Matigno,* a form found on a map of 1536, which may represent the original Carib name. Other early forms are *Madiana, Mantanino,* and *Matinino,* which last is believed to have been the name used or given by Columbus.

Maryland, one of the United States, was so named in honour of Queen Henrietta Maria, being termed *Terra Mariæ* in the charter given in 1632 to Lord Baltimore by Charles I. Probably the name was not selected without reference to the older name of *Bahia de Santa Maria,* which the Spaniards had bestowed on Chesapeake Bay, on whose shores Maryland lies. Lord Baltimore, who was a Roman Catholic, called the seat of his government St. Mary's. MARYBOROUGH was constituted the assize town of Queen's County, and named after the Queen by an Act of the 3rd and 4th of Philip and Mary, in whose reign the old Kingdom of Ossory was converted into shireland in consequence of a rebellion. MARYBOROUGH PORT and the RIVER MARY, in Queensland, were named in memory of the tragic death through a carriage accident of Lady Mary Fitzroy, the wife of Sir Charles Fitzroy, Governor of Australia. MARYLEBONE, now a London borough, was the parish attached to the chapel of St. Mary-le-bourne, so called because situated on the burn or brook now called the Tyburn.

Mascarene Islands (historically ILHAS MASCARENHAS), a group east of Madagascar, to which MAURITIUS and RÉUNION belong, were discovered in 1502 by Pedro Mascarenhas, a Portuguese seaman.

Massachusetts, one of the New England States, takes its name from the Puritan settlement of Massachusetts Bay, on which Boston stands. The old etymology explains it as the name of a tribe called after their chief, who took his name from a hillock in Boston Harbour on which he lived. This hillock resembled in shape the head of an arrow, and hence was called *mos-wetuset*, from *mos*, an 'arrow head,' and *wetuset*, 'a hill.' But, according to Roger Williams, Massachusetts meant 'the blue hills,' and this accords better with the modern philological conclusion that Massachusetts is an Anglicised plural or possessive meaning 'at the great hills,' from *massa*, 'great,' and *adchuash*, 'hills,' plural of *adchu*, 'a hill,' with the locative suffix *-it* or *-et*, meaning 'at' or 'near.' It is called MATTACHUSETTS BAY in the charter of Charles I. given in 1628, and Milton calls it *Massawachusett*. The final *s* is apparently superfluous.

Massacre Bay, New Zealand, is a free translation of the Dutch name *Moordenaars Bogt*, 'murderers bight,' given by Tasman, in 1642, to his first anchorage in New Zealand, because the natives attacked his boat without provocation, and killed three sailors. Since the recent discoveries of gold it has been renamed GOLDEN BAY, the old name being thought inauspicious. At the Patagonian RIVIÈRE DU MASSACRE Beauchesne's sailors in 1699 killed several natives in revenge for the murder of their comrades. MATANZAS, the 'slaughterings,' an inlet on the coast of Florida, near St. Augustine, takes its name from the massacre, in 1565, of all but five of the 150 Huguenot settlers, by the Spanish commander, Pedro Menandez de Avilès, whereby the French colony in Florida was exterminated. In 1513 Juan Ponce de Leon gave the name of ISOLA DE MATANZA, 'massacre island,' to a small island on the coast of Florida, where some of his men were killed by the natives. At MATANZAS, on the north coast of Cuba, the crew of a shipwrecked vessel having been massacred by the natives in 1511 or 1512, the Spaniards found the survivors, a Spanish woman and her daughter a girl of eighteen, both naked, or clad only in leaves.

Massena, a town east of Lake Tchad, is said to derive its name from a large tamarind tree (*mass*) growing in the market-place.

Massereene, a castle and two baronies near Antrim, giving a title to an Irish peer, is a corruption of *Masareghna*, the 'Queen's hill,' the Irish word *mas*, the 'thigh,' being applied to any long low hill.

Massowah, properly MEDSOUA, called Matzua by the Portuguese in 1542, is a town built on Base, a coral islet in the Red Sea. Medsoua is an Abyssinian word meaning 'to shout,' and it is supposed that the place was so called because it is within hail of the mainland. (*See* STRALSUND.)

Masulipatam, on the Coromandel Coast, was the first factory established by the East India Company in 1611. The name is a corruption of *Machli-patnam*, the 'town of fish.'

Matamoros, in Mexico, at the mouth of the Rio Bravo del Norte, was so called after a priest named Matamoros.

Matelotes, a group in the Carolines, was so named by Villalobos, in 1545, because the natives came out in canoes, crying *buenos dias, matelotes!* 'Good-day, sailors,' a proof of an earlier discovery by some Spanish ship.

Mathern, near Chepstow, is from the Welsh *merthyr*, 'a martyr'; the church having been built in memory of Tudric (St. Theodoric), king of Gwent, who died here of wounds received in a battle with the Saxons. (*See* MERTHYR-TIDVIL.)

Matterhorn, the most precipitous peak in the Alps, derives its lowly name from the meadow (*matt*) at its base, on which the village of Zermatt, 'at the-meadow,' is situated. The Piedmontese name, MONT CERVIN, is due to its resemblance to a stag's horn. The pass over the main chain at the foot of the Matterhorn is called either the MATTERJOCH, or the COL DE ST. THEODULE, from a legend which relates how St. Theodule, Bishop of Sion, compelled a devil, whom he had exorcised from a possessed person, to carry over it a church bell presented to him by the Pope.

Matto Grosso, a Brazilian province, is the 'great forest.'

Mauna Roa, or MAUNA LOA, the 'long mountain,' is the native name of a great volcano in Hawaii. A second volcano is called MAUNA KEA, the 'white mountain.' MAUPITI, one of the Society Islands, means the 'double mountain.' It is also called MAU-RUA, the 'long mountain.'

Maurienne, a county in Savoy, traversed by the Mont Cenis railway, is the district where a body of Moors who had landed near Fréjus, established themselves in the ninth century. The chief town is called ST. JEAN DE MAURIENNE.

Mauritius, one of the Mascarenhas Islands, was named in 1598 by the Dutch Admiral Van Neck, in honour of Prince Maurice of Orange, Stadtholder of the United Provinces. When the French acquired it in 1741 it was renamed ISLE DE FRANCE. The Dutch also gave the name of MAURITIUS to a settlement in Brazil; to an island and bay in the Straits of Magellan; and to the Hudson River, in the State of New York.

Maury Bay and MAURY CHANNEL, in the Arctic regions, bear the name of Lieutenant Maury, the American hydrographer.

May, Cape, in New Jersey, at the entrance to Delaware Bay, is also called CAPE CORNELIUS, both names being due to a Dutch skipper, Cornelius Jacobse Mey, who landed here in 1623.

Maynooth, in County Kildare, is a corruption of *Magh Nuadhat,* the 'plain of Nuadha,' a Celtic deity, represented in Irish legend as a king of Leinster.

Mayo, an Irish county, takes its name from the village of Mayo, where St. Colman, retiring from Northumbria with a number of English monks, after the synod of Whitby, erected a monastery at a place then called *Magh-éo,* the 'plain of the yew trees.'

Mayor and the Court of Aldermen, in the Bay of Plenty, New Zealand, is the name given by Cook in 1769 to a large island surrounded by numerous islets.

Mazampaha, 'universal sickness,' is the native name of an unhealthy place in Brazil.

Mazanderan, a Persian province, consisting of the lowlands between the mountains and the Caspian, means 'within the mountains' (*maz,* 'mountain,' and *anderun,* 'within').

Mearns, one of the seven old provinces of Scotland, representing approximately the modern county of Kincardine, is a corruption of the Gaelic name *Maghgirghinn,* the 'plain of Circinn,' one of the seven brothers who, according to the Pictish legend, ruled the seven provinces of Scotland.

Meath, anciently *Midhe,* the fifth Irish province, formed an appanage for the support of the overking of Ireland. The kingdom and diocese of Midhe, so called because of its 'central' position, comprised the modern counties of Meath, Westmeath, and Dublin.

Meaux, a city in France, preserves the tribal name of the Meldi. The name is probably derived from *Meldis,* the dative plural. The county of Meaux is called *Comitatus Meldensis* by Gregory of Tours.

Mecklenburg, now a small village, was formerly the capital of the two German States to which it has given a name. The old Wendish name was *Wiligrad,* the 'great castle.' In the tenth century we have the form *Mekelenborch* (O.H.G. *michel,* 'great'), a translation of the Slavonic name.

Medeah, in Algeria, is believed to occupy the site of a Roman town called *Mediæ* or *Ad Medias,* because 'midway' between two other towns.

Medína or EL MEDÍNA, 'the city,' is also called *Medínat Rasúl-Allah,* 'the city of the prophet of Allah,' or *Medínat al-Nabi,* 'the city of the prophet,' because it contains the tomb of Mahomet. MEDINAT HABU retains the name of Thebes (*q.v.*), whose site it occupies. Medina, 'the city,' is a common Arabic element in Spanish names, such as MEDINA SIDONIA, 'the city of the Sidonians,' believed by the Moors to occupy the site of a Phœnician city; MEDINA DEL RIO SECO, 'the city of the dry river bed'; MEDINA DE LAS TORRES, 'the city of the towers'; MEDINA DEL POMAR, 'the city of the apple orchard'; or MEDINA DEL CAMPO, 'the city on the plain.'

Mediterranean, the 'midland' sea, was called by the Hebrews and Greeks simply 'the sea,' or 'the great sea.' The Romans called it *Mare Internum,* or *Mare nostrum.* The term *Mare Mediterraneum,* of which our name is an adaptation, is not used by any early classical writer, being first found in Solinus, in the third century A.D. Isidore of Seville (570-636) is the first to use it as a proper name. The Germans have translated the name, and call it Mittelmeer, an abbreviation of Mittelländisches Meer. The Turks and modern Greeks call it by names meaning the 'White Sea,' as distinguished from the Black Sea.

Medway, the chief river of Kent, was formerly explained as the 'mid-way,' being the boundary between East and West Kent, an etymology which is not supported by the earliest forms of the name. But since the Meduana, now the Mayenne, is an old Celtic river name, it is possible that this may have also been the pre-Teutonic name of the Medway, which would be assimilated by the Saxons so as to make it intelligible in their own speech. The normal A.S. spelling *Medu-wæge* shows that it was thought to be the 'mead-wave,' the water flowing soft as metheglin, while the alternative spellings *Med-wæge* and

Mede-wæge are an indication that it was also supposed to be the meadow-wave, or 'river of the meads.'

Meelhaven, in Novaya Zemlya, is the name given by Barents to a bay where he found six sacks of rye meal.

Meiningen, the capital of Saxe-Meiningen, is the dative plural of a gentile name, as is shown by the old form *Meinungun.*

Meissen, a town in Saxony, lies between the Meissa and the Triebach, tributaries of the Elbe. The name is usually derived from that of the River Meissa, but both may be corruptions of the Slavonic *misni,* the 'key,' the name of a castle built by Henry I. in 930 at this spot, which forms the key to the plain of Dresden, lying as it does at the gorge of the Elbe.

Melanesia, the 'islands of the blacks,' is a modern name invented to designate those South Pacific Islands which are inhabited by the Papuan or Negrito race.

Melbourne, the capital of the Australian Colony of VICTORIA, was founded in 1837, when Lord Melbourne was Prime Minister, and Queen Victoria had just ascended the throne. MELBOURNE ISLAND and MOUNT MELBOURNE in the Antarctic Victoria Land also bear his name. Lord Melbourne took his title from MELBOURNE, a village in Derbyshire, called in Domesday *Mileburn,* the 'millburn,' where, as Domesday records, there was a mill of the annual value of three shillings. According to Kemble MELBOURNE in Cambridgeshire is from a proper name. The oldest form is *Meldulf's burh,* which became *Meldeburna,* and finally Melbourne. Several MELBOURNS and most, if not all, of the MELTONS and MILTONS are, however, corruptions of *Middelburn* and *Middeltun.*

Melun, a city twenty-five miles south-east of Paris, is the *Melodunum* of Cæsar, a Celtic name signifying a 'fort' (*dun*) on a rounded hill (*moel*). The same name recurs at MELDON in Peeblesshire, and perhaps at MALDON (*q.v.*).

Melville Island, where Parry wintered in 1819-20, was named in honour of Henry Dundas, Viscount Melville, then First Lord of the Admiralty. CAPE MELVILLE, MELVILLE LAKE, MELVILLE RANGE, and MELVILLE SOUND, in Arctic America, MELVILLE ISLAND and MELVILLE BAY on the Australian Coast, and MELVILLE ISLAND in the Low Archipelago, also bear his name. Lord Melville took his title from Melville in

Midlothian, the fief of one of the Norman adventurers in the time of David I. It is called in Latin documents *castellum puellarum,* a name which points to the A.S. *mæg,* a 'woman,' or to *mægth,* a 'maid.' In the thirteenth century we find Malavilla, 'bad township,' whence the modern name.

Memel, a town on the River Memel, which divides Russia from Prussia, was formerly called *Memelburg,* the 'castle on the Memel.'

Memphis, an important town on the Mississippi, in the State of Tennessee, repeats the name of the ancient capital of Lower Egypt, ten miles south of Cairo. Memphis was a Greek corruption of an old Egyptian name, either *Men-nefert,* the 'beautiful site,' or more probably *Ma-m-phtah,* the 'place of Phtah,' the chief deity of the Memphite triad.

Menai Strait is the 'Strait of Mona,' or Anglesey.

Menam, properly MEI-NAM, the great Siamese river, means the 'mother of waters' (Siamese *nam,* 'water'). It is also called *Menam Kong,* 'Menam river.' There is a place at the mouth of the Menam, below Bang-Kok, called PAK-NAM, which means 'water-mouth.'

Mendaña Archipelago, also called the MARQUESAS (*q.v.*), was discovered by Don Alvaro Mendaña, the nephew of the Viceroy of Peru, who in 1567 sent him with two ships to explore the South Sea. On this voyage he discovered and named various islands in the Salomon Group. In 1595 Mendaña again sailed from Callao with a squadron of four ships, and discovered the Santa Cruz Group as well as the Archipelago which bears his name.

Mendoza, an Argentine city, founded in 1559, bears the name of Don Garcia Hurtado de Mendoza, the Governor of Chili. MENDOCINO, a Californian cape, was so named by Ferrelo in 1543, in honour of Don Antonio de Mendoza, Viceroy of New Spain.

Mentone (French Menton), a town on the Riviera, is a name supposed to refer to the 'chin' or promontory east of the town.

Meon-Stoke, in Hants, preserves the name of a people, probably Jutes, called the *Meanware,* or dwellers on the River Meon. Bæda mentions the *Provincia Meanwarorum,* which we may recognise in the modern hundreds of East and West Meon.

Meran, in the Tyrol, bears a name commemorating the calamity which in the ninth century destroyed the Roman town on the site. In 1350 it is called *auf der Meran,* 'on the moraine.'

Mercury Bay, New Zealand, is the place where the transit of Mercury was observed on November 9th, 1769. In the immediate neighbourhood are MERCURY POINT and the MERCURY ISLES.

Mercy, Bay of, in Banks Land, marks the place where M'Clure's ship the *Investigator* was icelocked in 1851, and finally abandoned in 1853, after the discovery of the North-West Passage had been made. The HARBOUR OF GOD'S MERCY is a bay at the western entrance of the Straits of Magellan, where Davis twice took refuge from storms in his unfortunate expedition of 1592. This harbour seems to be that called *Puerto de la Misericordia* by Sarmiento a few years before. It is also called SEPARATION HARBOUR, Wallis and Carteret having here parted company in 1766.

Merida, a Spanish city containing magnificent Roman remains, represents the Roman colony of *Augusta Emerita,* the chief city in Lusitania. It was founded in B.C. 23 by Publius Carisius, the legate of Augustus, as a colony for *emeriti,* or 'veterans,' belonging to the fifth and tenth legions who had served in the Cantabrian war, and whose term of service had expired. The name has been transferred to MERIDA, the capital of Yucatan, and to MERIDA in Mexico and in Venezuela.

Merim is a native word meaning 'little.' LAGOA MERIM, the 'little lake,' forms the boundary between Brazil and Uruguay.

Merioneth, a Welsh county, bears the name of Meirion, a British saint, who, according to the Welsh legend, was the son of Cunedda, the Dux Britanniarum at the time of the departure of the Roman legions. Keredig, another son of Cunedda, gave his name to *Keredigion,* now Cardiganshire (*q.v.*).

Mermaid's Strait, MERMAID'S SHOAL, and MERMAID'S REEF, in Australia, were discovered by the cutter *Mermaid* in 1818.

Mersea Island, Essex, also spelt MERSEY, is the A.S. *Meres-ig,* the 'sea island.' The RIVER MERSEY has been explained as *Meres-ea,* the 'sea water' or river. It seems to be the *Mærse* mentioned in a charter of 1004 granting lands between 'Mærse and Ribbel.' This form, if correct, would imply a prehistoric *Marusia,* a Celtic name meaning 'dead, *i.e.* quiet water,' as contrasted with the open sea.

Merthyr-Tydvil, in South Wales, bears the name of the 'Martyr Tudfil,' who, according to a Welsh tradition, was here slain in a Pagan inroad. She was the daughter of Brychan, the Welsh prince who gave his name to the county of BRECON.

Merv, in Central Asia, is the *Antiochia Margiana* of the Greeks, which stood on the River *Margus,* now the Murgab or Merv. Margiana is the province called *Margu* in the cuneiform inscriptions. Spiegel connects the Margu of Darius with the old Bactrian word *meregho,* a 'bird,' and explains the MURGAB as the 'bird water,' in allusion to the numerous waterfowl by which it is frequented.

Meshed means a place of 'martyrdom' or 'witness,' hence the 'shrine' of a Moslem saint. Thus the tomb of Ali at Nejef near Kufa is called MESHED-ALI, and MESHED HUSSEIN is the place where Ali's sons were killed. MESHED-SAR, 'the tomb of the head,' is where Ibrahim, brother of the Imâm Reza, was beheaded. MESHED, one of the most important towns in Persia, is properly the Meshed of El-Reza, where in the ninth century the Imâm Reza, the eighth of the twelve Imâms, suffered martyrdom. It is a great place of pilgrimage, the Mecca of the Persians.

Mesopotamia, the Greek name of the country 'between the rivers' Tigris and Euphrates, is now known by the nearly equivalent Arabic name EL-GEZIRA, 'the island.' The Tigris and Euphrates, whose head waters are within five miles of each other, unite at their mouths.

Messina, a town in Sicily, gives a name to the straits which separate Sicily from the mainland. The old name *Messana* is probably a translation of the earlier Siculian name *Dankle* or *Zancle,* the 'sickle,' descriptive of the harbour which is formed by a long semi-circular spit of land. (*See* ANCONA.) The legend of the foundation of Messana by colonists from the Peloponnesian Messene probably grew out of the resemblance of the names.

Meteora is the name of the convents perched 'up in the air' on isolated peaks in the peninsula of Mount Athos (*q.v.*).

Metz is a corruption of the Celtic name of the *Matrici,* or *Mediomatrici,* a Belgic tribe, whose territory corresponded to that of the old diocese of Metz. Mediomatrici probably meant 'those placed in the middle.'

Mexico (in the modern Spanish spelling Mejico) took its name from a temple of

Mexitl, the Aztec war-god, the suffix *-co* being the Aztec locative postposition. The name of the city was extended to the whole of *Nueva España* (New Spain) of which it was the capital, and then to the great central American gulf. The older name of the city of Mexico was *Tenochtitlan*, the 'place of the cactus rock,' which is explained by the legend that when the Aztecs arrived they found a rock in a crevice of which a cactus was growing. On the rock sat an eagle holding a serpent in its mouth. The device of the rock and the cactus, with the eagle holding a serpent; became the tribal totem of the Aztecs, and has been adopted on the flag of the present Mexican republic.

Mexilliones (Mejilliones), which means 'muscles' or 'cockles' in Spanish, is the name of a bay in Peru, whose rocks are covered with the shells of a univalve, the *Concholepas peruviana*.

Michigan, one of the United States, nearly surrounds LAKE MICHIGAN, a name meaning the 'great sea,' from *missi* (*mitshaw*), 'great,' which appears in the names of the Mississippi and Missouri, and *sagiegan*, a 'sea' or 'lake,' which we have in SAGINAW BAY, the western arm of Lake Huron.

Michoacan, a Mexican province, is a native name meaning 'the land of fisheries.'

Middlesex, a tribe name which, like Essex, Wessex, and Sussex, has acquired a territorial significance, is the A.S. *Middel Seaxe* or *Middel Sexe*, 'the middle Saxons,' usually found in the dative plural Middelseaxon or Middelsæxum. MIDDELBURG, in Holland, is the 'town in the middle' of the Island of Walcheren. MIDDELBURG, one of the Friendly Islands, was named by Tasman in 1643 after Middelburg in Holland. It now usually goes by the native name Eoa. MIDDLE ISLAND, MIDDLE LAKE, MIDDLE MOUNT, MIDDLE POINT, and the like, common names in Australia and elsewhere, need no explanation. MIDDLETON, a common village name in England, has usually become MILTON or MELTON.

Midi, Pic du, one of the highest summits in the Pyrenees, is so called because at Pau it is seen due south. A similar name is that of the DENT DU MIDI, which lies due south from Vevay and other towns at the upper end of the Lake of Geneva.

Milan, the French and English form of the Italian MILANO, called *Mailand* in German, is a corruption of the Celto-Roman name *Mediolanum*, the capital of the Insubrian Gauls, which signified the town in the 'middle of the plain,' *lanum* being the equivalent of the Latin *planum.*

Milazzo, a fortified town in Sicily, near which Garibaldi gained a decisive victory in 1860, gives a name to a neighbouring cape. It was the *Milass* of the Arabs, a corruption of the Greek name *Mylæ*, 'the mills.'

Milford, a town in Pembrokeshire, which gives a name to MILFORD HAVEN, is not, we are told by Professor Freeman, an English *ford* or a Welsh *ffordd*, but a Scandinavian *fjord*, like Waterford and Wexford. This seems to be a mere guess, as the town is not named from the Haven, but the Haven from the town of Milford, which is merely the English translation of the Welsh name *Rhyd-y-milwr*, the 'ford over the Milwr,' a small brook falling into the Haven.

Milwaukee, in Wisconsin, is explained by Boyd as a native name meaning the 'good land.'

Minas Geraes, a Brazilian province with mines yielding diamonds, gold, silver, copper, and iron, means the 'general' or 'universal mines.' ELMINA, 'the mine,' or SAN JORGE DA MINA, was a Portuguese fort built on the Gold Coast in 1482, but ELMINA in Tripoli is an Arabic name meaning the 'haven.'

Minch, the name of the channel between Lewis and the mainland, is a corruption of the Gaelic *mionaich*, the genitive of *mionach*, 'gut' or 'bowel.' LA MANCHE, the French name for the English Channel, ostensibly from *manche*, a sleeve (Latin *manica*), may be an assimilated form of an older Celtic name.

Mincio, the river which drains the Lago di Garda, is the Roman *Mincius*, perhaps the 'little' river.

Mindanao is one of the Philippines, with numerous volcanic craters now filled with water, from which, or perhaps from the largest of them, comes the Malay name of the island, which means 'lake land.'

Minden or MÜNDEN in Hanover is at the confluence (*mündung*) of the Werra and the Fulda, but Minden in Westphalia, anciently *Mimida*, is seemingly from a personal name.

Minehead, Somerset, called in Domesday *Man-heved*, is probably the Welsh *Maenhafod*, the summer residence (*hafod*) on the rock. (*See* MAENTWROG.)

Minerva's Bank, between Australia and New Guinea, was discovered in 1818 by the ship *Minerva.*

Mingrelia, a Russian province in the Caucasus, is the Turkish *Mingreul*, the land of 'a thousand springs.' So MING-BULAK, a river in Turkistan, means 'the thousand sources.' MINGADARA, 'more than a thousand,' a mountain in Mongolia, is so called from its numerous Buddhist monasteries.

Minho, a river in Portugal, was the Roman *Minius*, probably the 'red' river, from *minium*, a Latin word of Iberic origin, which means 'cinnabar' or 'vermilion.'

Minnesota, one of the United States, is traversed by the RIVER MINNESOTA, a Dakota name meaning the 'blue water,' (*minnee*, 'water,' and *sota*, 'sky,' hence sky-colour or 'blue'). The state capital of Minnesota is designated by the barbarous hybrid name of MINNEAPOLIS. The Dakota word *minnee* appears in many names, among them MINNEHAHA, a river in Minnesota, the 'smiling' or 'laughing water'; MINISKA, the 'clear water'; MINNISNI, 'the cold water'; and MINNEKATA, the 'hot water.'

Minster, in the Isle of Thanet, is the site of a monastery built about 670 at Ebbes-fleet, where St. Augustine is supposed to have landed in 596. Minster, the M.E. form of the A.S. *mynster*, a corruption of *monasterium*, appears in many English names, such as Westminster, Kidderminster, and Axminster. The old Irish form was *Mainister*, now Monaster, as in MONASTEREVIN, formerly *Mainister-Eimhin*, the 'monastery of St. Eimhin,' the reputed author of the Tripartite Life of St. Patrick, or *Mainister-Buithe*, the 'monastery of Buithe (Boethius),' a disciple of St. Patrick, now MONASTERBOICE in Louth. MONASTERNALEA in Galway is *Mainister-na-liatha*, the 'monastery of the grey' (friars). MONASTERANENAGH in Limerick is *Mainister-an-aenaigh*, the 'monastery of the assembly place or fair.' MONEYSTERLING in Derry is *Monaster-lynn*, the 'monastery of O'Lynn.' In German we have MÜNSTER, the name of the chief town of Westphalia, and of a town in Canton Lucerne. A monastery founded by Charlemagne has given a name to the town of MÜNSTER in a picturesque valley of the Jura, now called the MÜNSTERTHAL in German, and VAL MOÛTIERS in French, Moûtier, Moustier, or Môtier being the French corruption of *monasterium*. NOIRMOÛTIER, the 'black minster,' is an island off the coast of La Vendée, so called from the chief town. MARMOÛTIER, near Tours, is a corruption of *Majus Monasterium*. PREMONTRÉ, in the Aisne, the chief seat of the Premonstratensian Order, does not mean the 'meadow of the monastery,' having been founded by St. Norbert in a place 'pointed out' to him in a vision, *locus præmonstratus*. MONTREUX, on the Lake of Geneva, is a corruption of *monasteriolum*, a diminutive of *monasterium*. MONASTER, the 'monastery,' is the name of a town in Macedonia, and of a seaport in Tunis.

Minstrel Shoal, Australia, was discovered in 1820 by the ship *Minstrel*.

Miramar, the 'sea view,' is the Spanish name of a castle in Mallorca, and of the castle of the late Emperor Maximilian near Trieste.

Mischabelhörner, the lofty rugged *grat* west of the Saas Thal, is believed to be a corruption of *Mist-gabel-hörner*, the 'fork peaks.' The word *mist-gabel* means strictly a 'dungfork' or 'mixen fork.'

Mississauga, a fort at the mouth of the Niagara River, the Mississauga Strait between Cockburn and Manitoulin Islands, and the Mississauga River in the district of Algoma, preserve the name of the Mississauga tribe which lived on the banks of the Trent, Kingston, and Napanee. The name, which is a corruption of *minzezageeg*, refers to the 'numerous streams' in the territories of the tribe.

Mississippi, one of the largest rivers of the world, is not, as frequently stated, the 'Father of waters,' but the 'great river' (Cree *missi, massa, masha*, 'great,' and *sepe*, 'water' or 'river'). De Soto, who in 1542 was the first to explore it, correctly translated by *Rio Grande* the native name, which first appears as *Mes-sipi*, the Sioux pronunciation, which was heard by Father Allouez, who in 1665 set forth from Canada and established a mission among the Sioux, returning in 1667. In 1673 it is called *Mescha-sebe*, and in Joliet's map of 1674 it is *Messa-sipi*. The State, which takes its name from the river, was admitted into the Union in 1817.

Missouri is a French spelling of the native name *Missuri*, the 'great muddy' river, as contrasted with the Mississippi, whose waters are clear. The State of Missouri was admitted into the Union in 1820. MISSINIPI is the native name of the CHURCHILL RIVER, so called because it enters Hudson Bay at Fort Churchill. In Cree *nipi* means 'water,' and Missinipi may be translated as 'much water.'

Mistaken Point, Newfoundland, is so called because liable to be mistaken for Cape Race, which is further to the East. So MISTAKEN CAPE is easily mistaken for Cape Hoorn.

Mitchell, Queensland, was named after a local surveyor.

Mitton or MYTON, the name of places near the confluences of streams, is probably from A.S. *mýthe,* the 'mouth' of a river.

Mobile is a town in Alabama from which MOBILE BAY takes its name. When, in 1539, Fernando de Soto landed in Florida, and made his wonderful march to the Mississippi, he had a desperate fight with the Creek Indians at a palisaded village called *Mauvila* or *Maubila* (probably the name of the tribe), at the junction of the Tombigbee and Alabama rivers. From this village the united stream acquired the name which in French became the RIVER MOBILE, at whose mouth the town of Mobile was built.

Modena, in the Emilia, was the Roman *Mutina,* probably an Etruscan name.

Mogador is a town in Morocco, founded by Mulai Ishmael in 1760, and called SUERAH or SHIRVAH, 'the beautiful.' Mogador is a European corruption of the name of a local saint, Sidi Mogodul or Mugdul, whose conspicuous shrine lies just outside the town.

Moghistan, a district in Persia, at the entrance of the Persian Gulf, is 'the land of palms.'

Mohawk River, in the State of New York, was named from an Iroquois tribe called MOHAWKS, an Algonquin name meaning 'cannibals,' applied to them by their enemies on the Lower Hudson. The Mohawks called themselves *Caniengas,* 'people at the flint.' The MOHICAN RIVER in Ohio is so named from the Mohegan tribe, a name meaning the 'wolves' (Cree *maheggun,* a 'wolf').

Moira, in County Down, whence the great Marquis of Hastings took the title of Earl, is a corruption of *Magh-rath,* the 'plain of the fort.'

Mokattam, Wadi, the 'valley of inscriptions,' in the peninsula of Sinai, is named from the numerous inscriptions engraved by pilgrims on the rocks. GEBEL MOKATTAM, the limestone range south of Cairo, is so called for a similar reason.

Moldavia is the Latinised form used in England for the Roumanian Province of Moldóva, which is traversed by the River Moldóva. The Polish and Bohemian name is Multany, which is derived from the Wallachian Muntany, a corruption of the Latin *montani,* 'mountaineers.' The people gave a name to the province, and the province to the river. It is curious that the name of a level plain should be derived from a range of mountains.

Moluccas, also called the SPICE ISLANDS because the native country of the clove, is the English spelling of the Portuguese corruption of the Malay form of an Arabic name. *Ilhas dos Molocos,* the Portuguese name of the group, may be traced back to the Malay-Arabic *Jazîrat-al-Muluk,* the 'islands of the kings,' so called because each of the five islands was ruled by its own petty prince.

Monaco, a principality on the Riviera, takes its name from the town of Monaco, built on a headland on which stood the Greek temple of Heracles Monœcus. The town is called by Roman writers *Monœci Portus,* or *Portus Herculis.*

Monaghan, an Irish county, is so called from the county town of Monaghan, a corruption of the old name *Muineachán,* 'the little thicket,' a diminutive of *muine,* a brake or shrubbery.

Mongolia is the land of the Mongols or Mungals, the 'braves' or 'invincibles.' This name, originally an honorific title of the Black Horde, became general in the time of Genghiz Khan, whose father, the Khan of the Black Horde, subdued the White Horde. MOGUL (MUGHAL) is a Perso-Arabic corruption of Mongol.

Monmouthshire takes its name from the county town of MONMOUTH (Monnowmouth), which stands where the Mynwy or Monnow joins the Wye.

Monroe, a city on Lake Erie, together with some 133 counties, towns, or townships, mostly in Indiana, Iowa, Ohio, and Pennsylvania, are named after James Monroe, the fifth President of the United States, 1817-1825. In his honour the capital of Liberia was named MONROVIA in 1824. Monroe is a territorial surname meaning in Gaelic the 'red bog.'

Montenegro is the Italian name of a principality on the Adriatic called TZERNAGORA or CRNAGORA in Servian and Montenegrin, KARADAGH in Turkish, and MAL-ZÉZE in Albanian. These names, all of which mean the 'black mountain,' refer to the dark pine woods which formerly clothed the hills.

Monterey, the chief town of the Mexican Province of Leon, bears the name of

Gaspar de Zuñiga, Count of Monterey, Viceroy of New Spain, who in 1598 also founded the town of MONTEREY in California from which the BAY OF MONTEREY takes its name.

Montevideo, the capital of Uruguay, is officially styled SAN FELIPE DEL PUERTO DE MONTEVIDEO. The name, which has been the subject of much controversy, is supposed to be the Spanish transformation of a Portuguese entry in the log of Ferdinand Magellan, who in 1520 sailed up the estuary of the Rio de la Plata in search of a passage to India. On the flat coast near the city there is a knoll, shaped like a sombrero. This Magellan, a Portuguese, would describe in his log as *Mont-vi-eu*, or in provincial Portuguese *Mont-vide-eu*, 'a mount saw I,' a phrase which must have found a place upon the chart. A Spaniard would have written *Monte vidi*, 'a hill I saw.' When the territory became a Spanish colony the name *Mont-vide-eu* would become Monte-video.

Montgomery, a Welsh county, constituted in 1533 by Henry VIII., was formerly a part of Powys land. The district was called Sirydd Tre Faldwyn by the Welsh, from the castle built in the eleventh century by Baldwin, lieutenant of the marches. This castle was taken by the Welsh, and then retaken by Roger de Montgomeri, so called from his lordship of Montgomeri, near Lisieux in Normandy. Roger gave his name to the castle, and the name of the castle passed to the town which rose around it, and which was made the county town when the shire was constituted by Henry VIII. MONTGOMERY, the State capital of Alabama, bears the name of General Montgomery, an American officer who was killed in the attack upon Quebec in 1775.

Montpellier, in the Hérault, called in the tenth century *Mons pestellarius*, the 'grinder's hill,' became *Mont-peslier* in the eleventh. MONTELIMAR, a town on the Rhone, took its name from the family of Adhémar or Aymar to which it belonged.

Monte Nuovo, the 'new mountain,' near Naples, was suddenly upheaved on September 29th, 1538. MONTEVERDE ISLANDS, a group in the Carolines, were discovered in 1806 by the Spanish Captain Don Juan Baptista de Monteverde.

Montréal. In 1535, Jacques Cartier, on his second voyage, ascended the St. Lawrence as far as Quebec, where he left his ship, and reached an Iroquois village called

Hochelaga, perched on an eminence, which from its splendid position he called *Mont Royal*, the 'royal mount,' now Montreal. MONREALE, a contraction of *Montereale*, is the 'royal mount' near Palermo, on which a palace and cathedral were built by Roger I. king of Sicily.

Montrose, in Forfarshire, appears in 1200 as *Munros*, which points to the Gaelic *moine t'ross*, the 'moor on the peninsula.'

Montserrat, in Spanish MONTE SERRATO (Latin *Mons Serratus*), is a serrated or sawlike ridge in Catalonia with jagged spires and pinnacles. Here was the celebrated convent in which Ignatius Loyola dedicated his sword to a black image of the Virgin. MONTSERRAT, one of the Antilles, was so named by Columbus in 1493, on his second voyage, because it reminded his chaplain, Father Boil, who had been a monk in the Benedictine monastery of Montserrat, of his Catalonian home. The island which he next discovered, being shaped like a rounded cone, he named *Santa Maria Rotunda*. It now appears on the maps as the Island of REDONDA.

Montt, or PUERTO MONTT, a port in Chili, bears the name of Don Manuel Montt, who in 1859 was President of the Republic.

Monument Bay, in the Lake of the Woods, is so called from the monument erected to mark the boundary between the Canadian Dominion and the United States.

Moore's Islands, MOORE BAY, and CAPE MOORE in Arctic America, and MOORE'S GROUP, Australia, bear the name of Sir Graham Moore, a lord of the Admiralty. CAPE MOORE, in South Victoria Land, is called after one of the officers of the *Terror*; and MOORE'S BAY, in Coronation Gulf, after Daniel Moore, of Lincoln's Inn. MOOR ISLAND, an isolated Pacific Island, south-east of Japan, bears the name of its discoverer.

Moravia is our Latinised name for the Austrian crownland, which is called in German MÄHREN or MARCHFELD, the plain of the River Mahr, March, Morava, or Mora.

Moray Firth takes its name from the old Scottish Earldom of Moray (whence the surname Murray), which is explained as *Mur-magh*, the 'plain by the sea.'

Morbihan, a department in Brittany, was so named from an inlet called Morbihan, 'the little sea' (Armorican *mor*, 'sea,' *bihan*, 'small').

Morea, the modern name of the Peloponnesus, is usually supposed to be due to the resemblance of its shape to the leaf of the mulberry (*morus*). The leaflike shape, *platani folio similis*, was noticed by Pliny. Hopf and Hertzberg think the name due to a transposition of letters, Romæa becoming Moræa, while Fallmerayer and Curtius maintain that the name is Slavonic, from *mor*, the 'sea.'

Morecambe Bay is usually explained as a Cymric name denoting 'the curved sea-shore.' But Ptolemy says that *Morikambé* was an estuary, probably that of the River Leven, or possibly of the Lune or the Ken. The name may consequently be compared with the Welsh word *morgamlas*, from *môr*, 'sea,' and *camlas*, a 'channel.' The name of Morecambe Bay, as now used, is a modern antiquarian figment, based on a misapprehension of Ptolemy's words.

Morembala, the 'high watch-tower,' is a lofty isolated hill on the River Shire, in East Africa.

Moresby Range, MOUNT FAIRFAX, and the MENAI HILLS, in Australia, commemorate the services of Captain Fairfax Moresby of the ship *Menai*.

Moreton Bay, Queensland, was called Moreton's Bay by Cook in 1770 for an unassigned reason, probably in compliment to some naval officer, places on either side of it being thus designated.

Morgan's Island, in the Gulf of Carpentaria, is a name recording the death from sunstroke in 1803 of Thomas Morgan.

Morges, a town on the Lake of Geneva, derives its name from a stony torrent bed, locally called *morge*, which is cognate with the obscure word *moraine*, and the Low-Latin *murenula*, a 'heap of stones,' or bed of river gravel. The word occurs in other names, such as LA MORGE DE MÖRILL and LA MORGE DE COUTHEY.

Morning Inlet, Australia, commemorates the time of day when it was entered by Stokes.

Morocco, more correctly MAROCCO, is the European name of the North African Sultanate called by the natives *Maghrib el Aksa*, 'the furthest west,' or *El Gharb*, 'the west,' an Arabic word which we have also in the Portuguese province of ALGARVE. Hence we have Maghribi, 'western,' as the name of the Morocco dialect and script. Morocco, the European name, is a Spanish corruption derived from the city of Maraksh, Marrakesh, or Marrakush, the capital, which means 'the adorned' city. In the sixteenth century the inhabitants of Marakesh were called by the Spaniards Maruecos or Marrocos, a name afterwards extended to denote the whole nation. This being supposed to be a plural form, the Italians invented the term Marocco as a name for the country.

Mortlock Islands, a group in the Carolines, were discovered in 1795 by James Mortlock, captain of the ship *Young William*.

Mosambique, a Portuguese territory in Eastern Africa, which gives a name to the MOSAMBIQUE CHANNEL between Madagascar and the mainland, took its name from a small coral island on which the capital is built, Mosambique being the Portuguese corruption of *Ma-sam-buco*, the native name of the harbour, which means literally 'the boats,' properly the seamed or sewn boats, like the Greek *Rhapta*, used by the natives.

Moscow, whence Muscovea or MUSCOVY, our old name for Russia, is called in Russian MOSKVA, from the small River Moskva on which it stands. The name of the river is probably Finnic, signifying a place for washing. In Mordwin, a neighbouring Finnic tongue, the stem *musk* means 'to wash clothes,' and in Tchermis *mosk* means 'to wash,' while the suffix has an illative force. The name has also been referred to the Slavonic *mokschow*, 'wet.'

Mosdok is a fort in the Caucasus, built in 1763, in a 'thick wood' on the River Terek.

Moselle, or Mosel River, is the *Mosella* of Tacitus, which is believed to be a diminutive of Mosa. Moselle would therefore mean the 'little Meuse' or Maas (*q.v.*).

Mosquito Coast, Nicaragua, is so called from a Sambo tribe, who were called *Moscas*, the 'flies,' by the Spaniards, Moustics by the buccaneers, and Mosquitos by the English.

Mossel Bay is the Dutch name of a bay in the Cape Colony which abounds in mussels.

Mosul, near the site of Nineveh, has given us the word *mussolino* or *muslin*, which, as Marco Polo records, was here first manufactured. The Arabic name *Al-Mausil* means the 'place of connection,' the Tigris being here crossed by a bridge and ford.

Mostar, the 'old bridge,' is the chief town of the Herzegovina. An ancient bridge, probably a Roman work, here crosses the River Narenta with a single arch of 95 feet span. The words *star*, 'old,' and *most*, 'bridge,' are both common components of Slavonic place names.

Mother and Daughters was the name given by Carteret in 1767 to three conspicuous mountains in New Britain.

Moubray Bay, in South Victoria Land, was named from an officer of the *Terror*.

Moulsey, in Surrey, at the mouth of the Mole, was the A.S. *Múleseige* (*Múlesíg*), 'Mole isle.'

Mo-Ussu, 'bad water,' is a caravan station in Mongolia.

Mouzon, in the Ardennes, is a corruption of *Moso-magus*, the field or plain by the Meuse.

Muck, one of the Hebrides, is in Gaelic *Eilean-nam-Muchad*, 'the island of the pigs,' perhaps porpoises or sea-pigs. So BEN-MAC-DHUI is 'black boar mountain.'

Mudge, Cape, in Arctic America, and MOUNT MUDGE, in Australia, bear the name of Colonel Mudge of the Board of Longitude.

Mühlhausen, MÜHLHEIM, MÜHLEN, MÜHLBACH, MÜHLDORF, from O.H.G. *muli*, a 'mill,' are common German names, corresponding to the English Melbourne (*q.v.*) and to the Irish *muilenn* (pronounced *mullen*), a 'mill,' as in CLON-MULLEN, 'mill-field.'

Mulgrave, in the North Riding, which gives the title of Earl to the Marquess of Normanby, was formerly *Grif*, which means a ravine or a deep narrow valley. Mulgrave would therefore be the 'mill ravine.' MULGRAVE ISLAND, PORT MULGRAVE, and POINT MULGRAVE were named from the first Earl of Mulgrave, who was First Lord of the Admiralty.

Mull, the *Malæus* of Ptolemy, the *Malea* of Adamnan, and the O.N. *Myl*, is from the Gaelic *maol*, a 'bald' or 'bare' hill. The MULL OF CANTIRE and the MULL OF GALLOWAY are bare headlands. In Ireland the word appears in modern names as MCYLE, as in the common name KNOCKMOYLE, the 'bald hill,' or KILMOYLE, which denotes a bare or dilapidated church. In Wales we have the corresponding word *moel*, as in the well-known mountain MOEL SIABOD.

Múltán, formerly spelt MOOLTAN, was the capital of the *Malti*, a people who were conquered by Alexander. The name has also been explained as a corruption of *Mulasthana*, from a temple of Mulasthani, a name of Párvatí.

Munich is the English name of the capital of Bavaria, which is called MÜNCHEN in German. Both forms have been independently obtained from the old name *Munichen*, found in 1058, which is from O.H.G. *munich*, 'a monk,' the town having been built on lands belonging to the monks of the convent of Schäftlarn. From *monachus*, 'a monk,' we have the Gaelic *manach*, the source of numerous names, such as KNOCK-NA-MANAGH, 'monks' hill,' or KIL-NA-MANAGH, 'the monks' church,' in Ireland, and AUCH-MANNOCH, 'the monks' field,' or MIL-MANOCH, 'the monks' hill,' in Scotland. MONJES, 'the monks,' is a group of four islands near the ANCHORITES, north of New Guinea, so named by Maurelle in 1781. The MÖNCH, one of the highest peaks in the Bernese Oberland, 13,044 feet high, was formerly called the Weiss-mönch, from its resemblance to the shaven head and white robe of the white monks, or Premonstratensians.

Munster, an Irish province, has, like Ulster and Leinster, the Danish suffix *-stadr*, 'place' or 'district,' appended to the old Irish name *Mumhan* (pronounced Mooan), the genitive of *Mumha*, the meaning of which is unknown. The Irish peerages of Ormonde, Desmond, and Thomond represented the old sub-king-doms of Munster; ORMONDE or Ormunde is a corruption of *Ur-mumhan*, which means East Munster; THOMOND, comprising the present counties of Tipperary, Clare, and Limerick, is a corruption of *Tuith-mumhan*, 'North Munster,' *tuith* (pronounced *tooa*) meaning the north, literally the left hand; and DESMOND, comprising the counties of Kerry, Cork, and Water-ford, meaning South Munster, from *deas* (pronounced *dass*), the south, literally the right hand (*see* DEKKAN), whence the name of the baronies of DEESE in Meath, at one time inhabited by the *Desi* or 'Southrons,' so called because they dwelt south of Tara. Expelled for not paying tribute to the overking, the Desi migrated further south, giving their name to a district, which being divided into two baronies acquired an English plural, and were called the DECIES, whence the title of an Irish peerage. So the Scotch names DUNDAS and FORDYCE mean 'south hill' and 'south land.'

Murchison Falls, on the Upper Nile, MOUNT MURCHISON, a peak 15,789 feet high, in the Rocky Mountains, and several Arctic, Antarctic, and Australian names were bestowed in honour of Sir Roderick Murchison, the geologist.

Murray is the principal river in Australia. In 1831 Captain Sturt by following the downward course of the Darling arrived at its junction with a great river which he called the Murray, in compliment to the Colonial Secretary, Sir George Murray. Its mouth, near Adelaide, is said to have been discovered in 1801 by Lieutenant John Murray in the brig *Lady Nelson*.

Muscat, or MASKAT, the chief town in Oman, is probably the *Moscha* of the Periplus.

Musgrave Islands, in the Caroline Group, were discovered in 1793 by Captain Musgrave of the ship *Sugarcane*.

Muskingum, 'moose eye' or 'elk's eye,' the native name of an affluent of the Ohio, was so called on account of the clearness of its waters.

Mustagh, 'the ice mountain,' is the Turkic name of a range in Central Asia.

Muttra, or MATHURA, is a very ancient and holy city on the Jumna, thirty miles above Agra. The name is a corruption of *Mathupura*, 'the city of Mathu,' a Rákshasa, who, according to the Indian mythology, was here slain by Krishna. The magnificent temple to which the town owes its name, was converted by Aurangzeb into a mosque. The sanctity of the name has caused it to be transferred to places in Ceylon, Java, Burma, and elsewhere.

Mysore (MÁISUR), the capital of the native state of the same name, is a shortened form of *Mahesh-úru*, which would ostensibly mean 'buffalo town'; but the name has with some probability been explained as mythological, *Mahesh-úru* being supposed to be a corruption of *Mahesh-asura*, the 'buffalo demon,' destroyed by the goddess Durga (Kali).

Mytilene, the capital of Lesbos, has now given its name to the Island.

Myvatn, in Iceland, means 'midge lake.'

Naas, the county town of Kildare, was the residence of the kings of Leinster. In Old Irish *nás* means a 'fair' or 'place of assembly.'

Nadejdi Strait, the best passage through the Kurile Islands, was discovered by Krusenstern in 1805, and named after his ship the *Nadejdi*, which means 'Hope.'

Naga Hills, in Assam, are inhabited by a group of uncivilised tribes called Nagas, who have been thought to be the Naga or 'snake' aborigines, but are more probably the 'naked' people (Sanskrit *nagna*, Hindi *nanga*, 'naked').

Nairn, a Scotch county, is named from the county town NAIRN, formerly called INVERNAIRN or INVERNARRAN, because situated at the mouth of the River Nairn, supposed to be from *amhuinn 'n Earnan*, 'the east flowing river,' or more probably from *amhuinn na' fhearn*, the 'alder tree river,' the *n* in both cases being a vestige of the prefixed article.

Nalsöe, 'needle isle,' is one of the Faröes. The sea has worn in the rocks a natural arch resembling the eye of a gigantic needle, through which vessels can pass. Several groups of pointed rocks bear the name of THE NEEDLES, among others, three pinnacles of chalk at the western end of the Isle of Wight, another group at the north end of Great Barrier Island, New Zealand, and a third on the Colorado River. (*See* FLAMBOROUGH.)

Namaqualand in the Cape Colony is inhabited by a Hottentot tribe called Namaqua or Namaga, a plural form meaning the 'Nama men.

Namur, in Belgium, is called NAMEN in Flemish, which represents the *Namon* of the Ravenna Geographer, who was probably a Goth who lived in the eighth century. The form Namur goes back to the seventh-century name *Namuco*, which becomes *Namurcum* in a tract of unknown date, called the 'Acts of St. Bertin,' who died in 698. The name is probably Celtic, signifying a 'temple' or 'sacred grove.'

Nancy, in Lorraine, is a corruption of the ninth-century name *Nanceiacum* derived from a hypothetical gentile name Nancius or Nantius.

Nanking or NANKIN, the 'southern capital,' or 'court of the south,' was the name given to the city of Kin-ling-fu when it became the capital of the Chinese Empire under the two first emperors of the Ming dynasty, who reigned from 1368 to 1410. It is officially designated as Keang-Ning, but is still popularly known as Nan-King. The third Ming Emperor returned to Shun-tien, which acquired the name of Pe-King, the 'court of the north.' *Nan*, the 'south,' is a common component of Chinese names, as NAN-HAI, the 'south sea,' or NAN-LING, the 'southern mountains.' HO-NAN is the province 'south of the river,' *i.e.* the Hoang Ho or Yellow River. AN-NAM is the 'peace of the south,' and YUN-NAN the 'cloudy south.'

Nantes, on the Loire, is the town of a Gaulish tribe called *Namnetes* by Cæsar.

Nant-Frangon, 'beaver's valley,' in Carnarvonshire, contains the Cymric word *nant*, a valley. In Cornwall we have

PENNANT, the 'head of the valley,' while NANT-Y-GWYDDEL, in the Black Mountains above Llanthony, testifies to an invasion of the Gael, and NANTWICH in Cheshire, called in Welsh *Halen Gwyn*, 'white salt,' is the *wych* or 'salt-house' in the valley. We have also NANTUA in Burgundy, and numerous Nants in Savoy and Brittany.

Napier, the capital of the province of Hawkes Bay in New Zealand, built on a peninsula known as SCINDE ISLAND, was named after Sir Charles James Napier, conqueror of Scinde.

Naples is a French corruption of the Italian NAPOLI, which preserves, with little change, the old Greek name *Neapolis*, 'the new city,' which in spite of its name is one of the oldest cities in Italy, having been founded by colonists from the still older settlement at Cumæ. NAPOLI DI ROMANIA in the Morea is merely a Venetian corruption of the Greek name *Nauplia*, the 'haven' of Argos, which is preserved in the modern name of the GULF OF NAUPLIA, while Nauplia has become ANAPLI. NABLOUS or NABLÛS in Palestine, which occupies the site of Shechem, is, like Naples, a corruption of *Neapolis*.

Narbonne in the Aube, anciently *Narbo Martius*, was the earliest Roman colony in Gaul.

Narim, a Siberian town on the Ob, founded in 1596, is from the Ostiak *nerim*, 'marshy.'

Narni, a town north of Rome, was formerly *Narnia*. It stands on a hill above the River Nera, formerly the Nar.

Narraganset Bay, which forms the port of Providence, Rhode Island, was so named in 1631, by Roger Williams, the founder of Providence, from the tribe inhabiting Point Judith, whose name *Naïganset*, or *Naiaganset*, means 'at the small point,' from *naigans*,' 'a small point of land,' and *-et*, the locative suffix, which we have in Massachusetts.

Nassau, till 1866 an independent Duchy, takes its name from the town of NASSAU, written in the tenth century *Nassaue*, the place on the 'wet meadow.' In 1564, Count William of Nassau succeeded to the principality of Orange, and was afterwards elected Stadtholder of Holland, whence sundry places named by Dutch seamen in honour of the House of Nassau-Orange, among them CAPE NASSAU, in the Straits of Magellan, so named in 1599 by Olivier de Noort, NASSAU HOEK,

a cape in Novaya Zemlya, named by Barents in 1594, and the NASSAU RIVER in the Gulf of Carpentaria, discovered by the early Dutch explorers of the Australian coast. NASSAU, the capital of the Bahamas, commemorates the English occupation in the reign of William III.

Nashville, the State capital of Tennessee, bears the name of a Colonel Nash.

Natal means 'Christmas Day' (*dies natalis*) in Portuguese. Vasco da Gama reached the coast of NATAL in South Africa on Christmas Day, 1497, and called it COSTA DO NATAL. CABO DO NATAL, in Madagascar, was discovered by Tristão da Cunha on Christmas Day, 1506. The Brazilian town of NATAL, at the mouth of the Rio Grande do Norte, was founded by Manuel Mascarenhas on Christmas Day, 1597. The corresponding Spanish name NAVIDAD usually signifies that a place was discovered, or a town founded, either on Christmas Day or on June 24th, the nativity of St John the Baptist. When the *Santa Maria* was wrecked on December 25th off the coast of Haiti, Columbus left forty sailors in a fort which he called NAVIDAD, from the day of the shipwreck.

Natchez, a city in the State of Mississippi, bears the name of a tribe which occupied the district when it was first explored by Europeans. Natchez is the French plural of the tribe name *Nache* or *Naktche*, from *naksh*, 'a warrior,' literally 'a hurrying man,' *i.e.* a man running to fight.

Natick, a town in Massachusetts, is a native name meaning 'our land.'

Naturaliste Channel, and CAPE NATURALISTE, West Australia, were named by Baudin in 1801 after the second ship of his expedition, the corvette *Naturaliste*.

Nautilus Shoal, in the Gilbert Archipelago, was discovered in 1799 by the ship *Nautilus*.

Navan, near Armagh, takes its name from the great palace of the kings of Ulster called *Eamhuin* (Latinised *Emania*), or, with the prefixed article, *n-Eamhuin*, of which Navan is a corruption. A very ancient legend connects the name with the golden brooch, *Eamhuin*, of Macha of the golden hair, from whom the name *Ard-Macha*, now ARMAGH, is traditionally derived.

Navarino in the Morea, on the site of the Greek Pylos, has been well called a barbarous word which history has immortalised, since here the battle was fought which secured the independence of Greece.

The older name, *Avarino*, is the Byzantine *Avarinos* or *Abarinos*, which recalls a settlement of Avars (*Abari*) who overran Greece in the sixth century. The form Navarino is due to a fragment of the Greek article prefixed to the accusative *Abarinon*.

Navarra (French NAVARRE), formerly an independent kingdom, is now a Spanish province. The Basque word *nava*, 'a plain,' enters into many of the names in the north of Spain, such as NAVA-HER-MOSA, the 'beautiful plain'; NAVA-DE-LOS-OTEROS, the 'plain of the heights'; PAREDES-DE-NAVA, the 'house on the plain'; NAVA DEL REY, 'the plain of the King.' Navarra probably means, like NAVARREUX, the 'plain among the hills.'

Navigators, a Polynesian group, now usually called the Samoa Islands, were named by Bougainville in 1768 *Les Iles des Navigateurs*, because on his arrival his ship was surrounded by a fleet of sailing pirogues.

Nazareth in Galilee, now En Nâsirah, was probably so named from a watch-tower (Hebrew.*nazar*, to 'watch').

Neagh, Lough, the largest Irish loch, is a corruption of the earlier name *Loch-n-Echach*, the 'lake of Eochy,' a chieftain of Irish legendary history.

Neath, a town in South Wales, takes its name from the River Neath on which it stands. It is believed to occupy the site of the Roman station of *Nidum* or *ad Nidum*, 'at the Neath.' Neath is supposed to mean the whirling or eddying river, from the Welsh *niddu*, to turn or twist. The NIDDA and the NIDDER in Germany, the NETHY and NITH in Scotland, and the NIDD in Yorkshire may be related names.

Nebraska, one of the United States, admitted in 1867, is watered by the River Nebraska, usually called the PLATTE, which is a French translation of the descriptive native name *Nebraska*, 'flat' or 'shallow' water, used by the Omaha and Otoe tribes who dwelt on its banks.

Neckar, a tributary of the Rhine, is believed by Förstemann to be a Teutonic name meaning the 'crooked' river. Zeuss contends that it is of Celtic origin, from an Aryan root meaning 'water,' whence the German *nix*, a water-spirit, the Irish *Nuada Necht*, a water-god, and *Nicor*, a water-monster, whence the name of Old Nick.

Necker Island, often wrongly spelt Neckar Island, is a barren isolated rock west of Hawaii, discovered in 1786 by La Pérouse, and named Ile Necker in compliment to M. Jacques Necker, the French Minister of Finance, after whom the NECKER ISLANDS off the coast of Oregon were named by La Pérouse in the same year.

Nejd, 'highlands,' is the Arabic name of Central Arabia.

Negrais, a cape and island at the extreme south end of Arakan, is believed to be a Portuguese corruption of the Burmese name, *Naga-rit*, the 'Dragon's whirlpool'; so called because ships are often wrecked by a strong current.

Negropont, the modern designation of the island of Eubœa, was the name of a Latin Barony which has been extended to the whole island, in the same way that the name Candia (*q.v.*) was extended to Crete. NEGROPONTE, which would mean the 'black bridge,' is an assimilated Italian form of the Neo-Greek name *Nevripo* or *N'Evripo*, 'the Euripus,' the old Greek designation of the channel between the island and the mainland. The initial *n* is a fragment of the article, which has become affixed, as in the case of NAVARINO (*q.v.*) or of Icaria, now NICARIA.

Negro, Rio, the 'black river,' is the name of an affluent of the Amazon, and of a river in Patagonia. Balboa, in 1511, gave the name RIO NEGRO to an affluent of the RIO ATRATO, which flows into the Gulf of Darien. PEDRAS NEGROS, the 'black rocks,' is a Portuguese name in Angola, and PIEDRAS NEGRAS is the Spanish name of a place on the Mexican side of the Rio Bravo del Norte. CERRO NEGRO, the 'black range,' is the name of a chain of hills in the Argentine Province of Catamarca.

Neill's Harbour, in Prince Regent's Inlet, was so named in 1825 from Dr. Samuel Neill, the surgeon of the *Hecla*.

Nellore, a town and district north of Madras, is explained by Hunter as *Nelliúru*, 'the town of the *nelli* tree' (*Phyllanthus emblica*). Burnell prefers the Tamil *Nall-úr*, 'good town.' The local interpretation is 'rice town,' from the Dravidian *nel*, 'paddy,' an explanation supported by local records in which the place is called by the translated Sanskrit name *Dhánya-puram*, which means 'rice town.'

Nelson, a town and province in New Zealand, is a companion name to those of Wellington, Napier, and Marlborough.

Nelson's name is also borne by PORT NELSON in De Witt's Land, and by CAPE NELSON in the Australian colony of Victoria. Thomas Button, who in the *Resolution* followed up Hudson's discoveries, wintered in 1612 at a place on the west coast of Hudson's Bay, which he called PORT NELSON after one of his officers who died there. The name has been extended to a large river, now called the NELSON, which here enters Hudson's Bay, and to LAKE NELSON which forms one of its sources.

Nemi, a lake in the Alban Hills, preserves the name of the 'grove' of Diana, *Nemus Dianæ.*

Nemours, in Algeria, bears the name of the second son of Louis Philippe, who took the title of Duc de Nemours from a town in the department of the Seine-et-Marne. (*See* NÎMES.)

Nenagh, in Tipperary, where a great fair is still held, is a corruption of *n-Aenach,* 'the assembly' or 'fair,' the initial *n* being the prefixed article which, as in other cases, has been incorporated into the name. The old name was *Aenach-Urmunhan,* 'the assembly place of Ormonde.'

Nennortalik, 'bear island,' is the Eskimo name of an island in Greenland, whose southern point is known as Cape Farewell.

Nepal, an independent State in the Himalayas, bears a name nearly equivalent to Piedmont, *nipa* meaning in Sanskrit 'at the foot' or base of a mountain, and *álaya,* 'seat' or 'place.'

Nepean Bay, South Australia, was named by Flinders, in 1802, after Sir Evan Nepean, Secretary to the Admiralty, whose name is also borne by POINT NEPEAN at the entrance of Port Phillip, CAPE NEPEAN in the Salomon Islands, and by NEPEAN ISLAND in Bass Strait.

Neptune Isles, at the entrance to Spencer's Gulf, Australia, is a far-fetched name given by Flinders, in 1802, because 'they seemed to be inaccessible to men.'

Nertchinsk, a town in Siberia, was founded in 1658 on the River Nertcha.

Ness, or NAZE (O.N. *nes*), a 'nose,' hence a cape, is a common element in Norse names. HOLDERNESS is the southeastern point of Yorkshire, and CAITHNESS is the northern point of Scotland. WALTON-ON-THE-NAZE stands on the Essex foreland called the NAZE. STENNIS, the 'stone ness,' in Orkney, takes its name from a great circle of standing stones. TROTTERNISH, in Skye, was called *Trouter-nes* in 1309. CAPE GRISNEZ, near Calais, with its cliffs of grey chalk, is the 'grey nose,' and CAPE BLANCNEZ, hard by, is the 'white nose.' LINDESNÆS, 'Linden-ness,' the southern point of Norway, is called the Naze by English sailors. The NESS, at the mouth of which stands the town of INVERNESS, is the river draining LOCH NESS, which is called in Gaelic *Loch an Eas,* the 'lake of the waterfall,' from the well-known Falls of Foyers, the inital *n,* as in NAVAN, NEWRY, NEAGH and other Gaelic names, being a fragment of the prefixed article.

Netherlands, which means the 'low lands,' is the English name of the Dutch Kingdom at the mouth of the Rhine which the French call LES PAYS BAS. Koningrijk der Nederlanden is the official Dutch name of the Kingdom as constituted after the war of 1830, when the Belgians acquired their independence. NETHERLAND ISLAND, in the Ellice Group, was discovered in 1825 by two Dutch ships.

Netley, the name of places on the borders of the New Forest, one of which is *Natanléah* in an A.S. charter, may be explained as the 'wet pasturage.' (*See* NASSAU.)

Neufchâtel, or NEUCHÂTEL, one of the Swiss Cantons, is a French translation of the older German name NEUENBURG, anciently *Nuvanburch,* given to the *Novum castrum* or 'Newcastle,' erected in the fifth century. From the castle the name passed to the town, then to the Lake on whose shores it stood, and finally to the Canton. NAUMBURG in Prussian Saxony, NIENBURG near Bremen, and NEUBURG in Bavaria are dialectic forms of the same name.

Neuwied, a town on the Rhine near Coblentz, was the 'New Wied,' founded in 1683 by Count Frederick of Wied near the site of the old village of Wied, which was destroyed during the thirty years' war. Old Wied stood on the Wiedbach, anciently the *Wida* (O.H.G. *wida,* 'withy' or 'willow'). There are in Germany between 4000 and 5000 places with the prefix *neu-,* of which there are more than 400 called either NEUHOF, NEUENHOF, or NEUHOFEN, 70 called NEUSTADT, 30 called NEUMARKT, while 160 bear the name of NEUDORF, NEUENDORF, NEUNDORF, or NIENDORF, equivalents of our numerous English Newtons. NEUSATZ, NEUHAUS, NEUSOHL, and similar forms are common ; NEUNKIRCHEN does not mean 'Nine churches' but 'New church,' as is shown by the older forms *Niuunchiricha* and *Niuwenchirgun*.

Nevada, one of the United States, admitted into the Union in 1864, but constituted as a territory and named in 1861, was originally a part of the Utah territory, which had been called Washoe from a native tribe. The new name was derived from the SIERRA NEVADA, the Spanish name bestowed on the 'snowy range' of California by an expedition despatched in 1542 by Mendoza, Viceroy of New Spain. This, as well as the SIERRA NEVADA in Mexico, were names adopted from the SIERRA NEVADA of Granada, whose snowy outline is such a conspicuous object to travellers voyaging eastwards from Gibraltar. (*See* SIERRA.)

Nevis, one of the Antilles, was passed by Columbus on his second voyage. It is not mentioned in his journal, but was doubtless entered on his chart, perhaps as *Nuestra Señora de las Nieves*, 'Our Lady of the snows.' It has been conjectured that the name was suggested either by the snow-white shore or by a cloud of steam floating, as is usually the case, from the summit of the conspicuous volcanic peak.

Newark - upon - Trent, in Nottinghamshire, from its position called the 'key of the north,' was the 'new work' or castle, rebuilt in 1125 by Alexander, Bishop of Lincoln, to replace a much earlier fortress, erected probably by Egbert, at a time when the Trent formed the boundary between the northern and southern provinces. NEWARK, the principal city in the State of New Jersey, was settled in 1666, the pastor being Abraham Pierson, from Newark-upon-Trent.

Newcastle-upon-Tyne, the county town of Northumberland, owes its name to the *Castellum novum*, the 'new castle' or precinct built in 1080 by Robert Courthose, Duke of Normandy, to replace that which had been destroyed by his father William the Conqueror. The rectangular Norman keep or *turris* was added to the precinct or *castellum* by Henry II. between 1172 and 1177. When coals had been discovered at Kingstown, on Port Hunter, in New South Wales, the name was changed to NEWCASTLE, since it was found that they could be shipped as readily as at Newcastle-upon-Tyne. NEWCASTLE-UNDER-LYME owes its name to the new castle under the forest of Lyme, rebuilt in the reign of Henry I. by Ranulf, Earl of Chester. NEWCASTLE BAY, near Cape York, Australia, discovered by Captain Cook in 1770, is believed to have been named after the first Duke of Newcastle-under-Lyme of the Pelham creation, prime minister from 1754 to 1762. NEWCASTLE WATER, in Australia, discovered in 1861, was named after the fifth Duke, who was Secretary for the Colonies.

Newfoundland was the earliest of the colonial possessions of Great Britain. The name originally applied to the regions discovered by the two Cabots, extending from lat. 67½° to 38°, thus including a great portion of the North American coast. The island to which the name is now restricted, is believed to have been the Island of St. John, so called because discovered by John Cabot on St. John's Day, June 24th, 1497. In an old Bristol record we read, 'In the year 1497, June 24th, on St. John's Day, was Newfoundland found by Bristol men in a ship called the *Matthew*.' In the privy purse expenses of Henry VII. for 1498, we have the entry, '10*l*. to him that found the new isle.' In 1503, it is called 'Newfoundland Isle,' and in an act of Parliament passed in 1540, it is called Newland. PORTUGAL COVE and CONCEPTION BAY in Newfoundland were discovered and named in 1500 by the Portuguese sailor, Gaspar de Cortereal. (*See* LABRADOR.)

New Guinea, discovered in 1526 by the Portuguese Jorge de Menezes, was so named in 1545 by Ortez de Rey, because of the resemblance of the Papuans, who are of Negroid type, to the Negroes of Guinea in West Africa. (*See* PAPUA.)

New Hampshire, one of the New England States, was granted in 1629 by a patent of Charles I. to Captain John Mason, who named it from the county in which as Governor of Portsmouth he had been resident. It was afterwards included in Massachusetts, but in 1679 the old name was revived, the four towns of Hampton, Portsmouth, Exeter, and Dorchester being taken from Massachusetts by Charles II., and made into the royal province of New Hampshire, on the ground that they were not within the boundaries of the original Massachusetts charter.

Newhaven, in Sussex, was formerly called Meeching. In the reign of Elizabeth the outlet of the Ouse was at Seaford, but the sea broke through the shingle barrier during a great storm, and formed what is now called the Old Harbour, which was enlarged and called The New Haven under an Act passed in 1713. NEWHAVEN in Connecticut was founded in 1638 by John Davenport, Theophilus Eaton, and others at *Quinipiac*, 'the land of the long water,' to which they gave the name of New Haven. The similar name of NEWPORT was given to the settlement founded in Rhode Island in 1639 by William Coddington and others. NEWPORT in Monmouthshire is called *Novus Burgus* by Giraldus Cambrensis, to distinguish it from Caerleon, the old Roman city, three miles distant. NIEWPORT in Belgium is the Flemish equivalent of Newport. NEWPORT in Salop was founded by Henry I. and called in the charter *Novo Burgo*, translated as Newport and Newborough, the word *port* being nearly a synonym of *borough*, as is shown by the title of portreeve. There are several inland Newports.

New Hebrides, so named by Cook in 1774, from the resemblance of the precipitous coasts to those of the Hebrides, were discovered in 1606 by Quiros and Torres, who supposing they had found the great Antarctic Continent, the *Terra Australis Incognita* of the old geographers, gave the land the name of *Tierra Austral del Espiritu Santo*, the 'Southern Holy Ghost land,' whence the name ESPIRITU SANTO, which is still retained by an island in the group. In 1718 Bougainville proved that the supposed continent consisted of a number of islands, to which he gave the somewhat fantastic name of *Archipel des Grandes Cyclades*.

New Jersey, one of the United States, is a part of the territory granted in 1664 to Lord John Berkeley and Sir George Carteret by the Duke of York ; and named in the conveyance *Nova Cæsarea* (New Jersey) as a compliment to Sir George Carteret, who had defended the island of Jersey against the Long Parliament.

Newmarket, on the borders of Suffolk and Cambridgeshire, was so called from the 'new market,' established in 1227, in lieu of the older market at Exning, a village two miles distant.

Newminster, in Northumberland, was a monastery established in 1138 by Cistercian monks from Fountains Abbey.

New River is the name of the aqueduct constructed in the reign of James I. by Sir Hugh Myddelton to supply London with pure water.

Newry, a town in County Down, which gives a second title to Lord Kilmorey, is a name which means 'the yew.' It was anciently called *Iubhar-cinn-tragha*, the 'yew at the head of the strand,' from a yew tree said to have been planted by St. Patrick when he founded the monastery. This was shortened to *Iubhar*, which with the prefixed article became *an-Iubhar*, 'the yew,' finally anglicised as Newry.

New South Wales was the name selected by Cook on August 21st, 1770, for the whole eastern coast of Australia, from Cape Howe to Cape York, on account of its supposed resemblance to the coast of South Wales. The western shore of Hudson's Bay, explored in 1631 by Captain James, was called by him NEW SOUTH WALES, in honour of the Prince of Wales, afterwards Charles II. who was born in the preceding year ; the contiguous district, to the north-west of Hudson's Bay, being styled NEW NORTH WALES. These names have now disappeared from the map.

Newton, the commonest of English village names, is generally represented by *Niwantune* in A.S. charters, *niwan* being the locative of *niwe*, 'new.' In some cases *Niwantune* has become NEWINGTON, or more rarely NEWNTON. *Niwanham* as a rule becomes NEWNHAM. Some Newtons are of more recent origin ; thus NEWTON STEWART, Wigtownshire, was founded in 1677 by the Stewarts, Earls of Galloway, and NEWTON STEWART in County Tyrone was built on the lands granted by Charles I. to Sir William Stewart.

New Year's Harbour and NEW YEAR'S ISLANDS in Tierra del Fuego, were discovered by Cook on January 1st, 1775. NEW YEAR'S ISLES, in Bass Strait, were discovered by John Black, commander of the brig *Harbinger*, on January 1st, 1801. The day of discovery also explains the names of NEW YEAR'S ISLANDS on the north coast of Australia, and NEW YEAR'S RANGE and NEW YEAR'S CREEK on the Upper Darling River.

New York, one of the United States, was a Dutch colony called the New Netherlands. In 1664 Charles II. granted the territory to his brother James, Duke of York and Albany, and when Nieuw Amsterdam had been surrendered by Stuyvesant to a squadron under the Duke's deputy governor, the name of the Dutch town was changed to New York, while the Dutch outpost of Fort Orange on the Hudson became ALBANY, now the State capital, the New Netherlands forming the nucleus of the colony, and ultimately of the State of New York.

New Zealand was discovered by the Dutchman Abel Tasman on December 13th, 1642, and called by him Staaten Land, as it was supposed to be a portion of the Antarctic continent, continuous with the Staaten Land (now STATEN ISLAND, Fuegia) which had been discovered and named by Le Maire and Schouten in 1616, in honour of the Dutch States-General. When the error was discovered, the name was changed to NIEUW ZEELAND, after the Dutch province of Zeeland. The Maori name of the North Island is *Te Ika a Maui*, 'the fish of the (god) Maui,' while the South Island is *Te Wahi Panamu*, 'the land of greenstone,' *i.e.* of the nephrite, out of which the stone axes of the Maoris were made.

Niagara is supposed to be an Iroquois name, *O-ni-aw-ga-rah*, or Nee-agg-arah, said to mean 'the thunder of the waters.' Boyd affirms that the Senecas called the falls *Date-car-sko-sa-sa*, 'the highest falls,' and that Niagara is an Iroquois word meaning the 'neck,' applied not to the fall, but to the river connecting Lakes Erie and Ontario, as the neck connects the head with the body.

Nias Islands, and POINT NIAS, in Arctic America, bear the name of Joseph Nias, one of Parry's officers.

Nicaragua, a city in Central America, was built on the spot where Nicaragua, a powerful native chief, received Gil Gonçales Davila in March 1523. The name has been extended to the State, and to the great lake called *Cocibolca* by the natives, and *Laguna de Nicaragua* by the Spaniards.

Nice, a town on the Riviera, is the French form of the Italian NIZZA, both corruptions of the old name *Nicæa*, a town built by the Phocæan colonists of Massilia to commemorate a 'victory' over the Ligurians. *Nicæa* in Anatolia, where the Council of Nice was held, is now ISNIK (*q.v.*). NICOPOLI in Bulgaria represents *Nicopolis*, the 'city of victory,' founded by Trajan after his victory over the Dacians. NICOSIA, the capital of Cyprus, is apparently a shortened form of the old name *Kallinikesia*, influenced by assonance with Lefkosia, the modern Greek form of *Leukosia*, also an ancient name of the place. NIKOLAIEVSH, a Russian port at the mouth of the Amur, was so named in 1851 in honour of the Czar Nicholas.

Nicholson Reef, east of the Friendly Islands, was discovered in 1818 by a Captain Nicholson.

Nicobar Islands, a group north of Sumatra, called *Necuvaram* by Marco Polo, appear in the great Tanjore inscription (*c.* 1050 A.D.) as *Nakka-varam*, a name probably referring to the nudity of the people (*nanga* or *nagna*, 'naked,' and *varam*, 'country'). An Arab historian writing in 1300 informs us that the men went entirely naked, while the women wore only a girdle of cocoa-nut leaves. The Nicobars are probably the *Nalo-kilo-chen* (=*Narikela-dvipa*, 'cocoa-nut islands') of the Chinese pilgrim Hwen T'hsang, and the *Nesoi Baroussai* of Ptolemy.

Nicoya, a gulf on the Pacific coast of Costa Rica, was named from *Nicoya*, a native village, where in 1522 Gil Gonçales landed to obtain provisions on his expedition to Nicaragua.

Niemesk, in Brandenburg, NIEMECZYN in Russia, and numerous village names in Eastern Europe, contain the word *nemec* or *niemiec*, the Slavonic designation of the Germans, literally 'the dumb,' 'those who cannot speak.' *Nemche*, the Turkish name of Germany, affords a curious proof that the Turks first acquired their knowledge of that country through a Slavonic channel.

Niger, the European name of the great river, 2000 miles in length, which traverses the Western Soudan, is not as is usually asserted the 'black river,' or the 'river of the negroes,' but a corruption of the Berber name *N-eghirreu*, derived from *ghir*, a 'river.' The native name of the lower part of the Niger is QUORRA (*Kowara*, or *Kuara*), a Yoruba word meaning 'river' or 'water.' In its upper course, above Timbuktu, it bears the Mandingo name JOLIBA, 'the great stream.' The Songhay people call it ISAI or YSSA, and the Fulbe call it MAYO, names meaning simply 'the river.'

Night Island, York Peninsula, is where King anchored for a night in 1819.

Nile was called in Old Egyptian either *Hapi* or *P-iero*, 'the river,' of which *Nehar Misraim*, 'the river of Egypt,' or simply *Nahal*, 'the valley' or 'stream,' were Semitic translations. The Greek name *Nilus* was probably a corruption of the Phœnician name *Nahal*. The Arabs now call it *Bahr*, 'the sea,' the two Niles being distinguished as BAHR-EL-AZRAK, 'the turbid,' or Blue Nile, and BAHR-EL-ABYAD, the 'clear' or White Nile. The Nile was also called *Sihor*, the 'blue' or 'dark' river, of which Nilus might conceivably be an Aryan translation, like the NILAB or 'blue water' in the Punjab.

Nilgherries (NÍLGIRI) is the modern name of a mountain spur at the southern end of the Mysore tableland, now much frequented as the Sanatorium of the Madras Presidency. The native name is *Malai-nádu*, the 'hill country.' The Sanskrit name *Nílagiri*, the 'blue mountain,' appears in the Hindu Cosmogony, and was applied to the Ootacamund range about 1820 by some ingenious European scholar. In the Punjab we have the NÍLA KOH, or 'blue mountains.' The BLUE MOUNTAINS in New South Wales are so named from their colour, as seen from Sydney at a distance of fifty miles.

Nimes, in Provence, is the Roman *Nemausus*, so called from the 'sacred grove' in which the Volcæ Arecomici held their assemblies. The Old Celtic word *nemetum*, which we have in *Augusto-nemetum*, now Clermont, meant a 'temple,' and Fortunatus tells us that *Ver-nemetis* meant the 'great temple.'

Ning-po means the 'repose of the waves' (Chinese *ning*, 'rest,' and *po*, a 'wave').

Nio, an island in the Ægean, is the ancient *Ios*, with a fragment of the prefixed article.

Nipimenan Sepesis, an affluent of the Qu'appelle River, means 'little cranberry river,' from the Cree words *Nipimenan*, 'summer berries' (*i.e.* cranberries), *sis*, 'little,' and *sepe*, 'water,' which we have in Mississippi.

Nipissing and NIPIGON, two lakes in the province of Ontario, are explained as 'the waters,' from *nippeash* and *nippeog*, the two forms of the plural of *nippe*, 'water.'

Nipon, or NIPPON, the largest of the Japanese Islands, means the Orient or 'land of the sunrise,' from the Japanese *ni*, 'fire,' 'sun,' and *pon*, 'land.' Nipon is also called HONDO, the 'mainland.' JAPAN (*q.v.*) is a Chinese equivalent of Nipon.

Nissa, or NISCH, in Servia, is the Greek *Naisos*, afterwards *Naisopolis*, so called from having been the 'birthplace' of the Emperor Constantine.

Nogoa, a river in Australia, was found dry by Leichardt, who called it the 'No go,' adding a final *a*, so as to give the name a sort of geographical respectability.

Nomansland is a district of Caffraria, south of the colony of Natal.

Nonnenwerth, the 'nun's island,' is a picturesque island in the Rhine above Bonn, with a convent founded in 1122 (O.H.G. *warid*, an 'island').

Noogsoak, 'great nose,' is the Eskimo name of a cape in Greenland on which a Danish colony was planted in 1758.

Nootka Sound is a large bay on the west coast of Vancouver's Island, discovered in 1774 by Juan Perez. Owing to some misconception the native word *nutchi*, a 'mountain,' has been transferred to the bay. It was called KING GEORGE'S SOUND by Cook, who visited it in 1778.

Nore, a sandbank in the estuary of the Thames, where the channel narrows, is the O.N. word *nór* (pronounced *nore*), an 'inlet' or 'sea loch,' which we have in the inlets called MON'S NOR and FALSTER NOR in Schleswig. The RIVER NORE in Ireland, a tributary of the Barrow, is called in 1645 'the Oure or Nore.' The initial *n* is an abraded relic of the definite article, *Avon n'Ore* representing the Old Irish *Avon An-Fheoir*, 'the grey river.' NORE, a hill name in Hants, Kent, and Surrey, is probably for Knore (M.E. *knor*, Old Dutch *knorre*, German *knorren*), 'a knob, hunch, or protuberance.'

Norfolk, in A.S. *Northfolc*, and afterwards *Norfolc*, signifying the northern division of the East Anglian folk, was at first, like Essex or Dorset, the name of the people, and not of the land they dwelt in. NORFOLK ISLAND, between New Zealand and New Caledonia, was discovered by Cook in 1774, and named in honour of the ninth Duke of Norfolk. NORFOLK BAY and MOUNT NORFOLK in Tasmania, discovered by Flinders in 1798, bear the name of his sloop the *Norfolk*.

Normandy, called Normandie in French, is the province occupied early in the tenth century by the Northmen, whose name on French soil gradually changed to Normans. The earliest form is *Terra Northmannorum*, followed by *Northmannia*, *Normannia*, *Normendie*, and NORMANDIE.

Normanton, Queensland, bears the name of Captain Norman, a Government Surveyor. NORMANTON, in Yorkshire, appears as *Norman-tone* in Domesday, indicating that it was the tun of some northman.

Noronha bears the name of a Portuguese seaman, Fernando de Noronha (*q.v.*).

Norrbotten, in Sweden, means North Bothnia. (*See* BOTHNIA.) NORRKÖPING, the 'north market,' is two miles north of SÖDERKÖPING, the 'south market.' NORDHAUSEN, 'at the north houses,' is now an important town in Prussian Saxony.

Norte means the north in Spanish and Portuguese. In Brazil we have the RIO GRANDE DO NORTE, or 'great river of the North,' so called with reference to the RIO GRANDE DO SUL, the 'great river of the South,' or to the neighbouring RIO PEQUENO, the 'little river.' RIO GRANDE DEL NORTE, the Spanish name of the river dividing Mexico from Texas, is also called RIO BRAVO DEL NORTE, 'the fierce river of the North,' from its violent summer floods. In its middle course it goes by the name of RIO PUERCO, the 'dirty river,' from its muddy waters.

Northallerton in Yorkshire, which gives a name to the district conventionally called Allertonshire, has received the distinctive prefix to distinguish it from Allerton Mauleverer. NORTHWICH, in Cheshire, is the northern *wych*, or salthouse.

Northampton is a name as to which nothing very definite can be said, since we have no early mention of the town or of the shire. In a forged or doubtful copy of a charter, professing to be dated in 664 A.D., but which cannot be earlier than the twelfth century (C.D. No. 984), we have *villa de Norhamtonne*. In a late and doubtful copy of a charter of 948 (C.D. No. 420) we have *Northamtonshire*; and *Norhamtun* in an undated charter (C.D. No. 1367). In the Saxon Chronicle, A.D. 917, we have *Hantun*, and *North-hamtun* in A.D. 1087. In Domesday the name appears as *North Antone*, and the forms Hantone and Amtune are also found. The name is probably to be explained in the same way as Southampton (*q.v.*), but it has been conjectured that the Nene on which it stands may be the misread *Antona* of Tacitus, in which case the town might have derived its name from the river.

North Cape is naturally a common name. The NORTH CAPE, on the Norwegian island of Mageroe, was so named by Chancellor, who rounded it in 1553. Somewhat farther to the east is the NORD KYN in Finmark, the northernmost point of continental Europe. NORTH CAPE, New Zealand, CAPE NORTH in Eastern Siberia, and in South Georgia, were named by Cook in the years 1769, 1778, and 1775. CAPE NORTH in South Victoria was named by James Ross in 1841.

North Sea is the English form of a name due to the Dutch mariners, who spoke of the *Noord Zee* as distinguished from the ZUIDER ZEE or 'southern sea.' The Dutch name has been adopted by the Germans, while the Danes call it *Vester-*

havet, the 'west sea.' In England, following the classical usage, we generally call it the GERMAN OCEAN, a translation of the Roman name *Oceanus Germanicus.*

Northumberland, originally the 'land north of the Humber,' was in the ninth century, at the time of its greatest extension, a kingdom stretching from the Humber to the Forth. The present county, between the Tees and the Tweed, is what remained after the shire of York, the Palatinate of Durham, and the Scotch earldoms of the Lothians had been carved out of it. It never included Cumberland or Westmoreland, which were no part of England, belonging to the Welsh kingdom of Strathclyde. NORTHUMBERLAND REEF in the Moluccas was discovered in 1796 by Captain Rees of the ship *Northumberland.* NORTHUMBERLAND SOUND, in the Parry Islands, was named by Belcher in 1852 after the Duke of Northumberland, First Lord of the Admiralty. In Australia we have the NORTHUMBERLAND ISLES discovered by Cook in 1770, and CAPE NORTHUMBERLAND named by Grant in 1800.

Norton Sound, Alaska, was named by Cook in 1778 'in honour of Sir Fletcher Norton,' Speaker of the House of Commons, who in 1782 was created Lord Grantley. NORTON (*North-tun*) is one of the commonest of English village names, *north,* except before a vowel, frequently becoming *nor,* as in Norfolk, Norwich, Norbury, Norcott.

Norway is the A.S. *Norweg* (frequently used in the dative plural, *Norwegum*), and the O.N. *Norvegr* or *Noregr,* which signified the 'Northern way or route of the Swedish Vikings, as distinguished from the *Vesturvegr* or 'Western route' across the German Ocean, and from the *Austrvegr* or Eastern route by the Baltic. The A.S. *Northriga* means a man of Norway. NORWAY HOUSE, on Lake Winnipeg, was so called because some Norwegians from Manitoba settled there.

Norwich is the county town of Norfolk. It is difficult to believe that there is no connection between the names of the city and the county, especially as there is no Southwick; but, as the name *Northwic* does not occur in the Chronicle before 1004, there may have been some earlier form of the name which would explain the difficulty, which is not diminished by the fact that SUDBURY was formerly a chief town of Suffolk, as is shown by its being the seat of one of the two Suffolk Archdeaconries. Norwich is the 'North wíc,' where *wic* probably does not mean a 'bay' or the 'reach' of a river, as is sometimes the case, but a 'village' or town, and may denote a considerable place, as is shown by London being called *Lundenwic* in the Chronicle.

Nòsy means island in Malagasy. Thus Nòsi-Bé, the 'great island,' lies off the coast of Madagascar. The word is also used for rising ground standing up in rice fields, as Nòsi-Vato, 'rocky island'; Nòsi-Zato, the 'hundred isles'; Nòsi-Arìvo, the 'thousand isles.' The old native name of Madagascar was *Nòsindàmbo*, the 'island of wild boars.'

Nottingham, the county town of Nottinghamshire, is called in the Chronicle Snotingahám, the 'ham' of the Snotingas, who are supposed, though without any direct evidence, to be the 'cavern-dwellers,' who inhabited the caves in the castle rock. Asser tells us that the British name was *Tigguocobauc*, signifying *speluncarum domus*. Tigguocobauc means a 'cave dwelling,' *tiggu* being an earlier form of the Welsh *ty*, a 'house' or dwelling, while *ogof*, a cave, gives the adjective *ogofawg*, cavernous.

Nova Scotia, or 'New Scotland,' was the pedantic name given by James I. to the French colony of Acadia, when he granted it by patent to Sir William Alexander, a Scotchman, on the pretext of its having been discovered by Cabot in the reign of Henry VII. In Cape Breton, which forms a part of the province of Nova Scotia, there are a large number of colonists from the Highlands and the Hebrides, nearly 30,000 emigrants having come out at the time of the clearances in the beginning of the nineteenth century. Gaelic is still spoken in the district around the places bearing the Scotch names of Mull, Skye, Glen, and Glendale, which formed the centres of the Highland colony.

Novaya Zemlya, the 'new land,' is the Russian name of a great island in the Arctic Ocean, already known to the Novgorod hunters in the eleventh century, and rediscovered in 1553 by Sir Hugh Willoughby, and hence at one time appearing on English maps as Willoughby's Land. Zemlya being feminine, the adjective *novaya* agrees with it. We have the masculine in Novgorod, the 'new town,' a name which occurs several times in Russia. Novgorod on Lake Ilmen was called *Holmgardr* by the Northmen. Novgorod on the Volga is distinguished as Nijni Novgorod, or Lower Novgorod. Novi-Bazar, the 'New Market,'

in Bosnia, is a Slavonic translation of the Turkish name Yenibazar. Nykoping in Sweden also means 'new market,' and Nyborg in Denmark is the 'new burg.' New is naturally the commonest adjectival component of local names. For Greek, Celtic, German, and French examples, *see* Naples, Noyon, Neuwied, and Neufchâtel.

Noyon in the department of the Oise, and Nyon on the Lake of Geneva are corruptions of the Celto-Roman name *Noviodunum*, the 'new dun' or fort. Nevers was the *Noviodunum Æduorum* of Cæsar. In the Antonine Itinerary it appears as *Nevirnum*, of which Nevers is a corruption, evidently so named from its position on the little river Nièvre which here joins the Loire. Neumagen near Trier, and Nimeguen in Holland, called Nijmegen in Dutch, are corruptions of the Celto-Latin name *Noviomagus* or *Noviomagum*, the 'new field.'

Nubia is from the Old Egyptian *nub*, 'gold,' being the land from which that metal was procured.

Nun, or Non, a cape on the west coast of Africa opposite the Canaries, is a corruption of the Portuguese name *Cabo de Não* (*Naon*) which became *Cabo Non*, popularly explained as 'Cape Nay,' because early in the fifteenth century it was the *Cabo non plus ultra* which they were unable to pass, saying No! to the wistful mariner. The Portuguese proverb ran *Quem passar o Cabo de Não ou voltarra ou não.* 'Whoever passes Cape Non will return or not.' Nun was the native name.

Nuñez, a West African river, north of Sierra Leone, formerly and more correctly called *Rio do Nuno*, was discovered in 1446 by Nuno Tristão, a Portuguese mariner who was killed here.

Nuremberg in Bavaria, the English form of the German Nürnberg, represents the older name which appears as *Nurinberg* in a document of 1050. It is usually said to have been a settlement of the Norici, who, flying from the Huns are supposed to have established themselves in this region in the middle of the fifth century. It is more probably from a personal name belonging to the same Celtic stem as the names of the Norici and the Noric Alps.

Nurska, a district, and Nureff a river, in Podolia, are believed to be derived from the name of the *Neuri* of Herodotus.

Nusa Kambangan, an island south of Java, is a Malay name meaning the 'island of flowers,' the flowers growing

O

on it being gathered only at the coronation of the kings of Surakerta.

Nuyts Land, NUYTS ARCHIPELAGO, POINT NUYTS, and CAPE NUYTS, on the southern coast of Australia, bear the name of the Dutch sailor Pieter Nuyts, who in the *Gulde Zeepaard* discovered this portion of the Australian coast in January 1627.

Nyanza, NYASSA, and NYANJA are dialectic forms of the Bantu word for a great lake or 'sea.'

Oakley, Hampshire; OCKLEY, Surrey; and ACLEY, Kent, all called in A.S. documents *Aclea,* 'oak pasture,' have given rise to numerous surnames, one of which, borne by an officer of the *Erebus,* has been transferred to Cape Oakley in South Victoria. OAKHAMPTON, in Devon, is the *tún* on the River Okement.

Ob or OBY, a great Siberian river, is usually explained as an Ostiak name, meaning 'the two,' two great branches, one milky and the other clear, uniting to form the main stream, and flowing for a considerable distance without intermingling. But it is possible that the name may be Zyrianian, in which case it might mean the 'grandmother' (*ob*) of waters.

Oban, the name of several places in the Western Highlands, is a diminutive of the Gaelic *ob,* a 'bay.'

Oberland, the name of several Swiss districts, means the 'high land.' The best known, the Bernese Oberland, is the mountainous part of Canton Bern.

Observation, Mount, in Banks Land, is a hill whence, in 1850, M'Clure, coming from the Pacific, discerned across Banks Strait the shores of Melville Island, where Parry had wintered thirty years before, thus ascertaining the actual existence of a North-West Passage. Never, he says, 'from the lips of man burst a more fervent "Thank God!" than now from those of that little company.'

Ocean Islands, a group in the Marshall Archipelago, were discovered by the ship *Ocean* in 1804.

Ochil Hills, Perthshire, bear a Cymric name, explained by the Welsh *uchel,* 'high.' So OCHILTREE may be *uchel-tre,* the 'high house,' and OGILVIE the 'high hill.'

Ocotal, a town in Nicaragua, takes its name from the *ocotl,* a local species of pine.

Oder, the *Viadus* of Ptolemy, afterwards called the *Odora, Oddara,* or *Adora,* is probably the Lithuanian *audra,* a 'flood,' or 'flow,' cognate with the Sanskrit *udra,* 'water,' in *sam-udra,* the 'sea.' The WEAR in Durham, the *Vedra* of Ptolemy, is referred by Pott to the same Aryan root.

Odinse, the capital of the Danish Isle of Fünen, formerly called *Odins oe,* 'Odin's island,' was a great heathen sanctuary, which became an episcopal see after the conversion of the Danes.

Odessa, a Russian port on the Black Sea, founded in 1796, was so named because it was built on a site then supposed to be that of *Odessos, Odyssos,* or *Odesopolis* (now Varna), a colony of Miletus connected by popular etymology with the Homeric hero.

Offa's Dyke bears the name of Offa, the great Mercian king, who constructed a vast earthwork, second only in magnitude to Hadrian's wall, to protect his dominions from the plundering inroads of the Welsh. The dyke, which in many places is still called either Offa's Dyke, or in Welsh *Clawdd Offa,* ran in a nearly straight line from the mouth of the Wye to the estuary of the Dee, passing by Oswestry and Mold. OFFLEY, in Herefordshire, has been supposed to be the place where Offa died in 796.

Ogdensburg, a city on the St. Lawrence, in the State of New York, was incorporated in 1817 and named after the proprietor, Samuel Ogden. OGDEN CITY, in Utah, bears the name of Major Edmund A. Ogden.

Ohio, one of the United States, is so called from the River Ohio, an Iroquois name, known to the early French colonists by the translated name *la Belle Rivière.*

Ohlsen, a cape in Smith Sound, was named in memory of Christian Ohlsen, who took part in Kane's expedition, and died here in 1855.

Oil City, on OIL CREEK, is in the petroleum district of Pennsylvania.

Okak, in Labrador, is situated in OKAK BAY, which is protected by two tongues of land (Eskimo *okak,* a 'tongue').

Okhotsk, Sea of, between Kamtchatka and Sagalien, takes its name from OKHOTSK, a town founded in 1639 on the river called OKHOTA, which is a Russian corruption of *okat,* a Tungusic word meaning a 'river.'

Oldenburg, a North German Grand Duchy, takes its name from the town of OLDENBURG, formerly *Aldenburg,* the 'old castle.' According to a popular tradition, the castle was built by Walbert, grandson of Wittekind, and named after his wife, Altburga.

Olenek, in Siberia, is the 'reindeer river.'

Oléron, near Pau, anciently *Iluro,* and the Isle of Oléron, anciently *Uliarus,* at the mouth of the Charente, are believed to be from the Basque *ilia,* a 'place' or 'town,' and *ura,* 'water.' (*See* ASTURIA.)

Olifant's Mountains, OLIFANT'S RIVIER, and OLIFANT'S VLEI, all in the Cape Colony, were so called from the elephants by which they were formerly frequented.

Olmütz, in Moravia, the German form of the Slavonic name *Olomouc, Holomauc,* or *Holomauce,* is believed to have been founded by the Emperor Julius Maximus, and called *Julii Mons* or *Julimontium,* of which the name is said to be a corruption, but is more probably Slavonic, meaning 'bare rocks.'

Olney, an island in the Severn, where Canute met Edmund in 1016 to divide the kingdom, is the A.S. *Olanég,* possibly for *Holenég,* 'holly isle.' There are also places called OLNEY in Bucks and Northants.

Olten, in Canton Solothurn, represents the Roman *Ultinum.*

Olyntorsk, a town on the River Olyntora, in Kamtchatka, gives its name to a neighbouring cape and bay.

Omaha, the state capital of Nebraska, perpetuates the name of a Dahcota tribe, explained by Boyd as those who live 'up stream.'

O-mei, the 'golden summit,' a great place of pilgrimage, is a mountain in Western China covered with Buddhist temples.

Ometepec, the 'double mountain,' is the native name of a volcano in the Lake of Nicaragua.

Omsk, a town in Siberia, stands on the River Om.

Onega is the name of a river which falls into the GULF OF ONEGA in the White Sea, and also of the great lake which discharges itself into Lake Ladoga. The name is doubtless Finnic, probably signifying the 'rough' or perhaps the 'noisy water.'

Oneida, the name of a lake, a river, and a county in the State of New York, is a corruption of *Onayoteka,* an Iroquois tribe-name, meaning, according to F. Müller, the 'granite people.' Cuoq derives the name from a certain 'standing stone.'

To another Iroquois tribe, the *Onundaga,* or 'hill people,' we owe the name ONONDAGA which has been given to a lake and county in New York State.

Ontario, one of the great North American lakes, which gives its name to a Canadian province, is a native name meaning 'the beautiful lake.' It was originally called Lac Frontenac, from Count Frontenac, the French viceroy. On Joliet's map of 1673 it is called *Lac Frontenac ou Ontario.*

Ootacamund (UTAKAMAND), a sanatorium in the Neilgherries, and the summer residence of the Governor of Madras, is from *Hotta-ga-mand,* 'stone house,' the Badaga name given to the first European bungalow erected in these hills.

Opelousas, in Louisiana, preserves the name of the tribe of the *Appalousa* or 'black heads.'

Oporto, the Roman *Portus Cale,* should be written in Portuguese fashion either O PORTO, 'the Port,' or simply PORTO, without the prefixed article which has been dropped in the derived name of Portugal (*q.v.*) and also in that of the 'Port' wine shipped from O Porto.

Opsloe, formerly *Ooslo,* a Norwegian town near Christiania, stands at the 'mouth,' *oos,* of a small river called the Lo.

Oran, in Algeria, is the European form of the Arabic name *Wahrán,* the 'ravine.'

Orange, a town in Provence with extensive Roman remains, · anciently called *Arausio* or *Arausion,* stands at the confluence of the River Araise and the Rhone. The principality of Orange, through the marriage of an heiress with a Count of Nassau, gave a title to the princes of the Orange-Nassau family who became Stadtholders of Holland, after whom, in 1777, the Dutch colonists at the Cape of Good Hope gave the name of ORANGE RIVER to the GARIEF, a Hottentot word which means the 'rusher' or 'rushing' river. The ORANGE FREE STATE lies between the Orange River and the Vaal. The well-known orange tree on the postage stamps of the Orange Free State is a punning cognisance, our *orange* being a corruption of *naranj,* the Persian name. The rivalry of the Dutch and Portuguese in South America is marked by FORT ORANGE, erected by the Dutch in 1631 on the Brazilian island of Itamarca, and by CAPE ORANGE, the northernmost point on the Brazilian coast. From the Orange-Nassau Princes we have ORANGE CAY in the Bahamas; the ORANGE ISLANDS at the north-east corner of Novaya Zemlya, discovered by the Dutchman Barents in 1594; and FORT ORANGE, the original Dutch name of Albany, now the State capital of New York. (*See* NASSAU.)

Oranmore in Galway, whence the title of an Irish peer, is a corruption of *Uaranmor*, the 'great spring.' At ORANMORE in Roscommon, the *uaran* or 'spring' is a holy well still frequented by pilgrims.

Oransay, one of the Hebrides, is the island of St. Odhran, a sixth century Irish missionary.

Ord, a word not uncommon in Scotch names, as ORD OF CAITHNESS, MUIR OF ORD, ORDHEAD, or ORDIQUHILL, is explained by Stokes from the Irish *ord* (Breton *orz*), a mallet or hammer. In modern Gaelic *ord* means a steep rounded height.

Oregon, one of the United States, is bounded on the north by the Oregon or Columbia River. The name formerly denoted the much larger territory which lies north of the parallel of 42°. It is uncertain whether the river was named from the territory or the territory from the river. In the former case it has been conjectured that the name is derived either from the Spanish word *oregano*, 'wild marjoram' or 'wild sage (*artemisia*), which grows abundantly in the region, or from the tribe - name *Orejones*, 'large eared,' applied by the Spaniards to the races which artificially enlarge the lobes of the ears. On the other hand the name Oregon is first mentioned by Carver, who started from Canada in 1766 to reach the Pacific, and returned in 1768. In his travels, published in 1778, he speaks of 'the Oregon or River of the West.' He can only have obtained the name from the Sioux, on the eastern side of the Rocky Mountains, who were hardly likely to have been acquainted with any Spanish name. It is therefore urged that Carver considered 'River of the West' to be a translation of the native name Oregon. The Flatheads call the river *Jakaïl Uimakl*, the 'great river.' (*See* COLUMBIA.)

Orellana, a name of the Upper Amazon, commemorates the exploit of Francesco de Orellana, who, starting from Peru, descended the whole course of the Amazon (*q.v.*).

Orenburg is a Russian town and province. In 1738 a military post was established at the confluence of the River Ural with the Or. Four years later the post was moved some 150 miles lower down the Ural River, the old name being retained, which has therefore only an historical connection with the name of the Or. The town of ORSK now occupies the former site of Orenburg.

Organ Mountains, in Portuguese *Serra dos Organos*, resemble organ pipes when seen from Rio.

Oriel was an Irish kingdom comprising the modern counties of Armagh, Monaghan, and Louth. A legend explains the name as the 'golden hostages,' *Oir-ghilla*, because of the stipulation that hostages should only be fettered with chains of gold. Oriel included two baronies called ORIOR, which is known to be a corruption of *Oirtheara*, the 'Easterns,' *i.e.* the Eastern people.

Orinoco is a corruption of the Tamanak word *orinucu*, the 'river,' a name obtained from the natives in 1531 by Diego de Ordaz.

Orissa, in Bengal, represents the ancient kingdom of *Odhra-desa*, 'the 'land of the Odhra' tribes.

Orizaba, an active Mexican volcano, 18,205 feet high, is locally called PICO DE ORIZABA, from the neighbouring town of Orizaba. The native name of the volcano is *Citlaltepetl*, 'the mountain of the star' (Aztec *citalin*, 'a star,' and *tepetl*, a 'mountain'), so called because the summit shines at night like a bright star.

Orkney Islands are the *Orcadæ* of Tacitus, and the *Orcades* of Ptolemy and Mela. The name is usually explained as the 'porpoise' or 'whale' islands, from a cetacean called *orca* by Pliny, which is probably the *Delphinus orca* of Linnæus. The Irish *orc*, a 'porpoise' or 'sea-pig' (whence the Latin loan word *orca*), is regarded by Stokes as a word cognate with the Latin *porcus*. The form Orkney is due to the Scandinavians, the suffix *-ey* meaning 'island' and *orkn* signifying in O.N. a kind of seal. On the other hand Ptolemy calls Duncansbay Head, the extreme cape of Scotland, by the name of *Orcas*, which has been referred to the Celtic *orch*, 'extreme' or 'limit,' and hence the Orcades might be the islands off the Orcas Cape.

Orléans on the Loire was the Celtic *Genabum*. It is called *Civitas Aurelianorum* in the Notitia. The Roman walls, of which traces remain, have been assigned to the Emperor Aurelian, to whom the name is supposed to refer. In the sixth century the name had become *Aureliani*, Orléans being a corruption of an oblique case *Aurelianos* or *Aurelianis*, which

we find in Gregory of Tours. NEW
ORLEANS in Louisiana was named in
1718 by Bienville, the French Governor,
after Philip, Duke of Orléans, Regent of
France during the minority of Louis XV.,
from whom the French Canadians gave
the name of ILE D'ORLÉANS to an island
on the St. Lawrence, below Quebec, which
had been called by Cartier *Ile de Bacchus*,
on account of the wild vines by which it
was overgrown.

Ormuz, a Portuguese city on an island at
the mouth of the Persian Gulf, acquired the
name of an older city on the mainland, the
Harmuza of Ptolemy. It was captured
by Albuquerque in 1507, and became an
emporium second only to Goa in importance till it was taken by the English East
India Company in 1622, when Baffin was
killed in the siege. Since MOGHISTAN
(anciently *Harmozia*) means 'the region
of date palms' it has been conjectured
that Moghistan was a translation of Harmozia, which may have been derived
from *khurma*, 'a date.' The STRAITS
OF ORMUZ acquired their name at the
time when Ormuz was a great centre of
Portuguese trade. FORMOSA, the name
used by Marco Polo for the plain near
Ormuz, is believed to be merely a corrupt
form of Harmuza or Harmozeia.

Orotava, in Teneriffe, is a corruption of
Taora, the Guanche name.

Orrery, a barony in County Cork, has
given a name to an astronomical toy purchased by an Earl of Orrery. The old
tribal name of the barony was *Orb-raige*,
meaning the descendants (*raige*) of Orbh.
Orbraige was pronounced Orvery, and
then softened to Orrery.

Orta, which means the 'garden,' is a
village on the LAGO D'ORTA, to which it
has given a name. HUERTA, the Spanish
form of *hortus*, is the designation of the
fertile plains near Valencia and Murcia.

Ortega, a river in Guadalcanar, one of
the Salomon Islands, bears the name of
Pedro de Ortega, who discovered it in
1567.

Ortler Spitz, a mountain in the Tyrol,
is from the Romansch word *ortle*, a 'point'
or 'needle.'

Orvieto in Italy, the *Urbiventum* of
Procopius, is the corruption of an oblique
case of *urbs vetus*, the 'old city.'

Orwell, a river in Suffolk, is called in the
Chronicle *Arewe* or *Arwe*, which, if not
pre-English, is apparently from *arewe*,
an 'arrow,' doubtless from its swiftness.
The name Orwell was probably formed

from the earlier name, and being a tidal
river, the last syllable may be compared
with the name of the WELLAND, into
which the tide 'wells' or flows.

Osage, a tributary of the Missouri, is so
called from the Osage tribe, whose name
means 'those on a mountain.' OSA-
WATOMIE in Kansas, the residence of
John Brown, the anti-slavery martyr, is a
barbarous compound formed by jumbling
together the names of the Osage and the
Pottowatomie tribes.

Osborne, in the Isle of Wight, was an
estate bought in 1848 by Queen Victoria
from Lady Isabella Blachford. It was
originally known as Oysterbourne, a name
changed by the Blachfords to Osborne, as
being a more aristocratic and dignified
designation.

Osborn Island, on the south coast of
Australia, was so named by King in
1819 after Sir John Osborn, a Lord of
the Admiralty.

Osnaburgh is an English mis-spelling
of Osnabrück, a city in Hanover on the
River Hase. The oldest form is *Asen-
bruggi*, connected by Zeuss, Grimm, and
Förstemann with *ans*, 'deus,' but is probably 'the bridge over the Hase.'
Frederick, Duke of York, second son of
George III., was made lay bishop of the
wealthy See of Osnabrück, and after him
were named OSNABURGH ISLAND in the
Low Archipelago, discovered by Carteret
in 1767, and OSNABURGH ISLAND (Maitea),
one of the Society Islands, discovered by
Wallis in the same year.

Ossian, Strath, in Perthshire, is probably *Srath Oisin*, 'fawn valley,' and not
from the proper name Ossian, which signifies the 'fawn.'

Ostende, in Belgium, called *Ostenda* in
the tenth century, is at the 'East End,'
and WESTENDE at the West End of a
sandbank about ten miles in length, which
stretches along the coast from the mouth
of the Yser as far as the Bruges and Ostende
canal. OSTENDE is a cape at the 'East
End' of the Danish island of St. Thomas,
in the West Indies.

Ostia is the port at the 'mouth' of the
Tiber.

Ostiaks, a Finnic people on the Obi, who
call themselves *Ass-yakh*, 'people of the
Obi,' are called by the Tartars *üschtak*,
'foreigners' or 'strangers,' of which Ostiak
is the Russian corruption.

Oswego, N.Y., a river which forms the
outlet of several lakes, means, according
to Boyd, the 'flowing out.'

Oswestry, in Shropshire, takes its name, according to an ancient legend, from a cross or 'tree' erected on the spot where in 642 St. Oswald, the Christian king of the Northumbrians, fell in a battle with Penda, the heathen king of the Mercians. The Welsh called the place *Croes Oswallt*, 'Oswald's cross,' and the English by the equivalent name *Oswaldstre*, and the town gathered round a monastery which was erected on the spot. But the identification of Oswestry with Maserfeld, where the battle was fought, has not been established, and may have been merely a guess suggested by the name *Oswaldstre*. There is no evidence that the Oswald of the cross was the same person as King Oswald.

Otaheite is Cook's spelling of the island now called TAHITI (*q.v.*).

Otranto, a town in Calabria, is the ancient *Hydruntum* on the River *Hydrus*, now the IDRO. From the town the STRAITS OF OTRANTO, leading from the Mediterranean into the Adriatic, take their name.

Ottawa, the capital of the Canadian Dominion, stands on the River Ottawa, which preserves the name of the Ottawa or Otaua tribe, an Algonquin term meaning 'traders,' literally 'he trades.'

Ottoman Empire, the official title of the realm subject to the Sultan, takes its name from Othman, the Emir under whom the Turks first advanced into Europe. Othman is the Tartar word *ataman*, which we have in the title of the Hetman of the Don Cossacks, and means a 'commander of horse' (*at*, a horse).

Otway, Port, on the west coast of Patagonia, bears the name of Admiral Sir Robert Waller Otway, commander-in-chief (1828) on the South American station. CAPE OTWAY, in the Australian colony of Victoria, was discovered and named by Grant in 1800.

Ouchy, on the Lake of Geneva, is the port of Lausanne. In charters it appears as *Ochie* and *Oschie*, explained by the O.H.G. *ezzesc*, N.H.G. *esch*, Latinised as *oscha* or *oschia*, which denotes an 'unenclosed field' or 'open pasture land.' The DENT D'OCHE, a mountain in Savoy, and CHATEAU D'OEX, in the Simmenthal, are from the same source.

Oudh (Awadh), often spelt OUDE, an Indian kingdom annexed in 1856, takes its name from the ancient sacred city called *A-yodhya*, 'the invincible,' literally 'not to be warred against.' It was the capital of Ráma, and its mag-nificence is described in the opening chapters of the Rámáyana.

Ouro Preto, officially called VILLA RICA DE OURO PRETO, the 'rich town of black gold,' now the capital of the Brazilian province of Minas Geraes (*q.v.*), was founded by Albuquerque in 1711, deriving its name from the black colour of the iron mica in which the gold is found. OURO FINO, 'fine gold,' in the same province, is so called because the gold is found only as minute specks of gold dust. A chain of auriferous hills in the Brazilian province of Goyaz bears the name of SERRA DOURADA, the 'gilded range.'

Ovens River, in Victoria, a tributary of the Murray, bears the name of Major Ovens, an Australian explorer.

Ovidiopol, the 'city of Ovid,' at the mouth of the Dniester, was founded and named in 1792 by the Empress Catherine II., because of an ancient tomb assigned to the poet Ovid, on the ground that it contained a bust which, it was conjectured, might be that of Julia, daughter of Augustus.

Owen Lake, Boothia Felix, and MOUNT OWEN, in Australia, bear the name of Sir Richard Owen, the palæontologist. OWEN'S ISLANDS, on the west coast of Patagonia, were named after Sir Edward Owen, R.N. OWEN STANLEY MOUNTAIN, New Guinea, which rises to a height of 13,205 feet, bears the name of Capt. Owen Stanley, R.N., who in the *Rattlesnake* surveyed Torres Straits in 1849-50.

Oxford, A.S. *Oxnaford*, the 'ford of the oxen,' is a name of the same class as Shefford, the 'sheep ford,' Hertford and Swinford in England, or OCHSENFURT and SCHWEINFURT in Germany. Oxford is not mentioned by Bæda, the first historical notice occurring in the Saxon Chronicle in the reign of Edward the Elder (A.D. 912), when it was already a city of importance, being coupled with London. In later A.S. charters we have the forms *Oxanaford*, *Oxoneford*, and *Oxneford*. In the ninth century, on coins of Alfred, we have *Oksnaforda* and *Orsnaforda*. The Welsh name *Rhyd-ychain* is not primitive, but merely the English name translated.

Oxley Town, Queensland, was named after Lieutenant Oxley, a Government Surveyor.

Paarl, a town and district in the Cape Colony, takes its name from a huge rounded block of granite called the

Pearl; a neighbouring angular block being called the Diamond.

Pachtussov, an island east of Novaya Zemlya, was discovered in 1835 by the Russian officer whose name it bears.

Pacific Ocean is the English translation of *Mar Pacifico* or *Oceano Pacifico*, the somewhat inappropriate name bestowed by Magellan in 1521 on the great ocean which he was the first to traverse. After battling with terrific tempests which had beset him in the straits which bear his name, he was so fortunate as to cross it without encountering a storm. The Pacific was at first known as the SOUTH SEA, a name even now not wholly obsolete, which, inappropriate as it may seem, is noteworthy as commemorating the opening of the new chapter in the history of exploration which dates from the day when Vasco Nuñez de Balboa, gazed from a 'peak in Darien,' on the waters of an unknown ocean spread out before him. At Darien he had heard, from a chief named Ponquiaco, of a mountain range, now known as the SIERRA DI QUAREQUA, from which another ocean could be seen. On September 1st, 1513, he left Santa Maria del Antigua with 190 Spaniards, 600 native porters, and nine canoes, and hewed his way through the matted forest which covered the Cordillera. On September 25th the native guides pointed to a ridge from which they said the ocean was visible. Balboa ordered his men to halt, and climbing the peak alone, gazed on the wide waters, and, falling on his knees, thanked God for His grace in permitting him to make such a discovery. On September 29th he reached an arm of the sea, into which he waded, taking possession of it in the names of King Ferdinand and Queen Juana. This gulf, from the day of the discovery, he named SAN MIGUEL. The isthmus approximately trends from east to west, and hence he called the ocean in front of him the South Sea, *Mar del Sur*, the Atlantic side being called *Mar del Norte*. In January 1514 he recrossed the isthmus and sent the news to Spain, whence he received a patent creating him Adelantado of the South Sea. Three years afterwards, at the age of forty, he was beheaded on a false accusation by order of Espinosa. PACIFIC CITY is a town founded in 1850 at the mouth of the Columbia or Oregon River, in the expectation, not yet fulfilled, that it would become the emporium of the Pacific,

Paderborn, in Westphalia, anciently *Padrabrunno,* derives its name from numerous springs which rise in, or near the town, forming the sources of the River Pader.

Padre é Hijo, 'Father and Son,' was the name given by Columbus in 1493 to a cape on the north coast of Haiti, distinguished by two great rocky needles, one larger than the other.

Padron (Portuguese *Padrão*) is a cape at the mouth of the Congo, so called from the stone pillar (*padrão*) erected in 1485 by Diogo Cam (Cão), in obedience to an order of King John II. of Portugal, that in future, instead of the usual wooden crosses, stone pillars, twice the height of a man, carved with the arms of Portugal, and inscribed with the names of the king and the discoverer, should be erected by explorers in conspicuous places. Diogo Cão erected the first of these pillars, which he called St. George, at the mouth of the Congo, which consequently appears in some maps as the *Rio de Padrão*. The second pillar was erected in lat. 13° S. at Cape St. Augustine, and a third near Walfish Bay, in lat. 22° S., at a cape which he called *Cabo do Padrão*. PONTAL DE SANTO ANTONIO, a spit in Brazil, was formerly called *Pontal do Pādrão*, from the stone pillar erected in 1531 by Martin Affonso de Souza.

Padua, a city in Venetia, called PADOVA in Italian, was the Roman *Patavium.*

Pae-choi, a range of hills forming the northern continuation of the Urals, derive their name from the Samoyed *choi*, 'a ridge,' and *pae* or *bae*, a 'rock,' two common elements in Samoyedic names.

Paestum, near Salerno, is a corruption, as old as the time of Ptolemy, of the Greek name *Poseidonia*, the town of Poseidon, whose magnificent temple is still standing.

Pagoda Island, the European name of an island off the coast of the Chinese province of Fo-kien, is so called from a conspicuous pagoda, a word believed to be a Portuguese corruption of the Persian *but-kadah,* 'idol habitation.'

Painted Cañon, on the Colorado River, and the PAINTED MOUNTAINS in North Carolina, were named from the variegated colours of the rocks.

Palaveram (*Pallávaram*), a town and cantonment near Madras, is a name explained as *Palla-puram*, 'the town of the Pallas,' a caste claiming descent from the Pallavas who ruled at Conjeveram,

Palencia, the capital of the Spanish province of the same name, is the *Pallantia* of Strabo and Ptolemy.

Palermo, in Sicily, is an Italian corruption of the Greek *Panormos,* the ‘ universal haven,’ so called because the old harbours, now filled up, afforded shelter from all winds.

Palestine is the Greek *Palæstina,* a name proving that the Greek mariners first knew Canaan as the land of the Philistines inhabiting the coast, who arrived, probably from Cyprus, after the Hebrew conquest and before the time of Rameses III., on whose monuments they appear as *Pulista.* They are not mentioned on the monuments of Rameses II., some seventy years earlier. They are the *Pilistê* or *Palastu* of the Assyrian annals. The early Greek knowledge of Palestine has recently been explained by an inscription of Sargon II., from which we learn that in 711 B.C., during the reign of Hezekiah, a Greek prince, probably from Cyprus, was king of Ashdod, a Philistine city.

Palestrina, in Central Italy, is a corruption of the old name *Præneste.*

Palk Strait and PALK BAY, between Ceylon and India, names sometimes explained from the Singalese word *palk,* a ‘ whirlpool,’ were named from Robert Palk, Governor of Madras (1763-7).

Palliser's Isles, in the Low or Dangerous Archipelago, CAPE PALLISER, the southern point of the North Island of New Zealand, and PORT PALLISER, in Kerguelen's Land, all discovered by Cook in the years 1774, 1770, and 1776, were named by him after his ‘ worthy friend,’ Sir Hugh Palliser, Comptroller of the Navy. CAPE PALLISER in Carteret's Straits, was discovered by Carteret in 1767.

Palma, the name of the chief town in the Balearic Islands, is explained by the palm branch on coins of the Roman period. There are towns of the same name in Italy, Sicily, and Spain. One of the Canary Islands is called PALMA ; and LAS PALMAS, ‘ the palms,' is the chief town in Great Canary. CAPE PALMAS, a West African headland, was named *Cabo dos Palmas,* ‘ cape of the palms,’ by the Portuguese in the fifteenth century. The RIO DE PALMAS in Mexico, discovered and named by Pineda in 1519, is probably to be identified with the modern Rio de Santander, and not with the modern RIO DE PALMAS, further south. Wilson's ‘ Isle of Palms,’ if it has any objective existence on the map, may be the ISLA DE LAS PALMAS, south-east of the Philippines. The PALM ISLES, at the entrance to Halifax Bay, Queensland, were discovered and named by Cook in 1770.

Palmerston, near Dublin, gave a title to Viscount Palmerston, a lord of the Admiralty, from whom CAPE PALMERSTON in Queensland, and PALMERSTON ISLAND in Cook's Group, discovered by Cook in 1770 and 1774, were named. He was the father of Lord Palmerston, the Prime Minister, whose name is borne by PALMERSTON in New Zealand, and by two Arctic capes. PALMERVILLE, Queensland, was named in compliment to Sir Arthur Palmer, a Prime Minister of Queensland. Two Arctic names, PALMER BAY and PALMER POINT, commemorate the services of Charles Palmer, an officer of the *Hecla.*

Palmyra, a Polynesian island, south of the Sandwich Group, was discovered in 1802 by the American ship *Palmyra.* The name of PALMYRA in Syria is a Greek translation of the Semitic name *Tadmor* (palms). It is now locally called TÛDMIR or TÎDMIR, the older name having outlived the Greek translation. PALMYRA POINT is a cape in Ceylon, on which grow conspicuously some lofty fan palms, called in Portuguese *palmeira,* of which *palmyra* is the English form. A headland on the Orissa coast, whose fan palms form an important landmark for ships bound from the South for the mouth of the Hugli, is also called POINT PALMYRAS. ·FALSE POINT, twenty-four miles to the south-west, is so called from its liability to be mistaken for Point Palmyras.

Pamir, a lofty plateau in Central Asia, is locally called *Bam-i-Dunya,* ‘ the roof of the world,’ a term recently invented.

Pampas, in Spanish *La Pampa,* is the name of the great South American treeless plain, 200,000 square miles in extent, between the Parana and the Colorado. Pampa is a Quichua word meaning an ‘ open plain.’

Pampeluna (in Spanish PAMPLONA), in the province of Navarra, is the ancient *Pompeiopolis* or *Pampelon,* so called because rebuilt by Pompey in 68 B.C. after the defeat of Sertorius. The name has been transferred to PAMPLONA in the United States of Columbia.

Panama was the native name of a village on the Pacific coast of the Gulf and Isthmus of Panama. Here, in 1518, Davila founded the oldest existing city in America. Panama is believed to be a Guarani word meaning a 'butterfly,' and also, according to Wüllerstorf, signifying a 'mudfish,' perhaps because the flaps of the mudfish resemble the wings of a butterfly. From the town of Panama the name was extended to the Isthmus and Gulf.

Pandora Entrance, leading through the Great Barrier Reef to Torres Strait, was first traversed in 1791 by the ship *Pandora*, which in the same year discovered the PANDORA REEF, north-east of the New Hebrides.

Panmure and PANBRIDE, in Forfarshire, seem to be Pictish equivalents of Llanmure and Llanbride, the 'great church' and the 'church of St. Bridget.'

Papéiti, the capital of Tahiti, stands on a brook of the same name, which means the 'small water.' The word *papa*, meaning in Maori a 'plain' or 'flat,' appears in such New Zealand names as PAPAROA, PAPANUI, or PAPAKURA.

Papua, usually supposed to be the native name of New Guinea, is merely a Malay adjective, *papuwah*, meaning 'crisped,' 'woolly,' or 'frizzled,' applied by Malay sailors to the woolly-haired Melanesian Negritos, and specifically to the people of New Guinea, where they form the chief race.

Para, 'water,' enters into numerous South American names. PARA is a Brazilian province, which takes its name from the town of PARA or Belem (*q.v.*), built on one of the mouths of the Amazon, called the Para. PARAHIBA, a seaport which gives its name to another Brazilian province, is built on the RIVER PARAHIBA, or 'bad water.' Another river called PARACATU means the 'good water.' PARANA, which means 'river,' is a stream which gives a name to a third province in Brazil. A town in the Argentine Republic is also called PARANA. The native name of the Rio de la Plata is PARANA-GUAÇU, the 'great river,' whence the name of the GUACOS who live on its banks. The RIVER PARAGUAY, which bounds the republic of PARAGUAY, is either the 'great water,' or possibly from a waterfowl called the *paragua*. PARANA-ASSU is the 'great river,' and PARANA-MIRUN the 'small river.' PARAMARIBO, the 'dwelling near the water,' the capital of Dutch Guiana, was formerly a native village. The PARIME is a tributary of the Rio Negro, PARATI is a Brazilian seaport, and in Venezuela we have the great Gulf of PARIA.

Pardo, a river in Brazil, is the 'brown' river.

Parenzo, a city in Istria, was the Roman *Parentium.*

Paris, the *Lutetia Parisiorum* of the Romans, preserves the name of the Celtic tribe of the *Parisii.* 'I have,' wrote the Emperor Julian, 'spent a winter (357-358) in dear Lutetia (for so the Gauls term the little town of the Parisii), a small island lying in the river, and walled all about.' According to a probable conjecture of Stokes, the reading *Lutetia* in Julian's letter, supposed to mean 'muddy,' should be corrected to *Lucetia*, the 'bright' city, a name which might refer to the white stone used in building. This emendation is confirmed by Ptolemy's form *Lukotckia*, which might mean the 'place of white houses.' The rise of Paris from being a 'little town' to her pre-eminent rank among the cities of Gaul was earned by her successful resistance to the Northmen in the great siege of 885-6; the gallant defence of the Count of Paris making him chief among the princes of the Franks, and raising his city to ducal and then to royal rank.

Parker River, Massachusetts, bears the name of Thomas Parker, the first Puritan pastor of Newbury. From Admiral Sir William Parker, a Lord of the Admiralty, an Arctic and an Antarctic MOUNT PARKER have been named.

Parma, a city in North Italy, preserves unchanged its ancient name.

Parry Islands, an Arctic group, of which Melville Island is the chief, were reached in 1819 by Captain Parry, whose services in the cause of Arctic exploration are also commemorated by CAPE PARRY, PARRY'S BAY, and other Arctic and Antarctic names.

Parsonstown, in King's County, was built on lands at Birr, granted in 1620 by James I. to Sir Lawrence Parsons.

Pascoal, a mountain near Porto Seguro, marks and dates Cabral's accidental discovery of Brazil (*q.v.*) on April 22nd, 1500, which was Easter Day, called *paschoal* in Portuguese.

Passamaquoddy, the native name of a bay between Maine and New Brunswick, refers to the productive 'pollack fishery.'

Passau was the station of a Batavian cohort, and hence called by the Romans *Castrum Batavum*, and then *Patavium.* (*See* BATAVIA.)

Patagonia is the country named by Magellan in 1520 *Tierra de Patagones,*

While in winter quarters at St. Julian, foot-marks in the snow, resembling those made by animals, attracted the notice of the sailors, who found that they were due to huge brogues, made of the skins of the guanaco, which were worn by the natives, who hence got the nickname of *Patagones*, the word *patagon* (from *pata*, the foot and leg of a beast) meaning in Spanish a large clumsy foot.

Patience Bay and CAPE PATIENCE, in the Island of Saghalien, are the English equivalents of the Dutch names given by de Vries in 1643 on account of his long detention by contrary winds.

Patino, an Ægean island, preserves the old name of *Patmos.*

Patná, in Bengal, was formerly *Pátali-putra*, a name which has been identified with the *Palibothra* of Megasthenes, which is supposed to mean the son (*putra*) of Bali, the 'mighty one,' while Pátaliputra means ostensibly the child (*i.e.* the town) of the *pátali* or bignonia flower. The modern name PATNA, seemingly a sort of echo of the older name, is merely a cor-rupted form of the Sanskrit *patana*, 'the town.'

Patos Bay, Patagonia, was named by Magellan in 1520 *Bahia de los Patos*, 'duck bay,' because some waterfowl were here killed by his sailors. ISLA DE LOS PATOS in the Gulf of California means 'duck island,' and LAGOA DOS PATOS in Brazil is 'duck lake.'

Patras, a town at the entrance to the Gulf of Corinth, hence called the GULF OF PATRAS, is an oblique case of the old Greek name *Patræ*, a Semitic loan-name referring to a local oracle.

Pau, formerly the capital of Béarn, was the birthplace of Henry IV. The name was derived from the 'pale' or 'palisade,' called *paü* in the langue d'oc, which sur-rounded the castle.

Pavia was anciently called *Ticinum*, because situated at the junction of the Ticinus (now the Ticino) with the Po. When admitted as a Roman *municipium* the citizens were enrolled in the Papian tribe, and hence it was called *Civitas Papia.* After the seventh century it ap-pears under the name *Papia*, which ulti-mately became Pavia.

Peabody, in Massachusetts, formerly called South Danvers, was renamed in 1868 in compliment to George Peabody, a native of the town, after whom PEABODY BAY, in Kane Sea, was named in recognition of his munificent donation of £10,000 to the Franklin search expedition.

Peace River is the English translation of the native name of a river flowing into Lake Athabasca. On its banks the Cree and Beaver tribes were accustomed to meet in order to settle their disputes. LA PAZ, a town in Bolivia, was founded in 1548 by Alonzo de Mendoza under the name of *Pueblo Nuevo de Nuestra Señora de la Paz*, the 'new town of Our Lady of Peace,' in memory of the peace which succeeded the bloody struggle between the partisans of Pizarro and Almagro.

Peakirk, in Northants, called *Pegecyrce, Peykirk, Peiekyrke*, and *Peichirche* in early charters, bears the name of St. Pega, who in 714 took up her abode in a cell afterwards converted into a monastery by Edmund Atheling.

Peard Island in the Gambier Group and PEARD BAY in Arctic America bear the name of George Peard, Beechey's first lieutenant.

Pearl Islands, in the Gulf of Panama, were called *Islas de las Perlas* by the Spaniards in 1515, a basket of pearls valued at 1200 ducats having been ob-tained from the cazique. On the PEARL AND HERMES REEF, west of the Sand-wich Islands, two English whalers, the *Pearl* and the *Hermes*, were wrecked.

Pe-Chi-Li, a Chinese province which gives a name to the great GULF OF PECHILI, appears on many maps simply as CHI-LI, the 'province of the court,' so called be-cause it contains PE-KING the 'northern capital.' The name PE-CHILI, 'northern court province,' was given to distinguish it from NAN-CHILI, the 'southern court province,' in which NANKING the 'southern capital' is situated. PE-LING is the pro-vince 'north of the mountains,' and HU-PEH the province 'north of the lakes,' HU-NAN being that 'south of the lakes.'

Peebles, the county town of Peebles-shire, is explained from the Cymric *pebyll* (plural of *pabell*), the 'tents.'

Peel, which means a 'tower' or 'keep,' is a name used to designate the small border strongholds on the Scottish march. Else-where we have PEEL in the Isle of Man, PEAL HILL, and the PILE OF FOUDREY, or PIEL-A-FOUDRY, a rocky island in Furness where the Abbots of Furness built a castle, from which comes the name of the neighbouring PILE or PEEL HARBOUR. The Welsh *pill*, a 'stronghold,' is believed to be borrowed from the English and French *pile*, which is the Latin *pila*, a 'pillar' or 'pile' of stone. From one of these 'peels' is derived the territorial sur-name of the English statesman which has been given to the PEEL RIVER in New South Wales, and to PEEL POINT, PEEL INLET, and PEEL RIVER in Arctic America. PEEL, a town in West Australia, bears the name of an early colonist who obtained large grants of land.

Pegu, a city and province in the Delta of the Irawadi, is one of the names which came through the Portuguese from the Malays, who call it *Pai-gu.* The Burmese name is *Bagó* or *Pagó,* a Talaing word of unknown etymology, but meaning, according to the local legend, 'conquered by stratagem.'

Pekin or PEKING, in Chinese *Peh-king,* the 'north court' or 'northern capital,' has been so called since 1421, when the third Ming Emperor transferred hither the residence of the court from NANKING, the 'southern court.' Marco Polo calls it *Cambaluc,* in which we may recognise the Mongolian name *Khan-baligh,* the 'city of the Khan.' KING - CHING, ' court town,' is the part inhabited by the Manchus, TSU-KING-CHING, 'red court town,' by the Emperor, while WAI - CHING, 'outer town,' is the Chinese quarter. The *Chandu* or *Xandu* of Marco Polo, which is the *Xanadu* of Coleridge's poem of Kubla Khan, is the Chinese *Shangtu,* 'Upper Court.'

Pellew Islands, a group in the Gulf of Carpentaria, were named by Flinders in 1802 in compliment to Sir Edward Pellew, R.N., afterwards Lord Exmouth. In some maps they appear as Sir Edward Pellew's Islands, in order to distinguish them from the PELEW ISLANDS east of the Philippines, so called because inhabited by the *Pelews,* an English corruption of the Spanish name *Palaos,* which was derived from the native name *Panlog* or *Panloque,* which means the 'islands.' The name Pelew Islands, which we find on the maps, means therefore the 'islands of the islanders.'

Pellegrino, Monte, the conspicuous hill overlooking Palermo, acquired the name of ' Pilgrim Mountain ' from the pilgrimages to a cave near the summit, in which Santa Rosalia is said to have lived and died.

Pelly Islands, at the mouth of the Mackenzie River, and LAKE PELLY, an expansion of the Great Fish River, bear the name of a Governor of the Hudson Bay Company.

Pelon, Cerro, the 'bald mountain,' in Costa Rica, was so called because it is treeless.

Pelsaert Islands, a West Australian group, bear the name of the captain of the *Batavia,* a Dutch ship wrecked on them in 1629. A neighbouring anchorage is called BATAVIA ROAD.

Pembroke, the county town of Pembrokeshire, is from *pen-bro* (Old Welsh *penbrog*), the end or 'head of the land.'

Pendulum Islands, on the East coast of Greenland, were selected in 1823 by General Sabine for experiments with the pendulum, in order to determine the figure of the earth. SABINE ISLAND is the largest of the group.

Penedo, the 'rock,' is the Portuguese name of a Brazilian town built on a sandstone cliff on the Rio San Francisco. From the Portuguese *pena* or *penedo,* and the Spanish *peña* or *peñasco,* a 'rock,' we have numerous names, such as PENAFIEL in Portugal, the GULF OF PEÑAS in Patagonia, and the VAL DE PEÑAS, or 'valley of rocks,' which gives a name to a delicate Spanish wine.

Penguin Islands, south of Newfoundland, were so called in 1536 by the English colonists from the multitude of penguins.

Penk, a river in Staffordshire, is a ghost-name invented by antiquarians to explain the name of the town of PENKRIDGE, which is the Celto-Latin *Penno-crucium* (Cymric *Pen-y-crug*), the 'head of the mount.'

Pennsylvania is the name of the immense territory granted in 1681 by Charles II. to William Penn, the Quaker, in discharge of a loan of £16,000. Penn wished it to be styled New Wales, but the king insisted that it should bear Penn's name, and the province being beautifully diversified with wood, it was called Pennsylvania, ' Penn's Woodland.' It is believed that the name was given in honour not of William Penn, but of Admiral Penn, his father.

Pennygown, in Mull, is the 'smith's peanyland,' *i.e.* land held at the rent of a silver penny, and PENNYGHAEL in Argyle is the ' Gael's pennyland.' LEFFENBEG, ' the little halfpenny land,' LEFFINDONALD, ' Donald's halfpenny land,' and LEFNOL, ' Olaf's halfpenny land,' are from the Gaelic *Leth-pheghin,* a halfpenny.

Penrith, in Cumberland, is a Cymric name meaning the ' red hill ' (*pen-rhudd*), or perhaps the ' head of the ford,' from *rhyd,* a ' ford,' which we have in *Augustoritum,* the ' ford of Augustus,' the Celto-Roman name of LIMOGES, or in *Camboritum,* the skew or ' crooked ford,' the Roman name of CAMBRIDGE.

Penryn, in Cornwall, and PENRHYN in Carnarvonshire are Cymric names meaning the 'head of the spit' or promontory. The PENRHYN ISLANDS, west of the Marquesas, were discovered in 1788 by the ship *Penrhyn*.

Pensacola, a bay and seaport in Florida, preserve the name of the tribe called *Pansha-okla*, 'hairy people,' literally 'hair people.'

Pentland Firth is a curious and valuable name, testifying to the extent of the old Pictish kingdom. It is a corruption of the O.N. name *Pettaland fjörth* or *Petlandsfiord*; the Scandinavians calling Caithness and Sutherland by the name of *Pettaland* or *Petland*, the land of the *Pechts*, *Pehts*, or Picts. The PENTLAND HILLS may perhaps mark the southern extent of the Pictish realm, but no forms of the name have been preserved of sufficiently early date to make it possible to determine whether the name is from *Peithland* (*Pethland*), or, as is more probable, from *Pen-lland*, where *pen* means a 'hill,' and *lland* is the word which we have in the name of the LANDES (*q.v.*). The name *Picti* has been supposed to be a Latin translation of the native name *Cruithnigh* or *Cruithne*, the tattooed or painted men, but since it can hardly be separated from the names of the *Pictones* and *Pictavia* (whence POICTIERS and POITOU) which are pre-Roman, the Latin *Picti* is probably only an adaptation of the name of the *Pechts*, which is derived by Stokes from the root **qvik*, to carve, hence to tattoo. PYTCHLEY (*q.v.*), in Northants, may mark the southern limits of an inroad of the Picts, and SPIKE ISLAND in Cork Harbour is a corruption of *Inis Pichht*, the 'Picts' Island.'

Penzance, in Cornwall, means 'Saint's head' or 'holy head,' from a chapel dedicated to St. Anthony, whose head is represented on the seal of the corporation.

Peoria, Illinois, preserves the name of a native tribe now extinct.

Pepandayan, the 'smithy' or 'forge,' is an active volcano in Java. Other Javanese volcanoes are called SUNDARA, the 'beautiful,' SUMBING, the 'notched,' MÁRAPI, the 'volcano,' MÁRBABU, the 'nurse,' BATAK, the 'bald.'

Pera, a suburb of Constantinople, bears a Greek name signifying that it lies 'beyond' the Golden Horn. PERA HEAD, in Arnhem Land, North Australia, preserves the name of the Dutch ship *Pera*, the consort of the *Arnhem*, the first to visit this coast.

Percy Isles, an outlying group of the NORTHUMBERLAND ISLANDS, Queensland, were so named by Flinders in 1802 in compliment to Hugh Percy, second Duke of Northumberland. MOUNT PERCY, South Shetland, was named in 1842 after Admiral Josceline Percy, naval commander at the Cape.

Perevosnaia Nos, 'Passage Cape,' is the point in the island of Waigatz nearest to the mainland. It gives a name to the neighbouring PEREVOSNAIA GULF.

Périgord, an old French province, and its capital, PÉRIGUEUX, preserve the name of the *Petrocorii*, a tribe whose territory is represented by the diocese of Périgueux.

Perm, a town and government of Russia, is the Biarmaland of Othere, the land of the *Biarmi* or Permian Finns.

Pernambuco, a Brazilian city, is built on a bay into which two rivers flow, whence the etymology, from *mbuco*, an 'arm' or 'branch,' and *parana*, a 'river.'

Péron Island and CAPE PÉRON, in West Australia, bear the name of the naturalist of the *Géographe*, one of Baudin's ships.

Pérouse, or LA PÉROUSE, the name of the strait between the islands of Yesso and Saghalien, commemorates the services of the brave but unfortunate French navigator La Pérouse, who first traversed it in 1787. His fate remained a mystery till 1825, when some wreckage from his ships was discovered on the reefs of Vanikoro, an island north of the New Hebrides.

Perpetua, a cape in Oregon, was discovered by Cook on St. Perpetua's Day, March 7th, 1778.

Persia, the European name of the country called *Irán* by its inhabitants, is the Latin form of the Greek name *Persis*, which originally denoted the small district of *Pársa*, now FARS or PARS, the cradle of the Persian monarchy. The name of the Aryan Persians who gave their name to the district of Pársa, where they settled about 600 B.C., does not occur in the Zend Avesta, and has not been explained from Aryan sources. It is probably a Semitic term meaning 'horsemen,' and connected with the Arabic *faris*, 'a horse.' Persian and Parthian are believed to be ultimately identical names. The PERSIAN GULF is the *Sinus Persicus* of Pliny, and the *Mar Parseo* of the early Portuguese navigators.

Perth, the county town of PERTHSHIRE, is explained by Stokes from the Welsh *perth*, 'bramble.'

Peru, a South American republic, is a name with a curious history. In 1515 Gaspar de Morales was sent to explore the coast of the Gulf of San Miguel. The Spaniards retreated after a fight with a warlike chief· whom they called Birú, whose territory lay on the banks of a small river called the *Birú* or *Pirú*, which enters the Pacific near the Punta de Pinas in 7° 30′ N. lat., at the mouth of the Gulf of Panama. Hence the whole region south of the Gulf came to be called the Birú or Pirú country, and here in 1522 Pascuel de Andagoga first heard tidings of the empire of the Incas which was reached by Pizarro in 1526. The River Pirú is 700 or 800 miles from the northern boundary of the modern republic of Peru.

Perugia, in Italy, preserves the Etruscan name *Perusia*.

Peshâwar, a city on the Indian frontier, bears a name attributed to Akbar, who is supposed to have changed the old name *Parashâwara* or *Parshâwar*, of which he did not know the meaning, to Peshâwar, the 'frontier town.'

Pesth, *see* BUDA.

Petchora, a river in Russia, is so named from the 'caves' in the cliffs near its mouth. In like manner PETCHORI, a monastery and town in Western Russia, takes its name from the 'caves' formerly inhabited by the monks.

Peterborough is an Episcopal See in Northamptonshire. We read in the Saxon Chronicle that in 655, Penda, king of the Mercians and Oswiu came together and agreed to erect a monastery at Medehamstede to the glory of Christ and the honour of St. Peter. From a later entry we learn that Abbot Kenulf in 963 built a wall round the minster, and gave the place the name *Burh*, which was before called Medehamstede (meadow-homestead). In early charters the place is called simply *Burh*, *Buruh*, or *Burch*, 'the Borough,' the name of St. Peter, to whom the church was dedicated, being afterwards prefixed by popular usage to distinguish it from other *burhs*, especially from Bury St. Edmunds, which is also called *Burh* and *Burch* in early charters.

Peterhead, a town on a promontory in Aberdeenshire, originally called Inverugie, acquired its present name from its church, dedicated to St. Peter, whence the place is called *Petri promontorium* in an old charter. The church at Petersfield, Hants, is also dedicated to St. Peter, as is that at PETERSHAM in Surrey, which,

however, seems to be only an assimilated name. (*See* BATTERSEA.)

Petermann Land, North of Franz Josef Land, the most northerly land seen by Payer in 1873, was so named by him in honour of the great German cartographer, Dr. Petermann of Gotha, whose name has also been given to PETERMANN BAY, in Grinnell Land, and to MOUNT PETERMANN, in the Southern Alps of New Zealand.

Petersburg, or ST. PETERSBURG, properly Peterburg or St. Peterburg, the capital of Russia, was founded by Peter the Great, who, having in 1702 taken the Swedish forts on the Neva, in the following year laid the foundations of a fort which he called Peterburg (Fort Peter), on an island in the Neva, the nucleus and now the most densely populated portion of the city. On this island, which retains the old name of *Peterburgskia Ostrov* (Peterburg Island), he also built a cathedral dedicated to St. Peter and St. Paul, whence the Russian name Sankt-Peterburg, which has replaced the older name of Peterburg. PETERSBURGH, one of the older towns in Virginia, is not, as might be supposed, a loan-name from Europe, but preserves the memory of the first settler, a man named Peters. PETROPAULOVSKI, a Russian settlement in Kamtchatka, was founded in 1740 by Bering, and named after his two ships, the *St. Peter* and the *St. Paul*. PETROPOLIS, a Brazilian town founded in 1844, bears the name of the Emperor Pedro II. PETERWARDEIN, called Peterwárad in Magyar, and Petrovaradin in Servian, a place on the Danube, north-west of Belgrade, is the spot where Peter the Hermit marshalled his levies for the first crusade. Peter is liable to be confused with similar names, as in the case of BATTERSEA (*q.v.*), or of PADSTOW, in Cornwall, called in the Saxon Chronicle Petrocstow, 'the place of St. Petroc.'

Petra, the rock-hewn city which gave a name to ARABIA PETRÆA, is a Greek translation of the older Semitic name *Sela*, the 'rock.'

Peyster Islands, in the Ellice Group, bear the name of the Captain of the American ship *Rebecca*, by whom they were discovered in 1819.

Pfäffikon, in Canton Zurich, whence the name of the neighbouring PFÄFFIKER SEE, was the grange or '*hof* of the fathers' of the Abbey of St. Gallen, to which it belonged. PFAFFENHAUSEN, PFAFFENHOFEN, and PFAFFENDORF, from *Pfaffe*,

O.H.G. *phafo*, a 'monk' (*papa*), are common names in Germany, corresponding to the numerous Prestons in England.

Pfalz, often Englished as the PALATINATE, was the name given to the fief held by the Pfalzgraf or Count Palatine, one of the ancient hereditary dignitaries of the empire. The two Bavarian provinces now known as the OBER-PFALZ and the RHEIN-PFALZ are fragments of the great fief of the Kur-pfalz or Elector Palatine. PFALZ-BURG, called PHALSBOURG in French, a fortress in Lorraine, was erected in 1570 by the Pfalzgraf George John, Duke of Bavaria.

Pfeffers, or PFÄFERS, a place with celebrated thermal springs, in Canton St. Gallen, was a monastery founded in the eighth century. In ancient documents it is called *Monasterium Fabariense, Fabaris,* or *Favaris*, from a *fabaria*. or plantation of beans.

Pfyn is derived from the Latin *fines* or *ad finem*, a term used in the Antonine Itinerary to denote boundaries. We find also *ad fine*, where *fine* has become an indeclinable noun. The village of PFYN, near Leuk, in Canton Valais, still divides the German-speaking population of the Upper Rhone valley from those who speak French. In like manner PFYN, in Canton Thurgau, marks the ancient boundary between the Celtic and Rhætian races.

Philadelphia, the city of 'brotherly love,' was founded in 1682 by William Penn, the Quaker, as the capital of Pennsylvania, and so named 'in token of the feeling which, it was hoped, would prevail among the inhabitants.'

Philæ, an island at the first cataract of the Nile, is a Greek corruption of the Coptic *pilak*, the definite article in the old Egyptian name *p-aa-lek*, 'the frontier,' having been incorporated.

Philippines, a Pacific group belonging to Spain, were discovered by Magellan on the Feast of St. Lazarus, 1521, and hence called by him *Archipelago de San Lazaro*, a name changed in 1542 to *Islas Filipinas* in honour of Philip II., in whose reign the Spanish colonisation of the islands was begun.

Phillip Island and PORT PHILLIP, in the Australian colony of Victoria, PHILLIP COUNTY in New South Wales, and CAPE PHILLIP in the Salomon Islands, bear the name of Captain Arthur Phillip, the first Governor of New South Wales. Port Phillip was discovered in 1801 by Lieutenant John Murray in the brig *Lady*

Nelson, and rediscovered ten weeks later by Flinders. CAPE PHILLIPS, in South Victoria, bears the name of an officer of the *Terror*, and PHILLIPS' ISLAND, in Arctic America, bears the name of Captain Charles Phillips, R.N., the neighbouring PHILLIP'S BAY being called after Professor Phillip of the Royal Academy. PHILIPS-TOWN, in King's County, was named in honour of Philip II. of Spain, husband of Queen Mary of England. PHILIPPOPOLI, in Rumelia, represents *Philippopolis*, founded by Philip of Macedon, from whom we have also the name of FELI-BEDJIK, in Macedonia, which stands on the site of *Philippi* visited by St. Paul, who wrote for his converts the Epistle to the Philippians. PHILIPPSBURG, in Baden, was fortified and renamed by Bishop Philip von Sötern in 1618, and PHILIPPS-BURG, in Lorraine, was built by Count Philip of Hanau in 1590. PHILIPPEVILLE, in Algeria, bears the name of King Louis-Philippe.

Phœnix Park, Dublin, is a corruption of the Irish *fionn-uisg*, 'clear water,' the name of a transparent spring near which, in 1745, Lord Chesterfield, then Lord Lieutenant, erected a pillar surmounted by a Phœnix rising from its ashes. The PHŒNIX ISLANDS are a Pacific group discovered by the ship *Phœnix*.

Piacenza, in Lombardy (called PLAISANCE in French), is the Roman *Placentia*, the 'pleasing' or pleasant place. PLACENTIA, in the Spanish province of Estramadura, retains unaltered the old Roman name. PLACENTIA BAY, in Newfoundland, is named from the French settlement of Placentia, founded in 1626.

Piasina, a 'woodless' district in Siberia, east of the Yenissei, gives a name to the Piasina Lake and River which traverses it.

Picardy, in French LA PICARDIE, one of the old provinces of France, is a name which does not appear before the thirteenth century. The etymology is unknown, but it has been conjectured that the district supplied *picards* or 'pikemen' to the French armies.

Pickering Lythe, a wapentake in the North Riding, was the *lythe* or district of the Pikerings, the 'men of the Pikes' or Peaks of the moors, at the foot of which lies the town of Pickering. DICKERING LYTHE, a wapentake in the East Riding, was the district inhabited by the Dickerings, the men whose place of assembly was at the great Dyke, now called the Danes' Dyke, which defends Flamborough Head.

Pickersgill Harbour, New Zealand ; PICKERSGILL ISLAND, South Georgia ; and PICKERSGILL COVE, Tierra del Fuego, were named by Cook after one of his officers.

Pico, properly O PICO, which means 'the peak' in Portuguese, is one of the Azores with a conical volcano 7613 feet in height. PICO is also the Spanish name of the Peak of Tenerife. PICO RUIVO, the 'red peak,' is the Portuguese name of the highest summit in Madeira.

Piedmont is the French form of the Italian name PIÉ DI MONTE or PIE-MONTE, the subalpine province at the 'foot of the mountains.' The name came into use at the end of the twelfth century.

Pietermaritzburg, the capital of Natal, now usually called MARITZBURG, was founded by two Boer leaders, Pieter Retief and Gerrit Maritz, who trekked hither from the Cape in 1837.

Pike's Peak, in the State of Colorado, is one of the loftiest summits of the Rocky Mountains, reaching an altitude of 14,216 feet. It was discovered and ascended in 1806 by Lieutenant (afterwards General) Zebulon Montgomery Pike, a surveying officer of the United States.

Pila, the 'saw,' is the name of a Siberian river which keeps sawing at its banks.

Pilatus, the mountain facing Lucerne, according to the well-known local legend derived its name from Pontius Pilate, who was believed to have drowned himself in a gloomy tarn near the summit. The legend may be due to popular etymology, in which case the original form of the name has to be discovered. One conjecture explains the name as a corruption of *pileatus*, since when the mountain is 'capped' with cloud, fine weather is usually foretold. But since the Romansch name is *Frakmont*, the 'cleft or broken mountain,' equivalent in meaning to the GESPALTENHORN in Canton Bern, it has been supposed that the primitive name of Pilatus was a derivative of the O.H.G. *billon*, 'to split,' thus meaning the 'fractured mountain,' a German translation of the older Romansch name Frakmont. This solution, however, is not free from philological difficulty.

Pinega, a Russian river, is a corruption of *Pint-ga*, the 'river of teeth,' so named from certain notched rocks. The suffix *-ga* is the Finnic word for a river, which we have in Palanga, Wolonga, Onega, Ladoga, and other names.

Pines, Isle of, New Caledonia, was so named by Cook because of sundry dark patches, at first taken for basalt rocks, which proved on nearer approach to be pine forests. On the ISLA DE PINOS, south of Cuba, the *Pinus occidentalis* grows abundantly.

Pinzgau, on the Salzach, appears in 798 as *Pinuzgaue*, meaning the 'rush district.' This is believed to be an early Teutonic folk-etymology, probably an adaptation of *Bisont-gaue*, derived from the Celtic name *Bisontium*.

Pioneer River, Queensland, was so named from the visit of H.M.S. *Pioneer* in 1862. PIONEER ISLAND, in Arctic America, bears the name of Belcher's ship, the *Pioneer*. PIONEER PEAK in the Karakoram Group of the Himalayas, was so named by Mr. Conway, being the highest altitude (23,600 feet) which has hitherto been ascended.

Piræus, the port of Athens, retains its old classical name, which implies that at one time it was an island to which it was necessary to 'pass over' by a ferry.

Pirahy, an affluent of the Uruguay, is the 'fish river' (Guarani *piro*, 'fish,' and *hy*, 'river'). The JACUHY RIVER has the same suffix, while the prefix is seen in PIRAPORA, 'fish-leap,' the name of a cataract on the Rio San Francisco.

Pisgah, a peak in Equatorial Africa, 4600 feet above the sea, was so called by H. M. Stanley in 1887, 'because after 156 days of twilight in the primeval forest we had first viewed the desired pasture lands.'

Pistoja in Tuscany was the Roman *Pistoria*, which became *Pistola*, and then *Pistoia*. A curious proof of the late date of the present name is afforded by the word *pistol*, which is the Italian *pistolese* or *pistola*, which originally designated a small dagger made at Pistola.

Pitea, a town in Sweden, is near the mouth of the River Pitea.

Pitlochrie, Perthshire, is one of the names exhibiting the prefix *pit* or *pet*, meaning a 'croft,' which is confined to the Pictish part of Scotland, especially to Fife and Perthshire where it is common. The old form of *pit* is *pette*, which may be compared with the Welsh *peth* and the Irish *cuit*, a 'portion.' From the Pictish region the Icelanders may have borrowed the word *petti*, which means in O.N. a small piece of a field. The Pictish word originally denoted a 'portion of land' and then came to mean a homestead, and finally a hamlet, being rendered *villula* in Latin documents, and replaced by *baile* in

Gaelic. In the Book of Deer the word is prefixed to personal names, as *Pette Mac Garmait*, *Pett Mac Gobraig*, *Pett Maldiub*, *Pittentaggart*, 'the portion of the priest' (*sacerdos*) or *Pittan-clerac*, the 'portion of the clergy.' PITTENWEEM, Fife, the 'land by the cave' (*uamh*), was the seat of an ancient monastery, near which is the cave, doubtless the habitation of a hermit, from which the name arose. PITGARVIE is the 'rough land,' PITGLAS, 'the grey land,' and PITFOUR 'the cold land.' PITSLIGO is the 'shelly land,' and PITTENCRIEF the 'land of the tree.' PITCAIRN, Perthshire, near which are two cairns, is the 'land by the cairn.' Hence the surname Pitcairn, given to PITCAIRN ISLAND in the Low Archipelago, discovered by Carteret in 1767, which bears the name of a midshipman who first descried it from his look-out at the mast head. Here, in 1790, the ship *Bounty* was burned by the mutineers, who, on April 28th, 1789, had taken possession of her, turning adrift in the launch her Commander, Lieutenant Bligh, and then, with native women from Tahiti, settled on Pitcairn Island.

Piton de Neige, the 'pin of snow,' is the highest summit in the Isle of Réunion.

Pitt Island, in the Santa Cruz Archipelago, was so named in 1791 from the ship *Pitt*.

Pittsburg, Pennsylvania, was originally called Fort Du Quesne, after a French Governor of Canada, and afterwards, in 1758, when the French had been driven out by Washington, it was renamed Fort Pitt, after William Pitt, Earl of Chatham, the name Pittsburgh being adopted in 1769. From the same statesman we have the name of the town PITTSFIELD, in Massachusetts, which was incorporated in 1761.

Plassy or PLASSEY, a village in Bengal, where Clive gained his decisive victory on June 23rd, 1757, is the English corruption of the native name *Palási*, probably so called from a grove of the *palás* or dawk tree (*Butea frondosa*).

Plata, Rio de la, 'river of the silver,' often Englished as the River Plate, was named by Sebastian Cabot in 1526 by reason of a few gold and silver ornaments, the earnest of the wealth of Peru, which he obtained by barter from the natives, and which he hoped were an indication of an El Dorado in the interior. It was previously called *Rio de Solis*, from Diaz de Solis, who visited it in 1508 and 1515, calling it *Mar Dolce*, the 'freshwater sea.'

The native names were *Parana-guaçu*, the 'great river,' and *Amara Mayu*, the 'snake river.' The ARGENTINE REPUBLIC on its banks is a Latinised formation from the Spanish word *plata*, 'silver.' MONTE DE PLATA, the 'mountain of silver,' on the north-east coast of Haiti, was so named by Columbus in 1493 from the silvery clouds resting on its summit. The name is preserved by the neighbouring town of PUERTO PLATA, 'port silver.' The RIO DA PLATA, 'river of silver,' is the Portuguese name of a river in the Brazilian province of Santa Catharina.

Platte, the 'flat' or 'shallow' river, is a French translation of the native name NEBRASKA (*q.v.*). When it joins the Missouri it is nearly a mile wide, but so shallow as to be impassable by boats except when in flood. PLATTE ISLAND, in French *Ile Plate*, the 'flat isle,' is one of the Séchelles. PLATTENSEE, in Hungary, is a German translation or corruption of LAKE BALATON, a Slavonic name from *blato*, 'mud,' 'bog,' 'marsh.' PLADDA, formerly *Flada*, in the Firth of Clyde, is the 'flat island,' as is FLADAY in the Hebrides, and FLATHOLM in the Bristol Channel.

Playgreen Lake in Winnipeg, is an English translation of the native name, given because certain tribes used to meet on an island in the Lake to celebrate festivals and sports.

Pleasant Island, in the Gilbert Archipelago, was discovered and named in 1798 by Captain Fearn of the ship *Hunter*.

Plettenberg Bay, in the Cape Colony, perpetuates the name of a Dutch governor.

Plimlimmon, a mountain in South Wales, is from the Welsh *pum-lumon*, the 'five hills,' literally, the 'five chimneys.'

Plymouth, Devon, is at the mouth of the River Plym. From here on September 6th, 1620, the *Mayflower* sailed with the Pilgrim Fathers, who landed on December 21st, and founded the town of PLYMOUTH in Massachusetts, the oldest settlement in New England. By a curious accident, five years earlier, in 1615, Prince Charles, afterwards Charles I., had already named the place Plymouth on Captain John Smith's map of New England. Prince Charles may have selected the name because by a charter given in 1606 the lands from 45° to 40° N. lat. had been granted to the Plymouth Company of Adventurers.

Po, the great river of Northern Italy, is a

corruption of *Padus*, a name said by Metrodorus to be Celtic, derived from the pine trees on its banks (Celtic *padi*, a 'pine tree'). Pliny tells us that *Bodincus*, the older Ligurian name of the river, meant 'deep' or 'bottomless.' The Greeks identified the Po with the heavenly river of the Babylonians, the constellation *Eridanus*, owing, it is supposed, to a geographical confusion between the Rhone and the Po, and to the resemblance of the names Rhodanus and Eridanus.

Poas, a volcano in Costa Rica, is so called from the plain at its foot called Poas or Puas, which is overgrown with thorns (Spanish *pua*, a 'thorn' or 'prickle').

Podolia, a government in Russia, means the 'lowland' (Slavonic *podolny*, 'low').

Pogorelaia Plita, a volcanic island in the Caspian, bears a Russian name meaning the 'burnt rock.'

Poitiers, formerly POICTIERS, the capital of the old province of POITOU or POICTOU (*Pictavia*), was the chief town of the tribe of the *Pictones*, afterwards called the *Pictavi*, a name probably related to that of the Pehts or Picts. (*See* PENTLAND). Poictiers was at first called *Civitas Pictavorum*, but appears on Merovingian coins as *Pectavis*; Poitou is called *Pectavus pagus* in the ninth century, and *le Poictou* in the fourteenth. POITEVIN is a corruption of *Pictavensis.*

Poland is the English corruption of the name of the country called POLEN or POHLEN in German, POLOGNE in French, and POLSKA in Polish. The older form, Polayn (or Polonia), was used in England till the time of Charles I., when it appears as Poleland, the syllable land being an assimilated form derived from Polayn. Polenland would have been better and more correct than Poland. The country, which is one vast plain, is named from the Slavonic *polë*, a 'plain,' and the Poles (*Poliani* or *Polaki*) are the dwellers in the plain. To the South Slavonic *poljana*, a 'field,' we may attribute the name of POLLA in Carinthia, and perhaps of POLA in Istria, a doubtful name, usually explained as a corruption of *Pietas Julia.*

Policastro, a town on the Calabrian coast, whence the name of the large bay called the GULF OF POLICASTRO, is an Italian corruption of the Byzantine *Palæokastron*, the 'old castle.'

Polk is the name of fifty-seven counties, towns, and townships, mostly in Missouri, Iowa, Indiana, and Arkansas, which were called after James Knox Polk, eleventh President of the United States (1845-7).

Polwarth, a county in Victoria, Australia, was named after Lord Polwarth, who assisted in passing the Australian Land Act of 1847.

Polynesia was a name invented by Malte Brun to designate the 'many-islanded' portion of the Pacific. MELANESIA is the western part, inhabited by the Negrito race, and MICRONESIA is the more northerly region of coral islands. The name Polynesia is now restricted to the islands inhabited by the brown race.

Pomerania, the Latinised form of the German POMMERN, is a name of Slavonic origin signifying 'on the sea' (*po*, 'by,' and *marya*, 'sea').

Pomona is a ghost-name which since the fourteenth century has been applied to the Mainland of Orkney, owing to a misunderstanding by Fordun of a passage in Solinus. The O.N. name of the island was *Hrossey*, 'horse island.'

Ponafidin, an isolated Pacific island, south of Japan, bears the name of a Russian lieutenant who discovered it.

Pond Bay in Fuegia, and POND'S BAY, a large inlet on the western side of Baffin Bay, were named in honour of John Pond, who from 1811 to 1836 was Astronomer-Royal.

Pondicherry (PONDICHÉRI), a French possession on the Coromandel coast, is a corruption of the Tamil *pudu-chéri*, the 'New Town' (*pudu*, 'new,' and *cheri*, 'a village').

Pontchartrain, a large lake north of New Orleans, was so named in 1698 after de Pontchartrain, the French Minister of Finance.

Pontefract in Yorkshire, pronounced POMFRET, the town at the 'broken bridge,' is a name later than Domesday, where the place is called *Tateshale.* According to the well-known legend the Latin appellation *de ponte fracto*, which has become Pontefract, arose from the breaking of the bridge over the Aire in 1153, when St. William of York returned to his see after exile, but this is disproved by the fact that the name is of earlier date, occurring in the *Gesta Stephani* (1137-1140), while it would seem that the bridge which broke on this occasion was that over the Ouse at York. Nor is there any reason for supposing that the 'broken bridge' by which, according to Ordericus, William I. was detained in 1069 was the bridge at Pontefract. It has also been suggested that the name is due to the fact that from a certain position the bridge, which is somewhat skew, looks as if one side had been broken away.

Pontoise, the 'bridge over the Oise,' translates the Gaulish name *Briva Isaræ*, the 'bridge over the Isara,' now the Oise. PONTE VEDRA, a town in Galicia, is the 'old bridge.' PONTE GRANDE, the 'great bridge,' is the chief place in the Val d'Anzasca. PORENTRUY or PRUNTRUT, in Canton Bern, is a corruption of *Pons Ragentrudis*, so called probably from a bridge built by Ragentrud, wife of Dagobert I. Pont, a loan-word from the Latin, appears in nearly fifty Welsh names. Thus PONT-Y-PRIDD, the 'brick bridge,' in Glamorganshire, also called NEWBRIDGE, is named from a bridge spanning the Taff with a single arch which was erected by William Edwards, a self-taught artificer. PONTYPOOL, in Monmouthshire, is the Welsh *Pont-y-pwl*, the 'bridge at the pool.' PONTFAEN, Pembrokeshire, is the 'stone bridge,' from *maen*, a 'stone.' PONT-Y-GLYN is the 'bridge in the glen,' and PONT-GLAS-LYN, the 'bridge at the grey pool.'

Ponza Islands, off the Gulf of Gaeta, also called the Pontian, Pontine, or Pontinian Islands (Italian ISOLE PONZE, Latin *Insulæ Pontiæ*), are named from the ISOLA DI PONZA, the largest of the group, which preserves the Greek name *Pontia*, the 'Ocean' island. On the mainland, opposite the Pontine Islands, are the PONTINE MARSHES (*Paludes Pomptinæ* or *Pontinæ*), named either from the Islands, or, it is said, from a town called *Pometia*, 'the orchards.'

Popham Bay, on the north coast of Australia, was named in 1818 after Admiral Sir Home Popham. FORT POPHAM, the first English settlement in New England, was founded in 1607 by George Popham, captain of a ship despatched by the Plymouth Company, of which Sir John Popham, Lord Chief Justice of England, was the master spirit.

Popocatepetl, the loftiest volcano in Mexico, 17,783 feet high, means the 'smoking mountain' (Aztec *popoca*, 'he smokes,' and *tepetl*, a 'mountain'). So NAUAMPATEPETL, also in Mexico, is the 'square-shaped mountain,' and CITLALTEPETL is the 'mountain of the star.'

Portobello, in Spanish PUERTO BELLO, 'the fair haven,' on the eastern side of the Isthmus of Panama, was so named by Columbus in 1502 on account of the beauty of the densely populated and well cultivated shores. PORTOBELLO, a favourite watering-place near Edinburgh, was for-

merly a piece of waste ground on which a house was built in 1742 by a retired sailor who had served under Admiral Vernon at the capture of Puerto Bello in 1739.

Porto Praya, the capital of the Cape Verd Islands, where Suffren attacked the English fleet in 1781, is from the Portuguese *praia*, 'shore' or 'strand.' There are several Brazilian names from the same source.

Porto Rico, in Spanish PUERTO RICO, the 'rich port,' one of the Antilles, takes its name from its chief harbour, *San Juan de Puerto Rico*, a name which has been split, the town being now called San Juan, while the island is known as Puerto Rico.

Port Said, at the northern entrance to the Suez Canal, was founded in 1859, and named by Lesseps in honour of Saïd Pasha, Viceroy of Egypt, the chief promoter of the enterprise. The common Arabic name Saïd means 'fortunate,' and has no etymological connection with the title Sayyid, which meant primarily a prince, but has come to denote a descendant of the Prophet. The Cid of Spanish romance exhibits the word in its original signification of 'prince.' PORT JERVIS, in the State of New York, bears the name of John B. Jervis, the engineer of the Delaware and Hudson Canal.

Portsmouth, Hampshire, is the town at the mouth of the port called Portsmouth Harbour, which was the *Portus Magnus* or 'great port' of the Romans; PORCHESTER (A.S. *Portceaster*) occupying the site of *Portus*, the Roman station, while PORTSEA forms a sort of island in the great port. PORTSMOUTH, in the state of New Hampshire, repeats the name of Portsmouth in the English county, and there is also a PORTSMOUTH in Virginia, and another in Ohio. PORTLAND, Dorset, A.S. *Portland*, is from the A.S. *port*, a 'haven,' an early Latin loan word. The ISLE OF PORTLAND, on the New Zealand coast, was so named by Cook in 1769 from its resemblance to the Isle of Portland in Dorset. CAPE PORTLAND, in Tasmania, and the PORTLAND ISLES, New Britain, were named in honour of the third Duke of Portland. The name of PORTLAND in Maine only dates from 1786. The native name was *Machigonne*. In 1658 it was called Falmouth, probably because of the inlet forming the harbour resembling that at Falmouth in Cornwall. From the A.S. words *port* and *loca*, 'a place shut in,' we have PORLOCK or PORTLOCK in Somerset, called *Portloca* in the A.S. Chronicle. PORTLOCK'S REEF, in Torres' Strait, was discovered in 1792 by Lieutenant Nathaniel Portlock. PORTRUSH in Antrim is the port or landing-place at a basaltic spit (*ros*), which here runs out into the sea, and PORTUMNA, Galway, is the landing-place at the oak. PORTREE, in Skye, is the Gaelic *port righe*, 'harbour of the king.' James V. STOCKPORT was once *Stockford*.

Portugal is a corruption of *Portus Cale*, the Roman name of PORTO, which we call OPORTO. The fief of the *Terra Portucalensis* or County of Portu-Cale was bestowed in 1094 by Alphonso VI. of Castile on Count Henry of Burgundy, who became the first Count of the district round Oporto, which by conquest from the Moors gradually grew up into the present Kingdom of Portugal.

Posen, now a Prussian province, but formerly the nucleus of the Kingdom of Poland, derives its name from the town of Posen, a Germanised corruption of the Polish name *Poznán*.

Posilipo, a hill near Naples, took its name from a Roman villa to which the Greek name of *Pausilypon*, equivalent to *sans souci*, was given by the owner Vedius Pollio. Beneath the hill the road to Baiæ passes through a tunnel called the GROTTO DI POSILIPO.

Possession Bay, South Georgia, is the place where Cook, in 1775, with the usual ceremonies, took possession of the country in the name of George III. At POINT POSSESSION, near the mouth of Cook's river, Alaska, Cook took possession in 1778. On POSSESSION ISLAND, Torres Straits, he took possession of the whole eastern coast of Australia, 'with all the bays, harbours, rivers, and islands situated upon it.' On POSSESSION ISLAND James Ross took possession of South Victoria Land. In POSSESSION BAY, Baffin Bay, John Ross took possession of the neighbouring lands. RIO DE LA POSESION (now called Rio Tinto), in Honduras, is where Columbus, in 1502, on his fourth voyage, took possession, in the name of Ferdinand and Isabella, of that part of the continent which he had discovered. The usual ceremonies consisted in erecting a flagstaff, unfurling a flag, and depositing a bottle with current coins and records of the proceedings, at the foot of the flagstaff, generally followed by a salute, and drinking to the health of the sovereign. The Spaniards erected a wooden cross, the Portuguese a stone pillar. (*See* PADRON.)

Potenza, in Southern Italy, represents the Roman *Potentia*, a name of the same class as Valentia, Florentia, and Placentia.

Potocki's Islands are a group in the Yellow Sea, the existence of which Klaproth prided himself on having discovered, without leaving his study, from the writings of Chinese authors, and as he boasts, 'without having exposed himself to the tempests and typhoons so frequent in the Chinese seas.' He tells us that he bestowed 'aux îles que j'ai decouvertes,' the name Archipel de Jean Potocki.

Potomac, a river in Virginia, is believed to bear the name of a native tribe.

Potosi, in Bolivia, is the Spanish corruption of the native name *Jatum Potochi.*

Potscherfstrom, in the Transvaal Republic, is a name manufactured, in the objectionable South African fashion, by combining syllables from the names of three Boer leaders, Potgieter, Scherf, and Stockenstrom. The place had previously been called *Mooi Rivier Dorp*, because it stood on a tributary of the Vaal called the MOOI, a native name meaning the 'fine river.'

Potsdam, near Berlin, formerly written *Pozdupimi*, is a German corruption of the Slavonic name *Pod-dubami*, 'under the oaks.'

Pottsville, Pennsylvania, bears the name of John Pott, who in 1827 here erected a smelting furnace.

Poverty Bay, New Zealand, where Cook anchored on October 8th, 1769, was so called by him on account of his being unable to obtain provisions from the natives, a contrast to a neighbouring bay which he visited in 1770, and named the BAY OF PLENTY, from the prosperity of the natives.

Pozzuoli, on the Bay of Naples, represents *Puteoli*, 'the wells,' where St. Paul landed in Italy. POZOBLANCO, in the Spanish province of Cordova, is the 'white pool.'

Prague, the capital of Bohemia, is the English form of the German PRAG, locally called *Praha*, which in Czech means the 'threshold,' referring, it is supposed, to a reef of rocks in the bed of the Moldau. The suburb of Warsaw on the right bank of the Vistula similarly goes by the name of PRAGA, the 'threshold.'

Prainha, the 'strand' or 'shore,' is the Portuguese name of a town on the Lower Amazon, the older settlement OITEIRO being on the hill. (*See* PORTO PRAYA.)

Prätigau, a valley in the Canton Graubünden, is the Germanised form of the Romansch name VAL PRATENS, or VAL PRATENSA, the 'meadow dale.' The

Bardo at Tunis is believed to be a corruption of the Spanish name *Prato*.

Predpriate, an island in the Low Archipelago, was discovered by Kotzebue in 1824, and named after his ship, the *Predpriatie*, a Russian name meaning the 'Enterprise.'

Presburg, on the Danube, formerly called *Bresisburg*, is believed to be the town of Brazilaus.

Prestonpans, near Edinburgh, where Prince Charles Edward won a victory in 1745, was a Preston (priest's tun), distinguished from other places of the same name by the existence of salt pans.

Pretoria, the capital of the Transvaal, was named in honour of Andries Pretorius, a Boer leader whose son became the first President of the Republic.

Pribylov Islands, in the Bering Sea, bear the name of a Russian pilot who discovered them in 1786.

Priestholme, Anglesea, is now usually known by the translated name PUFFIN ISLAND. The Puffin, from its black and white plumage, is locally termed the priest, and elsewhere the pope.

Prima Vista, probably Cape Breton, was the land 'first seen' by John Cabot in 1497.

Prince Edward Island, in the Gulf of St. Lawrence, was formerly called *St. John's Island*. In 1798 the local legislature passed an Act, confirmed in 1799 by the king in Council, changing the name to Prince Edward Island, in compliment to Prince Edward, afterwards Duke of Kent, and father of Queen Victoria, who was then commander of the forces in British North America. In 1776 Cook had given the name of PRINCE EDWARD'S ISLANDS to a group, of which Marion Island is the largest, lying south-east of the Cape of Good Hope.

Prince of Wales' Cape, Alaska, was the name given by Cook, in 1778, to the westernmost point of America, in honour of George, Prince of Wales, afterwards George IV., from whom PRINCE OF WALES' FORELAND, in Kerguelen Land, was also named by Cook in 1776. In 1774 he had given the same name to the south-west point of New Caledonia. In 1770 he called a group in Torres Strait PRINCE OF WALES' ISLANDS. PRINCE OF WALES' STRAIT, in the Polar Archipelago, was named by M'Clure in 1850 after Albert Edward, Prince of Wales.

Prison Island, in the Indian Ocean, is one of the Keeling or Cocos Group, on which Hare, an English adventurer, settled in 1823, and built a sort of prison for the natives he had enslaved.

Procida, an island in the Bay of Naples, preserves the old Greek name *Prochyte*, given because it appears to be thrown out or 'ejected' from Ischia.

Prome, in Pegu, is a corruption of *Prohm* or *Brun*, a Talaing name believed to mean the 'city of Brahma.' The Burmese call it *Pyé* or *Prémyo*, the 'city.'

Promise, Plains of, the name of the rich prairie lands south of the Gulf of Carpentaria, was given by Stokes in 1841.

Provence is the *Provincia* of Cæsar, a name reminding us that it was the first Province acquired by Rome beyond the Alps. The Provence rose did not, however, come from Provence, but from PROVINS, a town fifty miles from Paris, whither the crimson rose of Sharon was brought from Palestine by Thibaut, Count of Champagne, on his return from the fourth Crusade. Edmund of Lancaster having married the widow of Thibaut's son, the red rose of Provins became the cognisance of the House of Lancaster.

Providence, the capital of Rhode Island, was founded by Roger Williams and five companions, who in 1636 were expelled from Salem on account of their opinions, and after wandering for fourteen weeks in the wilderness, were hospitably received by the Wampanoags at a place he named Providence, in recognition of ' God's merciful providence to him in his distress.' CAPE PROVIDENCE, at the south end of Melville Island, was so called by Parry in 1819, 'in humble gratitude' for the preservation of an exploring party which had been for three nights absent from the ship. POINT PROVIDENCE, in Banks' Land, was so named by M'Clure in 1851 in recognition of his providential escape from the ice-locked coast. PROVIDENCE HILL, near TREACHERY BAY, North Australia, marks the providential escape of Stokes in 1839 from an attack by the natives. PROVIDENCE ISLE, north of New Guinea, marks Dampier's deliverance from danger in 1700. CAPE PROVIDENCE, in Corea, takes its name from Broughton's ship the *Providence*. PROVIDENTIAL CHANNEL is an opening in the Great Barrier Reef which enabled Cook in 1770 to resume his survey of the Australian coast. PROVIDENTIAL COVE, New South Wales, is an inlet where in 1795 Bass and Flinders in the boat *Tom Thumb* took refuge from a storm.

Prussia is our Latinised form of the German name PREUSSEN, itself a corruption of an older Lithuanian name. Old Prussia was the Duchy formed in the eastern corner of the modern kingdom out of the possessions of the Teutonic knights, whose inhabitants in the tenth century were called *Prutheni* or *Pruzzi*, which, according to Zeuss, is a Lettish name meaning 'neighbours.' The Latin form *Porussia* or *Borussia*, which is not found before the fifteenth century, was probably influenced by a popular etymology explaining it either as Po-Russia, the land 'near Russia,' or as the northern or boreal land. Old Prussia, being Polish territory, and hence beyond the limits of the Holy Roman Empire, the Electors of Brandenburg, to whom as Dukes of Prussia the sovereignty had fallen, were able, in 1701, to take from it a royal title, just as the Austrian dukes styled themselves kings in virtue of their Slavonic possessions. Hence Prussia, a non-Teutonic name, has been shifted westward so as to include a great part of Germany; such an anomalous term as Rhenish Prussia reminding us of the long history which has brought a Polish designation from the east of the Vistula to the west of the Rhine.

Puan, 'island,' is common in Brazilian names, as PARANA-PUAN, 'river island.'

Puebla, a Mexican province, takes its name from a mission founded in 1531 by a Franciscan monk, and called *Puebla de los Angeles,* the 'town of the angels,' from the popular belief that two angels assisted in the building of the church, adding every night to the walls as much as the workmen had accomplished during the preceding day. The name was shortened to Puebla, the 'town,' and this became the designation of the province of which it was the capital.

Puisortok, 'the place where something shoots up,' is the Eskimo name of a dangerous calving glacier on the east coast of Greenland, for which the natives entertain the greatest dread and veneration, believing that large masses of ice may suddenly dart up out of the depth of the sea and annihilate a boat and her crew.

Pulicat, on the Madras coast, once an important Dutch factory, is usually explained as a corruption of *Paliyáverkádu,* the 'jungle of old mimosa trees,' but according to Burnell the old form was *Pala-velkádu,* 'old Velkadu.'

Pulo Penang, correctly Pulo Pinang, in the Straits of Malacca, is a Malay name meaning the 'island of the areca' (betel nut), probably because the shape of the island resembles the shape of the nut. It is often ignorantly called PENANG, the 'betel nut,' just as Brazil, the name of a dyewood, is used instead of the correct term Terra do Brazil. The official name is PRINCE OF WALES' ISLAND, given in honour of the Prince of Wales, afterwards George IV., when the island was ceded in 1786. Pulo, 'island,' is common in Malay names, as PULO REKATA, 'crab island,' in the Straits of Sunda; or PULO CONDORE, 'gourd island,' at the mouth of the Mekong River. Six islands in the Malay Archipelago have acquired the name of PULO PISANG, 'banana island,' and several are called PULO PANJANG, or 'long island.' LAUT PULO off Borneo is 'ocean island,' PULO WAY is 'water island,' PULO GAIA, between Singapore and Borneo, means 'elephant island,' and PULO CABALLE, one of the Moluccas, is 'pot island,' earthenware being obtained from it for a great distance around.

Punjab (PANJ-ÁB) is the district of the 'five rivers,' the Sutlej, the Beás, the Rávi, the Chénáb, and the Jhílam, all affluents of the Indus, which is not usually reckoned among the five, though it sometimes takes the place of the Sutlej in the enumeration.

Putney, in A.S. *Puttan-ig,* in Domesday *Putelei,* afterwards *Puttenheth* and *Pottenheth,* was originally 'the isle of Putta,' a personal name, subsequent corruptions being due to popular etymology.

Puy-de-Dôme, a French department, bears the name of an extinct volcano in Auvergne, 4800 feet high, with a dome-shaped summit. The post-classical Latin loan word *podium,* an 'elevation,' from which Puy is derived, originally denoted the foot rail which surrounded the arena in an amphitheatre, and has been the source of numerous names in the South of France, as PUCH, LA POUA, PUGET, and PUITS - HAULT (*podium altum*). Puy appears in Catalan as PUIG, a 'hill,' as PUIG DE CEBOLLA, 'onion hill,' near Valencia.

Pylstaart, an island south-west of the Friendly Group, was so named by Tasman from the abundance of 'divers,' a sea fowl called *pijlstaart* in Dutch.

Pyrénées, the chain separating France from Spain, is the *Mons Pyrenæus* of the Greek and Roman geographers. The name first appears in Herodotus, who supposed *Pyrene* was the name of the place whence the Danube flowed. The etymology is unknown, being probably pre-Aryan. Many guesses have been made, from Basque, Celtic, and Greek sources, explaining the name as the ' high,' ' steep,' ' pineclad,' or ' burnt ' mountains. The most probable derivation is from *biren* or *pyren*, a local Béarnais word, doubtless ultimately Basque or Iberian, which signifies a ' summit ' or ' ridge.'

Pytchley, or PITCHLEY, in Northamptonshire, well known from the kennels of a favourite pack of foxhounds, is believed to be a name marking the southern limit of an inroad of the Picts. In an A.S. charter we have the form *Pihtesleá*, which implies that Pytchley was the *leá* or field of a Peht or Pict. Henry of Huntingdon records an incursion of the Picts as far as Northamptonshire, and their bloody repulse at a place in the neighbourhood of Stamford, which is about twenty miles from Pytchley. At Pytchley quantities of bones have been turned up, indicating that it was an early battlefield. In the churchyard rude kistvaens or stone coffins have been found at a great depth, and there is a large funeral barrow near the church.

Quail Island, in Clarence Strait, North Australia, was so called because quails incubated here in immense numbers. At PORTO QUAGLIO, near Cape Matapan in Greece, the quails congregate in preparation for their flight to Crete or Tripoli (Italian *quaglia*, a ' quail ').

Qualöen, ' whale island,' near Hammerfest, was so called because frequented by the rorqual, or fin whale.

Qu'appelle is a Canadian town and district on the River Qu'appelle, a French translation of the Cree name *Katapaywie Sepe*, from *sepe*, ' river,' and *katapaywie* ' who calls,' the cry of the native navigating its winding course in his canoe, hearing a distant hail, and shouting in reply, ' Who calls.'

Quatre Bras, a Belgian hamlet, gives a name to the battle fought on June 16th, 1815, at the ' four arms ' formed by the intersection of the road from Nivelles to Namur with that from Brussels to Charleroi. In the centre of the city of Oxford we have the similar name CARFAX, a corruption of *Quatrevoies*, the place where four roads meet.

Quebec, the former capital of Canada, arose round a stockhouse built by Champlain in 1608. In his book, published in 1613, there is a view of this solitary house, which is labelled *Abitation de Quebecq*. In 1535, Jacques Cartier had visited the

site, where he found a small collection of native wigwams called *Stadacoma*. It is often asserted that Champlain's name *Quebecq* was transferred from a village in Brittany, but there is no such village-name in France, and Champlain distinctly asserts that it was the native name. In the first edition of *Les Voyages du Sieur de Champlain* (1613), he says, that advancing up the river from the Isle d'Orleans ' je cherchay lieu propre pour nostre habitation, mais je n'en peu trouver de plus commode, n'y mieux situé que la pointe de Quebecq, ainsi appellé des sauvages, laquelle estoit remplie de noyers.' In the edition of 1633 we read ' trouvant un lieu le plus estroit de la riviere, que les habitans du pays appelent Quebec, j'y fis bastir et edifier une habitation.' The name Quebec is believed to refer to the ' narrowing ' of the river at this point, to which Champlain alludes.

Quedda, a town on the west coast of the Malay peninsula, which has given its name to the kingdom of which it is the capital, is the Portuguese form of the Malay *kádah* (Indian *kheda*), an ' elephant trap.'

Queenborough, in the Isle of Sheppey, was the A.S. *Cyningburh*, which meant ' Kingsborough,' the name being changed to Queenborough by Edward III. in honour of Queen Philippa. QUEENSTOWN was the new name given to the Cove of Cork in honour of the visit of Queen Victoria in 1849. QUEENSFERRY is the place where Margaret of England, Queen of Malcolm III., embarked to cross the Firth of Forth on her way to Dunfermline. QUEENHITHE, Middlesex, is the A.S. *Cwénhýth*, the ' woman's wharf.'

Queensland, in Australia, was constituted as a separate colony in 1859. The name Cooksland, from Captain James Cook, who had surveyed the coast, was at first proposed, but it was finally decided to name it after Queen Victoria. QUEEN'S COUNTY, formerly called Ossory, was made shire-ground by Act of Parliament (3rd and 4th of Philip and Mary), the assize town being called MARYBOROUGH. The adjacent territory of the O'More's was at the same time called KING'S COUNTY (*q.v.*). QUEEN CHARLOTTE ISLANDS, lying off the coast of British Columbia, were so named by Captain Dixon, who visited them in 1787 in the ship *Queen Charlotte*.

Quemoy, an island at the eastern opening to the harbour of Amoy, is a corruption of *kin-man* or *kin-mui(n)*, the ' golden door.'

Querfurt, in Prussian Saxony, is the ford on the QUERNE, or 'mill stream.'

Quilimani, a town on the River Quilimani, one of the mouths of the Zambesi, is a Portuguese corruption of the native name, of which the first portion is the Bantu word *kilima*, a 'hill,' which we have in Kilima-njaro (*q.v.*) and other mountain names, while the last syllable is probably *ny*, 'water' or 'river,' the town taking its name from the Kilima-Ny or 'hill river.' According to another explanation the river took its name from the town Kilima-ni, signifying a place 'on a hill.'

Quillebœuf, in Normandy, is doubtless a Scandinavian name. Depping and Cocheris* affirm that the old form was *Kilbœ*, which would correspond to the English Kilby, as CRIQUEBŒUF corresponds to Kirkby, DAUBŒUF to Danby, while MARBŒUF would be the 'horse village.' Brachet however explains the suffix *-bœuf* in these names as equivalent to *both* or *bothie* in English names.

Quilon, a town in Travancore, is the Portuguese form of *Kaulam*, an Arab corruption of the Tamil *Kollam*, believed to signify 'Palace' or Royal residence.

Quimper in Brittany, the capital of the department of Finistèrre, at the 'confluence' of the rivers Odet and Steir, as well as QUIMPERLÉ, at the 'confluence' of the Isole and the Ellé, are from the Breton *kem-ber*, a 'confluence' (Gaelic *comar*), a Celtic word which, in the form of *cumber* or *cumper*, occurs in several Scotch and Irish names, as CUMBER-TREES or BALLYCUMBER.

Quisisana, which means in the Neapolitan dialect 'here one is well,' is the name of a residence of the late king of Naples near Sorrento.

Quito, the capital of Ecuador, was founded about 1439 by the Inca Tupac Pachacutec, the great hero of Peruvian history, in the country of the Quitus, a tribe whose territory he had conquered. Pachacutec means 'he who changes the world.'

Radama Islands, north-west of Madagascar, were so named in 1824 by Captain Owen in compliment to Radama, king of Madagascar.

Radepont (Eure) is explained by de Jubainville as a hybrid Celto-Latin name meaning 'ford bridge.' The Celtic name was *Ritumagus*, the field or 'plain of the fo·d,' which became Radepont when the ford was replaced by a bridge.

Radnorshire, made into shire-land by Henry VIII., takes its name from NEW RADNOR, formerly the capital of the county. The name was transferred from the neighbouring village of OLD RADNOR, partly in Herefordshire, which was burnt by King John in 1216. It is probably the *Readanora*, 'red shore,' of a charter.

Radolfzell, on the Lake of Constance, called *Ratoltescella* in the ninth century, was a cell or church built by Ratold, bishop of Verona.

Raffles Bay, North Australia, was so named by King in 1818 in compliment to Sir Thomas Stamford Raffles.

Rafti, a port in Attica, is so called from a colossal statue on a rock at the entrance, which resembles a 'tailor' (*raptes*, pronounced *rafti*) sitting at his work.

Ragatz, in Canton St. Gallen, is from Regenzo, a personal name.

Ragusa, a Dalmatian port, is called *Dubrovnik* in Slavonic, and *Paprovnik* in Turkish. The older forms of the name, *Labuda, Labusædum, Lavusa, Raugia, Rausium, Raousion,* and *Ragusium* vary so greatly that no certain etymology can be given. The huge carracks of Ragusa, a town known in England in the sixteenth century as Aragouse or Arragosa, have given us the word *argosy*.

Rájputána is a great territorial circle, including twenty autonomous states, which formed the refuge after the Moslem conquest of the pure blooded Hindus, and is named from the Rájputs (Sanskrit *Rája-putra*, a 'king's son'), the honorific title of the great warrior caste.

Rakiura, the Maori name of Stewart Island, New Zealand, means 'dry weather' island, the southerly winds which blow from it usually bringing clear skies.

Raleigh, the State capital of North Carolina, has been appropriately named after Sir Walter Raleigh, the projector of the colony. The ill-fated colonists he sent out settled at RALEIGH BAY in North Carolina. MOUNT RALEIGH and the neighbouring CAPE WALSINGHAM in Davis Strait were discovered by Davis in 1585, and named after his friends Raleigh and Walsingham. Raleigh is a territorial surname (found in Somerset and Devon) supposed to mean the 'roe's field' (A.S. and O.N. *rá*, a 'roe deer').

Ramos, Isla de, one of the Salomon Islands, was discovered in 1567 by Mendaña on Palm Sunday, which is called in

Spanish *Domingo de ramos*, the 'Sunday of branches.'

Ramsgate is the chief town in the Isle of Thanet, whose British name, as we learn from Asser, was *Ruim*. In East Kent the gaps in the line of cliffs which lead to the foreshore are called 'gates,' and hence Ramsgate might be the gate of Thanet (*Ruim*) as MARGATE is the 'mere gate.' According to Dr. Stokes, the word *rumn*, genitive *ruimm*, is cognate with the Greek word *rumbos* or *rombos*, a 'lozenge.' Ruim, the old name of Thanet, is usually said to mean a 'foreland,' but may have been named from its shape, as well, possibly, as RUM (*q.v.*), formerly Ruim and Rumn, a lozenge-shaped island near Skye. ROMNEY MARSH is also lozenge-shaped.

Ranger Island, one of the Navigator Group, was discovered by the English whaler *Ranger*. It is also called NASSAU ISLAND, from the American whaler *Nassau*, by which it was subsequently visited.

Rangitoto is a volcanic island of recent formation near Auckland, New Zealand. The reflection on the clouds of the red-hot lava explains the expressive Maori name, which means 'bloody sky.'

Rangoon, the chief town and port of Pegu, is called in Burmese *Ran-kún*, 'end of the war,' literally 'enmity exhausted,' a name given in 1763 by Alompra, the founder of the Burmese dynasty, who, after the destruction of the city of Pegu, established the capital of the kingdom near the famous golden pagoda called Da-gun, with which Ran-kun may probably be connected by assonance.

Rannoch, the name of a moorland tract in Perthshire, in which lies LOCH RANNOCH, is explained from the Gaelic *raithneach*, 'bracken' or fern.

Raphoe, in Donegal, is a corruption of *Rath-both*, the 'fort at the huts.' The word *rath*, 'a fort,' is found in about 1100 Irish names, RATHMORE, the 'great fort,' being the name of more than forty townlands. Another common name is RATHASPICK, the 'fort of the bishop.' The second element is frequently a personal name, as in RATHKENNY, RATHKIERAN, RATHRONAN, or RATHBARRY.

Rappahanoc is a river in Virginia. In the earliest records of the colony the Rapahannock and the Susquehannock are mentioned in 1603 as the names of two native tribes. But, according to Boyd, Rappahannoc means 'tidal river,' literally the place where the tide ebbs and flows.

Rapperswyl, in Canton Zürich, is called in a document of 972 *Rapprehtswillare*, 'Rátbert's dwelling.'

Rascals' Village, a name more expressive than elegant, was given in 1793 by Mackenzie to a settlement on the north-west coast of America where he was plundered by the natives.

Rat Island, in the Aleutian Chain, and RAT ISLAND in Houtman's Abrolhos, West Australia, were, when discovered, overrun with rats.

Ratisbon is the French name of the city called by the Germans REGENSBURG (*Reganesburg* in the eighth century), because it stands at the confluence of the Regen and the Danube, whence also the Roman name *Reginum* or *Castra Regina*. The German name seems to be unconnected with the French name *Ratisbon*, which preserves the Celtic name *Ratisbona* or *Radespona*, 'the embanked town.' Old Celtic *ratis*, Irish *rath*, 'an earth-wall.' (*See* BONN.)

Ratmanoff, an island in Bering Strait, and CAPE RATMANOFF, on the Island of Saghalien, bear the name of one of Krusenstern's officers.

Rauparaha, an island in Cook's Strait, New Zealand, was the dwelling of Rauparaha, a Maori chief. It is also called MAYHEW'S ISLAND, from an American who made it a whaling station.

Reading, the county town of Berkshire, is a patronymic or clan name, as is shown by the A.S. name *Readingas*, which appears in the dative plural *æt Readingan* in the will of Queen Æthelflæd, *c.* 972.

Rebecca Island, in the Ellice Group, was discovered in 1819 by the American ship *Rebecca*.

Recherche Archipelago, off NUYTSLAND, on the south coast of Australia, was discovered by the Dutchman Nuyts in 1627, and revisited in 1792 by the French Admiral Entrecasteaux in the ships *La Recherche* and *L'Espérance*. (*See* ENTRECASTEAUX.)

Recife, the 'reef,' is a Brazilian coast town. The ILE AUX RÉCIFS, 'reef island,' is one of the Séchelles.

Record Point, Port Essington, is where Captain Bremer, in 1824, deposited in a bottle a record of his having taken possession of Arnhem Land.

Reculver, Kent, was the Roman *Regulbium*. This became in A.S. *Ræculfceaster*, *Raculf*, and *Ræculf*. From the dative

Ræculfe, through the M.E. *Raculvre*, we have Reculver.

Redonda, one of the Lesser Antilles, a round dome of rock, was called by Columbus *Santa Maria de Rotunda.* ESCOLLO REDONDO, one of the Galapagos, was also named from its shape.

Red River, a tributary of the Lower Mississippi, is so called from its colour, due to beds of red clay and sandstone over which it flows. The RED RIVER OF THE NORTH, which gave its name to the Red River settlement, now Manitoba, flows into Lake Winnipeg.

Red Sea translates the unexplained classical names *Erythræan Sea* and *Mare Rubrum.* To the early Portuguese mariners the name *Mar Vermelho* seemed to be appropriate because of the red streaks of water, due probably to floating infusoria. The name ERYTHREA or ERITREA has been revived for the Italian protectorate established in 1890-91 on its western coast.

Refuge Harbour, in Smith's Sound, afforded refuge to Kane in 1853 during a thick fog. In REFUGE INLET, near Point Barrow, a boat's crew of the *Blossom* found refuge from the pack ice in 1826. In the same year REFUGE COVE on the same coast sheltered Dr. Richardson from a storm.

Regent's Inlet, or PRINCE REGENT'S INLET, a channel leading southwards from Lancaster Sound, was discovered by Parry in 1819. PRINCE REGENT'S BAY, at the head of Baffin's Bay was discovered by John Ross in 1818. These names, together with REGENT'S PARK and REGENT STREET, London, date from the regency of George IV., February 6th, 1811, to January 29th, 1820. PRINCE REGENT'S RIVER, Australia, was named by King in October 1820, after the Regency had ceased, but before the news had reached Australia.

Reggio, a Calabrian town on the Straits of Messina, was the Greek colony of *Rhegium,* founded at the 'rent' dividing Sicily from the mainland. REGGIO near Parma, on the Via Æmilia, was *Regium Lepidi,* founded by Æmilius Lepidus at the time of the construction of the Æmilian way.

Reichenhall, on the SAALE, or 'salt river,' in Bavaria, is so called from its rich brine springs. (*See* HALLE.) REICHENBACH, a waterfall in Canton Bern, is so named from the copious supply of water. REICHENAU in Saxony is the

'rich meadow.' REICHENAU, an island in the Lake of Constance, is the 'rich meadow' occupied by a wealthy Benedictine Abbey, founded in 724.

Reigate, the 'ridge-gate,' in Surrey, is the Anglo-Norman name of a gate or passage through the ridge of the North Downs, the Norman castle at Reigate, which gave a name to the town, commanding the defile. Above Reigate is the disfranchised borough of GATTON, apparently the *tún* at the gate or opening through the chalk cliff.

Reindeer Island, in the Great Slave Lake, was so named by Mackenzie because on it seven reindeer were killed, at a time when his expedition was in great straits for food. REINDEER HILLS, near the mouth of the Mackenzie River, and REINDEER MOUNTAINS near the Peace River, are translations of the native names.

Reliance, Fort, on the Great Slave Lake, formed Back's winter quarters, 1833-1835. It was so named, he tells us, in token of his trust that a merciful Providence would protect him in his difficulties and dangers.

Remagen, a town on the Rhine near Bonn, preserves the Celto-Latin name *Rigimagus* or *Rigomagus.*

Rembo, the name of a river in the Fan country, West Africa, means simply 'the river.' It is a dialectic form of the word for river seen in LIMPOPO and other African river names.

Rencounter Bay, Newfoundland, was the scene of a murderous conflict between the natives and the early colonists.

Rendsburg, Holstein, was the castle of Reinhold, as is shown by the old form *Reinholdsburg.*

Rennell Island, in the Salomon Group ; CAPE RENNELL and MOUNT RENNELL, in Arctic America, bear the name of Major Rennell, the eminent hydrographer.

Rennes, formerly the capital of Brittany, is a tribal name, having been the chief city of the Redones. It was called *Condate Rhedonum,* or simply *Condate,* the 'confluence.'

Rensselaer Harbour, in Kane's Sea, bears the name of Stephen Van Rensselaer, a promoter of the Grinnell Expedition.

Repulse Bay, in Rowe's Welcome, lies beyond CAPE HOPE, where Middleton in 1741-42 'hoped' to find a North-West Passage, but was 'repulsed' by finding the supposed strait was a closed bay. REPULSE BAY in Queensland, and REPULSE BAY in Kerguelen Land, are bays which Cook explored in the vain expectation that they would prove to be navigable channels. At REPULSE POINT, North Australia, one of King's officers was driven back by a sudden storm.

Rescue, Cape, in Wellington Channel, bears the name of the *Rescue*, a vessel of the first Grinnell Expedition despatched for the rescue of Franklin.

Reshd, or RESHT, a town on the Caspian, is explained by Spiegel as a Persian name, referring to the material with which the houses are washed or daubed.

Resolution Island, at the entrance to Hudson Strait, bears the name of the *Resolution,* one of the ships in Button's Expedition of 1612. RESOLUTION ISLAND, New Zealand, RESOLUTION ISLAND in the Low Archipelago, and PORT RESOLUTION in the New Hebrides, discovered in 1773-74, all bear the name of the *Resolution,* the principal ship in Cook's second and third voyages.

Rest, Bay of, North Australia, is one of the places where in 1818 King's crew rested, because they were tired.

Restoration Island, North Queensland, was discovered by Bligh in 1789, on May 29th, the anniversary of the Restoration of Charles II.

Return Reef was the most westerly point reached by Franklin on his expedition down the Mackenzie River to explore the coast of the Polar Sea.

Réunion was the name given in 1793 by a decree of the Convention to the ISLE DE BOURBON, between Mauritius and Madagascar. In 1809 the name was changed to Isle Bonaparte. It was taken by the English in 1810, and restored to France by the Treaty of Vienna in 1815.

Reuss, a Thuringian principality, was created in the thirteenth century by Henry the Pious, in favour of his son who was nicknamed *der Russe* (the Russian), from his Russian grandmother.

Revel, a Russian port on the Baltic, was founded by the Danes in the thirteenth century. The name is explained by the Danish *rev* or *revle,* Swedish *räfvel,* a 'sandbank' or 'reef.'

Revilla-Gigodo Islands, a Pacific group west of Mexico, bear the name of a Spanish Viceroy of New Spain (1789-94).

Reyes, a Californian cape at the entrance to the bay of San Francisco, retains the old name of the bay, called by the Spaniards *Puerto de los Reyes,* because discovered in 1542 on Twelfth Night, January 6th, the festival of the Three Kings. The RIO DOS

REYS, the 'river of the (three) Kings' (also called RIO DE COBRE, from the copper implements obtained from the natives by barter), is a river north of Natal which was discovered by Vasco da Gama on Twelfth Night in 1498. According to a local tradition ISLA DEL REY, the 'island of the King,' is the place where Alphonso III. landed when he visited Minorca.

Reykiavik, 'reek-bay,' and REYKIANES, 'reek-cape,' in Iceland, are so called from the steam arising from the hot springs.

Rhætic Alps is the name given to a part of the main chain which was held by the *Rhæti,* a name explained by Zeuss from the Celtic *rait,* a 'mountain region.'

Rhaiadr or RHAYADER, a town in Radnorshire, was formerly called *Rhaiadyrgwy,* the 'fall of the Wye,' from a small waterfall on the Wye, removed in 1780. *Rhayadyr* or *Rhiader,* a 'cascade,' is a common term in Welsh nomenclature.

Rheims, more correctly REIMS, the metropolitical city of France, is a corruption of *Remis,* dative plural of *Remi,* a Belgic tribe-name equivalent to *primi,* and signifying 'princes' or 'rulers.'

Rhenoster, a river in the Orange Free State, was so named before the 'rhinoceros' was driven to the north.

Rhine is the English spelling of the German name RHEIN, which was the Latin *Rhenus* and the Celtic *Renos,* a form better preserved in the name of the RIVER RENO in Cisalpine Gaul, near Bologna. The name is explained as a participle derived from the verbal root *ri,* to 'flow' or 'run.' The upper valley of the Rhine in Canton Graubünden is called the RHEINWALD, a German corruption of the Romansch name *Rin-val,* 'Rhine valley.'

Rhode Island, the smallest of the United States, is not itself an island, but takes its name from the nucleus of the colony, a small island in Narragansett Bay called *Aquednek,* which was purchased from the natives by Puritan dissidents from Massachusetts (*see* PROVIDENCE), who first settled in the north of the island at a place called *Pocasset* by the natives. The reason why Aquednek was renamed Rhode Island is unknown, the only contemporary statement being the assertion of Roger Williams that it was so named 'by us' in 1636. This disposes of the conjecture that Rhode Island was a corruption of an older Dutch name *Roodt Eylandt,* 'red island.' The name may have been taken from the Ægean island of Rhodes, or from the name of one of the early settlers, but more probably from the excellent anchorage or 'roadstead' between the island and the mainland, an etymology supported by the early spelling Road Island, which appears in 1647 on the title-page of the earliest, or one of the earliest, books printed in the colony. On the other hand the official order, made in 1644, for the change of name, decrees that the island shall be called 'the Isle of Rhodes or Rhode Island,' which favours the theory that the name was from that of the Ægean island, if it were not that the change from Rhodes to Rhode is left unexplained.

Rhodes or RHODIS, anciently *Rhodos*, is an island in the Ægean. The rose, which appears on early local coins, shows the signification attached by the inhabitants to the name, which is very old, the Rhodians appearing in the Ethnological Table in Genesis as *Rodanim* (erroneously *Dodanim* in the A.V.).

Rhodesia, the name of a territory on the Zambesi, acquired by the Rt. Hon. Cecil Rhodes, and administered by the Chartered Company.

Rhone, the great river known to the Romans as the *Rhodanus*, is still locally known, near its source, as the *Rhodan* or *Rotten*. According to Zeuss the name means violent or rapid stream.

Rhymney, Monmouthshire, bears the name of the river on which it stands.

Ribchester, Lancashire, is shown by the Domesday name *Ribelcastre* to be the chester on the River Ribble.

Richardson Bay, RICHARDSON RIVER, and other names in Arctic America, commemorate the services of Dr. (afterwards Sir John) Richardson, R.N., who shared with Franklin the perils and hardships of the two overland expeditions to the Arctic Ocean in 1819-20 and 1825-26.

Richborough, in Kent, was the Roman *Rutupiæ* or *Ritupiæ*, whence Bæda's *Reptaceaster*. In the twelfth century it is called *Richeberg* by Alured or Alfred of Beverley, and *Ratesburg* by Leland in the time of Henry VIII.

Rich Island, on the coast of New Guinea, was so named by Dampier in 1700 after Sir Thomas Rich. ISLA RICA, the 'rich island,' was the name given by Bilboa to the pearl island of Terarequi, on the Pacific side of the Isthmus of Darien. From its beautiful flowers Gaspar Morales in 1515 named it Flores, but the Spaniards have preferred Bilboa's name. RICA DE ORO, 'rich in gold,' is the Spanish name of a North Pacific island, South of Japan,

rediscovered in 1788 by Meares, who named it LOT'S WIFE. A neighbouring island called RICA DE PLATA, 'rich in silver,' is believed to be identical with CRESPO ISLAND, discovered in 1801 by Captain Crespo of the Spanish ship *El Rey Carlos.*

Richmond, the 'rich mount,' in Yorkshire, is the Norman-French name of the town which grew up under the castle built in Swaledale by Alan of Brittany, nephew of William the Conqueror. Henry VII. gave the name of the Yorkshire earldom, which he had inherited through John of Gaunt, to his Surrey palace at SHEEN (A.S. *Sceon*, the 'beautiful place'). The name has been transferred to RICHMOND in Virginia, founded in 1737, and to numerous towns in Canada, and the United States, Australia, and the Cape Colony.

Rideau Canal, which connects Lake Ontario with the Ottawa River, is fed by the RIDEAU RIVER, so called from a cascade which, as the French name implies, falls like a 'curtain' over a rock forty feet in height.

Riffel, a jagged ridge near Zermatt, is from the M.H.G. *riffel*, a 'saw.'

Riga, a Russian port on the Baltic which has given a name to the GULF OF RIGA, was founded by merchants from Bremen. It stood on one of the mouths of the Dwina (or Düna) now silted up, called the *Ryghe* or *Rige*, probably from the ridge of sand, *Righ-ö*, which separated it from a neighbouring channel.

Rigi, a mountain near Lucerne, is locally called *d'Rigi*, a patois form of *der rik'*, 'the back,' a term used to denote a steep path over a 'ridge.' An early popular etymology made it the 'mountain queen,' the name *Regina Mons* appearing on a map of 1478.

Riley's Bay and CAPE RILEY, in Arctic America, and POINT RILEY in Spencer's Gulf, South Australia, bear the name of Mr. Richard Riley of the Admiralty.

Rimnik, a cape on the Island of Saghalien, was named in commemoration of Suwarrow's victory over the Turks at the River Rimnik in Wallachia.

Rio, the capital of Brazil, means 'river,' being a colloquial abbreviation of RIO DE JANEIRO, 'January River,' the name given by Amerigo Vespucci to a bay, one of the finest in the world, which he entered on January 1st, 1502, and supposed to be the entrance to a great river which has no existence. In 1565 a city was founded on this bay and called *São Sebastião do Rio* *de Janeiro*, from the name-saint of the young King Sebastian of Portugal, grandson of Charles V., born in 1554, King in 1557, killed in 1578. RIO RICO, the 'rich river,' in the Brazilian province of Goyaz, was so called because of its auriferous sands. RIO GRANDE, the 'great river,' is a common name, occurring in Senegambia, Brazil, Mexico, San Salvador, Panama, the Mosquito Coast, and Texas. The RIO GRANDE DO NORTE, the 'great river of the North,' and the RIO GRANDE DO SUL, the 'great river of the South' give their names to Brazilian provinces. We have a RIO NEGRO, or 'black river' in Uruguay and Brazil, a RIO COLORADO, or 'ruddy river' in Texas and in the Argentine Republic, a RIO BRANCO, or 'white river' in Brazil, a RIO DULCE, or 'sweet river' in Guatemala, and a RIO TINTO, the coloured or 'vermilion river,' at the Rio Tinto quicksilver mines in Spain. RIO DE LA PLATA is the 'river 'of the silver.' (*See* PLATA.)

Riom (Puy-de-Dôme) was the Roman *Ricomagus* or *Ricomum*. (*See* REMAGEN.)

Ripon, a city in Yorkshire, which stands on the banks of the Ure, grew up around a monastery, which Bæda tells us was founded in 660 *in loco qui dicitur in hrypum.* In the Chronicle we have *to Ripum* (A.D. 709), *abbot in Hripum* (A.D. 785), and *æt Rypon* (A.D. 948). In early charters we have Rippon and Ripon. The name has been supposed to be an English corruption or assimilated form of the Latin designation, *Monasterium ad ripam,* 'the minster on the bank' of the Ure, but this is untenable. The date given by Bæda cannot be reconciled with a Danish etymology, or the name might be explained from the O.N. *ripum,* 'at the crags,' but a cognate Anglian word may have existed, enabling us to explain Bæda's name as 'among the clefts' or crags. We may compare the name of REPTON in Derbyshire, which appears in the Chronicle and elsewhere as *Hreopandún, Hreopadún, Hreopedún,* and *Hrypadún.*

Ripon Island, at the mouth of the great Fish River, was named by Back in 1834 after the first Earl of Ripon, then Secretary for the Colonies. MOUNT ROBINSON, in Arctic America, was named by Franklin in 1826 after Sir F. G. Robinson, Chancellor of the Exchequer, afterwards the first Earl of Ripon. The RIPON FALLS, near the exit of the White Nile from the Victoria Nyanza, were named by Speke, 1860-63, after the second Lord Ripon, who

was President of the Royal Geographical Society when his expedition was organised.

Riviera means in Italian 'shore' or 'coast land.' The narrow strip of coast at the foot of the Maritime Alps, west of Genoa, is called the RIVIERA DI PONENTE, the 'west coast' or 'coast land of the setting sun,' while the coast land at the foot of the Apennines, between Genoa and Spezzia, is called the RIVIERA DI LEVANTE, the 'east coast' or 'coast land of the rising sun.' RIBEIRA, in the Azores and in the Cape Verd Islands, and RIBERA in Spain are the Portuguese and Spanish equivalents of the Italian Riviera. RIVA, a town occupying a small delta at the head of Lago di Garda, is the place on the 'shore.' The RIVERINA, in Australia, is a barbarous term invented to designate the fertile lands which border the River Darling.

Rivoli, Venetia, a corruption of *Ripula,* a diminutive of *ripa,* a 'bank,' well describes the steep shore of the Adige, where Napoleon gained his victory over the Austrians in 1797. Hence the name of the. RUE DE RIVOLI in Paris, and of RIVOLI BAY in South Australia which was discovered in 1802 by the French expedition under Baudin.

Roanne, a town on the Loire, is the *Rodomna* of Ptolemy.

Robben Island is the Dutch name of an island in Table Bay formerly frequented by seals (*robben*).

Robbin Passage, between Tasmania and ROBBIN ISLAND, was discovered in 1804 by Lieutenant Charles Robbin, R.N., in H.M.S. *Buffalo.*

Robertsville, Liberia, was named after Joseph Roberts, a negro born in Virginia, who became the first President of the Negro Republic. ROBERTS ISLAND, one of the Marquesas, was visited in 1792 by Captain Roberts of the American ship *Jefferson.*

Robertson Bay, South Victoria, bears the name of the surgeon of H.M.S. *Terror.*

Rocca, 'the rock,' is the name of more than fifty places in Italy, and ROCHE or LA ROCHE, from the Low-Latin *rupica,* is nearly as common among French names. We have ROCHEFORT, the 'strong rock,' both in France and Belgium. ROCHE-SUR-YON, a town in France, is named from a castle built on a rock above the River Yon. LA ROCHELLE, 'the little rock,' is a French seaport, whose name appears in the tenth century in the Latinised form *Rupella.* The dialectic form *roque* is seen in ROQUERONDE, called *Rocca rotunda* in 1135, as well as in ROQUEFORT, CAPE LA ROQUE, and other names, but CABO DE SAN ROQUE in Brazil was discovered by Vespucci in 1501 on August 16th, the festival, in the Roman calendar, of St. Roch, from whom SAN ROQUE, a town near Gibraltar, also takes its name. The Portuguese form ROCA is seen in CABO DA ROCA, 'rock cape,' near Lisbon, the extreme western point of the continent of Europe, and in AS ROCAS, 'the rocks,' a group of small islands near Fernando de Noronha in the South Atlantic.

Rochdale, Lancashire, is in the dale of the River Roach or Roche. ROCHFORD, Essex, is the ford over the River Roche. ROCKFORD, Illinois, stands on the Rock River.

Rochester, a city in Kent, was, according to Bæda's belief, the chester of a settler called Hrof, an etymology supported by the oldest A.S. form, *Hrofes ceaster,* which we have in the Saxon Chronicle, and in a charter of 673, while in a charter of 789 it is *Civitas Hrofi.* Hence the name should be pronounced Ro-chester and not Roch-ester, as if it were the chester on a rock. It was the Roman station of *Durobrivæ,* a Celtic name meaning the 'bridge over the water'; but it must have been called simply *Brivæ,* 'at the bridge,' as appears from the name *Hrofi-brevi* which we have in a charter. A new light has been thrown on the etymology by the Peutinger Tables, in which the Roman station appears not as *Durobrivæ,* but as *Rotibis,* seemingly a duplicate name, which enables us to dispense with Bæda's *Hrof,* and yet to explain the *Hrofes-ceaster, Civitas Hrofi,* and *Hrofi-brevi* of the charters. HIGH ROCHESTER in Northumberland, occupying the brow of a rugged eminence, is on the site of *Bremenium,* the strongest of the Roman stations on the wall. Like ROCESTER, near Uttoxeter, in Staffordshire (formerly *Rocetter* and *Roucestre*), it may be the 'rock chester' (Cymric *rhwg,* Gaelic *roc,* a 'rock'). ROCHESTER, a city in the State of New York, with a population of 115,000, derives its name from Colonel Nathanael Rochester, who projected the settlement in 1818.

Rockhampton, Queensland, was a fancy name given by Commissioner Wiseman from a rock at the entrance to the River Fitzroy.

Rockingham Bay, Queensland, was named by Cook in 1770 in honour of Charles Watson Wentworth, second Marquess of Rockingham, who became Prime Minister in 1765. The title was taken from ROCKINGHAM in Northamptonshire. The A.S. names *Rocgingaham* and *Rocing,* though both probably in Kent, suffice to show that the Northamptonshire name may be from a patronymic *Hroccing,* like ROCKING and RÖCKINGHAUSEN in Germany.

Rocky Mountains has now supplanted the older name *Stony Mountains* as the designation of the central chain of North America.

Rocroi, in the Ardennes, was formerly *Croix-de Rau,* which became *Rau-Croix,* and finally ROCROI.

Rodney, a place in Somerset, gave a territorial surname to Sir Edward Rodeney, who held the estate of Stoke Rodney in the time of Charles I., to whose family Admiral Lord Rodney, also a Somerset man, is believed to have belonged. In his honour Cook, in 1769, named POINT RODNEY, in New Zealand, and afterwards gave the same name to a Cape in the Bering Sea.

Rodosto, near Adrianople, was the ancient *Rhædestus.*

Rodriguez, also called DIEGO RUY'S ISLAND, in the Indian Ocean, is a dependency of Mauritius. It was discovered by the Portuguese in 1645, and doubtless named from the discoverer. It appears on a map of 1752 as *Insula Jacobi Roderici,* the island of James (Diego) Rodrigo (Ruy). It belonged at one time to the French, to whom the present form of the name may be attributed.

Roermonde, 'Roer-mouth,' in the Netherlands, is situated at the confluence of the River Roer with the Maas.

Roe's Welcome bears the name of the eminent traveller and diplomatist Sir Thomas Roe, who in 1631 promoted the expedition of Luke Fox (North-west Fox). Sir Thomas Roe's Welcome was originally a name given either by Fox or Button to an island at the mouth of a channel leading northwards from Hudson's Bay, the name being subsequently transferred to the channel in which the island lies. ROE'S GROUP, Tasman Land, bears the name of Lieutenant Roe, R.N., and ROE'S RIVER that of his father, the Rector of Newbury.

Rogers Strait, Tasman Land, was named by King after Captain R. H. Rogers, R.N.

Roggefeld, 'rye plain,' is an extensive upland district at the Cape, so called because suited to the growth of rye. It is intersected by a chain of hills called the ROGGEFELD BERGEN.

Rohilkhand is a district west of Oudh, inhabited by the Rohillás or 'highlanders' (Balúchí, *rohelá*, a 'mountaineer,' from *rohu*, a 'mountain'). In the seventeenth century the name Rohelá was applied to the Afghans who came from their hills to take service under the Mogul Emperors at Delhi. Early in the eighteenth century some of these adventurers established themselves in the province of Katehur, which came to be known as Rohilcund or Rohilkhand (*khand*, a 'district').

Rohrbach, 'reed beck,' is the name of thirteen rivers in Germany.

Rolland, an island near Kerguelen Land, was named by Kerguelen from his ship the *Rolland*.

Rome is the French name of the city called ROMA in Latin and Italian. Among the various guesses as to the meaning of the name, the most probable refers it to the word *gruma* or *groma*, a technical name given to the point in a city or camp where the *cardo* crossed the *decumanus*, the two cross roads spreading themselves at their junction into a sort of forum. Constantinople was called NEW ROME when it became the seat of Empire. The ROMAGNA, an Italian province which ultimately became part of the patrimony of St. Peter, acquired its appellation not from Rome, but from its long adherence to the Eastern Empire of New Rome, whence also the names of ROUMANIA (*q.v.*) and RUMELIA. The imperial name of Rome has been absurdly given to more than twenty insignificant places in the United States. ROMANS (Drôme) was the *Monasterium Romanum*, founded by St. Bernard. Dedications to St. Romanus explain the names of the French villages ST. ROMAIN, (Yonne), and ST. ROME and ST. ROMAND (Hérault). On August 9th, the feast of St. Romanus, the CABO DE SAN ROMAN at the entrance of the Gulf of Maracaybo was discovered by Alonso de Hojeda in 1499. The name of the Russian chancellor, Count Romansoff, has been given to CAPE ROMANSOFF at the northern end of the Japanese island of Yesso, to two Polynesian islands, and to a chain of hills in Arctic America. ROMANSHORN, in Canton Thurgau, was called *Romanicornu* and *Rumanishorn* in the eighth century, either from the personal name Romanus or from the Teutonic name Ruman (*Hruommannu*, equivalent to *Ruhmesmann*). ROMA, a town in Queensland, was named after Countess

Roma, who married Sir George Bowen, the first Governor of Queensland. ROMSDAL in Norway is the 'valley of the Rauma.'

Romford, Essex, perhaps the 'roomy' or 'wide ford,' is pronounced Rumford, the spelling having probably been altered because it was supposed to mean the Roman ford. Romford is now usually said to be the ford over the Rom, a name bestowed of late years on the brook at Romford, the river-name having been evolved out of the town-name, in the same way that the river names Cam, Eden, and Penk have been evolved out of the town names Cambridge, Edenbridge, and Penkridge. (*See* RUNCORN.)

Rona, an island off Lewis, and RONA or RONAY, an island in the Sound of Skye (both called *Rögney* in O.N.), bear the name of St. Ronan, a bishop who died in 737, from whom Sir Walter Scott invented the name St. Ronan's Well.

Ronaldshay is the name of two of the ORKNEYS, distinguished as North and South Ronaldshay. South Ronaldshay is called in the Orkney Saga *Rögnvalsey*, the 'isle of Rögnvald,' brother of Sigurd, who was Earl of Orkney in the ninth century. The name of North Ronaldshay has been assimilated; in the Orkney Saga it is called *Rinansey*, the 'isle of St. Ringan' (Ninian) of Whithorn, who lived in the fourth century.

Rook's Island, between New Guinea and New Britain, was named by Dampier, in 1700, after Sir George Rook.

Roosey, one of the Orkneys, was called in the thirteenth century *Hrolfsey*, 'Hrolf's island.'

Rosalgat, a cape forming the most easterly point in Arabia, is a Portuguese corruption of the Arabic name *Ras-al-hadd*, which signifies the 'Cape of the End' or boundary.

Rosas, a town on the Catalonian coast, is a corruption of the classical name *Rhoda* or *Rhodos*. According to Strabo, it was a colony of Rhodians who had previously settled in Sicily.

Roscommon, which means 'Coman's wood,' is an Irish county taking its name from ROSCOMMON, the county town, where St. Coman built a monastery in the eighth century. The Irish *ros* (Welsh *rhos*) signifies in the South of Ireland a 'promontory,' and in the North a 'wood,' being glossed *nemus*. It is believed that it originally signified a 'rough plain,' and was applied to any rough promontory, such as the ROSS OF MULL. The Scotch county of ROSS was originally only the peninsula of EASTER ROSS, of which the mountainous part was called ARDROSS, the 'height of Ross,' to distinguish it from MACHAIR ROSS, the level sea-board. ARDROSS is also the name of a district in Perthshire, and ROSS is a district in County Monaghan. ROSNEATH is a corruption of *Ros-neveth*, the 'promontory of St. Nevydd,' a Welsh bishop in the sixth century.

Ross Bay, ROSS POINT, and other names testify to the services of Sir John Ross and his nephew, Sir James Clark Ross, in Arctic and Antarctic exploration.

Rotherham, in Yorkshire, stands on the River Rother, and ROTHERFIELD, Sussex, takes it name from another River Rother, but ROTHERFIELD in Hants (A.S. *Hrytheran-feld*) and elsewhere is the ' cattle field ' (A.S. *hryther*, an ' ox,' M.E. *rotheren* and *rutheren*, ' cattle '). The Scotch name RUTHERFORD is doubtless the ' cattle ford,' being analogous to such names as HORSEFORD in Norfolk, and SWINFORD in Leicestershire.

Rotherhithe, Surrey, pronounced and sometimes spelt Redriff, is in A.S. *Ætheredes hýth*, also *Retheres hithe*, *Retherhithe*, *Rethra hith*, and *Hrýthra hyth*. It seems to have been originally so called from the personal name Ethered, and subsequently assimilated so as to signify first the ' boatman's or rower's wharf ' (A.S. *rethra*, a ' rower ' or ' sailor,' and then the ' ox wharf ' (A.S. *hryther*, an ' ox '). The place seems to have given its name to the brook called the Rother, which here joins the Thames.

Roto, which means a ' lake ' in Maori, is a common element in New Zealand names. Thus ROTO RUA, a lake which lies in a deep circular crater, means ' hole lake '; ROTO KAWA, whose waters hold alum in suspension, is the ' bitter lake ' ; ROTOMA is the ' white lake'; ROTO MAHANA is the ' warm lake '; ROTO MAKARIRI is the ' cold lake '; and ROTO KAKAHI, the ' mussel lake.'

Rotterdam, in Holland, a name of the same class as Amsterdam, Saardam, and Edam, was so called from the dam or embankment at the confluence of the River Rotte with the Maas. In 1643 Tasman gave the name of his native town to Annamocka in the Friendly Group, which he called ROTTERDAM ISLAND.

Rouen, the chief town in Normandy, is a corruption of the Celto-Latin name *Rotomagus*, which became *Rotomum*, *Rodumum*, and finally ROUEN.

Roumania is a modern kingdom on the Lower Danube, comprising the former Turkish principalities of Wallachia and Moldavia. The kingdom was so named because the people, who speak a Neo-Latin dialect derived from the colonists settled by Trajan in Dacia, designate themselves as Rumeni or Romani (Romans). RUMELIA or ROUMELIA, a principality lying on either side of the Balkans, is the Latinised form of the Turkish *Rum-ili*, 'the land of Rûm,' that is of Constantinople or New Rome. The Turkish word *ili* means a ' tribe ' or ' district '; Bosnia, for instance, being called in Turkish Ili-Bosna, the ' district on the Bosna. ROUM or RÛM is the Turkish name for European Turkey, Europe being supposed to be subject to the Emperor of Constantinople or New Rome. The last seat of Greek Empire was ERZEROUM (*q.v.*) called by the Turks *Arzi-rum*, the 'lands of Rum,' from *arazi*, plural of *arz*, ' land,' an Arabic loan word.

Rousillon, one of the old French provinces, derived its name from a small bourg near Perpignan, formerly called *Castel Rossello* or *Roscelione*, now RUS-CINO.

Roventhal, the easternmost cape in the Falkland Islands, bears the name of a Dutch officer who first sighted it in 1721.

Roveredo, a town in the Trentino, on the Brenner route, is from the Low-Latin *roboretum*, an ' oak grove.'

Rowlett Narrow, on the west coast of Patagonia, and CAPE ROWLETT, Tierra del Fuego, bear the name of the purser of H.M.S. *Adventure*.

Rowley Shoals and IMPÉRIEUSE SHOALS, West Australia, were discovered in 1800 by Captain Rowley of H.M.S. *Impérieuse*.

Roxburgh, the county town of Roxburghshire, is probably from a proper name, and not, as often supposed, the ' castle on the rock,' since in the twelfth century, when we find the name as *Rokesburch* and *Rochisburc*, it is doubtful whether the English word *rock* had been borrowed from the French *roche*, or the Celtic *roc* had survived.

Ruabon in Denbighshire, also called RHUABON or RHIWABON, is a corruption of *Rhiw-Fabon*, 'the ascent of St. Mabon,' *m* changing to *f*, according to the laws of Welsh phonology. The word *rhiw*, an ' ascent,' is common in Welsh names, as RHIW, RHIWLAS, or RHIWBACH.

Ruad represents the Greek *Aradus*, and

the Phœnician *Arvad*, the 'refuge,' so called because built on a rocky island off the coast.

Rüdesheim, opposite Bingen on the Rhine, anciently *Hruoidinesheim*, is from a personal name.

Rudolf, Lake, was the name given in 1887-8, in honour of the Austrian Crown Prince Rudolf, by Count Teleki to an East African lake, called by the natives *Basso Narok,* the 'black water.' A smaller neighbouring lake called *Basso Ebor,* the 'white water,' he named LAKE STEPHANIE after the Crown Princess.

Rudston is a village in the East Riding of Yorkshire. In the churchyard there is an enormous block of millstone grit, on which a rood or cross must have been erected, as is indicated by the Domesday name *Rodestan,* or *Rodestein,* 'rood stone.'

Rufus River, an affluent of the Murray, was foolishly named by Sturt in allusion to the red hair of his companion MacLeay.

Rügen, an island in the Baltic, anciently *Rugium,* is supposed to have been a stronghold of the *Rugii* of Tacitus.

Rum, one of the Hebrides, is said to be a Scandinavian corruption of *I-dhrvim,* 'ridge island,' the *d* being silenced by aspiration. (*See* RAMSGATE.)

Runaway, Cape, New Zealand, is where some armed 'Indians,' who approached Cook's ship in 1769, hastily paddled off when a cannon shot was fired over them.

Runcorn, Cheshire, on the Mersey, is a corruption of *Rumcofan,* the dative of the A.S. *Rumcofa,* the broad or roomy cove. In A.S. *cofa* meant a 'chamber' or 'cave,' and afterwards a 'cove' or 'bay.'

Rupert's Land, an immense territory on RUPERT'S RIVER, south-west of Hudson's Bay, was discovered in 1668 by Captain Zacharias Gillam, and named after Prince Rupert, the first governor of the Hudson's Bay Company, constituted in 1670 by Charles II., who granted Rupert's Land to Prince Rupert and other noblemen. RUPERT ISLAND, in Magellan Strait, was also named in his honour by Sir John Narborough in 1670.

Rurick Straits, a passage through the Aleutian chain, RURICK STRAIT in the Marshall Archipelago, and the RURICK GROUP in the Dangerous Archipelago, were discovered in 1815-17 by Kotzebue, commander of the Russian ship *Rurick.*

Russell Point, Banks Land, was named by M'Clure, in 1850, after Lord John Russell. RUSSEL INLET, in Arctic America, was named by Richardson, in 1826, after Professor Russel of Edinburgh.

Russia is a name not older than the close of the seventeenth century, when it began to be used instead of the name MUSCOVY, derived from Moscow, the old capital. The name Russia was constructed from the name given to the Swedish Vikings or Varangians, who established themselves at Novgorod, and were called *Rôs, Rus, Russ,* or *Russi,* which are Slavonic and Greek corruptions of *Ruotsi,* a name applied by the Finns to the Swedes, derived from the Swedish *Rodsen* or *Rothsmenn,* which means 'rowers' or seafarers. The Swedes are still called *Ruotsi* by the Finns, and *Rôts* by the Esths.

Ruthven, in Forfarshire, was called in the thirteenth century *Abirruotheven,* the place at the 'mouth of the red river.'

Rutland, the smallest of the English shires, bears a name which has not been satisfactorily explained. When Domesday was compiled it had not been constituted into a shire, a part being included in Northamptonshire, and the rest being a detached portion of Nottinghamshire, separated from it by Leicestershire. In the fifth year of King John, *Roteland* first appears as a county in a document assigning a dowry to Queen Isabella. The name Roteland had previously denoted the district round Oakham, which was a detached portion of Notts. The soil being red, Rutland is usually explained as the 'red land,' but in this case the early form of the name should be Rodeland, and not Roteland, as in the case of ROTHWELL, Lincolnshire, where the red chalk is conspicuous, which is called *Rodewell* in Domesday. Since the older Rutland designated a detached portion of Notts, the Old French *rôte* (from the Latin *rupta*) which denotes a division or separated portion, whence the German *rote,* the Danish *rotte,* and Dutch *rot,* would be satisfactory, were it not for the difficulty of supposing that an old French word could have become vernacular in England before the date of Domesday, not to speak of the statement, whose date is uncertain, that in 702, Coenred, afterwards king of the Mercians, was king of the Northumbrians, of Lindseye, Hoiland (Holland), Kesteven, and Roteland. The greater part of the older Rutland was forest, as shown by the phrase 'foresta de Roteland Broyl' in the Hundred Rolls, where Broyl denotes a bushy plain. Hence the name might be 'rootland,' signifying a forest in which the trees had been felled, but the stumps left standing. On the whole, this is the most probable etymology, since the O.N. (*w*)*rót* or *rót* makes the plural *rót*, so that Roteland might be the land of stumps. Phonetically *rút*, 'cheerful,' would do, but such a name would be meaningless. An equally impossible etymology is that from *hrot*, 'slime,' the older Rutland being heavy clay land. It is, of course, possible that the first part of the name may be Celtic, and it has been plausibly conjectured that the name originally denoted a larger district, the capital of which was the Roman town of *Ratæ* (Old Celtic *rāti*, an 'earthen-wall'), the long *ā* becoming *ō* by phonetic law.

Ruwenzori, the 'cloud king,' a snow-clad volcanic range, nearly 19,000 feet in height, north of the Victoria Nyanza, is identified by H. M. Stanley with the 'mountains of the Moon.'

Rye, one of the Cinque Ports in Sussex called *La Rie* in medieval French chronicles, is perhaps, like PECKHAM RYE, the 'rough' place. RYDE, in the Isle of Wight, occupies the site of a village called *La Rye* or *La Rithe,* destroyed by the French in the reign of Edward II. (A.S. *rithe,* a 'rivulet.')

Ryke Yse, a group of islands on the east coast of Spitzbergen, were discovered in 1640 by a Dutch whaling captain, Ryke Yse, of Vlieland.

Saar, a tributary of the Mosel, is called *Saravus* by Ausonius. The meaning is unknown, but the name is probably from a primitive Aryan root *sravati* meaning 'to flow,' seen in the Sanskrit *srava,* a 'stream,' or in the Gaelic *sruth,* 'a river.' SAARBURG is the castle on the Saar; SAARBRUCK, called *Sarbrucca* in the second century, and *Pons Saravi* in the fifth, is the 'bridge over the Saar'; SAARGEMUND is at the junction of the Saar and the Blies ; and SAARLOUIS was the frontier fortress on the Saar built by Vauban in 1687 for Louis XIV. SAARDAM is properly ZAANDAM (*q.v.*).

Saas, a village in Canton Valais which gives a name to the SAASTHAL, was called *Sausa* in 1397 ; doubtless from the Middle Latin *saucea* or *saucia* (French *saussaie*), a corruption of *saliceta,* 'osier beds' or 'willow plantations.' In Spanish America we have SAUCES, the 'willows,' RIO SAUCE, 'willow river,' and CAPE SAUCE-LITO, 'little willow cape.'

Sabine Island, on the east coast of Greenland, is one of the PENDULUM

ISLANDS (*q.v.*) on which Captain Sabine, R.A., made observations with the pendulum for the purpose of determining the configuration of the earth. Several Arctic and Antarctic names commemorate the services of this distinguished officer, who as General Sabine was one of the Secretaries of the Royal Society.

Sable Island, ninety miles south-east of Nova Scotia, bears a French name meaning 'sand island.' Its dangerous shoals have been the scene of many shipwrecks. Sable or Les Sables are naturally common elements in French names.

Sabrina Land, due south of New Zealand, and probably a portion of the Antarctic continent, was discovered in 1839 by the cutter *Sabrina.* A new island in the Azores was thrown up in June 1811, and the eruption being witnessed by Captain Tillard of H.M.S. *Sabrina,* he gave the island, which has since disappeared, the name of his ship.

Suchau, a city which is the Chinese outpost at the eastern verge of the great desert, means 'sand district.'

Sacramento, the State capital of California, was founded in 1819 on the river called by the Spaniards, doubtless from a mission, RIO DEL SAN SACRAMENTO, the 'river of the holy sacrament.'

Sacred Isles, in the Strait of Belle Isle, is an English mistranslation of the French name *Iles Sacrés,* 'the accursed islands,' so called because dangerous to navigation. SACRED ISLAND, in the Delta of the Mackenzie, was used as a burying-place by the Eskimos.

Sacrificios, Isla de los, near Vera Cruz, was so called by Grijalva in 1518, because he found on the island a temple with corpses which had been recently sacrificed.

Saffron Walden, Essex, formerly Chepping Walden, derives its appellation from the former cultivation of Saffron.

Saghalien, also spelt SAGALIN and SAKHALIN, is the name now given to KARAFTU, a large Russian island opposite the mouth of the Amur (*q.v.*), whose Manchu name is SAGALIN ULA, the 'black river.'

Saginaw is a city in Michigan, on the SAGINAW RIVER, which discharges its waters into SAGINAW BAY, an arm of Lake Huron. The river derived its name from the bay, which means a 'lake' or 'sea.' (*See* MICHIGAN.)

Sahara, the great desert of Northern Africa, is an Arabic word meaning 'deserts' or 'wildernesses,' being the plural of *sahra*, literally an 'extension,' and hence a widely extended plain, and then used to denote a plain destitute of herbage, a moor, heath, or desert. In the form SIERRA (*q.v.*) the Spaniards borrowed the word from the Arabs, and applied it to the desolate moorlands separating the great valleys of Spain, such as the SIERRA MORENA.

Saïda, in Palestine, preserves the old Phœnician name of *Tsidon* (Sidon), the 'fishing' town, or the 'fishery.'

Saigon, the capital of French Cochin China, stands on the River Saigon, one of the mouths of the Me-kong. SAGAING, the 'gold sieve,' a town on the Irawadi, is so called from the auriferous sands, formerly washed for gold.

St. Abb's Head, a promontory on the coast of Berwickshire, is so called from a neighbouring monastery founded in the seventh century by the first abbess, St. Æbba, daughter of Æthilfrith, king of Northumbria.

St. Albans, now an episcopal see in Hertfordshire, appears in early charters either by the Celto-Roman name of *Verulamium*, or as *Watlinga-ceaster*, 'the chester on Watling Street.' It acquired its present name from the great Benedictine Abbey, dedicated to St. Alban, founded in 793 by Offa, king of the Mercians, on the spot where he claimed to have discovered the remains of Albanus, the reputed British protomartyr.

St. Amand-les-Eaux (Nord) derives its name from a monastery founded in the reign of Dagobert by St. Amand (Amandus), bishop of Tongres.

St. Andrews, the metropolitical see of Scotland, was originally called *Mucross*, the 'boar's head' or promontory. The dedication is due to supposed relics of St. Andrew, which gave the church its importance, and were probably brought by Acca, bishop of Hexham, from Hexham in Northumberland, where they had been deposited. Hexham had been dedicated to St. Andrew by Wilfrid, bishop of York, who believed that he had received the gift of eloquence in answer to prayers offered in the Church of St. Andrew at Rome. In 732, Acca, probably owing to the invasion of the Danes, fled from Hexham, and there is a legend that he founded a see among the Picts, and the Chronicle of the Picts and Scots relates the transference of the relics of St. Andrew to Scotland in 761, in the reign of Angus mac Fergus, one of the most powerful of the Pictish kings. Hence St. Andrew became the patron saint of the Picts, and afterwards of Scotland.

St. Anthony, a city in Minnesota, now incorporated in Minneapolis, stands on the FALLS OF ST. ANTHONY, discovered in 1680 by Father Louis Hennepin, a French missionary, and named by him after his patron saint St. Anthony of Padua, to whom Father Serra also dedicated a mission which is now the town of SAN ANTONIO in California. SAN ANTONIO, the Spanish capital of Texas, founded in 1714, stands on the SAN ANTONIO RIVER. SAN ANTONIO, one of the CAPE VERD ISLANDS, was discovered in 1462 on St. Anthony's Day, but the CABO DE SAN ANTONIO at the entrance of the Rio de la Plata, discovered in 1520, is believed to bear the name of the *San Antonio*, one of Magellan's ships.

St. Asaph, an episcopal city in Flintshire, bears the name of a disciple of St. Kentigern, who is believed to have founded the see.

St. Augustine, a town in Florida, is the oldest European settlement in the United States. Don Pedro Menendez de Aviles, sent by Philip II. of Spain in 1565 to drive out the French Protestant refugees who, three years before, had reached Albemarle Sound, arrived off the coast of Florida on St. Augustine's Day, August 28th, and gave the name of the saint to the city which he founded shortly afterwards. On the same day, August 28, 1501, Amerigo Vespucci arrived at CABO SANTO AGOSTINHO in Brazil on his famous voyage. It had already been visited by Pinzon, and also by Cabral, who had named it *Cabo da Santa Cruz.*

St. Bartholomew, an island in Bougainville's Passage, was discovered by Cook on St. Bartholomew's Day, August 24th, 1774. SAN BARTOLOMÉ, one of the Radack Islands, was discovered by Loaisa in 1526, on the Eve of St. Bartholomew. ST. BARTHOLOMEW ISLAND in the Straits of Magellan, discovered by Drake in 1574, and the PUERTO DE SAN BARTOLOMÉ in California, discovered by Vizcaino, also owe their names to the day on which they were discovered.

St. Bees, in Cumberland, has an Irish origin, the priory from which the town derives its name having been founded about 650 by St. Bega or Begogh, an Irish virgin, whose shrine became a noted place of pilgrimage.

St. Bernard is the name of two Alpine passes near Mont Blanc, called the

Great and Little St. Bernard, which commemorate the labours of St. Bernard of Menthon, a Savoyard cleric of noble family who about 960 founded hospices near the summit of the passes for the reception of pilgrims. MONT ST. BERNARD, on the South Australian coast, was so named by Baudin in 1802 in commemoration of the passage of the Great St. Bernard by Napoleon and the French army. SAN BERNARDINO, a pass in the Eastern Alps, is so called from a chapel at the foot of the pass dedicated to St. Bernardino of Sienna.

St. Brieuc, the capital of the Côtes du Nord, grew up round a monastery founded by St. Brieuc (Briocus), the apostle of Brittany, who came from Wales in the fifth century. The monastery afterwards attracted crowds of pilgrims to his tomb.

St. Cloud, near Paris, takes its name from St. Chlodovalde or Clodoald, son of King Chlodomire or Clodomir, and grandson of Clovis, who here founded a religious house in which he died.

St. Davids, an episcopal see in Pembrokeshire, was the burial-place of St. David, the patron saint of Wales, who died in 601.

St. Denis near Paris has arisen around the Abbey Church, founded by Dagobert in the seventh century, in which the French kings were buried. According to Gregory of Tours, St. Denis (Dionysius) was the first bishop of Paris, and was beheaded in 272, and buried at St. Denis. A late legend identified him with St. Paul's convert, Dionysius the Areopagite. St. Denis became the patron saint of France, and after him St. Denis, the capital of the ISLE DE BOURBON (now RÉUNION), was named.

St. Dié, a town in Lorraine, called in Latin documents *Sancti Deodati oppidum*, takes its name from St. Dié (Deodatus), bishop of Nevers, who resigned his see in 664, and retired to a Benedictine monastery he had founded in the Vosges, around which the town of St. Dié afterwards arose.

St. Gallen (in English ST. GALL) is a town which, since 1803, has given its name to the Swiss Canton formed out of the territory belonging to the great Abbey founded by St. Gall (Gallus), an Irish missionary, who on the destruction of Bangor in the seventh century, left Ireland with Columbanus, and settled in the great forest south of Lake Constance, with the object of converting the heathen Alemanni. The Abbey, and afterwards the town, grew up around his cell.

St. George's Channel is the name of the southern part of the Irish Sea, but it does not appear when it was given. The name is not recognised in any of Camden's Editions of his *Britannia*, 1586-1607, but in 1578 it occurs in the record of Frobisher's second voyage. CAPE ST. GEORGE in New Ireland was discovered and named by Dampier in 1700. The neighbouring opening which he called ST. GEORGE'S BAY, having been proved by Carteret in 1767 to be a strait separating New Britain from New Ireland, has now received the appropriate name of ST. GEORGE'S CHANNEL. CAPE ST. GEORGE, New South Wales, was discovered by Cook on St. George's Day, April 23rd, 1770. ST. GEORGE'S BRIDGE on the Darling River was named by Mitchell on St. George's Day, 1845. SAN JORGE, one of the Salomon Islands, is believed to have been discovered by Mendaña on St. George's Day, April 23rd, 1595.

St. Germain-en-Laye, near Paris, takes its name from a monastery built by King Robert in the forest of Layce, and dedicated to St. Germain (Germanus), bishop of Paris. There are several French villages called St. Germain from churches with the same dedication.

St. Goar, a town on the Rhine, is said to take its name from St. Goar, a hermit from Aquitaine who here took up his abode (519-575).

St. Gobain (Aisne) is best known from its famous glass works. The commune bears the name of an Irish priest who, in the seventh century, came to the forest by the Oise, where he built himself a cell, replaced by a church erected in the reign of Clothair III. (656-670).

St. Gotthard, the chief pass over the Central Alps, takes its name from a chapel and hospice erected in 1374 by the Abbot of Disentis, and dedicated to St. Godehardus, bishop of Hildesheim, who died in 1038.

St. Helena, an island in the South Atlantic, was discovered on St. Helen's Day, 1502, by the Portuguese navigator, João da Nova, on a return voyage from India. ST. HELEN'S SHOAL, south of the Pelew Islands, was discovered in 1794 by the English ship *St. Helen*. ST. HELEN'S, near Liverpool, was formerly a small village with a church dedicated to St. Helen.

St. Imier, a town in the Jura, takes its name from a cell built by St. Himerius in the seventh century.

St. Ives in Cornwall, formerly called.

Pendenis or Pendunes, takes its name from St. Hya, Jia, or Ia, an Irish virgin who is said to have landed in the bay about 460 A.D., and from whom the place was called Porth Ia. St. Ives, in Huntingdonshire, is called *Slepe* in Domesday. In the eleventh century the Abbot of Ramsey, to whom the manor belonged, built a church dedicated to St. Ivo, a Persian archbishop, who is said to have travelled to England as a missionary, and to have died here in 600, a story probably fabricated by the Ramsey monks.

St. Jans, an island east of New Britain, was discovered by the Dutch seamen Le Maire and Schouten on St. John the Baptist's Day, June 24th, 1616.

St. Jean d'Angely, in France, takes its name from a Benedictine Abbey dedicated to St. John on the site of *Angeriacum*. The Ilots de St. Jean, in the estuary of the St. Lawrence, were discovered by Jacques Cartier in 1534, on August 29th, the feast of the beheading of St. John the Baptist. St. Jean d'Acre, in Palestine, was held by the Hospitallers or Knights of St. John. (*See* Acre.)

St. John, the chief city in New Brunswick, was formerly called Parr Town, in honour of Governor Parr, but was incorporated in 1785 under the name of St. John from the St. John's River on which it stands. St. John's is also the name of the capital of Newfoundland (*q.v.*). St. Johnsburg, Vermont, founded in 1786, was named in honour of St. John de Crèvecour, French consul at New York. Saint John is a nautical corruption of several Oriental names. St. John's Islands is the chart name and the popular European name of two islands six miles south of Singapore, the chief of which is properly Pulo Sikajang, of which St. John's Islands is a European corruption. St. John's is an English sailors' corruption of *Sajana* or *Sanján*, the *Sindan* of the old Arab Geographers, which was the first settlement of the Parsees when they emigrated to India in the eighth century. St. John's Island is also a corruption of San-Shan, the Chinese name of an island at the mouth of the Canton River, where St. Francis Xavier died, and was originally buried.

St. Katharine, one of the peaks of Sinai, is so called from a monastery near the summit dedicated to St. Katharine of Alexandria, whose body, according to the legend, was borne thither by angels. The Cabo de Santa Catharina, south of the Gulf of Guinea, was discovered by the Portuguese on St. Catharine's Day at the close of the reign of Alfonso V.

St. Kitts is the English name of one of the Antilles, which was passed by Columbus in his second voyage, and though, owing to the loss of his chart and log, we have no evidence of the fact, may well have been named by him San Cristoval, after his own name-saint St. Christopher, a name which would naturally suggest itself as appropriate, Mount Misery resembling a giant stooping under a burden, or, to the vivid imagination of Columbus, St. Christopher bearing the infant Christ.

St. Lawrence, the great Canadian river, was discovered by Cartier, who, on his second voyage, in 1535, ascended it as far as Montreal. Cartier gave the name not to the river, but to the channel between the island of Anticosti and the mainland, which he called *Baie de St. Laurent*, having discovered it on St. Lawrence's Day, August 10th. The name was afterwards extended to the *Golfo Quadrado*, or 'Square Gulf,' now called the Gulf of St. Lawrence, and subsequently it came to denote the great river which enters it, originally called *Rivière de Canada*. St. Laurens Bay, since found to be a strait, on the south-west coast of Novaya Zemlya, was discovered by Barents in 1594 on St. Lawrence's Day. The Bay of St. Lawrence, on the western side of Bering Sea, was discovered by Cook on St. Lawrence's Day, 1778. It is curious that Bering, on the same day in 1775, sailed past the Bay without discovering it, giving the name of St. Lawrence to a neighbouring island. Cook, in 1778, sighted its eastern cape, and, supposing he had discovered a new island, gave it the name of Charles Clerke, captain of the *Discovery*, his second ship. Hence it usually appears on the map as St. Lawrence or Clerke's Island. Lawrence, a town in Massachusetts, was so called from a Boston family of that name. Lawrence City, in Kansas, founded in 1854, was named after Amos A. Lawrence, then Governor of Massachusetts.

St. Leonard's, now a part of Hastings, was, at the beginning of the century, an outlying hamlet with a chapel dedicated to St. Leonard.

St. Lô (La Manche), formerly *Briovira*, a Celtic name meaning the 'bridge over the Vire,' was the patrimony of Laudus (St. Lô), bishop of Coutances, who in the sixth century endowed his see with his patrimonial estate, where he built a church which acquired the name of St. Lô from the veneration paid to his relics, afterwards translated to Thouars.

St. Louis is the name of several towns named after Louis IX., the canonised king of France. (*See* LOUISIANA.) SAN LUIS REY, California, was a mission founded by Father Peyri in 1798, by the name of *Mission de San Luis Rey de Francia*. SAN LUIS OBISPO, a town and cape in California, are named from a mission founded in 1771 by Father Serra, and dedicated to St. Louis, bishop of Toulouse, under the name of *Mission de San Luis Obispo de Tolosa de Francia*.

St. Malo, a town in Brittany, takes its name from St. Malo (Maclou, Maclovius, or Malovius), a Cambrian priest, who came to Brittany in the sixth century, and became Bishop of Aleth, a see afterwards transferred to the larger town now called St. Malo. (*See* ST. SERVAN.)

St. Maur (whence the name Seymour), properly St. Maur-sur-Loire, the first Benedictine Abbey established in Gaul, became the western home of Benedictine learning. It was founded in 543 at a place then called Glanfeuil, by Maurus (St. Maur) the first abbot, who had been a pupil of St. Benedict.

St. Maurice, a town in Canton Valais, lies below an abbey founded in 515 on the traditional site of the martyrdom of St. Mauritius, commander of the Theban legion, put to death, according to the legend, by Maximinian.

St. Nazaire, on the Loire, called *Sancti Nazarii vicus* by Gregory of Tours, is so named from a dedication to St. Nazarius, a martyr of Milan.

St. Neots, a town in Hunts, grew up near a Benedictine monastery founded in 974, which possessed relics of a brother of King Alfred, brought from ST. NEOT in Cornwall.

St. Omer (Pas de Calais) bears the name of St. Audomarus, Audomare, or Omer, the great Swiss bishop of Thérouanne, who, in the seventh century, evangelised North-Eastern Gaul, and was buried in a monastery which he founded, around which grew up the town which, in the ninth century, acquired the name of the Saint.

St. Paul, Minnesota, a city which in 1885 had a population of 111,334, has grown up near a log chapel erected in 1841 by a Jesuit missionary, and dedicated to St. Paul. SAN PAULO, a Brazilian province, takes its name from its capital, SAN PAULO, where, in 1554, a Jesuit College was founded, in which the first mass was celebrated on January 25th, the feast of the Conversion of St. Paul, to whom the college was dedicated. ST. POL DE LÉON, in Brittany, is called in Latin documents *Fanum Sancti Pauli Leonini*, the Church of St. Paul in the Barony of Léon.

St. Quentin (Aisne), a town on the Somme, bore the Celtic name *Samarobriva*, the 'bridge over the *Samara*,' now the Somme, where, in the third century, Caius Quintinus is said to have been martyred. In the reign of Dagobert the reputed tomb of the martyr had become a place of pilgrimage, and in the twelfth century we find the name Samarobriva replaced by *Municipium Beati Quintini*.

St. Servan, in Brittany, is opposite St. Malo. Its first bishop was St. Malo, but, after the see had been removed to the place now called St. Malo, it was placed under the patronage of St. Servan, the Apostle of the Orkneys.

St. Thomas, an island in the Gulf of Guinea, properly called the *Ilha de São Thomé*, was discovered by the Portuguese on St. Thomas' Day, December 21st, 1470. The CABO DE SÃO THOMÉ, Brazil, north of Cape Frio, was reached by Vespucci on St. Thomas' Day, December 21st, 1501. ST. THOMÉ, near Madras, the earliest Portuguese settlement on the Coromandel coast, was so called from a supposed discovery of the bones of St. Thomas, reputed to have been the Apostle of India. ST. THOMAS, a Portuguese settlement in Madagascar, is now called TAMATAVE.

St. Vincent, one of the Antilles, was discovered by Columbus in 1498. SAN VICENTE, one of the Cape Verd Islands, was discovered in 1492 on St. Vincent's Day (January 22nd). On the same day in 1502 Vespucci discovered the PORTO DE SAN VICENTE in Brazil. CAPE ST. VINCENT (in Portuguese *Cabo de San Vicente*), the south-west corner of Portugal, derives its name from a monastery perched on the lofty promontory, which is dedicated to the martyr St. Vincent, who is said to have lived there. After the victory of Admiral Jervis, on February 14th, 1797, over the Spanish fleet at Cape St. Vincent, he was created Earl St. Vincent, and was first Lord of the Admiralty from 1801 to 1804. In his honour Flinders, in 1798, gave the name of POINT ST. VINCENT to a Tasmanian Cape, and in 1802 to the great gulf in South Australia, on whose shores the city of Adelaide was afterwards built.

St. Waast, near Arras, is the site of an Abbey built over the tomb of St. Vedast (Vadasius), bishop of Arras, and afterwards of Cambrai, to whom, after the victory ot Clovis at Tolbiac in 495, was assigned the duty of teaching the Frankish king his catechism.

Saintes, the capital of the old French province of SAINTOGNE, was the chief town of the Santones. It was called by the Romans *Mediolanum* (*see* MILAN), which, as in other cases, has been replaced by the tribe-name. The town is called *Civitas Santonas* by Gregory of Tours. SAINTOGNE is a corruption of *Santonica*.

Sain Ussu, 'good water,' is the Mongolian name of a station in the Gobi.

Saldanha Bay, South Africa, bears the name of Admiral Antonio de Saldanha, who in 1503 was attacked and wounded by the natives while taking in water at Table Bay, which, for nearly a century, was known as *Aguada de Saldanha,* 'Saldanha's watering - place.' In 1601 the Dutchman Joris Spilbergen renamed it *Tafel Bay,* now TABLE BAY (*q.v.*), and the name of Saldanha Bay was thereafter transferred to a bay some eighty miles further north.

Salem, 'peace,' was the Biblical name given in 1628 by the Puritan colonists to their settlement at Naumkeag ('eel-land '), in Massachusetts, 'from the peace they had and hoped in it,' after the amicable adjustment of rival claims under charters which had been granted to Gorges and Endicott. Some forty places in the United States have received the same name. (*See* JERUSALEM.) SALEM (*Shelam*), a town and district in the Madras Presidency, is supposed either to be a corruption of Chelam, the 'rocks,' or derived from *Chera*, the name of the old monarchy.

Salisbury, or NEW SARUM, is the county town of Wiltshire. Hither in 1218 Bishop Poore removed the see from Old Sarum, the *Sorbiodunum* of the Romans. In the Saxon Chronicle Old Sarum is called *Searoburh, Seareburh, Searburh,* and *Seresburh.* From the dative *Seresbyrig* came the Domesday form *Sarisberie,* and this on Norman lips became Salisbury. According to Dr. Maunde Thompson, Sarum, the signature of the bishop, arose out of a contrac-

tion for Sarisburia, which was misread Sarum. FORT SALISBURY, the capital of Mashonaland, was founded in 1890, and named from the British Prime Minister.

Salkitu, the 'stormy,' is a Mongolian mountain.

Salomon Islands, in the South Pacific, were so named by Alvaro de Mendaña in 1567, because, having obtained some gold by barter, he imagined that he had discovered the land of Ophir, whence Solomon procured his treasures.

Saloniki, in European Turkey, is a corruption of *Thessalonica,* a city renamed by Cassander after his wife Thessalonica, half sister of Alexander the Great. The city gives a name to the GULF OF SALONICA.

Sal si puedes, 'get out if you can,' is the Spanish name of a dangerous channel in the Gulf of California.

Salvator Valley, MOUNT SALVATOR, LAKE SALVATOR, the CLAUDE RIVER, and MARTIN'S RANGE are fanciful names scattered by Major Mitchell over a picturesque district in Central Australia, where the scenery reminded him of the pictures of Salvator Rosa, Claude Lorraine, and John Martin.

Salzkammergut, an imperial domain in Upper Austria, is rich in deposits of salt, the manufacture and sale of which forms a valuable monopoly of the crown. Hence the name, which means 'salt exchequer property,' literally 'property of the salt chamber.' HALLSTADT (*see* HALLE) is in the same district, as well as SALZBURG, which stands on the SALZACH or 'salt river.' Here, in the eighth century, Rupert, bishop of Worms, the Apostle of Southern Bavaria, established a mission, and enriched his starving converts by showing them how to work the salt mines. Hence the town which grew up around his church and monastery acquired the name of *Salziburg,* 'salt town,' now Salzburg. SALZBRUNN, in Silesia, possesses saline springs. At SALTCOATS in Ayrshire bay salt was extensively manufactured in the last century. SALT LAKE CITY, Utah, founded in 1847, was called New Jerusalem by the Mormons. It stands near the lake to which Fremont in 1842-44 gave the name of the GREAT SALT LAKE: its chief affluent is called the JORDAN by the Mormons. LAS SALINAS, in California, Mexico, and elsewhere, are places with deposits of salt. RIO SALADO, 'salt river,' is the name of several South American rivers. SAALE is the name of three 'saline' rivers in Germany, on one of which stands the town of SAALFELD.

Samana Bay, in Haiti, was called by Columbus *El Golfo de las Flechas,* 'Gulf of the arrows,' because the natives were armed with arrows as large as assegais and powerful bows.

Samarang Islands, a Polynesian group, were discovered in 1840 by Capt. Scott of the ship *Samarang.*

Samarkand, in Central Asia, occupies the site of *Marcanda,* the capital of Margiana, a city destroyed by Alexander the Great. After the Arab conquest in 643, Marcanda reappears in history under the name of Samarkand, probably a revival of the old name, in which case Samar, who is said to have been an Arab leader who gave his name to the town, must be considered only as an Eponymus.

Samo, an Ægean island, preserves the old name *Samos,* obtained by the Greeks from the Phœnicians, in whose tongue it meant the 'lofty' island, or, as Strabo puts it, the 'height.' The mountainous island of Cephalonia also bore the name of Samos in Homeric times. SAMO-THRAKI is the modern form of the ancient *Samothrace,* the 'Thracian Samos.' Seen from the sea, it stands out like one great mountain mass broken into several peaks, and rising to the height of 5240 feet.

Samoa, or HAMOA, is the largest of the Samoa or Navigator Group in the Pacific. The name is a corruption of *Sa-ia-Moa,* 'sacred to Moa,' a Samoan deity or hero, under whose guidance, according to the native legend or tradition, the people claim to have arrived in the island.

Samoyeds, a people near the White Sea, bear a name probably of Finnic origin, and related to that of the Finns (*Suomi-laiset*) and of the Lapps (*Same-lads*), meaning 'marshmen' or 'people of the tundras.' The Russian form in which the name has come to us is due to a folk-etymology, the Russians supposing the Samoyeds to be cannibals, literally 'eaters of themselves.'

Sanderson's Tower, near Cape Walsingham, on the western side of Davis Strait, was named by Davis after his patron William Sanderson, a wealthy London merchant. SANDERSON'S HOPE, in lat. 72° N., the most northerly point reached by Davis on his third voyage, is a mighty cliff on the west coast of Greenland, rising 850 feet above the sea; this he quaintly named *Sanderson his Hope of a North-West Passage,* a designation too cumbrous

for modern maps, and now clipped down to SANDERSON'S HOPE.

Sandusky, a town in the State of Ohio, stands on the shore of Lake Erie at the mouth of the Sandusky River, a native name meaning the 'cold brook.'

Sandwich, the 'sandy bay,' in Kent, is the descriptive name of one of the Cinque Ports which gave a title to Lord Sandwich. The fourth Earl, who was First Lord of the Admiralty, and afterwards Secretary of State, despatched Cook on his memorable voyages of discovery. Carteret in 1767 had given the name SANDWICH ISLAND to a small island south of New Ireland. On his second voyage, in 1774, Cook gave the same name, 'in honour of his noble patron,' to Vaté, one of the New Hebrides, anchoring in PORT SANDWICH in the island of Mallicolo ; and in 1775 he discovered SANDWICH LAND, an Antarctic group of Islands, and named SANDWICH BAY in New Georgia. In 1778, on his third voyage, he gave the name of the SANDWICH ISLANDS to the great North Pacific group, now usually called the HAWAIIAN ISLANDS, already known to the Spaniards as LOS MONJES, 'the monks.' HINCHINBROOK ISLAND, on the Queensland coast, discovered in 1770 on Cook's first voyage, was so named from the second title of Lord Sandwich, its north-eastern point being called CAPE SANDWICH. SANDWICH SOUND, in Torres Strait, was discovered and named in 1791 by Captain Edwards of the ship *Pandora.*

Sandy Cape, on GREAT SANDY ISLAND, Queensland, so called by Cook in 1770, is a descriptive name, like the numerous SANDY BAYS, SANDY POINTS, SANDY LAKES, SANDY ISLANDS, SANDY HILLS which dot our maps. SAND-HURST is the 'sandy wood.' SANDRING-HAM, Norfolk, is called in Domesday *Sant-dersincham.* It adjoins DERSING-HAM (Domesday, *Dersincham*), and was the -ham of those of the Dersingas who inhabited the sandy part of the district.

San Esteban, Islas de, Lower California, were discovered by Francisco de Ulloa at the end of December 1539, doubtless on the 26th, which is St. Stephen's Day.

San Francisco, the commercial capital of California, bears the Spanish name of St. Francis d'Assisi. The Presidio or fortified settlement was founded on September 7th, 1776, and the *Mission de los Dolores de San Francisco* in October, probably on the 4th, which is the Festival of St.

Francis in the Roman calendar. The mouth of the RIO DE SAN FRANCISCO, a large Brazilian river, was reached by Vespucci on St. Francis' Day, October 4th, 1501.

San Joaquin, a Californian river which joins the Sacramento, is a Spanish name probably derived from a mission dedicated to S. Joachim of Sienna.

San José, a town in California, was founded in 1777 by Don Felipe de Neve, the Spanish Governor of California, under the name of *Pueblo de San José de Guadalupe,* and placed under the protection of Our Lady of Guadalupe. ST. JOSEPH, an important city in the State of Missouri, was founded in 1843 by Joseph Robidoux, a French Canadian trader, and called after his name-saint.

San Julian, or PUERTO DE SAN JULIAN, is the Patagonian haven to which Magellan shifted his winter quarters on March 31st, 1520, and where the three captains mutinied. It had probably been discovered on St. Julian's Day, March 16th, when the fleet was lying in an exposed inlet a few miles further north.

San Marino, a minute but ancient republic on the Adriatic coast of Italy, surrounds the reputed hermitage of St. Marinus, a Dalmatian mason.

San Martino, or ST. MARTIN, one of the Antilles, was discovered by Columbus in 1493 on November 11th, the festival of St. Martin of Tours. TUXTLA, a volcano in Mexico, is also called SAN MARTIN, from the name of a soldier of Grijalva who first sighted it in 1518.

San Matias, Bahia de, a great Patagonian Gulf, was discovered in 1520 by Magellan, on February 24th, the feast of St. Mathias.

San Miguel, a gulf on the Pacific side of the Isthmus of Panama, is a name which may remind us that it was on September 25th, 1513, that Vasco Nuñez de Balboa crossed the isthmus, and gazed at the Pacific from 'a peak in Darien,' and four days later, on Michaelmas Day, reached the coast of the gulf which he therefore called Golfo de San Miguel. The RIO DE SAN MIGUEL in Brazil was discovered by Vespucci on September 29th, 1501. SAN MIGUEL, one of the Azores, was discovered in 1444 by Cabral on May 8th, which in the Roman calendar is the feast of the apparition of St. Michael.

San Nicolao, one of the Cape Verd Islands, was discovered by the Portuguese in 1461 on December 6th, the feast of St.

Nicholas. SAN NICOLAS, a harbour in Haiti, was discovered by Columbus on December 6th, 1492.

San Raphael, California, was a mission founded in 1817 under the protection of St. Raphael.

San Remo, a town on the Riviera, was called till the fifteenth century by the name *San Romulo,* from its sixth century bishop, the day of whose death is still a local festival. How Romulus came to be supplanted by Remus is not known, possibly from a confusion with the better known saint St. Remigius, from whom ST. REMI and DOMREMI the birthplace of Joan of Arc are named, but more probably the change of name was due to the full title of the Hermitage of St. Romulus, called *Sancti Romuli in Eremo,* being contracted to San Remo.

San Roque, a Brazilian cape, was Amerigo Vespucci's landfall on August 16th, 1501, the festival of St. Roque in the Roman calendar.

San Salvador, the Holy Saviour, was the name given by Columbus on his first voyage to the first island he discovered (October 12th, 1492). Its native name was *Guanahani.* It was formerly supposed to be CAT ISLAND, one of the Bahamas, which is marked as San Salvador on many maps. But recent investigations have made it probable that the real San Salvador of Columbus is WATLING ISLAND (*q.v.*), somewhat further to the east, though the claims of Mayaguana and of Samana or Atwood's Cay, have been stoutly maintained. Columbus also gave the name of SAN SALVADOR to the first harbour which he reached in Cuba (now called Puerto de Nipe) in the belief that he had reached the coast of Japan; the natives telling him that in ten days he would reach the mainland, which he thought was China. SAN SALVADOR is also the name of one of the Central American Republics, so called from its capital, the city of SAN SALVADOR, placed by the first settlers under the protection of the Saviour.

San Sebastião, an island on the Brazilian coast, was discovered in 1502 by Amerigo Vespucci on January 20th, the feast of St. Sebastian. St. Sebastian being supposed to give protection against the arrows of pestilence, we find his cult in various pestilential spots in Southern Europe.

Santa Cruz, one of the Antilles, near Puerto Rico, was discovered by Columbus in 1493. In 1494, on his second voyage, he called a cape on the south coast of Cuba CABO DE SANTA CRUZ, the ' cape of the Holy Cross.' The RIO DE SANTA CRUZ in Patagonia, discovered by Magellan in 1520, and SANTA CRUZ on the Isthmus of Darien, founded in May 1515, are only a few of the places named SANTA CRUZ or VERA CRUZ by the Spaniards and Portuguese.

Santa Fé, the capital of New Mexico, was founded as a Franciscan mission under the name of *Santa Fé de San Francisco,* ' the holy faith of St. Francis.' SANTA FÉ is the name of five other towns.

Santa Izabel, a recent German colony in Brazil, was so named in compliment to the Princess Imperial, Donna Isabel, Countess of Eu.

Santa Lucia, one of the Cape Verd Islands, was discovered in 1461 on St. Lucia's Day, Dec. 13th, on which day in 1498 Columbus is supposed to have discovered SANTA LUCIA, one of the Antilles. The mouth of the RIO DE SANTA LUCIA, a Brazilian river, was discovered in 1501 by Vespucci on St. Lucia's Day.

Santander, a Spanish province, takes its name from the city of SANTANDER, which arose round a fortress built by Alfonso the Catholic, near a hermitage dedicated to San Andreo (St. Andrew).

Santarem, in Brazil, is a name which has been transferred from SANTAREM near Lisbon, so called from Sant Yrene (St. Irene), about whom there is a local legend.

Santiago, the capital of Chili, was founded in 1541 by Pedro de Valdivia, and placed under the protection of the patron saint of Spain. Iago is a form of Jacobus, and Santiago of Spain was St. James the Great, the elder brother of St. John. His name has been as freely bestowed on towns of Spanish foundation, as have those of St. George, St. Denis, and St. Louis by the English and French. The Spanish devotion to St. James arose at a place in Galicia now called SANTIAGO DE COMPOSTELLA, where in 835 Theodomir, Bishop of Iria, discovered, as we are told, in a wood near Iria the body of St. James, being guided to ' the invention of the body' by an accompanying star, and hence the place was called *Campus stellæ* or COMPOSTELLA, the ' plain of the star.' The discovery stirred all Christendom, and Compostela took rank with Jerusalem, Rome, and Loreto as one of the four chief places of European pilgrimage. As a token of their visit the pilgrims took home with them scallopshells from the shore, the scallop in so many coats of arms testifying to the pilgrimage of some ancestor to the famous shrine, which was endowed with a grant of a bushel of corn from every acre of corn-land in Spain. The annual value of this tax, finally abolished in 1835, is said to have amounted at one time to £200,000. SANTIAGO, one of the Cape Verd Islands, was discovered by the Portuguese in 1456 on May 1st, the festival of St. James the Less.

Santorin, a volcanic island in the Ægean, was formerly called by the Greeks *Calliste,* the ' most beautiful,' but after the desolating eruption in 196 B.C. the name was changed to *Thera,* the ' beast.' The chief town still goes by the name of PHERA, a corruption of Thera. The name Santorin is derived from its dedication by the Latins to St. Irene. In the harbour there are three small islands called *Palæa Kaumene,* ' old burnt' island, which is the cone of the volcano formed at the time of the eruption of 196 B.C.; *Mikra Kaumene,* ' little burnt' island, formed during the eruption of 1573 ; and *Nea Kaumene,* ' new burnt' island, due to the eruption of 1707.

Santos, in Brazil, correctly TODOS OS SANTOS, ' All Saints,' was founded in 1545 by Braz Cuba. PORTO SANTO, the ' blessed harbour,' one of the Madeira group, was so named by the early Portuguese navigators from its safe harbour. Four small islands near Guadalupe, discovered, it is believed, by Columbus, on Nov. 1st, 1493 (All Saints' Day), still bear the Spanish name of LOS SANTOS.

San-tash, the ' counted stones,' is a pass in Central Asia, on which stands a cairn said to record Timur's losses in a battle previous to which every man was ordered to place a stone upon the heap, one being removed by each survivor as he returned after the victory, so that by counting the remaining stones the number of the slain was ascertained.

Saône, a broad, tranquil river, joined at Lyons by the impetuous Rhone, is a corruption of the Gaulish name, *Sauconna* or *Savona.* The older name was *Arar* (Cymric *araf,* ' gentle' or ' slow ').

Saquish Head, near Plymouth, Massachusetts, is a native name referring to the ' clams ' (*saquish*) found upon the rocks.

Saracen is a term loosely used by medieval writers to denote the Moslem races, and especially the foes of the Crusaders.

It is a Greek corruption of the Arabic *sharkeyn*, 'eastern' people, as opposed to the *maghribe*, or 'western' people. Hence it is an error to apply it, as Prof. Freeman has done in his book on the Saracens, to the Maghribe, or Moors of Spain.

Saratoga, in the State of New York, where Burgoyne surrendered to Gates in 1777, is now a fashionable watering-place. The name is said to be derived from a Mohawk word meaning a 'hill-side.'

Sarawak, Borneo, is a corruption of the Malay name, *Sarakaw*, 'the Cove.'

Sardinia (Italian SARDEGNA) bears the name of the *Sardi*, its early inhabitants, who may possibly be identified with the Shardina or Shardana, one of the northern races who attacked Egypt in the reign of Meneptah. The prehistoric bronze figures discovered in Sardinia show that the warriors wore a curious helmet, with horns on either side, resembling the helmet with two spikes with which the Shardina are represented on the Egyptian monuments. But as similar horned helmets are seen on a fragment of pottery found by Schliemann at Mycenæ, it is possible that the Shardina may be the men of Sardis.

Sarepta, on the River Volga, was a settlement founded in 1765 by the Moravian brethren, on which they bestowed the somewhat inappropriate Sidonian name of *Zarepta*, now SARFEND, which means the 'smelting-house.'

Sargans, 'the rock on the Saar,' is the Romansch name of a town in Canton St. Gallen.

Sarmiento, a conspicuous snow-clad volcanic peak in Tierra del Fuego, 7330 feet high, bears the name of Pedro Sarmiento de Gamboa, an intrepid explorer, and also a scholar who wrote a history of the Incas. Sent by Don Francisco de Toledo, Viceroy of Peru, to intercept Drake in the Straits of Magellan, he sailed from Callao in 1579, and, after surveying the Straits, returned to Spain, whence he was despatched by Philip to found a settlement in the Straits. After landing 400 colonists with 30 women at a place he called SAN FELIPE, he was captured by Sir Walter Raleigh as he was returning to Spain. The fate of the colonists was lamentable. Cavendish in 1587 found 18 starving wretches, whom he left to their fate, calling the place PORT FAMINE (*q.v.*), all the rest had perished by hunger. In 1590 Chudleigh found a solitary survivor, whom he took on board. The PUERTO DE MISERICORDIA of Sarmiento at the western end of the

Straits is the HARBOUR OF GOD'S MERCY of Davis. The volcano which now goes by the name of Sarmiento had been named by Magellan *Campana de Roldan*, 'Roldan's bell,' after one of his officers. Sarmiento named it *Volcan Nevado*, the 'snowy volcano.' A strait on the western coast of Patagonia has been called SARMIENTO CHANNEL.

Sarnen, the chief town in Canton Unterwalden, takes its name from the black poplar, *Populus nigra*, locally called the *Saarbaum*, which formerly grew on the banks of the Aa. The earliest form of the name is *in sarnono*, which occurs in a document of 848, and this has become *Sarnon* in 1210.

Sarratt, Hertfordshire, has been doubtfully identified with the *Scergeat* of the Saxon Chronicle, a name aptly describing the passage up the steep chalk cliff or 'scar' which here borders the River Chess.

Saskatchewan, a province in the Canadian Dominion, is watered by the Saskatchewan, a river flowing into Lake Winnipeg. Its native name was *Ki-sis-kah-che-wan*, 'the river which flows rapidly.'

Sasso del Ferro, a picturesque mountain, 5918 feet high, on the Lago Maggiore, is the 'rock of iron.' The Italian *sasso* (Latin *saxum*) is a common element in mountain names, especially among the Dolomites, as GRAN SASSO, SASSALBO, SASSOFERRATO, SASSANDRO, and SASSO S. MARTINO.

Saugor Island, a place of pilgrimage at the mouth of the Hugli, is a corruption of the native name *Ganga Ságara*, 'Ocean Ganges.' Formerly populous, the island is now a tiger-haunted jungle.

Saul, in County Down, was formerly called *Sabhall Patrick*, 'Patrick's barn,' from a barn given to St. Patrick as a place of worship by Dichu, an Irish chief, his first convert. DRUMSAUL, in Monaghan, is the 'barn-ridge'; and CAIRNTOUL, Aberdeenshire, is said to be *Cairn-t-Sabhall*, the 'cairn of the barn.' There is a mountain in the North of Scotland called, from its shape, SAVAL MORE, the 'great barn.'

Saumarez Island, Patagonia, as well as CAPE SAUMAREZ and the SAUMAREZ RIVER, in Arctic America, bear the name of Lord de Saumarez, a British admiral who served with distinction under Rodney and Nelson.

Saunders Island, near Sandwich Land, in the South Atlantic, was so named by Cook after his friend Sir Charles Saunders, whose name he also gave to a prominent cape near Dunedin, in New Zealand.

Savage Islands, in Hudson's Strait, were so named by Baffin in 1615 because he here encountered a party of savages (Eskimos). In 1774 Iniue, east of the Friendly Islands, was named SAVAGE ISLAND by Cook from 'the conduct and aspect of these islanders.'

Savana-la-Mar, the 'seaside plain,' is a coast town in Jamaica. The Spanish word *sabana* and the Canadian French *savana*, which mean a 'prairie,' are derived from the Low-Latin *sabana*, for *sabanum*, a 'napkin' or 'table-cloth.' SAVANNAH, the chief seaport of Georgia, U.S.A., takes its name from the river on which it stands, the Savannah, probably so called from the Shawenu, better known as the Shawnee tribe, or possibly it may be a Spanish name, which it received from the prairies through which it flows.

Savoy (French SAVOIE) is a corruption of the old name *Sapaudia*, which denoted originally the district round the Lake of Neufchâtel. According to Gatschet the name refers to the forests which clothe the hills, the Latin *sapinus* and French *sapin*, a 'spruce fir' explaining the Swiss dialect words *za-au*, a 'forest,' and *za-u*, an alp or 'upland forest.' The SAVOY in London obtained its name from the palace built by Peter, Count of Savoy, uncle of Eleanor of Provence, Queen of Henry III.

Saxony, a modern German kingdom, called SACHSEN in German, is a Wendish land, inhabited not by Saxons, but by Germanised Slavs. It has nothing but the name in common with Old Saxony or Nieder-Sachsen, which lay at the mouth of the Elbe, whence the Saxons, or most of them, crossed to Britain, establishing the kingdom of the East Saxons, now ESSEX, of the Middle Saxons, now MIDDLESEX, of the South Saxons, now SUSSEX, and of the West Saxons, or WESSEX, now cut into shire land. The Old Saxon dukes gradually extended their dominions by the conquest of Thuringian and Wendish lands, at the same time losing the Old Saxon territory. Their Thuringian conquests, which were called Ober-Sachsen, as distinguished from Nieder-Sachsen, were ultimately divided into the four Saxon Duchies, SAXE-MEININGEN, SAXE-COBURG-GOTHA, SAXE-ALTENBURG, and SAXE-WEIMAR-EISENACH. Henry the Fowler, the first Saxon Emperor, established his dominion on the upper Elbe in the modern kingdom of Saxony. In 1485 the dominions of the Saxon dukes were divided between Ernest and Albrecht (whence the so-called Ernestine and Albertine lines), the first keeping Thuringia, now divided into the four so-called Saxon duchies, and the second taking the Slavonic conquests on the Elbe, with Dresden as his capital. Hence the Saxon duchies, and still more the Saxon kingdom, are Saxon only in a dynastic sense, the one being ethnologically Thuringian, and the other Slavonic. The Saxons, according to Grimm and Zeuss, were so called from their characteristic weapon, the *sahs* or *seax*, a short sword, originally a stone weapon, the word being cognate with the Latin *saxum*, as is shown by such ancient names as the *Sahsbach* and the *Saxaha*, which mean the 'stony brook' and the 'stony river.' The name *Saxones* dates from the second century, being found in Eutropius, Ammianus Marcellinus, and Claudian. In the Life of Altman, Bishop of Patavium, we have an excellent exposition of the name, *Gladiis utebantur qui lingua eorum sahs dicebantur, a quibus Sahsones, non Saxones, appellantur.* In like manner, Nennius (*Hist. Brit.* c. 48) represents Hengist as calling to his men, '*Saxones nimeth eure Saxes,*' 'Saxons, take your swords.'

Saxon, a watering-place in Canton Valais, is a corruption of the Latin *saxum*, as is indicated by the name of a certain Miles de Saxo.

Saybrook, a town at the mouth of the Connecticut River, was founded in 1631 by colonists sent out by the patentees, Lord Say and Sele and Lord Brooke, from whose titles was compounded a name which is the earliest instance of the vicious practice followed in such South African names as POTSCHERFSTROM or ZWELLENDAM (*q.v.*). (*See* p. 26.)

Scaletta, the 'ladder,' is the name of a steep pass in Canton Graubünden. The SCHÖLLENEN in Canton Uri take their name from the *scaliones*, or ladder-like steps in the rock.

Scanderoon is the English corruption of ISKANDERÛN, the Turkish name of the port of Aleppo, called ALEXANDRETTA by the Italians. It was one of the towns founded under the name of Alexandria (*q.v.*) by Alexander the Great, who is called Iskander in Turkish.

Scandinavia, a convenient name for the Swedish and Norwegian Peninsula, has been adopted from a passage in Pliny where the correct reading is probably *Scadinavia*, which Mr. Bradley refers to the Teutonic **skadino*, 'dark.' Scadinavia, the 'land of darkness,' was possibly at first a mythical name for the dark North which was afterwards applied to the Swedish Peninsula.

Scarborough, a name not found in Domesday, appears in 1209 in a charter of King John as *Scardeburgh*, a form which would point to an O.N. name *Skardhaborg*, the burg at the clefts or gaps. The O.N. *skardh*, a 'gap' or 'place cut,' is a common element in Icelandic names. The name must originally have denoted not the modern town but the castle on the projecting and broken cliff. The SCARBOROUGH RANGE, a chain of islands in the Gilbert Group, south of the Marshall Group (*q.v.*), bears the name of the ship *Scarborough*, commanded by Captain Marshall by whom they were discovered in 1788.

Scesaplana, a mountain between the Vorarlberg and the Graubünden, bears a Romansch name equivalent to *Saxa piana*, 'smooth rock.'

Schaffhausen, a Swiss canton, takes its name from the town at the falls of the Rhine, which necessitate the debarkation of all merchandise. *Scefhusin, id est navium domus*, is the old explanation of the name. These 'ship houses' were the warehouses or sheds in which the cargoes of vessels coming up the Rhine were stored.

Schams, in the Graubünden, is the valley of the 'six streams,' as appears by a tenth century document in which it is called *Sex Amnes*.

Schapenham Bay, Fuegia, was discovered in 1624 by the Dutch Admiral Gheen Huygen Schapenham.

Scheideck, the 'dividing ridge,' is a pass in the Bernese Oberland between Grindelwald and the Haslithal. Hardly less familiar to Swiss travellers is the RIGI SCHEIDECK.

Scheldt, or SCHELDE, a Belgian river, called L'ESCAUT in French, is the *Scaldis* of Cæsar, a name which has been explained as the 'divided' river, in reference to the two mouths by which it enters the North Sea. The root *sgal*, 'to divide,' is found both in Teutonic and Celtic.

Schiedam, in Holland, takes its name from the dam or embankment at the confluence of the Schie and the Maas.

Schleswig (Danish SLESWIG), usually spelt Sleswick in English, formerly a Danish crownland, is so called from its capital, which stands on a long narrow inlet of the Baltic called the Schley,

Schlei, or Sley. The tenth century form was *Slia*. which means a 'pool' or 'swamp.' The last syllable is probably the Old Saxon *wik* (O.H.G. *wich*), a 'village' or 'town,' and not the O.N. *vik*, Danish *vig*, a 'creek' or 'bay,' as is indicated by the fact that in the ninth century the place was called *Sliesdorf*, or *Sliesthorp*, which was translated in the eleventh century by *Sliaswig* and *Sliaswic*.

Schlüsselburg, 'key castle,' is the German name given by Peter the Great to the fortress he built at the mouth of the Neva, regarding it as the key giving the command of the river.

Schmalkalden, a town on the River SCHMALKALD, called in the ninth century *Smalacalta*, meaning probably the 'small stream.'

Schönbrunn, near Vienna, the suburban residence of the Austrian Emperors, so called from a 'beautiful spring' in the grounds of the palace, was erected in 1744 by Maria Theresa on the site of a former hunting-seat.

Schouten Islands, north of New Guinea, were discovered in 1616 by the Dutch explorers Le Maire and Schouten. SCHOUTEN ISLAND, east of Tasmania, was discovered by Tasman in 1642, and named after his illustrious predecessor.

Schreckhorn, one of the highest summits in the Bernese Oberland, is probably the 'riven' or 'shattered' peak (O.H.G. *scric*, a 'cleft'), and not the 'peak of terror,' as is affirmed in the Swiss guidebooks.

Schuylkill, Pennsylvania, retains its Dutch name, 'skulk-creek,' the skulking creek, or creek that hides itself.

Schwaben, now a Bavarian province, preserves the name of the great Swabian Duchy, the South German land conquered by the *Suevi* or *Suebi* of Tacitus. The meaning of the name is doubtful, but probably signifies 'freemen.'

Schwalbach, a watering-place in Nassau on a stream of the same name, is not, as usually said, the beck frequented by swallows, but, as is shown by *Sualabah*, the eighth century spelling, from the O.H.G. *swal*, cognate with our verb to swell. The SWALE in Kent and Yorkshire may be from the same source, as well as the German river the SCHWALE, formerly the *Suala*.

Schwarzburg, a Thuringian principality, ultimately derives its name from a castle on the SCHWARZA or 'black river,'

a tributary of the Saale. From the castle the name passed to the family which possessed it, and from them to the principality over which they ruled.

Schwerin, the capital of Mecklenburg-Schwerin, is the German form of the Slavonic name *Zwarin* or *Swarin*, given to a 'game preserve' of the Wendish princes. SCHWERIN, in Posen, is a name of the same signification.

Scilly Isles, a Cornish group, have been doubtfully identified with the island called *Silura* in the compilation of Solinus, which, he tells us, is separated from the land of the Dumnonii (Devon) by a stormy sea. Silura, which may be South Wales and not Scilly, is doubtless the land of the Silures, the dolichocephalic race which occupied parts of Britain before the arrival of the Celts. Sulpicius Severus speaks of *Sylina*. The O.N. name Syllingar may mean the islands of herrings or of conger eels (Cornish *sillis*). In Malory's Arthurian legend we have *Surluce*, which seems to be related to the French name SORLINGUES. It is not easy to connect any of these forms with the modern name SCILLY, which, strictly speaking, denotes not the whole of the group, but only a small inaccessible outlying rocky islet one acre in extent to the north-west of the rest, which is called Scilly, a name which may be compared with two lofty skerries off the coast of Kerry called the SKELLIGS (Old Irish *sceilig*, a 'skerry' or rock in the sea). Probably the modern name of the group has been assimilated to that of this Scilly rock, which is the nearest to passing ships. Captain Wallis in 1767 gave the name of SCILLY ISLANDS to a dangerous cluster of the Society Islands, on account of their resemblance to the Cornish Group.

Scio, an island in the Ægean, is an Italian corruption of the old Greek name *Chios.*

Scoresby Sound, on the east coast of Greenland, and other Arctic names commemorate the services of an English scientific whaling captain who in 1822 surveyed 400 miles of the unexplored eastern coast of Greenland.

Scotland, as the designation of the northern part of Britain, is a term of comparatively recent origin. Till towards the close of the tenth century, the term Scotia or Scotland does not denote any part of what is now called Scotland, but is always applied to Ireland. Not till after the twelfth century does it become the name of the whole of the modern kingdom, previously denoting part of the lowlands

north of the Firth of Forth. The Scots, an Irish sept, invaded Argyll in the fourth century, and in 360 A.D. we hear of them as having passed the Roman walls in conjunction with the Picts. In the sixth century they occupied only Argyll. In the ninth century Kenneth Macalpine united the royal lines of the Picts and Scots, and absorbed the kingdom of the Picts, and to this kingdom were afterwards added the English earldoms of the Lothians, south of the Forth, the northern part of the British kingdom of Strathclyde, and the Norwegian earldom of Caithness. The meaning of the name Scot is doubtful. Isidore of Seville, writing in the sixth century, says the Scotti were so called because they tattooed their bodies with various figures ; and Professor Rhys explains this explanation by the help of the Welsh word *ysgwthr*, a cutting or sculpturing, making the Scots a people who were cut or scarred. On the other hand Dr. Stokes has suggested that the name means 'rulers,' or 'possessors.' An old explanation, now rejected, points out that in the Pictish Chronicle the Scots are called *Secotti*, a name resembling that of the *Attecotti*, which is explained as 'ancient inhabitants' or 'aborigines,' by help of the Cornish *coth*, 'old' or ancient, *at* being a formative prefix meaning 'those who are.' Hence it has been argued that *Se-cotti* might be for Siolcotti, *siol* being a common prefix in tribe names, meaning 'seed, progeny, or tribe,' which we have in such names as SHILLALAGH or SHELBURNE (*q.v.*).

Scutari, the capital of Albania, was the Roman *Scodra*, probably an Illyrian name, supposed to mean the 'hill town.' But SCUTARI on the Bosphorus is from the Persian *Uskudar*, a 'messenger,' because, being opposite Constantinople, it was the station from which the Turkish couriers started for Anatolia and the East.

Seaton, in South Devon, is supposed to be the Roman station of *Moridunum*, the 'dun by the sea,' of which the modern name would be a sort of translation or adaptation. LOCH SEAFORTH, 'sea firth,' is the reduplicated Scandinavian name of a salt-water loch in the Isle of Lewis, whence the chief of the Mackenzies, attainted in 1716, took the title of Earl. Mr. W. E. Gladstone's father, whose mother was a Mackenzie, borrowed the name for his estate near Liverpool on which the Lancashire watering-place called SEAFORTH is built.

Sebald's Islands, in the Falkland

Group, were discovered in 1600 by Sebald de Weert, a Dutch seaman.

Sebastopol, the 'august' or 'imperial city,' was founded and named by Potemkin soon after the conquest of the Crimea in 1783. SEBASTIEH, the modern name of *Samaria,* which meant a 'watch tower,' preserves the name *Sebaste,* the Greek translation of *Augusta,* bestowed on the town by Herod in honour of the Emperor Augustus, from whom also was named the city of *Sebasteia* in Cappadocia, called *Sevaste* by Marco Polo, but now corrupted by the Turks to SÍVÁS or SÍWÁS.

Séchelles is an East African group of islands often wrongly spelt SEYCHELLES, and sometimes on English maps called The SEYCHELLE ISLANDS, owing to the erroneous supposition that Seychelles is a plural form. The group is usually said to bear the name of Count Hérault de Séchelles, an officer of the French East Indian Fleet, afterwards Minister of the French Marine. Colonel Yule has, however, shown that the true godfather of the group was Moreau de Séchelles, Con-trôleur-Général des Finances in 1754-56. One of the islands bears the name SIL-HOUETTE, from M. de Silhouette, who succeeded Moreau as Controller of the Finances; and another is called PRASLIN, from the Duc de Choiseul-Praslin, who was Minister of Marine from 1766 to 1770. The name ILES SÉCHELLES was adopted in 1767, first appearing on a chart made in 1756. The group is sometimes called the MAHÉ ARCHIPELAGO, from the largest island, which bears the name of M. Mahé de Labourdonnais, a governor of Mauri-tius, who in 1744 despatched a vessel to ex-plore the archipelago. In 1756 M. Magon, Governor of Mauritius and Bourbon, sent the frigate *Le Cerf* to take possession of the Isle de Mahé.

Se-chuen, the largest province in China, is the 'land of the four rivers.'

Secunderabad (SIKANDARÁBÁD), in Bengal, the 'place of Alexander,' was named after Nizam Sikander Jah. SECUNDERABAD, in the North-West Pro-vinces, was founded in 1498 by Sikandar Lodhi of Jaunpur, who belonged to the Lodhi dynasty of Afghan princes who reigned from 1450 to 1526. SIKANDRA, near Agra, and SIKANDARPUR date also from his reign.

Seelisberg, the 'hill of the little lake,' overlooking the Lake of Lucerne, takes its name from a mountain tarn called SEELI, the Swiss dialectic form of the diminutive *See-lein,* a 'lakelet.'

Seguro, Porto, in Brazil, is the 'safe harbour' in which Cabral in 1500 took refuge from a storm.

Seine is the *Sequana* of Cæsar, which became *Sigona* in the seventh century, *Signe* in the ninth, and *Seigne* or *Seine* in the fourteenth.

Seistan (Sístán), a contraction of *Sejistán* or *Segistán,* a district in Afghanistan, is a corruption of the old Persian name *Sagas-tán* or *Sakastána,* the 'land of the Sacæ,' a Scythian people who overran Irán in the second century B.C.

Selefkeh, in Cilicia, represents the ancient *Seleucia,* one of the cities named from Seleucus Nicator.

Selinunto, in Sicily, represents the Greek city of *Selinus,* on the River Selinus, ap-parently a Greek name derived from the 'wild parsley' which grew on its banks and is represented on its coins. Ulti-mately, however, the name may be from the Phœnician *sela,* 'a rock,' which is no doubt the source of the rock-perched Phœnician city of *Solœis* near Palermo, now called SOLANTO.

Selkirkshire, a Scotch county, takes its name from SELKIRK, the county town, anciently written *Seleschirche* and *Schales-chyrche,* denoting a church (erected before the twelfth century) among a collection of forest huts (shiels or shealings). (*See* SHIELDS.) The SELKIRK SETTLEMENT, founded in 1812 on the Red River, was named from Lord Selkirk.

Selsey, Sussex, called *Seolesíg* in the Chronicle and in a charter of 683, is rightly explained by Bæda as the 'seal's island' (A.S. *seoles,* gen. of *seol,* a 'seal').

Seltz, which has given a name to Seltzer-water, was the Roman *Saletio,* 'at the saline spring.'

Selwood, often tautologically called Selwood Forest, is a tract of ancient woodland near Frome. The A.S. name, *Sealh-wudu,* ostensibly signifying the 'sallow wood' (A.S. *sealh,* 'sallow,' *salix*), may be an accommodated name from the earlier Roman designation *silva,* or from the British name *sauel-coed,* which we have in the *Caer Pen-savel-coit* of Nennius.

Semigallia, a district adjoining Cour-land, signifies the 'end of the earth' (Lithuanian *zeme,* 'land,' and *galas,* 'end').

Seminole, towns in Georgia and in South Carolina, are named from the Seminole tribe, who were originally located in Florida. The name *Semanole,* meaning 'runaways' or 'fugitives,' literally 'those who are separated,' was given to them

GLOSSARY

because they had separated from the Creek Indians.

Semipalatinsk, the 'seven palaces,' a town on the Irtish, was so called from the ruins of ancient buildings in the neighbourhood.

Sempach, in Canton Lucerne, which gives a name to the neighbouring lake called the SEMPACHER SEE, is the place where, owing to the marshy ground, Leopold of Hapsburg was defeated in 1386 by the Swiss. According to Gatschet, the town took its name from a brook overgrown with rushes and sedge (O. H.G. *semida*).

Senaar or SENNAR, a region in the Soudan, is sometimes referred to the Turkish *sinir*, a 'boundary' or 'frontier,' but the name is properly Dar-Sennár, the 'land like fire,' or, if Nubian, 'land of the river isle.'

Seneca Falls, oh the SENECA RIVER which drains SENECA LAKE, all in the State of New York, preserve the name of the Senecas, an Iroquois tribe whose name is said to mean 'people of the great hill.'

Senegal, a West African river, bears a ghost-name which we owe to a misconception of the Portuguese. It formed the division between the negroes and a Berber tribe called the *Azanague,* a name corrupted into *Zanaga* or *Senaga.* At the mouth of the river, discovered in the fifteenth century by Lançarote, he put on shore one of these people, a Moor who was called the Sanaga, from whom the river came to be called the Senegal, a name which the native tribes do not recognise as that of the river, which is formed by the junction of the BA-FING, or 'black river,' with the BA-KHOY, or 'white river.' Its principal tributary is the BA-ULE, or 'red river.'

Senegambia is a modern compound invented to denote the district between the Rivers Senegal and Gambia.

Senlis (Oise) was a town in the territory of the *Silvanectes,* a Gaulish tribe.

Sens, a French city on the Yonne, was the capital of a Gaulish tribe called the *Senones,* whose name is better preserved by the surrounding district, called in the sixth century *Senonensis pagus,* and now styled LE SÉNONAIS.

Septimer, a pass over the Alps, is believed to owe its name to a road constructed by the Emperor Septimius Severus.

Sequeira Islands, sometimes called LOS MARTIRES, a group in the Carolines, were accidentally discovered in 1527 by Gomes de Sequeira, who had been driven out of his course by a storm.

Sergipe, a Brazilian province, is so called from the town of SERGIPE DEL REY, on the RIO DO SERGIPE, which bears the name of a native chief.

Seringapatam, a corruption of *Sri-ranga-patnam,* was the capital of the kingdom of Mysore during the reigns of Hyder Ali and his son Tippu. *Sri-ranga-pattana* would mean 'the town of Sri-Ranga,' one of the names of Vishnu, but it is possible that *ranga* stands for *lanka,* in which case the true meaning would be the 'town on the Holy Isle.' The SERINGAPATAM SHOAL, Tasman's Land, was discovered in 1840 by the ship *Seringapatam.* The town and island of SERINGHAM (*Sri-rangam*) owes its name to a temple of Vishnu, worshipped here under his name of Sri-ranga, 'celestial pleasure.'

Sermesut, correctly SERMESOK, near Cape Farewell, means 'ice island' in Eskimo.

Serrana, a lonely island in the Caribbean Sea, bears the name of Pedro Serrano, a shipwrecked Spaniard, who existed on it for seven years.

Servia, a Danubian kingdom, is the land of the Serbs, a national Slavonic name signifying 'the people.'

Sesheke, the 'white sandbanks,' is a town on the Zambesi.

Setubal, a Portuguese seaport, miscalled St. Ubes by English sailors, was the ancient *Cetobriga.*

Sevenoaks, Kent, formerly *Seovan-áccan,* is a name which must have been derived from a clump of 'seven oaks' growing on the hill.

Severinowka, a town near Odessa, was founded by Count Severyn Potocky.

Severn, the largest river in England, bears a Celtic name of uncertain origin. The English form Severn descends directly from the A.S. *Sæfern,* the Welsh name being *Hafren,* and the Roman *Sabrina.* Some scholars connect the name Sabrina with the Irish *sabhrann,* a 'boundary,' and consider that the river obtained its name because it formed the western boundary of the Belgic kingdom of Cunobelin. The Romans would take this Celtic name and transform it into Sabrina, while in Welsh it would become Hafren, the *s* being softened into *h* according to phonetic law. This theory is supported by the name of SAVERNAKE FOREST, called in A.S. *Safernoc,* which points to a British *Sabrinacon*, signifying a border or boundary forest. Moreover, the River Lee at Cork, which divided two tribes, is called *Saverennus* by Giraldus Cambrensis, apparently meaning the 'boundary river.' The name of the RIVER SÈVRE in France might be explained in the same way. Another theory connects the Welsh name Hafren with that of Somerset, called in Welsh *Gwlad-yr-Hâf*, the 'southern land,' or 'land of summer,' the Welsh *haf*, 'summer,' answering to the Sanskrit *sama* and the Zend *hama*. The Hafren would thus be the river of Hâf (Somerset), or possibly the river of the south.

Seville is called in Spanish SEVILLA, a form which has kept close to the Phœnician name *Sephela*, which signified a 'plain' or 'lowland,' being used in the Old Testament to denote the plain between Joppa and Gaza (Joshua v. 16 and 1 Macc. xii. 38). The Roman name *Hispalis* explains the Moorish corruption *Ishbíliya*.

Shaftesbury, Dorset, which appears in the Chronicle in the dative case, *æt Sceaftesbyrig*, is ostensibly from the A.S. *sceaftes*, gen. of *sceaft*, a 'pole,' or the 'shaft' of a spear.

Shan States, between Siam, Burma, and China, are inhabited by a people belonging to the Tai family, who speak a monosyllabic language intermediate between Chinese and Burmese, into which Pali and Sanskrit words have been introduced. In the compound names of this region the substantive comes first, followed by the adjective, and there are perplexing mutations among the consonants. Thus from *Loi, Doi*, or *Noi*, a 'mountain,' we have LOI-KOM, the 'golden mountain,' and LOI-KOM-NGAM, the 'beautiful golden mountain.' LOI-CHAN is the 'steep hill,' and TAT-LOI, the 'hill pagoda.' *Nong* is a 'lake,' whence NONG-CHANG, the 'elephant lake,' and LOI-CHANG-MOO, the 'mountain of the crouching elephant,' so called from its shape. A 'ford' or 'ferry' is *ta*, whence TA-PA, the 'rock ferry,' and TA-KWAI, the 'buffalo's ford.' WUNG-HOO-A-KWAI, from *wung*, a 'pool,' is the 'pool of the buffalo's head.' LOI-HOO-A SOO-A is the 'tiger head mountain,' so called from its aspect, and LOI-WUNG-NGOO is 'snake pool hill.' *Meh* means a 'river,' whence MEH-KOM, the 'golden river,' MEH-PIK, the 'pepper river,' and MEH-SAI, the 'variegated river,' quartz and sandstone cropping out in its bed. A smaller stream is *huay*, whence HUAY-

BAU-KYOW, the 'stream of the ruby mines.' *Ban* or *Man* is a 'village,' whence BAN-NONG-LONG, the 'village of the lake of the monk's coffin.' LOI-KAUNG-HIN is the 'hill of the stone heap,' from a cairn on its summit. LOI-PAH-KHOW is the 'mountain of the white cloud,' its head being usually shrouded in mist. (*See* SIAM.)

Shantar Islands, in the Sea of Okhotsk, derive their pleonastic name from Shantar, the largest of the group, which signifies 'island' in Gilyak.

Shan-tung, in China, is the district 'west of the mountains,' as SHAN-SI is that 'east of the mountains.' The main chain in Formosa is called TA-SHAN, the 'great mountain.' KIN-SHAN, 'golden mountains,' is the Chinese translation of the Turkic name ALTAI, whose eastern continuation is called in Chinese IN-SHAN, the 'silver mountains.' HOANG-SHAN means the 'yellow mountain,' YEN-SHAN the 'salt mountain,' while the snowy range between Manchuria and Corea is called the CHANG-PEI-SHAN, or 'great white mountains.' THIAN-SHAN, 'celestial mountains,' is the Chinese name of the great range of Central Asia, known to the Turkic tribes as the TENGRI-TAGH, or 'mountains of heaven.' THIAN-SHAN-NAN-LOO is the 'country south of the Thian-Shan,' while THIAN-SHAN-PE-LOO is the 'country north of the Thian-Shan.'

Shark Bay, West Australia, is a descriptive name given by Dampier in 1699.

Shaw River, West Australia, was named by Gregory, in 1861, after the Secretary of the Royal Geographical Society.

Sheffield, Yorkshire, called *Scafeld* in Domesday, stands at the confluence of the Sheaf with the Don, but SHEFFIELD, Sussex, means the 'sheep field.'

Shelagskoi, a Siberian cape on the Arctic Ocean, took its name from the Shelagi, a tribe now extinct.

Shelburne in County Wexford, which gives a second title to the Marquess of Lansdowne, is an Anglicised form of the Irish tribal name *Siol-Brain*, the 'descendants of Bran.' Another tribal name *Siol-Elaigh*, the 'descendants of Elach,' is the source of the name SHILLELAGH, a barony in County Wicklow, once celebrated for its oak woods, whence we have the Irish dialect word *shillelagh* for an oak cudgel.

Shenandoah River joins the Potomac at Harper's Ferry, draining the fertile Shenandoah Valley in Virginia, which was the scene of such obstinate fighting during the Civil War. The name is believed by the Virginians to mean the 'Father of the floods,' and has also been explained as the 'Daughter of the Stars,' but is probably the 'spruce pine river.'

Sheppey (A.S. *Sceáp-íg*) is the 'isle of sheep.' The Northern SKIPTON which corresponds to the Southern SHIPTON or SHEPTON is usually from the A.S. *sceáptún*, an 'enclosure for sheep.' SHEPTON MALLET in Somerset obtained the distinctive suffix from having belonged to the Barons Malet. SHEEPWASH, in Worcestershire, is *Sceáp-wæsu* in an A.S. charter, a 'place for washing sheep.'

Shetland Isles, otherwise the ZETLAND ISLES, north of the Orkneys, so called from the largest island of the group, which is an English corruption of the Norse name *Hjaltland* (afterwards *Hetland*), probably the 'land of Hjalti,' a ninth century Viking, nicknamed from the O.N. *hjalt*, the boss or knob of a sword, whence our word *hilt*. It is possible that Hjaltland may be a descriptive name derived from the characteristic knobs or bosses of rock. The SOUTH SHETLANDS, an Antarctic group, were discovered in 1819 by William Smith, and named from their resemblance to the northern islands.

Shield, Cape, in the Gulf of Carpentaria, was named by Flinders in 1803 after Capt. W. Shield, a commissioner of the navy.

Shields is the name of two towns at the mouth of the Tyne. NORTH SHIELDS, on the Northumberland shore, in the parish of Tynemouth, probably takes its name from some fishermen's huts or 'shiellings.' SOUTH SHIELDS, on the Durham shore, in the parish of Jarrow, was called St. Hild's from a chapel dedicated to St. Hilda. The similar names of the two contiguous towns were inevitably assimilated, Shiels becoming North Shields, and St. Hild's becoming South Shields. Two centuries ago South Shields was officially designated as St. Hilds, commonly called Sheelds. The *d* in North Shields is intrusive, and is absent in SELKIRK (*q.v.*) and in GALASHIELS, the 'huts on the River Gala.' The O.N. *skáli*, a 'wooden hut,' becomes *scale* in Cumberland, as in SCALES, BONSCALE, or GUDDERSCALE.

Shiloh, in Tennessee, a Biblical name derived from a log meeting-house, was the scene of one of the most desperate battles of the American Civil War.

Shíráz, in Persia, is said by Edrisi to signify the 'lion's paunch,' because like

the lion it consumed much but produced nothing. Another etymology hardly more probable, derives the name from *shir*, 'milk,' because of the rich pastures round the town.

Shireoaks, in Notts, stands at the point where the three shires of Nottingham, York, and Derby meet. SHERWOOD or SHIREWOOD FOREST, Notts, formed an almost impenetrable barrier between the northern and southern provinces. But SHERBORNE in Dorset, and SHIRBURN in Yorkshire, are from the A.S. *scir-burne*, the 'clear brook.'

Shoalwater Bay, west of the mouth of the Mackenzie River, is where Franklin's boats in 1826 ran aground, and were pillaged by the Eskimos. There are many similar names, such as SHOAL BAY, SHOAL RIVER, or SHOAL POINT, which need no explanation.

Shoeburyness, Essex, is a cape which takes its name from a *burh* or earthwork constructed by the Danes in 894. In the Saxon Chronicle the name appears as *Sceobyrig*, which seems to be Scandinavian, and may be compared with the Shetland word *skaw*, 'a promontory,' which we have in the SKAW OF UNST. This is the O.N. *skagi*, a 'ness' or 'promontory,' from *skaga*, 'to jut out,' whence CAPE SKAGEN in Denmark, and the SKAGER RACK (*q.v.*), called THE SKAW by English sailors. The township of SCAGGLETHORPE (Domesday, *Schachetorp*), in the East Riding, lies at the extremity of a projecting spur of the chalk escarpment, and at the foot of the next projection of the chalk we have the village of KNAPTON (Domesday, *Cnapetone* and *Cnapton*), an English equivalent of the Danish Scagglethorpe, from the A.S. *cnæp*, O.N. *knappr*, a 'knob,' whence the KNAB on Windermere and NAB-SCAR, Rydal.

Shoreham, Sussex, is usually explained as the 'ham at the shore,' a plausible and appropriate name. But the word *shore* first appears in Middle English, and its existence in A.S. can only doubtfully be inferred from *Scorham*, the name of Shoreham in a charter of 822 A.D. In A.S. *scoru* means a 'notch.'

Shrewsbury, the county town of SHROPSHIRE, was a seat of the Welsh Princes of Powys, and bore the Welsh name of *Pengwern*, 'alder hill,' while the forest which covered the greater part of the county was called *Argoed Bowys*, the 'Powys woodland' (*ar*, 'at,' and *coed*, a 'wood'). Pengwern, when taken by the English, was called *Scrobbesburh*, or in the dative

Scrobbesbyrig, either from a personal name, or, as explained by Professor Skeat, the town of underwood, scrub, or shrub. *Scrob* was converted by Norman scribes, who could not pronounce *scr,* into *srob, sirop,* and *slop,* which was euphonised into SALOP, which is properly the name of the town and not of the county; while the English form *Scrobbesbyrig* became SHREWSBURY. The people of the district were called *Scrobsǽte,* the 'settlers in the scrub,' and the county name might easily have become Shrubset, like Dorset and Somerset, but it so happened that the shire finally took its name, not from the people, but from the county town, and *Scrobbesbyrigscir* became *Scrobbescyr,* whence the Domesday name *Sciropescire,* which finally became SHROPSHIRE.

Siáh-Koh or KOH-I-SIÁH, in Afghanistan, is the 'Black Mountain.' The people called the SIÁH-POSH KAFIRS, the 'black-clothed unbelievers,' in the north of Afghanistan, derive their name from their black cloaks.

Siam is the European corruption, through the Portuguese *Sião,* of the Malay *Siyam,* which is identical with the name SHIAN or SHAN (*q.v.*) given by the Burmese to their eastern neighbours. The Shans and the Siamese call themselves *Tai* or *Thai,* which means 'free,' of which the name Shian or Shan is a translation, or rather a dialectic form. F. Müller, however, considers that Shan is a corruption of the Sanskrit *shyama,* 'brown.' Siam being the name of a people and not of a country, the term Siamese is as anomalous as our reduplicated name of Dutchmen (*q.v.*). The parallel term Shan States is correct, but the people should be called Shan, and not Shans, as is usual.

Sibbald, a cape in South Victoria, bears the name of an officer of the *Erebus.*

Siberia, in Russian SIBIR, is so called from *Sibir* or *Ssibir,* a town on the Irtish near Tobolsk, which no longer exists. Sibir was the capital of a Tartar Khanate of the same name, which was conquered in the sixteenth century by Yermak, the Hetman of the Don Cossacks. A group of islands off the mouth of the Lena, discovered in 1770, goes by the name of NEW SIBERIA.

Sicily is the English form of *Sicilia,* so called from the *Siculi,* who possessed a great part of the island when the Greek colonists arrived.

Sidi Ibrahim, in Algeria, is so called from the tomb of a Moslem saint of that name. In village names derived from the tombs of Moslem saints a common prefix is *Sid-i,* 'my lord,' which answers to the Christian prefix *Saint* or *San.* (*See* PORT SAID.)

Sidlaw Hills, in Forfarshire, is a pleonastic form, Sidlaw meaning 'fairy hill.' (Gaelic *sith,* a 'fairy').

Siebenbürgen is the German name of an Hungarian crownland usually called TRANSYLVANIA (*q.v.*) by English writers. It denotes the land of the 'seven burghs' or fortified towns which were settled in the twelfth century by German colonists from the Lower Rhine. As early as 1242 we find these burghs called by the collective name of *Septem urbes, Septem castra,* or *Terra septem castrorum.* Rösler, who is followed by Professor Freeman (*Historical Geography,* p. 435) arbitrarily proposed to derive the name from *Cibinburc,* an imaginary name of Hermanstadt, which stands on the River Cibin, and whose classical name was *Cibinium.* The name has also been derived from the Zibin mountains, on the northern frontier, which, it is alleged, were called *Zibin-Bergen* by the Saxon colonists.

Siena, in Tuscany, preserves the old name *Sena,* supposed to be Etruscan, which afterwards became *Sena Julia.* SINIGAGLIA, a town on the Adriatic coast north of Ancona, was also called *Sena,* and was distinguished from the Tuscan *Sena* as *Sena Gallica* (in Pliny *Senogallia*), being a town of the Galli Senones, a Gaulish tribe.

Sierra Leone (Spanish *Sierra Leona*; Portuguese *Serra Leão*), an English settlement on the Guinea coast, was named in 1462 by the Portuguese navigator Pedro de Cintra, who called it the 'lion range,' the roaring of the surf on the reef at the end of the rocky promontory formed by the Kong mountains being supposed to be the roaring of lions in the forest. The word *Sierra* (Portuguese *Serra*) is often supposed to denote a toothed or sawlike range of mountains, but is probably a corruption of the Arabic *sahra,* which we have in the name SAHARA (*q.v.*). The SIERRA NEVADA in Spain is the 'snowy range,' and the SIERRA MORENA is the 'dark,' or 'brown range.' In the New World the word was used to denote the lower ranges of the Andes and of the Rocky mountains. Thus the SIERRA MADRE in Mexico is the central chain or 'mother range,' and the coast range in Brazil is called SERRA DO MAR, or 'sea range.'

Sigmaringen, the capital of a German principality, appears in the eleventh century as *Sigimaringen,* a clan name derived from the personal name Sigmar.

Sihánaka, the province in Madagascar which contains Lake Alaotra, is from the Malagasy *hánaka,* a 'lake.'

Sikhs, a warlike sect or brotherhood in the Punjab, are the 'disciples' of Nának Sháh, their Guru, 'lawgiver and prophet,' who was born in 1469.

Silchester, the Roman *Calleva Atrebatum,* is a name of unknown meaning, related perhaps to that of the great earthwork called SILBURY HILL. It has been variously referred to the A.S. *sel,* 'good,' 'noble,' 'great,' to *sigel,* the 'sun'; to the people called the Silures, and to the Latin *silva,* Silchester being on the border of Pamber Forest· but it probably preserves a fragment of a more ancient name, as it is the *Caer Segeint* or *Caer Segont* of Nennius, and according to Henry of Huntingdon, was called *Segontium,* while British coins with the legend *sego* are assigned to it.

Silesia is the Latinised name of the Prussian province called SCHLESIEN in German (Czech, *Slézsko,* Polish, *Szlask).* The form *Slezin* dates from the eleventh century. Dietmar of Merseburg mentions the *Pagus Silensis,* which he says was so called from a certain mountain, doubtless the Mons Zlenz or Mons Silentii, afterwards the Zobtenberg. Ptolemy mentions the Silings (*Sliusli*), a Vandal tribe who occupied Lower Silesia in the second century, and afterwards wandered into Spain.

Silistria, a fortress on the Danube, was the Roman *Durostolum* or *Durostorum,* a name made by the Bulgarians into *Drster,* of which SILISTRIA is believed to be a Turkish corruption.

Sils, a village in the Graubünden, which gives a name to the Silser See, is called *Seillia* in 1161 and *Silles* in 1216, forms which point to the word *seglias,* equivalent to the *selliones* or tilths so frequently mentioned in English charters, the Romansch *seglia* corresponding to the German *zelge.*

Siluan or SILWAN, a village close to Jerusalem, preserves the old name of *Siloam* or *Siloah,* so called from the subterranean 'conduit' or tunnel constructed by one of the Jewish kings, probably either Manasseh or Hezekiah, in order to bring water from the Pool of the Virgin, as is recorded in the celebrated inscription.

Silvaplana, 'the wood on the plain,' is a village in the Engadine, which takes its Romansch name from a wood, now destroyed, on the plain above the Lake of Silvaplana.

Simbirsk is a town on the Volga founded in 1648, and so called from *Sinbir,* a neighbouring Tartar settlement. It is the capital of a Russian Government of the same name.

Simmenthal, Canton Bern, is the valley of the RIVER SIMME, so called, it is said, from its 'seven' sources.

Simplon, the Alpine pass selected by Napoleon for his great military road into Italy, takes its name from Simpeln, a village at the foot of the pass.

Simpson Strait and SIMPSON RIVER in Arctic America, bear the name of Sir George Simpson, Governor of the Hudson Bay territories.

Sinai is usually supposed to have been named from the Hebrew *seneh,* the 'acacia tree,' but is more probably the mountain of Sin, the moon-god of the Babylonians, who, about the time of the sixth Egyptian dynasty, worked turquoise and copper mines at Sinai. At Telloh, in Chaldæa (4500-2500 B.C.), a diorite sculpture has been found with an inscription recording how the stone was brought from Sinai, which was then probably the name of one of the mountains of Midian, east of the Gulf of Akabah. The present traditional site, to which early Christian anchorites transferred the name, is later than the apostolic age.

Sind, SCINDE, or SINDH, is the name of the lower valley of the Indus. The Sanskrit word *sindhu,* the 'sea,' was applied to the great sealike river, and then to the country on its banks. In Persian, Sindhu became Hindu, whence HINDUSTAN, a Persian form ; and from the Persians it passed to the Greeks, and then to the Romans, giving us the names INDUS for the river, INDIANS for the people, and INDIA for their country, afterwards extended to the valley of the Ganges.

Singapore (SINGAPUR), the 'lion city, is the name of an island and city in the Straits Settlement. The form Singapore was adopted by Sir Stamford Raffles for the city which he founded in 1819 on an island which since the Middle Ages had been called Sinhapura, from a town of that name built in the fourteenth century by Malay or Javanese settlers.

Sion, the capital of Canton Valais, is called in German SITTEN, which preserves better than the French form Sion the Celto Roman name *Sedunum.*

Sioux City, in Iowa, and SIOUX RIVER, a tributary of the Missouri, preserve the name of the great Sioux confederation. (*See* DAKOTA.)

Siphanto, an island in the Ægean, retains the old Greek name *Siphnos.*

Siwálik Hills, the Anglo-Indian name of the outer tertiary range of foot-hills running parallel to the main chain of the Himálaya, is the twelfth century Moslem name *Siwálikh,* which denoted a territory embracing Nágore and Jodhpur, derived from the *Saiválas,* a national name found in the Vishnu Puranas. In 1834 this name was bestowed on the foot-hills by Falconer, who called a huge Saurian, whose remains were found in the tertiary strata, the *Sivatherium,* under the mistaken belief that the name was derived from the god Siva, and not from the Saiválas.

Skager Rack, the channel between Norway and Jutland, means 'cape strait.' The word *rack* denotes a crooked channel, and the Skager Rack is so called from the town of SKAGEN, situated on Cape Skagen (O.N. *skagi,* a 'promontory'), the SKAW of English sailors, which forms the northern point of Jutland. (*See* SHOEBURY.)

Skalafell, Iceland, is a descriptive name signifying 'saddle mountain' (O.N. *skál,* a 'hollow,' whence the English word *scales*).

Skeleton Point, Tasman Land, is where Stokes in 1838 found under a tree the skeleton of a native.

Skene Bay and SKENE ISLANDS, in Arctic America, bear the name of an officer who served under Parry and Ross.

Skibbereen, County Cork, signifies a place frequented by small boats, in Irish 'skribs,' in English 'skiffs.' SKEPPS-HOLM, the naval arsenal at Stockholm, means 'ship's holm' or island.

Skirmish Bay, Chatham Islands, was the scene of a skirmish with the natives when Lieutenant Broughton visited it in 1795. At POINT SKIRMISH, in Moreton Bay, Queensland, Flinders was attacked by the natives in 1799.

Skye, one of the Hebrides, is called in Gaelic *Ealan - skianach,* the 'winged island,' from its shape. It is the *Sketis* of Ptolemy, and the *Scia* of Adamnan, names which represent the Gaelic *sciath,* a 'shoulder-blade.'

Slatington, a Pennsylvanian town with extensive slate quarries, exhibits a barbarous and ignorant attempt to fabricate a name of the Old English type.

Slaughter Point, on the WALLABY ISLANDS, West Australia, commemorates an event which had better have been forgotten—the wanton slaughter by Stokes in 1840 of a great number of kangaroos belonging to a small species called the Wallaby.

Slave River, in the Canadian Dominion, has given a name to the GREAT SLAVE LAKE, of which it is the chief feeder. It was so called from the Slave Indians, whose name translates the opprobrious designation given to the Hare and Dog-rib tribes by their hereditary foes the Crees, by whom they were driven northward as far as the river to which their name has been attached.

Slavonia, an Austrian crownland on the Danube and the Drave, is a Latinised form denoting the land of the SLOVANE, or 'speakers.' The name Slav or Slavonic is referred to the stem *slovo,* a 'word,' the Slavs designating themselves as the 'speakers'—literally, 'people of the word,' as distinguished from the Germans, whom they called NIEMEC or NIEMEZ, which means 'dumb' or 'unintelligible.'

Sleaford, Lincolnshire, is called *Sliowaford* in the Chronicle, and *Slioford* and *Sliowaford* in A.S. charters. It stands on the SLEA, formerly the *Sliowa,* or 'slow' river.

Sledge Island, in the Bering Sea, was so called by Cook because a sledge was found near the landing-place.

Sligo, whence the name of an Irish county, is the town on the River Sligo, which was called in Old Irish *Sligeach,* the 'shelly' river.

Slinger Bay, New Britain, is where Dampier, in 1700, was attacked by natives armed with slings.

Småland, the little or 'small land,' is a Swedish province.

Smith Sound, the strait leading from Baffin Bay into the Polar Ocean, was discovered by Baffin in 1616, and named by him after Sir Thomas Smith, the foremost English merchant of his time, who was the chief founder and first governor of the East India Company, incorporated in 1599. He was a great promoter of maritime research, and despatched Hudson and Baffin to discover a new passage to China, either by a north-eastern or a north-western route. In attempting the first, Hudson, in 1610, discovered SIR THOMAS SMITH'S INLET, separating the two chief islands of Spitzbergen. The SMITH ISLANDS, a small North Pacific group, south west of the Sandwich Islands, were discovered in 1807 by Captain Johnstone in the ship *Cornwallis*, and named after his first lieutenant. They are sometimes called either JOHNSTONE ISLANDS or CORNWALLIS ISLANDS. SMITH INLET, South Victoria, bears the name of an officer of the *Erebus*. CAPE SMITH, in Fury and Hecla Strait, was named by Parry after Captain Matthew Smith, R.N. SMITH RIVER, West Australia, bears the name of Frederick Smith, who accompanied George Grey in the expedition of 1838. SMYTH'S ISLANDS, in the Gambier Group, and CAPE SMYTH, on the northwest coast of America, bear the name of William Smyth, one of Beechey's officers. SMYTH ISLAND, near the Antarctic circle, was named after Captain William Henry Smyth, R.N., President of the Royal Astronomical Society.

Smoky Cape, New South Wales, and SMOKY BAY, Alaska, were so named by Cook, and SMOKY BAY, South Australia, by Flinders, because smoke was seen arising from fires kindled by the natives.

Smyrna is one of the few cities which has retained unaltered the ancient name, derived, according to the Greek legend, from Smyrna, an Amazon. It is now supposed that the name is cognate with Myrina, one of the appellations of the great Asiatic goddess.

Snake River, a tributary of the Oregon, bears the name of the Snake tribe which inhabited its banks.

Sneehätten, the 'snow hat,' 7620 feet high, is one of the summits of the Norwegian Dovre Fjeld. SNEEUWBERGEN, the 'snow mountains,' near the source of the Great Fish River in the Cape colony, rise to the height of 8500 feet.

Sniaul, the highest summit in the Isle of Man, is a modern corruption of the Norse name *Snaefell*, which means 'snow mountain.' SNAEFELLS-JÖKULL, an extinct volcano, is the highest summit in the west of Iceland. In modern Icelandic Jökull signifies a glacier, in O.N. it meant an icicle, corresponding to the A.S. *gicel*, whence *ísgicel*, the parent of our word icicle.

Society Islands, also called the Tahiti Archipelago, were so named by Cook in 1769 in compliment to the Royal Society on whose recommendation his expedition was despatched to observe the transit of Venus.

Socotra is an island in the Indian Ocean, east of Cape Guardafui. The name has been traced to a Sanskrit original, *Dvipa-*

Sukadara, the 'fortunate island,' literally the 'abode of bliss island,' out of which, contracted to *Diuscatra*, the Greeks manufactured the name *Dioscorida* used by the ancient geographers. *Dvipa-Sukadara* became *Diu-Zokotora*, *Sokotora*, and finally SOCOTRA.

Sodor is an Old Norse name which has curiously survived in the title of the Bishop of Sodor and Man. It is a corruption of the O.N. plural *Suthr-eyjar*, or 'south islands,' a name applied to the Hebrides as distinguished from the Orkneys and Shetlands, which were called *Northr-eyjar*, the 'North islands.' According to the Manx Chronicle, after a battle, fought in 1156, between Goddard, king of Dublin, and Somerled, Lord of the Isles, the heritage of Olaf, king of Man, was divided, Somerled taking the northern and Goddard the southern isles, after which he was styled King of Man and the Sudereys (Sodor and Man), instead of *Rex Manniæ et Insularum* as before. The See of Sodor being on Peel Island, that island acquired the name of the See, being designated as *Sodor vel Pile* in a bull of Gregory IX., dated in 1231. The full title of the Bishop in the patent appointing him is Bishop of the Isle of Man, of Sodor, of Sodor and Man, and of Sodor of Man, thus embracing the Isle of Man, the adjacent islet of Sodor, and the old Hebridean diocese of Sodor now included in the See of Argyll and the Isles.

Sofala, a district north of Zanzibar, on the East African coast, is an Arabic name meaning the 'lowland.' The full name is *Sofalatu' l Dhahab*, the 'lowland of gold.'

Sofia, the capital of Bulgaria, is a modern name which in the fourteenth century replaced *Sredetz*, a Bulgarian corruption of the Roman name *Serdica* or *Sardica*.

Soissons (Aisne) was the chief town of the *Suessiones*, a Belgic tribe. The Romans called it *Augusta Suessionum*, abbreviated in the sixth century to *Suessiones*, and in the thirteenth to *Soyssons*.

Sokoto, a town in the Soudan, is 'the market-place' (Arabic *suk* or *sok*, a 'market').

Solander Island, south of New Zealand, bears the name of Dr. Solander, a Swede, who accompanied Cook as botanist in his first voyage.

Soledad, in New California, represents the *Mission de Nuestra Señora de Soledad*, 'Our Lady of Solitude,' founded in 1791. A Brazilian settlement in the Province of

Rio Grande do Sul, is called *Nossa Senhora da Soledade do Passo Fundo*, 'Our Lady of Solitude at the deep ford.'

Solent, the channel between the Isle of Wight and the mainland, is a name possibly related to that of the Solway (*q.v.*). Bæda speaks of it as the sea 'which is called Solvente in which the two ocean tides daily meet and conflict.' Hence the name of the Solent has been explained from the Celtic *sul-want*, the 'battle of the *sul*,' where *sul* signifies the salt water or incoming tide. But if, as is probable, Hampshire was called Gwent, the Solent might be *sul-gwent*, the 'sea of Gwent.'

Solimoens, also called the Alto Amazonas (Upper Amazons), was so named from the Sorimóas or Yarimaúas, an extinct tribe related to the Passés, who, when the district was explored by Texeira in 1637, inhabited the banks of the river from Peru to the mouth of the RIO NEGRO, or 'black river,' so called from its dark colour as contrasted with the turbid yellow water of the Solimoens.

Solitary Isles, New South Wales, discovered by Cook in 1770; SOLITARY ISLAND, West Australia, discovered by Stokes in 1841; and ISLA SOLITARIA, north of the Navigators, discovered by Mendaña in 1595, were named from their isolation.

Solothurn, in French SOLEURE, a town which gives its name to a Swiss Canton, is a corruption of the Celto-Latin name *Salodurum*.

Solway Firth is a name which has been much discussed, but without positive result. About 1300 we have the form *Sulway*, and it was also called *Scottiswathe*, the 'Scots ford' (*wath*, a 'ford'). The last syllable in Solway may mean a channel or passage, as in Conway and Medway (*q.v.*), or a 'bay' (*vagr*), as in Scalloway. The first syllable may be *sul*, 'salt water,' or incoming tide (*see* SOLENT), or it may be connected with the name of the *Selgovæ*, a British tribe inhabiting its shores. Professor Rhys thinks the Selgovæ were the 'hunters' (Irish *selg*, Welsh *hela*, 'hunting'), and he maintains that the Selgovæ left their name on the Solway Firth and the Solway Moss. Mr. Bradley, on the other hand, considers that the name of the tribe was derived from that of the estuary, the Selgovæ being the Solway men. Dr. Guest thinks Solway is either the ford (*wath*) or the channel (*wyth*) of the incoming tide (*sul*). Mr. Johnston thinks the name may be Scandinavian, and explains it as the 'muddy bay' (*sol*, 'mud,' and *vagr*, 'bay'). But the chief characteristic of the Solway being the sands exposed at low tide when the channel is fordable, the probable meaning is either 'tidal channel' or 'tidal ford.' In the absence of earlier forms the question is probably insoluble.

Somali, 'blacks' or 'negroes,' is the name given to the tribes occupying the East African coast north of the district of the SWAHILI, or 'coast-men.'

Sombrero is the Spanish name of one of the Lesser Antilles, which resembles a broad-brimmed hat, the central hill being encircled by a strip of flat coast. The SOMBRERO CHANNEL in the Nicobar Islands is a name originating with the Portuguese, who called the Nicobars by the name of Somerara Islands, because of an umbrella-shaped hill on the largest island.

Somerset (A.S. *Sumersǽte*) was originally like Dorset, Essex, or Norfolk, a tribal name, denoting not the land, but its inhabitants. The chief place in the county was the royal *tún* of SOMERTON (A.S. *Sumer-tún*), which denoted a summer residence, like the Welsh HAFOD. If Dorset signifies the settlers near Durnovaria, Somerset might signify the settlers around Somerton, although Somerset is not a contracted form of Sumertúnset as Wiltshire is of Wiltun-scir. In Welsh Somerset was called *Gwlâd-yr-Haf*, the 'land of Summer,' but it is not known whether Somerset is a translation of the Welsh name, or whether the Welsh name is merely a twelfth century translation of Somerset. Professor Rhys inclines to the former view, believing that *Gwlâd-yr-Haf*, the 'land of summer,' was a term of mythical origin, which afterwards became attached to a definite locality, the region beyond the Severn, known in Welsh as *Hafren*, the summer or 'southern river.' In any case the Welsh names of the Severn and of Somerset are etymologically related. In Latin documents Somerset is translated by *æstiva regio*, the 'land of summer.' NORTH SOMERSET, in Arctic America, was so named by Parry in 1822 from his native county.

Somers Town, a suburb of London, was built on the property of Lord Somers.

Sömmering, a pass in the Eastern Alps, crosses a mountain formerly called the *Semernick*, which is explained by the Slavonic word *semerek*, 'fir' or 'pine.'

Somvix, the 'highest village' on the

Upper Rhine, appears in the thirteenth century under the name *in Summo Vico.*

Songi is a Malay word meaning a 'river,' which we have in SONGI RAJA, the 'Raja's river,' SONGI PAKU, the 'river of the paku-tree,' or SONGI PALIMBANG, the 'river of the kingdom of Palimbang.

Sorbonne, in Paris, was founded in 1253 by Robert de Sorbonne, the Almoner of St. Louis.

Sorel, a town in Canada, bears the name of a French captain of engineers who erected a fort here in 1665. CAPE SORELL, Tasmania, was named by King in 1819, after Colonel William Sorell, the Lieutenant-Governor of Tasmania, whose name is also borne by PORT SORELL, LAKE SORELL, and the town of SORELL.

Sorge Bay, Spitzbergen, which means the 'Bay of Sorrow,' was so called by the Dutch from the numerous graves of their countrymen on its western shore.

Sorrento, on the Bay of Naples, was the Roman *Surrentum.*

Soudan, an undefined region in Central Africa, is a name derived from the Arabic appellation *Belád-es-Súdán,* the 'district of the blacks' or negroes. So Media is called *Bilád-ul-jebel,* 'the mountain districts,' *bilád* being the plural of *belád,* a city, town, or country.

Southampton was so called to distinguish it from Northampton. As it stands on the River Anton or Ant, it has been supposed that the name is equivalent to *Súth-Ant-tún,* but in a charter of Æthelred, dated in 985, and supposed to refer to Southampton, we read *in loco qui dicitur æt Heántúne,* where *Heántúne* is the dative case of *Heáh-tún,* the 'high tún.' Southampton Island, north of Hudson Bay, was discovered in 1613 by Button, and doubtless named by him after the Earl of Southampton.

Southend, Essex, is a comparatively modern name, denoting the houses built at the 'south end' of the parish of Prittlewell.

South's Bay, Dolphin and Union Strait, bears the name of Sir James South the astronomer. The SOUTH CAPES in Tasmania, New Zealand, Spitzbergen, and elsewhere, were named from their position.

Southwark, called *Súthgeweorc* in the Saxon Chronicle, took its name from an earthwork made to defend the southern approach to London Bridge. (*See* NEWARK.)

Spa, a watering-place in Belgium, is from the Walloon word *espa,* a 'spring' or 'fountain.' From the chalybeate waters of the Belgian Spa, which, at the end of the last century was the most fashionable continental watering-place, many mineral springs have been called Spas.

Spain is the English name of the country called ESPAÑA by the Spaniards, and ESPAGNE by the French. It was called *Iberia,* the land on the *Iberus,* now the EBRO (*q.v.*) by the Greeks, and *Hispania* by the Romans. In Plutarch we find the form Spania, which is also used by St. Paul (Romans xv. 24, 28). Bochart, followed by Niebuhr, considers it a name of Phœnician origin, signifying the land of rabbits, from *shaphan,* a 'rabbit,' and Strabo gives an account of the great plague of rabbits which infested the whole coast from Cadiz to Marseilles. Asterloa, followed by W. von Humboldt, derives the name España from the Basque *ezpaña,* which means a 'lip,' 'border,' or 'edge' of anything. The modern kingdom of Spain has been built up of successive kingdoms wrested from the Moors. We have (1) LEON, including the two kingdoms of Leon and Galicia; (2) CASTILE, including the five kingdoms of Old Castile, Toledo or New Castile, Jaen or Cordova, Seville and Murcia; (3) ARAGON, including the three kingdoms of Aragon, Valencia, and Majorca.

Spalato, a Dalmatian town, nestles among the vast ruins of the *Palatium* built by Diocletian. The old form of the name of the town is *Aspalathum,* which points to *as palatium,* 'at the palace,' as the source of the modern name.

Spanish Head, in the Isle of Man, was so named, according to the local tradition, from the wreck of one of the vessels of the Spanish Armada. SPANISH TOWN was the former capital of Jamaica, and is also the name of one of the Virgin Islands, the rocks at a distance resembling the towers of a city. The SPANISH MAIN was the name of the mainland of Central America, as distinguished from the Antilles.

Spartivento, the southern point of Sardinia, is the 'divider of the wind,' an appropriate name, as travellers passing it by sea cannot fail to remember. For a similar reason the southern point of Calabria and a cape between the Gulf of Salerno and Policastro bear the same name.

Spear Point, North Australia, is where King narrowly escaped being speared by the natives.

Speedwell, Cape, Novaya Zemlya, is where the ship *Speedwell* was wrecked in 1676.

Speen, in Berkshire, was the Roman *Spinæ,* the 'thorns.' No other place in England has retained a pure Roman name.

Speeton, on the Yorkshire coast near Filey, is a place where a spring in the cliff has worked a deep gully leading to the shore. The Domesday form *Spet-ton* explains the name as the 'tun by the spout' (O.N. *spyta,* a 'running sore,' that which spits ; A.S. *spittan,* 'to spit'; Dutch *spuit,* a 'spout' or squirt).

Speicher, a Swiss village-name, is from the Low-Latin *spicarium,* a word used to denote a monastic 'grange,' used for storing the 'spikes' or ears of corn.

Spencer Gulf, South Australia, CAPE SPENCER, and ALTHORPE ISLANDS were discovered by Flinders in 1802, and named, he tells us, in honour of the 'respectable nobleman' John Spencer, Viscount Althorpe, and second Earl Spencer, who was first Lord of the Admiralty at the time when his ship was commissioned.

Spessart Wald is a range of wooded hills in Northern Bavaria. The older forms, *Spehteshart* and *Spechtshard,* show the meaning to be the 'woodpecker's wood.'

Spey, a Scotch river, was anciently the *Spe,* which is regarded by Stokes as the Pictish equivalent of the old Celtic **squeas,* a 'vomit.'

Spiers, the French form we have adopted of the German name SPEYER or SPIER, was called *Spiraha* or *Spira* in the eighth century. It stands at the junction of the River Speyer or Speyerbach, formerly the *Spiraha,* with the Rhine.

Spitzbergen was discovered in 1596 by the Dutchman Willem Barents. It was visited by Hudson in 1607 and by Baffin in 1612. At first the Dutch called it *Nieuwland,* a name which Fotherby in 1614 proposed to change to *King James his New-land.* But the descriptive name *Spitzberghe,* the 'peaked mountains,' which was used by the Dutch as early as 1613, has fortunately held the ground.

Splügen, a village which gives its name to the SPLÜGEN PASS, leading from Canton Graubünden into Italy, is a German corruption of *speluga,* the Romansch form of the Latin *specula,* a 'watch-tower.'

Spree, the river on which Berlin stands, was formerly called *Spriawa,* a name apparently Slavonic, meaning 'sorb-tree river.'

Springfield, Massachusetts, is the chief arsenal of the United States. The first European settler, William Pynchon of Springfield in Essex, came in 1635. In 1640 he changed the native name Agawan to Springfield. There are sixty places of the same name in the United States, among them the State capital of Illinois.

Spurn Head, in Yorkshire, was formerly called *Ravenspur* or *Ravenspurn,* being the spur or cape near the lost town of Ravenser or Ravenore. It was at Ravenspur that Edward IV. landed when he invaded England before the battle of Barnet. The form *spurn* is derived from *spuran,* the dative of the A.S. *spura,* a 'heel' or 'spur.'

Squillace, in Italy, is a corruption of the Roman name *Scylaceum.*

Stade, in Hanover, was anciently called *Statho,* a word which in Old Saxon meant a shore, bank, or landing-place. STAITHES, near Whitby, is a name of the same signification (A.S. *stæth,* a 'shore,' M.E. *stathe,* a 'wharf'). STETTIN, the capital of Pomerania, has been explained from the Slavonic *Zytyn,* which would mean the 'place of green corn,' but as a suburb of Stettin is called LASTADIE, the 'lading-place,' the name may be Teutonic. There are seven places in Germany called STETTEN, of which the old forms *Steti* or *Stetin* show that the name means simply 'place' or town, like the English *sted* or *stead.* (*See* WALLENSTAD.)

Staffa, one of the Hebrides, is the O.N. *Staf-ey,* 'step isle,' a descriptive name referring to the stumps of the basaltic columns at the entrance to the cave.

Staffordshire takes its name from the county town of STAFFORD, which grew up at a ford over the River Sow. The older name *Berteliney* signifies the 'eyot of Bertela,' a personal name. It is called *Stæf-ford* in the Chronicle. The coins struck at Stafford by the moneyer Godwin bear the legend *Godwinne on Stæf.* The A.S. *stæf* means a 'staff,' 'stick,' or 'pole,' and the ford may have been defended by stakes, or marked by poles stuck in the stream for guidance, or, as has been thought, it may have been crossed by aid of stilts. How fords were defended by stakes is well seen at Coway Stakes near Halliford, where Cæsar crossed the Thames, the stakes by which the ford was fortified having been discovered. They were driven into the bed of the river, all over the shallows, leaving a narrow un-staked passage, which, as Cæsar dis-covered, was easy to defend, since only one man could pass at a time.

Staines, in Middlesex, is a town near the stone which marks the river jurisdiction of the city of London. In the Chronicle it is called *Stán*, the 'stone,' the oblique cases *Stána* and *Stáne* occurring in A.S. charters. The form Staines seems to be a later plural formation.

Stalimene and STANKO, the modern names of *Lemnos* and *Cos*, are the ancient names with a fragment of a Greek pre-position and article attached.

Stamford, Lincolnshire, is the A.S. *Stanford* or *Stænford*, 'stone ford,' from a ford over the Welland, probably paved with stones. STAMFORD BRIDGE, in Yorkshire, is called *Stanford Brycg* in the Chronicle. After Harold's victory it was long called *Pons Belli*, 'battle bridge.' Where only a small stream is crossed STAMFORD or STANFORD, usually *Stan-ford* in charters, may denote a ford with stepping-stones rather than a paved ford. STEINFURT is a common name in Germany.

Starastschin, a cape in Spitzbergen, bears the name of a Russian hunter who, for thirty winters, was the sole inhabitant of the island. His hut, in which he died of old age in 1826, stood on the cape now called by his name.

Stargard, the 'old fortress,' is the Sla-vonic name of two Prussian towns. (*See* MOSTAR.)

Start Point, in Devon, sometimes more correctly called THE START, is from the A.S. *steort*, 'a tail,' hence a 'spit' or 'point' of land, a word which is preserved in the name of the *redstart*, a bird distin-guished by its red tail. According to the popular nautical etymology it is the point from which vessels 'start' from the English coast to cross the Bay of Biscay. STAART-VEN in the Netherlands is the fen at the spit.

Starvation Cove, in King William Island, records the fate of Franklin's last expedition. Here a boat and thirty or thirty-five skeletons were found, evidently the remains of a party which had aban-doned the icebound ships.

Staten Island, south-east of Tierra del Fuego, from which it is separated by LE MAIRE STRAIT (*q.v.*), was discovered in 1616 by the Dutch seamen Le Maire and Schouten, who named it *Staatenland* after the Dutch States-General. In 1643 it was found to be an island, having pre-

viously been supposed to be a part of the great Antarctic continent, the *Terra Aus-tralis Incognita* of the old geographers. New Zealand, when first discovered, was also called *Staatenland* by Tasman, who supposed it to be part of the same con-tinent, as represented on the maps of Mercator and others. STATEN ISLAND, near New York, was also named in honour of the Dutch States. STAATEN ISLAND, in Waigatz Strait, reached by the Dutch in 1594, was named, we are told, in 'eternal memory' of the Sovereign States. STAATEN RIVER, in the Gulf of Carpen-taria, discovered by the Dutch in 1623, received its name for the same reason.

Staubbach, the 'dust beck,' falls 900 feet over a lofty cliff near Lauterbrunnen, and disappears in fine spray. A water-fall in Canton Uri is called the STAUBI, from the cloud of spray which envelops it.

Stellenbosch, a town in the Cape Colony, was founded in 1670 by the Dutch Governor Simon van der Stell, in compliment to whom SIMON'S VALLEY was named, as well probably as SIMON'S BAY, on whose shores SIMON'S TOWN has been built.

Stelvio, in German the STILFSER JOCH, is an Alpine pass leading from the Tyrol to Lombardy, which takes its name from Stilfs, a Tyrolese village, called Stelvio in Italian.

Stephen's Range, North Australia, bears the name of Sir James Stephen, Under Secretary for the Colonies. PORT STEPHEN, New South Wales, CAPE STEPHEN in Norton Sound and in New Zealand were named by Cook after one of the Secretaries of the Admiralty. MOUNT STEPHEN, one of the highest peaks on the Canadian Pacific Railway, was named after a Canadian statesman, Sir George Stephen. From it he took the title of Lord Mountstephen.

Stepney, Middlesex, was formerly *Steben-hithe*, from the A.S. *stebb*, a 'stub' or 'stump' of a tree, or from *stefn*, the stem of a tree. It was probably a wharf with a stump to which ships were moored, or perhaps a wharf at which timber was stored.

Stewart Island, New Zealand, called in Maori RAKIURA (*q.v.*), is separated from the South Island by Foveaux Strait, which was missed by Cook, and only dis-covered in 1816 by a sealing captain named Stewart.

Stockholm, the capital of Sweden, is often said to have been so called because built like Venice on stocks or piles. According to the local legend a stock or log floating up the Malar lake from Sigtuma guided the first settlers to the granite rocks on which Stockholm is built. But the older form *Stäkholm* explains the name as a *holm* or 'island' in a *stäk* or 'sound.' The local word *stäket* or *stäk*, an 'inlet,' is supposed to be of Finnic origin. STOCKTON, a common name in England, seems to have denoted a *tún* or inclosure fenced with logs (A.S. *stocc*, a 'log' or tree trunk). To the A.S. *stoccen*, 'made of logs,' we may refer such names as STOKENCHURCH, Oxon, or STOKENHAM in Devon.

Stonehenge is the name of a megalithic monument on Salisbury Plain, where the upper stones of the great trilithons overhang (M.E. *hengen*, to hang). The name seems to be identical with that of STEINHANG in Germany, where there is a precipice with overhanging stones. STENNIS in Orkney, a cape with two circles of great standing stones, is the 'Stone-ness.' STANTON DREW in Somerset, where there is a group of stone circles with avenues, was supposed by Stukeley to mean the 'Stonetown of the Druids,' an etymology which still continues to be repeated and copied. The affix Drew, which is later than Domesday, where the name is *Stan-tune*, was doubtless derived from Drogo or Dreux, a former owner. CARNAC, in Brittany, with extensive avenues of standing stones, is from *cairn*, a 'heap of stones,' with the Celtic formative *ac*.

Storm Bay forms the approach to Hobart Town, Tasmania. The name records a furious storm by which Tasman was blown out to sea during the night of November 29th, 1642. In like manner STORMY ISLE, North of New Britain, records a violent tornado encountered by Dampier in 1700.

Stornoway, a seaport in the island of Lewis, is probably the 'great bay' (O.N. *stor*, 'great,' and *vagr*, a 'bay'). If the *n* is not intrusive, the name must be explained from O.N. *stjörn*, a 'rudder.' STOORHOLM, the largest island in Yell Sound, Shetland, means the 'great island.' The great cliff at the entrance of the Bay of Portree, Skye, is called THE STORR, and the two islands called PAPA are distinguished as PAPA STOOR and PAPA LITTLE, the great and little 'priest's isle.'

Stour is the name of six English rivers, all called *Stur* in A.S. charters, one of them being the *Sturius* of Ptolemy. There are also two rivers in Italy called *Stura*. Hence, as the name cannot be Teutonic, but is probably Celtic, it may be cognate

with the word *staer*, a 'river,' which has been preserved in Armoric. STOURBRIDGE, on the Worcestershire Stour, is called *æt Sture* in a charter in 855, and STOURMINSTER, on the Dorset Stour, is *Stureminster* in a charter. STOURMOUTH, in Kent, now five miles from the sea, marks the place where the Kentish Stour formerly entered the navigable channel of the Wantsum, now silted up.

Stowborough, Dorset, is a curious corruption of the Domesday name *Stanberge*, 'stony hill.'

Stralsund, a Pomeranian town, was founded in 1209 by Jaromar, Prince of Rügen, on the Strelasund, a narrow arm of the Baltic dividing the Isle of Rügen from the mainland. STRELASUND means the 'arrow sound' (Lithuanian *strela*, an 'arrow'), probably because the width was only a bowshot.

Strangford Lough, in Ireland, obtained its name from the tidal currents at the entrance which make navigation dangerous, the name Strangford meaning in Danish the 'strong fiord' or inlet.

Strassburg, Elsass, the 'burg on the street' or Roman paved road, was the Roman *Argentoratum*. It is called *Stratiburgum* in 728, *Stratisburgum* by the Ravenna Geographer, and *Strasburg* in 859. A Vatican codex, quoted by Förstemann, makes the German name translate the Celtic name. *Argentoratum, i.e. Stratiburgo, teutonice namque strati argentum, burgo civitatem significat.*

Stratford-on-Avon is called in an A.S. charter *Ufera Strétford*, 'Upper Street ford.' STRATFORD is a common name in the Saxon parts of England, and usually appears in early documents as *Strétford* or *Strétford*. The Saxons must have learned on the Continent the post-classical Latin term *strata* for a paved Roman road, and have brought *street* with them as a naturalised word. The name Stratford only occurs where a river is crossed by a Roman road, as is the case at STRATFORD, on the Bedfordshire Ivel, and STRATFORD-LE-BOW, where a 'bow' or arched bridge was built over the Lea near the ford on the Roman street. The Strattons, Strettons, Streathams, and Stratfields, which are so numerous in England, often help to mark the courses of the Roman roads. Thus STREATHAM in Surrey, called *Strétham* in a charter of 737, marks the continuation of Stone Street, which connected *Regnum*, the old capital of the Regni, now Chichester, with London. STRAT-

TON near Bath, STRATTON near Leamington, and STRETTON in Warwickshire are all on the Fossway. STREATLY, in Bedfordshire, is on the Icenild-way, and LONG STRATTON, in Norfolk, is on another Roman Road.

Strathclyde is the Gaelic equivalent of Clydesdale, STRATHEARN is the valley of the Earn, ANNANDALE was formerly called *Strathannan*, and STRATHMORE is 'the great valley.' *Strath* is the Gaelic *Srath*, which primarily denoted not a dale but the flat meadow-land bordering on a river. In Ireland the primitive meaning has been retained, STRABANE, in Tyrone, being anciently *Srath - ban*, 'the white holm,' or riverside flat. *Srath*, being unpronounceable by English lips, has been made into *strath* by the insertion of a euphonic *t*, as in the case of other Gaelic words beginning with *sr*. Thus STROAN, in Antrim, Cavan, and Kilkenny is the Old Irish *Sruthan*, 'a streamlet,' the diminutive of *sruth*, a 'stream,' while from *sron*, a nose or ness, we get STRONE, and possibly STRANRAER. YESTER, in Haddingtonshire, was formerly *Ystrad*, the Cymric form of the Gaelic *srath*, which we have in many Welsh names, such as YSTRADVELLTEY or YSTRADYFODWG.

Strelitz, the capital of the Duchy of Mecklenburg-Strelitz, is believed to have been a hunting-seat of the Dukes. The Slavonic word *strelitzi* means an 'archer,' whence the name of the Streltzi, the famous bodyguard of Peter the Great, who mutinied in 1682. STRELKA, the 'arrow,' is the Russian name of an island in the delta of the Petchora, so called from its shape. (*See* STRALSUND.)

Strokkur, the 'churn,' is one of the Icelandic Geysers.

Stroma, 'stream island,' in the Pentland Firth, lies in the strong current running between Caithness and the Orkneys. STROMAY, a name of the same meaning, is one of the Outer Hebrides. STROMNESS, a town in Orkney, takes its name from a ness past which the current runs. STRÖMOE, one of the Faröes, the 'island of the stream' or current, is either from the ocean current, or possibly from a small stream near Thorshavn, the chief town.

Stromboli, one of the Lipari Islands, is a volcanic cone, whose name is a corruption of the descriptive Greek name *Strongyle*, the 'round' island. Edrisi, writing in the twelfth century, calls it *Strangelo*.

Strong Island (Ualam), in the Carolines, was discovered in 1804 by the American Captain Crozer, and named after Governor Strong of Massachusetts.

Stroud and STROOD are common names in England. There is a STROOD near Rochester, a STROUD in Gloucestershire, and a STROUD GREEN near Croydon. STRUDWICK, Northants, is the A.S. *Stród-wíc*. The A.S. *stród* probably meant a waste place overgrown with scattered scrub. (Cf. O.H.G. *struot*, a 'wood.') The Stroud water, on which STROUD in Gloucestershire stands, doubtless takes its name from the town.

Strzelecki, a mountain range in Victoria, commemorates the services of Count Strzelecki, an Australian explorer.

Stuttgard, the capital of Würtemberg, grew up around a 'stud-yard' or enclosure for horses belonging to the Würtemberg Counts.

Styria is the Latinised form we use for STEYERMARK, an Austrian crownland, erected into a marquisate by Otto I. in 955, and named from the castle of STEYR, which stands at the confluence of the River Ens with the STEYR, in Slavonic *Schtyra*.

Suanetia, an inaccessible district in the Caucasus, is believed to mean a 'place of refuge.'

Suarez, or DIEGO SUAREZ, more correctly DIEGO SOARES, a bay in the North of Madagascar, containing a French port of the same name, is believed to bear the name of a Portuguese captain, the brother of Fernão Soares, the Portuguese Admiral by whom the island was discovered in 1506. The names of Portuguese captains are also commemorated in Madagascar by the bay called ANTONGIL (Antonio Gil), and by the island of JUAN DE NOVA.

Subiaco is an Italian town on the Anio, where Nero had a villa called by Frontinus *Villa Neronis Sublacensis*. The name afterwards became *Sublaqueum*, which denotes its position below the three artificial lakes formed by damming the Anio in order to obtain a continuous head of water for the Aqua Claudia, the great aqueduct which supplied the palaces on the Palatine hill in Rome.

Sucre, a city in Bolivia, bears the name of General Sucre, the first President of the Republic.

Suez, a place at the head of the Red Sea, is a Portuguese corruption of *Bir Suweis*, the Arabic name of a fortified well of brackish water about an hour's journey from the town, where the pilgrims waited to embark for Mecca. From this well, by a curious accident, the Gulf and Isthmus of Suez, and the Suez Canal take their names.

Suffolk (A.S. *Suthfolc*), a tribal name which has become territorial, is the land of the Southern folk of the East Angles. (*See* NORFOLK.) SUDBURY, the old capital of Suffolk, is the 'South burgh.' SUDREY, the 'South isle,' is one of the Westmanna Islands. The plural of Sudrey is *Sudrey-jar*, 'south islands,' the Norse name of the Hebrides, which became SODOR (*q.v.*).

Sugar Island, SUGAR POINT, and the like, are names given to places in the U.S.A. where the sugar maple grows abundantly. SUGAR LOAF is a common name of conical hills, like PAN DE AZU-CAR (*q.v.*) in Spanish.

Sul, which answers to the Spanish *Sur*, means the 'south' in Portuguese, as in the Brazilian RIO GRANDE DO SUL, or 'great river of the South.'

Suláimán Range (Persian, *Koh-i-Suláimán*), west of the Indus, was so named, according to the tradition, because here the progress of the armies of the Caliph Suláimán was stayed. The highest point is called TAKHT-I-SULÁIMÁN, 'Solomon's throne,' a name repeated elsewhere.

Sulphur Island, in the Lew-Chew group, emits strong fumes of sulphur from a volcanic vent.

Sumatra, the European name of the great island which is called by the Malays *Pulo Partcha*, or *Pulo Indalas*, is derived from the name of the place where the Moslem Sultans resided when the Portuguese first visited the island. The site is now marked by a village called SAMUDRA. Ibn Batuta (*c.* 1346) visited the Court of the Sultan at a place which he calls *Samothrah*, *Samuthrah*, or *Samuthra*. In one MS. of Marco Polo it is called *Samarcha*, in another *Samara* (probably for Samatra), and it is called *Sumatra* by Ludovico Barthema, an Italian, who visited it in 1505. There is no evidence that it ever bore the conjectural Sanskrit name of *Dvipa Samudra*, the 'island in the ocean' (Sanskrit *samudra*, 'the sea'), which has been inferred from the name *Isola Siamotra*, which appears on Fra Mauro's map.

Sumburgh Roost, the channel dividing the Orkneys from the Shetlands, takes its name from a cape on which stood a castle called SUMBURGH, meaning 'Sweyn's castle,' as is shown by the oldest forms *Swynbrocht* and *Svinborg*. The Orkney

dialect word *roost*, signifying a 'strong current' (O.N. *röst*, a 'whirlpool'), appears also in ROUSHOLM HEAD, a cape on the Island of STRONSAY, the 'stream island,' past which a strong current flows.

Sumter, a fort at the entrance to Charleston Harbour, South Carolina, where the Civil War began, was named after General Thomas Sumter, a Colonial leader in the War of Independence.

Sunda Islands is the European name of the group extending from Timor to Sumatra. When the Portuguese first visited the Eastern Seas, Sunda was the name of a small state in the western part of Java, in which a language different from the Javanese proper was spoken. Hence Java and Sunda were supposed to be separate islands. Consequently the adjoining Strait dividing Java from Sumatra came to be called the *Boqueirão da Sunda*, of which the STRAITS OF SUNDA is the English translation. The name of the SEA OF SUNDA was then given to the neighbouring portion of the ocean, the islands in which, including Timor, Floris, Java, and Sumatra, came to be called the Sunda Islands.

Sunday Cove, New Zealand, SUNDAY STRAIT and SUNDAY ISLAND, Australia, were named from the day of the week on which they were discovered.

Sunderbunds, the name given to 3000 square miles of jungle and swamp in the Delta of the Ganges, is an Anglicised form of the native name *Sundarban*, which may either mean the 'beautiful forest' (*sundar*, 'beautiful,' and *ban*, 'forest' or 'brake') or the forest of the 'beautiful' tree, *sundrí* or *sundari* (*Heritiera littoralis*), which grows abundantly in the jungle. Among other etymologies which have been proposed are *Samudraban*, the 'forest near the sea,' or from *Súndari*, which is believed to have been an old name of the Hugli.

Superior is the 'uppermost' of the five great American Lakes. Champlain in 1632 called it *Grand Lac*, a translation of the native name *Kichi Gummi*. The name *Lac Superieur* first appears in 1674 on Joliet's map.

Surat was the chief English factory in India from 1612 to 1687. The old name was *Surath*, which Sir H. Elliot identifies with the name of the ancient kingdom in Gujarát called *Surashtra*, variously explained as the 'good region,' or the kingdom of the Sah dynasty.

Surrey, an English county, is usually explained as *Súth-ríce*, the 'South kingdom,' but this etymology is not supported by the early forms. In the Chronicle (A.D. 823) we have *Súthríg* for Surrey, while *Súthríge* is a nominative plural denoting the people of Surrey, *Súthrígea* or *Súthrígena* being the genitive plural, and *Súthrígum* the dative plural. The Latin forms *regio Sudergeona* or *Sudregiona* do not mean the 'south region,' but are adaptations of *Súthrígena*, the A.S. genitive plural. *Súthríg* might be divided as Súth-ríg or as Súthr-íg. In the former case the name has been referred to the most characteristic feature of the county, the great escarpment of the chalk downs which traverses it from east to west, the A.S. *hrycg* or *rig* meaning a ridge or line of hills. But, though *suth* is more usual than *suthr*, we are justified by the analogy of Sutherton and Westerham in dividing the name not as *Súth-ríg*, but as *Súthr-íg*. In A.S. *íg* denotes an island, but the parallel form *íg* usually means the shore or coast of a sea or river, Chertsey, for instance (A.S. *Cerotes-íg*), meaning 'Cerot's shore,' and not 'Cerot's island.' *Súthr-íg* would thus mean the 'southern shore' of the Thames opposite Middlesex, while *Súthríge* would be a nominative plural denoting the inhabitants of Súthríg. This explanation agrees best with the early forms Súthrígum and Súthrígena. Another explanation has been suggested which derives the name from that of the Regni, the British tribe who occupied Surrey and Sussex, and whose capitals were at Chichester and at Noviomagus, probably Woodbury near Croydon. The form *Suthregena* has been appealed to as meaning the South Regni. But the Regni of Surrey were the northern and not the southern division of the tribe, so that the modern name should have been Norrey and not Surrey.

Susa, in Piedmont, is a corruption of the Celto-Roman name *Segusio*, afterwards *Seusia*, derived from a tribal name which probably meant the 'strong' or 'victorious' people. SUSA, in Persia, is a Semitic name from *susa*, a 'lily,' whence the personal names Susan and Susannah.

Susquehanna, a river which flows into Chesapeake Bay, contains the native word *hanne*, a 'river.' It was formerly called CROOKED RIVER, which has been supposed to be a translation of the native name. Boyd, however, explains it as 'long reach river.'

Sussex, an English county, is a tribal appellation which became territorial, as is shown by the A.S. name *Súth Seaxe*, the 'south Saxons.' SUSSEX LAKE, in Arctic America, the source of the Great Fish River, was named in honour of the Duke of Sussex.

Sutherland, a Scotch county, from its position south of Caithness, was called *Sudrland* or 'south land' by the Norsemen who occupied it after the conquest by Thorfinn in 1034. SUTHERLAND POINT, Botany Bay, bears the name of Forby Sutherland, one of Cook's seamen, who was buried here on May 1st, 1770. The SUTHERLAND FALLS, on the Arthur River, in the South Island of New Zealand, are among the highest in the world, descending for 1904 feet in three leaps. They bear the name of a mineral prospector who discovered them in 1885 or 1886.

Sutlej (SATLAJ), one of the five rivers of the Punjab, is the river with the 'hundred bends.' Either the Sutlej, or more probably the BEAS, was the river known to the Greeks as the *Hyphasis*, a name explained from the Sanskrit *Vipasa*, which is descriptive of its 'breaking through' or 'bursting out' of a gorge of the Himalaya.

Sutton, one of the commonest English village-names, is the A.S. *Súth-tún*. SUTTON, a town in Queensland, was named from a merchant in Sydney.

Suwarrow Islands, east of the Navigators, bear the name of a Russian ship, named after the great Russian general, which discovered them in 1814.

Sviatoi Nos, 'holy cape,' in Siberia, was the name given by the Russian explorers in 1736 to the furthest point they reached.

Svinavatn is a 'lake' in Iceland, where a man called Svin was drowned.

Swabia is the Latinised form we have adopted for *Schwaben*, an ancient duchy in South-Western Germany, representing the territory of the Suevi, one of the great Teutonic tribes. The name is now restricted to a Bavarian province, whose capital is Augsburg. The older name of Swabia was *Alémannia*, whence ALLEMAGNE, the French name for Germany. In the fifth century the Suevi poured into the region, and amalgamating with the Alemanni, gave their name to the country, in the same way that the land occupied by the Saxons has come to bear the name of the Angles, though the older Saxon name continues to be used in Wales, like the older Alemannian name in France.

Swahíli, or SEWAHÍLI, the name given

to the Arabs of the African coast near Zanzibar, means the 'coast men,' from the Arabic *sewáhil*, 'coasts,' 'shores,' a plural of *sahil*, the 'sea-shore' or 'bank of a river.' Swahíli, the *lingua franca* of South Eastern Africa, is the trade language spoken by the Arab traders on the coast, who are called in Bantu speech *Wa-Swahíli*, 'the men of the coasts.' Es-SAHEL, 'the coast,' is a name given to a coast region near Tunis, and to another near Algiers, whence the favourite Algerian vintage called Sahel.

Swain County, North Carolina, bears the name of Daniel Lowry Swain, Governor of the State from 1832 to 1835. SWAIN, a coral island north of the Navigators, bears the name of the discoverer, the boatswain of a whaler.

Swallow Bay, Egmont Island, and SWALLOW HARBOUR, Fuegia, were discovered by the ship *Swallow* in 1766.

Swan River, West Australia, was visited in 1696 by the Dutch seaman Willem van Vlaming in the ship *Geelvink*, and named from the abundance of black swans, two of which he brought home alive.

Swanage, in Dorset, is probably to be identified with *Swanawic*, where, as the Chronicle tells us, a Danish fleet was defeated. Sweyn, a common Danish name, is probably found in the name of SWANSCOMB, formerly *Swenes-camp*, near Northfleet, where Sweyn, king of Denmark, is supposed to have landed. Names like SWAINBY, SWAINTON, or SWANTON, probably denoted a *tún* inhabited by 'swains' or farm servants (O.N. *sveinn*, A.S. *swán*, a lad or servant).

Swaziland, in South Africa, is the country of the AMA-SWAZI, or 'people of Swazi,' a former chief whose name meant 'the rod.' The prefix *ama-* is the same as that which we have in MA-SHONA, BECHUANA, or BA-NTU (*q.v.*).

Sweden is the modern English name of the kingdom called Swedeland in England till the Thirty Years' War, when we adopted the German name SCHWEDEN, an ethnic term originally denoting the Swedes, and, in a secondary sense, their country. Schweden is from *Sui-theod*, which means the Svea-people. The Swedish name of Sweden is SVERGE or SVERIGE, a corruption of *Sve-rike* or *Svea-rike*, a name which survived till the sixteenth century, and means the 'Svea realm.' The central province of SVEA-LAND was the nucleus of the Svea-rike, and came gradually to include the dependent provinces, just as

France includes its kernel, the Isle de France, as Switzerland includes the Canton of Schwyz, and the Austrian Empire the small Austrian duchy. In the earliest times there were two distinct races, the Göta or Geats in the South, and the Svea or Swedes in the North, just as England includes the Angles of the North-East, and the Saxons of the South-West.

Switzerland is the English name of the Federal State called SCHWEIZ in German, and LA SUISSE in French. The name Switzerland, which goes back to 1617, when it appears as Sweitzerland in Fynes Moryson's travels, means the land of the Swiss (in German *Schwyzer*), a name originally designating the people of the small Canton of Schwyz, which was the first to assert its independence, and was afterwards extended to their confederates of Uri and Unterwalden, and finally to the inhabitants of the other Cantons which successively joined the league. Only in 1803 do we find any official recognition of the distinctive spelling, previously adopted by historians, of Schwyz for the Canton, and Schweiz or Schweitz for the confederation. The Canton takes its name from the village of SCHWYTZ, called *Swites* in 970, and *Switz* in 1281. A local legend refers the name to a settlement of Swedes. Hardly more probable is the modern guess that the village was built on a spot where the forest had been 'burnt' (O.H.G. *suedan*, 'to burn').

Sydney, the capital of New South Wales, was founded on January 26th, 1788, in Sydney Cove, Port Jackson, by Captain Arthur Phillip, R.N. (*see* PORT PHILLIP), the first Governor of New South Wales, who, in May 1787 had sailed from England with 11 ships and 200 marines, in charge of 776 convicts, and named PORT JACKSON had been named by Cook after a Secretary to the Admiralty, then known as Mr. George Jackson. SYDNEY COVE was named by Captain Phillip after Thomas Townshend, first Lord Sydney, who as Home Secretary drew up, in 1786, a scheme for the transportation of convicts to New South Wales. Sydney, a territorial surname, may be from an unidentified place in Kent called in a late A.S. charter *Sudaneie*, the 'south isle.' CAPE SYDNEY, in the Salomon Islands, was discovered in 1788 by Captain Shortland, on a voyage from Sydney to England.

Sydra, Gulf of, on the coast of Tripoli, preserves the classical name of the *Syrtis*, or 'sandbank.'

Sylhet, in Assam, locally pronounced

Chhilat, signifies 'the market of good fortune' (*srí-hatt*).

Sylt, an island off the coast of Schleswig, is a corruption of the Old Frisian name *Silendi*, 'sea-land.'

Syracuse (in Italian, *Siracusa*; in Greek, *Syracusæ*), the greatest Greek colony in Sicily, is believed to have replaced an older Phœnician trading post which obtained its name from a marsh at the mouth of the Anapus called *Syraco*, a name explained from the Phœnician *serach* or *sarach*, 'to stink.'

Syria, now called *Súristan* by the Turks and Persians, is the classical name which replaced the older name *Aram*, 'the highlands.' The name Syria first appears in Herodotus, and is doubtless a modification of the name Assyria, adopted by the Greeks at the time when Aram was included in the Assyrian Empire. Assyria was thought to be the land of the eponymous deity Assur oᵣ Asshur, but it is now believed to have taken its name from the former capital ASSUR, a city on the Tigris, represented by the mounds of Kalah Shergat. Assur is supposed to be an Accadian name meaning 'the water bank,' the deity deriving his name from that of the sacred city.

Szent-Kercsyt, in Hungary, is a Magyar name equivalent to Santa Cruz, the town of the 'holy cross.' So SZENT-GYÖRGY is 'St. George's,' MIND-SZENT is 'All Saints,' SZENDRO is 'St. Andrews,' and SZENTES or SZENTA means 'holy' town or 'saints' town.

Tabasco, a town in Mexico, capital of the province of the same name, stands on the RIO TABASCO, also called RIO DE GRIJ-ALVA, on whose banks in 1518 Juan de Grijalva met Tabasco, a friendly Cacique. QUAREQUA and POCOROSA are also towns which preserve the names of native chiefs.

Table Bay at Cape Town, when first discovered by the Portuguese was called *Angra da Concepção*, from the day of its discovery. The later name, *Angra de Saldanha* (*q.v.*), is now shifted to a bay further north. The name Table Bay is due to the Dutchman Joris Spilbergen, and dates only from 1601, but the conspicuous flat-topped mountain which lies behind the bay had already been named *A Meza*, 'the Table,' by the Portuguese. CAPE TABLE in New Zealand, TABLE CAPE in Tasmania, TABLE HILL in North Australia, TABLE MOUNTAIN in Wicklow and in South Carolina, the TABLE HILL near San Francisco, as well as TREBIZOND (*q.v.*), are descriptive names of the same class.

Tabriz, the commercial capital of Persia, was the classical and medieval *Tauris*. A local legend explains the modern name as the 'fever-expelling' place, relating how Zobeideh, the wife of the Khalif Harun-er-Rashid was here cured of a fever. The real etymology refers to the 'hot springs' for which Tabriz is noted, being from the word *teb* or *tap*, 'warm,' which we have in TIFLIS (*q.v.*), and the verbal root *rez*, *riz*, or *rest*, 'to flow.'

Tabun Aral, in the delta of the Volga near Astrakhan, is a Kalmuck name meaning the 'five islands.' TABUN TOLOGOI, in Mongolia, means the 'five hills.'

Tagus was the Roman name of the river called TAJO in Spanish and TEJO in Portuguese. According to Martial and Strabo it was celebrated for its fish, which confirms the usual explanation that the name is Phœnician, meaning the 'Fish' river.

Tahiti (the *Otaheite* of Cook), in the Society Group, is probably a tribal name, from *taitu*, 'the men.' It was discovered by Quiros in 1606, and named *Isla Sagiaria*, 'archers' island.' In 1767 it was visited by Wallis, who called it *George the Third's Island*.

Takhtipul, the seat of government in Afghán Turkistán, means the 'city of the throne.' So TAKHT-I-SULÁIMÁN, the highest summit in the Suláimán range, is 'Solomon's throne.'

Talaing, the name by which the chief race inhabiting Pegu is known to the Burmese, probably means 'slaves,' literally 'those who are trodden under foot.'

Talavera is the name of three towns in Spain, one of which, TALAVERA DELLA REYNA, has been doubtfully identified with the Roman *Talabriga*. But, as the prefix occurs in several Spanish names, it is probably the Arabic *talah*, from *atallah*, a 'look-out place.'

Talbot, Cape, North Australia, was named by King, in 1819, after Earl Talbot, Lord-Lieutenant of Ireland.

Talk-on-the-Hill is a mining town in Staffordshire. A local legend refers the name to a council of war held here by Charles I. The name is probably from the Welsh *twlch* (Gaelic *tulach*), a 'small hill' or 'knoll,' seen in numerous Irish and Scotch names, such as TULLOCH (*q.v.*).

Tallahassee, the state capital of Florida, is a native name meaning the 'old town.' (Creek *italua* or *talwa*, a 'town' or 'village,' and *ahassi*, 'old,' 'waste,' 'deserted.')

Tamaulipas, a coast province of Mexico, means the 'place of Indian-rubber,' from the Aztec *tam*, a 'place,' which we have in TAMPICO and other Mexican names, and *olli* or *ulli*, 'caoutchouc.'

Tamworth, Staffordshire, a residence of the Mercian kings, is the 'estate on the River Tame' (A.S. *Tama-weorthig*). The name of the TAME, like those of the THAMES and the THAME, is referred to the Celtic *tam*, 'spreading, quiet, still.' TAMERTON, Devon, is the *tún* on the River Tamar. TAMAR and DOLPHIN, two headlands at the entrance of Falkland Sound, were named by Byron in 1765 after his two ships.

Tananarivo, the capital of Madagascar, is more correctly called ANTANANARIVO (*q.v.*).

Tanganyika, the name of one of the great African lakes, is doubtless compounded with the Bantu word *tanganya*, to 'gather' or 'collect.' The Europeans who first visited its shores thought it was so named from the gathering or mingling of the waters of the numerous streams flowing from the surrounding hills, while others maintained that it was named from the gathering of the various tribes on its banks. Subsequent researches have shown that *nyika* is the local name of the waterchestnut (*Trapa natans*), a floating water plant producing edible nuts which 'gather' in great masses, and it is now believed that Tanganyika means the place where the nyika nuts gather or collect. The lake bears several names. The Wa-kawendi call it *Msaga*, 'the tempestuous,' while the Wa-rungu name is *Kimana*.

Tangiers, in Morocco, properly TANGIER, is an English corruption of the Portuguese name *Tanger*, and this again was a corruption of the Arabic *Tanja*, which transmits the old Numidian name made by the Romans into *Tingis* or *Tinge*.

Tanjore is a city and district in Southern India. In the eleventh century inscription on the great Tanjore Pagoda the name appears as *Tanjávúr*, which is believed to mean the 'Low Town.'

Tankerville is an English earldom, the title of which is derived from the Norman earldom of TANCARVILLE bestowed by Henry V. on Sir John Grey of Heton, who fought at Agincourt. TANCARVILLE, in Normandy, may be referred to Tanchard, a Teutonic personal name.

Taormina, on the eastern coast of Sicily, is a corruption of the classical name *Tauromenion*, which was given to the town built in 397 B.C. on Mount Tauros,

the hill above Naxos, after the destruction of that city in 403 B.C. According to Diodorus Siculus the name denoted the intention of the settlers to 'abide on Tauros.'

Tapajoz, Rio, a great affluent of the Amazons, bears the name of a tribe found on its banks by Texeira in 1639.

Tara, in Meath, the seat of the Overking of Ireland, is a corruption of the Old Irish name *teamhair*, which denotes an elevated spot commanding an extensive prospect. The same word appears in the Anglicised form *tower* in such names as TOWERMORE and TOWERBEG.

Tarái, the name of the strip of fever-haunted jungle at the foot of the Himálaya, means the 'moist land.'

Taranaki, a province in New Zealand, takes its name from Taranaki, the Maori name of the volcano called by Cook MOUNT EGMONT (*q.v.*). The Maori word *tara*, 'rock,' is also found in the name of LAKE TARAWERA, which means the 'burnt rocks,' while TE TARATA means the 'tatooed rocks.'

Taranto, the town which gives a name to the GULF OF TARANTO, was the Roman *Tarentum* and the Greek *Taras*, a name derived from the Taras, a small stream on which the Greek colony stood.

Tarbert, TARBAT, or TARBET is a common Scotch name derived from the Gaelic *tairbeart*, an 'isthmus,' which popular etymology explains as a contraction of *tarruing-báta*, meaning literally a 'drawboat' or 'boat draught' place, used to denote a narrow neck of land across which the *curachs* or skin canoes could be dragged from bay to bay. Thus at TARBAT NESS in Ross-shire, called in Gaelic *Rugha Tarbait*, the 'Tarbat Promontory,' there is such a narrow neck of land separating the Moray Frith from the German Ocean.

Tarifa, a town on the Straits of Gibraltar, is believed to bear the name of Tarif-Ben-Malik-Abu-Zarah, the first Berber chief who effected a landing in Spain, but may perhaps be the Arabic *taraf*, a tract or district. CABO TARIFA is the most southern point on the continent of Europe.

Tarragona, a city and province in Catalonia, preserves the Roman name *Portus Tarraconis, Colonia Tarraconensis*, or *Tarraco*, which has been explained by Bochart from the Phœnician *tarchon*, a 'citadel.'

Tartary is the old name, now falling into disuse, for Turkistan, the parts of Central Asia which are inhabited by the nomads of Turkic race called Tartars or Tatars. The name is said to have arisen out of the designation *Tha-ta*, 'robbers,' applied by the Chinese to the Mongols, and when the hordes of Genghis Khan appeared in Eastern Europe the name was applied to the Turkic tribes which followed him. The spelling ' Tartar ' arose from the detestation of these desolating hordes, who were held to be a brood issuing from the bottomless pit, the realm of Tartarus. The GULF OF TARTARY was a name applied by La Pérouse in 1767 to the sound which separates the island of Saghalien from the coast of Mongolia. (*See* TURKEY.)

Tasmania, the modern name of Van Diemen's Land, commemorates the geographical exploits of Abel Janz Tasman, who was despatched on a voyage of discovery by Antony Van Diemen, Governor-General of the Dutch East Indies. Sailing from Batavia in August 1642 with two ships, the *Heemskirk* and the *Zeehahn*, he sighted Tasmania on November 24th, and sailing from the west round the south of the island, practically established the fact that Australia did not form part of the supposed South Polar continent which geographers had hypothetically named *Terra Australis Incognita*. Tasman, however, did not discover that Tasmania was an island, but supposed that it formed part of New Holland, as Australia was then called. The island retained the name of VAN DIEMEN'S LAND, bestowed by Tasman in honour of his patron, till 1855, when the name was officially changed to Tasmania, partly in honour of the discoverer, and also because the colonists thought the old name opprobrious, the island, as a penal settlement, having become a pandemonium. On December 13th, 1642, Tasman sighted the high mountains on the west coast of New Zealand, in lat. 42° 10', and anchored in TASMAN BAY. In 1644, on a second voyage, Tasman explored a part of the north-western coast of Australia which, in his honour, has been called TASMANLAND. Flinders, in 1802, gave the name of ABEL TASMAN'S RIVER to a stream which flows into the Gulf of Carpentaria, believing that Tasman had visited the coast in 1644. TASMAN'S PENINSULA, in Tasmania, was discovered by Tasman, and called Abel Tasman's Island, afterwards receiving its present name when it was found to be united to the mainland by a narrow neck.

Taunton, Somerset (A.S. *Tan - tún*), is the *tún* on the River Tone.

Taunus, a range of hills in Nassau, is a modern revival by German scholars of the Roman name, which is unknown to the peasantry, by whom these hills are called DIE HÖHE.

Taviers in Belgium, called *Tavernæ* in the twelfth century, as well as TABERNAS in Andalusia and ZABERN in Elsass, called *Zaberna* in the seventh century, are from the Latin *taberna*, a ' tavern.'

Tavistock, Devon, is the *stoc* or ' place on the Tavy.' The name appears in a charter of 1042 as *Tæfingstoc*, and in a forged charter of later date as *Tavistoc.*

Tay, the largest river of Scotland, flows from LOCH TAY, where, probably, was the *Tamia* of Ptolemy, a name explained by the Gaelic *tamh*, ' tranquil ' or ' smooth,' the equivalent of the Pictish *tau* and the Cymric *taw*, of which an oblique case may be the source of the name *Tava*, given by Tacitus to the Firth of Tay.

Taylor's Isles, in Spencer Gulf, were so named by Flinders in 1802 in memory of William Taylor, one of his officers who was drowned in the wreck of the cutter.

Tchad, CHAD, or TSAD, more correctly TSÁDÉ, is a great swampy lake in Central Africa, whose name is a dialectic form of *Ssághi*, the ' water.'

Tchao Sien, ' Morning Serenity,' the oldest name of Corea, is still in use. According to Terrien de Lacouperie it dates from about 1100 B.C., when it was bestowed by a member of the Shang-yu dynasty of China, who had established himself there. The later name, COREA or KOREA, a corruption of *Kao Li*, ' Kao's Elegance,' was used officially in 918 A.D.

Teddington, Middlesex, cannot mean, according to the popular etymology, ' Tide-end-town,' since the form *Tudingtún*, which is found in an A.S. charter, proves that it is derived from a personal name. TEDDINGTON, Worcestershire, called *Teottingtún* in a charter, is also from a personal name.

Tee Bee, near Washington, U.S.A., is not, as might be supposed, a native name. The letters T.B., believed to be the initials of Thomas Blandford, an early owner of the soil, were found cut upon a tree, whence the place was known as T.B., converted, for euphony or convenience, into TEE BEE by the Post Office officials of the United States. Of similar origin is the name of the famous JENOLAN Stalactite Caves in the Blue Mountains, New South Wales, the initials of the discoverer, J. E. Nolan, carved in the rock at the entrance having become part of the name by which the caves are known.

Teheran, correctly TEHRAN, the capital of Persia, is a name of unknown etymology, the usual explanation as the 'pure' place, and the proposed identification with the *Tahors* of the Theodosian Tables being both untenable.

Telega signifies a 'lake' in Malay. Hence such Javanese names as TELEGA-PASIR, the 'mountain lake,' or TELEGA-BODAS, the 'white lake.'

Tel el-Maskhutah, the 'mound of the image,' marks the site of the city of Pithom, the image being the colossal statue of Rameses II. now in the garden at Ismailia. Close by is TEL EL-KEBIR, the 'great mound,' where Arabi Pacha was defeated on September 13th, 1882, which conceals the ruins of some still larger town. A hillock or mound is *tel* in Egyptian Arabic and *tell* in Syrian Arabic, words used to denote the mounds which usually cover the sites of deserted cities. Thus TELL EL-HESY is the name of the mound which covers the site of Lachish, and TEL EL-AMARNA that of the mounds on the eastern bank of the Nile, between Assiout and Miniah, covering the city built by Khu-n-Aten to supersede Thebes as the capital of Egypt.

Temisconata, a lake and district in Canada, is a native name believed to mean 'the wonder of water.'

Templemore, in County Derry, is the 'great church,' the Old Irish *teampull*, a 'church,' being derived from the Latin *templum*. TEMPLE in English names, such as TEMPLE HURST or TEMPLE NEWSAM, denotes a preceptory of the Knights Templars. A preceptory founded by David I. has given a name to the parish of TEMPLE in Midlothian.

Tenasserim, a district in Lower Burma, is so called from an insignificant hamlet, once an important city, of the same name, which is a corruption of *Tana-sari*, 'betel leaf island.'

Tenby, a watering-place in Pembrokeshire, is a Flemish corruption of the Welsh name *Dynbych-y-Pyscod*, 'fish cliff.' (*See* DENBIGH.)

Tenerife, one of the Canaries, is a Portuguese corruption of *Chinerfe* or *Tinerfe*, the name of the last Guanche chief. From its snow-clad peak the Romans called it *Nivaria*, the 'snowy.'

Tengri-Khan is the Mongolian name of the highest mountain in the Thian-shan range. It consists of a cluster of some twenty snowy ghost-like peaks, thus accounting for the name, which may be translated the 'ghost king,' or perhaps the 'heaven king.' TENGRI-NUR, a lake in Central Asia, discovered in 1872, is a Mongolian name meaning 'Sky Lake' or 'Sea of Heaven.'

Tennessee, one of the United States, is traversed by a tributary of the Ohio, called the Tennessee River, usually explained as a descriptive name meaning 'the crooked spoon'; but it may be a tribal name from *tena* or *tinneh*, which means 'people' or 'the men.'

Tennyson's Monument is a lofty isolated pillar of rock on the eastern coast of Kane Sea, which to Kane's vivid imagination seemed, he says, to resemble the poet's Genius, rising like a lofty rock in the solitudes of a wilderness.

Teramo, in Italy, was formerly the capital of the Prætutii, and hence called *Interamna Prætutiana*, a name clipped down to *Teramne*, and then to *Teramo*, 'between the rivers.' TERNI, in Umbria, which lies between two branches of the Nera, is a corruption of the old name *Interamna*.

Terek, a river flowing into the Caspian, is believed to mean the Turks' river, from a Turkic tribe living on its banks.

Terhalten is a Fuegian island, named in 1624 from Johan Ter Halte, captain of the ship *Mauritius*.

Termini, in Sicily, has saline springs with a temperature of 110° Fahr. Hence the ancient name of *Thermæ*, the 'hot springs,' which has become Termini. So the Piazza di Termini, at Rome, now called PIAZZA DELLE TERME, which fronts the railway station, is named from the *Thermæ* of Diocletian, and not from the railway terminus. But the LAGUNA DE TERMINOS, a gulf in Yucatan, was so named by Grijalva in 1518 because, thinking Yucatan was an island, he imagined that he had found the channel dividing it from the mainland.

Termonde (German DENDERMONDE) is at the 'mouth' or confluence of the River Dender (anciently the *Tenera*) with the Schelt.

Terror Bay is the name which has been given to a place in King William Island, which was the scene of the final catastrophe in Franklin's last fatal Arctic expedition. In 1848 the two ships, the *Terror* and the *Erebus*, having been abandoned in the ice, the survivors of the crews seem to have struggled on to Terror Bay, where the Eskimos reported that they had found a tent, 'the floor of which was completely covered with the bodies of white men.' The *Terror* had been one of the ships of the Antarctic expedition of James Clark Ross, whence the Antarctic names of TERROR REEF, TERROR COVE, and MOUNT TERROR. (*See* EREBUS.)

Tersoos, in Asia Minor, represents the ancient *Tarsus*, which is to be explained as the 'strong place,' since the name is presumably Phœnician, like the *Tarshish* of the Bible (the *Tartessus* of Herodotus), whose site must probably be sought near the mouth of the Guadiana.

Tetas de Cabra, the 'goat's teats,' is the descriptive Spanish name of a mountain near the Gulf of California.

Tetuan, in Morocco, is from the Arabic *tewawin,* a dual form signifying 'the two springs' or wells, literally the 'two eyes.'

Tetuara or TETIAROA, the island in 'the distant sea,' belongs to the Society Group.

Tewkesbury, Gloucestershire, is supposed to take its name from a monastery founded in 715 on the site of the hermitage of Theoc, a Saxon monk.

Texas, one of the United States, was the territory of the Assinaes, a native tribe called by the Spaniards Tiguas, Tejas, or Texas, a name which is believed to have arisen from a curious blunder of Father Damian, who visited the coast at the end of the seventeenth century. Asking one of the Assinaes their tribal name, the reply *texia,* which means 'good friend,' was assumed to be the name of the tribe.

Texel, an island at the entrance to the Zuider Zee, was called *Texela* and *Texla* in the ninth century, and may possibly be the *Tekelia* of Ptolemy. The etymology is doubtful, the most probable explanation being from the Frisian *têk* or *thêk* (Old Frisian *thekke*), which denotes the line of sea wrack thrown up by the tide, marking its highest reach.

Thames, the *Tamesis* of Cæsar, is a Celtic name meaning the 'tranquil' or 'smooth' river (*see* TAMWORTH and TAY). In Saxon charters it appears as *Tæmese, Tamese,* and *Temis.* It is *Tamisia* in one MS. of Nennius, *Tamisis* in another. The RIVER THAME which joins the Thames some fifteen miles below Oxford is called *Tame-strém* in an early charter. The name ISIS (*q.v.*), given to the Upper Thames, is thought to be an early ghost-name. The WAIHO (*q.v.*), a river in New Zealand, was renamed the THAMES by Cook in 1769, because it was as broad as the Thames at Greenwich.

Thanet, Isle of, in Kent, is called *Tenet* and *Tænet* in the Chronicle, and in A.S. charters *Tenid, Tænet, Tenatorum Insula,* and *Thanet.* The name *Tanatus,* as Mommsen has shown, has been preserved in a misread passage of Solinus, who is believed to have written in the third century, and it appears as *Tenet* in the Peutinger Tables, and hence the name is probably pre-Teutonic, in spite of the fact that it is the *Coünnus* of Ptolemy, and the *Ruim* of Asser. The name may be compared with that of LE TANNEY (Eure), which appears in a document of 1138 as *Tanetum.* TANNOIS (Meuse) was *Tannacum* in 992, and we have places called TANAY and THENAY in Brittany, doubtless from the Low-Latin *tannetum,* a 'place of oaks.' This, as well as our verb 'to tan,' is explained by the Armorican *tann,* an 'oak-tree,' which, if allied to the German *tanne,* a 'fir-tree,' may have had the primitive meaning of a 'forest tree.' Hence Thanet may mean an 'oak-wood,' or simply a 'wood' or 'forest.'

Thank God Bay, in Smith Sound, is the place where Captain Hall in the *Polaris* took refuge from the ice in 1871, and found safe winter quarters.

Thayet-myo, a district in Pegu, takes its name from its capital THAYET-MYO, ostensibly meaning 'mango city,' but believed to be a corruption of *That-yet-myo,* the 'city of slaughter,' so called, according to the local legend, from the slaughter of his sons by an early king. The Burmese *myo,* a town, is seen in ALLAN-MYO and other names.

Thebes in Bœotia, the Greek *Thebæ,* is now called PHEBA or PHIBA. The site of the acropolis was a small hill, and we learn from Varro that *teba* meant a hill. In the name of the Egyptian THEBES we have a Greek corruption of the popular Egyptian designation of the city, which was called *t'ape,* 'the capital,' the initial *t* being the feminine article. The old name is preserved by the village called MEDINET ABU, the 'city of Ape,' which occupies the site of ancient Thebes.

Theresienstadt in Hungary was named after the Empress Maria Theresa, and THEREZOPOLIS in Brazil after the Empress Thereza, wife of Pedro II.

Thetford, formerly the capital of the East Angles, is at the junction of a stream now called the Thet with the Little Ouse, which divides Norfolk from Suffolk. It is called *Theod-ford* in the Chronicle and *Theth-ford* in an A.S. charter. The name is usually explained either as the ford over the Thet, or as the 'people's ford' (A S. *theod*, 'folk' or 'nation'), an etymology so improbable that we may prefer the A.S. *theote*, a 'watercourse' or conduit. A parallel name is that of the German DIETFURT, formerly *Theot-furt*, which is supposed to be the 'ford of the people.'

Thibet or TIBET is the European form of an Arabic corruption of the Mongolian name of a country which is called BOD, 'the country,' by the natives, BHOTIJA by the Indians, and THU-PIIO by the Chinese. The oldest Chinese form is said to be *Tu-bat* or *Tu-pat* (fifth century), the Mongolian is *Tü-bet*, and the Arabic *Tibat*, *Tobbat*, and *Tibet* (ninth and tenth centuries). Rabbi Benjamin in 1165 has *Thibet*, and Marco Polo has *Tebet*. The second syllable means 'land' or 'country,' and the first probably signifies 'high,' 'great,' or 'strong.' According to a legendary story reported by Terrien de Lacouperie, a Chinese prince named Tapöt Fanni conquered the country in 434 A.D. and gave it his name, Ta-pöt, which means 'prince of the land.'

Thieves Sound, in Fuegia, was so named by Fitzroy in 1830, because one of his boats was stolen by the natives.

Thingwall, in Cheshire, was the meeting-place of the *thing* or judicial assembly of the Scandinavian colony in the Wirral. The O.N. *thinga-völlr* is from *völlr*, a plain, field, or inclosure, and *thing*, a council or parliament. The Manx laws are still promulgated at TYNWALD HILL on July 5 (St. John's day, old style), without which ceremony they are not valid, and till recently the Icelandic Thing was held on the plain called THING-VÖLLR. The Things of other Scandinavian settlements seem to have been held at TING-WALL in Shetland, at DINGWALL, the county town of Ross-shire, and at TIN-WALD HILL near Dumfries.

Thionville, a town on the Mosel, is an ancient French translation of the German name DIEDENHOFEN, anciently *Thioden-hove*, 'Thiod's hof,' from a personal name.

Thirsty Sound, Australia, was so called by Cook because he found no fresh water.

Thirteen Islands, a cluster in the Caroline Group, were so named by Wilson in 1797 from their number.

Thistle Island, at the entrance to Spencer Gulf, and THISTLE COVE, South Australia, bear the name of John Thistle, an officer of Flinders' ship the *Investigator*.

Thorny Passage, between Dirk Hartog's Island and the Australian coast, was so named by Dampier on account of the sharp rocks by which it is beset.

Thousand Isles, a group of islets in the St. Lawrence, are said to number 1600. The THOUSAND LAKES, west of Lake Superior, a translation of the French name *Mille Lacs*, is a sheet of water so thickly studded with islands that it seems to consist of innumerable small lakes.

Throndhjem, a town in Norway, often spelt TRONDHEIM or DRONDHEIM, and explained as the 'throne home,' was originally the name of a district which was the home of a people called Thronds. The town built by King Olaf Tryggvason in this district at the mouth of the Nidar was at first called Nidaros (*i.e.* 'Nidar-mouth'), or Kaupstad, the 'merchant's town,' but ultimately obtained the name of the surrounding country.

Thule, Southern, Sandwich Land, was so called by Cook in 1773, because it was then 'the most southern land that has ever yet been discovered.' The locality of the *Thule* of Pytheas has been much disputed. Possibly the name may be preserved in that of the Scandinavian district of TIELEMARK.

Thun, a town in Canton Bern, gives a name to the Thuner See or LAKE OF THUN, which is called *Lacus Dunensis* in 595, proving that the early form of the name Thun was *Dun*, the well-known Celtic designation of a hill fortress. In the twelfth century the name had become *Tuno* and *Tuna*.

Thurgau is a Swiss Canton, consisting of the district called in the eighth century *Duragowe*, the *gau* or 'district' on the River Dura, now the Thur. There is also a RIVER THUR in Elsass. The THÜRINGER WALD, in Central Germany, preserves the name of the powerful Thur-ingian nation, whose territory is now divided among the so-called Saxon duchies, which are Saxon only in a dynastic sense.

Thurles, an episcopal see in Tipperary, anciently called *Durlas O'Fogarty*, was the *dur-lios* or 'strong fort' of O'Fogarty.

Thurso, called in Gaelic *Inbhir-Theòrsa* (Inver Thursa), is a town in Caithness at the mouth of the River Thurso, called in the twelfth century *Thórsá*, a Norse name meaning 'Thor's water' or river, but not necessarily from the Scandinavian deity, since Thor was a common personal name among the Northmen, as in the village-names THURSTON or THORESBY.

Thusis, in Canton Graubünden, is called

in Italian TOSANA, a form found as early as 1156, and explained by Gatschet as an adjectival form from the Romansch *dutg*, *duch*, or *duoch* (Low-Latin and Italian *doccia*), which denotes a duct or aqueduct of wooden pipes through which water is led. The RIVER TOSA, in Italian TOCCIA, is from the same source.

Tiber (Italian TEVERE) was the Roman *Tiberis*. From the name of the river was derived the Roman name Tiberius, whence we have TABARIEH, on the Sea of Galilee, which preserves the name of *Tiberias*, given by Herod Antipas in honour of the Emperor Tiberius. TIVOLI, on the River Teverone, is a corruption of *Tibur*, the Roman name.

Tiburon, a large island in the Gulf of California, is called in Spanish ISLA DEL TIBURON, 'shark island.' CABO TIBURON, 'shark cape,' at the south-west corner of Haiti, was named by Columbus *Cabo de San Miguel*. Magellan named an island south-west of the Marquesas ISLA DE LOS TIBURONES, 'island of the sharks.'

Ticino, or TESSIN, a Swiss canton, takes its name from the River Ticino, anciently the *Ticinus*.

Ticonderoga, a summer resort on Lake Champlain, N.Y., bears a native name said to mean the 'noisy' place, from the roar of the falls at the outlet to Lake George.

Tien-Tsin, a Chinese town at the mouth of the PEI-HO or 'white river,' means the 'celestial place,' the name being correctly translated by Marco Polo as *Città Celeste*.

Tiflis, a town in the Caucasus with thermal springs, was founded in 469 A.D. It is a corruption of the Georgian name *Tbylysys-Kalaky* or *Tphilissi-Kalaki*, the 'hot (water) city.'

Tigris is a name rightly explained by Strabo, who says that it was so called from its swiftness, 'for among the Medes *tigris* means an arrow.' The primitive Accadian name *Idiqla*, the 'encircling' river (the *Hiddekel* of Genesis), was changed by the Semites to *Idiglat*, with the feminine suffix, out of which the Aryan Persians, by a play upon words, constructed *Tigrâ*, the swift or arrowy (Zend *tighri*, an 'arrow'), whence also the name of the *tiger* or swift beast. It is now locally called *Shat*, the 'river.' BOCCA TIGRIS (*q.v.*) or BOCA DO TIGRE, the European name of the mouth of the Canton River, is of Portuguese origin, derived from the ILHA DO TIGRE, an island on whose eastern side is a rock resembling the head of a tiger.

Tîh is the name of the desert between Palestine and Sinai. The Arabs call it *et-Tîh-beni-Israel*, 'the wanderings of the children of Israel,' or simply *et-Tîh*, 'the wanderings.'

Tilsit, in East Prussia, was a castle built in 1288 by the Teutonic knights at the junction with the Niemen of the TILSE, or 'marsh' river (Lithuanian *tilszus*, 'marshy').

Timbuktu, formerly spelt TIMBUCTOO, in Central Africa, is the Arabic form of the native name, which is *Timbutu* in Surhai, the language of the place, *Tumbutu* in Somrai, and *Tumbutku* in Berber, words which mean a 'hollow,' the city being built in a depression in the sand-hills, and also overlooking a marshy hollow which was the former bed of a creek branching from the Niger.

Timor, or TIMUR, a Malay word signifying the 'east' or the 'orient,' is the name of the easternmost of the Sunda Islands. Apart from the rest, and still further to the east, lies the island of TIMUR LAUT, which may be translated 'seaward Timur' or 'east sea island.' (*See* LAUT.)

Timsah, a lake on the Suez canal fronting the town of Ismailia, is locally called *Bahr-el-Timsah*, 'crocodile lake.'

Tinnevelli (*Tiru-nel-véli*), a town giving a name to a district in Southern India, is explained by Burnell as meaning the 'sacred Rice hedge,' or the 'sacred Bamboo hedge.'

Tinto, Rio, in Spain, is the 'coloured river,' so called because its waters are tinted by the copper ores in its bed.

Tipperary, a town which gives a name to an Irish county, was called in Old Irish *Tiobraid-Arann*, 'the well of Ara,' from a famous well, now closed, in the main street of the town. Arann is the genitive of *Ara*, the name of the district, and *tiobraid* is the Gaelic *tobar*, a 'well,' whence TOBERMORY, 'St. Mary's well,' in Mull; TIPPERMUIR, the 'great well,' in Perthshire; and TOBERMORE, the 'great well,' in Mayo, which, according to the legend, was blessed by St. Patrick. TIPPERKEVIN is the 'well of St. Kevin,' and TOBER-NA-CLUG is the 'well of the bell.' TIPPERSTOWN is a translation of the older name BALLINTOBAR (*Baile-an-tobar*), the 'town of the well.' In the Isle of Man *tobar* becomes *chibber*, as in CHIBBER VOIRREY, 'St. Mary's Well,' or CHIBBER UNJIN, the 'ash well,' so called from a sacred ash tree on which votive offerings were hung, Unjin being the

Gaelic *uinnsinn*, as in CROOK UNJIN, 'ash tree hill,' in the Isle of Man.

Tiree, one of the Hebrides, a low and fertile island, is a corruption of *Tir-eth*, meaning either the 'land of corn,' or the 'land of Ith,' an Irish tribe.

Titlis, a well-known Swiss mountain, was so called because its slopes are overgrown with a dock (*Rumex acutus*) locally called *Ditt*, or *Tittiblache*.

Tiverton, Devon, is a corruption of the old name *Twy-ford-tún*, the 'tun at the two fords.' The town is at the confluence of two rivers, the Exe and the Lowman, each of which is now crossed by a bridge, replacing the 'two fords' from which the place takes its name. TWYFORD is the name of several places where there were 'two fords.'

Tlaxcala, formerly *Tlascala*, is a town and province in Mexico, believed to mean in Aztec the 'house of bread.'

Tobago or TABAGO, one of the Antilles, was discovered in 1500 by Vicente Yañez Pinzon, and called *Mayo*, a name replaced by Tabago, which, if not the native name, may be a corruption of an older form *Tra-bajo*, meaning the island of toil, labour, or trouble. The BAHIA DE LOS TRABAJOS, or 'Bay of Troubles,' in Patagonia, was a name given by Magellan in 1520 on account of the increasing perils and difficulties he encountered.

Tobolsk, the capital of Western Siberia, was founded in 1587, the year after Siberia had been conquered by Tchulkoff and his five hundred Cossacks. It stands at the confluence of the Tobol and the Irtish, not far from the Tartar town of Ssibir, to whose proximity to Tobolsk the name of SIBERIA (*q.v.*) is due. The river TOBOL derived its name from the 'willows' growing on its banks.

Tödi, a stumpy mountain in Canton Glarus, formerly called the *Töddi* or *Döddi*, is a name derived from the Romansch word *detti* (*digitus*), a 'finger.'

Todos os Santos, 'All Saints,' is a common Portuguese dedication. CABO DE TODOS OS SANTOS, Brazil, was discovered by Diego Leite in 1531, doubtless on All Saints' Day, November 1st. The RIO DE TODOS OS SANTOS in Brazil is a tributary of the Mucuri River. The BAHIA DE TODOS OS SANTOS in Brazil, discovered by Vespucci on November 1st, is now called simply BAHIA (*q.v.*).

Tokio (formerly called Yeddo), the capital of Japan, is the 'Eastern capital,' in contradistinction to SAIKIO, the 'Western capital.'

Toledo, the capital of Gothic Spain, was the Roman *Toletum*, a name of unknown etymology, wildly supposed to be of Phœnician origin, meaning the city of 'generations' (Hebrew *toledoth*, 'genealogies').

Tomsk is a Siberian Town founded in 1604 on the River Tom.

Tongariro, New Zealand, is the Maori name of the volcano 'to the south' of Lake Taupo.

Tongatabu, the *tabu* or 'sacred island,' is the largest in the Friendly Group. It was discovered by Tasman in 1643, and called *Amsterdam Eylandt*, but is now known by the native name.

Tongres, in Belgium, preserves the name of the Teutonic tribe called *Tungri* by Tacitus.

Tonquin or TONG-KING, called *Dong-King* by the Annamese, means the 'Eastern capital.' The name was originally applied to the city of Hanoi, the capital of Tong-King, but afterwards became the designation of the whole country. From *tong*, 'east,' we have many Chinese names, such as TONG-HAI, the 'eastern sea.'

Torcello, the mother islet of Venice, takes its name from the conspicuous campanile of the ancient cathedral. TORRES VEDRAS, in Portugal, means the 'old towers,' and TORQUEMADA, in Spain, is believed to be a corruption of *Turris cremata*, the 'burnt tower.'

Torment Point, North Australia, is one of the foolish names given by Stokes. It records the annoyance he suffered from mosquitoes in 1838.

Toronto is now the capital of the Canadian province of Ontario. The name at first denoted the country of the Huron tribe to which the BAY OF TORONTO gives access. Here a French trading post was built on the site of the present city, and called *Fort Toronto.* In 1793 the name was changed to *York* in honour of the Duke of York, but in 1834 the old name Toronto was revived.

Torquay, Devon, is the quay in TORBAY, so called from Torre Abbey, founded in 1196. At TOR-MAHON is the old church of the village from which the Abbey took its name. The numerous Tors in Derbyshire and Devon are from the British word *tor*, 'a hill,' cognate with the Latin *turris*. TORY ISLAND, off the coast of Donegal, is from the Old Irish *Toraigh* (pronounced *torry*), an oblique case of *Torach*, the old name, which means 'towery,' from the tors or towerlike rocks. TORY CHANNEL, in Queen Charlotte's Sound, was first surveyed by Captain Chaffers in the ship *Tory*.

Torrens River, LAKE TORRENS, and MOUNT TORRENS in Australia, bear the name of Colonel Torrens, one of the founders of the Colony of South Australia.

Torres Strait, between Australia and New Guinea, was discovered in 1606 by the Spanish navigator, Luis Vaez de Torres, second in command of an exploring expedition despatched from Peru to the Moluccas, in the course of which the New Hebrides and New Guinea were discovered. In 1770 Cook, ignorant of the discovery of Torres, gave the Strait the name of his ship the *Endeavour*, a name which has been retained for the Passage between Prince of Wales Island and the mainland. It was not till after Cook had passed through the Strait that a letter of Torres, describing his voyage, was discovered at Manila.

Tortugas, in the Gulf of Mexico, are the turtle islands. ISLA DE LA TORTUGA, 'turtle island,' north of Haiti, was discovered and named by Columbus in 1492. In 1513 Ponce de Leon gave the same name to an island off the coast of Florida which he found inhabited only by waterfowl and turtles.

Toul, on the Mosel, was the Roman *Tullum*, a Celtic word meaning a 'hill,' which we probably have in the name of TOULOUSE, the *Tolosa* of the Romans, still locally called TOLOSO. The diminutive *tulach* gives us numerous Scotch and Irish names. (*See* TULLOCH.)

Toulon, the great French arsenal, was the Greek *Telonion*, and the *Telo Martius* of the Itineraries.

Tournai, in Belgium, is called in Flemish DOORNIK, which preserves better than the French form the old name *Turnacum*, which d'Arbois de Jubainville derives from the proper name Turnus, with the possessive suffix -*ac*. It was the *Civitas Nerviorum* of Cæsar, and its coins bear the legend *Durnacos*.

Tours, the capital of the Old French province of TOURAINE, bears the name of the *Turones* or *Turoni*, a Gaulish tribe.

Towcester, in Northants, called in Domesday *Tovecestre*, is the chester on the River Tove.

Townshend Island, Queensland. Its northern point was named CAPE TOWNSHEND by Cook in 1770 from the family name of Lord Sydney, from whose peerage title came the name of the capital of New South Wales. (*See* SYDNEY.) In 1802 Flinders extended the name of the cape to the island, whose existence had escaped Cook's observation.

Townsville, Queensland, bears the name of Captain Town, a local shipowner.

Traitor's Head, Erromango, was so called by Cook in 1774 because of a treacherous attack by natives who had feigned friendship. At TREACHERY BAY, Arnhem Land, Stokes in 1839 was struck by the spear of a treacherous native.

Trafalgar is a cape in Andalusia, where the cliffs have been hollowed by the waves into caverns, whence the Arabic name *Taraf-al-ghar*, from *taraf*, a cape, side, or district, and *ghar*, a 'cave,' which we have in the Maltese name GARBO, the 'cave.' MOUNT TRAFALGAR, in New South Wales, and PORT NELSON, a neighbouring bay, were so named by Mitchell in 1836 because of his arrival on October 21st, the anniversary of Nelson's decisive victory at Cape Trafalgar in 1805.

Tralee, the county town of Kerry, formerly called *Traigh-Li* (in Latin documents *Littus Li*), is said to be the strand of a man named Li mic-Dedad, but more probably is the strand or shore of the River Lee. TRALEE, in Derry, formerly *Traigh-liath*, is the 'grey strand,' and TRAMORE, in Waterford, is the 'great strand.' BALLANTRAE (*bail-an-traigh*), in Antrim and Ayrshire, is the 'village on the shore.'

Tranquebar, formerly a Danish factory in Southern India, is a corruption of *Tarangam-bâdi*, the 'Sea town' or 'Wave town.' The Danish missionaries use the Latin form *Trangambaria* on their title-pages.

Transvaal, officially styled the South African Republic, is the territory beyond the Vaal (*q.v.*).

Transylvania, 'the land beyond the forest,' is a sort of Latin equivalent, used as early as the thirteenth century, for ERDÉLY, the 'woodland,' the Magyar name of the Hungarian crownland called by the Germans SIEBENBÜRGEN (*q.v.*).

Trapani, in Sicily, is a corruption of the descriptive Greek name *Drepana* or *Drepanon*, which refers to the 'sickle' shaped tongue of land forming the harbour.

Tras-os-Montes is a Portuguese province lying 'beyond the mountains.'

Travemünde, the port of Lübeck, is,

as the name implies, at the mouth of the River Trave.

Trebizond, on the Black Sea, is a corruption of the Greek name *Trapezus,* the 'table,' the old Greek city being built on a sloping tableland, with steep rocky precipices on two sides. The coast hills behind the modern town exhibit the same table-shaped outline. The modern form Trebizond has been influenced by *Tirabzûn,* the Turkish corruption of the Greek name.

Tremola, Val, in Canton Ticino, is the 'valley of aspens.'

Trent, one of the largest English rivers, has been identified by Mr. Bradley with the *Trisantona* of Tacitus. By the laws of Welsh phonology *Trisantona* would become *Trihanton* and then *Tryhannon,* and Nennius, when describing the Eagre rushing up at Gainsborough, calls the Trent *Trahannon.* There is a RIVER TARANNON in Wales. The ARUN was formerly called the *Tarant,* a corruption of Ptolemy's name TRISANTON. (*See* ARUNDEL.) The Dorset TARRANT is called *Tarente* in Domesday, and the PIDDLE, on which stands the village of Piddletrenthide, must also have borne the same name, as Asser and Florence speak of Wareham, which is at the junction of the Frome and the Piddle, as lying *inter duo flumina Fraw et Terente.*

Trent, the capital of the Italian Tyrol, called TRIENT in German, and TRENTO in Italian, was the Roman *Trientum* or *Tridentum,* a name supposed to refer to three neighbouring pointed rocks or teeth. From the Latin name the decrees of the Council of Trent are called *Tridentine.*

Tribulation, a name given by Cook to a cape in Queensland, commemorates the great calamity which befel him in his first voyage. Having safely navigated the dangerous channel between the Great Barrier Reef and the mainland, it was here, he tells us, that he first 'became acquainted with misfortune,' his ship, the *Endeavour* (*q.v.*), striking on a rock on June 10th, 1770.

Trier, on the Mosel, in French TRÈVES, the capital of the *Treveri,* was called by the Romans *Augusta Trevirorum* or *Colonia Treverorum.* Under the later empire the name became *Treviri,* from which, with the stress on the second syllable, came the modern German name TRIER, the French form TREVES being, as in other cases, from the dative *Treviris,* with the stress on the first syllable.

Trieste, an Adriatic port called TRIEST in German and TRST in Slavonic, represents the *Tergeste* of Pliny. The name, which is probably Illyrian, is supposed to be from *terst,* a 'reed.'

Trim, in Meath, is a corruption of *Ath-Truim,* the 'ford of the elder tree' (Irish *ath,* a 'ford,' and *truim,* genitive of *trom,* an 'elder tree').

Trinchinopoly is a famous rock-fort in Southern India. According to Burnell the oldest form of the name, which occurs in an inscription of 1520, is *Tiru-ssitapalli,* which would mean the 'town on the sacred rock.' So TRAVANCORE, a native state in Southern India, is explained as *Tiru-varán-kodu,* the 'sacred prosperous kingdom,' and its modern capital TRIVANDRUM as *Tiru-vánantapuram,* the 'city of the holy eternal one,' but TRINCOMALEE, a harbour in Ceylon, is believed to be a corruption of *Tri-konamalai,* 'three-peak-hill.'

Trinidad, a large West India island, was discovered by Columbus on his third voyage. On July 31st, 1498, the look-out at the masthead saw three separate flat summits, which were afterwards found to be united, so as to form one island. Hence Columbus called it *Ilha de la Trinidad.* In like manner a triangular island on the western coast of India was regarded by the Portuguese as a symbol of the Trinity, and hence called *Divo,* now DIU. TRINITY BAY, Queensland, was discovered by Cook on Trinity Sunday, 1770. TRINITY ISLAND, Alaska, and the neighbouring CAPE TRINITY were discovered by Cook on June 14th, 1778, and were named from the date of the discovery.

Tripoli in Syria, called TARÂBLUS by the Turks, was the Greek *Tripolis,* the seat in Persian times of the federal council of the three cities of Sidon, Tyre, and Aradus, each of which had its special quarter in the 'triple town.' TRIPOLITZA in the Morea, called *Tarâbolus* by the Turks, and now officially styled TRIPOLIS, is the capital of Arcadia, representing the three ancient cities of Mantinea, Pallantium, and Tegea. TRIPOLI, a North African vilayet of the Ottoman Empire, called in Arabic *Tarâbolus-al-Gharb,* 'Western Tripoli,' represented also the district of three Greek cities.

Tristan d' Acunha, correctly TRISTÃO DA CUNHA, is a rocky island in the South Atlantic, accidentally discovered in 1507 by the Portuguese navigator Tristão da Cunha on a homeward voyage from India,

The ANGRA DE DONA MARIA DA CUNHA, a bay in Madagascar, was named after his mother by Nuno da Cunha, son of Tristão da Cunha.

Trolhatta, a waterfall in Sweden, means the 'abyss of trolls' or demons, whence the neighbouring town is called TROL-HÄTTA.

Troppau, in Silesia, stands on the River Oppa, an affluent of the Oder. The eleventh century Slavonic name *Opawa* became *Troppowe* in the fourteenth century, owing to the German article *der* being prefixed.

Troyes, a town in Champagne, on the Seine, was the Roman *Augustobona*, a hybrid Celto-Latin name meaning the 'town of Augustus.' (*See* BONN.) It was the chief city of the Tricasses or Tricassii, a Belgic tribe, whose name probably means the 'very swift.' The name Augustobona became successively *Augusta Trecorum*, *Tricassi*, *Tricasi*, and *Troyes*. Our Troy weight is derived from the standard used at the great thirteenth century fair held at Troyes.

Truns or TRONS in the Graubünden, where the oath of the Grey league was sworn, appears in 1290 as *Trunnes*, a name explained by the Romansch *drun*, a 'torrent' (Latin *torrens*).

Truro, Cornwall, anciently *Triuera* and *Treuru*, is supposed to be a corruption of the Cornish *Tre-rhiew*, the 'dwelling on the slope.'

Truxillo, now spelt TRUJILLO, a city in the Spanish province of Estramadura, is a corruption of the Roman name *Trogilum* or *Turris Julia*. Here Pizarro was born, and he gave the name of his native place to TRUXILLO in Peru, which he founded in 1535. The name of the Spanish city has also been bestowed on towns in Honduras and Venezuela.

Tryal Rocks, West Australia, are so called from the wreck of the ship *Tryal* in 1622.

Tshuktskoi Nos, one of the easternmost points in Asia, called CAPE TSHUKT-SKOI on English maps, was discovered in 1728 by Bering, and named after a tribe calling themselves *Tshuktski*, 'the people.'

Tso or CHO, a 'lake,' is a common element of names in Tibet, as TSO-KUR, 'white lake'; TSO-GAM, 'dry lake'; TSO-PANJ, 'green lake'; TSO-RUI, 'bitter lake'; TSO-MAGNALARI, 'sweet [water] mountain lake,' or LONG-TSO, 'ox lake.'

Tuam, an episcopal see in Galway, is called in the Irish annals *Tuaim-da-ghualann*, the 'tumulus of the two shoulders,' from the peculiar shape of an ancient sepulchral mound. The word *tuaim*, a 'mound,' or tumulus, usually becomes *Toome* in modern Irish nomenclature.

Tuamotu, an archipelago called by the Tahitians PAUMOTA, 'the cloud of islands,' is the native name of the extensive group of coral islets otherwise known as the LOW ISLANDS or DANGEROUS ARCHIPELAGO.

Tuareg, the 'renegades,' is the name given by the Arabs to a nomad tribe in the Sahara.

Tucker Inlet, South Victoria, bears the name of an officer of the *Erebus*.

Tuhua, 'obsidian,' is the Maori name of a volcanic island in Tauranga Harbour, New Zealand, which is also called Maydr Island.

Tula, a town forty miles north-west of the city of Mexico, was a pueblo called *Tollan*, meaning in Aztec 'the place of the sun,' a name given to various places with temples to Quetzalcoatl, the Aztec sun-god.

Tulare, a lake and valley in New California, is so called from *tule*, the native name of a rush (*Scirpus palustris*) which grows in the lake, and is used for thatch.

Tulloch in Perthshire and TULLOW in County Carlow, with many other Irish and Scotch names, are from the Gaelic diminutive *tulach*, a 'knoll' or small hill. TULLIBARDINE in Perthshire is the 'bard's knoll'; TULLAMORE is the 'great hillock'; KILTULLAGH the 'church on the hillock'; and TULLYALLEN is the 'beautiful hillock.' (*See* TOUL.) The TULLOCK REEF in the Azores bears the name of an American seaman who discovered it in 1808.

Tummel, a Scotch river which gives a name to Loch Tummel, whence it flows, derives from the falls in its short course the appropriate Gaelic name of the 'plunging stream,' *tum-allt*.

Tunguska, a tributary of the Yenissei, is so named from the Mongolian tribe known as the TUNGUS, which is believed to be a Europeanised form of the native name *Donki*, which means the 'people.' The Tungus on the coast are called LAMUT, a plural form often wrongly written LAMUTS, meaning the 'sea dwellers,' from *lama*, the 'sea.' (*See* YAKUTSK.)

Tunis, in North Africa, preserves the ancient name of a fortified town called *Tunês* by Polybius and Diodorus, and *Tunis* by Strabo, dedicated, it is supposed, to the Phœnician goddess Tanith, identified by the Greeks with Artemis, to whom several inscriptions have been found at Carthage.

Turin, in Italian TORINO, the capital of Piedmont, was the chief city of the *Taurini* or *Taurisci.* Under Augustus it became a Roman colony called *Augusta Taurinorum.* In the Itineraries the honorific prefix Augusta is already dropped, and the city is called *Taurini.* The tribe name is probably Celtic, meaning the people of the ' tors ' or hills. (*See* TORQUAY.)

Turk, in Irish and Scotch names, such as BEN TURC, BRIG O' TURK, or ALTATURK is from the Gaelic *tuirc,* a ' wild boar.'

Turkey, the English name of the Ottoman Empire, appears to have been derived from *Turcia,* the Latinised form of the Arabic name, written by Ibn Batuta *Al-Turkiyah,* the ' land of the Turks.' TURKESTAN in Central Asia is a Persian form of the same name, denoting the land occupied by the Usbeks, the Kirghis, the Turcomans, and other Turkic races. TURCOMAN is a collective form meaning Turkdom, from which we have manufactured the erroneous plural form Turcomen, like Mussulman and Mussulmen from Moslemin the plural of Moslem. The name TURK has been supposed to be a corruption of the name *Tu-kiu* of the Chinese historians, or from the Arabic *turkur,* ' robbers.' It is probably a Tartar word meaning ' brave.'

Türkheim, a corruption of *Thuringoheim,* is the name of five places in Germany, which must have been settlements of Thuringians, whose name is better preserved by the range of hills called the Thüringer Wald (*q.v.*).

Turk's Island, properly TURK ISLAND, in the Bahamas, was so called from a local species of cactus, known from its peculiar shape as the Turk or the Turk's head.

Turnagain Island marks the point where, in 1793, two English ships, the *Chesterfield* and the *Hormusier,* abandoned the attempt to penetrate Torres Strait. At TURNAGAIN RIVER, a small stream flowing into Cook's Inlet, Alaska, Cook in 1778 gave up the exploration of the inlet which bears his name. At CAPE TURNAGAIN, New Zealand, Cook, in 1769, when exploring the coast southwards from Poverty Bay, had to return northwards, having failed to find a harbour. POINT TURNAGAIN was the easternmost point on the coast of Arctic America reached by Franklin on his descent of the Coppermine River in 1821. At this point he was obliged to turn again to the west on August 22nd. REPULSE BAY, the point reached at the same time by the relief expedition commanded by Parry, is 539 miles further east.

Turtman, a village in Canton Valais at the foot of the TURTMAN THAL, is so called from an ancient tower, *Turris Magna.* The French name of the village is TOURMAGNE, which indicates the etymology more plainly than the form Turtman.

Tuscany, in Italian TOSCANA, called *Tuscia* in the Notitia, bears the name of its ancient inhabitants the *Tusci* or *Etrusci.* The Etruscans were called *Tyrrheni* by the Greeks, whence the name TYRRHENIAN SEA given to that part of the Mediterranean which lies between the mainland and the islands of Corsica and Sardinia, the Greeks of Cumæ and of Sicily encountering them by sea and the Romans by land.

Twickenham, Middlesex, appears as *Tuicanhom* in a charter of 704, and in 783 we have the name in the dative singular as *Tuicanhamme.* Hence the suffix is -*ham* or -*hom,* an ' enclosure,' and not -*hám,* a ' home.' The prefix is usually explained from the A.S. *twycene* or *twicina,* which denotes a place where two roads meet (*bivium*), but it is more probably from a personal name, or possibly from *twiccen,* a ' circuit' (*ambitus*), the name referring to the eyot surrounded by a palisade which is near the old church, and not to the junction of the Hampton and Hounslow roads, which is remote from the spot at first designated by the name.

Twining, near Tewkesbury in Gloucestershire, occupies a spit of land at the junction of the Avon and the Severn. The Latinised name *monasterium Bituinæum,* which is found in a charter, shows that the name signifies ' between the rivers' (A.S. *bi-tweon,* ' between,' and *eaum,* dative plural of *ea,* a ' river ').

Twizel, in Northumberland, is at the junction of the Till and the Tweed, and HALTWISTLE at the junction of a large burn with the Tyne. In Lancashire we have ENTWISTLE at the junction of two brooks, the Bradshaw Brook and the Broadhead Brook. The suffix -*twisle* or -*twizle* is not uncommon in Northumbrian names, and denotes a place at the junction of two rivers (A.S. *twisel,* a ' fork '). We have ZWIESEL in Germany, and WIESELBURG, a town in Austria, which was called *Zwisila* in the tenth century.

Tyndall, Mount, in the Southern Alps of New Zealand, was so named by Haast in 1861 in compliment to Professor Tyndall.

Ty-Newydd, Glamorgan, the 'new house,' and TY-GWYN, Monmouthshire, the 'white house,' are from *ty*, a house, which is common in Welsh names. It corresponds to the Gaelic *teach*, a house, cognate with the Latin *tectum*, whence such Irish names as TAGHBOY, the 'yellow house,' or TEEBANE, the 'white house.' TYNDRUM, Perthshire, may be the 'house on the ridge.'

Tyre, in the State of New York, has borrowed the name of the great Phœnician city, built on a rocky coast islet now called ES SÛR. The name Tyre denotes the 'rock' (*zor*) on which Old Tyre was built. An Egyptian traveller about the time of the Exodus tells us that water had to be brought to Tyre in boats. The Ægean island of *Syros*, now SYRA, is supposed to bear a Phœnician name from the same source.

Tyrol, or TIROL, an Austrian crownland, takes its name from a castle near Meran called Tirol, which belonged to the Tyrolean Counts.

Tyrone, an Irish county, is a corruption of *Tir-Eoghain*, the 'land of Owen,' who was the son of Niall of the nine hostages, the ancestor of the great clan of the O'Neills.

Uganda, the country north-west of the Victoria Nyanza, offers a familiar example of the Bantu prefix *u-*, signifying 'land' or 'country.' (*See* BANTU.) U-ganda is the land of the WA-GANDA, or 'people of Ganda.' So U-NY-ORO, north of Uganda, on the Albert Nyanza, is inhabited by the Wa-ny-oro, and U-JIJI, on Lake Tanganyika, by the Wa-jiji. U-NYA-MWEZI is the 'country of the moon,' and U-NYA-NYEMBE is the 'country of hoes.' In such names the intermediate syllable *nya*, *nga*, or *ny* is an abraded preposition forming the sign of the case, usually the instrumental or the genitive.

Uig, a bay in Skye, is probably an assimilated Gaelic form of a Norse name. In the sixteenth century it was written *Wig*, which points to the O.N. *vík*, a 'bay.' In Gaelic *uig* means a nook, cove, or cave. In Lewis there is a bay called UIG, which may be either a Gaelic or a Norse name. The town of WICK, on the RIVER WICK, is called in modern Gaelic *Inbhir Uig*, plainly the town 'at the mouth of the River Wick.' In the Isle of Man a cave is called *Ooig*, as OOIGDOO, the 'black cave,' or OOIGVEG, the 'little cave.' EIGG, one of the Hebrides, was anciently *Ega* or *Egea*, apparently a Norse name meaning the 'creek island' (O.N. *ögr*, a 'small bay'), though the well-known cave suggests a derivation from the Gaelic *uig*. NIGG, at Aberdeen, and NIGG, near Fearn, in Ross-shire, are believed to be from the Norse *vík*, a 'bay,' with the Gaelic article prefixed.

Uitenhage, the capital of a district of the same name at the Cape, bears the name of a Dutch official.

Ujung-Tanah, the Malay name of the extreme end of the Malay peninsula, means the 'land's end' (Malay *ujung*, a 'point' or 'promontory,' and *tanah*, 'land'). JAVA HEAD, the western point of Java, is called by the Malays UJUNG-KULON, the 'West Cape.' JUNK-CEYLON, an island off the west coast of the Malay peninsula, is a curious European corruption of the Malay name *Ujung-Sâlang*, 'Salang headland.'

Ukraine (Polish *ukraina*, a 'boundary' or 'frontier') was the name of the frontier district of Little Russia, comprising the governments of Karkov, Kiev, Podolia, and Pultowa. So the UKERMARK in Brandenburg was the 'mark' or frontier of a Wendish people whose Slavonic name proclaims that they were the men of the 'border' or Slavonic frontier.

Uleåborg, a town in Finland, takes its name from a *borg* or 'castle,' built in 1570 on the River Uleå.

Ulloa, properly SAN JUAN DE ULLOA, is the name of the island and fort in front of Vera Cruz in Mexico. Ulua or Olua is a corruption of *Culhua*, the native name of this part of the coast, which was discovered in 1518 by Juan de Grijalva on June 19th, shortly before the festival of St. John the Baptist, from whom the island was named, though doubtless not without reference to the name saint of the discoverer.

Ulm, a city in Bavaria, is first mentioned in the ninth century by the names *Ulma* and *Hulma*. The etymology is unknown, but the Latin *ulmus*, an 'elm tree,' and the Low-Latin *hulmus*, referred to a doubtful O.H.G. *ulma*, a *holm* or 'river island,' have been suggested.

Ulster, the northern province of Ireland,

has a hybrid name, Celtic and Norse. The suffix -ster, seen also in the names of Leinster and Munster, is the Scandinavian word stadr, 'a place' or 'district.' Ulster, a contraction of Ula-ster, is the district of Uladh (Uluidh) (pronounced Ulla), which signifies a 'cairn' or 'tomb.' The district anciently called Uladh is said to have taken its name from a great cairn raised over the body of Fothadh Airgtheach, king of Ireland, who in 285 A.D. was slain at the battle of Ollarba (Larne Water) in County Antrim, where his uluidh was erected, and became a place of pilgrimage, thus giving a name to the district.

Umballa (AMBÁLA), in the Punjab, was founded, probably in the fourteenth century, by an Amba Rajput.

Umbria, an Italian province, was the land of the Umbrians (Umbri), explained as the 'dwellers by the water,' umber being a word cognate with the Latin imber.

Unst, one of the Shetlands, was formerly called Ornyst, seemingly a Scandinavian name meaning an 'eagle's nest.'

Unterwalden, one of the Swiss cantons, is the land 'below the forest' called the Kernwald. OBWALDEN, a division of the Canton, lies 'above the forest.'

Unthank, the name of townships in Norfolk, Derbyshire, Northumberland, and Cumberland, denoted the dwelling of a squatter who had settled on some one's land 'without leave,' thæs hlafordes unthances. Hence the surname Unthank.

Uppernavik, the northernmost Danish settlement in Greenland, is an Eskimo name meaning 'summer dwelling.' OPPERNAVIK, the northernmost cape of Labrador, is a dialectical form of the same word.

Upsala, the see of the primate of Sweden, in whose cathedral Swedish kings were formerly crowned, bears a name transferred from Old Upsala, two miles further north, which is believed to take its name from a great heathen temple called Ubsala, the 'lofty hall.'

Ural, the chain dividing Europe from Asia, means the 'girdle' or 'belt,' ural-tau, being a Turkic word meaning a 'mountain chain,' while urr means a 'chain' in Ostiak. The Russians call the Ural mountains by the translated name POYAS, the 'girdle.' The mountains have given their name to the RIVER URAL, which flows from them into the Caspian. URALSK is a town on the River Ural.

Urbino, in Italy, the birthplace of Raphael, occupies the site of Urbinum Hortense, a Roman town.

Urga, a town in Mongolia, is the 'residence' of the Khutukhtu, or Kutucha, the 'resplendently divine' Lama, who is the Metropolitan of the Khalka tribes, and ranks third among the Buddhist dignitaries.

Uri, one of the Swiss forest cantons, is usually supposed to have taken its name from the wild ox called the urus or aurochs (ur-ox). The antiquity of this popular etymology is shown by the head of the Urus which appears in the armorial bearings of the Canton. It would, however, appear that the name did not originally apply to the whole district now called Uri, but merely to the territory immediately surrounding Altdorf, the capital of the Canton. As early as 853 the Gemeinde of Altdorf was called Pagellus Uronie, whence Uronia and Vallis Urania, later names denoting the plain at the head of that arm of the Lake of Lucerne which is known as the Bay of Uri. This name, as Gatschet contends, meant 'shoreland,' since in Romansch ur (Latin ora) means 'shore,' while -aun (Middle Latin -onus) is an adjectival suffix. ALTDORF, the capital of the Canton, cannot at first have been called the 'old village,' a name which may have been given to the village 'on the shore' of the Lake when the Alemannic invaders took possession of the country. Uri therefore would be the older name of Altdorf, and the Vallis Urania would be the valley of Uri or Altdorf. The name of the Urus is preserved in many local names, if not in that of Uri. The old name of the RIVER AURACH was Uraha, 'Urus river.' Both EUERDORF and AUERDORF are corruptions of Uri-dorf, and the UHRBACH, the EUERBACH, and the AUERBACH are the 'Urus beck.'

Uruguay, often called BANDA ORIENTAL, is a South American republic, officially styled Banda Oriental del Uruguay, the 'eastern side of the Uruguay,' a great river which bounds it on the west. In Guarani the word uru-guay means a 'bird's tail,' from uru, 'bird,' and guay, 'tail.' It is believed that the river got its name from the SALTO GRANDE, or 'great waterfall,' which spreads out like the tail of a bird.

Urumiah is the European name of a large lake in north-western Persia, ten miles from the city of URUMIAH. This name is not used by the Persians, who call it Daria-i-Shahi, 'the royal sea.' It is the *Kapauta* of Strabo (Persian *kabuda*, 'blue'). The city of URUMIAH, as well as URUM SERAI in Armenia, are supposed to be from Urum (Rûm), the name given by the Turks to the Greeks of the Lower Empire.

Usdum, on the Dead Sea, traditionally conserves the name of Sodom, one of the cities of the plain. USEDOM, a Pomeranian town on an island of the same name, is said to be the German corruption of a Slavonic name meaning the 'place of learning.'

Ushant, the English form of the French name OUESSANT, is the westernmost island off the French coast. It was the Roman *Axantos, Uxisana,* or *Uxantis Insula.* The modern French name Ouessant is an assimilated form of the Roman name, derived by folk-etymology from *ouest,* the 'west.'

Uskup, a town in Rumelia, is a Turkish corruption of the Greek name SKUPIA (*skopi*), the 'outlook.'

Ustica, an isolated island north of Palermo, bears a Phœnician name signifying the 'low' or 'flat' island.

Ust-Usa is a place at the 'confluence' (*ust*) of the Usa and the Petchora. So UST-POSA, UST-PINEGA, UST-NAFTA, and UST-ILGINSKOI lie at the confluences of the Posa, the Pinega, the Nafta, and the Ilga with other rivers.

Utah, a territory of the United States, ceded by Mexico in 1848, was the land of the Utah or Otoe tribe, whose name is said to mean 'mountaineers' or 'highlanders.'

Utrecht, a Dutch city on the Old Rhine, is called in medieval Latin documents *Ultra Trajectum,* 'beyond the ford' or passage, and is also explained as *Oude Trecht,* the 'old ford.' These are only popular etymologies, the true source being the Old Frisian *drecht,* which answers to our thorpe, meaning a 'settlement,' 'assemblage,' or 'family,' whence the name of DORDRECHT, called in the eleventh century *Thuredrecht.* The primitive name of Utrecht seems to have been *Vulta-drecht,* the 'settlement of the Vultæ,' a Frisian tribe whose name we also have in WILTENBURG, near Utrecht, anciently called *Viltaburg* and *Vultaburch,* the 'burg of the Vultæ.'

Uttoxeter, in Staffordshire, formerly *Utoc-cester,* was, as the name implies, a Roman town, whose alleged name, *Utocetum,* is merely an antiquarian figment.

Vaal, the South African river beyond which lies the TRANSVAAL REPUBLIC, is the 'yellow' river (Dutch *vaal,* 'yellow' or 'tawny'). VAALPENSE, 'yellow bellies,' is a scornful name given by the Dutch Boers to a degraded race living in the Kalahari desert.

Vaduz, the 'sweet valley,' is the capital of the Principality of Liechtenstein (*q.v.*).

Vai-Levu, 'the great water,' is the largest stream in the island of Viti-Levu, 'great Fiji.' A lake in the same island is called VAI-KALAU, the 'water of the gods.' (*See* FIJI.)

Valais, or LE VALAIS, a Swiss Canton, occupies the great 'valley' of the Upper Rhone, called by the Romans *Vallis Pœnina.* The modern names of the canton, IL VALLESE in Italian, LE VALAIS in French, and WALLIS in German, descend directly from the names *Vallesia* and *Vallesium* used in documents of the thirteenth and fourteenth centuries. Gatschet has suggested that an inscription given by Mommsen commemorating a *civis Vallinsæ* implies *patria Vallensis* or *territorium Vallense* meaning the 'valley country,' as adjectival formations which would yield the names *Vallensia* and *Vallensium* as the sources of the documentary forms *Vallesia* and *Vallesium,* which are the parents of the modern names. PORT VALAIS, the old *Portus Vallesiæ,* a village now nearly two miles from the Lake of Geneva, is a name which curiously marks the rapid advance of the shore line. The German name CANTON WALLIS has been thought to be an assimilated form equivalent to Canton Wales, the Welsh or non-German district.

Valdivia, the capital of the province of VALDIVIA in Chili, was founded in 1551 by Pedro de Valdivia, the conqueror and viceroy of Chili, who in 1558 fell in battle with the Araucanian Indians.

Valencia, a Spanish city, was the Roman *Valentia Edetanorum,* the strong place or 'strength of the Edetani.' The city gave its name to the kingdom, now the province, of Valencia. The name of the Spanish city has been transferred to VALENTIA in Kerry, and to NUEVA VALENCIA in Venezuela. VALENCE, on the Rhone, was a Roman city called *Valentia Segalaunorum urbs* or *Valentia Colonia Julia.*

Valenciennes (Nord) is supposed to have been founded or restored by the Emperor Valentinian I. There is, however, no early mention of the name, and it is only in 693 that we meet with it as *Valencianis*, and in 771 as *villa Valentiana*. The formation may have been similar to that of ORLÉANS (*q.v.*).

Valetta, or LA VALETTE, the capital of Malta, commemorates the heroic defence of the island under the Grand Master of the Hospitallers or Knights of St. John, Jean Parissot de la Valette, who built the new fortress after the repulse of the Turks in the great siege of 1565 and 1566.

Valientes, or ISLAS DE LOS VALIENTES, 'the islands of the brave,' a group of the Carolines, were discovered in 1773 by the Spanish seaman Don Filipe Tomson, and so named, it is believed, from the bravery of the natives.

Valladolid, a town and province in Castile, is first mentioned in 1072 as *Vallisoletum*. The etymology is doubtful, but is usually referred to a personal name, *Valle de Lid* or *Valle de Olid*. The name was transferred to VALLADOLID in Yucatan, founded in 1543, and perhaps to VALLADOLID in Mexico, which, however, is said to have been founded in 1536 by Christobal de Olid.

Vallejo, the former capital of California, bears the name of M. G. Vallejo, a Mexican General, who in 1835 took the country from the native tribes.

Vals, in Canton Graubünden, is from the Romansch *vals*, 'the valley.' VALS, in the Ardèche, famous for its alkaline waters, is also the 'valley.' VALPARAISO, in Chili, was founded in 1536 by Juan de Saavedra, who named it after his birthplace, Valparaiso, 'Paradise Valley,' near Cuença in Spain.

Valtellina (German VELTLIN), the name given to the valley of the Adda before it enters the Lake of Como, is a corruption of *Val di Teglio*, so called from the town of TEGLIO (from *tilia*, a 'lime-tree'), the former capital of the district.

Valtüsch, in Canton St. Gallen, is the 'waterfall valley' (Romansch *tüsch*, a 'waterfall').

Vancouver, a rising city which forms the western terminus of the Canadian Pacific Railway, bears the name of Captain George Vancouver, R.N., who, as a midshipman in Cook's last voyage, visited the coast in 1776, and surveyed it in 1792. VANCOUVER ISLAND, which fronts it, was visited by Juan de Fuca in 1592, and by Juan Perez in 1774. Vancouver shares with Galiano and Valdez, who had been sent by Don Quadra, Governor of Nootka, the honour of discovering the strait which

separates the island from the mainland, a fact which Vancouver acknowledged by naming the island jointly after himself and Quadra. Hence in some maps it is called ISLA CUADRA. FORT VANCOUVER, on the Oregon River, was built in 1824 as a fur trading post, and named after Captain Vancouver.

Van Diemen's Land is now called TASMANIA (*q.v.*). Another VAN DIEMEN'S LAND, on the north coast of Australia, was discovered in 1618 by the Dutch navigator Zeachen, who had been sent on a voyage of discovery by Van Diemen, Governor of the Dutch East Indies. KAAP VAN DIEMEN, the eastern extremity of Mornington Island, in the Gulf of Carpentaria, is believed to have been discovered by Tasman. KAAP MARIA VAN DIEMEN, at the north-western extremity of New Zealand, was discovered on January 6th, 1643, by Tasman, who believed it to be the northern extremity of a great Antarctic continent, *Terra Australis Incognita*, and named it after a daughter of Governor Van Diemen. VAN DIEMEN GULF, on the north coast of Australia, was discovered by three Dutch ships in 1705. VAN DIEMEN STRAIT, south of Japan, was discovered at the beginning of the seventeenth century by a Dutch ship which was driven through it in a storm.

Vannes, the capital of the Morbihan, a town in the territory of Cæsar's *Veneti*, was called in the sixth century *Venetensis* (*civitas*), which became successively *Vannetais*, *Vanes*, and VANNES. The tribe name is also the source of GUENET, the Breton name of the town.

Vansittart Bay, West Australia, and VANSITTART ISLAND in Bass Strait and in Arctic America, as well as CAPE BEXLEY, were named in compliment to Nicholas Vansittart, Chancellor of the Exchequer in 1812, afterwards Lord Bexley.

Var, a French department, was named from the RIVER VAR, which, however, no longer flows through it, the eastern portion having been lopped off when Nice was acquired from Italy, in order to make up the department which goes by the name of the Alpes-Maritimes.

Varna, a Bulgarian port on the Black Sea, is a Turco-Hungarian name meaning 'castle' or 'fortress.'

Vaucluse, a French department, is named from Vaucluse, Petrarch's fountain in the *vallis clausa* or 'closed valley.'

Vaud, a Swiss Canton, is called in French

Pays de Vaud, and in German Die Waadt, Der Waldgau, or Das Waadtland. It probably means the 'woodland,' though the etymology is uncertain. In the ninth century it is called *Waldensis comitatus*, 'the forest county.' The eastern portion is called LA VAUX, the district of 'the valleys,' *vaux* being the plural of *val*. It has also been maintained that Waadtland is a corruption of Wälschland, 'the land of the foreigners' (*walas* or *Welsh*), but this is not supported by the early forms of the name.

Velas, the 'sails,' is the Spanish name of a rocky island in the North Pacific, so called from the resemblance to a ship in full sail. The more usual modern name is DOUGLAS REEF, from a Captain Douglas, who sighted it in 1789.

Vellore (VELLÚR), in Arcot, is a name of doubtful meaning. Fra Paolino explains it as the 'town of the lance,' and Colonel Bramfill derives it from *vel*, a 'benefaction,' since, according to a local tradition, the fortress was 'given' by the founder to the Raja of Vijayanagar.

Vendée, a French department, takes its name from a small affluent of the Charente.

Vendôme (Loir et Cher) is a corruption of the Roman name *Vindocinum*. VENDOM OE, 'return island,' was the northernmost point on the east coast of Greenland reached by the Danish Captain Graah in 1829.

Vendres, or PORT-VENDRES, a town in the Hérault, appears in the twelfth century as *Terminium de Veneris* and as *Portus Venere*, which is supposed to represent a Roman *Portus Veneris*.

Venezuela, 'little Venice,' is a later formation from the older name *Venecia*, given in 1499 by the sailors of Alonso de Hojeda to a native village built, like Venice, on piles, in the Gulf of Maracaybo. The town has given its name to one of the South American republics, as well as to the Gulf by which it is approached.

Venice, called VENEZIA in Italian and VENEDIG in German, is the French name we use for the city founded by fugitives from the Roman province of *Venetia*, who, in the fifth century A.D. took refuge in the islands of the lagoons from the barbarian invaders. About the fifth century B.C. Venetia was peopled by the *Veneti*, who, according to Pauli's researches, were Illyrians, whose language is now represented by the Albanian.

Ventry, in Kerry, is the place with the

'white strand' (*Fionn-traigh*), a name still admirably descriptive.

Venus Bay (otherwise ANDERSON'S INLET), in the Australian Colony of Victoria, was named after Bass' ship the *Venus*. The northern cape of Tahiti, where, on June 4th, 1769, the transit of Venus was observed on Cook's first voyage, was hence called POINT VENUS.

Vera Cruz, in Mexico, was the name given by Cortez to the city which he founded in 1520 on the spot where he had landed the year before, calling it *Villa Rica de la Vera Cruz*, the 'rich city of the true cross.' The site being found unhealthy, the town has been removed a few miles further to the south. There are twenty places which bear the name of Vera Cruz or Santa Cruz.

Vera Paz, 'true peace,' was the name given to Tuzulutlan, a district in Central America, north of Guatemala, after it had been pacified by Las Casas and the Dominican missionaries in 1537-1539. From the constant conflicts with the natives it had previously been called the Land of War.

Verd, Cape. (*See* CAPE VERD.)

Verden, an episcopal see in Hanover, is the place 'at the ford' over the River Aller. The old names *Ferde*, *Ferdia*, and *Fardium* (eighth century) point to the Old Frisian *ferd* (O.H.G. *fart*), a 'road,' and hence a passage over a river. VERDUN, a fortress on the Meuse, represents the Celto-Roman *Virodunum*, afterwards *Veredunum*.

Vermont, one of the New England States, is traversed by the 'Green Mountains,' a range of wooded hills about 4000 feet in height, from which the State takes the name bestowed on the district in 1731 by French settlers from Canada.

Verona is one of the few places which retains its Roman name unaltered. (*See* BERN.)

Vesuvio is the Italian and VESUVE the French form of the Roman VESUVIUS, which, according to Benfey, is an Oscan name from the root of *Ves-ta*, signifying the 'emitter of smoke.'

Vevay, on the Lake of Geneva, is the modern form of the old name *Vibisco*, erroneously supposed to denote a place at the *bivium* or parting of the two roads leading respectively to Lausanne and Moudon. It stands on the VEVAYSE, a small stream usually said to derive its name from the town. It is more reasonable to suppose that this stream was formerly called *Vibiscus*, whence the name *Vibisco*, 'at the Vibiscus,' used in the Antonine Itinerary for the place where it was crossed.

Via Mala is the 'evil road' through the wild gorge of the Hinterrhein which leads to the Splügen Pass.

Viborg, in Jutland, is the 'sacred hill' where the kings of Jutland and afterwards of Denmark were elected.

Vicenza, in Northern Italy, was the Roman *Vicentia*.

Victoria is a name which the enormous extension of the colonial empire of England during the reign of Queen Victoria has caused to be repeated on our maps with inconvenient and perplexing frequency. VICTORIA, the wealthiest of the Australian colonies, was separated from New South Wales in 1851, the name of Victoria having been bestowed upon it in 1847. The district had previously been known as PORT PHILIP (*q.v.*), a name given at the beginning of the century in compliment to Captain Philip, Governor of New South Wales. The settlement began in 1836, when the name Australia Felix was proposed on account of its natural advantages. VICTORIA, a settlement at Port Essington, North Australia, was so named in 1838. VICTORIA RIVER, Arnhem Land, was named by Stokes in 1839. VICTORIA RANGE and MOUNT VICTORIA, in West Australia, were so named by Grey in 1838. VICTORIA EAST is a district in the Cape Colony. VICTORIA, the capital of British Columbia, was incorporated in 1862. VICTORIA, the capital of Hongkong, was founded in 1842. PORT VICTORIA, in Mahé, one of the Séchelle Islands, was so named in 1841. SOUTH VICTORIA, an Antarctic region of unknown extent, was named by James Ross in 1841. The VICTORIA ARCHIPELAGO, in Belcher Channel, was named by Belcher in 1853. VICTORIA AND ALBERT MOUNTAINS, in Grinnell Land, were named by Kane in 1853. The VICTORIA NYANZA, the largest of the African lakes, called *Ukerewé* by the natives, was discovered and named in 1858 by Speke. Nyanza is a general term meaning a 'sea.' The VICTORIA FALLS on the Zambesi, discovered and named by Livingstone in 1855, send up columns of spray visible for twenty miles. The native name is MOSI-OA-TUNYA, 'smoke sounds there.' VICTORIA, the capital of the Brazilian province of Espirito Santo, was originally called Espirito Santo, and took the name of Victoria in 1558 in commemoration of a defeat of the natives by Fernando de Sa. ILHA DA VICTORIA, Bahia, was so named because of a victory over the natives about 1537. CABO VICTORIA, at the west extremity of Magellan Straits, was named after Magellan's ship the *Victoria*, the first vessel to circumnavigate the world. CIUDAD VICTORIA, in the Mexican province of Tamaulipas, was so named in 1825 after Guadelupe Victoria, the first president of the Mexican confederation.

Victory Point and VICTORY HARBOUR, in Arctic America, bear the name of Ross' ship the *Victory*.

Vienna, the capital of the Austrian Empire, is the Latin form of the German name WIEN. It stands at the confluence with the Danube of a small river called the Wien, which, however, may have obtained its name from the town. It is called *Wienna* in a document of the twelfth century. The Roman name *Vindobona*, which becomes *Vindomona* and *Vindomina* in the Itineraries, may mean either the 'town of the Wends,' the 'town on the River Vindus,' or, as Zeuss maintains, the 'white town.' (*See* BONN.) *Vienna*, the chief town of the Allobroges, is now *Vienne* (Isère).

Vierwaldstätter-See, the 'Lake of the Four forest Cantons,' Uri, Schwyz, Unterwalden, and Luzern, is the German name of the Swiss lake which, following the older French usage, we call the Lake of Lucerne.

Vigo, in Spain, was the *Vicus Spacorum* of the Romans and the *Vica* of Ptolemy. VICH or VIQUE, in Catalonia, the ancient *Ausa*, the chief town of the Ausetani (or people of Ausa), afterwards came to be called *Ausona*, then *Vicus Ausonensis*, corrupted into *Vic d' Osona*, and finally shortened to *Vic* and VICH. VICHY in France is also from *Vicus*.

Villefranche (Aveyron) obtained the name of the 'free town' because of the immunities granted in the thirteenth century by Alphonse of Poictiers, Count of Toulouse. VILLEFRANCHE-SUR-SAÔNE, a town near Lyons, was so called from privileges granted by Guichard I. of Beaujeu. VILLAFRANCA DE PANADES in Catalonia was so called from franchises granted by a Count of Toulouse. VILLEFRANCHE, near Nice, and many other places possessed similar privileges. (*See* FREIBURG.)

Vincent-pyramide, one of the peaks of Monte Rosa, was first ascended by the brothers Vincent of Gressonay.

Vintschgau, in the Tyrol, a name given to the valley of the Adige near Meran, is a German translation of *Vallis Venusta,* so called from the tribe of the Venostes.

Virgin Islands, a group in the Antilles, were discovered and named by Columbus on his second voyage. Leaving Guadalupe on November 10th, 1493, he sighted on the 14th a swarm of small islands, about one hundred in number. He called them *Las Virgines,* and the largest island SANTA URSULA. The RIO DAS VIRGENS in Brazil was discovered by Amerigo Vespucci in 1501 on October 21st, the Festival of St. Ursula and the eleven thousand virgins. CAPE VIRGINS, Patagonia, was sighted by Magellan on October 21st, 1520, and named by him *Cabo de las Virgines,* from the day of discovery.

Virginia, one of the United States, is a small remnant of the vast territory, extending to Lake Erie, included in the original colony of Virginia, which originated with the despatch of two small vessels sent out by Sir Walter Raleigh in 1584, when Roanoke Island and adjacent parts of the North American coast were discovered. This first attempt at settlement ended in disaster, and the colony was practically founded by the Virginia Company, constituted by patent in 1606 and reconstituted in 1609. A tradition asserts that Virginia was so named by the Virgin Queen 'in honour of herself.'

Visp (French VIÈGE), formerly *Vesbia,* is a village in Canton Valais, where a stream called the Vispach or the Viège joins the Rhone. VISPACH is a corruption of *Wiesbach,* the 'meadow beck,' coming from the pastures which give a name to Zermatt (*q.v.*).

Vistula was the Roman name of the river called WEICHSEL by the Germans. Pomponius Mela calls it *Vistula,* and Pliny *Vistilla sive Vistula.* The Lithuanian name *Isla* means the 'river,' but the Polish name *Wisla* is believed to refer to the great 'waterfall' in its upper course at the village of Wisla, near its source in the Carpathians.

Vizcaino, a bay on the west coast of the Californian peninsula, is properly called BAHIA DE SEBASTIAN VIZCAINO, from a Spaniard who discovered it.

Vladimir, before the rise of Moscow the capital of Russia, was founded in 1110 by Vladimir Monomakh. It gives a name to VLADIMIR, a Russian Government.

VLADIVOSTOK, the chief port and naval station of the Russians on the Pacific, bears a name signifying the 'dominator of the East.' VLADIKAUKAZ, the 'dominator of the Caucasus,' is a Russian fortress founded in 1785, and so called because it commands the military road leading through the Caucasus to Tiflis.

Vlaming's Land, West Australia, bears the name of a Dutch seaman, who discovered this coast in 1696.

Vliegen Eylant, the 'island of flies,' in the Low Archipelago, was so called in 1616 by the Dutch mariners Lemaire and Schouten, because they were pestered by swarms of insects.

Volcano, one of the Lipari Islands, still an active volcano, was called *Vulcania* or *Hiera* by the Romans, because deemed to be the sacred isle of Vulcan. The name VOLCANO has also been given to one of the Santa Cruz islands, and to an island in the Queen Charlotte Group.

Volga, the greatest European river, bears a name which is comparatively modern. It is the *Rha* of Ptolemy, a Finnic name retained by the Mordwins and other Finnic tribes on its banks, who call it *Rhau,* the 'river.' The Tartar name was *Atal, Adal, Adel,* or *Idel,* the 'river,' a name by which it was known to Ibn Batuta and Edrisi, and which is still used by the Tchuwash, a Turkic tribe, who call it the *Adal.* The name Volga may be from the Old Slavonic *wolkoi* or *wolkoia,* 'great.' According to F. H. Müller, the name is Ugric, meaning 'the great river,' the first syllable being the Finnic *wol-as,* 'strong,' 'mighty,' and the suffix *-ga* being the Finnic *ga* or *ja,* 'river,' which we have in the name of the Pinega, One-ga, Wa-ga, Molo-ga, and other rivers. The theory that the Bulgarians (*q.v.*) were the 'people of the Volga' is now given up, but it is possible that the Volga may be the river of the Bol-gari.

Voltas is the name of a cape and bay in South Africa, near the mouth of the Orange River. In 1486 Bartolomeo Diaz gave the bay the name *Angra das Voltas,* either because the coast here trended to the east, or in memory of his many 'turnings' or 'tackings' whilst beating up for five days against contrary winds.

Volterra, in Italy, was the ancient *Volaterræ,* a Roman form accommodated from the Etruscan *Velathri.*

Vorarlberg is an Austrian crownland lying 'in front of the Arlberg' (*q.v.*).

T

Vosges (German VOGESEN), a range of wooded hills now forming the frontier between France and Germany, are Cæsar's *Mons Vogesus* (*Vosegus*), probably a Celtic name.

Wabash, a river which joins the Ohio, is a name said to mean the 'Bear River' (Osage, *wasauba*, a 'bear').

Wager Inlet, in Arctic America, was named in 1742 in honour of Sir Charles Wager, First Lord of the Admiralty.

Wagram is a village ten miles from Vienna, where the Austrians were defeated by Napoleon in 1809. The ninth century form *Wagreine* means the 'pool shore' (O.H.G. *wâg*, a 'lake' or 'pool,' and *rain*, a 'bank' or 'steep shore').

Waiblingen, near Stuttgard, whence the nickname of the GHIBELLINES, is a patronymic, as is shown by the old forms *Weibilinga* and *Weibelingen*.

Waigatz Strait, the passage into the Kara Sea, takes its name from Waigatz, an island between Novaya Zemlya and the mainland, discovered in the sixteenth century by Ivan Waigatz.

Waikato, a New Zealand harbour, takes its name from the WAIKATO or 'flowing water,' a large and rapid river running into it from Lake Taupo, which is fed by the WAIMARINO, or 'still water.' The WAIPA, another New Zealand river, is the 'quiet water.' The river WAITAKI or WAITANGA in Otago is the 'crying water,' and the river WAITETUMA is the 'eel water.' WAIKARE, the 'welling water,' is a lake in which a spring wells up. WAI-UKO, 'white clay water,' is an inlet with cliffs of white clay. WAIKAN-PANAPA, the 'water of changing colour,' is a valley with boiling springs. WAIANI-WANIWA, 'rainbow water,' is the expressive Maori name for a waterfall.

Wainwright Island, in the Gambier Group, and WAINWRIGHT INLET, in Arctic America, bear the name of one of Beechey's officers.

Wakashian or WAKASHAN, a collective name given to the tribes on the coast of British Columbia, is from the word *wakash* (*waukas*), 'good,' frequently used by the natives of Nootka Sound when visited by Captain Cook.

Wakefield, in the North Riding, is usually explained from the A.S. *wæg*, a 'way' or 'road,' as there are some faint traces of a Roman road. But in this case the modern name would have been Wayfie!d. The Domesday form *Wachefeld*

suggests as a possible etymology the A.S. *wâc*, 'weak' or 'soft.' On phonological grounds 'watchfield' would be more probable, but the meaning is not so obvious.

Walcheren, an island at the mouth of the Scheldt, was called *Walacria* in the seventh century, and afterwards *Walacra* or *Gaulacra*, 'the foreigner's plain,' from *walh*, a 'foreigner' (Welshman), and *accar*, a 'plain' (acre).

Waldeck, a German principality, was so called from the castle of the reigning family, which, as the name implies, stood at a 'forest corner.' WALDSHUT, in Baden, was built by Rudolf of Hapsburg for the protection (*hut*) of the Schwarzwald or Black Forest. IM WALD is a common German name for woodland villages.

Walenstad, in Canton St. Gallen, sometimes incorrectly written Wallenstadt, was the *stad*, 'staith' or 'landing-place' of the *Walen* or Welsh, as the Germans called the Romansch-speaking people to the south of the lake, which at one time formed the boundary between Romansch and Alemannic speech. From the town which grew up near the staith, the lake is called the Walenstatter See, the Walensee, or the Lake of Walenstad. The Romansch people called the landing-place RIVA (*ripa*) 'the shore,' and not the Stad, and hence in old documents the lake is called *Lacus Rivanus*.

Wales is derived from *Wealas*, 'foreigners' or 'Welsh,' a name given by the Anglo-Saxon invaders to the natives of Britain. Wales is a plural form denoting the people, which, like Sussex or Dorset, afterwards acquired a territorial significance. (*See* CORNWALL.)

Walfisch Bay, South Africa, was discovered by Diaz in 1486, and called *Angra dos Ilheos*, the 'Bay of the Islands,' a name still partly preserved in the neighbouring PUNTA DOS ILHEOS, 'Cape of the Islands.' The bay, being at one time the resort of American whalers, acquired from the Boers the name of Walfisch or 'Whale' Bay.

Walker Islands, a Polynesian Group, were discovered in 1814 by a Captain Walker. WALKER'S BAY, in Arctic America, was named after Admiral Walker. WALKER'S PASS, in the Californian Sierra Nevada, bears the name of one of Fremont's exploring party. CAPE WALKER, in Arctic America, was named after an Admiralty clerk.

Wallachia, on the Lower Danube, is a Latinised form of the German name

WALLACHEN, which is derived from the Slavonic *vlach* or *wlach*, a 'foreigner,' which corresponds to the Teutonic *walah*, whence the names WALES and WALLOON.

Wallis Island (UEA), west of the Samoa Group, was discovered in 1767 by Captain Wallis, whose name has also been given to two other Pacific islets.

Wallsend, in Northumberland, stood at the eastern end of the Roman wall; as CARLISLE, a British name of similar signification, protected the western end.

Walsingham, a cape on the west shore of Davis Strait, was discovered by Davis in 1585, and named after his patron, Sir Francis Walsingham, Secretary of State.

Waltham, a common English name, is usually *Wealtham* in A.S. charters, meaning an 'enclosure in the weald' or forest. WALTHAM ABBEY or WALTHAM HOLY CROSS takes its name from the Holy Cross found at *Leogares-burh* (now Montacute) in Somerset, and carried by the oxen of Tofig from Wessex to Essex, where Tofig reared a minster, now Waltham Abbey, which was enlarged by Harold. The adjoining parish of WALTHAM CROSS takes its name from one of the Eleanor crosses erected by Edward I. WALTHAMSTOW, Essex, though not far from Waltham Abbey, seems to be an unconnected name. The Domesday name is *Walamestún*, and T.R.E. it belonged not to the Abbey but to a person named Waltheof.

Walton, Surrey, was a *tún* on the defensive dyke or wall which stretched from the Thames to the camp on St. George's Hill. WALLSCOMBE, near Wells, was on the dyke or 'wall' which guarded Somerset against the Welsh. In some cases, as in Suffolk and Northants, WALTON (A.S. *Wealton*) may be the *tún* enclosed by a wall (*weal*). WALTON ON THE NAZE, Essex, is believed to take its name from a sea-wall. The reclaimed land between Wisbeach and King's Lynn in Norfolk lies beyond the ancient sea-wall from which the landward villages of WALTON, WALSOKEN, and WALPOLE take their names, WALPOLE being named from a 'pool' of water near the wall. WALPOLE ISLAND, one of the Loyalty Group, was discovered in 1794 by Captain Butler in the ship *Walpole*. WALWORTH, Surrey, called in a charter *Wealawyrth*, was an estate belonging to Welshmen or Britons (*weala*, gen. pl. of *wealh*).

Wanborough, near Swinton in Wilts, is called *Wenbeorge* in a charter of 854, and *Wemberge* in Domesday (A.S. *wen*,

a tumour or swelling). The *Wodnesbeorge* of the Chronicle is not Wanborough as often asserted, but Wednesbury (*q.v.*).

WANSDIKE (A.S. *Wodenesdíc*), the great entrenchment which defended Bath against the Welsh, is 'Woden's dyke,' a name explained by the fact that Woden was regarded as the protector of boundaries.

Wandsworth, Surrey, is a corruption of *Wandelworth*, the 'estate on the Wandel' River, as Tamworth (*q.v.*) is the estate on the Tame.

Wanganui, a river in New Zealand, is the 'great valley'(Maori, *wanga*, a 'valley,' and *nui*, 'great').

Ware, in Hertfordshire, takes its name from a 'weir' or dam across the River Lea constructed by the Danes in 964.

Warrender Bay and CAPE WARRENDER in Arctic America were named after Sir George Warrender.

Warsaw, formerly *Varsovia* (Polish *Warszawa*), takes its Slavonic name from a castle (*var*) built in the ninth century by Conrad, Duke of the surrounding palatinate of MAZOVIA (Polish *Mazowsze*), in which originated the Mazurek, a dance of the Polish peasantry, which we call the Mazurka.

Warwick, a town which gives its name to a Mercian shire, is *Wæringawic* or *Wæringwic* in A.S. documents, the shire being called *Wærincwic-scir* or *Wæringscir*. Warwick was therefore the abode of the Wærings, a Teutonic clan whose name is identical·with that of the Scandinavian *Væringjar*, who furnished the Varangian guard to the Byzantine Emperors. WARWICK, in Rhode Island, was so named in honour of the Earl of Warwick, who in 1643 was appointed head of the Parliamentary Board of Commissioners for Colonial affairs.

Wasen, or AUF DEM WASEN, a village in Canton Uri, is situated at the striking point where the St. Gothard Railway begins to climb in spiral tunnels. In a document of 1365 it is called *Wasson*, which means 'at the steep' (O.H.G. *hwas*, M.H.G. *waz*, 'steep').

Washington, the name of two places in England, one in Durham, the other in Sussex (A.S. *Hwessingatún* and *Wassingatún*, signifies the *tun* of the Hwessings or Wassings. From the Durham village the ancestors of George Washington, the first President of the United States (1789-1797), are believed to have derived their territorial surname. In his honour the city of Georgetown, in Maryland, selected in 1790 for the federal capital, was re-named WASHINGTON, the district around it being taken out of Maryland, and called COLUMBIA, in honour of Columbus. One of the north-west territories, now a State, was named WASHINGTON in 1853, and there are 318 cities, counties, and town-ships, chiefly in Virginia, Pennsylvania, Missouri, Illinois, Indiana, Iowa, and Kansas, which have thus indirectly come to bear the name of the little Durham village.

Wasp Rapids, on the River Aruwimi, a tributary of the Congo, were so named by H. M. Stanley in 1887, his expedition passing them with great difficulty, owing to the trees overhanging the river having numerous pendent nests of wasps which attacked his men.

Wa-sukuma, a tribe in Equatorial Africa, are the 'northmen,' *sukuma* mean-ing the north, and *wa* being the plural prefix. So the WA-GWABA are the 'knob-nosed people,' the WA-NYIKA the 'wilder-ness people,' and the WA-TONGA or BA-TONGA the 'independent people.' (*See* BANTU.)

Waterford, an Irish county, is named from Waterford city, whose old Celtic name was *Cuan-na-groith*, the 'haven of the sun.' The Danish name *Vadrefiord*, of which Waterford is a corruption, might signify the 'ford over the fiord,' the fiord being the estuary of the Suir, and the word *vadre* being the equivalent of what in northern English is called a 'wath,' a word seen in the Yorkshire parish of WATH-UPON-DEARNE, and other places called WATH.

Waterloo, a village on the skirts of the forest of Soignies, near Brussels, was about three-quarters of a mile behind the British position on June 18th, 1815. Names in -*loo* or -*lo* are numerous in the Nether-lands, as Venloo, Beverloo, Hengloo, and Tongerloo, where *loo* is the phonetic equi-valent of the A.S. *leáh,* and the O.H.G. *lôh,* a 'woodland pasturage' while in Flemish the word *loo* must have meant a moor or marsh. There is no ancient form of the name Waterloo to determine the etymology, which must therefore de-pend on the topographical features. There is no marsh near the village, which lies on rising ground near the forest, and therefore the probable meaning is 'watery wood' or 'wet pasture.' The names in *lo* or *loo* usually refer to places in forests. Wellington's victory has caused the trans-ference of the name of the Belgian village to places in Lancashire, Lanark, Perth-shire, Iowa, New York, and to several in Canada.

Watford, in Northants, is a ford on Watling Street. WATFORD in Herts, though not far from Watling Street, is not the actual ford by which Watling Street crossed the Colne. We have no old form of the name, as Watford is not mentioned in Domesday, being included in the manor of Cashio. The name has been referred to the A.S. *wath,* 'a way,' 'course,' or 'journey,' or to *wét,* 'wet,' but is more probably from *wadan,* 'to wade.'

Watling Island, one of the Bahamas, is probably to be identified with GUANA-HANI, the landfall of Columbus in his first voyage (October 12th, 1592), which he named SAN SALVADOR (Holy Saviour). The modern name is referred to John Watling, a famous buccaneer, who was killed in 1681.

Wavre, in Canton Neufchâtel, was anciently *Waura,* whence the Low-Latin *waureia* or *wauriacum,* 'untilled' or 'fallow land.' WAVRE, near Brussels, probably to be explained in the same way.

Weald, commonly called The Weald of Kent, is the Teutonic name of the great forest of Anderida (*Andredes-leáh*). There are other Wealds, such as NORTH WEALD and SOUTH WEALD, both on the skirts of the great Essex forest. (*See* WALDECK.)

Wear, a river in Durham, the *Vedra* of Ptolemy, is from a widespread Aryan word denoting 'water' (Sanskrit *udra*). BISHOP'S WEARMOUTH and MONKS' WEARMOUTH (A.S. *Wierimutha*) stand on either side of the mouth of the Wear.

Wednesbury, in Staffordshire, is 'Woden's hill,' and WEDNESFIELD, in the same county, is 'Woden's field.' Wednesbury is called *Wodnesbyri* in a charter of 1004, and *Wednesberie* in Domesday, forms which render probable its identification with the *Wodnesbeorge* of the Chronicle, where great battles were fought in 592 and 715. (*See* WAN-BOROUGH).

Weenen is a town in Natal whose name commemorates the 'weeping' caused by the massacre of the Boers in 1838 by the Caffre chief Dingan.

Weil, or WYL, is the name of several places in Germany, and -*weiler,* -*weil,* or -*wyl* forms the suffix in 271 German names. The word -*wila,* now -*weil* or -*wyl,* de-noted a single house, while -*wilare,* now -*weiler,* signified a hamlet or collection of houses. On the Meuse and the Mosel -*wila* mixes with the Latin -*villa,* now

-ville, and *weiler*, now VILLIERS, with the Latin *vilare*. The Latin words are now supposed to have been borrowed by the Teutons.

Weimar, the capital of SAXE-WEIMAR, anciently written *Wimari* and *Wehmari*, is supposed to be equivalent to *wech-mar*, meaning a 'morass,' literally a 'soft moor.'

Weisshorn, a conspicuous snowy pyramid in Canton Valais, as well as the WEISSMIES, MONT BLANC, the DENT BLANCHE, and the TÊTE BLANCHE are named from their snow-clad peaks.

Wellesley Islands, a group in the Gulf of Carpentaria, the largest of which is MORNINGTON ISLAND, were named by Flinders in 1802 after Richard Wellesley, Earl of Mornington and Marquess Wellesley, then Governor-General of India.

Wellingborough, in Northamptonshire, was the A.S. *Wendlingburh*, 'the burh of the Wendlings.'

Wellington, a common village name, occurring in the counties of Somerset, Hereford, Wilts, and Salop, is a patronymic, as is proved by the A.S. forms *Weolingtun* and *Welingtun*, meaning the tun of the Weolingas or Welingas. Wellington, in Somerset, gave a ducal title to Sir Arthur Wellesley, in whose honour WELLINGTON, New Zealand, the first settlement of the New Zealand colonists, and now the seat of the Colonial Government, was named. CAPE WELLINGTON and WATERLOO BAY, in Bass Strait, were surveyed and named by Stokes on June 18th, 1842, the anniversary of the battle of Waterloo. WELLINGTON CHANNEL and WELLINGTON STRAIT, in the Arctic Archipelago, together with an Australian lake, a Patagonian island, a district in New South Wales, and a town in the Cape Colony, are among the places which bear the name of the English general.

Wells, an episcopal see in Somerset, is called in A.S. charters *Wyl, Willan, St. Andrea æt Welles*, and in Latin charters *Fontanetum* and *Fontanensis*. The name refers to a spring in the Cathedral Close called St. Andrew's Well. WELLS, in Norfolk, is in A.S. *Wyl, Welle*, and *Welles*. WELHAM, in Yorkshire, is an assimilated form from *Wellun*, a locative plural meaning 'at the wells.'

Welshpool, in Montgomeryshire, formerly called Pool, stands on a wide pool formed by the Severn. It was called the Welsh Poole in the time of Henry VIII., no doubt to distinguish it from POOLE in Dorset, which stands on a large inlet or pool at the mouth of the Frome.

Wengern Alp, in the Bernese Oberland, is the alp or mountain pasture belonging to a hamlet in the valley of Lauterbrunnen called WENGEN, 'at the wang.' From the O.H.G. *wang*, a 'field' or 'plain,' we have several German villages called WANGEN, and the word appears as a suffix in the name of WETWANG, a village in Yorkshire.

Weser, a large German river, was the *Visurgis* of Tacitus. The oldest Teutonic form is *Wisaraha*, which became *Wisara*, and then Weser. The suffix *-aha* means water, and the name would signify in German the 'western water,' *i.e.* the river west of the Vistula, *westar* and *wisar*, 'western,' being parallel formations from *wis*, the 'west.' Another proposed etymology is from *wisa*, 'meadow' or 'pasture,' but the German names are doubtless only assimilated forms of an older Celtic designation.

Wessel Island and CAPE WESSEL, North Australia, commemorate the visit to this coast in 1636 of the *Wezel*, a Dutch ship.

Westall, Point, and MOUNT WESTALL in Australia bear the name of the well-known artist who accompanied Flinders.

Westeras, on the Malar Lake in Sweden, is a corruption of *Vestra-Aros*, the 'western mouth' or inlet.

West Indies is a name which perpetuates the misconception of Columbus, who imagined that Haiti was Cipangu (Japan), that Cuba was China, and that Costa Rica was Malacca. Hence he named the lands which he had discovered *las Indias Occidentales*, 'the Western Indies,' to distinguish them from the East Indies which Vasco da Gama had reached by sailing eastward round the Cape of Good Hope. The term INDIANS has thus become established as the collective name of the Aboriginal American races.

Westmanna Islands, off Iceland, obtained the name of *Vest-manna-eyar*, because some fugitive Irish slaves, called 'Westmen' by the Norwegians, were there slain.

Westminster Hall was the name given in 1670 to an island in the Straits of Magellan by Sir John Narborough from a fancied resemblance of its outline to that of Westminster Hall in London.

Westmoreland was the land of the *Westmoringas* or people of the Western Moors. Higden speaks of 'Appelbyshire cum Westmereland,' showing that the Barony of Appleby, east of the Fells, was not then considered to belong to the county.

Weston's Island, in James Bay, Hudson Bay, was so named by James in 1631 in compliment to Lord Weston, after whom LORD WESTON'S FORELAND in Fox Channel was named by Luke Fox in the same year.

Westphalia is the Latinised form we have adopted for the German WESTFALEN or WESTPHALEN, which primarily denoted the inhabitants and not their territory. In the eighth century we have *Westfalun* and *Westfalahi*, which afterwards became *Westfalen* and *Westfali*. According to Grimm, *falah* meant a person employed in tillage, and hence a settler or occupier. The Ostfali lived on the eastern bank of the Weser, and the Westfali on the western bank, afterwards extending themselves to the south-west far beyond their original seat, the western field or plain of the Weser. The modern Westphalia is a hilly district remote from this plain.

Wetterhorn, the 'storm' or 'weather peak,' is a conspicuous buttress in the Bernese Oberland, on whose crest gathering clouds are believed to foretell the approach of bad weather.

Wetumpka, the native name of a town in Alabama, is the place at the 'rapids' which here stop navigation on the River Coosa.

Wexford, a Scandinavian settlement, gives its name to an Irish county. The etymology is uncertain, but the older form *Weisford* suggests that it may be from *veisu-fjördhr*, the 'firth of the stagnant pool.'

Weymouth, in Dorset (A.S. *Wægemuth*), stands at the mouth of the RIVER WEY, a name which must not be classed with that of the WYE, as we learn from Ptolemy that the pre-Teutonic name was the Alaunus. The name *Wæge* shows that it must be referred to the A.S. *wæge*, which means a 'wave,' and also a way or passage. The WEY, in Surrey, whence the name WEYBRIDGE (M.E. *Waigebrugge*). is doubtless from the same source, as well as that of the Medway (*q.v.*), and perhaps those of the Conway and the Solway.

Whaingaroa, a harbour and river in New Zealand, is a Maori name meaning 'long pursued,' in reference, it is supposed, to the great length of the inlet.

Whale Sound, Baffin Bay, is an inlet where Baffin in 1616, taking refuge from a storm, sighted several whales.

Whangape, a New Zealand lake, means in Maori 'expanse of water.'

Whare-kahu, in New Zealand, is the 'house of the falcon.'

Whipple, Mount, on the Colorado River, bears the name of Captain Whipple, who explored the district in 1854.

Whithorn, in Wigtownshire, the *Candida Casa* of Bæda, appears in the twelfth century as *Hwiterne*, the 'white dwelling.'

White Sea, a translation of the Russian name BIEL OSERO or BJELOJE MORE, is appropriately so called, because the ice in winter becomes covered with a sheet of snow. WHITE ISLAND, in the Bay of Plenty, New Zealand, is an active volcano, so named by Cook in 1769 from the column of white smoke emitted from the crater.

Whitsun Island, in the Low Archipelago, was discovered by Wallis on Whitsun Eve, June 6th, 1767. WHITSUN ISLAND, in the New Hebrides, was discovered by Bougainville on Whitsunday, May 22nd, 1768. Cook discovered WHITSUNDAY PASSAGE, leading out of Repulse Bay, Queensland, on Whitsunday, June 3rd, 1770, and CAPE WHITSUNDAY and WHITSUNTIDE BAY, Alaska, on Whitsunday, June 7th, 1778.

Wickham's Range and WICKHAM HEIGHTS, North Australia, bear the name of an Australian explorer.

Wicklow, a town which gives a name to an Irish county, was anciently *Wykynglo*, the place of the vikings, so called because they mostly came from the great *vik* or bay between Sweden and Norway, now called the Skagerack. The *lo* in *Wykynglo* may be a Celtic corruption of the O.N. *lôn*, a 'sea-loch' or 'firth.' From the O.N. *vik*, a 'creek' or 'bay' (Danish *vig*, Old Saxon *wik*, A.S. *wîc*), we have the names of WICK, the county town of Caithness, and of WYK, the principal harbour of Föhr, one of the North Frisian islands, usually called DE WYK, 'the bay,' and indirectly of Nantwich, Northwich, and Droitwich (*q.v.*), all of them places where 'bay salt' was made. From the O.H.G. *wich*, A.S. *wîc* (Latin *vicus*), we have VIGO (*q.v.*), HAMPTON WICK, ALNWICK, BERWICK, and other places; while to the O.N. *veikr*, M.H.G. *weich*, English *weak*, we may probably refer WYKE, in Yorkshire, WEIMAR (*q.v.*), and other names of places on boggy sites.

Wielicza, a town near Cracow with salt works, is said to bear the name of a shepherd who, in the thirteenth century, discovered the salt deposits.

Wiesbaden, a watering-place in Hesse-Nassau, appears as *Wisibadum* in 965, and as *Wisebadon* in 1043, forms which point to the O.H.G. *wisa* (N.H.G. *wiese*), a meadow. The dative plural *Wisibadum* would therefore mean 'at the meadow baths,' a name which would translate the Celto-Latin names *Fontes Mattiaci* or *Aquæ Mattiacæ* of Tacitus and Pliny.

Wiesensteig, near Ulm, anciently *Wisuntes-steige*, 'the auroch's ascent,' WIESENDANGEN, anciently *Wisunt-wangas*, 'the auroch's plains,' in Canton Zürich, WIESENFELD in Hesse, WIESENT near Ratisbon, WIESENTHAL near Spier, WIESENTHAU near Forchheim, and WIESENSCHWANG in the Tyrol, are interesting names taking us back to the times when the huge extinct aurochs, the *wisent* of the Niebelungen Lied, roamed over the plains of Germany.

Wight, an island in the English channel, is Ptolemy's *Vectis*, a name which became *Wiht* in A.S., whence the modern English Wight. The form *Mictis* in Pliny is a misreading for *Vectis*, the letters *ve* in the Roman cursive being easily mistaken for *mi*. Nennius speaks of *With*, which the Britons call *Gueid* or *Guith*, which he says may be translated in Latin by *divortium*. The Welsh *gwyth* means a 'channel,' and *divortium* may be rendered as a 'turning' or 'passage.' Nennius evidently supposed that the Isle of Wight took its name from the Solent, the channel which divides it from the mainland. The Welsh name *Ynys-yr-wyth* means the 'island of the channel.' It may be noted that the changes from the Latin *Vectis* through the Welsh *Guith* and the Saxon *Wiht* to the modern Wight are parallel to the corresponding forms—Latin *Picti*, Celtic *Peithi*, Saxon *Pyhtas*, and O.E. *Pights*.

Wilberforce Falls, on the Arctic Hood's River, and CAPE WILBERFORCE, in the Gulf of Carpentaria, bear the name of the philanthropist William Wilberforce.

Wildkirchli, the 'little church in the wild,' a place of pilgrimage in Canton Appenzell, was a cave in which a Capuchin monk established an oratory in 1621.

Willems Eylant, Novaya Zemlya, discovered by Barents in 1594, and WILLEMS RIVER, North Australia, discovered by the ship *Mauritius* in 1618, bear the name of William II., Prince of Orange, the Dutch Stadtholder.

Williamsburg, named after King William III., replaced Jamestown in 1696 as the capital of Virginia. The ground-plan of the city was laid out in the shape of a W, the initial letter of the king's name. KING WILLIAM'S CAPE, in New Guinea, was also named by Dampier in 1700 in honour of William III.; PRINCE WILLIAM'S LAND, on the west coast of Baffin Bay, discovered by Ross in 1818; PRINCE WILLIAM'S SOUND, Alaska, discovered by Cook in 1778; KING WILLIAM'S LAND, Boothia Felix, discovered by Ross in 1830; WILLIAM THE FOURTH'S LAND, at the mouth of the Great Fish River, discovered by Back in 1834; and WILLIAMS-TOWN, Port Philip, were named after King William IV.

Wilson's Promontory, the southernmost point of Australia, discovered by Bass in 1798, was named in compliment to Thomas Wilson, Esq., of London.

Wiltshire is first mentioned in the Chronicle (A.D. 799) under the name of *Wilsæte* or *Wilsætan*, which would have given us a modern form Wilset, like Somerset or Dorset, meaning the district of the settlers on the Willy. The *t* in Wiltshire is accounted for by a later entry in the Chronicle (A.D. 870), where we find *Wiltún-scir*, which means the shire of which WILTON (A.S. *Wiltún*), the 'tún on the River Willy,' was the county town.

Wimbledon, in Surrey, is commonly identified with a place called *Wibban-dún* in the Saxon Chronicle, meaning possibly 'Worms hill' (A.S. *wibba*, a 'worm'), but more probably from the proper name Wibba, which is doubtless preserved in the name of WHIPSNADE (formerly *Wibba-snade*), in Bedfordshire, which is not far from Berkhamstead, where Wibba, one of the Mercian kings, had a palace, and which remained a royal manor till the present century. The suffix -*snade* means a 'detached piece of land,' or perhaps a 'clearing in a wood.'

Wimborne Minster, Dorset, is the A.S. *Winburnan*, the place on the Winburne, now the Wimborne.

Winchester was the Roman *Venta Belgarum*, where Venta is the Latin form of the British *gwent*, usually said to denote an open champaign country, such as the treeless Hampshire downs as contrasted with the neighbouring Andred forest. There were three places called Venta or Gwent: *Venta Silurum*, the Gwent of the Silures, now CAER-WENT, the 'city of Gwent,' in Monmouthshire; *Venta*

Icenorum, the Gwent of the Iceni, now CAISTOR, in Norfolk; and *Venta Belgarum,* the Gwent of the Belgae, now Winchester. In the Chronicle Winchester, as well as Chester, is called simply *Ceaster,* 'the chester,' but to distinguish it from other Chesters, such as CHESTER in Cheshire, CAISTOR in Norfolk, or CASTOR in Northamptonshire, the prefix derived from the Roman name was added. From the Roman *Venta* the Saxons made a genitive *Wintan,* whence we have the form *Wintan-ceaster,* the 'chester of Venta,' while from the later form *Winte-ceaster* the modern name of Winchester is derived. We have a curious French corruption of the name in the BICÊTRE at Paris, which was a Carthusian house held in 1290 by the Bishop of Winchester.

Win-de-go, near Rainy Lake, Canada, also known by the translated name CANNIBAL LAKE, was the scene of an act of cannibalism perpetrated in 1811 by a band of Ojibways.

Windhonds Bay, Fuegia, bears the name of a Dutch ship which discovered it in 1624.

Windisch, near Zürich, preserves the name of the Roman station of *Vindonissa.*

Windsor, Berks, a contraction of the A.S. name *Windlesofra, Windlesora, Wendlesore,* or *Windelesore,* is usually explained as the place by the 'winding shore.' In A.S. *windel* (genitive *windles*) means a thing twined, hence a basket, and *Windel-treow* means a windle tree, willow, or osier, from which windels or baskets were made. For 'winding shore' we should expect to find the form *Windel-ora,* and for 'shore of osiers' we should expect *Windela-ora.* The place may have been named from some single windletree, but most probably from some special kind of fixed basket, such as an eel trap or salmon corve, or the first element may be a personal name, as in the case of EDENSOR, which is 'Eadnoth's shore.'

Winnipeg City, the capital of the Canadian province of Manitoba, is built on a spit at the junction of the Red River and the Assiniboine, whose united waters after a course of forty-five miles reach LAKE WINNIPEG, which bears an Algonquin name meaning 'the muddy water' (*wi* or *win,* 'muddy' or 'dirty,' and *nipi,* 'water'), the water being discoloured by the Saskatchewan, which brings down much clay in solution. LAKE WINIPEGSIS is the 'little Winipeg,' the Cree suffix *-sis* being a diminutive, as in the name

SEPE-SIS, the 'little water.' LAKE WINNEBAGO, or LAC DES PUANS, is named from a dirty Indian tribe, whose malodorous nickname the French translated as Les Puants.

Winter Harbour, Melville Island, sheltered Parry's ships in the winter of 1819-20. In WINTER HARBOUR, Kerguelen Land, Robert Rhodes, a whaling captain, passed eight months in 1799. At WINTER ISLAND, in Fox Channel, Parry wintered in 1821-22. At WINTER LAKE, near the Coppermine River, Franklin built Fort Enterprise, where he wintered in 1821-22.

Winterthur, a city in Canton Zürich, is the Germanised form of the Celto-Latin name *Vitudurum,* which is older than the third century, and might mean the 'forest fortress.' The modern name is plainly due to an Alemannic folk-etymology, the form *Winturdura* occurring in 865.

Wirral, a hundred in Cheshire, comprises the tongue of land between the Dee and the Mersey. It was the territory of the Cornavii, a Celtic tribe, who, like the *Cornwealas* (*see* CORNWALL), probably took their name from this projecting corner or 'horn' of land, to which the Teutonic name Wirral, spelt *Wirhal* in 1004, may also refer. The people were called *Wirhealas,* Chester being described in the Chronicle as 'a waste chester *on Wirhealum,*' where Wirhealum is the dative plural of the name of the inhabitants. In A.S. *heal* or *healh* signifies a corner, angle, or slope, and *wir* means myrtle, probably bog-myrtle, a plant with which this boggy flat was doubtless overgrown.

Wisbeach, Cambridgeshire, is written *Wisebec* in the Chronicle and also in a charter, meaning perhaps the 'dry beck' (A.S. *wis-nian,* 'to become dry,' whence the modern word *wizen,* 'to dry up').

Wisconsin, one of the United States, takes its name from its chief river, the WISCONSIN, called the *Miskonsing* by Joliet in 1674, a name said to mean the 'wild rushing channel.'

Wissant, near Calais, formerly *Witsant,* 'white sand,' is one of the names which prove the existence of a Saxon settlement on the further side of the Straits of Dover, where we find such familiar Teutonic forms as WIMILLE (Windmill) and SANGATTE (Sandgate).

Woiwodina, or VOIVODINA, a district in Austria, means the 'Duchy,' from the Slavonic *voivode,* a 'commander' or 'duke.' (*See* HERZEGOVINA.)

GLOSSARY

297

Wolfe Islands, in the Gambier Group, bear the name of James Wolfe, one of Beechey's officers.

Wollaston Land, and several islands in Arctic America and Australia, bear the name of Dr. W. Hyde Wollaston, a distinguished man of science, who died in 1828.

Wollombi, a common Australian name for places at the confluence of streams, is a native term signifying the 'meeting of the waters.'

Wolstenholme Sound and WOL-STENHOLME ISLAND in Baffin Bay, discovered by Bylot and Baffin in 1616, and CAPE WOLSTENHOLME in Hudson Channel, discovered by Hudson in 1610, bear the name of Sir John Wolstenholme, a munificent promoter of Arctic research in the reign of James I.

Wolverhampton, Staffordshire, takes its name from the collegiate church founded by Wulfruna, sister of King Ethelred II. In the oldest documents the place is simply called *Hantune*, 'high tun' (*see* HAMPTON). In a charter of 996 it has acquired the name of *Wulfrune Hantune*, of which Wolverhampton is the later euphonic corruption.

Wombat, Point, in the Furneaux Islands, is the place where the first known specimen of the wombat (*Phascolomys fossor*) was found by Flinders in 1798.

Women's Island, in Baffin Bay, is where Baffin met with some friendly Eskimo women.

Wood's Bay, in the Antarctic South Victoria, bears the name of an officer of James Clerke Ross. CAPE WOOD, also in South Victoria, bears that of Sir Charles Wood, afterwards Lord Halifax. WOOD LAKE and the LAKE OF THE WOODS, in the Canadian Dominion, are surrounded by dense pine forests.

Woolwich, Kent, appears in Domesday as *Hulviz*. Hence the name has usually been explained as *hyl-vik*, 'hill bay' or 'hill village.' But in earlier charters the name is written *Uuluwich, Wulewic*, and *Wulewich*, forms which point to the A.S. *wull* or *wulle*, 'wool,' or possibly to the proper name Wulf.

Worcestershire takes its name from the city of WORCESTER, a name of doubtful etymology. Worcester is the *Wigornia* or *Vigorna* of Bæda, and appears in an eighth century Latin charter as *Weogorna civitas*, and later as *Wigranceaster*. In the later portion of the Chronicle we have *Wigeraceaster*,

Wigraceaster, and then *Wireceaster*, whence Worcester, the pronunciation of which has now lapsed to Wooster. In Nennius we have *Kaer Gorangon* (or *Cair Guoranegon*) *id est Wigornia*, which may be only a translation into Welsh of the English name, or, as Mr. Bradley has suggested, may be a corruption of a genuine Welsh name, probably from *wegorn-*, the conjectural Old Celtic form of the Welsh *gwern*, a 'marsh.' Worcester was the capital of the tribe of the Hwiccas, and hence it has been supposed that the name was a corruption of *Hwicca ceaster* or *Hwiccwara ceaster*, like Cantwarabyrig or Wihtgaraburh. The objection to this is that it is based on the late and probably corrupt form *Wigera-ceaster*, and not on the earliest forms, which are better explained by Mr. Bradley's conjecture. The same objection applies to Mr. Eyton's explanation of the late form *Wireceaster* as the chester near Wire Forest.

Wormhill, in Derbyshire, is a curiously assimilated name. The Domesday form *Vurvenele* points, as Mr. Bradley ingeniously conjectures, to an A.S. *hweorfanhealh*, which would mean the 'haugh of the water mill.'

Worms, a city in Hesse Darmstadt, was the Celto-Roman *Borbetomagus* or *Bormitomagus*, which as early as the second century became *Wormatia* and *Wormacia*. Borbetomagus is supposed to be from the Celtic *magos* (*magh*), a 'field' or 'plain,' and *borbaith*, 'high,' or from **Borvetos*, conjecturally the primitive name of the River Worms on which it stands, but which may, however, have derived its name from the town. In the eighth century it was called *Wangionum civitas* or *Wangiona*, being in the territory of the Vangiones (*vang*, a 'field' or 'plain' being the Teutonic equivalent of the Celtic *magh*). In the tenth century we have *Episcopus Vangionum quæ nunc dicitur Wormatia*. BORMIO in Italy is also called Worms by the Germans, and the WORMSER JOCH is the Teutonic name of the pass leading across the Alps to Bormio.

Wörth, one of the battlefields in the Franco-German war of 1870, is a corruption of the old name *Warida*, from the O.H.G. *warid*, an 'island,' which is common in German names, such as KAISERSWERTH, the 'emperor's island,' DONAUWÖRTH, the 'island in the Danube,' or NONNENWERTH, an island in the Rhine with a convent for nuns.

Wrangel Land, in the Arctic Ocean, bears the name of Admiral Wrangel, a Russian explorer, who discovered it in 1823.

Wrath, Cape, in Scotland, is believed to be a Norse name meaning the cape at the *hvarf* or 'turning.'

Wreck Reef, between New Caledonia and Australia, was the scene of the wreck, on August 17th, 1803, of the *Porpoise* and the *Cato*. Flinders and Franklin were returning to Europe on board the *Porpoise* after their survey of the Australian coast. (*See* FLINDERS.)

Wrottesley, Cape, in Banks' Land, was named by M'Clure in 1881 after Lord Wrottesley, President of the Royal Society.

Wroxeter, the 'chester by the Wrekin,' was the Roman *Uriconium* or *Viroconium* (Vrikin-ium), hence the WREKIN must have been called Uricon or Virocon. The English colonists in the neighbouring lands called themselves *Wroken-sæte*, and would call the Roman town *Wroken-ceaster*, which would become *Wrokceaster*, and finally WROXETER.

Würtemberg, or WIRTEMBERG, a south German kingdom, officially styled WÜRTTEMBERG, takes its name from the castle of WIRTINEBERG near Stuttgart, which is first mentioned in 1092 as *Wirtinisberk*, plainly from a personal name.

Würzburg, a city in Bavaria, is called *Wirziaburg* in 704. In the eleventh and twelfth centuries the name is Latinised as *Herbipolis*, probably a correct translation of the name.

Wycliffe-on-Tees, in Domesday *Witclive*, the 'white cliff,' is interesting as having given a territorial surname to John Wycliffe, the reformer.

Wyoming, U.S.A., a corruption of the native name *Maughwauwame*, 'the large plains,' is the name of a territory admitted in 1890 into the Union as a State.

Xalpa, in Mexico, means 'upon the sand' (Aztec *xalli*, 'sand,' and *pan*, 'upon'). The word *xalli*, 'sand,' is found in numerous Mexican names, as XALTEPA, from *xaltetl*, 'sandstone'; XALTOCCAN, the 'sandy maize field,' from *toctli*, a 'maize plantation'; and XALAPA, usually spelt JALAPA (*q.v.*).

Xeres, near Cadiz, in the modern spelling JEREZ, whence the white wine called *Sherry* was shipped, has been identified with the Roman *Asido Caesariana*. The Moors turned *Caesaris Asidona* into *Caeris Sidonia*, whence we get *Xerez Sidonia* in documents of the thirteenth century.

Yahuar-cocha, in Peru, is the 'lake of blood,' where the Inca Huayna Capac (*c.* 1475-1523) massacred hundreds of prisoners, whose bodies were thrown into the lake. (*See* COCHA.)

Yakutsk, a Siberian town in the Yakut territory on the Lena, was founded by the Cossacks in 1632. The *sk*, as in Tomsk or Tobolsk, is the Russian formative. The syllable *ut* in the tribe-name Yakut is the Mongolian plural suffix, as in BURUT, a plural tribe-name from Bur or Bor. Hence to speak or write of Yakuts or Buruts, as is often done, is as much a pleonasm as to speak of Englishmens.

Yampee Point, on the coast of Tasmanland, Australia, is a curious instance of how a waterless spot may receive a name meaning water. Here Stokes found a native dying of thirst, who was only able to ejaculate *yampee! yampee!* 'water! water!'

Yankton, before 1883 the capital of Dakota, and the YANKTON RIVER, an affluent of the Missouri, bear the name of the Yankton tribe, a division of the Dahcotas. Yankton is a corruption of the native name *Ihanktonwe*, the 'dwellers at the end.'

Yarkand, a town in Central Asia, would mean in Persian the 'place of friends' (*yar*, a 'friend,' and *kand*, 'place'). More probably the name is Kirghiz, in which case it would mean the 'place on the cliff' or bank of the Zerafshan or Yarkand River.

Yarmouth, or GREAT YARMOUTH, Norfolk, anciently *Gernemuta*, is at the mouth of the Yare, the *Garrienus* of Ptolemy, afterwards called the *Gerne*, *Yerne*, or Yare. YARMOUTH, Isle of Wight, is at the mouth of the Yar, formerly the Yaver. The RIVER YARE, with the YAIR and the YARROW, both in Selkirkshire, bear the same Celtic name as the Perthshire GARRY (*q.v.*).

Yaroslav, or JAROSLAV (*q.v.*), a town on the Volga, the capital of a government of the same name, was founded between 1026 and 1036 by Yaroslav Vladimirovitch.

Yarra-Yarra, the river on which the city of Melbourne stands, is a native name believed to mean 'flow-flow,' that is the river which always flows, most of the Australian rivers becoming mere chains of ponds in the dry season.

GLOSSARY

299

Yason, a cape on the south coast of the Black Sea, is the Greek *Iasonion*, where the myth of Jason was localised.

Yedo, or YEDDO, in Japan, now called TOKIO (*q.v.*), means the 'river door' or 'estuary gate.'

Yell, one of the Shetlands, is a sterile island, consisting mostly of peat bog. In the Shetland dialect *yell* means 'barren.' The name was formerly written Jala or Jella, the 'barren isle' (O.N. *gall*, 'barren').

Yellow Knife River, a tributary of the Great Slave Lake, was named from a tribe living on the Atnah or Coppermine River, who were called the 'Yellow Knives' by the English. YELLOWSTONE, a tributary of the Missouri, is a translation of the French name *Roche Jaune*, so named from the colour of the cliffs. YELLOW RIVER is a translation of the Chinese name HOANG-HO (*q.v.*).

Yemen, properly THE YEMEN, the name of Southern Arabia, is curiously translated by Arabia Felix. The Arabic *yemin* signifies an 'oath,' and also the 'right hand,' oaths being taken by holding up the right hand. Then it came to mean the 'south,' the south being on the right hand of one who swears facing the east. For this reason 'The South' of Arabia came to be called EL-YEMEN. But the right hand being considered more lucky than the left, the word came to signify 'fortunate' or 'prosperous,' so that ARABIA FELIX is a sort of Latin translation of Yemen.

Yenikale, the 'new castle' built by the Turks in 1702 at the entrance to the Sea of Azov, gives a name to the Straits of Yenikale or Kertch. *Kale*, a 'castle,' is an Arabic loan-word in Turkish (*see* KELÁT), while *Yengi* or *Yeni*, 'new,' common in Turkish names, as YENI-BAZAR, the 'new market,' or YENIKEUI, 'Newton,' appears in the word Janissary, a corruption of *yengi-cheri*, the new formation of the former Turkish army which replaced the former feudal levies by an embodied militia (*cheri*, 'bold,' 'brave,' and hence 'troops').

Yenisei, the great river of Siberia, also written *Jenissy*, *Geniseia*, or *Gelissy*, has been absurdly explained as the 'New River,' from the Turkic *yeni*, 'new,' and *su*, 'water.' The Koibals, a Turkic tribe, call it simply Kem, 'the river.' The name Yenisei, by which it is known to Europeans, seems to have been acquired from Samoyed or Ostiak sources by Dutch sailors, and has been explained as 'the water which flows down,' or the river

which 'brings down ice.' In Samoyed *yi* is 'water,' and *nëser-nak* means 'I flow down,' while in Ostiak, an allied language, *yi* means 'ice,' and 'water' is *yink*.

Yeovil, in Somerset, stands on the Ivel, sometimes called the YEO, a name invented to explain the name of Yeovil, supposed to be the 'ville on the Yeo.' IVEL is a corruption of the older name *Givel* (once probably *Geovel*, whence YEO-VIL), as is shown by the fact that IL-CHESTER or Ivelchester, which also stands on the Ivel, is called *Givelchester* by Florence. Yeovil was formerly designated as the burh or borough of Yeovil, and according to the analogy of other names, should now be called Yeovilbury or Ivelbury. A suffix has, however, been retained by the village of YEOVILTON, formerly Evilton, close to Ilchester. In Bedfordshire there is another Ivel, which must also at one time have been called the *Givele*, as appears from the names of two villages on its banks now called Northill and Southill, assimilated forms which appear in Domesday as *Nortgivele* and *Sudgivele*.

Yerba Buena is a suburb of San Francisco, where in 1835 the first house in the city was built. The name, meaning in Spanish the 'good herb,' refers to a vine with a small white flower, esteemed as a medicinal plant, which grew wild on the spot.

Yester, Haddingtonshire, is believed to be a corruption of *Ystrad*, the *strath* or 'valley.'

Yokohama, now the chief port in Japan, was before 1854 a small fishing village. The name is believed to mean the 'cross shore.'

York was the capital of Roman Britain. The Celto-Latin name, found in an early inscription, was *Eburacum*, which, about the time of the Emperor Severus, became *Eboracum*. In the Chronicle we find the Roman name transformed into *Eoforwíc* or *Eoferwíc*. In the A.S. translation of Bæda it is *Eoferwíc-ceaster*, and the men of York are called *Eoferwícingas*. The Danes made Eoferwíc into *Jorvík*, whence the transition to York is easy. The Teutonic forms were evidently influenced by folk-etymology, the Anglian Eoforwíc meaning 'wild boar town.' The Welsh name *Caer-Ebroc* or *Caer-Ebrauc* was derived from the primitive British name *Ebur-ác-on*, where *ác* is plainly the common Celtic formative, leaving *to* be determined the meaning of *Ebur*. To do this the numerous similar names must be taken into account. There were three places called *Eburodunum*, one of which is now YVERDUN in Switzerland, and another is EMBRUN in the Hautes Alpes. *Eburobriga* has become BRIMONT, *Eburobritium* is now EBORA, and *Eboriacense monasterium* became FAREMOUTIERS. EVREUX was the capital of the *Eburovices*, and IVRY in Normandy was *Eburovicus*. To these names we may perhaps add that of the *Iberus*, now the EBRO. Some of these names may be derived, as d'Arbois de Jubainville has suggested, from Eburos, a Celtic personal name which is found in several inscriptions; but IVRY, formerly *Eburovicus*, must be from the name of the EURE, formerly the *Ebura*, on which it stands. York seems to be an analogous case. The river above York is called the Ure, a name probably identical with that of the French Eure, formerly the Ebura, in which case *Eburac*, the Celtic name of York, might mean the place on the Ebura or Ure (*see* YVERDUN). York being a royal duchy has been the source of numerous colonial names, first among which comes NEW YORK (*q.v.*), the name given to *Nieuw Amsterdam* in honour of James, Duke of York, afterwards James II. CAPE YORK, the northernmost point of Australia, whence the name of the great territory called the YORK PENINSULA, was sighted by Torres in 1606, but received its present name from Cook on August 21st, 1770, five days after the celebration of the birthday of the Duke of York, second son of George III. CAPE YORK, at the corner of Prince Regent's Bay, Greenland, was discovered by Ross in 1818, on August 16th, the birthday of the Duke of York. CAPE YORK, at the entrance to Prince Regent's Inlet, was discovered by Parry on August 17th, 1819. CAPE YORK, south-east of Prince of Wales' Cape, Alaska, was discovered by Beechey in August 1827. The DUKE OF YORK'S ARCHIPELAGO, at the mouth of the Coppermine River, was discovered by Franklin in 1821. The DUKE OF YORK'S BAY, Southampton Island, was entered by Parry on August 16th, 1821. The DUKE OF YORK'S ISLAND, one of the Navigator Group, was discovered by Byron in 1765. Another DUKE OF YORK'S ISLAND, in St. George's Channel, was discovered by Carteret in 1767. YORK ISLAND (Eimeo), one of the Society Group, was discovered by Wallis in 1767. YORK SOUND, in De Witt's Land, was named by King in 1820. YORK RIVER, which flows into Chesapeake Bay, was so named in 1607 after the Duke of York, afterwards Charles I. YORK SOUND, in Frobisher Bay, was so named by Frobisher in 1577 after Captain Gilbert York who explored it. The YORKE PENINSULA, between Spencer Gulf and St. Vincent Gulf, South Australia, was so named by Flinders in 1802 in honour of Charles Philip Yorke, first Lord of the Admiralty, after whom CAPE YORKE in Arctic America was named by Parry.

Yoruba, a country in Western Africa, was populated by refugees from various tribes speaking different dialects, *Yo-ru-ba* meaning a 'meeting-place,' literally 'I go meet.' (*See* ABBEOKUTA.)

Yosemité Valley, in the Rocky Mountains, is the 'valley of the grisly bear' (*osoamit* or *uhumati*).

Youghal, County Cork, is from the Old Irish *Eochaill*, a 'yew wood.'

Young Nick's Head was the first point in New Zealand sighted by Cook (October 6th, 1769). It was descried by Nicholas Young, nicknamed Young Nick, a boy who happened to be stationed at the masthead.

Young's Island, in Barrow Strait, was named by Parry in 1819 in honour of Dr. Thomas Young, an eminent man of science, after whom CAPE YOUNG in Dolphin and Union Strait was named by Richardson in 1826. MOUNT YOUNG, on the west coast of Spencer Gulf, bears the name of Admiral Young. YOUNG ISLAND, a coral island on the coast of York Peninsula, was so called by King in 1819 because it seemed to him to be 'in an infant state,' and appeared likely to grow larger. This is perhaps the silliest name on record.

Ypres, or YPEREN, a town in Belgium, stands on the River Yperlea, which is supposed to derive its name from a species of elm locally called *Ypereaux*.

Ysabel, the largest of the Salomon Islands, was discovered by Mendaña in 1567, and called by him Santa Isabel.

Ysselmonde is a town in Holland at the mouth of the Yssel, called *Isela* in the eighth century.

Yucatan was discovered by Hernandez de Cordoba on March 1st, 1517. The real name of the country is Maya, Yucatan being a ghost-name which arose from misunderstanding a native, who, being asked the name of the country, replied, according to Gomara, *tectican*, 'I do not understand thee,' or according to another account, *jucatan*, 'what do you say?' or 'listen to what they say,' an answer which was supposed by the Spaniards to be the name of the country.

Yu-Ho, the 'emperor's river,' is the name of the Grand Canal of China, which is also called YUN-HO, 'transport river,' or YUN-LIANG-HO, 'corn transport river,' because by it Peking is chiefly supplied with grain.

Yule Bay, South Victoria, bears the name of an officer of the *Erebus.*

Yuma, a town on the lower Colorado River, bears the name of an Indian tribe.

Yverdun, on the Lake of Neufchâtel, is a corruption of the Celto-Roman name *Eburodunum,* the dun or hill fort on a brook which still bears the name of the BURON. (*See* YORK).

Yvorne, in Canton Vaud, signifies a place for wintering cattle (Italian *inverno,* 'winter,' Latin *hibernare*).

Zaandam, Holland, sometimes incorrectly written SAARDAM, is on the dam or embankment at the confluence of the Y and the Zaan.

Zagan, 'white,' is a common element in Mongolian names, as ZAGAN ULA, the 'white mountain,' 'ZAGAN NUR,' the 'white lake,' or ZAGAN BALGASSU, the 'white town,' a place outside the Great Wall of China.

Zaiman, Laguna di, in Costa Rica, means the 'turtle lake,' the Mosquito tribe having thence procured turtles.

Zaire, an old name of the Congo, is said to have originated in a question as to the name of the river asked by the King of Portugal of a native who had been brought to Lisbon. The negro replied *zeroco,* 'I don't know,' and this, as the story runs, was the source of the name found on the old maps. It is more probable, however, that Zaire is the real name, the *za* of Zaire being a root meaning 'river,' which we have in the Za-mbesi and other African river names. CONGO (*q.v.*) is not properly the name of the river, but of a negro kingdom on its banks. Thus Camoens speaks of the '*grande Reino de Congo . . . por onde o Zaire passa claro.*'

Zambesi is the 'great river' of Eastern Africa, whose upper waters and chief affluents are called Jambaji and Luambezi, dialectic forms of the same name. The largest affluent of the Congo is called the CHAMBESI. The first element in the names of the Lualaba, the Luapula, the Lukugu, the Lulongo, the Lulua, the Loangwa, and the Lungebuno is a dia-

lectic form of the Bantu word for 'water' or 'river.'

Zanesville, a city in Ohio, was founded in 1799 by Ebenezer Zane, a noted trapper.

Zante, one of the Ionian Islands, is an Italian corruption of the old Greek name *Zacynthus,* derived from the Phœnician *zachuth,* a 'height.'

Zanzibar, the name of an East African island, was used before the fifteenth century in a more general sense to denote the East African coast south of the River Jubb. Zanzibar is a Portuguese form of the Arabic *Zanjebar,* which is itself a corruption of the Persian *Zangibar* or *Zenquebar,* which means the coast or 'region of the blacks,' the name being formed like *Hindubar,* the land of the Hindus, or *Malabar,* the land of the mountains. The ancients knew the coast from the River Jubb to Cape Corrientes as *Zinguis* or *Zingium.* The people now known by the Arabic name Swahili or Sawahili, 'the men of the coast,' were formerly called *Zengui* or *Zenj,* 'the blacks,' a name variously written *Ha-zine, Ka-zain, Zanui,* and *Zendje.* The island to which the name of Zanzibar is now confined is called U-NGUGA by the natives, Zanzibar being the Arab and European name.

Zara, in Dalmatia, is a Venetian corruption of the Slavonic name *Zadar,* which was the Byzantine *Diodora* and the Roman *Jadera,* the town on the River Jader.

Zarafshan, the river on which Bokhara stands, is the 'distributor of gold.'

Zaragoza, or SARAGOSSA, in Aragon, was walled by the Emperor Augustus B.C. 25, and made a *colonia immunis* under the title *Cæsarea-Augusta.* This became *Cæragusta,* which the Moors converted into *Saracosta,* and the Spaniards into Zaragoza, of which Saragossa is an English spelling.

Zealand (Danish SJÄLLAND) is the name of the largest of the Danish islands, and ZEALAND (Dutch ZEELAND), of a Dutch province intersected by arms of the sea, and hence called the 'Sea land.' From the second of these we have the name of NEW ZEALAND (*q.v.*).

Zeehan, a mining township in Tasmania, stands at the foot of MOUNT ZEEHAAN, so called by Tasman in 1642, and named after one of his ships.

Zeekoe Rivier, the hippopotamus or 'sea-cow river,' is a Dutch name which occurs repeatedly in the Cape Colony.

Zeewyk Passage, in Houtman's Abrolhos, West Australia, was first traversed in 1727 by a boat constructed by the shipwrecked crew of the Dutch ship *Zeewyk.*

Zeitz, in Prussian Saxony, is believed to take its name from the Slavonic goddess Ciza.

Zell, or ZELLE, from the Low-Latin *cella,* is a frequent name in Germany and Switzerland, denoting a village which has grown up round a monastic cell. The lake of Zell, for instance, is so called from the island of Zell, on which a convent stands, and the Swiss Canton of APPENZELL (*q.v.*) takes its name from a town which arose round a cell of the Abbey of St. Gallen. There are nine places named ZELL in Germany, and many more with -*zell* as an affix. It corresponds to *kil-* in Irish names. (*See* KILDARE.)

Zendah-Rud, a river in Persia, means 'the living stream.' (*See* HERAT.)

Zerbst, in Slavonic *Sserbski,* signifies a place inhabited by Serbs or Wends.

Zerka, a stream in Palestine, from the Arabic *Nahr-az-Zerka,* which means 'blue river,' was formerly called 'Crocodile River,' and is still a habitat of crocodiles, which conceal themselves in the thick tangle of papyrus. According to a legend which is as old as the thirteenth century, the crocodiles were brought from Egypt by a Lord of Cæsarea in order that his brother might become their victim, but the wicked lord being the first to bathe in the stream, was devoured, while his brother escaped.

Zermatt is a Swiss village at the foot of the Matterhorn (*q.v.*) and the Matterjoch. In the local patois *ze* corresponds to the German *zu,* and hence Zermatt, a contraction of *ze der mâd,* is equivalent to *zur matte,* 'at the mead' or meadow. In the same neighbourhood we have the dialectic form *ze* in ZENHÄUSERN, ZENSCHMIEDEN, ZERPLETSCHEN, and other names. Elsewhere we have the names ZUMHOF, ZUMLOCH, ZUMSTEIN, ZUMBACH, ZUMRIED, ZUMRODA, ZUMSEE, ZURHEIDE, and ZURMÜHLE, in which the first syllable is the preposition *zu,* combined with the article. Similar names are AMWALDE, 'at the wood,' AMBACH, 'at the brook,' ANDERMATT (*q.v.*), ANHALT (*q.v.*), and AMSTEG (*q.v.*).

Ziegen Insel, 'goat island,' in the Marshall Archipelago, was stocked with goats in 1817 by Kotzebue.

Zimbabwe, the chief site of the ancient ruined cities of Mashonaland, means the 'great kraal.' The name is not uncommon, being used for the head kraal at which a chief resides.

Zout Rivier, the 'salt river,' and ZOUTPANSBERG, the 'saltpan mountain,' are Dutch names in the Cape Colony.

Zug, a Swiss lake and canton, take their names from the town of ZUG, which stands on the lake. In the twelfth century there were several villages on the shelving shores of the lake called Honzug, Godelzug, Huirwilzug, and the like, each denoting a *zug* (*cf.* English *tug*), or place where nets might be drawn or tugged ashore. One of them called *Fischzug* is believed to represent the modern town of Zug.

Zuider Zee is the 'Southern Sea,' so called by the Dutch in contradistinction to the Noord Zee, which we call the German Ocean.

Zumstein-Spitze, one of the peaks of Monte Rosa, was repeatedly ascended for scientific purposes by Joseph Zumstein.

Zürich, a Swiss lake and canton, are so called from the town of ZÜRICH, the corruption of a Celto-Roman name which appears as *Sta*[*tio*] *Turicen*[*sis*] in a Roman inscription, and as *Turicum* and *Turigum* in later documents. We have the first syllable of the name in TURIN (*q.v.*), the suffix -*ic* being the common Celtic formative.

Zutphen, near Flushing, where Sir Philip Sidney fell, is shown by the old name *Sudvenum* to mean the 'South fen' or marsh.

Zwarte Bergen and ZWARTE RIVIER, Dutch names at the Cape, are the 'black mountains' and the 'black river.'

Zweibrücken, called DEUX PONTS in French, is a town in Rhenish Bavaria named from a castle standing between the 'two bridges' over the Erbach.

Zwellendam, a town in the Cape Colony founded in 1740, is an odious compound constructed out of the names of Swellengrebel, a Dutch governor, and of his wife, whose maiden name was Ten Damme.

Zwolle, a town in the Netherlands, stands at 'the swell' of the waters.

APPENDIX

WITH the object of keeping the length of the Glossary within moderate limits, it has been thought expedient to treat compendiously, in the following pages, certain classes of names which could not be left wholly without notice, but yet are of minor interest or importance. It has seemed that large numbers of Indian, Turkish, Magyar, and Slavonic names, with many village names in France and England, may thus be most advantageously discussed, the more important names having been treated at greater length in the Glossary.

PART I

INDIAN NOMENCLATURE

Names in India are formed on the same model as in England, the qualifying element coming first. In the South of India they are mostly derived from the Dravidian languages, such as Tamil or Canarese; in the North from the Prakrit or neo-Sanskrit dialects, with intrusive elements from various sources, Persian, Arabic, Pushtu, Turkic, Portuguese, and English, testifying to successive invasions or conquests of foreign races. The elements of most frequent occurrence may be briefly enumerated.

From Sanskrit or Prakrit sources we have *-nagara(m)*, a 'city,' whence the abraded suffixes *-nagri*, *-nagram*, or *-nagore*, now officially spelt *-nagar*, as Chandernagore (Chandarnagar), or Farukhnagore (Farukhnagar). In Ceylon the derived form *nuvara* denotes a city, as Nuvara Panduas, and Nuvara Eliya. The usual word for a village is *gráma*, whence the suffix *-gaon*, *-goum*, *-gao*, or *-gama*, which is now spelt *grám*, as Sátgáon (Saptagrám), the 'seven villages,' in Bengal. Another word is *pind*, as Pind Dádan Khán, built in 1623 by Dádan Khán, or Ráwal Pindi in the Punjab, which means the 'village of the chief priest.' The word *pura(m)*, cognate with the Greek *polis*, means a town. Formerly spelt *pore* or *poor* the form *pur* or *pura* is now used, as Serampore (Serampur), Singapore, Nagpoor (Nágpur), Cawnpore (Kánhpur), or Bhurtpore (Bhartpur). In the South of India we have *palli*, a town or village, formerly spelt *poli*, *polly*, or *pully*, as Isakapalli, the 'sandy village,' or Trichinopoli (Tirusirápalli). Another Dravidian form is *úru*, a town, whence the suffix *-ore*, now usually spelt *-úr*, as in Mysore (Maisúr), Vellore (Vellúr), Nellore, and Tanjore. Another word for a town is *pattana(m)*, whence the suffix *-patam* or *-pata*, in the modern spelling *-patnam*, as Masuli-patam (Machli-patnam), or Seringapatam (Srírángapatnam). In the South *patta* becomes *petta* or *pet*, and signifies a town as opposed to a citadel, and hence it is used to mean a suburb, as Adrampet or Ránípet. A Tamil word for a village is *cheri*, corrupted to *cherri* or *cherry*, as Pondicherry, Tangacheri, or Tellicherri (Tallacheri). The suffix *wár* or *bár*, which is of obscure origin, means a district or country, as Káthiáwár or Márwár. Bábriáwár is the district inhabited by the Bábriá tribe, and Bánswára is the 'forest country.' In Southern India *kovil* or *koil* is used to denote a temple or place of worship, from the Dravidian *ko*, a king, hence a god, whence *ko-il*, a temple, literally 'god-house,' as Koilpatti, and Nachiakovil. For a holy place or shrine we have *prayága*, corrupted to *praag*, as Vissenpraag, the holy place of Vishnu.

A fortress is *kódu*, whence the suffix *-cotta*, *-kotta*, and *-cot*, now spelt *-kot*, as Gunjicotta (Gandikot), the 'fort at the gorge,' Palámkottá, the 'camp fort,' or Sealcote (Siálkot). A fort is *garh*, corrupted to *ghar*, *ghur*, *gore*, and *gar*, as Chanárgarh, the fort of the Chanár district; Alígarh, the fort of Alí; or Chatísgarh, the thirty-six forts. The Sanskrit *durga*, corrupted to *durg* or *droog*, now spelt *drúg*, means a rock fort, literally that which is hard to approach, as Viziadrúg. A rock is *kal* or *gal*, as Nidugal, the 'high rock.'

The word *ganj* means a 'market' or market town, whence the suffixes *-gunga*, *-gunge*, *-gange*, and *-gong*, as Fatehganj, the 'mart of victory,' or Sháhganj, the 'king's mart,' but *gangá* is a river, whence the names of the Ganges, of the Nilgangá, or 'blue river'; the Kishangangá, or 'black river'; the Bángangá, or 'arrowy river'; the Gorigangá, the Viswagangá, and the Ramgangá. A river is also *nadí*, corrupted to *nuddy*, as Mahanuddy (Mahánadí), the 'great river,' and the Rangánadí. A *ghát* is a passage either to a river or through hills, whence the name of Ghauts or Gháts. The Bálághát is an upland district 'above the gháts,' while Payanghát is the lowland 'below the gháts.' The word *giri*, corrupted to *gherry*, means a mountain, as Dhawálágiri, the 'white mountain'; Pulgiri, the 'peaked hills'; or Bráhmagiri in Malabár. A Dravidian word for a mountain or hill is *malai*, whence Pachamálai, the 'green hill'; or Malabár, the 'mountain country.' Another Dravidian name for a mountain is *betta*, as Gopálswámi-betta in Mysore, or Doda-betta, the 'great mountain,' the highest summit of the Nilgherries (Nílgiris) or 'blue hills.'

From the Persian loan-word *koh*, a 'mountain,' we have in the Punjab Nílakoh, the 'blue mountains,' and the mountainous district called Kohát. In Afghanistan, Koh-i-Siáh is the 'black mountain,' and Koh-i-Safed, the 'white mountain.' The Koh-i-Suláiman, on the Afghan frontier, is usually translated as the Suláiman range, while one of the highest summits of the Elburz range goes by the name of Sháh Koh, the 'king's mountain.'

An island is *dvípa* or *dwípa*, corrupted to *dipa*, *diva*, *dive*, *deep*, or *deeva*, as the Maldives, the Laccadives, Agradwíp or Sandwíp. From *bhúm*, land or country, we have Singhbhúm and Dhalbhúm, while Beerbhoom (Bírbhúm) in Bengal is the 'jungle land.' The word *khand*, corruptly *cund* or *kund*, means literally a division, hence a district, province, or country, Rohilcund (Rohilkhand), Bundelcund (Bundelkhand), and Baghelkhand, signifying the country of the Rohillas, the Bundelas, and the Baghelás. The word *mandala*(*m*), whence *mandel*, is a circuit or country, as in Coromandel

(Cholamandalam) or Púlivendala (Púli-mandalam). *Mahal,* from *mahil,* an Arabic loan-word, means an 'estate' or district, as Bárámahal, the twelve estates.

Some Persian loan words are common in Indian nomenclature. Thus from *sitan,* 'one who takes possession,' we have the common suffix *-stán,* 'possession,' 'country,' as in Afghanistan, Beluchistan, Hindustan, or Turkistan. Equally common is the suffix *-ábád,* a dwelling, abode, or place, usually used to denote a place which some one has helped to found, as Abbasábád, built by Abbas the Great, or Aurangábád, built by Aurangzeb. In Firozshahr or Bulandshahr we have the Persian *shahr, shayr,* or *shehr,* a village or town, in Mughalsarai we have *serai,* a halting-place or mansion, and in Alumbagh we have *bagh,* a garden.

The first or adjectival element in Indian names usually denotes size, age, colour, situation, or productions, but is often a personal or a divine name. Thus Mahában is the 'great forest'; the Mahánadí in Orissa is the 'great river'; the Mahá welliganga in Ceylon is the 'great sandy river'; and the Maráthas were the people of the great kingdom. Perumbaucum (Perambákam), a town near Conjeveram, is explained as *perum-pákkam,* the 'big village.' From the Dravidian *dodá,* great, we have Dodábetta, the 'big mountain'; and Dod-ballápur is Great Ballápur as distinguished from Chikballápur, little Ballápur. Chikakotta is the 'little fort,' and Chittúr in Arcot is the 'little town'; but Chitor in Rájputána is a corruption of Chitrapur, the 'variegated city,' and Chitaldrúg in Mysore is the spotted or variegated fort. Naiakot is the 'new fort,' Hoskot and Hosdrúg also mean the 'new fort' in Canarese, and Hospet the new village. Alut-gama in Ceylon is also the 'new village,' and Alut-nuvara is the 'new city.' The Burmese name of Old Arakan is Myo-haung, the 'old town.'

Chengalpat (Chingleput), the 'brick town,' gives a name to a district in the Madras Presidency, and Káthmándú means the 'wooden building'; Atúr *(Attin-úr),* a common name in Southern India, is the 'town by the river,' and Badágara *(Vadákara),* a town in Malabár, means 'the north bank.' Angádipuram, also in Malabár, is the 'market town,' Argaum *(Argáon)* in Berár is 'the village of wells,' and Manjarábád in Mysore is 'the abode of fog.' Badvel *(Baddelu vailu)* is the 'town of cloths.'

From numerals we have in Bengal Tribeni, the 'three streams,' Daspur, the 'ten towns,' Dasnagar, the 'ten cities,' Dasgáon, the 'ten villages,' Daspara, the 'ten houses.' Sátára, a district in the Deccan, is named from a fort which had 'seventeen' gates and towers. Sátgáon *(Sapta-grám),* is the 'seven villages,' and Chittagáon the 'four villages.' Arcot is from the Tamil *ár-kad,* the 'six forests,' and Bárámahal in Arcot means the 'twelve estates.' The Panchmaháls in Gujarát are the 'five districts,' Háshtnagar in the Punjab is the district of 'eight cities,' Ikkeri in Mysore means the 'two streets,' Satásgarh means the 'sixty towers,' Nálatwár in Bijápur is the 'forty gardens,' and Chhatísgarh in the Central Provinces means the 'thirty-six forts.' Panchánnagrám, the name of the suburbs of Calcutta, signifies the 'fifty-five villages.' In Bengal we have the Anglo-Indian name of the 'twenty-four Parganahs,' while the Laccadives are the 'hundred thousand islands,' and the Maldives are said to be the 'thousand islands.' The Punjab is the district of the 'five rivers' which join the Indus, and Doab is a name applied in several instances to a district lying between 'two rivers.'

From animals, or from personal names derived from animals, we have Sinhgarh near Poona, a Marátha fort which was the scene of the exploits of Shivaji, who in 1647 gave it the appropriate name of the 'lions' den' or fort. Singhbhúm is the 'lion land,' and Singapore is the 'lion city.' Bhagalpur is the 'tiger city,' and Púlivendala (Púli-mandalam), a district in the Madras Presidency, is the 'haunt of tigers.' Bárnagar (Varáha-nagar) is the 'city of the boar,' and Kadúr in Mysore is the 'elk town.' Máyaveram (Mayúram) in the Tanjore district, is the 'peacock town,' and Cocanáda (Káki-náda), in the Godávari district, is the 'crow country.' Magar Taláo, a village near Karáchi, takes its name from a 'crocodile tank,' which affords a wonderful spectacle when the sacred crocodiles are fed. Negapatam (Nágapatnam) in Tanjore is the 'snake town,' and Nágpur, the 'snake city' in Central India, testifies to the serpent-worship of the Gonds. The Nagadi is the 'serpent river,' and the Pambam passage between India and Ceylon takes its name from the Pambam or 'snake' island, so called from its form. Nagur, Nagar, and Nagari are, however, corruptions from the Sanskrit *nagara*, a 'city.'

Among the names from the character of the vegetation we have in Bengal Nalbaná, the 'reed forest,' and the Sundarbans, probably the forest of the Sundri tree, while the Sálandi (Sálnadí), a river in Orissa, is so named from the *sál* forests which it traverses. Bednore is the 'bamboo town,' and Balgáum (Vennugrámá) means 'bamboo village' in Canarese. Anjengo (Anju-tengu), on the Travancore coast, signifies the 'five cocoa-nut trees,' and Kamalpur is the 'town of water-lilies.' Monghyr in Behar is 'bean hill,' and Bangalore (*Bengal-úr*) is named from the *bengalu*, a kind of bean, whence also the name of Bangali, a city and district in Mysore which is said to have been so named from the beans supplied to its founder, a Ballala king, when hunting. Arrah, a city in Behar, is from the Sanskrit *aranya*, 'jungle,' while from *irina*, a 'salt marsh,' we have the Runn (Rann) of Cutch, the Kach States being almost surrounded by salt marshes.

Laudatory epithets, not unknown in Europe, are common elements in Indian names, though these are difficult to separate from mythological or personal names having the same meaning. For example, Oodeypore (Udaipur) in Rájputána was founded in 1568 by Udai Singh, but in other cases Udaipur might mean either the 'city of good fortune' or the 'city of sunrise.' Mangalore (Mangal-úr) in Canara, as well as Mangalkot and Mangaldái, may be from *mangala*, 'fortunate,' or *mangal*, 'felicity' or 'bliss,' or may be due to the worship of Vishnu under the name of Mangala Devi, as in the case of Mangalagiri, which has two shrines of Vishnu. Jaipur (Jayapuram), in the Madras Presidency, is 'the city of victory,' and Jaigarh, south of Bombay, is 'Fort Victory,' while Jeypore (Jaipur) in Rájputána was founded by Jai Singh II. in 1728. Fatehgarh doubtless means the 'fort of victory,' but Fatehábád in the Punjab was founded by the Emperor Firoz Sháh, and named after his son Fateh Khán, while Fatehábád in the Agra district is known to mean 'the place of victory,' the name having been given by the Emperor Aurangzeb to the battlefield where he gained a victory over his brother Dárá in 1658. He built a mosque on the spot where he rested after the battle. Fatehganj, the 'mart of victory,' is the name of two towns in the Bareli district, commemorating British victories over the Rohillás, one gained in 1774, and the other in 1794. Fatehkhelda, the 'field of victory,' in Berár, commemorates a decisive victory gained by the Nizám in 1724. Fatehpur or Fatehpur Síkri, where the Emperor Jahángír was born, is a town twenty-two miles from Agra, which was built by Akbar in 1569, on the site of the village of Síkri, and named by him the 'city of victory' in commemoration of his conquest of Gujarát.

Vizagapatam (Vísákha-patnam) is the city of Visákha, the 'victorious,' the Hindu war-god, while Viziadrúg is the 'fort of victory.' Vizianagram (*Vijaya-nagaram*) in Orissa is the city of Vijaya, the founder, and Bisnagar, once a great city, but now in ruins, was at first called *Vijaya-nagara*, the 'city of victory,' afterwards becoming *Vidyá-nagara*, the 'city of learning.' Rangpur, a city and district in Bengal, may mean the 'city of pleasure,' but like Seringapatam the name may be derived from *Sri-Ranga*, 'celestial happiness,' one of the epithets of Vishnu. Periápatam is the 'chosen city,' while Kásipur and Kásinagar mean the 'illustrious town.' Channapata (Chennapatnam) in Mysore is the 'handsome city,' and the usual native appellation of Madras is Chennapuri or Chennapatana, which signifies the same. Kalyánpur is the 'beautiful city,' and Ellore is the 'ruling town.' Ichápur, in the Gamjam district, is the 'city of desire.'

Suvarndrug, the 'golden fortress,' stands on an island north of Goa. The name of the great diamond called the Koh-i-Nur or 'mountain of light' may serve to remind us that such names as Nurnagar, Nurábád, and Nurpat signify the 'town of light.' Conjeveram (Kánchipuram), a sacred city near Madras, is the 'golden' or 'shining city.'

Saugor (Ságar) is a common name for places near a 'lake,' and Ságargarh south of Bombay is the 'sea fort.' Cuddalore (Kúdalúr) in South Arcot is explained by Burnell as *Kadal-úr*, the 'sea town,' and by Hunter as *Kudla-úr*, 'the town at the confluence' of the rivers. Tranquebar, in the Tanjore district, is a corruption of *Taragambádi*, the 'sea town,' literally the 'village on the wave.' Reha, the 'bitter water,' is the Burmese name of a salt lake near Ava.

Indian rivers often bear poetical names. The three rivers called the Banás are the 'hope of the forest'; the River Kabadak (*Kapotáksha*) in Bengal is 'the Dove's eye'; the Subarnarekhá in Bengal means the 'streak of gold,' and the Son (Soane or Sone), a tributary of the Ganges, is the 'golden' or 'crimson' river (Sanskrit *sana*, 'crimson'). The Beypur (Pauna-puya) in Malabár is the 'golden river.'

The Nerbudda (Narbadá), a large Indian river, the Na(r)mados of Ptolemy, is explained as the 'river of delight' (Sanskrit *narma*, delight), and the Kalyání Ganga is the 'beautiful river,' the Chitra in Bengal signifying the 'glancing waters.' The name of the Godavery (Godávari) is explained as the 'cattle giver,' but may probably be a corruption of some older name. The

Pálár in the Carnatic bears a Tamil name which signifies the 'milky river,' the Vasadhárá is the 'bamboo stream,' the Sharavatí in South India is 'the arrowy,' and the Burábalang in Orissa is the 'old twister.' The Beas (Biás), the Hyphasis of the Greeks, one of the five rivers of the Punjab, is the 'unchainable'; the Adjai (Ajaya) in Bengal is the 'invincible,' but the Baleswar, or 'lord of strength,' in Bengal is probably named from one of the titles of Siva. In its middle course it is called Madhumatí, 'honey flowing,' and at its mouth it is called the Haringháta, 'where the deer drinks.'

Mountain names, as a rule, are simply descriptive. Agastya Malai, 'Agastya's Hill,' in Southern India, is a conical peak where Agastya, the legendary Sage and Teacher of the Tamil race is believed to sleep. The Nalla-malái in Karnúl are the 'black hills,' the Yellamala (Yerramalai) in South India are 'the red hills,' and Madgiri in Mysore is 'Honey Hill.' Trincomalee (Trikonomalli), a harbour in Ceylon, is explained as a corruption of Tri-kona-malai, 'three-peak hill,' or the hill with three summits, and the Pacha-málai Hills in Trichinopoli are the 'green hills.' The Ana-malai, a range of hills in the Travancore and Coimbatore districts, are the 'Elephant mountains.' Malabar is the 'hill-country.' The Santáls, a Kolarian tribe in Bengal, are said to be the 'lowlanders,' while the Khands, Kondhs, or Khods are the 'hill-men,' from the Telegu *konda* (Tamil *kundru*) a 'small hill.' An allied name is Conoor (Kunn-úr), a hill station in the Neilgherries, which means 'hill-town.' Coorg (Kurg), an Indian province, consisting of a picturesque mountain region, is a corruption of Kodagu, the 'steep highlands.' Girnár, a sacred hill in Gujarát, is believed to be a corruption of Giri-nagara, the 'hill-town,' while Pahárpur, 'hill-town,' and Pahárgarh, 'hill-fort,' are common Indian names. Damán, a name occurring in the Punjab and elsewhere, denotes the 'skirt' of a hill. Karnala in the Bombay Presidency is the 'funnel hill.' The Vindhya Range in Central India is explained as the 'rent' mountains, so called because of the numerous passes through them. Nidugal, a hill-fort in Mysore, is the 'high stone' or 'long stone,' and Nurelia (Nuvara Eliya) in Ceylon is so called from its position on a 'flat' place among the hills. Nanga Parbat, the 'naked mountain,' is a conspicuous peak in the Himalayas.

Naturally we find in India many names corresponding to such English names as Kingston. Such are Rájapur, Rájpur, or Rájnagar. Rájgarh and Rájkot mean 'royal fort,' and Rájmahál, at one time the capital of Bengal, is the 'royal domain.' Mahárájpur is the town of the Mahárája, and Maheswar (Mahesvra) in Malwá is the land of the great lord. Ránípur is the Queen's town; Rániganj the Queen's market; Ráníghat the Queen's pass; Ráníkot the Queen's fort, and Ráníserai the Queen's palace. To the Mughal emperors we refer Sultánpur, a common name, as well as Sultánganj, Kot-i-Sultán, and Sultánkot. From the Persian sovereign titles Sháh and Padisháh we have Sháhpur, in the Punjab, founded by Sháh Shams, with the common names Sháhbunder, the 'King's port,' Sháhábad, Sháhbazar, Sháhganj, Sháhgarh, and Sháhkot, as well as Pádsháhpur and Pádsháganj. Bhopál or Bhopálpur in Malwa is the town of the *bhopál* or 'regent.' Nizampur, Nizampatam, and Nizamábád are the towns of the Nizam, an Arabic loan-word signifying 'one who puts in order,' a regulator. Wazírábád, Wazírpur, Wazírgarh, and Wazírganj are the town, fort, or market of the Vizier, another Arabic loan-word signifying a prime minister, literally 'one who bears the burden' of the State. From the Arabic *emir*, a 'prince,' or from *mirza*, its Persian form, we have Kot-i-Amir in the Punjab, Mirgarh, Mirganj, Mirzapur and Mirzagarh. Malikpur is from the Arabic *malik*, a king.

The rulers of India have naturally left on the map numerous personal traces of their reigns in the names of cities or fortresses which they erected. Many of the Rajput states, such as Jodhpur, Jaipur, Udaipur, Jaisalmer, Bikaner, Dholpur, and Bareli, take their names, as has been explained in the Glossary, from their capitals, which are called after the princes by whom they were founded.

The Moghul, Persian, and Afghan Emperors have freely scattered their names over Northern India. Thus there are several places called Akbarpur, by which the name of Akbar is commemorated directly, and also indirectly by such names as Jelalabad (Jalálábád) in Afghanistan, which means literally the place of fame or glory, Akbar having gone by the name of Jalál-ud-dín, the 'glory of the faith.'

Among the cities built by Akbar's successor Jahángír (1605-1628), whose name signifies the 'conqueror of the world,' were Jahángírábád and Jahángírpur, while Jahánábád and Jahánpur were built by his successor, Sháh Jahán (1628-1658), who has also left his name at six places called Sháhjahánpur. After Sháh Jahán came Aurangzeb, the 'ornament of the throne,' in whose reign (1658-1707) the two cities called Aurangábád were founded. Murád, another son of Sháh Jahán, has left his name at Murádábád. Murád is, however, one of the commonest Moslem names, being an Arabic word meaning 'desired' or 'wished for,' and hence we have Murádnagar, Murádkot, and many other names, among them one of the two rivers whose junction forms the Euphrates, which is called the Murád, from the Turkish Sultan Murád (Amurath IV.), because of the bridges and roads which he constructed.

Another common Moslem name is Ahmád, an Arabic word meaning 'the praised,' which is applied to Mahomet. Ahmádábád in Gujarát (p. 40), was founded in 1413 by Ahmád Sháh, king of Gujarát (1413-1443), and Ahmádnagar in the Bombay province was founded in 1494 by Ahmád Nizám Sháh, and other towns such as Ahmádpur contain the same name.

From the personal name Muzaffar, which means the 'victorious,' we have Muzaffarnagar in the North-West Provinces, founded by a son of Muzaffar Khán about 1633 in the reign of Sháh Jahán. Muzaffarghar, a fort in the Punjab, was built by Náwáb Muzaffar Khán ; Muzaffarábád and Muzaffarpur also bear the name of their founders ; Jafarábád is a corruption of Muzaffarábád.

The Persian loan-word *firuz*, which also means victorious, fortunate, or successful, was used as a personal name, being borne by the Emperor Firozsháh (1351-1387), whence Firozábád near Delhi, and Firozpur, a city and district in the Punjab. In the district of Firozpur there is a place now called Firoz-sháh which was the scene of the hard-fought battle with the Sikhs on December 21st and 22nd 1845. This name is not, however, due to the

Emperor Firoz-Sháh but is a corruption of Pharú Shahr, the 'town of Pharú' being named after Bhai Pharú, a Sikh saint, the assimilated form Firoz-sháh being doubtless due to its being within the district of Firozpur. The Lodhí, an Afghan dynasty, reigned at Delhi from 1450 to 1526. Ludhiána, a city in the Punjab, was founded in 1480 by Yusaf and Nipanj, two of the Lodhí princes. Secunderabad (Sikandarábád), in the North-West Provinces, was founded in 1498 by another Lodhí prince, Sikandar (Alexander) of Jaunpur, in whose reign Sikandra, near Agra, and Sikandarpur were also founded. But Secunderabad (Sikandarábád) in the Nizám's dominions bears the name of the Nizám Sikandar Jah.

Dera Ghází Khán and Dera Ismáil Khán, towns in the Punjab, were founded in the fifteenth century by two Beluch adventurers, Ghází Khán Mahrani and Ismáil Khán. Gházípur, in the North-West Provinces, was founded about 1330 by the Sayyid chief Masaúd, from whose title of Málik-us Saádat-Ghází the city takes its name. Gháziábád near Meerut was founded in 1740 by the Wazír Ghází-ud-dín, 'champion of the faith.' Hoshangábád, a town in the Central Provinces, was founded about 1405 by Hoshang Sháh, king of Málwá. Shujábád, in the Punjab, was built by Shujá Khan, Nawáb of Múltán, about 1750. Murshid Kulí Khán, a Brahmin apostate to Islam, who was Nawáb of Bengal at the beginning of the eighteenth century, transferred the Moslem capital of Bengal from Dacca to a place which he named Murshid-ábád, after himself.

Hyderabad (Haidarábád), the capital of the Nizám's State, was founded in 1589 by Muhammed Kúlí and named from his son Haidar, the 'lion.' From the same personal name we have Haidarábád in Sindh, while Haidar-ábád in Oudh was founded about 1700 by Haidar Khán, and Haidarnagar by the famous Haidar-Alí. Alí, which means high or exalted, is a common Moslem name, owing to its having been borne by the son-in-law of Mahomet, and has become the source of numerous town names, such as Alíbandar, Alípur in Bengal, or Alíganj in Bihar. Alíbágh, the 'garden of Alí,' near Bombay, bears the name of a wealthy Moslem, who, some two centuries ago, here constructed several wells and gardens. Alígarh, the 'fort of Alí,' in the North-West Provinces, was built by Kachak Alí, who was made governor of Koil by the Emperor Bábar in 1526. Hassan (Hasan), the 'beautiful,' was the son of Alí, whence Hasanpur in Oudh, founded by Hasan Khán in the reign of Sher Sháh, and Hasanganj, also in Oudh, founded by Hasan Rezá Khán at the end of the eighteenth century. Omar is also a common name, whence Omarkot and Omargarh. From Mubárak, the 'blessed,' we have Mubárakpur in the North-West Provinces, and from Daud (David), Daudpur and Daudnagar. From Nasír, the 'helper,' come Nasírpur and Nasírábád. From Jalál, which means 'fame,' we have Jalálpur in the Punjab and Jalálábad in Afghanistan ; Khairpur, Khairábád, and Khairágarh are from the personal name Khairá, the 'good' one. Ratanpur, Ratanganj, Ratangarh, and Ratnágiri are from *ratna*, a 'jewel' ; and Farídpur, Farídkot, and Faríd-ábád from Faríd, the 'pearl' or the 'incomparable.' From Núr Jahán, wife of the Emperor Jahángír, we have Núr Mahal (*mahal*, 'an estate') in the Punjab, and the famous Alumbagh is the garden of the lady Alum.

Kishni in Oudh was founded in the fifteenth century by Rájá Kishan Chand, and Kishangarh, a State in Rajputana, takes its name from a fort built in 1594 by Kishan Singh. Jaisinghnagar was founded about 1690 by Rájá Jai Singh. In 1822 Hari Singh, a Sikh, founded Haripur, a town in the Punjab. Devaraydurga, in Mysore, is the 'hill' taken and fortified in 1608 by Deva Rájá, while Azamgarh, the 'fort of Azam,' in the North-West Provinces, bears the name of Azam Khán, a landowner, by whom the fort was built in 1665. According to a local tradition Asírgarh was a fort erected in the fourteenth century by one Asá Ahir, a herdsman, and Ajmere, the favourite residence of Akbar, was founded, according to the legend, by a Rájá Aja in the second century A.D., but the dubious character of such traditions is shown by the name of Darbhangah in Behar, which the local legend assigns to an eponymic Darbhangí Khán, whereas the name is really a corruption of *Dar-i-bangála*, the 'gateway of Bengal.'

The latest layer, so to speak, in the stratification of Indian names dates from the British occupation. From Governors-General we have Amherst in Tenasserim, founded in 1826 ; Dalhousie, a hill sanatorium in the Punjab; Port Canning at the mouth of the Ganges ; and the Palk Straits from a Governor of Madras. Montgomery, a station in the Punjab, was so named in 1864 in compliment to Sir R. Montgomery, Lieutenant-Governor of the Punjab ; Edwardesábád in the Punjab was founded by Sir Herbert Edwardes ; Campbellpur was named after Sir Colin Campbell, afterwards Lord Clyde ; Jacobsábád in Sindh was founded by General John Jacobs ; Abbottábád, the northernmost frontier station in the Punjab, was established by Lieutenant, afterwards Major James Abbott ; Daltonganj in Bengal bears the name of Colonel Dalton, Commissioner of Chutiá Nágpur ; Cox's Bázár in Bengal that of Captain Cox, stationed there in 1799 ; Allan-myo in Burma, of a Major Allan ; Perkinsganj and Thurburnganj, of two Deputy-Commissioners ; and Colonelganj, a town in Oudh, takes its name from the Colonel commanding a British force stationed here in 1802.

A few names arise from occupations. Shikárpur, a common name, is the town of the *shikári* or huntsman ; Malibhum is the 'gardener's land,' and Malipura and Maligáon the gardeners' town or village ; Khavaspur, in the Punjab, is the town of a *cawass* or servant ; Dinajpur is the 'town of beggars' ; Toomkoor (Túmkúr) in Mysore means 'a tabret,' the town having been granted to the herald of the Rájá. Such names as Gopálnagar, Gopálgarh, Gopálpur, and Gopálganj may be from *gopál*, a herdsman, or in many cases from temples erected to Krishna in his character of the infant cowherd. We have here an instance of a feature of so many Indian names, their marked mythological character. As in Europe many towns bear the names of Christian saints, having grown up round places of pilgrimage, shrines, monasteries, or churches, so Indian cities like Bombay or Seringapatam owe their names to shrines or temples of special veneration, towns or villages growing up round places of pilgrimage, or round temples dedicated to some deity whose name or title has become part of the name of the place, or has ousted some older name. Thus Pápanásham, a noted place of pilgrimage in the Tinnevelli District, means

'removal of sin,' and Pápaghni, a sacred river in Southern India, means the
' sin destroyer.'

More numerous are the towns containing the names of Indian deities, due
to temples erected for their worship. Thus from Rudra, the 'roarer,' who is
the storm-god of the Vedas, we have Rudra Prayág, and Rudrapur, the 'city
of Rudra.' In the later mythology Rudra has developed into Siva, the
destroyer and reproducer, who is the third person of the Brahman triad, and
is called Bhíma, the 'dread one.' Sivagangá in Mysore is a hill with
numerous temples to Siva. Siva-Samudram, literally the ' sea of Siva,' is an
island in the River Cauvery (Káveri). Among Siva's many titles, Ambarnáth,
the 'immortal lord,' has given a name to Amarnáth, a place in the Bombay
Presidency which has a celebrated group of ancient temples, and also to
Amarnáth, a great place of pilgrimage in Kashmir, where there is a cave held
to be the special dwelling-place of Siva. Nanjangad in Mysore is the town
of ' the swallower of poison,' one of the attributes of Siva. Trimbak
(*Tryambak*), a great place of pilgrimage, means the 'three-eyed,' another title
of Siva. He is called Mahabaleswár, the 'lord of great strength,' whence the
name of the River Baleswar. Siva is also the Mahádeva or 'great god,'
and at Deogarh in Bengal are numerous temples dedicated to him under
this name. Siva's wife, called Durgá or Párvatí, also Kálí, the 'black one,'
Chandi, the 'fierce,' Gauri, the 'brilliant,' Umá, the 'light,' and Deví, the
'goddess,' has a prominent place in Hindu mythology. To her we owe the
names of the River Párvatí, and of Párvatípur. Mahákálídurga in Mysore
is the ' rock of the great [goddess] Kálí.' Kálíghát, on the old course of the
Ganges, a mile from Calcutta, has a temple of Kálí, whose finger, according
to the legend, fell here when she was cut to pieces. The nearest village
to this ghát where bodies were burnt was the Moslemised *Kalikata* of the
Aín-í-Akbarí, a name now Anglicised as Calcutta (*q.v.*). As Kumárí, the
'damsel,' she has given a name to Cape Comorin (*q.v.*). Chamúndibetta in
Mysore is the 'hill of Chamúndi,' another name of Kálí, whose temple stands
on the summit of the hill. From her name Nanda, 'happiness,' we have
Nandapur and Nandpara. Nanda Deví is a lofty conical peak in the Himá-
layas, and the cloud which usually rests on the summit is regarded as the
smoke from Nanda's kitchen. Nandidrúg, Nandiál, and Nandigáma take
their names from Nandi, the sacred bull of Siva. Chilambaram, believed to
mean the 'bliss of virtue,' is a place in South Arcot celebrated for temples
dedicated to Siva and his wife Párvati, who is called Deví, 'the goddess,'
whence the name of the River Deví in Orissa. Kálí is also called Umá, 'the
light.' Hence Siva's name Umánda, 'he whose delight is in Uma,' has been
given to an island in Assam which contains a temple of Siva.

Vishnu, the preserver, is styled Vardhamána, the 'increasing,' whence the
name of the town and district of Bardwán in Bengal. He is also called
Sri-Ranga, 'celestial pleasure,' whence the names of Seringapatam (*q.v.*),
and Seringam (Srírángam). From his titles Hari and Náráyana we have the
towns Haripur, Náráinpur, Náráinpatam, Náráyanganj, Náráyanavanam in
Arcot, Náráinpet, and Náráingangá or ' Vishnu's river.' Harihar in Mysore
is a compound of the names Hari (Vishnu) and Hara (Siva).

Vishnu, in his eighth incarnation as Krishna, plays a great part in popular Hindu mythology, endearing epithets being lavished upon him. Kirstnapatam in the Carnatic is 'Krishna's city,' Kishannagar, Kishanpur, and Kishapur are all 'Krishna's town,' Kishenganj is 'Krishna's market,' and Kishenganga is 'Krishna's river.' Krishna Bái, the source of the great Kistna River, is a great place of pilgrimage. Krishna is called Mádhava, the 'sweet one,' whence the town of Mádhapur, and Mádhapollam (Mádhaváyapalem), where there is a temple of Krishna. Kahn, 'the beloved,' is a Prakrit form of Krishna, whence Cawnpore (*q.v.*), and Cannanore (Káhnanúr) in Malabar. From the title Mohana, 'sweetheart,' we have Mohanpur, Mohanganj, Mohangarh, and Mohankot, the town, market, and fort of Mohana. Krishna is also the Bala Gopala, or 'infant cowherd,' whence Gopálswámi-betta, in Mysore, a hill which has a temple of Vishnu on the summit. Rádhá is the mistress beloved of Krishna, whence Rádhápuram in Tinnevelli. Muttra (Mathura), a great centre of Krishna worship, takes its name from a Rákshasa slain by Krishna. *See* BURDWAN (p. 78).

From Narsingh, the 'man-lion,' regarded as the fourth incarnation of Vishnu, we have Narsingha, Narsinghpur, Narsinghnagar, Narsinghgarh, and Narsinghpetta, while Sinháchalam in the Vizagapatam district takes its name from a temple dedicated to Vishnu in his leonine incarnation.

The curious name of Alawa-kháwa in Bengal is derived from a fair held in honour of Krishna, who is worshipped with offerings of dried rice (*kháwá*, to 'eat,' *alawa*, 'dried rice').

Ráma, the national hero of India, is regarded as the seventh incarnation of Vishnu. Hence the name of Serampur in Bengal, the station where the early missionaries Carey and Marshman laboured, formerly spelt Serampore, which is a corruption of *Sri-ráma-pur*, the 'city of the holy Ráma,' Seringapatam being in like manner from Srírángapatnam, the city of Srí-Ránga, the 'holy Ranga,' one of the forms of Vishnu. Adrampet (*Adrampatnam*) in Tanjore is a name ultimately derived from the designation *Adi(víra) Rámapatnam*, signifying 'the town of the great hero Ráma,' and a celebrated shrine of Ráma has given the name Rámeswaram to an island between India and Ceylon. Rámpur, the 'city of Ráma,' gives its name to a feudatory state of which it is the capital, and is the name of several Indian towns. We have also Rámgangá or 'Ráma's river' in the North-West Provinces, besides Rámnagar, Rámgarh, Rámghát, Rámdrúg, Rámgiri, and other similar names, while from Sítá, the wife of Ráma, we have such names as Sítápur, Sítákund, and Sítámarhí. Coringa (Koringa), in the Godávari district, takes its name from *kurangam*, the golden 'stag' of the Rámáyana.

Mahábalipur, on the Carnatic coast, a place with wonderful temples, is the 'city of the great Bali,' one of the kings of Hindu legend. Sealkote (Siálkot) and Karnál, both in the Punjab, owe their foundation according to the legend to two heroes of the Mahábhárata, Rájá Sál and Rájá Karna, who, however, may merely bear eponymic names.

From temples to Lakshmi or Lakhim, the goddess of luck or good fortune, we have Lakshmipur in Bengal, and Lakhipur and Lakhimpur in Assam. Máyapur and Máyakot refer to Máyá, a title of Lakshmi, but Máyavaram

314   NAMES AND THEIR HISTORIES

(Mayúrám), is from *mayúra*, a 'peacock.' Trichinopoli (*Trisarapalli*) in the
Carnatic is the town of the giant Trisara, the three-headed Rákshasa, a
god of wealth. Vizagapatam (Visákha-patnam) on the Coromandel coast is
the town of Visákha, a name of Karttíkeya, the Indian Mars or god of war.
There are three towns called Madanpur, the 'city of Madan,' the 'cheerer,'
an epithet of the god Kámadeva, and Madanapalli is the village of Madan.
Jellasore (Jaleswar) in Bengal is the town of Jalesvara, the 'lord of the
water,' a title of Varuna.

Gautama Buddha is believed to have died in a *sál* forest at Kasia (Kusiná-
gara), the 'city of the holy grass,' and there is a legend that at Arkalgad,
the 'abode of the sun,' in Mysore, he performed penance to the sun. Temples
to Súrya the sun have given names to Súrajpur, Súrajgarh, Súrajgang, and
probably to Srínagar, the capital of Kashmir, a corruption of Súrjyanagar,
the 'city of the sun.' From Chandra the moon we have Chandarnagore
(Chandra-nagar) and Chandrapur, but Chandragiri the 'moon hill' in the
Carnatic, like Chandra-gutti, the 'moon obscuring,' a peak of the Western
Gháts, has probably no mythological significance. The same may be said of
Tárápur, the 'town of the star,' which is not an uncommon name, and may be
due, like Tárágarh and Tárághat to the female proper name Tárá, the 'star.'

The name of Hassan, a district in Mysore, is explained as a corruption of
Hásin-amma, the 'smiling goddess,' and that of Trivandrum in Travancore
as Tiruvánanta-puram, the 'city of the holy eternal one.' From *amara*, the
'immortals,' we have Amarápura, the 'city of the gods,' the former capital of
Burma, founded in 1783; Amartal, the 'lake of the gods'; Amarkantak, the
'hill of the gods'; Amritsar, the 'pool of immortality,' in the Punjab (see
p. 47), as well as Amarapattan, Amarkot, and similar names. Tájpur in
Bengal is the 'city of sacrifice,' Amantápur in the Ballary district is the
'eternal city,' and Amalápúram in the Madras Presidency is the 'sinless
city.' From *pír*, a 'saint,' we have Pír Panjál, the 'saint's mountain' in
Kashmir, Pírnagar, the 'city of the saint,' and Pírganj, the market of the saint.
Tásichozong in Bhutan is the 'sacred town of instruction,' *i.e.* of religious
teaching. Kanárak in Orissa is the 'black pagoda,' Combaconum (Kum-
bhakonam) in Tanjore means the 'brim of a waterpot,' a name explained by an
idol in the temple, which is called Kumbhesvaran, the 'Lord of the water-pot.'
Dindigal (Dindú-kal) in Madura is the 'rock of Dindu,' an Asura or demon.

A Buddhist monastery was called *Vihára*, whence the name of the province of Behar (Bihár), the most important early seat of Buddhism, as well as
of Cooch Behar (Kúch Bihár), a state in the north-east of Bengal adjoining
Assam, so called from the Koch or Kúch, a forest tribe which founded the
state in the fifteenth century, and from some *Vihára* or monastery whose
site is now unknown. Kacha Vihára in Bhutan signifies the 'monastery in
the marsh.'

Of Moslem origin are such names as Islámpur, Islámábád, Islámkot, and
Islámnagar. Dingarh, in the Punjab, is the 'fortress of the faith' (of Islam);
Rasúlpur and Rasúlábád, are the 'town of the prophet' (Mahomet); Sidh-
pur, is the 'city of the saint' (sidi). The Hindus religiously avoid pronounc-
ing the name of Allahábád, the abode or 'place of Allah,' which was the

new Perso-Arabic name given by Akbar in 1575 to the city at the confluence of the Ganges and Jumna, and where he erected the fortress. The situation explains the name Preág (Prayága), the 'place of junction' at the union of the two sacred rivers, by which the city is always designated by the Hindus.

PART II

Turkish Nomenclature

Turkic names are scattered over an immense region, which stretches from the Adriatic to the Arctic Ocean. We find them among the Yakut, a Turkic tribe at the mouth of the Lena, as well as in European Turkey and the Danubian Provinces, but chiefly in Asia Minor, the Khanates of Central Asia, the north of Persia, and the Pamirs.

These names are for the most part of comparatively recent origin, and hence of simple construction; a substantival element such as *keui*, 'village,' or *su*, 'water,' being preceded by an adjective or qualifying word such as *yeni*, 'new,' or *kara*, 'black.' Thus the common Turkish names, Yeni-keui and Kara-su, correspond in structure and meaning to such English forms as Newton and Blackwater.

The usual substantival elements are *dagh*, *tagh*, or *tau*, a mountain, plural *daghlar*; *tepe*, a summit, hill, heap, or mound, plural *tepeler*, hills, diminutive *tepejik*, a hillock; *tabiya*, a battery or bastion; *korum*, a range of hills; *sirt*, the back, hence a ridge; *yokush*, an ascent; *kaia*, a rock; *dere*, a valley; *su* means water, also a river, *chai* or *chay*, a brook or streamlet; *ermak* or *irmak*, a stream or larger river; *gol*, *kul*, or *gheul*, a lake or pool; *dengiz* or *tengiz*, a sea; *kurfez*, a gulf, bay, or inlet; *yali*, shore or coast; *ghechid*, a ford, ferry, pass, or defile; *yol*, a roadway or channel; *keupri* or *kupri*, a bridge; *kum* means sand, hence a sandy desert; *kir* is moorland or uncultivated ground; *tal*, a pasture; *toprak*, earth, territory; *sinir*, a boundary or frontier; *orman*, a wood or forest; *kapu*, a gate or pass; *batak*, a marsh; *bunar*, a spring; *kuyu*, a well or pit; *dil* is a tongue, spit of land, isthmus; *kirman*, a town; *keui*, spelt *köi* in German books, a village or hamlet; *ev*, a house; *yurd* (*yurt*), a habitation, tent, country house; *kule*, a tower; *kulube*, a hut; and *deghirmen*, a mill.

Of the adjectival elements or qualifying words the more frequent are *kara*, black; *ak*, white; *kok*, *kuk*, or *gok*, blue; *yeshil*, green; *al*, scarlet; *kizil*, red; *sari*, yellow; *ala*, spotted, variegated, beautiful; *eski*, old; *yeni* (*yengi*), 'new'; *kutchuk*, little; *ulu* or *biyuk*, great; *uzun*, long; *issik*, warm; *suk* (*soghuk*), cold; *kuru*, dry; *duz*, smooth, flat; *dar*, narrow; *doghru*, straight, upright; *fena*, bad, dangerous; *demir* or *timur* is iron; *altin* is gold; *tuz*, salt; *bati* is west; *doghu*, east; *yildiz*, north; *jenub*, south; *chinar*, a sycamore; *meysheh*, an oak; and *meyshelik*, an oak forest,

A considerable number of Persian and Arabic and a few Greek and Italian loan-words have also found place in Turkish topography, and these are commonly combined with genuine Turkish elements. Among the more usual topographic words of Persian origin are *bagh*, a vineyard or garden; *serai*, a mansion or palace; *bázár*, a market; *shahr*, a town; *khane*, a house; *kend*, a village; *bala*, high; *abad*, a city; *juy*, a stream; *stán*, a country; *der*, a gate or door, whence *derbend*, a place easily guarded, as a bridge, pass, or mouth of a valley; and *derbar*, the court (*i.e.* the gate) of the sovereign. Among the Arabic loan-words may be enumerated *hissar*, a castle or fort; *hammam*, a bath or bathing place; *suk*, a market; *menzil*, a station-house or halting-place; *meydan*, an open place; *vilayet*, a county or district; *maden*, a mine; and many more, beside numerous personal names of Arabic origin, as Amurat, a corruption of Murad, which means 'wished for,' or desired; or Mustafa, the 'chosen one,' an appellation of Mahomet.

In some cases we have homonyms of diverse origin, which have to be carefully distinguished. Thus *suk*, 'cold,' is Turkish, while *suk*, a 'market,' is Arabic; *mersa*, a 'port,' is Arabic, while *merz*, a 'frontier,' is Persian; *dere*, a 'valley,' is Turkish, *deyr* or *dar*, a 'house' or 'convent,' is Arabic; *der*, a 'gate' or 'pass,' is Persian, and *dar*, 'narrow,' is Turkish; *khara*, 'hard' (stone), is Persian, while *kara*, 'black,' and *kar*, 'snow,' are Turkish; *chai*, a 'brook,' is Turkish, and *chah*, a 'well,' is Persian; *ala*, 'highest,' an 'elevation,' is Arabic, and *ala*, 'beautiful,' is Turkish; *shehr*, a 'town,' and *shir*, a 'lion,' are Persian, while *sur*, a 'rampart,' is Arabic; *sari*, 'yellow,' is Turkish, and *sahra*, a 'desert,' is Arabic.

A few examples, many of which occur repeatedly, may now be given of the way in which Turkish names are constructed of these elements. Among the names of mountains we have the Ak-Tagh, or 'white mountain,' in Turkistan; the Kara Dagh, or 'black mountain'; and the Kara-Daghlar, or 'black mountains'; while the Kara Tau in Central Asia is a dialectic form of Kara Dagh. The Ala Tagh, or 'variegated mountain,' in Asia Minor, is the same word as the Ala Tau in Central Asia, which is so called from being streaked with snow. Yeshil Dagh is the 'green mountain,' and Kizil Dagh the 'red mountain.' The Mustagh, a lofty range in Central Asia, is the 'ice mountain' (*buz*, 'ice'); the Belur Tagh is the 'crystal mountain' (Arabic *billur*, 'cut glass,' 'crystal'); the Suk Dagh, in Asia Minor, is the 'cold mountain'; the Sultan Dagh, in Asia Minor, is the 'royal mountain'; the Baba Dagh is the 'chief or father mountain' (*baba*, a 'father'); and the Sunderlik Dagh, a nearly extinct volcano on the Upper Euphrates, is the 'oven-shaped mountain.' Aghri Dagh, the Turkish name of Ararat, is the 'painful mountain' (*aghri*, a pain, an ache); and Uzunja Dagh, in Asia Minor, is the 'longish mountain.' The Beshtau are the 'five mountains'; while Daghestan, in the Caucasus, is a Perso-Turkic name meaning the 'mountainous country'; and Bala Dagh (the hill behind Troy, a part of Ida), a Perso-Turkic name, is the 'high mountain.' Durzi-daghi, the Turkish name of Lebanon, means the 'mountain of the Druses' (Durzi).

The Kara-koram, north of Kashmir, is the 'black range'; Kara-Tepe is the 'black hill'; Gok-Tepe, or Geok-Tepe, is the 'blue hill'; and Kizil-

Tepe the 'red hill.' There are villages in Asia Minor called Tepeler Keui, the 'village of the hills,' and Tepejik, the 'hillock.'

From *tash*, a stone, we have Tashkend, the 'stone tower'; Tash-bunar, the 'stone well'; and Tash-kapu, the 'stone gate.' Tash-Keupri is a village in Asia Minor with a 'stone bridge.' From *kaia*, a rock, we have Kizil-kaia, the 'red rock'; Kara-kaia, the 'black rock'; Sari-kaia, the 'yellow rock'; Kaiajik, the 'little rocks'; Kaialy, the 'rocky' place; Kaia-dibi, the 'bottom of the rock'; Kaia-bashi, the 'head of the rock'; and Kaia-bunar, the 'rock fountain.' Kapukaia, the 'gate rock,' and Kapukaily Dagh, the 'gate rock mountain,' both in Asia Minor, contain the word *kapu*, a gate, door, and hence a mountain pass. A pass through the Alai range, in the Pamir, is called the Kara Kazik, the 'black post,' or 'black sentinel,' because it is flanked by needle-like peaks, too steep to allow the snow to lie (*kazik*, a 'wooden post'). Kizilbel is the 'red height.' *Bash*, a 'head,' (whence *pasha*), is also applied to mountain peaks, like the Celtic *pen*, as well as in other names like Bunarbashi, near Smyrna, which means 'the head of the spring.' Bunarbashi is also the name of one of the rival sites of Troy.

From *dere*, a dale or valley, we have the common village name Derekeui, which translates the English Dalton or Compton. Buyukdere, on the Bosphorus, is the 'great valley' (*biyuk*, great); Kurudere, in Asia Minor, being equivalent to our Dryden, or 'dry valley,' while Suludere is the 'watery' or 'wet valley.' Karadere is the 'black vale,' and Gokdere the 'blue' or 'green valley.' Ak-su-deresi, in Asia Minor, is the 'vale of the white river.'

A lake is *kol*, *kul*, *gol*, *ghul*, or *gheul*, whence Ak-kul, the 'white lake,' and Kara-kol, on the Pamir, the 'black lake.' The Ala-kul would mean literally the 'variegated lake,' but probably takes its name from the Ala-Tau, to the north of which it lies. North of the Ala-Tau we find also the Issik-kul, the 'warm lake,' warmer, that is, than Lake Balkash, never being frozen over. The Koko-nor in Eastern Tibet, 230 miles in circumference and 10,000 feet above the sea, a Mongolian rather than Turkic name, meaning the 'azure sea' or lake, is the same word as the Guku Nur, in Eastern Turkistan. The Gheuljik, in Armenia, is the 'little lake,' so called because smaller than the neighbouring Lake Van. The Araxes is called the Bingol-chai, or 'river of the thousand lakes or sources,' rising in the Bingol Dagh, or 'mountain of the thousand lakes.'

A river is called *chai*. In Asia Minor, besides the Bingol-chai just mentioned, we have the Kum-chai, or sand river, the Kuru-chai, or dry river, the Ulu-chai, or great river, and the Kuchuk-chai, or little river. The Sari-chai is the yellow river, the Ak-chai the white river, while Chai-keui means the village on the river. A large river is called *irmak*. The Halys, in Asia Minor, which brings down great quantities of red mud, forming a large delta, is now appropriately termed by the Turks the Kizil-Irmak or 'red river.' The Yeshil Irmak is the green river, the Gok Irmak the blue river, while the Kizil Usun in Persia bears a Turkic name meaning the 'red water,' or river. The most usual name for a river is *su*, which properly means 'water.' Ak-su, 'white water,' and Kara-su, 'black water,' are common river names. Kara-su-Bazar, a town in the Crimea, is the market on the Black River, and both the Melas and the Cydnus are now called the Kara-su, while the petrifying stream by Colossæ is now the Ak-su. The Kizil-su, or red river, flows through one of the valleys of the Pamir, and Gok-su or Kok-su, the 'blue river,' is the Kirghiz name of a river which rises in the Ala-tau. The Suk-su, in Asia Minor, is the 'cold water,' Aji-su is the 'bitter water,' and Uzun-su is the 'long river.' The Chamur-su, in Asia Minor, is the muddy water, and there is a place called Chamur, which means 'mud.' Sulu-serai and Sulu-owa, in Asia Minor, mean the well-watered palace and the well-watered plain. There is a place in Bulgaria called Batak, the marsh, and Kara-batak is the 'black marsh.' Yildiz Kiosk is the 'Northern palace.'

From *keupri* or *kupri*, a 'bridge,' we have Keupri-keui, 'bridge village,' and Keupri-su, 'bridge river.' Keupris is the 'place at the bridge,' and Vezir-keupri is the 'bridge of the Vizier'; *vizir*, a prime minister, being a person charged with the burden of the state, from the Arabic *vizr*, a 'load' or 'burden.'

From *deghirme*, 'round,' we have *deghirmen*, a 'mill,' whence Deghirmen-keui, which is as common as Milton, the English equivalent, while Deghirmen-su or Deirmen-su corresponds to our Melbourne (Mill-burn), and Deghirmen-deresi means the 'mill valley.' Deghirmenlik, the Turkish name of the Ægean island of Melos, is a translation of a folk etymology of Milo, the neo-Greek name of the island.

Demirchi-keui or 'forge village' (*demir*, 'iron'), is a common village name in Asia Minor. So Demir-Hissar in Rumelia is the 'iron castle.'

The word *kum* means 'sand.' The Kara-kum, or 'black sand,' and the Kizil-kum, or 'red sand,' are the names of two sandy deserts which adjoin the sea of Aral. Kum-chai, in Asia Minor, is the sandy river, and Kum-burun, in Rhodes, is the 'sandy nose' or cape.

From *tuz*, 'salt,' we have the Tuz-su or 'salt river' on the Pamir. Tuz-kol, in Central Asia, means the 'salt lake,' as does Tuz-gol in Asia Minor, near which we find Tuzassar, 'salt castle,' and Tuz-keui, which answers to our Salton. There are two villages near saline springs called Tuzla, a name which denotes 'salt works.'

Kadilar and Delilar are not uncommon names. They are Turkish plurals—the first meaning 'the judges,' denoting places where two or more Kadis have resided, while Delilar is the plural of *deli*, a fool, chatterer, or madman, also a kind of irregular trooper in the old time. Delibaba, the 'crazy father,' is a village in Asia Minor, doubtless so called from some dervish who lived there. A similar name is Papaskeui, the 'priests' village.'

Places are often named from conspicuous trees. Thus Sughud, in Asia Minor, means the 'willow tree.' Kara-aghaj in Bulgaria means 'the elm,' literally the 'black tree' (*kara*, 'black,' and *aghaj*, 'tree'). Selvi, also in Bulgaria, means the 'cypress.' Kavak, the poplar tree (or plane tree) is a common local name, as well as Kavaky and Kavak-keui. Chamkeui is 'pine tree village,' Chamly-Dagh is 'pine tree mountain,' and Cham-chai is the 'pine tree river.' In Asia Minor we find Katran-Dagh, 'pitch mountain,' and Katran-su, 'pitch river.' In Asia Minor we have Chakal-su, 'jackal river,' and Sungurlu, 'the place of falcons.' There are villages called Kara-kechi, the 'black goat,' and Kara-arslan, the 'black lion.'

The Turks call the Bosphorus Boghaz, a word which means a throat, pass, channel, strait, or gorge. Kuchuk Boghaz is the 'little strait,' and Kara Boghaz, the 'black mouth' or opening. Boghaz Keui, in Cappadocia, famous for its rock carvings, is 'the village at the gorge.'

From *turmak*, to settle, we have *tura*, which denotes a settlement, whence Tura, a town in Hungary, and the River Tura in Russia, so called from a Tartar settlement on its banks.

The most frequent element in Turkish names is *keui*, a 'village,' which is as universal as the English equivalents *ton* or *ham*. To take a few instances, Yenikeui, Eskikeui, and Ortakeui answer to our Newton, Alton, and Middleton, Keuprikeui is Bridgeton, Akkeui and Karakeui are the white and black villages, Bazarkeui designates a village with a market, and Kadikeui a village of a kadi or judge.

The commonest Persian loan-words are *bazar*, a 'market'; *serai*, a 'palace'; and *bagh*, a 'garden.' Yenibazar, in Bulgaria, answers to our Newmarket. Karabagh, the 'black garden,' is a district in Armenia, so called from its dark forests, Balabagh, in Afghanistan, is the 'lofty garden,' and Baghchi-serai, the Tartar capital of the Crimea, means the palace in the garden, all from the Persian *bagh*, a 'garden,' which we have in Baghdad and many other names, such as Alumbagh and Alibagh in India. The Persian loan-word *serai* signifies a halting-place, a building for travellers, hence a house, mansion, or palace. The Turkish formation, *saraili*, denotes a person who belongs to the palace, and hence we have the Italian word *seraglio*, meaning the household of the Sultan. Bosnaserai, the capital of Bosnia, is the palace on the Bosna, the river on which it stands. In Asia Minor we find Suluserai, the well-watered palace, and Akserai, the white palace. From *serai* and the Persian *kervan*, our caravan, a 'crowd of men,' a 'company of travellers,' we have *kervan-serai*, a caravansery, the eastern inn being a building for travellers. A mountain in Asia Minor is called Kervan-serai Dagh, the hill of the caravan house. The holy city of Kairwan in Tunis, a great place of pilgrimage, was so named from the crowd of pilgrims.

A caravansery is also called a khan, as Yeni-khan, the 'new inn.' This is the Persian *khane*, a house or dwelling, whence the name of the village of Kyaghid-khane near Constantinople, so called from a paper factory (Persian *kyaghid*, 'paper'). When the word *khan* forms part of the name of a village, as in the case of Hekim Khan or Ailaja Khan, we may assume that a khan was first erected, round which a village has grown up.

The Persian loan-word *shehr*, a dwelling-place, and hence a 'town,' which we have in Shiraz and Bushire, appears also in such Turkish names as Eski-shehr, the 'old town,' which stands on the site of Dorylæum, Yeni-shehr (Newton), or Kadi-shehr, the town or dwelling of a judge. The site of Philadelphia, in Asia Minor, so named from Attalus Philadelphus, is now marked by a Turkish village called Allah Shehr, the town of Allah, while the site of Antioch in Phrygia is called Ak-shehr, the white town.

From *kend* or *kand*, a Persian loan-word, which means a village or town, we have Yarkand, Samarkand, Khok-kand, the town of pigs, and Tash-kand, a hybrid name from the Turkish *tash*, stone.

More widely spread than any other Persian loan-word is *-stán*, a country, properly a possession, from the Persian *sitan*, 'one who takes possession.' Servia is called by the Turks Sarpistan (Serpistan), the country of the Serbs; and Frangistan is Western Europe, the country of the Franks, a term dating from the time of the Crusades. We have also Turkistan, the country of the Turkic nomads north of Persia, as well as Afghanistan, Beluchistan, and Hindustan.

The Arabic loan-word *hisar*, a castle, is common. Eski-Hissar, the 'old castle,' marks the site of Stratonicæa in Caria, so named by Antiochus Soter, from his wife, Stratonica; and another Eski-Hissar stands on the site of Laodicea ad Lycum in Phrygia. Hissarlik marks the site of Troy. Ak-Hissar, the 'white castle,' is the Turkish name of Thyatira, one of the seven churches of Asia, and the home of Lydia. The ruins of Synnada, in Phrygia, go by the name of Eski-Kara-Hissar, the 'old black castle.' The centre of the opium trade is at Afium-Kara-Hissar, the 'opium black castle,' which represents Philomelium, the city of nightingales, in Phrygia. Selvi-Hissar, or 'cypress castle,' represents Pessinus in Phrygia. There are three places called Zervi-Hissar, or Sevri-Hissar, 'peak castle'; Demir-Hissar, in Rumelia, is the 'iron castle'; Bala-Hissar, the 'lofty castle'; Ghuzel-Hissar is the 'handsome castle'; and Kizil-Hissar is the 'red castle.'

Another Arabic loan-word is *kale* or *kaleh*, a castle or fortress, whence Yenikale, the 'new castle' in the Crimea, which gives a name to the Straits of Yenikale between the Black Sea and the Sea of Azov. Redut-kale, redoubt castle, is on the eastern coast of the Black Sea; and Toprak Kaleh, in Armenia, is 'earth castle.' Aklat Kalessi, on Lake Van, is the 'castle of Aklat'; but Aklat is itself a corruption, probably due to the Kurds, of the older Arabic name Kal'at, the 'castle.' There is a town in Asia Minor called Kassaba, a loan-word from the Arabic *kasbah*, a 'citadel.'

The Arabic loan-word *ma'den*, a 'mine,' which is familiar in the name of Almaden in Spain, is also found in the Turco-Arabic name of Maden Dagh, the 'mine mountain,' in Asia Minor. Karamaghara, the 'black cave,' is also a Turco-Arabic formation from the Arabic *maghera*, a 'cave,' which we have in the Wâdi Maghera, or 'valley of caves.' Uzun-burj, in Asia Minor, means the 'long tower,' from *burj*, 'a tower on a wall,' a loan-word adopted immediately from the Arabs, who obtained it from the crusading Franks.

There are also loan-words from the Greek, such as Ilidcha, or Lidcha, which appears repeatedly in Asia Minor and the Balkan Peninsula as the designation of places with thermal springs, and seems to be a Turkish corruption of the Greek *loutra*, 'baths.' Even more frequent is the word *kalissa*, a Christian church, a corruption of ecclesia, whence Bin-bir-Kalisseh, the 'thousand and one churches,' which marks the site of Lystra in Lycaonia, evidently a revered Christian site, from the numerous ruins of churches—perhaps two score in number. Eski-Kalese, the 'old church,' is the Turkish name of Perga (Acts xiii. 13). Kizil-kalisse, in Asia Minor, is the 'red church,' and Kizil Liman, also in Asia Minor, means the 'red haven' (Greek λιμήν). In Kuchuk Mendere, the 'little Mæander,' which is the Turkish name of the Caystrus, we have a survival from the prehistoric speech of Asia Minor, which has found its way into English. Changeli, the 'place of bells,' from *chang*, a bell, is a name given to monasteries and churches which have been allowed to retain their bells.

PART III

MAGYAR NAMES

The dominant race in Hungary being the Magyars, a Ugro-Altaic people, we find a predominance of Magyar names intermingled with others of Slavonic, German, Roumanian, or Turkish origin. Just as in Wales and Ireland we find places with two names, Celtic and English, one being usually a translation of the other, so in Hungary we find Magyar names in current use together with their German or Slavonic equivalents. Thus the Magyar *varos*, a 'town,' is translated by the German *stadt*, and *var*, a 'fortress,' by *burg*; Szasz-varos, the Saxon's town, being called Sachsenstadt in German; while Vas-var, the 'iron fortress,' and Kolosvar, the 'enclosed fortress,' are respectively called in German Eisenburg and Klausenburg. So Petervarad is Peterwardein, and Szekes-Fehervar is Stuhlweissenburg.

The most usual substantival components of Magyar names are *falu* or *falva*, a village; *varos*, a town; *var* or *varad*, a fortress; *hely*, a place; *haza*, a house; *föld*, land; *hago* or *hegy*, a hill; *füred*, a bath; *banya*, a mine; words which are commonly preceded either by a personal name or by an adjective, such as, *uj*, new; *kis*, little; *nagy*, great; *fel*, high; *al*, low; *feher*, white; *fekete*, black.

Thus we have Uj-falu, the new village; Uj-varos, new town; Uj-var, new castle; Uj-banya, the new mine; Nagy-banya, the great mine; Nagy-varad, also called Grosswardein in German, the great fortress; Fel-föld, the high land; Al-föld, the low land; Al-varos, low town; Also-varos, lower town; Felso-varos, upper town; Föld-var, the land castle; Feher-var, the white castle; the former capital of Dacia is called Var-hely, the castle place; Udvar-hely is the court place; Uj-hely, the new place; Fekete-halam, the black hill; and Nád-falu is reed village (*nád*, a reed).

Many places are named from the rivers on which they stand. Thus Temesvar, the capital of the Banat, is the 'fortress on the River Temes,' the Roman Tibiscus. Tisza-Füred is the bath or watering-place on the River Tisza or Theiss; while Balaton-Füred signifies the baths on Lake Balaton. Abrud-banya is the mine on the River Abrud; Szamos-Ujvar is the new castle on the River Szamos, and Nagy-Körös is the great [place] on the Körös, or 'red river.'

Many places in the kingdom of Hungary bear Slavonic or German names, as Buda-Pest, Kremnitz, Schemnitz, Pressburg or Oedenburg.

Personal names are also common, as Hanus-falva, the village of Hans (John); Nagy-Karoly, great Charleston; or Nagy-Szent-Miklos, great Saint Nicholas; Szar-hegy, the hill of the Tsar or Kaiser.

Naturally we have numerous loan-words. Thus in Kishissar, 'the little castle,' the suffix -*hissar*, a castle, is an Arabic word which has found its way through Turkish into Magyar. In Maros-vasar-hely, which means the market-place on the River Maros, *vasar* is the Persian word *bazar*, a market, also introduced through Turkish; while in Sarivar, the palace fortress, *sari* is the Persian *serai*, a palace, adopted into Turkish and so introduced into Magyar. In Szombath-hely, Saturday (market) place, Szombath is the Magyar form of the Hebrew word Sabbath.

PART IV

SLAVONIC NOMENCLATURE

In Eastern Europe the local names belong for the most part to languages of the great Slavonic family of speech. We find them as far west as the Elbe and even in the Netherlands, as far south as the Balkan peninsula, while to the east they are scattered over the whole of Asiatic Russia. Mingled with Magyar names they are numerous in Hungary. In Mecklenburg, Brandenburg, Saxony, Prussia, and generally in the region between the Vistula and the Elbe, Wendish names contend with German ones for predominance. In Bohemia, Moravia, and the south of Poland the names are Czech (pronounced *Chekh*). Ruthenian or Little Russian names prevail in Galicia and in South-Western Russia, while in many of the Austrian crownlands, Styria, Croatia, Carinthia, Dalmatia, and Bosnia, as well as in Servia, Bulgaria, and Roumania, they are of the Servian, Slovenian, or South Slavonic type. Polish names are not confined to Poland, but extend into Silesia and Russia, while Russian names are scattered over Siberia, and in Russia proper are mingled with Finnic and Teutonic names.

It would manifestly be impossible, within any reasonable limits, to give an account of the many thousands of names which are scattered over these vast regions. The names of a few important towns, such as Moscow, Dresden, Leipzig, Berlin, Novgorod, Buda-Pest, Prag, Belgrade, and the two Mecklenburg duchies, Schwerin and Strelitz, have already been discussed in the Glossary; all that can now be done is to give some brief account of the general principles on which Slavonic names, whether Polish, Czech, Wendish, Servian, or Russian, are constructed, and a list, with a few illustrative examples, of the chief Slavonic words which enter into the composition of the names of villages, lakes, rivers, islands, plains, mountains, and other natural features. This list is a mere summary of the results of the researches of a few specialists, more especially of Miklosich, who is the chief authority on the subject of Slavonic nomenclature. The task is simplified by the fact that

Slavonic names are mostly compounded of a few simple elements. One peculiarity is that the first element is frequently a preposition, and the last an
adjectival formative. Thus the preposition *za* or *sa*, which means 'beyond'
or 'behind,' is very common. Sabor, for instance, signifies a place 'beyond
the wood,' Sabrod is 'beyond the ford,' Zadol, 'beyond the valley,' Zablatt,
and Zablotow, a town in Galicia, mean 'behind the marsh'; Nablatt, on the
other hand, signifying 'near the marsh.' Another common preposition is
pod, 'under' or 'below.' Thus Podbor is a place 'below the forest,' Podlesi
is 'below the moor,' Podgora and Podgorica are 'below the mountain,'
Podgrad is 'below the castle,' Podlipa is 'under the lime-tree,' Podulchin
is 'under the alder,' Poddub, 'under the oak,' Potsdam (see p. 227) being a
German corruption of a cognate Slavonic name. Of similar significance are
such names as Podolia (see p. 225), Podoly, Podolec, and Podal, which however are formed not from the preposition, but from the Polish adjective
podolny, 'low.'

Even more characteristic of Slavonic names are the suffixes. The possessive
suffix, which takes the forms *-skoi*, *-skia*, and *-ski*, and dwindles to *-sk*, *-sch*,
or *-itz*, means 'belonging to' or 'annexed to.' This and the similar suffix
-ow, *-ov*, *-owa*, also used as a patronymic like the English *-ing*, enters into the
names of a host of towns and villages, sometimes being appended to a personal name, as Janow, the 'town of John,' Alexandrovsk, the 'town of
Alexander,' or is appended to a substantive, as Studnitz, the place of the
fountain, Kamnitz, 'the stony' place, or Lipsk, the place of the lime-tree.
Appended to the names of rivers this suffix in the form *-sk* is seen in a multitude of names of important Russian towns, more especially of those newly
founded in Siberia. Thus we have Tobolsk on the River Tobol, Tomsk on
the Tom, Irkutsk on the Irkut, Udinsk on the Uda, Yansk on the Yana,
Selinginsk on the Selinga, Neviansk on the Neva. Omsk was built in 1756
on the Om, Nertchinsk in 1658 on the Nercha, Irbitsk in 1633 on the Irbit.
Kansk stands on the Kan, a tributary of the Yenissei; Argunsk on the
Argun, a tributary of the Amur. Penjinsk Bay, Kamtchatka, takes its name
from the town of Penjinsk, which stands on the River Penjina. Tigilsk,
a town in Kamtchatka, was built in 1744 on the banks of the Tigil.
Tagilsk, in the Ural, stands on the Tagil; Miask, also in the Ural,
stands on the Mias. On the Kolima, in Siberia, there are two towns
called Kolimsk, of which the older, now called Nijni-Kolimsk, or 'lower
Kolimsk,' was founded in 1644 by Michael Stadirchin, a Cossack from
Yakutsk, the capital of the Yakut tribe and country. Ischiginsk stands at
the mouth of the Ischiga, Pinsk is on the Pina, Vitepsk on the Viteba, Ber-
diansk on the Berda, Okhotsk on the Okhota, Ilginsk on the Ilga, Olekminsk
on the Olekma, Olensk on the Olenek, Lugansk on the Lugan, Bielitz on the
Biela, Bobroninsk on the Bobronia, Jarensk on the Jarenga or 'strong river,
while Kupiansk and Kupiszki are towns so named from their situation on 'a
promontory,' *kupa*. This suffix is often undistinguishable from *-witz*, *-wes*, or
-viz, meaning a 'village,' like *-ton* or *-ham* in English names. Thus Karlowitz
is equivalent to our Charleston, Janowitz to our Johnston, and Mitrovitz or
Dmitrovsk is the town of Demetrius. Zerkowitz answers to our Kirby, Bilowes

to Whitton, and Jeloviz means ' fir-tree village.' Another common suffix is *-ec*, *-ik*, *-ica*, which is merely a diminutive. The first component of a name is usually an adjective. Thus the Old Slavonic *staru*, ' old,' becomes *stary* in Polish, whence Stargard (for Starigrad) in Pomerania, which signifies the ' old fortress ' (see p. 265). From the same source we have Starysedlo and Starasiolo, the ' old settlement,' Starwitz, Staritz, Staritzen, Stariza, Staritza, Starin, Starinka, and Starova, meaning the ' old village ' ; while from *mlady* or *mlody*, ' new,' we have in Bohemia, Mladiza, Mladowitz, and Mladzowitz ; and in Silesia, Bladen and Bladow, answering to our English Newton. In Russia, Novgorod is the ' new fortress,' Nova Cerkev is the ' new church,' Nova Vas and Nova Wies the ' new village,' and Novoselo the ' new settlement.' Novytarg is ' new market,' and Novigrad is Newbury.

Bolskaia Zemlya, the ' great land,' and Malaia Zemlya, the ' small land,' are Russian translations of the Samoyedic names Arka-Ya and Nuwey-Ya, which designate the districts on either side of the mouth of the Petschora. So Bolskaia Reka, in Kamtchatka, is the ' great river,' and Bolskoi Ostrov is the ' great island.' Bolskoi Osero is the ' great lake,' and Bolskaia Luka the ' great marsh.' From *velik*, *velky*, *velika*, or *veliki*, which also means ' great ' in sundry dialects, we have Velikaia (Reka), the ' great river,' Welkawes, the ' great village,' Wiligrad and Welehrad, the ' great castle,' with many similar names, such as Welkau, Welchow, Welka, and the hybrid name Welkendorf, while from *maloi*, ' little,' we have Malinek, Malenz, Malkow, Malkowitz, Malowitz, and Malkendorf, answering to our English Littleton.

From the Old Slavonic *dlugy*, Servian *dilji* or *dulgi*, and Russian *dolgi*, ' long,' Germanised as *dolge*, comes Dolgoi Ostrov, the ' long island,' a name which occurs repeatedly in Russian waters. The Dolgen See, near Potsdam and elsewhere, is a hybrid Slavo-German name meaning the ' long lake.' Dlugimost is the ' long bridge,' Dlugibrodt and Dolgenbrod the ' long ford,' Dlugiwoda the ' long water,' while Dolgow, Dolgen, Dolgenow, Drugy, Dlouha, and Dolha are long places or villages. A very common element is *dobro* or *dobra* (Old Slavonic *dobr*), ' good,' whence the Dobrudcha, at the mouth of the Danube, a hybrid name signifying the ' good district.' Dobropul and Dobropole mean the ' good plain.' Dobrawoda is the ' good water,' Dobberbus the ' good dwelling,' Dobbergast the ' good inn,' to which may be added Dobrezin, Dobrawitz, Dobrau, Döbra, and Döbern.

Teplitz, Töplitz, Toplice, Topla, and similar names of places with hot springs in Hungary, Bavaria, Illyria, and elsewhere are from the Slavonic *teply*, *tepl*, *tepel* or *topel*, ' warm.' Tepel stands on the Tepla or ' warm river,' and there are places called Teplik and Teplovka in Russia. From the Old Slavonic and Czech *studen*, ' cold,' or the Polish *studnia*, a spring or well, we have such local names as Studenz, Studena, Studenitz, Studnitz, and Studnic.

Wisoka, a ' height,' is from *vysok*, ' high,' which becomes *wysoki*, *vysoky*, *visok*, *ossick*, and *osisch*, all common elements in Slavonic names. Wyschehrad in Bohemia, as well as Visegrad and Wissegrad, mean the ' lofty castle '; Wyssokaia Gora is the ' high mountain '; while Ossagh, Wissek, Wisowice, Wisnica, and Vysokow are high places or villages. Werchni

Ostrov is the 'upper island,' Nijni-Novgorod is the 'lower new fortress,' Nijni-Neviansk the 'lower town on the Neva,' Nijni-Devitzk the 'lower town on the Devitza,' and Nijni-Tagelsk the 'lower town on the Tagel.' From *miedzy*, 'middle,' we have Misdroi in Silesia, a place in the 'middle of the wood,' Mediasch in Hungary, a place in the middle of the water, while Meseritz in Moravia stands in the middle of a stream. The words *sreda, sredina, scrodak*, and *sredni* also mean the 'middle,' whence Srednia Vas, the 'middle village,' Seredovoi Ostrov, the 'middle island,' and places called Seredne and Serednica.

From *mokre, mokry, mokar* or *mokryi*, 'wet' or 'moist,' we have the Polish word *moczara* a 'marsh,' whence Moczary, Mokro polje, the 'wet plain,' and scores of other names, such as Mokrau and Mokra. Sucha Gora is the 'dry mountain,' and Suchadol, the 'dry valley,' from *suchy*, 'dry,' whence also several places called Suka and Zauche.

The word *niemetz* means 'foreign' (see p. 206), and is frequently applied to German towns. Thus Niemitch, Niemez, and Niemtchiz are German towns in Bohemia, and Nemet-uj-var, a hybrid name in Hungary, signifies the 'new German fortress.' Niemesk, in Brandenburg, must date from the period when the Germans were the intrusive and the Slavs the dominant race.

From colours we have numerous names. White is *bel, biala, biélo*, and *bely*, whence Belgrad (see p. 65), the 'white castle,' and Bialgorod, a translation of the Turkish Ak-kerman, the 'white town.' Bielagora is the 'white mountain,' Bilowes, Bilowitz, and Belowiz all mean the 'white village,' and the Bialy, in South-West Russia, is the white (river), as is the Biala in Silesia, on which stand the towns of Biala and Bielitz. Similar names are Bielau, Bülow, Biele, and Belitz. Black is *czarny* in Polish, *czerna* in Czech, and *cerny* in Wendish. Montenegro is the Italian translation of the Slavonic Tzernagora (see p. 196) called the 'black mountain' from the dark firs that clothe it. Czernahora is the Czech form of the same name. From the feminine *tchernaya* we have the battlefield of the Tchernaya Reka, or 'black river,' in the Crimea, while the Tchernaya Dolina is the 'black valley.' The Czarny Staw and the Tcherno Osero mean the 'black lake.' Czarnilasz is the 'black forest,' Tchornegosda, the 'black inn,' Zarnowice and Zarnowitz are the 'black village,' to which we may add such Germanised names as Sarnow, Sarne, Zschorne, Sarnovo, and Sarnaki. Zielonagora and Zelonahora mean the 'green mountain,' from the Polish *zielony*, 'green' (Czech *zeleny*, Wendish *seleny*). The Selinga and the Zielona are the 'green rivers,' and Zielengbrod is the 'green ford.' We have also places called Zielonka, Zielonken, Zielontkowo, and Zelenitz, with hybrid names like Zelendorf. Zielenzig is a town in Brandenburg. The Sinaya Gora, one of the highest points in the Ural chain, is the 'purple mountain,' and the Sinaie Morze, a gulf of the Caspian, is the 'purple sea.' Zerniz and Tcherna are from *zereny* or *czereny*, 'red.' The Old Slavonic *sweti* (Czech *swetly*) means bright, shining, or clear, whence Swetlaya Gora, the 'shining mountain,' Swetloi Osero, the 'clear lake,' and such names as Zwettl or Zwidlern. The word *krasna*, 'beautiful,' frequently means 'red' in Russian names. Thus the Krasnavoda, a river in Croatia, is the 'beautiful water'; Krasnapol is the 'beautiful plain,' and Krasnabrod is the the 'fair ford.' Krasna, Krasne, and Krasnitz all mean beautiful place. Krasnoyarsk, on the Yenissei, one of the most important towns in Siberia, was founded in 1627 by Dubenskoi, the Cossack Attaman, and named from the cliff of red clay on which it was built.

From the preceding examples it will be seen that the adjectival element is followed by a substantive. Those most frequently found in composition may be now enumerated.

The Bohemian Czernahora and Tzernagora the Slavonic name of Montenegro, both mean, as we have seen, the 'black mountain,' the second element being *gora*, a 'mountain,' whence Sinaya Gora, the 'purple mountain' in the Ural, as well as Görlitz in Silesia, Göritz near Trieste, Gorica, Goriza, Goranica, and many other names. From the Czech *chlum*, the Polish *chelm*, or the Russian *cholm*, a 'hill,' a word cognate with the German *kulm* and the Latin *culmen*, we have numerous names, such as Kulm, a town in West Prussia, standing on a hill, Kulm on the Saale, as well as Chelm, Chlumetz, Golmitz, Colmüz, and Chelmo. From the diminutive of this word we have Chlumek, Chelmek, Chumek, and Chlomek, all meaning the 'little hill.' A summit is *vrh* or *werch*, whence Vrhe-Veliky, the 'great hill,' Werche, Virchow, Werchau in Prussia, and the Russian Werchni-Ostrov, the 'upper island,' and Werchne-Dnieprevosk, the 'high town on the Dnieper.' The Russian and Polish *mogila* and the Bohemian *mohila* mean a tumulus or grave, whence Mogilnoi Osero, the 'grave lake,' as well as Mugeln, Mügliiz, Mogielnica, and Mohilev. The word *rog* means a 'horn' or 'cape,' as in Taganrog on the sea of Azov, but a more usual word is *nos*, a nose or ness, as in Sviatoi Nos, the 'holy cape.'

From *pole*, a 'plain,' we have the name of Poland (see p. 225), and such names as Polla, Pöllaw, Poljice, Policka, and Polanka, while as far west as Holstein, from the Wendish *plön* or *plun*, a 'plain,' we have the town of Plön, which gives a name to the Plöner See. From *ravan*, 'level or flat' (Polish *rowny*, Czech *rovny*), we have Raven, Ravna, Ravnica, Rovna and Raunach. The Old Slavonic *pust*, Czech and Polish *pusty*, signifies waste or desolate, whence Pusava, Pusca, Pustina, Pusina, Pustin, Pustitz, and the hybrid names of the Pusterthal and the Pusterwald. From *dolina*, a valley (Czech *dol*), we have Dolzen, Dolau, Dehlau, Dolich, Dol, Dolsk, and many similar names. The Old Slavonic *lanka* means a 'meadow,' whence the Polish *laka*, the Ruthenian and Wendish *luka*, and the Czech *louka*, while *lug* is a 'moor' in Wendish. Hence Dobrilugk, the 'good meadow,' Luckau, Louka, Lucknitz, Loukowitz, Lacka, and Lanky. From *luza*, a 'marsh' or 'bog' (Czech *luh*), we have the district called Lausitz (see p. 169), as well as Louzek, Louzna, Lusnitz, Luze, and Luhy. From the Wendish *para*, which signifies a 'swamp' or soft marshy district, we have Parchim in Mecklenburg Schwerin, and Barsh or Bars in Hungary. Paretz, Paaren, Parchen, Parchau, Partwitz, and Barduz are all on swampy ground, and Baireuth has been referred to the same source. From *grjasnyi*, 'marshy' or 'muddy,' we have the Grijasnaya Reka, or 'muddy river,' and Grjasnoi Osero, the 'muddy lake.' Stolpe, the name of several villages in Pomerania and Hungary, and Stolpen in Saxony are from *stolpe*, which means a rising ground in a marshy place, like the English *holm*.

Rega, Reka, and Regen, three rivers in Germany, are from the Slavonic *reka*, a river. Reika, the 'river,' also called Welika Reika, the 'great river,' is the largest stream in Montenegro. Fiume, near Trieste, is an Italian translation of Reka, the Slavonic name of the stream on which it stands (see p. 125). We have also the Rieska, and the Recknitz, or 'little river.' The Bistra and the Bistrica, the 'rapid' rivers, are from *brz*, or *bister*, quick, rapid ; while Bistraw and Bistritz are towns on rivers named from their swiftness. A brook is *potok*: whence Potocac, Potocska, Potoko, and many other names. Water is *voda* or *woda*: whence Czernawoda, the 'black water,' Dlugiwoda, the 'long water,' Vodno, Wodna, and Vodnic. The prefix *ust-* or *ustje-* denotes the mouth or confluence of a river, as Ust-Nafta, at the 'mouth of the Nafta,' Ust-Pinega, at the 'mouth of the Pinega' (see p. 285). But Zlatoust, 'golden mouth,' the name of several Russian villages, arises from the dedication of their churches to St. John Chrysostom, of whose name Zlatoust is the Russian translation (*zlato*, 'gold').

A fertile source of local names is *brod*, which signifies a 'ford.' Isenbrod is the ford over the River Iser, and there are five places in Bohemia and Galicia called Brody. Dolgenbrodt is the 'long ford,' Zabrod denotes a place 'beyond the ford,' while Brodkowitz, Brodsack, Brodden, and Brodowen are names of the same class. Jamlitz, Jamnitz, and Jamno are from *jama*, a ditch ; Riez, Rieze, Riezov, and Riezig, are from *rysch*, a dam or embankment. The Wendish *jasor*, a 'marsh,' is related to *jezioro*, which means a lake in Old Slavonic and Polish, whence several places called Jehser, Jeserig, Jesero, Jezer, and Jezera. In Russian this word becomes *ozero* or *osero*, as Bieloi Osero, the 'white lake,' near Novgorod ; Nishnaya Osernaya, the 'lower lake,' and Werchnaya Osernaya, the 'upper lake.' Pustoje Osero, literally the waste or desert lake, is a lake without fish.

In Russian *ostrov*, plural *ostrova*, means an island. The island in the delta of the Volga, on which Astrakhan is built, bears the name of Dolgoi Ostrov, the 'long island,' and Dolgoi Ostrov, south of Novaya Zemlya, is the Russian translation of the older Samoyedic name Jambu-ngo, meaning the 'long island.' Bolgoi Ostrov is the 'great island,' and Pustinnyi Ostrov the 'desolate island.' Ostrova is the name of an island in the Danube, and Ostrova is a Russian town, standing on an island in a river. Similar names are Ostrau, Ostrovec, and Ostrowy.

Many names are derived from the nature of the soil. There are thirty-two villages in Eastern Germany called Glienicke, from the Wendish *glina*, clay (Czech *hlina*) ; whence also Glinsk in Russia, Gliniany in Austria, Glina on the River Glina in Hungary, Glienek, Gliny, Glien, Glinzig, Glintsch, Glindow, and Glinow. Mutilated forms such as Lindow, Lintha, and Hline are also found. From *pisch*, 'sand,' Wendish *pesk*, Czech *pisek*, and Polish *piasek*, come such names as Pisek, Peschow, Peckska, Pshov, Peschkowitz, Peschen, and perhaps Pesth. From the Old Slavonic *kamen*, 'stone,' we have Chemnitz in Prussia, Camenz in Saxony, the birthplace of Lessing, Kemmen and Cammin in Pomerania, Kemnitz in Saxony and in Prussia, Kemenz in Saxony, Schemnitz in Silesia, as well as Kaminietz the capital of Podolia, several towns in Bohemia called Kamenitz, and many similar names such as Kamengrad, the 'town on the rock,' and Pusta Kaminica, the 'stony waste,' from *pusty*, a waste place. From *pec*, a 'rock' (Servian *pecina*), come Peca, Pecska, Petschin, and Petschek. Lomnitz, Lomice, and Lomec are from *lom*, a 'quarry' or cliff (Old Slavonic *lomiti*, to break). Rudawa, Rudno, Rudka, and Rudina are from *ruda*, 'ore,' 'metal'; Zelesno and Zelezny from *zeleso*, 'iron'; Zlatnik and Zlatina are from *zlato*, 'gold.' The word *srebro*, 'silver,' is used to designate clear streams, as Serebrenka, the silver or clear river. To *sol*, *ssol* or *sul*, 'salt,' *slan*, *solne*, 'saline,' or *slatina*, a 'saline spring,' we may refer Slana, Slanik, Slatinak, Slatna, Solin, Soletz, and Solonka, Maidenoi Ostrov, 'copper island,' in the Bering Sea, was so named by Bering in 1728.

Other names refer to the nature of the vegetation. The vast pine forests of Eastern Europe and their products have naturally been the source of many names. Smolensk, Smolkau, and Smolnitz are among the names which may be referred to *smola*, 'pine-wood' and 'pitch,' whence *smolin*, asphalte. Smrcek, Smerek, and Smrkova, as well as the Alpine pass called the Sömmering (see p. 262) are from *smrk* or *smerek*, a 'fir-tree.' Pekla, Peklina, and Pekeletz are from *pekel* or *paklina*, 'pitch.' Iglau, a town in Moravia, stands on the River Iglau, a corruption of Jihlawa, the 'fir river,' from the Lithuanian *jehla*, a 'fir-tree'; in Czech *jedla*, in South Slavonic *jela*, in Russian *iga* or *jega* : whence Jela, Jelovice, Jeloviz, Jedle, Jedlow, and Jeletz, a large city in Russia. The word *bor* properly means a pine or fir-tree; and from the prevalence of this tree in the vast forests of Northern and Central Europe it has come to signify a wood or forest. A very common name is Bohrau, which means the woody place, and we have also Borau in Bohemia, Borek in Posen, as well as Borow and Borovsk in Russia, Borowa in Hungary, Bohra, Borowitz, Borovna. Sabor means 'behind the wood,' and Brandenburg is an assimilated German corruption of the Wendish name Brannibor, the 'forest fortress' (see p. 74). From *drowo* or *drzewo*, a 'wood,' a word connected with our *tree*, we have Drewiz, Drehnow, Drehna, Drebkau, Drewitsch, and Drohobicz. Gollnow in Pomerania, Gollin, Gollwitz, and Golschow in Prussia, as well as Goltzen and Kolkwitz, are referred to the Wendish *gola*, a wood, though some of these may be from *gol*, bare, naked, as is probably the case with the Golaia Gora and Gologory, which mean the 'bare hill,' as well as with Golk, Golo, Golsovo, and Golice.

Lützen, the battlefield near Leipzig, Lissa in Posen, Leschnitz in Silesia, Leizig in Saxony, as well as Lützow, Lieske, Leske, and Leskau are assigned to *lesso* or *lesse*, bush, scrub, or thicket. Leschkirch in Transylvania is the church in the wood, and Liezegorike is the bushy little hill. Sakrau and Sakrow mean 'behind the coppice,' from *kre*, a coppice. From *trebez*, a 'clearing' (*trebiti*, to clear land), we have Trebesch, Treboc, Trebitz, Trebija, and Tribuny. A cleared place is also called *laz* : whence Laze, Lazina, and Lazec. A clearing is *paseka* in Czech, whence Pasek, Pasieka, and Posiecz.

An oak is *dabu* in Old Slavonic, *dab* in Polish, and *dub* in Czech, whence

Dubrau, the name of 200 places in Germany, meaning an oak-wood or place of oaks. Dubrowa, Dubrawa, Dobrau, Doubraw, and Dubrow are variant forms. Teuplitz, of which the Wendish name was Dublize, as well as Duba, Dubovic, Dubovka, Dubenec, Dublicza, with Duben and Düben which are common names in Prussia, and Potsdam, near Berlin (see p. 227), are all called from the oak. From the Russian *berésa*, the ' birch' (Old Slavonic *breza*), we have the rivers Beresowka and Beresina, the last an accommodated form of the Greek Borysthenes (see p. 67). Bresegard is 'birch town,' Priebus in Silesia is 'birch house,' Presinitz in Bohemia is 'birch village.' We have also six places called Breesec, as well as Britz, Bresow, Briesnitz, Beresek, Bries, Beresoff, Briesen, Berezow in Galicia, Berezov and Berezna in Russia. To *brasa*, the Wendish form of the word, we may refer Braslef and forty other places in Germany.

The adjectival form *bukowy*, ' buccny,' is formed from the Old Slavonic *buky*, Czech *buk*, a 'beech-tree,' whence the Austrian province called the Bukovina (see p. 78), or 'beech land.' In Prussia there are twenty-two places called Buckow, as well as Bukow in Mecklenburg, to which we may add Buk in Posen, Bukovacz and Buken in Hungary, Bukowosko in Bohemia, and many other names elsewhere, as Bukowa, Bukowice, Bukowitz, and Bockwitz. From the 'white beech,' called *grabu* in Old Slavonic, *grab* in Polish, and *habr* in Czech, we have Grabow, Grabowna, Grabina, Gabre, Gaberk, Gabernik, Grabkow, Grabitz, and Grabig. From *vrba*, *verba*, or *werba*, a 'willow,' we have Werben, a town in Prussia, Verbas, a Bosnian river, and many other names, as Werbnov, Verbovo, Verbovac, Verbica, and Verbace. Tismitz, Tissa, and Tisina are from *tis*, a 'yew,' and Jessen, Jessern, Jasen, Jasenik, Jasionow, Jesenica, and Jessnitz from *jesin* or *jassen*, an 'ash-tree.'

From *sliva*, a 'plum-tree,' we have Slivina, Slivno, and Slivniak. Names from *topol*, a 'poplar,' are liable to confusion with those from *tepel*, 'warm,' which usually attach to places with hot springs, but Topola, Topolau, Topoly, and Topolnice are doubtless from the former source. The Wendish *wolscha* or *oelza* an 'alder,' Ruthenian *olcha*, Polish *olsza*, Servian *jelsa*, are the source of many names, such as Olsnitz in Saxony which stands on the River Elster, whose Slavonic name was Wolschinka, 'alder-tree river,' Oels in Silesia, which stands on the Oelse, another 'alder-tree river,' Wolschau, Wolchen, Olchowa, Olchowiec and Olesza in Galicia, Olszany, Olesnic, Olschi, Jelsa, and Jelsovik.

Glogau in Silesia, anciently Glogów, is the 'place of whitethorn,' from the Polish *glog*, 'whitethorn,' whence we have also Glognitz, Glogoviza, and other names. Tarnograd, 'thorn castle,' Tarnopol, 'thorn field,' Tarnogora, 'thorn hill,' Tornau, Tornow, Tarnow, Tornitz, Türnov, Terne, Ternova, Ternjak, Tarnowce, and Tarnowitz are to be referred to *tarn* or *tarnik*, a 'thorn-tree.' Gablenz, a common name in Prussia, is from *jablon*, an 'apple-tree,' whence also Gablona, Jablonetz, Jablona, Jablonka, Jablunka, Jablon, Jublon, Jablonow, and Jablonec. From *jawor*, a 'maple,' come Jawer in Silesia, Jauer, and Jauerwitz. In Czech a maple is *klen*, whence Klenak, Klenau, Klenovica, Kleny, and Klenovik. A hazel is *laska* in Polish, and *liska* in Czech, whence Leskau, Leska, Leskowitz, Lisko, and Laskowa. The lime, *lipa*, gives a name to Leipzig, and to 600 places in Germany, with many more in Eastern Europe, among them Lipa, Lipau, Lipkov, Lipnik, Lipsk, Liepe, and Lipnitz (see p. 170).

From *rogocha*, *rogoz*, or *rohoz*, rushes, reeds, or water-plants, we have Rogoza and Rohova, with Rogattazn in Poland, Rogozno in Posen, and Rogatchev in Russia. Praprot, Prapetna, and Prapatnica are from *praprot*, *praprat*, or *prapet*, 'fern.' Zittau in Saxony is a German corruption of the Slavonic name Chytawa, from *zyto*, green corn or rye, and Seddin and Settin are referred to the same source. Werben on the Elbe is from the Wendish *werba*, pasture, and Traunik and Trawitz from *trawa*, grass.

From the Wendish *sweré*, a wild beast, Old Slavonic *zvér*, we have Schwerin (see p. 253), the capital of Mecklenburg Schwerin, and Schwersentz in Posen. Volhynia is the Latinised form of the Polish name Wolyn, which signifies the 'land of cattle,' from *wol*, an ox, which is the source of numerous names primarily denoting inclosures for cattle, such as Wollin at the mouth of the Oder, Wolla, Wohlau, and Wollau. From the Old Slavonic *svinija*, swine (Czech *svine*), we have Swina, Swinarek, Swinsko, and many more. There are two groups of Siberian islands which are called Medveji Ostrova, the 'bear islands.' Cape Medweschi is 'bear cape,' Medzibor in Silesia is 'bear forest,' which, as well as Medvedak, Nedvezi, and Niedzwiada, are from *medved* or *nedved*, a 'bear.'

The wide diffusion of the beaver (Russian and Polish *bovr*, ~~~ .. . ʲ ɪɪɪ Eastern Europe is shown by the number of names derived from it, such as Bobersberg in Brandenburg on the River Bober ; another Bober river in Silesia, the Bobrka or 'beaver river' in Galicia, Bobritsch in Saxony, Bobrocz in Hungary, Bobrov in Russia, Bobrow in Moravia, Bobrinetz and Bobruisk in Russia, as well as Boborow, Bobera, Bobrau, and Boberwitz.

To *koza* or *kosa*, a goat, *kosel*, a stag, or *kosuta*, a hind, we may refer the names of Koslin in Pomerania, the River Koselo, a lake called Kozjak, and places called Kozy, Kozica, Kosutina, Kozli, and Kozlow, while Lossewo, Lossewa, Lossenki, and Lossino are from the Russian *loss*, Polish *los*, a 'stag'; Lisowic, Lissagora, and Lisicina from *lis* or *lisika*, a fox ; Vlkow, Wlkonic, and Wilcza Gora, the 'wolf mountain,' are from *vlk*, a wolf. From *krak*, a raven, either directly or through a personal name, we have Krakov, Krakovcic, and Krakowan.

From *golb* or *gulb*, a dove, we have Gulben, Güben, and Golembki ; from *rak*, a crab, Rakov, Rakwitz, and Rakowa ; and from *ryba*, fish, Rybna, 'fish river,' Ribnica, Rybnik, and Ribniza, denoting fish-ponds, with Rybenitz, Rybinsk, and Riba.

We have already met with numerous names exhibiting the suffix *-witz* or *-ves*, which is as common in Slavonic names as *-ton*, *-ham*, or *-by* in England, being derived from the word *vas*, *ves*, or *vez*, a 'village.' We find it alone, or as a diminutive, in the places called Vesce, Wesce, Vesca, and Vesnica, Nova-Was and Nova-Wies corresponding to our English Newton, and Knezeves to our Princeton. Liable to be confused with this is *wiki*, *wice*, or *wisek*, a 'market-town,' whence the names of Zwickau in Saxony and in Bohemia, and of several places called Wieck. Jazlowiec, in Galicia, is the 'market-town on the marsh.' Torgau on the Elbe, and such names as Torgelow in Pomerania, Targowitz, Torgowitz, and Torgovitza are from *torgau*, a 'market-place.'

A settlement or seat is *sedlo* or *selo*, whence Sedletz, Sedl, Sedlo, Sela, Siela, Selze, Sedlatitz, and Sielnica. Zarskoi Sselo, 'the seat of the Czar,' is an imperial palace near St. Petersburg. Stanow, Stanowitz, Stanowna, and Staniza are from *stan*, a hut or dwelling. From *bus*, a building or dwelling, we have such names as Dobberbus, the 'good dwelling,' Putbus, equivalent to our Netherby, Trebus, the 'three houses,' Lebus and Kottbus. Bautzen, Budin, Budow, Budau, Budkau, and Buda are from *buda*, a 'hut,' or *budka*, a 'little hut.' Jassy in Roumania, as well as Jäschen and Jäschwitz are probably from *jaza*, a house.

Many frontier names, such as Straza in the Bukovina, Strassnitz in Moravia, Straschic in Bohemia, and Strasschische in Carniola, are from *strassa*, a watchtower. Mlyn, Mlyny, Mlinek, Mlynask, and many similar names in Eastern Europe, are from *mlyn*, a 'mill.' The Old Slavonic *plavu*, Czech *plav*, Wendish *plaw*, denote a place for floating logs, or a river down which logs are floated. Hence the names of Pleva, Plava, Plauen, Plaue, Plavic, and Plevna. Mostar (see p. 199), the capital of the Herzegovina, is the 'old bridge,' derived like Maust, Mostje, Mutz, Mustin, and Motzen, from *most*, a bridge. Dolgemost is the 'long bridge,' Priedemost in Silesia is the 'first bridge,' Bomst or Babimost means the 'fragile bridge,' literally the 'old woman's bridge.'

Ostrog in Volhynia, Ostrozec, and Ostroznik are from *ostrog*, which means primarily a 'wall,' also a palisaded place, and hence a fort or fortress, in which sense it is common in Siberian names. Thus Okhotskoi Ostrog is the 'fort on the Okhota' river. The Old Slavonic *grad*, a 'wall,' is the source of some of the most important Slavonic names. It is the Russian *gorod*, the Wendish, Polish, and Bohemian *grad*, *grod*, and *hrad*, with the diminutives *gradec* and *hradec*, which signify a castle, fortress, fortified place, or town, equivalent to the English borough or bury. In Russia we have the two Novgorods meaning 'Newcastle' (see p. 209), one of them, Veliki-Novgorod, 'great Novgorod,' was the cradle of the Russ; the other Nijni-Novgorod, 'lower Novgorod,' is the great emporium on the Volga. There is also a Novigrad in Hungary and in Russia; Belgorod, also in Russia, is the 'white fortress,' and Belgrad (see p. 65), the capital of Servia, is a southern form of the same name. Ekateringrad and Elizabethgrad were fortresses built by the Empresses Catherine and Elizabeth. Grodno in Russia, Hradec and Hradisch in Bohemia, Graudenz in West Prussia on the Vistula, and Grätz (see p. 137) the capital of Styria, are all fortified places. Königgrätz is a hybrid Slavo-Teutonic name. The Hradschin is the name of the royal castle at Prag. A stone building is *krem* or *krim*, whence the name of the Kremlin, the stone castle of the Tsar at Moscow. Similar names are Kremnitz in Hungary and elsewhere, Kremmen, Kremenetz, Kremmenaia and Kremenskaia.

The Slavonic *zerka*, *cirkev*, or *zerkwa*, a 'church,' is a loan-word from the Greek, the numerous places called Cerkovic, Zerkwitz, Zerkowitz, Zerknitz, or Zerkovo answering to the Northumbrian Kirby. Another Greek loan-word is Stavropol, the 'city of the cross,' the name of a town and government in the Caucasus, and of a town on the Volga where the Christian Kalmucks were settled in 1730. Several places in Russia are called Stavro, the 'cross.' Krestovaia, a river in Kamtchatka, is so called from the 'cross' erected in 1697 by the Cossacks at its mouth. Similar names are Krizna, Krizanka, Krizek, Cape Krestovi, and Krestovi Island on the coast of Siberia near the mouth of the Kolima. From the Czech *svaty*, Russian *sviatoi*, 'holy,' are Svaty Kriz, the 'holy cross,' in Carinthia and in Croatia ; Sviatoi Nos is the 'holy cape,' and Sviatiye Gori, a great place of pilgrimage, means 'holy mountains.' Several Russian towns called Troitsk or Troitskoi have gathered round convents or churches dedicated to the 'Trinity.'

From *pop*, a 'priest,' we have Popowitz, Popowo, Poppow, Poppendorf, and similar names, equivalent to the English Preston. From the Polish *król*, Wendish *kral*, a 'king,' we have Krolevetz in Russia, Kralowitz in Bohemia, Kralowka in Galicia, and Kralitz, Kralic, Kralka, Kraliewa, Krolow, which answer to our English Kingstons. From the Czech *knez*, a prince (Russian *kniaz*), we have Knezpol, the 'princes' field,' Knezdol, the 'princes' valley,' Knez in Hungary, Knezic, and Knezina. From *strela*, an arrow, come *strelici* or *strelitz*, an archer or hunter, whence the Strelitzi or life-guards of Peter the Great, and the town of Strelitz, which gives its name to one of the Mecklenburg duchies, as well as the places called Strelitzkaia, Strielinskaia, Strelna, Strelov, and Strehlen.

Zobten in Silesia, called Sabat in the twelfth century and Soboth in the thirteenth, refers to a market held on the Sabbath or Saturday.

There are a few names which are believed to be memorials of Slavonic heathendom. Ratibor is supposed to have been a forest sacred to Razi, Juterbogk to have been named from a temple dedicated to the god of spring, Mittau from a temple of Mita, another Slavonic deity, and Sviatskaia is believed to mark the site of a temple of the god Sviativid.

PART V

French Village Names

In France, as elsewhere, village names are largely derived from the personal names of early possessors of the soil. The personal name is either followed by a possessive suffix, or by some word denoting the nature of the possession, such as *-court*, from *curtis*, which originally denoted an enclosure for animals, then a farmstead, and lastly a country-house. A familiar instance is that of Agincourt, but there are others whose ancient forms are known, as Rembercourt, called *Raginberti curtis* in 848 ; Bettancourt, formerly *Bettonis curtis* ; Liencourt, formerly *Leonii curtis* ; and Magnicourt, formerly *Manii curtis*.

More usual is *villa*, now *ville*, which is the commonest of French suffixes, being found in more than a thousand village names in France, taking the form *wyl* or *weil* on the German frontier, and retained as *villa* in Italy, Spain, and Portugal. It denoted a tenement with the surrounding land, and in early documents interchanges with *mas*, *meix*, and *mex*, from *mansus* (the Scotch manse), which means the same, the diminutive *maisnil*, or *menil*, being from *mansionile*. Thus Gibeaumeix, called *Gibodi villa* in 707, appears in 965 as *Gibonis mansus*, whence the modern name. But *mansus*, although retained in such names as Mazas or Mansac, was usually replaced by *villa* as a suffix. Hence such names as Theonville, from *Theodonis villa*, Orgeville, from *Otgeri villa*, Flouville, from *Flogeri villa*, Ermenonville, from *Herminulfi villa*, signify respectively the house and land of Theodo, Otger, Hlodger, and Irminwulf. Grandville in Belgium, formerly Grenvilhe, the source of sundry English surnames, is a corruption of Gerenne-vilhe. Villiers, Villers, or Villars is usually from *vilare* or *villaria*, a word signifying a hamlet of a few houses, which on the Eastern frontier has become -*weiler*.

But these designations were commonly interchangeable with possessive suffixes of Celtic or Latin origin. Of these the most important is the Gaulish suffix -*acos*, Latinised as -*acus* or -*acum*. This formed adjectives, which after-wards became substantives, denoting the dwelling or possession of the person to whose name it was affixed. Thus we learn from Ausonius that his father Julius possessed a property which was called indifferently either *Villa Julii* or *Juliacum* (see p. 158). In like manner Chaouilley (Meurthe) is mentioned as *Chilulfi villa* in the eighth century, and in the eleventh as *Caulei-villa* and *Cheuliacum*, while Acquigni (Eure) was *Accini-curtis* in 844, and *Aciniacum* in 876. This Celtic suffix -*aco-s* corresponds in meaning to the Latin suffix -*i-anus*, with which it is frequently interchanged. Thus (fundus) Lucianus and (fundus) Luciacus, meaning the farm or estate of Lucius, are terms used indifferently to denote the same property. These possessive suffixes have usually become almost unrecognisable in the modern names. Thus Joigny (Yonne) is a corruption of *Joviniacum*, the 'estate of Jovinius,' probably of the Flavius Jovinius who in 364 A.D. was *magister equitum* under Valentinian ; and Payerne, Canton Vaud, was called in 962 *Paterniacum*, which signifies the property of Paternus or Paternius.

But these changes were not wholly arbitrary, since in various parts of France this suffix normally assumes special forms. In the South and in Brittany the syllable *ác* has usually been preserved owing to the accent falling upon it, *Albiacus*, the 'estate of Albus,' becoming Albiac, and *Calviacum*, the 'property of Calvus,' becoming Calviac. In Guienne, Auvergne, and the Lyonnais, owing to local phonetic laws, the suffix -*ac* became -*as*, -*at*, and -*a*, *Marciacum*, the 'property of Marcus,' becoming Marsas and Marsat, *Berciacus* becoming Berchat, while *Gisiacus* is now Gizia. In the Nord -*iacum* became -*ecque*, *Sperliacum* becoming Eperlecques. The same suffix becomes *é* in the West, *ey* and *ay* in the East and West, and *eu* and *eux* in the Burgundian region. In the centre of France the accent fell on the *i*, and hence *íacus* became -*i*- and *y*. As examples of these variations we find that *Floriacum* is now Fleuré, *Fiacum* is Fié, *Poliacum* is Pouilley, *Vinciacus* is Vincey,

Malliacum is Maillet, *Cassiniacus* is Chasnay, *Ursiacum* is Urçay, *Floriacus* is Fleurieux, *Ambariacus* is Amberieux, *Gaudiacus* is Jouy, *Antoniacus* is Antony, *Alligniacum* is Alligny ; while *Albiniacum* has variously become Aubinac, Aubeney, Aubigny, and Aubigné. In accordance with the rule we find that in different provinces the name *Cotiacum* has become Cussac, Cuissiat, Cusset, Cuissay, Cussay, Cussey, Coisy, Cuissy, Cossé, Cuzieu, Cuzieux, and Cuisia. *Sabiniacus* has become Savignac, Savenay, Savigny, and Sévigné ; *Aniciacus* has become Anisy, Anizy, and Aigné ; *Marcelliacus* is Marcilly, Marcillat, Marcillac, and Marsilly ; *Martiniacus* is Martigny, Martigné, Martignac, Martignat, and Martigna (see p. 189); *Latiniacus* is now Lagneu, and *Lucaniacus* is Loigny. *Tauriacus* is now either Tauriac, Thorey, Thoiré, or Thurey ; and *Tauriniacus* is Thorigné and Thorigny. The communes of Chaillac in the South, Chaillé in the West, and Chailly in the centre, are from *Calliacus*, the 'estate of Callius.' Charencey was the estate of Carantius, Choisy of Caucius, Clichy of Cleppius, Crécy, Cressy, and Cressac of Crixsius, Crépy of Crispius, Foissac and Foissy of Fuscius, Mailly of Mallius, Romilly and Rumilly of Romilius, Vitry and Vitrac of Victorius. This suffix is occasionally equivalent to the Latin -*etum* ; thus *Betuliacum* is used for *Betuletum*, 'a birch wood,' *Ratinacum* is the equivalent of *Filicetum*, a 'place of ferns,' and Madrid, in the Bois de Boulogne, is a corruption of *Madriacus*, a 'place abounding in timber.' Fontenoy (Meurthe) was *Fontiniacum*, perhaps from a proper name, while Fontenay (Yonne) was *Fontanetum*, signifying a place abounding in springs (see p. 127).

Names denoting the character of the vegetation had, as a rule, the suffix -*etum*, or in many cases the plural *eta*. The oak, French *chêne*, Old French *chesne* (dialectically *qien* and *chien*, Picard *quesnes*), has given rise to more French village names than any other tree. For an oak-wood we have the modern *chênaie* and *quenaie*, representing an older *casnetum*, *quesnetum*, *quercetum*, or *tannetum* (from *tann*, an oak). Hence we may explain such village names as Chenois, Chenay, Chenailles, Quesnoy, Quenay, Quennois, Quenne, Xenois, Tanay, Tannec, Tannois, Thenay, and Thenailles. In Béarn the dialectic name of the oak is *cassou*, whence the names Cassan, Chasnay, and Chassenay ; while *roboretum* from *robur*, gives Rouvray, Rouvroy, and Rouvret, and Jarrey, Jarret, and la Jarrie are from *jarro*, a special kind of oak. La Blaquière and la Blachère are from *blacha*, a 'young oak.' More than 200 names, such as Frassinet, Frasnay, Fresney, Franay, and Fraisnes are from *fraxinetum*, an ash wood ; Boulay, Boulais, and Belloy are from *betuletum*, a birch grove ; Châtenet, Castenet, Châtenay, and Châtenois from *castanetum*, a chestnut grove. One hundred and sixty names, such as la Fayette, la Fage, le Fay, Fagès, Feyt, Fou, and les Fayaux, are from *fagetum*, a beech wood (see p. 123), while the lime (*tilia*) explains Teil, Theil, They, Thil, Thilay, Thillières, and Thilleux. From *alnetum*, an alder grove, we have 100 names like Aulnay and Launay (called *Alnetum* in 1139), while *vernetum*, from the Celtic *vernos* (*gwern*), an alder, gives Verney, Vernet, Vernoy, and Vernon. From *salicetum*, a plantation of willows, we have Saulcy, Saussy, Saule, Sauliac, Saulx, and Sausses (see p. 241). Charme, Charmes, Charmoy (called *Charmetum* in 1070), and Chalmettes are from the hornbeam (*carpinus, carpinetum,* French *le charme*); Pinet, Pinay, and Pinas from the pine (*pinus, pinetum*). The elm (*ulmus, ulmetum,* French *orme*) gives Ulmoy, Olmet, Ormoy, Lormoy, Olme, Ulmes, Ormes, and Ormeteau. The aspen (*tremulus, tremuletum,* French *le tremble*) gives Tremblay and Tremel; and to the walnut (*le noyer*) we may refer Noyers, Nozay, and Nogarède. Cornet and Corneuil are from the dogwood (*cornuil-liers*). Coudry, la Coudray, and 240 similar names are so called from the hazel (*corylus, coryletum*), and Buxières, Boussey, and Boussière (called *Buxarias* in 862), from the box. From the maple (French *érable,* Armoric *arabl*) we have Arblay, Herblay, and Rablay. Apple orchards have given names to numerous villages, such as Pommerey, Pommiers, Pomay, and Pomaret, in addition to a few Celtic names like Avallon (see p. 56). Names denoting vineyards (*vinetum, viniacum,* or *vineale*) are naturally numerous, as for example Vigny, Vignol, Vignac, Vignon, Vignet, Vignolle, Vigneaux, and la Vignette. Ligniers, Lignières, and Liniers are corruptions of *linarias,* which denoted places where flax was grown or prepared. From *cannabis,* hemp, we have Chenevières (anciently *Canavarias*), Chanvre, Chenevrey, with Cambo and Cambon in the south, where *cambones* signified hemp fields. Espiers (called *Spicariæ* in 1040) and Epieds (*Spicarias* in 1031) derive their names from wheat (*spica*), Favières and Faverolles are from beans (*faba*); while Fougères, Feuchères, and Falguière were places overgrown with fern (*filicaria, fulgariæ*), and Cardonnet, Cardonne, and Chardogne with thistles. Roncières, Roussay, Rousset, and Roussey are from brambles (*roncia,* French *les ronces*). Some 200 names, such as Bruère and la Bruyère are from *brugariæ* (French *bruyères*); Epinay, Epineux, Epinoy, and Epine are from thorns (*spinæ, spinetum,* French *l'épine*), and Jonchère and Jonquière from rushes (*juncus, juncariæ*).

Many village names refer to wooded districts. La Silve, Selve, Sauve, Servas and Servais (Aisne), called *Silvagium* in 846, may be explained from the Latin *silva, silvacum,* or *silvagium*; Cailly, Chaley and Chailey point to the Celtic *caill,* ' wood '; while the Armorican *koat* or *koad* (Welsh *coed*), a wood, will explain Coetbo, les Couëts, Er Hoët, Coetmaen, and Coetmieux; the Low-Latin *boscus* (bush) or *bosquetus* explains le Bois, le Bosc, le Bost, Boissay, Boissy, Bouchat, Bussy, and Buxy. Barrault is a corruption of *Boscum Raaudi.* The Low-Latin *broca* or *brossa,* a place covered with brushwood, gives Brossay, Broussy, Broxelle, and Bruxelles, while from *brogilum* or *brolium* (French *breuil,* Italian *broglio*), an ' enclosed park for game,' we have Breuil, Bruel, Bruillet, les Brules, and many more. From *concisa,* ' a felled wood,' we have Concise, Conceze, and la Concie; and from *sartus* or *assartum,* a ' grubbed wood,' come Essart, les Essards, Assars, Certaux, and Essertaux; while Rhode, Roye, and Rœux are from *rode,* a Teutonic word of the same meaning. Hollebecke, formerly Holtbecke, Wormhout, and Houtkerque are from the Flemish *holt,* a wood.

From *pratum* or *pratellum* we have eighty-three names as le Prat, les Prats, le Pras, Prez, Prey, Pray, Prads, Pradel, Pradou, Bras, Brasles, Bré, Brec, Bréal, Préau, Presles, and Bresles. Premol is *pratum molle,* and Prabert is *pratum Alberti.* From the Low-Latin *bessa* or *baissa,* a low or marshy place, we have Baix, Bais, Besses, Bessey, Bessins, Bessons, and Bessac. From the Low-Latin *riparia*, which means a plain for hunting birds, primarily one on the banks of a river, we have Rivière, Rivery, la Rivier, and la Ripara. From the Low-Latin *olca* or *oschia* (French *oche* and *osche*), which denoted a cultivated piece of land amid forests, we have Ouche and Ouches.

Other names express the nature of the soil. The battlefield of Gravelotte, Gravelle, le Crau near Arles, Gravioc, la Grée and la Graverie are gravelly places, from a root ultimately Celtic, while Gresse, Grez, and Gressey signifying the same, are from the Low-Latin *gresum* (O.H.G. *griez*). Sable, le Sablon, and la Sablier (see p. 241), are sandy places (French *sable*), while Marne, Marné, Marle, Marly, and Morlay are from marl (French *la marne*), and Argilly, Argilliers and Argilès from clay.

The names from animals are not so numerous as in England. Asnières, called *Asinarias* in the ninth century, denoted an enclosure for asses ; Vaquerie and Vacherie were for cows ; Bouverie, Bouvets, Bouviers, and Bouvigny for oxen (*boveria*) ; Bergerie, Bergières, and Brevières for sheep (*bercaria*) ; Chevregny (called *Capriniacum* in 893), Chèvrey, Chèvres, Chevreux, Chabris, and Cabrials for goats ; Etaves, called *Stabulæ* in 1045, Establet and Etables, were stables.

Ferrières, near Paris and elsewhere, is from the Low-Latin *ferraria*, a 'smithy,' while Fabrèques, Faverges, Faur, la Faurée, Forge, and Forgues, are from *fabrica*, a smelting-house or forge. Tiles were made at la Tuilerie and Thuilières. Muison and Mudaison were *mutationes*, a name given to the post-houses on the great Roman roads, where horses were changed. Taviers in Belgium is from *Taberna* (see p. 273) ; Espiers, Epiais, and Epieds are from *spicarium*, a grange for storing spikes or ears of corn (see p. 264) ; Aire, Airel, les Aires, and Airon, are from the Low-Latin *aera*, *aria* (area), a threshing-floor. There are several villages, mostly in Burgundy, called Abergement, from the Low-Latin *habergamentum*, a habitation or house. Cambray, Cambre, and Chambre, are from *camera*, a house or chamber ; while from *casa*, a house, and its derivatives *casalis* and *casella*, we have Cas, Caze, Casal, Cazelles, Chaise, Chaʒoy, Chazelet, and Chazeuil. From *vicus* we have Vinneuf, formerly *Vicus novus*, as well as Neuvy, Vicnau, and Vichet. From the Low-Latin *foleya*, a pleasure-house, we have Feuilly, Feuilles, and la Folie-Herbault near Chartres, called in 1123 *Stultitia Herebaldi*.

Ferté, or Fermité, is a common French village name denoting a 'strong place,' from the Latin *fermitas*, or more directly from *firmitate*. From the Low-Latin *bastida*, a fortified place, we have Bastide, la Bastie, and Bastille, while from *castrum*, or the diminutive *castellum*, we have seventy-two French village names, such as Châtres, Castres, Cassel, Chastel, Castels, le Châtelet, Châtillon and Chatellot (see p. 90.) The Low-Latin *warenna* or *garenna*, a Teutonic loan-word meaning an inclosure for game, gives Varenne, Varesnes, and la Garenne, while the numerous places called Plessis, Plessin, or Plessie signify an enclosure surrounded by woven boughs ; and thirty-nine places called Mazère, Mezeray, Mazeras, Mazerolles and the like, are referred to the

Low-Latin *maceriæ*, which signifies a garden or vineyard surrounded by a wall.

Chaumont, a common village name, appears in early documents as *Calvus mons*, the bald mountain; corresponding to the Italian Monte Calvo. Le Montheu was *Mons acutus* in 875. Montigny, Montaigné, and Montagnac are names of the same class, while Le Moncel, Moussel, and Monteil are from *monticellus*, a little mountain. Le Puy, Puget, and Poey are from the Latin *podium*, which came to mean a ridge or elevation (see p. 229). Champagne, Champigny, Champey, and Champel are from *campus* or *campellus*, and La Frette, Frettes, Fretoy, and Fretin from *frecta* or *freta*, which signifies uncultivated land ; while to *magus*, the Celtic word for a plain, we may refer names like Maing and Magnac, as well as Rouen, formerly *Rotomagus*, and Riom, formerly *Ricomagus*. Meung-sur-Loire was formerly *Magus*, and Cranton near Cahors was *Carantomagus*, the field of a person called Carantos.

From the Latin *strata*, whence the English street and the Italian *estrada*, we have Lestret, Estrade, Estra, Etrées, and Estrée, while the names of Poncey, Poncet, Poncelle, Pons, Pont-Audemer, Pont-à-Mousson, Pontoise, and Pont de l'Arche, are derived from bridges (see p. 226). La Planquay, les Planches, and Planchette were named, like County Clare in Ireland, from bridges formed by planks thrown across a brook. Boué was formerly *Bonum vadum*, like our English Bungay ; and le Gua, le Gué, Vay, and many similar names are also from fords. Aix (see p. 40) is from *aquis*, and Maupas (Aisne) may compare with Malpas in Salop (see p. 185.) Courbevoie, near Paris, is a corruption of *Curva Via*, the crooked road, and Treviers was called *Tres viæ* in 1280. Vanoise (Nièvre) was formerly *Vallis noxia*; Sexeles was *Sicca vallis* ; Champenoux was *Campus Spinosus* ; Montjoux was *Mons Jocosus* ; Entrains was *Interamnium* in the second century, *Interamnis* in the sixth, and *Interannis* in the twelfth. From the suffix *-gilum*, which seems to have meant a water-course of some kind, we have *Arcogilum*, now Arcueil, *Antogilum*, now Anteuil, *Altogilum*, now Auteuil, *Argentogilum*, now Argenteuil, *Spinogilum*, now Epinay-sur-Seine, *Diogilum*, now Deuil, *Riogilum*, now Rueil, *Bonogilum*, now Bonneil, and *Vinogilum*, now Vignols.

French villages often bear simply the name of the patron-saint, which is usually recognisable in the modern form, as in the case of St. Pierre, St. Maurice, or Ste. Agnès, but is occasionally so disguised as to be inexplicable without documentary evidence as to the older forms. Thus Ste. Aulaire and Ste. Eloi are S. Eulalia, St. Berain is S. Benignus, St. Branché is S. Pancratius, St. Brès is S. Brixius, St. Bris is S. Priscus, St. Calais is S. Carileffus, St. Celerin is S. Serenicus, Ste. Cerise is S. Sirica, St. Chaffre is S. Theothfredus, St. Chef is S. Theuderius, St. Chinian is S. Anianus, St. Cloud is S. Clodoaldus, St. Cyr, St. Cirq, and St. Chartres are S. Cyricus, St. Cyran is S. Sigirannus, St. Dizier and St. Géry are S. Desiderius, St. Escobile is S. Scubiculus, St. Estève and St. Esteben are S. Stephanus, St. Eusoge and St. Haruge are S. Eusebius, St. Ferjus and St. Forget are S. Ferreolus, St. Galmier is S. Baldomerus, St. Gengoux is S. Gengulphus, St. Gilles and St. Gely are S. Ægidius, St. Hellier and St. Ylie are S. Hilarius, St. Jory and

Y

St. Jores are S. Georgius, St. Léger is S. Leodegarius, St. Lezer is S. Licerius, St. Lot is S. Laudus, St. Malo and St. Maclou are S. Maclovius, St. Mard is S. Marcus, St. Mard, St. Mars and Cinq-Mars are S. Medardus, St. Mayme is S. Maximus, St. Moré is S. Moderatus, St. Mury is S. Mauricius, St. Nitasse is S. Anastasia, St. Nom is S. Nonnius, Ste. Offange is S. Euphemia, Ste. Olive and Ste. Allire are S. Illidius, St. Oyen, St. Yan and St. Héan are S. Eugendus, St. Oury is S. Udabricus, St. Parize is S. Patricius, St. Pey and St. Péare are S. Petrus, Ste. Pole is S. Paulus, who, like S. Illidius and S. Anastasia, has changed his sex, St. Polgues is S. Sepulchrum, St. Pons and St. Point are S. Pontius, St. Priest is S. Prejectus, St. Python is S. Piatus, St. Saens is S. Sidonius, St. Saire and St. Saulge are S. Salvius, St. Simple, St. Souplet and St. Sulpin are S. Sulpicius, Ste. Solange is S. Solemnia, St. Sorlin and St. Sernin are S. Saturninus, St. Ustre is S. Adjutor, St. Xist is S. Quiritus, St. Ytaire is S. Eustadius, and St. Ythaire is S. Eptadius.

The church at Chamond or St. Chamond (Loire) was founded in the seventh century by St. Annemundus or Ennemond, Archbishop of Lyon. The *Ch* is due to the prefix *Sanctus*, locally pronounced *chanctu'ch*; Chanctu'ch Annemond becoming Chamond. So Sanctus Amantius became Chamand, whence the village names of Saint Chamand (Cantal) and Saint Chamas (Bouches-du-Rhône). Dammartin and Dommartin are the names of several French villages whose churches are dedicated to St. Martin of Tours, Domnus Martinus. So Dammarie and Dommarie are from Domna Maria, Domaloain is Domnus Alanus, Domvallier is Domnus Valerus, Damplou is Domnus Lupus, Domptail is Domnus Stephanus, Doncières is Domnus Cyriacus, Domcevrin is Domnus Severinus, and Dammard and Damas are both Domnus Medardus, Dampière, Dompière, and Dompaire being from dedications to Domnus Petrus (see p. 103).

The names of imaginary saints have sometimes been evolved out of place names. Thus Saint-Plovoir in Belgium is from *simplex-via*, which became Semplovei, Semplovoir, and finally Saint Plovoir, while Saint Fontaine is from *Terra de centum fontanis*. St. Peraville is a corruption of *S. Petrus in Villa*, St. Peravy of *S. Petrus in Via*, St. Tron of *Centro*, St. Igny and St. Ignet of *Sentiniacus*, and St. Remimont is *S. Remigii mons*. The contrary sometimes happens, and the saint-name has been effectually disguised. Thus Sandweiler in Luxemburg is a corruption of Sanct-Valer, Samer of S. Vulmarus, Strenquels of S. Tranquillus, Senneterre of S. Nectarius, and Sommecaise of S. Casius.

Coming to ecclesiastical edifices we have several names from *basilica*. Bazoches (Aisne) was *Basilicæ* in 1153, and from the same source came Bazeille near Sedan, Basoge, Bazeuge, Bazolles, and Bazoilles. Ouroux, Ourouer, Oradour, Loreux, and Orrouq are corruptions of *oratorium*. L'Eglise is naturally a common name, while Églisolles, Egriselles, and Glisolle are from *ecclesiola*. In Basque *ecclesia* becomes *eliza*, whence such names as Eliça-berria and Elissa-garay. From *monasterium* and *monasteriolum* we have numerous names, such as Moûtier, Moûthiers, Munster, Monestier, Montreux, Montreuil, and Musturole (see p. 195). In Brittany hermitages were distinguished by the prefixes *loc-* or *kill-*, usually followed by the name of a saint, as Locmalo, Locmaria, Locminé, Loktudi, with Quillignon, Quillinen, and le Quillio. Chaudé and Chandai, both corruptions of *Campus Dei*, were cemeteries. Locdieu was *Locus Dei*, and Dilo (Yonne) was *Dei locus*, while Montdaie (Calvados) was *Mons Dei*. A few pre-Christian names of this class survive : Famars being from *Fanum Martis* (see p. 123), Templemars and Talemars from *Templum Martis*, Alajou and Jouare from *Ara Jovis* (see p. 157), and Jeumont from *Jovis mons*. The names of the Gaulish deities Esus and Borvo are found at Oisemont from *Esi mons*, and Bourbon from *Aquæ Borvonis* (see p. 73). The capitals of the old Provinces mostly bear the names of the Gaulish tribes whose chief towns they were ; the names of Paris, Chalons, and Bourges, for instance, repeating the tribe names of the Parisii, the ' valiant' or well placed (see p. 217), of the Catalauni, 'glad to fight' (see p. 89), and of the Bituriges, the 'world kings (see p. 73). To this category, as already explained, belong also the names of Amiens, Angers, Arras, Bayeux, Beauvais, Cahors, Chartres, Nantes, Poitiers, Rennes, Rheims, Sens, Troyes, Vannes, and several more.

In addition to these great cities, a considerable number of village names, mostly in Brittany and the adjacent parts, are also from Celtic roots. Thus from *ker*, a ' village' (Welsh *caer*, Irish *cahir*) we have Kerbel, Kermarier, Kerdeff, Kergal, and Carheix. Carnac, however, is from *carn*, a cairn or heap of stones. From *bot*, a dwelling (Cornish *bod* in Bodmin) we have Botmel and Botsorhel. From *cab*, a cabin (Neo-Celtic *caban*, Low-Latin *capanna*, French *cabane* and *cabinet*) come Cabane, Cabanac, Chavanac, and Chavannes. In Bod-kneû or Bod-kanô, as well as in Ker-gneû or Ker-ganô, and Ros-kneû or Ros-kanô, we have the word *knaoun*, a ' nut-tree.' From *tref*, a village or habitation (Cornish *tre* in Truro and Tredegar), we have Treux, Treffrin, and Trevarn, while *plou*, a tribe, territory, or village, explains the names of Pleumeur, Plouec, Ploulech, Ploemal, and le Plouy. Balme and Baume are from *balma*, a ' cave,' whence also the Col de Balme near Chamounix. From *comba*, a combe or valley (Welsh *cwm*), we have Combas, Combet, and la Combe ; from *kon*, a 'hill between valleys,' we have Cognac, Coigny, and Cugny ; from *kember*, a 'confluence,' we have Quimper and Kemper (see p. 231) ; and from *condate*, which means the same, we have Condé, Cosne, Condat, and Condas (see p. 97) ; while Clapiers, la Clapy, and Clichy are from *clap* (Gaelic *clach*), a ' stone.' From *lann* (Welsh *llan*), a ' plain,' we have Lannbihan, Lannbel, Lannec, and Lanne, many names being also due to the Celtic *caill* and *koad*, a ' wood' (see p. 335).

From the Teutonic *stein* we have Steene, Steenbecque, and Steenwoorde ; from *wast* (Low-Latin *gascaria* for *wastaria* ; French *gâtine*), meaning waste or ravaged land, we have le Gast, le Gat, les Gats, Gastine, Gâtine, le Vast, and la Wattine. The Low-Latin *borda*, a house, is derived from the O.H.G. *bort*, O.N. *bord*, a ' plank ' ; hence the places called Bord, Bordet, Bordeau, les Bordiers, les Bourdeaux, Bordeaux-Saint-Clair. From the O.H.G. *bûr*, a 'cottage' (French *buron* a cabin) we have the names Bure, Bures, Buron, Burey, and Bœurs.

In Normandy we naturally find many names from Danish sources. A common suffix is -*tot*, answering to the English toft. Thus Yvetot means the toft or farm of Ivo, and we also find Prétot, Sassetot, Appetot, Plumetot, Valletot, Criquetot, and Routot. The suffix -*by* (Danish *boe*), so common in England, takes the form -*beuf*, the older forms showing that the final *f* is merely euphonic. Thus Quillebeuf, answering to an English Kilby (see p. 231), was formerly Kilbœ, Paimbeuf was formerly Pentebœ, Lindebeuf was Lindebue, Criquebeuf was Criquebœ, and we have also a Marbeuf and Quittebeuf. In Harfleur, anciently Herosfluet, as well as in Barfleur, Fiquefleur, and Vittefleur, we may recognise the Danish suffix -*fliot* (English *fleet*) denoting a channel (see p. 142). The O.N. *beckr* (English *beck*) is seen in Caudebec (Coldbeck) and Houlbec (Holbeck); *gardr* (English *garth*) in Fisigard (Fishgarth), and *thorpe* in le Torp.

PART VI

German Nomenclature

A brief notice of the chief elements in German local names may here suffice, partly because they have been admirably explained in such an accessible little book as Förstemann's *Die Deutschen Ortsnamen*, and partly because the greater number of German topographic words are identical with those used in England, and presently to be discussed. A good instance is the German *berg*, a hill, which is confused and interchanged with *burg*, a fortified place, a castle, or town, in the same way that the A.S. *beorh*, a hill, and *burh*, a town, are confused, both becoming *borough* or *bury* in modern English names. So *stone* (A.S. *stán*), as in Stanton, is the German *stein*, and the Dutch *steen*, as in Hauenstein or Lahnstein. It often refers to boundary stones, as at Staines; and in Germany and the Netherlands, and in the Flemish settlement in South Wales, though not in England, it denotes a stone castle. Among designations of uncultivated ground we have the O.H.G. *lôh*, which answers to the A.S. *léah*, now -leigh, a woodland pasturage, while *feld*, as in Feldberg, which denotes a more open tract, is the A.S. *feld*, now *field*, as in Sheffield. The O.H.G. *witu*, now -*wede* or -*wied*, as Langwieden, is the A.S. *widu*, afterwards *wudu*, and now *wood*, as in Woodford; and the German *holz* is the A.S. *holt*, denoting a copse. The usual German name for a forest is *wald*, as in Schwarzwald, which is the same word as the A.S. *weald*, as in Walden or Waltham. This is now *wold*, which has come to denote a more open tract, the word *wood* having replaced the older *weald*. The A.S. *hyrst*, now *hurst*, as Lindhurst, is the O.H.G. *hurst*, now *horst*, as Tannenhorst or Ellerhorst, which denotes a thicket or clump of trees. The A.S. *sceaga*, now *shaw*, as in Bradshaw, is the same word as *schachen*, which is used in Swabia and Bavaria to denote the remnant of a larger wood, as in Geisschachen. The O.H.G. *struot*, now *strod*, *strut*, or *struth*, as in Eichenstruth or Eschenstruth, signifying open ground overgrown with brake and bushes, is the A.S. *strod*, as in Strudwick or Stroud. The A.S. *gráf*, a 'grove,' does not appear in Germany, but *græf* or *graf*, a trench or grave, which we have in Gravesend, is the German *graben*, a ditch, which appears in several hundred names, as Mühlgraben or Coppengrave, and in the Netherlands as Vloedgraven or Bisschopgraaf. In the Netherlands we have also Delft and Assendelft (A.S. *delf*, a ditch), a word which does not appear in South Germany.

The German *matte*, a meadow, as in Alkemade, Zermatt, or Steinmatt, is cognate with the A.S. *mæd*, now *mead*, as in Runnymede. The O.H.G. *angar*, now *anger*, as in Rabenanger or Moosanger, also means a grassy field, corresponding to the A.S. *hangra*, a meadow, or village green, whence Ongar in Essex. This is not to be confused with the O.H.G. *hang*, a steep slope, as in Steinhank or Reilhäng, which is the English *hanger*, signifying a steep wooded slope. The German *hügel*, a hill, as in Haidhügel, is not related to the English *hill*, but is a diminutive of the O.H.G. *houg*, cognate with the English *howe*. The A.S. *hrycg*, now *ridge*, as in the Ridgeway in Wilts, is more common in local names than the corresponding German word *rücken*, which we have in the Hausrück and the Hundsrück. A more usual German word for a ridge is *balken*, as in Griesenbalken or Meesbalken, answering to the English *balk*, which in England is rare, except in field names. The A.S. *clif*, now *cliff*, as in Clifton or Trotterscliff, is the O.H.G. *cleb*, now *clippe*, as in Klebheim or Kleedorf. The Scotch *brae* is the German *braue*, as in Braubach or Brauweiller.

The German *boden*, originally meaning soil or ground, has come to mean a 'meadow,' as in Grasboden. It is the English *bottom*, as in Broadbottom, Sidebottom or Longbottom. The A.S. *haga*, English *haw*, signifying ground enclosed by a hedge, which we have in the places called Haigh, is the German *hag*, as in the Hague or Hildenhain, formerly Hildenhagen. The contracted form *hain*, as in Wildenhain, signifies a place overgrown with thorns. Another related word is the O.H.G. *heida*, now *haide*, as in Hohenhaid or Falkenheide, meaning a place overgrown with brushwood. It is the A.S. *hǽth*, now *heath*, as in Blackheath or Hatfield. The German *moos*, a marsh or moss, as in Tegernmoos, whence the Swiss diminutive *mösli*, reappears in England in such names as Chatmoss. The suffixes in such names as Edelsitz, Fürsatz, Elsass, Neusass, Neusiedel, Brockzettel, and Holstein, all from the root *set*, to sit, and denoting seats or settlements of some kind, are allied to the A.S. *sæta*, a settler, whence Dorset, Somerset, and Ambleside. The German *gasse*, a street (A.S. *geat*), is the O.N. *gata*, whence the word *gate* used for the streets of northern towns, as Micklegate or Stonegate in York. Our *street*, a Latin loan-word, is the German *strasse*, as in Strassburg, while the German *weg* has become *way* in English, as in the Fossway; their *brücke* is the A.S. *brycg*, now *bridge*, and their *-furt*, as in Frankfurt, is our *-ford*, as in Stratford, Bedford, and innumerable English names. A town at the 'mouth' of a river, as Plymouth, is similarly designated in German, as in Travemünde. The German *zwiesel*, the 'fork' of a river, as in Zwieselen, is the Northumbrian *twisle*, as in Birchtwisle. The German *bach*, a 'brook,' as in Schwalbach, is our *beck*, as in Pinchbeck and numerous northern names, while *thal*, as in Rosenthal, is our northern *dale*, as in Rochdale, Kendal, or Dalton; and the German *deich*, a 'bank,' is the A.S. *dîc*, a rampart, as in Wansdike. In many parts of Germany *heim*, a home, is as frequent in local names as the A.S. *hâm* is in England ; but the A.S. *ham* or *hom*, with a short vowel, is only found in the Frisian districts and along the coast of the North Sea, as in Hamburg. The English *stead* or *stede*, a 'place,' as in Hampstead, is the O.H.G. *stat*, a 'place,' whence the later form *stadt*, which has replaced *burg*, and is now used to denote a ' town,' as in Darmstadt or Halberstadt. The German *dorf*, a village, is the O.N. *thorp*, whence the suffix *-thorpe* so common in the north of England. The A.S. *bûr* (now *bower*), a ' chamber,' whence Burcott, is the O.H.G. *bûr*, a chamber or house, whence the later *buren*, a dwelling, as Amelsbüren. From the O.N. *bûa*, 'to dwell,' comes the German *bude* or *baude* (our *booth*), a hut or building, whence *büttel*, a ' dwelling,' as in Wolfenbüttel or Brunsbüttel, which is our *bottle*, *battle*, or *bold* (A.S. *bôld*, Frisian *blod*), as in Newbottle or Bolton. The German *kote* or *kothe*, a 'hut,' as in Hinterkothen, is the A.S. *cote*, as in Prescot ; and the O.H.G. *wîch*, now *wiek*, is the A.S. *wîc*, now *wich* or *wick*, as in Norwich, Harwich, Berwick, or Alnwick.

The common English suffix *-ton* does not occur in Germany, where it is replaced by *hof*, a word of the same meaning, occasionally found in England, as at Hove. The A.S. *hûs*, as in Lofthouse, is the German *haus*, as in Mühlhausen, corresponding to an English Millhouse or Milsome, where we have a German word for a ' mill ' which only appears in names of recent origin. The Greek loan-word *kirk* or *church*, as in Churchill, Kirkwall, or Selkirk, is in German *kirche*, as in Kirchditmold or Feldkirch, and the *minster* in Westminster is the German *münster*.

The adjectival elements of names also agree to a great extent in Germany and England. The German *breit*, ' broad,' as in Breitenbach, is the A.S. *brâd*, as in Bradford ; their *lang* is our *long*, the A.S. *lang* being retained in such local names as Langton ; the *mittel* in Mittelmark is the *middle* in Middlesex ; *lützel*, as in Lützelburg, now Luxembourg, is our *little*, as in Littlehampton ; *roth*, as in Rothbach, is our *red*, as in Ratcliffe ; and *neu* js our *new*. The tree-names largely agree, *buche* being a *beech* ; *dorn*, a *thorn*; *birke*, a *birch* ; *erle* is the A.S. *âlr*, English *alder* ; *binse* as in Binsfeld, is our *bent*, as in Bentley ; *eiche* is the A.S. *ac*, English *oak*, as in Acton ; and *esche*, as in Eschweiller, is an *ash* (A.S. *æsc*), as in Ashton.

Several A.S. words which in England have disappeared from common parlance, though surviving in topographic nomenclature, have been retained in the vernacular speech of portions, or even of the whole, of German territory. Conspicuous among such words is *ufer*, a shore or strand, which is the A.S. *ôfer*, now supplanted by shore, but preserved in such local names as Over near Cambridge, Windsor (A.S. *Windles-ôfer*), or Hever (A.S. *Heân-ôfer*). The German *snaid* (O.H.G. *sneida*), signifying a piece of land ' cut off ' or separated, as in Eckschnaid or Hinterschnaid, is the A.S. *snâd* or *snæd*, which appears in such names as Wipsnade or Snaith. The A.S. *rîthe*, denoting running water, survives in a few local names such as Leatherhead (A.S. *Leôdrithe*), Shottery (A.S. *Scottarith*) or Hendred (A.S. *Hennarithe*).

In North Friesland it is still current in the form or *ride*, or *rie*, while Reide is the name of numerous streams in Northern Germany. The A.S. *seath*, a 'stream,' which appears in such local names as Roxeth (A.S. *Hróces-seath*), is the German *sod*, M.H.G. *sôt*, a well or fountain, *i.e.* a place where water seethes or bubbles up, seen in the names Soden or Ostersode. The German *leit*, a watercourse, now obsolete, is the A.S. *láde*, as in Cricklade, which survives in our dialect word *lode*, used to denote the great drains in the fens.

Some English words, cognate or identical with German words, are used in a somewhat different sense. Thus the English brook (A.S. *bróc*) signifies a 'stream,' as in Cranbrook, while the German *bruch*, which is the same word, means a 'marsh,' or 'wet meadow,' as Eichenbruch. It is *broek* in Dutch, as Aabroek, *brok* in Low German, as Uhlenbrok, and *broich* on the Lower Rhine, as Grevenbroich. Our *burn* is the German *brunn*, *bronn*, or *brunnen*, a 'well.' The German *quelle*, a 'well,' corresponds to the O.N. *kilda*, which we have in Kilburn, Kilham, and other Northern names. The English dialect word *wath*, A.S. *wad*, a ford or wading-place, appears in such local names as Wath-upon-Dearne. The corresponding German word is *wat*, a provincial term signifying a shallow or ford, but as a topographic term *watt* denotes a holm or river-island, literally a place reached by wading, as Wurstenwatt. A river-island or sandbank is also denoted by *sand*, as in the names Neidersand, Nordsand, or Estesand. The O.H.G. *warid*, an 'island,' whence the suffix in Kaiserswerth, Donauwörth, Saarwerden, or Poppenwurth, is probably not connected with the A.S. *wyrth* or *wurth*, an 'estate,' as in Tamworth or Walworth, but in the Low German dialects the word *worthe* signifies an 'inclosed homestead,' the meaning in both cases being a guarded or protected place.

Some topographic terms are used in Germany which do not reappear in England. Among them is the suffix *-morgen*, as in Zehnmorgen or Nonnenmorgen. It is practically equivalent in meaning to the English acre, both primarily signifying the amount of land constituting a morning's work in ploughing. In those parts of Germany settled by the Thuringians a common suffix, hardly found elsewhere, is *-leben*, which occurs in about two hundred and fifty names, as Hadersleben or Ritzleben. It has been the subject of much discussion, but most probably means an 'inheritance,' that which is 'left behind' by a deceased person, whose name usually forms the first portion of the word. A similar suffix, also absent from England, is *-eigen*, a 'possession,' that which is one's own, as Ruhmannsaigen or Frondeigen. The word *gut* still denotes a property, and also appears in such local names as Salzkammergut. It is strange that we do not find in England the common German word *gau*, a province or district, as Aargau or Rheingau. A common suffix in German village names is *fleck*, a patch or spot of land, as Flecken, Pfaffenfleck, or Weisfleck, which does not appear in England. A word now obsolete, and found only in local names in the suffix *-esche*, which signifies a 'sowed field,' as Dannesch. The word *billig*, a level space or plain, is also confined to local names, such as Wasserbillig. The word *gaden*, which now signifies a room or apartment, is used in local names for a cottage, probably a one-roomed cottage, as Steingaden. In Westphalia and Hanover we find the suffix *-lage*, signifying a low-lying field, as Hondelage. A 'gorge' is -*kehle*, as Bergkehle or Langekehle. From the German verb *roden*, to grub up or root out, we have the topographic term *rode* or *rade*, a clearing in a wood, as in Wernigerode. In England this is found only in such local names as Huntroyd. The obsolete word *schwand* also denotes in local names a clearing in a wood, as Schwandorf. The word *schlag*, which is still in use, signifies a clearing in a wood effected by cutting down the trees, as Grafenschlag. When the clearing has been made by fire the living words *brand* and *brunst* are used, as Oberbrand, Neuenbrand, or Fernbrunst. Such a clearing is also denoted by *sang*, now obsolete, except in local names, as Absang (*cf.* our verb to singe). The suffix *-fang*, as in Aalfang or Entenfang, denotes a place where something is taken or captured. The word *lauf*, used for a rapid in a river, literally a 'run,' as in Braunlaup or Laufen, is the Dutch *loop*, as in Beekloop. The German *stad*, a landing-place or bank, as in Wallenstad or Stade, is the A.S. *stæth*, a shore or bank, surviving locally as stade or staith. It appears in Staithes, but is usually replaced by *hithe*. The word *bogen*, an elbow or corner, seen in Langenbogen, is related to the English *bow*, as in Bowness.

A few words, found in the topographic nomenclature both of Germany and England, are now obsolete in both countries. Chief among these is the O.H.G. *aha*, 'water,' which appears as *-ach* or *-a* in such local names as Erlach, Salzach, Fulda, or Werra. This is the A.S. *eá*, 'water,' which we have in Eaton, Eton, Cerney, or Mersey, and the northern names Greta and Rotha. The O.H.G. *hleo*, a 'hill,' now obsolete, but the probable source of Kirchlehen, is the A.S. *hléw* or *hláw*, a grave-mound or tumulus, common as *law* or *low* in such English names as Hounslow or Marlow. Golf players are familiar with the word *link*, while *linch* is still a local term for the ridges left in ancient plough-lands. This is the A.S. *hlinc*, a slope or ridge, as in the name Moorlinch, which is not the same word as the German *klinge*, signifying a hill or a narrow valley, which is cognate with the English *clough*. The A.S. *-hó*, a hock or heel, seen in Hoo, Hutton, or Holland, is not used in Germany; the word *höhe*, a height, being from another source. The A.S. *bearo* or *bearu*, dat. *bearwe*, denoting an oak or beech-wood producing acorns or mast for fattening swine, whence the names in -bere, -bear, and -barrow, though common in England is not represented in German names. While among the commonest of English village names are Knighton, Charlton, Chorlton, Carlton, and Hinton, which denote hamlets inhabited by servants, such names are curiously scarce in Germany, though occasionally we find places called Schalksdorf, Schalkendorf, Schallstadt, or Schalkheim, from *schalk* (O.H.G. *scalch*), a servant.

The numerous topographic names of Slavonic origin in Northern and Eastern Germany, such as Dubrau, Glienicke, Chemnitz, or Potsdam have been already noticed. Such names are naturally absent in England, where, on the other hand, we have many Celtic and Scandinavian terms unknown in Germany. One of these is the common suffix *-don* (Celtic *dún*), a hill, and the related suffix *-ton*, A.S. *tún*, which would correspond to the German *zaun*. The A.S. *denu*, now *den*, denoting a swine pasture in a sheltered valley, as in Tenterden and other Kentish names, is also probably Celtic, and is absent from Germany. Nor do we find the English suffixes *-by*, *-thwaite*, and *-toft* (German *zumpt*), which are due to Scandinavian settlement.

PART VII

ENGLISH VILLAGE NAMES

In the Glossary the names of the English counties, of the county towns, and of some other places of importance have been discussed, but something remains to be said respecting the component elements commonly found in the names of villages and the smaller towns. While the older forms of such names in Ireland and Scotland have been collected and explained, no attempt has been made to examine systematically those of England. The names in a few counties or districts of limited extent have been dealt with in monographs of greater or less excellence, and a few sporadic names have been explained in learned periodicals or in the Transactions of local Societies.

But for any general description of the ordinary elements found in English village names we have to fall back on a short essay by Mr. Kemble in the third volume of the *Codex Diplomaticus*, and on an Appendix to the *Rectitudines Singularum Personarum* in which Prof. Leo of Halle examined the names occurring in the first two volumes of the *Codex.*

A great difficulty in the way of any such attempt lies in the absence of an Index identifying the names in Mr. Birch's *Cartularium Saxonicum*, and in the unsatisfactory nature of the identifications of ancient names in the indices to the collections of charters published by Thorpe and Kemble, not to speak of the dubious authenticity of many of the charters themselves. Moreover, when dealing with the Domesday names, considerable uncertainty arises from the difficulty of getting behind the capricious orthography of the Norman scribes, and so recovering the probable form of the underlying Anglo-Saxon name. A good example of this difficulty is seen in Mr. Bradley's ingenious restoration of the older form of the Domesday name of Wormhill in Derbyshire (see p. 297 *ante*). Hence the materials for a systematic treatise on the topographic nomenclature of England are so defective that all that can be here attempted is to give a few examples from Domesday and the published charters of the older forms of typical names of frequent recurrence, so as to disclose the usual elements which enter into our village names, and the principles on which they have been constructed.

§ 1. *Survivals of Grammatical Inflexion*

In modern English the old case signs have been discarded, lingering only among the personal pronouns. Their influence is however apparent in the modern forms of many local names, which, owing to the meaning having become obscured, retain not unfrequently traces of the oblique cases in which they usually occur in ancient documents. In such documents, in Germany as well as in England, local names appear only exceptionally in the nominative case, being as a rule in the dative, governed by a preposition. This came to be omitted, and the name in the dative, either the singular or the plural, is treated as if it were an indeclinable nominative singular. The same was the case with Roman names, Aix for example being from *aquis*, and Amiens from *Ambianis*, both dative plurals. So in Germany the names Bergen and Baden, which are dative plurals meaning 'at the hills' and 'at the baths,' are treated as if they were nominatives in the singular. In the Saxon Chronicle the city of Bath is called *æt Bathum*, 'at the baths,' and afterwards *Bathum*, which is really a dative plural. Like Baden in Germany this dative plural might easily have been retained as the modern name, as has been the case in other instances, such as Bury St. Edmunds. The Anglo-Saxon *burh*, a walled town, would normally become burgh or borough in modern English, as in such names as Edinburgh or Peterborough, but the more usual form -*bury*, which we have in Salisbury or Canterbury, can only come from *byrig*, the dative singular. In the Chronicle the name of Canterbury occurs only once in the nominative as *Cantwara-burh*, but repeatedly in the dative as *Cantwarabyrig*, which is the source of the modern form of the name.

The preposition governing these cases has usually disappeared, but in a few somewhat doubtful instances seems to have been incorporated into the name. Thus Byfleet in Surrey is apparently the place 'by the fleet' or shallow stream of the Wey, as appears from the A.S. form *Bi-fleót*, which, however, might mean a 'side-stream' or backwater. In the Boldon Book Biddick in Durham is called *Bedic* and *Bydyk*, 'by the dike.' Bewick in Holderness is called in Domesday *Bi-wich*, the place near or by the *wíc* or inlet, now a marsh, whose former existence is also indicated by the name of the neighbouring village of Withernwick, called in Domesday *Widfornewic*, which, if not from a personal name, may incorporate the obsolete preposition *with-foran*, 'in front of,' which is analogous to *bi-foran*, which we retain in the preposition *before*. So Binney in Kent is called in an A.S. charter *Binnan-eá*, 'between the waters.' Twynham, the old name of Christchurch in Hants, appears in early charters as *Tweon-eá* and *Tweoxn-eá*, afterwards becoming Twyneham (Domesday *Tuinam*). It stands at the junction of the Avon and the Stour, whence the name *Tweon-eá*, 'at the two waters,' *tweon* being the dative of *tweo*, two. In the parallel form *Tweoxn-eá* we have the form which gives our word betwixt (A.S. *be-tweox*). More doubtful cases are Etton, Northants, A.S. *Et-tun*, 'at the tun,' and Ayton and Acaster in Yorkshire, called *Atun* and *Acastra* in Domesday, probably 'at the tun' and 'at the chester.' There is a place called Attwell in Salop, and an Etwell in Derbyshire, called *Etewelle* in Domesday, while Atlow in Derbyshire is *Etelawe*, 'at the grave-mound.' Abridge in Essex is apparently the hamlet 'at the bridge,' but the old forms *Affebruge* and *Affebregge* suggest that there may have been an 'off bridge' or side bridge, not on the main road, but, as is the case, on a side road. Allerton Bywater in Yorkshire is called *Alretune* in Domesday, but in 1284 it has become *Allerton juxta Aquam*, doubtless a translation of the vernacular descriptive designation which has come down to us as Bywater, and suggesting an explanation of the name of Attwaters in Kent.

In Yorkshire we find a number of names derived from the dative plural in -*um*, which in Domesday usually appears as -*un* or -*on*, and in the modern names has been frequently assimilated to the familiar suffixes -*holm* or -*ham*. Thus from *húsum*, 'at the houses,' the dative plural of *hús*, a house, we have the township of Howsham, in the East Riding, which appears in Domesday as *Huson*, while Housham in Lincolnshire is called *Husum* in the Hundred Rolls. Newsham, in the parish of Appleton-le-Street, is called in Domesday *Newehusun*, 'at the new houses.' Another Newsham, in Gilling Wapentake, is *Newhuson* in Domesday, and Newsham in Durham is *Newsom* in the Boldon Book. There are three Yorkshire villages now called Newsholme, a form which must have been derived from the dative plural, although in all three cases Domesday has the nominative plural *Newhuse*. In other cases the Domesday form is in the dative plural, while the modern name has reverted to the nominative singular. Thus there are three places in Yorkshire called Lofthouse, all of which appear as *Loctehusum* or *Locthusum*, in Domesday, while Loftsome, in the East Riding, which was called *Lofthusum*, still retains a vestige of the case ending. It may be noted that Lofthouse represents the Danish *lopt-hús*, which denoted a house with a loft or upper story, the mention of which shows that such houses were unusual. In Domesday Moorsholm in Cleveland appears as *Morehusum*, 'at the moor-houses,' while Wothersome, a name in which the case ending has not been assimilated, was *Wodehusum*, 'at the wood-houses.' Somewhat doubtful are the names of Huddleston in Yorkshire, called *Hunchilhuson* in Domesday, and Bewsholme, also in Yorkshire, in Domesday *Begun*, possibly 'at the bigs' (*bys*) or buildings, but the names Stenson and Milson may probably be regarded as corruptions of *Stanhusum* and *Mylnhusum*, 'at the stone-houses' and 'at the mill-houses.'

The dative plural of the A.S. *cot* or *cott* (O.N. *kot*), a 'cottage,' is *cotum* or *cottum*, which explains the name of Coatham in Durham, of which the earliest recorded form is *Cotum*, which afterwards became *Cothome*, and then Coatham. West Coatham, in Yorkshire, was formerly spelt *Cotum* and *Cottum*, 'at the cottages,' and a place now called Cottam was formerly *Cotum*. Cotton in Derbyshire, called *Cotun* in Domesday, explains the origin of the surname Cotton. Beadlam, Yorkshire, is called in Domesday *Bodlum*, 'at the bottles,' bottle being from *botl*, 'a timber building,' whence the names Newbold and Newbottle. There are two places in Yorkshire called Hillam, both of which appear in 1284 as *Hillum*, 'at the hills.' Ilam in Staffordshire is called *Hilum* in a charter of Ethelred, dated in 1004, though here the long vowel in the modern name presents a difficulty. Welham, a township in the East Riding, appears in Domesday as *Wellun* and *Wellon*, and in the fourteenth century more correctly as *Wellom* and *Wellum*, 'at the wells,' of which there are several, yielding a supply of water sufficiently copious to supply the waterworks of the neighbouring town of Norton. The suffix in Wellam, Notts (Domesday *Wellum*), has not, however, been assimilated to the familiar -*ham*. At Kilham in the East Riding the river Hull issues from the chalk hills in copious streams. The Domesday form is *Chillon*, and other early forms are *Killom* and *Kyllum*, which we may explain from the A.S. *cylum*, 'at the springs' or sources. Cowlam is a Yorkshire village which stands on the summit of the wolds, which are here crowned by conspicuous neolithic tumuli. In old documents the name is spelt *Cullum*, and in Domesday it is *Colnun*, the first form pointing to *killum*, 'at the knobs,' the dative plural of the O.N. *kúla*, 'a knob,' and the second to *kollunum*, the dative plural with the article, of the O.N. *kollr*, 'a summit.' Near Cowlam is a place called Croom, where two deep, crooked dales traverse the chalk hills. The Domesday name *Crognum* may be explained from *krógunum*, the dative plural with the suffixed article, of the O.N. *krókr*, a nook, bend, crook, or winding. In these, as in some other cases where the names are of Norse origin, the suffix may be the sign of the dative plural with the O.N. suffixed article. Laytham (Domesday *Ladon*) is probably from the dative singular of the O.N. *hladar*, 'a barn.' The name of Lathom House, which the Countess of Derby defended for four months against the forces of the Parliament, and which gives a title to an English earl, may probably be explained in the same manner. The same word is seen in the name of Lade, formerly *Hladir*, the old capital of the Throndhjem district in Norway, and as *lathe*, a barn, it still survives as a dialect word in the North of England. Kirkleatham, in Yorkshire, must be referred to another source, since it appears in Domesday both as *Westlid* and *Westlidum*, and as *Letham* in the fourteenth century. It may be from *hlid*, a slope or hillside, or perhaps from the O.N. *hlid*, a gate. From *hrísum*, dat. plur. of *hrís*, bush or brushwood, we have Riseholme in Lincolnshire, called *Risum* in Domesday, while Rysome and Rise in Yorkshire are both called *Rison* in Domesday, one of which has now thrown off the suffix which the other has retained. Thornholm, near Bridlington, is in Domesday *Thirnon*, 'at the thorns.' Askham is the name of a place in Notts and of two places in Yorkshire, all of which appear in Domesday as *Ascam*, possibly for *Ascum*, 'at the ashes,' while Acklam in Yorkshire is called in Domesday *Achelum*, which may be explained as *ác-healum*, 'at the oak slopes,' and Acomb was *Acum*, 'at the oaks.' Hallam, from which the district round Sheffield acquired the name of Hallamshire, is called in Domesday *Hallun*, probably for *healum*, 'at the slopes,' like Halam in Notts and Hallam in Derbyshire, called in Domesday *Halun* and *Holun*. The A.S. *holum* would mean 'at the hollows' or holes, which enables us to explain the names of Hulam or Holom in Durham, which is called *Holome* in the Boldon Book.

These names in the dative plural are easier to recognise than those in the dative singular, because the vocalic suffix in the latter case is more liable to disappear. There are, however, a few names, chiefly on the coast of Holderness, where, owing to false analogy or to assimilation, the suffix of the dative singular may have been retained. Thus Hornsea lies on the border of Hornsea Mere, to which the suffix *-sea* is supposed to refer. But Hornsea appears in Domesday as *Hornesse* and as *Hornessei*, forms which point to *nesi*, the dative singular of the O.N. *nes*, a nose or promontory. Hornsea would thus be the place 'at the ness' which here juts into the mere. So Kilnsea, near Spurn Head, is *Chilnesse* in Domesday, also meaning 'at the ness,'

Withernsea, near Hornsea, appears in Domesday as *Widfornessei*, which may be explained as *withforan-nesi*, 'in front of the ness,' *withforan*, as already explained, being an obsolete preposition which we have also in the name of Withernwick.

In the foregoing cases it is the case sign of the substantive which has left traces in the modern name, but there are many instances in which we may detect a vestige of the case sign of the first or adjectival component of the name.

Thus Newton, the commonest of English village names, normally appears in A.S. charters as *Niwantúne*, which is the dative singular. This has now usually been replaced by the nominative, in the same way that the datives Langandúne and Bradanforde have now become Langdon and Bradford. But occasionally the *n* of the dative case has been retained, as in the instances of the A.S. *Niwantune* in Wilts and Bucks, which are now Newnton, instead of the usual form Newton. An abnormal spelling is exhibited by Neenton in Salop, which appears as *Newentone* in Domesday. Not uncommon is the assimilated form Newington, the origin of which is made clear in the case of Newington, Oxon, called *Newintun* (for *Newantúne*) in a charter. In the case of Newnham, a name which occurs eleven times, the sign of the dative survives, as is shown by the old form *Niwanham* which occurs in Kent, Oxon, Northants, and Warwickshire. It is not only in names like Newnton, Newington, or Newnham that the sign of the dative is retained by the adjective, but also in such names as Hampton, Hanbury, Hampstead, or Hanley, where the medial *m* or *n* is usually due to the retention of the case sign of the dative of *heáh*, 'high,' which makes *heán* in the dative singular of the definite declension. Hampton (see p. 141) is usually a corruption of *Heántúne*, 'at the high *tún*.' So Hampstead in Middlesex, A.S. *Heámsteáe* (for *Heánstede*) is probably 'at the high place,' and Hanbury would mean either the 'high hill,' or the 'high town,' and as a matter of fact we find that Hanbury in Hants, Worcestershire, Gloucestershire, and Warwickshire, are called *Heánbyrig* or *Heánbyri* in A.S. documents, while Henley, Hanley, and Handley would mean the 'high pasturage,' Henley in Hants, Henley-on-Thames in Oxon, Hanley in Worcestershire, and Handley in Dorset appearing in A.S. charters as *Heánleáh*. Hennor in Herefordshire is probably to be identified with a place called in a charter *Heánofer*, 'at the high shore,' and Hever in Kent has been identified with a place called *Heánofre* in a charter of 814.

Patronymic or clan names not unfrequently appear in the charters in the dative plural. In the majority of instances the case sign has been thrown off; *Godelmingum* being now Godalming, and *Ciwingum* being Cheving, but its nfluence has occasionally transformed the name, destroying the patronymic suffix. Thus in Herts *Wellingum* has become Welwyn, and *Brahcingum* has become Braughin, while *Beadingum* in Gloucestershire is now Beden. A personal name forming the first element of a local name was in the genitive. As will be shown in the next section, traces of the genitive in -*s* very commonly survive, as, for instance, in such names as Amersham, Aylesbury, Rolleston, Burstock, Oswestry, Ellesmere, Silksworth, and

Evesham.   Of the genitive in *n* the traces are less persistent, including, however, such names as Banbury, Wembury, Bamborough, Lavenham in Suffolk,
Dagenham in Essex, and others presently to be enumerated (see p. 352).
Owing to the influence of assimilation the genitive in *n* has not unfrequently
lapsed into the patronymic suffix -*ing*; thus Bullingdon in Hants is a corruption of *Bulandún*, Chillington in Somerset of *Cylfantún*, and Huntingdon
of *Huntandún*.   Traces of the names of animals in the genitive singular are
seen in Hounslow, Gateshead, Ramsey, Gaddesden, and Cransley.

§ 2. *Personal Names*

In most countries, notably in England, Germany, and some parts of France,
personal names are the most usual source of local names.   Naturally the early
Teutonic settlers 'called the lands after their own names,' our village names
being usually the sole existing memorials of the unknown adventurers from
across the ocean, who, according to the Teutonic practice which Tacitus
records, either established themselves in the waste—discreti ac diversi, ut
fons, ut campus, ut nemus placuit—or took possession of the lands of British
owners.

In such cases the personal element of the name becoming meaningless in
after times has been so disguised by contraction or assimilation as to be
beyond recognition where the evidence of early documents is wanting.

Occasionally, as in the case of Édinburgh, Glasgow, Oswestry, Malmesbury, Chichester, Bamburgh, Bibury, Amesbury, Merthyr-Tydvil, Wolverhampton, Brighton, Bridgewater, or Montgomery, names already discussed in
the Glossary, we possess historical knowledge, more or less precise and trustworthy, as to the person from whom the name was derived.   This is
frequently the case with towns and villages which have acquired distinctive
suffixes derived from Norman lords who obtained the manors.   Thus Bolton
Percy and Wharram Percy were among the Yorkshire Manors which belonged
to the great fee of Percy, and serve to remind us that the Percys were a
powerful Yorkshire house before they obtained the Northumberland Earldom
and the wardenship of the Scottish march.   In the reign of Henry 1.
Melton Mowbray in Leicestershire belonged to the Mowbrays, from whom
also the great central plain of Yorkshire takes its name of the Vale of
Mowbray.   Burton Constable was the capital manor of the hereditary
Constables of Scarborough Castle.   From the twelfth to the fourteenth
century Ashby de la Zouch belonged to the family of La Zouch.   In 1213
Stanford, Essex, passed by marriage to Richard de Rivers, and so acquired
the name of Stanford Rivers.   The neighbouring parish of Willingale was
owned, when Domesday was compiled, by Hervey of Spain (*de Ispania*), and
hence it acquired its present name of Willingale Spain.   Thorpe-Arch or
Thorpe Arches, Yorkshire, obtained its distinctive suffix from Osbern de
Arcis, who holds it in the Domesday record.   Stanton-Harcourt, near Oxford,
passed by marriage in the thirteenth century to Robert de Harcourt.   We
learn from Domesday that Hooton Roberts, in Yorkshire, which as early as
1284 appears as Hoton Roberts, was held of the king *in capite* by Robert, son

of William. Such nominal affixes are found in every county, mostly commemorating families which have long passed away, or whose possessions have been merged in those of other lords.

In a few cases we have manorial names of more recent origin. Thus Audley End in Essex takes its name from the great house built by Thomas Audley, Lord Chancellor. Castle Howard, in the North Riding, was the new name given to Hindershelfe by Charles Howard, third Earl of Carlisle, and the neighbouring Duncombe Park is a distinctively Southern form inappropriately transferred to Yorkshire by the Duncombes, Earls of Feversham.

But cases in which historical recognition is possible are rare, though not unfrequently we recognise familiar Anglo-Saxon or Scandinavian names without being able to say that the place was called from any personage bearing that name who is known to history. Thus from the common Scandinavian name of Ivar or Ingvar, we have Jurby in the Isle of Man, formerly Ivorby, Irby in Lincolnshire and in Yorkshire, as well as Ivory in Lincolnshire.

The invaluable Domesday record often makes it possible to detect such personal names, as well as to correct errors into which it otherwise would be easy to fall. Thus it might be supposed that Adlingfleet and Adlington were names of similar etymology. But a reference to Domesday will show that while Adlingfleet is the 'creek of the Ætheling' or prince, Adlington was the *tún* of some person who bore the name of Eadwulf. To take a few instances of names now disguised beyond recognition, which may be detected by the Domesday record, we find that in Lincolnshire Addlethorpe was the thorp of Ardulfr, and Woolsthorpe of Ulfstan, while in Yorkshire Barlby took its name from Bardulf, Anlaby from Olâfr, Onlaf, or Anlaf, Ganthorpe from Gamel, Sewerby from Siward, Thirkleby from Thorkill, Thornthorpe from Thorgrimr, Tholthorpe and Thurlstone from Thorulf, Osgodby from Osgod, Gunby from Gunnr, Amotherby, now pronounced Amerby, from Edmund, Armthorpe from Ernulfr, Ellerby from Alward, and Foggathorpe from Fulcar. We also learn from Domesday that Burstock in Dorset was formerly *Burwinestoch*, that Bescot, near Walsall, was *Bresmundes-cote*, that Osmaston in Derbyshire was the *tún* of Osmund, that Woolfardisworthy in Devon, now locally pronounced Woolsery, as at some future time it will probably be spelt, was the *worth* or estate of Wulfheard, that Almesworthy in Somerset was the estate of Edmund, and Edington was the *tún* of Edwin. A Yorkshire manor called *Ianulfestorp* in Domesday, became *Ulvesthorp* in the fourteenth century, and is now Owsthorpe, a name whose etymology it would be vain to guess without documentary evidence. Alderley in Cheshire has nothing to do with alder-trees, but was the *leáh* or field of Ealdred, Abberley, Worcestershire (D.B. *Edboldlege*), was the field of Eadbold, and Ambaston in Derbyshire was the *tún* of Eanbald. *See* Edmonton and Epsom (pp. 116, 119).

The names in Domesday have frequently been so corrupted by the Norman scribes that no certain conclusions can be drawn from them. But when the name chances to be preserved in an early charter it is generally possible to detect the original form. Thus in Kent we find that Sibbertswold, now

pronounced Sheperdswell, was anciently *Swythbrihtesweald*, meaning the
wood of Swythbriht, while Harrietsham appears in documents as *Hærigeardes-
ham*, Aylesford as *Ægelesford*, and Aylesthorpe as *Æglesthrop*. In Buckinghamshire Aylesbury was *Ægelesbyrig*, and Amersham was the A.S.
Agmondesham. In Surrey Windlesham was *Hunewaldesham*, the 'home of
Hunewald'; in Gloucestershire Calmsden was *Calmundesden*, the swine
pasture of Calmund, and Dowdeswell was *Dogodeswell*. In Somerset Baltons-
borough was *Baldheresberg*, and Congresbury was *Cungaresbyrig*, the 'burgh
of St. Cungar,' who was buried there. Cuckamsley Hill in Berks was
Cwichelmeshlæw, the 'grave-mound of Cwichelm.' Wolverley in Worcestershire was *Wulfweardingled*; while from Wilburg, a woman, we have *Wil-
burgeham*, now Wilbraham in Cambridgeshire; and from the lady Ælfgyth
we have *Ælfgythe Cyric*, now Alvechurch in Worcestershire. In Salop
Albrighton was the *tún* of Ealdbricht or Aldbriht; Chelmick (A.S. *Cheil-
mundewik*) was the *wic* or village of Ceolmund, and Broseley, called *Bure-
wardesley* in a charter, was Burhweard's pasture. Bromsgrove in 804 was
Bremesgræf, the 'grove of Breme'; and in 722 Willenhall, Staffordshire, was
Willanhalch, the *healh* of Willa. From other charters we learn that Barlaston
and Burslem, both in Staffordshire, are corruptions of *Beorelfestun* and
Burwardes-lyme; while in Derbyshire Alvaston and Breadsall were called
Alewaldestun and *Bregdeshall*. Kynaston and Kinnerton in Salop are both
from the personal name Cyneweard, appearing in charters as *Kineverdeston*
and *Kinevardon*. Darlaston in Staffordshire was *Deorlafestun*, the 'tún of
Deorlaf,' and Harleston in the same county was *Heorelfestun*, the 'tún of
Heorowulf.' Dauntsey in Wilts was *Domecesíg*, the 'isle of Domec,' and
Hankerton, also in Wilts, was *Honekynton*. Beenham, Berks, was *Bennan-
hám*, the 'home of Benna,' and Kelvedon in Essex was *Kynleveden*, the
'swine pasture of Cynlaf.' Denchworth, Berks, was *Denicheswyrth*, and
Droxford, Hants, was *Drocelesford*. Shitlington, Beds, is *Scillingtune* in
a charter of 1066, in 994 Bilston was *Bilsetnatín*, the '*tún* of the *Bilsæte*,'
and Alconbury, Hants, is *Alkemondebiri* in the Hundred Rolls.

As in some of the foregoing instances, the genitive singular, in which the
personal names appear, has often left vestiges which may be traced in the
modern forms. Thus the A.S. *Daccanham*, the 'home of Dacca,' is now
Dagenham in Essex; *Feccanhom*, Worcestershire, which belonged to Fecca,
is now Feckenham; *Lauanham*, Suffolk, the 'home of Lava,' is now Lavenham; *Toccanham*, Wilts, the 'home of Tocca,' is now Tockenham; *Todanham*,
Gloucestershire, the 'home of Toda,' is now Todenham; and *Hædanham*,
Cambridgeshire, the 'home of Hæda,' is now Haddenham. But the *n*
of the genitive has often disappeared. Thus *Bleddanhlæw*, Bucks, is now
Bledlow; *Corsantun*, Wilts, is now Corston; *Eóppanwyllanbroc*, Oxon, is
now Epwell; *Teobbanwyrth*, Beds, is now Tebworth; and Bakewell, Derbyshire was *Badecanwylle* in 924. Vestiges of the genitive in *-es* are usually
more persistent than those of the genitive in *-n*. Thus *Belesham* and *Bodeke-
sham* in Cambridgeshire are now Balsham and Bottisham; *Beolmesthorp*,
Rutland, is now Belmisthorpe; *Corigescumb*, Dorset, is now Corscombe;
Doddesthorp, Northants, is now Dogsthorpe; *Eadesbyrig*, Cheshire, is

now Eddisbury; *Egonesham*, Oxon, is now Ensham; *Hunesworth* and *Egbaldeston* are now Handsworth and Edgbaston near Birmingham; *Sylceswyrth*, Durham, is now Silksworth; *Sidelesham*, Sussex, is now Sidlesham; *Rolfestún*, Staffordshire, is now Rolleston; *Posentesbyrig*, Salop, is now Pontesbury; *Ormisby*, Norfolk, is now Ormesby; *Fremesham*, Surrey, is now Frensham; Eddleston, near Peebles, was *Edolveston*, and Middlesborough, Yorks, pronounced Millsborough, was formerly *Medellesburghe*.

As a general rule the syllable *ing* is a patronymic, denoting in local names the settlement of a descendant or of the family of some person. Thus in the Chronicle *Ælfréd Æthelwulfing* denotes Alfred, the son of Ethelwulf, and *Pending* signifies the son of Penda. In the translation of St. Luke's Gospel, *Seth Adaming* is Seth, the son of Adam. So the Æscings were the royal family of Kent, the Azdings were the royal race of the Vandals, and the Bal'things of the Visigoths. That *ing* is a patronymic is the rule, but occasionally it has a topographic significance, the men of Kent being called *Centings*, the men of Britford are *Brytfordings*, the men of Bromley *Bromleagings*, while the *Catmæringas* are the men of Catmere, the *Coedmawr*, or 'great forest,' and *Orkneyingar* is the name given to the men of Orkney. We also find Dartington on the Dart, Torrington on the Torridge, Leamington on the Leam, and Ermington in the valley of the Erme, just as in Germany we have Bodungen on the Bode, or Tyrungen on the Tyra.

The syllable *ing* is sometimes merely the equivalent of the genitive or possessive, which is also the generative case. Thus *Æthelwulfinglond* is equivalent to Æthelwulfeslond, the 'land of Ethelwulf'; Alfreton, Derbyshire, was *Ælfredingtún*, equivalent to Ælfredestun, the '*tún* of Alfred'; Barlavington was *Beorláfingtún*, 'the *tún* of Beorláf'; Wool-Lavington, Somerset, was *Wulflávingtún*, the '*tún* of Wulfláf'; and Woolbeding, Sussex, was *Wulfbædingtún*, the '*tún* of Wulfbæd.' The true patronymics are not always easy to distinguish. They may generally be recognised by being in the plural, either without a suffix in the nominative or dative, or in the genitive followed by a suffix such as -*tún* or -*hám*. But even in these cases we meet with uncertainties, as the sign of the genitive plural is specially liable to fall out in charters carelessly written, or in those of late date. Thus Lakenheath, Suffolk, is called *Lakingheth* in a charter of Cnut, and *Lacingahith* in a somewhat earlier charter of Eadmund. Walsingham, Norfolk, is written *Walsinghám* in a charter which must be later than 1055, and *Wælsingahám* in one of earlier date. Hence many names which we first meet with in charters comparatively late may be really patronymics, though there are no means of actually determining whether they are so, or are merely possessives. To take a few examples which are undoubtedly tribe names or patronymics we have from nominatives plural Birling, A.S. *Bærlingas*; Cooling, A.S. *Culingas*; Halling, A.S. *Hallingas*; Malling, A.S. *Meallingas*, all in Kent. In Sussex we have Brightling, A.S. *Byrhtlingas*; Ditchling, A.S. *Dicelingas*; Patching, A.S. *Pæcingas*; Steyning, A.S. *Stæningas*. In Surrey we find Poynings, A.S. *Puningas*; Eashing, A.S. *Ascengas*, also *Æscingum* in the dative plural; Tooting, A.S. *Totingas*; Woking, A.S. *Woccingas*; and Wittering, A.S. *Wihtringas*. In Essex we have Barking, A.S. *Berecingas*; in Middle sex Yeading, A.S. *Geddingas*, also in the dative plural *æt Geddincggum* ; in Gloucestershire Avening, A.S. *Æfeningas*, and also in the dative plural *to Æfeningum* ; in Hants Worting, A.S. *Wyrtingas* ; and in Oxon Bensington, A.S. *Banesingas.*

Occasionally we have forms apparently in the genitive singuiar, but these, if they occur in late charters, are more probably nominative plurals.   Instances are Charing, Kent, A.S. *Cerringes* ; Tarring, Sussex, A.S. *Terringes* ; Roothing, Essex, A.S. *Rodinges* ; and Terling, Essex, A.S. *Terlinges* ; while Worthing, Sussex, is *Ordinges* in Domesday.

Among the dative plurals we have Angmering, Sussex, A.S. *Angermeringum*, also *Angemæringtun* ; Godalming, Surrey, A.S. *Godelmingum*, a patronymic from Godhelm ; and Reading, Berks, A.S. *Reddingan*.   The dative plural, instead of disappearing as in the foregoing cases, has often come down curiously disguised.   Thus, as already mentioned, Beden, Gloucestershire, was formerly *Beadingum*, manifestly a dative plural ; Welwyn and Braughin in Herts being *Wellingum* and *Brahcingum*.   The ancient forms of nearly a thousand of the German patronymic names are known.   The usual terminations are *-ingum*, *-ingun*, *-ingan*, or *-ingen*, which are dative plurals, or *-inga*, the dative singular.

The most general test of a patronymic is when we have the genitive plural *-inga* followed by some such syllable as *-ton* or *-ham*.   Such are Catherington, Hants, A.S. *Cateringaham*, the 'ham of the Caterings' ; Gillingham, Dorset, A.S. *Gillingaham* ; Mottingham, Kent, A.S. *Modingaham* ; Hoddington, Hants, A.S. *Hodingatun* ; Waldingfield, Suffolk, A.S. *Wældingafeld* ; Effingham, Surrey, A.S. *Effingeham* ; Beddingha n, Sussex, A.S. *Beadingaham* ; but Beddington, Surrey, is *Bedintun*, probably a possessive ; Coldred, Kent, is *Colredinga gemere* ; Keston, Kent, is *Cyŝtaninga mearc* ; Lakenheath, Suffolk, is *Lacingahith* ; Pangbourne, Berks, is *Pegingaburn* ; Petworth, Sussex, is *Peartinga-wyrth* ; Rainham, Kent, is *Roegingaham* ; Athelney, Somerset, is *Æthelinga-ig* ; Wateringbury, Kent, is *Wothringaberan* ; and Lastingham, Yorks, is called *Lastinga-eu.*

In some of the cases just enumerated, such as Pangbourne, Petworth, Rainham, or Welwyn we should not suspect the existence of a patronymic if we did not possess the ancient form of the name.   The syllable *-ing* has not unfrequently disappeared in the modern name.   Thus Patton, Salop, was *Peattingtun* ; Kemerton, Gloucestershire, was *Cyneburgingctun* ; Powick, Worcestershire, was *Poincgwic* ; Troston, Suffolk, was *Trostingtun* ; Chilbolton, Hants, was *Ceobaldingtun* ; Grittleton, Wilts, was *Grutelingtone* ; Elton, Hunts, was *Ayllington* ; Mongeham, Kent, was *Mundelingham* ; Nettleton, Wilts, was *Netelingtun* ; Peckleton, Leicestershire, was *Pakintun* ; Frittenden, Kent, was *Efrethingdenn* ; Wolverley, Worcestershire, is *Wulfweardig lea* in one charter, and *Wulferdin leh* in another ; Harden Huish was *Heregeardinge hiwisc* ; and Wantage, Berks, appears in Ælfred's will as *Waneting.*   On the other hand the syllable *-ing* is sometimes intrusive, either replacing an equivalent genitive or from assimilation.   Thus Billingsley, Salop, was A.S. *Bilgesley* ; Seckington, Warwickshire, was *Seccandun* or *Sæcandun* ; Bullington, Hants, was *Bulandun* ; Chadlington, Oxon, was

Cadandun ; Chillington, Somerset, was *Cylfantun* ; Edington, Wilts, was *Ethandun* ; Allington, Wilts, was *Ellendun* ; Abingdon, Berks, was *Æbbandun* ; Aldington, Worcestershire, was *Aldandun* ; Harvington, Worcestershire, was *Hervertonne* ; Itchington, Warwickshire, was *Icenantun*; Wennington, Hants, was *Wythentun* ; Withington, Gloucestershire, was *Wudiandun* or *Widiandun* ; Warrington, Lancashire, is *Walintune* in Domesday ; Covington, Lanarkshire, was in 1262 *Colbayniston,* the 'tún of Kolbeinn,' an O.N. name ; and Lamington was *Lambinistun.* In the Scandinavian districts the O.N. *eng*, a 'meadow,' occasionally appears as the prefix *ing-*, as in Ingham, Ingthorpe, and Inkset.

§ 3. *Occupations and Status*

In many cases it is not the names of early inhabitants that are recorded by our village names, but their occupations, or the civil or ecclesiastical status of the owners or the manorial lords.

From Domesday we learn how considerable was the number of royal manors. Such royal ownership is sometimes signified by a distinctive affix, as in the case of King's Langley, King's Norton, or Lyme Regis. Lynn in Norfolk is known either as King's Lynn or Lynn Regis. Such affixes are usually later than Domesday. Some, such as Kingsgate, Thanet, where Charles II. landed in 1683, or Princes Risborough, Bucks, which was a residence of the Black Prince, and others enumerated on p. 164, are of historic or recent date. The older names are usually such compounds as Kingston-on-Thames, where so many of the Saxon kings were crowned, or Kingsclere, Hants, a residence of the West Saxon kings. In this class we may include Kingsbury in Middlesex and in Somerset, both called *Cyngesbyrig* in A.S. charters, while Kingsdown, Kent, was *Cyninges dún*, Kingswood, Gloucestershire, was *Kynges wudu*, and Kennington, Berks, was *Cenigtún*. In the Scandinavian districts the vowel changes, Coningsby in Lincolnshire and Yorkshire appearing in Domesday as *Cuningesbi*, Conisbrough as *Coningesburg*, Coneysthorpe and Coneythorpe as *Coningestorp*, and Coniston as *Cuningestone*, but Conybeare, Conisholme, and Coniscliffe and a few similar names may denote rabbit warrens (M.E. *cony* or *conig*, a rabbit). Some names which may be referred to Queens have been enumerated on p. 230, while to the A.S. *cwén*, a woman, whence the word queen, we may refer Quinton in Northants, Worcestershire, and Gloucestershire, the last of which appears in a charter as *Cwéntún*, which must signify the woman's tún. The related A.S. word *cwěne*, a wench or harlot, (Gay's 'scolding quean') explains Quinbrook, Gloucestershire, A.S. *Cwenenabróc*, as well as Quina Brook in Salop. Very curious is the assimilated name of Westow, Durham, called *Wivestona* in the Boldon Book, which, as well as the Yorkshire names of Westow, formerly *Wivestow*, and Winestead, called *Wifestad* and *Wivessted* in Domesday, must be from the A.S. *wífes*, genitive of *wíf*, a woman. Weaverthorpe, Yorkshire, was *Wifretorp*, from *wifre*, a weaver, and Wibtoft, Warwickshire, was *Wibbetoft*, from *webbe*, a webster.

Manors owned by Bishops were as numerous as those belonging to the King, but many of them have only gradually acquired a distinctive prefix of ownership. Thus Bishopsbourne in Kent, a manor belonging to the See of Canterbury, appears in an early charter as *æt Burnan*, 'at the burn.' Bishopthorpe, the residence of the Archbishop of York, is called *Torp* in Domesday, and among his manors Bishop Wilton is entered merely as Wilton, and Bishop Burton as Burton, but Biscathorpe in Lincolnshire is called *Biscopetorp* in Domesday, and Bishton, Staffordshire, is *Bisopeston* (for Biscopestún) in a charter. There is another Bishton in Gloucestershire, and there are places called Bishopton in Durham, Yorks, and Warwickshire. There are forty-nine places called Preston (A.S. *préost*, a priest), and many more called Prestwick, Prestwich, Prestcot, and Prestbury, doubtless denoting places with a resident priest, which, as we learn from Domesday, was quite exceptional.

Fifteen villages are called Knighton, in addition to others called Knight-wick, Knightcote, Knightleigh, and Knightsthorpe. Knighton-upon-Teme in Worcestershire, appears as *Cnihtatun* in a charter, and Knightwick, in the same county, as *Cnihtawic*, names plainly from *cnihta*, the genitive plural of *cniht*, which like the German *knecht* meant a 'servant' or 'youth,' and not a knight in the modern sense of the word. Charlton is a common village name in the South, corresponding to Carlton in the North. Charlton occurs twenty-nine times, Carlton forty times, and Carleton twelve times. Five of the Charltons, all in Southern counties, Sussex, Hants, Berks, Wilts, and Worcester, with Carlton in Norfolk, have been identified with places mentioned in charters as *Ceorlatún*, a name explained by *ceorla*, genitive plural of *ceorl*, a peasant or husbandman, whence the modern word churl. In other cases the Domesday forms point to a cognate etymology, Carlton in Notts, for instance, being *Carlatona*, Charlston, Sussex, being *Carletone*, while Charlcombe, Somerset, was *Cerlacuma*. The same explanation applies to such names as Charlecote, Charley, Chorley, and Chorlton. It may be noted as a dialectic peculiarity that the eight places called Chorlton and the five called Chorley are all in the Mercian region. In Lincolnshire and York-shire there are places called Caythorpe, the first of which is *Carltorp*, and the second *Caretorp*, in Domesday. There are twenty-seven English villages called Hinton. When, as in the case of Great Hinton in Dorset, the Domes-day form is *Hineton*, the name may be referred to the A.S. *híne* or *hína*, a servant, whence *hind*, the northern word for a farm servant. But when Hinton is represented in Domesday by *Hantona*, as in the case of the three Somerset Hintons, Hinton Blewitt, Hinton St. George, and Charterhouse Hinton, the name must be explained as a doublet of Hampton, from *heán*, dative of *heáh*, 'high.' Hinton in Somerset is *Hyneton* in the Hundred Rolls. Hinstock, Salop, called *Stoche* in Domesday, becomes in he thirteenth century *Hinestok*, probably for *Hinastoc*, the hinds' place.

There are several villages in the Danish districts whose names indicate a settlement of vikings, pirates who came, not from the northern fjords, but, as the name implies, from the *Vík*, or great bay between Norway and Sweden, now called the Skagerack. In Domesday Wigganthorpe, Yorks, is *Wickena-*

torp, Wigston, Leicestershire, is *Wickingestone*, Whissendine, Rutland, is *Wichingdene*, Wickenby, Lincolnshire, is *Wichingebi*. Close to Wickenby is Westleby, called in Domesday *Westledebi*, the home of the westward sailor. A *sumerlida* or 'summer sailor,' was a viking who in spring started forth for an annual plundering expedition. One of them must have settled at Somerby in Leicestershire, called *Sumerlidebie* in Domesday, another at Somerleyton in Suffolk, called *Sumerledetún* in a charter. There are several places called Somerby, which, as well as Somersby, Lincolnshire, the birthplace of Tennyson, may be probably explained in the same way. Flotmanby and Hunmanby in Yorkshire were the dwellings of a *floteman* or sailor, and of a *hundman* or dogkeeper. The six places called Woodmancott or Woodmancote refer to the cot of a woodman. Smisby, Derbyshire, called *Smidesby* in Domesday, is the smith's dwelling, while Smethcot in Salop, and Smethick or Smethwick (Smith-wick) in Derbyshire and Staffordshire, may be explained in the same way, but the four places called Smeaton in Yorkshire, all of which appear as *Smidetune* or *Smedetone* in Domesday, may be either the 'smithy tun,' or from A.S. *sméthe*, a smooth place. Wrexham, Denbighshire, is called *Wrightes ham* in the Chronicle, probably from a personal name, since *wyrhtan* would be the genitive of *wyrhta*, a wright or workman.

The A.S. *céap* meant cattle, saleable commodities, sale, business, or market. Hence Chepstow, Monmouthshire, in A.S. *Céapstów*, means a place of sale. Chipstead, Surrey, called in an A.S. charter, *Chepstede*, the 'market-place,' is doubtless the same name as Chepstead in Kent. Kippax, Yorkshire, in Domesday *Chipesche*, must have denoted at one time an ash-tree at which a market was held. Cheapside was the south-side of the great open market-place of London, the northern portion of which is now built over. The prefix Chipping, from the A.S. *cýping* or *cíping*, a market-place or market, is used to denote a market-town. We have Chipping Camden and Chipping Sodbury in Gloucestershire, Chipping Lambourn in Berks, Chipping Wycombe in Bucks, Chipping Warden in Northants, Chipping Barnet and Chipping in Herts, Chipping Ongar in Essex, Chipping Norton in Oxon, and Chippenham in Wilts and Cambridgeshire. The A.S. *stapol*, *stapel*, or *stapul* denoted a post or pillar of wood or stone. Such staples were often erected to mark places where markets were held or where merchandise could be exposed for sale. Thus Dunstable would be a staple on the chalk downs; Whitstable, Kent, must have taken its name from a white pillar, erected either for a market or as a guide to ships entering the harbour. A similar name is Barnstaple in Devon (see p. 62). There are nine places called Stapleford, but as none of them are market-towns the name must signify a ford marked out by posts. So also of the eight places called Stapleton, none of which are market-towns. The two Stapletons in Yorkshire are *Stapledun* and *Stapletona* in Domesday. Stalbridge, Dorset, in Domesday *Staplebrige*, probably refers to a trestle bridge.

§ 4. *Hundreds, Shires, and Parishes*

The Hundred is the oldest and in many respects the most interesting of English institutions. It is so ancient that we do not know its origin. Of the original settlers a hundred families, or a hundred warriors, or the holders of a hundred hides, constituted themselves into groups for self-defence, with powers of local self-government. Unlike the hundreds the shires and counties were formed at very different periods, and owe their origin to a variety of causes, some representing ancient kingdoms, and others divisions of ancient kingdoms, or aggregated fragments of such kingdoms. We do not hear of Rutland as a county till the reign of King John, when certain hundreds of Nottinghamshire and Leicestershire were formed into a county, apparently as a dowry for the Queen. In the twelfth century Lancashire was formed into an earldom by uniting the Mercian lands between Ribble and Mersey with the northern hundreds of York, Amounderness, and part of Richmond-shire, with the addition of Furness, originally a part of Cumberland, which was the English share of the old Cumbrian or Strathclyde kingdom, West-moreland being the Cumbrian march or frontier. Northumberland was the small remnant left of the great Northumbrian kingdom stretching from the Humber to the Forth which was left after the Lothians had gone to Scotland, after the patrimony of St. Cuthbert had been constituted into a county pala-tine, and the sub-kingdom of Deira had become the great shire of York, con-taining the subordinate shires of Cravenshire, Richmondshire, Borgheshire, now Claro Wapentake, Riponshire, Norhamshire, Howdenshire, Islandshire, and Hallamshire, with the districts of Holderness and Cleveland. Norfolk and Suffolk were the northern and southern 'fylkes' or folks of the East Angles. Essex was one of the primitive kingdoms, of which the capital was London, whose importance caused the surrounding district to become the county of Middlesex. Mercia was divided into five regions none of which was called a shire, and it was only after the reconquest of Mercia from the Danes in the reign of Edward the Elder that the Mercian shires were created and named after the chief towns. In Wessex, perhaps in 880 after the treaty between Alfred and Guthrun, we have the division into the primitive tribal settlements of Dorset, Wilset, Somerset, and Sussex, with Hamptunscir, Defnascir, and Bearrocscir. The sees of Rochester and Canterbury long continued to represent the kingdoms of East and West Kent.

The wapentakes found in several northern counties were aggregations, each consisting of three hundreds, formed for the purpose of naval defence against the Danes, each wapentake having to furnish a ship. In some southern counties these divisions were afterwards called hundreds, as in Buckingham-shire, where the original eighteen hundreds are now combined into six new hundreds. The names of the wapentakes and hundreds are often of consider-able historical interest, preserving a sort of record of the places at which the assemblages of the moots or hundred courts were held either for civil or military purposes. The meeting-places were usually at some conspicuous or well-known object : a hill, a ridge, a dyke, a ford, or a bridge, or very often an ancient tree, a monolith (*stán*), a preaching cross (*cros*), a post (*stapol*), a

barrow, a pre-historic grave-mound, either a law (*hláw*) or howe (*haugr*).
The localities of many of these moots, especially the trees, the monoliths
and the staples, are now lost, although occasionally preserved by the names
of adjacent houses. The older names of the hundreds are usually to be found
in Domesday Book (D.B.), or in the Hundred Rolls (H.R.), compiled about
a century later in the reign of Edward I. in an English form more easy to
recognise. The trees at which the moots were held occasionally bear the
names of the persons near whose dwellings they doubtless grew. Such are
the Hundreds of Edwinstree (H.R. *Edwinestre*) in Hertfordshire; of Thedwestry (H.R. *Thedwardistre*) in Suffolk, and Grumbald's Ash (H.R. *Grim-
boldesasse*) in Gloucestershire. Naturally, trees with peculiarities of growth,
appearance, or situation were often selected as the meeting-places. Thus in
Herefordshire we have the Hundreds of Greytree (H.R. *Greytre*) and Web-
tree (H.R. *Webetre* or *Welbetre*); in Worcestershire, Doddingtree (H.R.
Dodintre or *Dudintre*) and Wodingtree; in Kent, Toltingtrough or Toltingtrow (H.R. *Toltyntre*), in Salop, Brimstry (H.R. *Brimestree*); in Beds,
Wixamtree; in Dorset, Cullifordtree (H.R. *Culfordestre*, D.B. *Cufertstroue*);
in Gloucestershire, the lost Hundred of *Burnetre* (H.R.). In Essex we have
Becontree (H.R. *Bekentre*) and Winstree (H.R. *Wenstre*); in Sussex,
Gostrow (H.R. *Gosetreu*); and in Yorkshire *Gerlestre*, now lost. There is
a Langtree Hundred in Oxon, and a Longtree Hundred in Gloucester-
shire, both anciently *Langetre* (H.R.). In Lincolnshire and in Leicester-
shire there are Hundreds called Gartree, anciently *Gayrtre* and *Gertre*
(H.R.), meaning the 'fir-tree'; in Derbyshire we have Appletree Hundred
(D.B. *Apultre*, H.R. *Appeltre*), and in Notts there was the lost Domesday
Hundred of *Plumtre*. Wellow Hundred in Somerset is the 'willow-tree'
(H.R. *Welowe*). A curious corruption is the Gloucestershire Hundred of
Slaughter, the 'sloe-tree' (H.R. *Sloutre*). An assimilated name, nearly
as curious, is that of Manhood Hundred in Sussex (H.R. *Manewode*).
Several Hundreds are named from conspicuous ash-trees, among them Brox-
ash or Brocash in Herefordshire, Barkstone Ash in Yorks, Grumbald's Ash in
Gloucestershire, and Catsash in Somerset (H.R. *Cattesass*). From oaks we
have the Hundreds of Tipnoak in Sussex (H.R. *Tipenoc*), and of Skyrack in
Yorks (H.R. *Schyrayk*, D.B. *Siraches*), the 'shire-oak.' Thorns are the most
common, giving names to the Hundreds of Elthorne (H.R. *Elethorn*) and
Spelthorne (H.R. *Spelethorn*) in Middlesex: Copthorne in Surrey; Eythorne
in Kent; Crowthorne in Gloucestershire; and Horethorne in Somerset; as
well as to the lost Domesday Hundred of *Nachededorne* in Berks, and the
doubtful case of *Godernthorn* Hundred in Dorset. From staples or posts we
have the Hundreds of Staple in Sussex, with Barstaple (H.R. *Berdestapel*),
and Thurstable (H.R. *Thurstaple*) in Essex.

From crosses, probably either preaching or memorial crosses, we have in
Berks the Hundred of Faircross; in Sussex Singlecross; in Hunts Norman-
cross (H.R. *Normancros*); in Norfolk Brothercross (H.R. *Brotherescros* or
Broserescros) and Guiltcross (H.R. *Gildecros*, *Geldecros*, or *Gyldecros*), where
some accustomed geld or payment must have been made. In Yorkshire
are the wapentakes of Staincross, the 'stone cross' (H.R. *Staincros*), Ewcross,

the 'yew cross'; Buckrose, the 'beech cross' (H.R. *Buc-cros*); Osgoldcross (H.R. *Osgotescros*, D.B. *Osgotcros*) and *Sneculfcros*, now lost; and in Lincolnshire, Walshcroft, a corruption of *Walescros*, and *Walecros* in Derbyshire, now lost.

From stones, probably monoliths of pre-Teutonic date, we have the Hundreds of Stone in Bucks (D.B. *Stanes*); Stone in Somerset (H.R. *de la Stane*); Staine in Cambridgeshire (H.R. *Stane*), and the lost Domesday Hundred of *Stane* in Dorset.   Ossulston Hundred in Middlesex (H.R. *Ousolvestan*, D.B. *Osulvestone*, 'Oswulf's stone') was so called from a Roman stone of geometric shape, supposed to have been a milestone, which stood at Tyburn Gate, now the Marble Arch, Hyde Park.   Whitstone Hundred, Staffordshire (D.B. *Witstan*), was the 'white stone,' and there is also a Whitstone Hundred in Gloucestershire.   From personal names we have the Hundreds of Cuddlestone in Staffordshire (H.R. *Cuthulfestan*); Kinwardstone in Wilts (H.R. *Kynewardestan*); Tibbaldstone (H.R. *Thebaldestan*), and Dudstone (H.R. *Duddestan*), in Gloucestershire; and two lost Hundreds called *Dudestan* and *Hamestan* in Cheshire; as well as Bishopstone in Sussex; Washingstone in Kent (H.R. *Wackelestan* or *Wachelestan*); Hurstingstone in Hunts (H.R. *Hirstingstan*); Bemptone in Somerset (H.R. *Bemestan*), and Axton in Kent (H.R. *Acstane.*)

Hundreds were also often named from sepulchral mounds or tumuli (A.S. *hláw* or *hléw*), which may sometimes conserve the name of the hero or chieftain over whose remains the mound was raised.   Such are the Hundreds of Bassetlaw in Notts (D.B. *Bernedeslawe*, H.R. *Bersetelawe*); Beltisloe in Lincolnshire (D.B. and H.R. *Belteslawe*); Blidesloe in Gloucestershire (H.R. *Blideslawe*); Bledisloe in Essex; Baldslow, Sussex (H.R. *Baldeslowe*); Oswaldslow in Worcestershire (A.S. *Oswaldeslawe*); Huxloe, Northants (H.R. *Hokeslawe*); Offlow, Staffordshire (H.R. *Offelowe*); Triplow, Cambridgeshire (H.R. *Tripelawe*); Munslow and Purslow in Salop (H.R. *Munselawe* and *Posselawe*); Segloe and Cotteslow or Cotslow in Bucks (H.R. *Segelawe* and *Coteslau*); Harlow in Essex (H.R. *Herlawe*); Radlow and Wormelow in Herefordshire (H.R. *Radlow* and *Wormelaye*); Ringslow, Kent (H.R. *Ringeslo*); Botloe in Essex and Botloe in Gloucestershire (H.R. *Botlowe*); Knightlow, Warwick (H.R. *Knytelawe*); Bucklow in Cheshire (D.B. *Bochelau*); Hadlow in Kent; Totmanslow in Staffordshire, and the lost Hundreds of *Tremalau* and *Pattelawe* in Warwickshire.   Broxtow Hundred in Notts is, however, a name of another class, appearing in Domesday as *Broculestou*, and in the H.R. as *Broxholestowe*, signifying the 'place at the badger's hole.'   In the Danish districts those grave-mounds or tumuli which are not distinguished by the suffix *-low* or *-loe*, from A.S. *hláw*, may usually be recognised by the suffix *-hoe* or *-oe*, which is the M.E. *howe* (O.N. *haugr*), not to be confused with the A.S. *hógh*, *hóh*, or *hó*, denoting a projecting heel of land.   The names of Hundreds are usually from the former source, a *howe* forming a more recognisable object than a *hoo*.   These names are as a rule confined to the Danish shires, occurring chiefly in Norfolk, Lincolnshire, and Yorkshire.   In Norfolk the moot of the Hundred now called Forehoe (H.R. *Fourhowe*) was held on four adjacent howes or

tumuli, and the moot of Greenhoe Hundred (H.R. *Grenehowe*) must have
been held on a green howe. Gallow Hundred in Norfolk (H.R. *Galhowe,
Galehowe, Galleho,* and *Galehoge*) may be the gallows howe. We have also
the Hundreds of Grimshoe, Norfolk (H.R. *Grimeshowe*), and Thingoe, Suffolk
(H.R. *Thinghowe*), where a Thing was doubtless held at some earlier time;
with Staploe, Cambridgeshire (H.R. *Stapelhowe* or *Stapilho*), a howe marked
by a post, while Spelhoe, Northants (H.R. *Spelho*), may be 'speech howe.'
In Leicestershire we have Sparkenhoe Hundred; in Yorks Claro Wapentake
(H.R. *Clarhou* and later *Clarhowe*); and in Lincolnshire the Wapentakes or
Hundreds of Aslacoe (H.R. *Aslachow*, D.B. *Aslacheshou*), Haverstoe (H.R.
Haywardeshou, D.B. *Harwardeshou*), Candleshoe (H.R. *Candelshoue*, D.B.
Calnodeshou), which apparently contain proper names, as well as Graffoe
(H.R. *Graffhow* or *Graffhou*), the 'grave howe'; Langoe (H.R. *Langhou,*
D.B. *Langehou*), the 'long howe'; Elloe (H.R. *Ellowe*, D.B. *Elleho*),
Wraggoe (H.R. *Wraghou*, D.B. *Waragehou*), and Threo or Treo (D.B.
Trehos, H.R. *Trehou*, Plac. Abb. *Trehowes*), the 'three howes' like Forehoe
in Norfolk. The Wapentake of Lawress, called *Lagulris* in Domesday, and
afterwards *Lagolfris*, may have been from the cairn or raise (O.N. *hreysi*),
erected over some viking named Lagúlfr. Other moots were held on con-
spicuous hills, as in the case of the Hundreds of Tintinhull, Somerset (H.R.
Tintehille), Pimhill, Salop (H.R. *Pemehul* and *Pemenhull*); Buttinghill,
Sussex (H.R. *Bottinghull*); Brownshall, Dorset (H.R. *Broneshull*); Hill,
Lincolnshire (H.R. *Hulle*); Calehill, Kent (H.R. *Kalehull*); Harthill and
Tickhill in Yorkshire (H.R. *Herthill* and *Tykehull*).

From *berwe*, dative of *bearo*, a 'barrow' or wooded hill, we have in Dorset
the hundreds of Hundreds-barrow (H.R. *Hundredes berewe*), Row-barrow
(H.R. *Ruber'*), and Loose-barrow (H.R. *Lesseberwe*). In Gloucestershire we
have Brightwells-Barrow (H.R. *Bristewaldeberewe*), and in Kent Bewsborough
(H.R. *Bewesberwe*). With these names from barrows those from *beorge*,
dative of *beorh*, a 'hill,' are liable to be confused. Thus we have the
Hundreds of Swanborough, Wilts (H.R. *Swaneberge*); Swanborough,
Sussex (D.B. *Soanberge*); Hawkesborough, Sussex (H.R. *Havekesberge*);
Flexborough, Sussex (D.B. *Flexeberge*, A.S. *fleax*, flax); Loningborough,
Kent (H.R. *Lonebergh*); Felborough, Kent (A.S. *Feldbeorge*); Hounds-
borough, Somerset (H.R. *Hundesberge*); Branch, Wilts (H.R. *Brenches-
berge*); Babergh, Suffolk (H.R. *Badberge* and *Balberge*); Roborough, Devon
(D.B. *Rueberge*); and the Wapentake of Langbargh, Yorks, formerly
Langeberge.

Assimilated to these Hundred names in -borough, from *beorge*, are others
from moots held at ancient earthworks. Thus the Dorset Hundreds of
Badbury and Modbury appear in Domesday as *Bedeberia* and *Morberga*;
Ramsbury Hundred, Wilts, is *Rammesbyre* in the H.R., and the Hundred
of Guilsborough in Northants is called *Gildeburg* and *Gildesburg* in the H.R.,
indicating, like Guiltcross Hundred in Norfolk (H.R. *Geldecros* and *Gildecros*), a place where a geld or payment of some kind had to be made. The
curious name of Sixpenny Hundred in Dorset (D.B. *Sexpena*), and that of
Sixpenny Handley Hundred in Wilts, so called from the village of Sixpenny

Handley in Cranbourne Chase, must have arisen from some custom of the Hundred Courts, probably the payment of a fine of sixpence from each manor in the hundred. In Devon Hundreds are named from ridges and tors, as the Hundreds of Coleridge (H.R. *Colrig*); Hayridge (H.R. *Harrigge*); or Witheridge (D.B. *Witric*, H.R. *Wytherigg* and *Wyrigge*), as well as Haytor (H.R. *Hartorr* and *Haytorr*). Elsewhere we have names from duns, cliffs, or hills, as the Hundreds of Smithdon, Norfolk (H.R. *Smethedune*); Cawden, Wilts (H.R. *Cawedone*); Cleeve, Gloucestershire (H.R. *Clive*); Rushcliffe, Notts (H.R. *Riseclive*); and Hartcliffe, Somerset (H.R. *Hareclive*). Dikes were also used for moots, as in the Hundreds of Launditch, Norfolk (H.R. *Laundiz*); Wrangdyke, Rutland (H.R. *Wrangedik*); Flendish, Cambridgeshire (D.B. *Flamindic*, and H.R. *Flemdich*); Coomsditch, Dorset (H.R. *Cumebusdich*), probably the same as D.B. *Concresdic*; and Dickering Wapentake, Yorks, where the moot was at the great Danes' Dyke at Flamborough Head.

Among the commonest Hundred names are those from fords and bridges, the most curious of which is Cashio Hundred, Herts, called in the H.R. *Caysford*, apparently a ford over the River Chess. Many names denote moots by the water side, such as the Hundreds of Mere, Wilts (H.R. *Mere*); Broadwater, Herts (H.R. *Bradewatre*); Willybrook, Northants (H.R. *Wylebrok*); Condover, Salop (H.R. *Condovere* and *Conedovere*); Overs, Salop (H.R. *Overes* and *Oures*); Hasler, Dorset (D.B. *Haselora*, H.R. *Haselore*); Lewknor, Oxon (H.R. *Leukenore* and *Leweknore*); Pershore, Worcestershire (H.R. *Persore*). Blackbourn Hundred in Suffolk seems to be an assimilated name, being called *Blakebroue* in the H.R., where, however, the true reading may be *Blakebrone*, *n* being easily misread for *u*.

There are many names like Moat Hill, which may have been places of popular assembly, either hundred moots or shire moots. Such perhaps was Landmoth in Yorkshire, which is called *Landemot* in Domesday. The chief manor of the Falconbergs, Lords of Holderness, was at Rise, and in Rise Park there is a mound called Moat Hill, where probably the Holderness moot assembled. The name of Rise itself may refer to this mound, if, as is possible, it means a 'raise' that is a cairn or heap of stones. In Domesday Rise is called *Rison*, which might be explained by the O.N. *hreysum*, from *hreysi*, a raise or mound, whence Dunmail Raise. Occasionally these names point to Scandinavian rather than to Anglo-Saxon institutions. Such, as a rule, are names like Walsoken in Norfolk, or Thorpe le Soken in Essex, which retained the local jurisdiction (*sócn*) of the Danish freeholders.

Still more unmistakable are names like Thingoe Hundred in Suffolk, called *Thinghowe* (H.R.) and *Thinghow* in a charter, which points to a *howe* on which the Danish Thing was held. Taingoe Hundred, also in Suffolk, may be a variant form of the same name. Dengie Hundred, Essex, formerly called *Danesey*, is the Danes' island; and Dacorum Hundred in Herts also takes its name from the Danes who were left on the Saxon side of Watling Street in Alfred's division of the kingdom. In these, and some other hundreds, the population seems to have been wholly or mainly of Scandinavian origin. But in other districts the Anglo-Saxon population was not dispossessed by the Danish invaders, who seem to have settled down side by side with them in a manner not unfriendly. Local names furnish a curious support of this theory. Thus parishes in the North of England frequently comprise two or more townships, possessing distinct rights of self-government and taxation. In many cases the name of one of these townships, generally the older and larger, which gives its name to the whole parish, has an Anglian suffix, such as *-ton* or *-ham*, while the subsidiary township has a Danish ending, like *-thorpe* or *-by*. To take a few instances from the East Riding, the Parish of Settrington contains the two townships of Settrington and Scagglethorpe, one Anglian, the other Danish; the contiguous Parish of Langton contains the townships of Langton and Kennythorpe; the Parish of Burton Agnes contains the townships of Burton and Haisthorpe; the Parish of Cayton contains the townships of Cayton, Killaby, and Osgodby; the Parish of Bishop Wilton contains the townships of Wilton, Belthorpe, Youlthorpe, and Gowthorpe; the Parish of Brantingham contains the townships of Brantingham and Thorpe; the Parish of Catton contains the townships of Catton and Kexby; the Parish of Cottingham contains the townships of Cottingham and Willerby; the Parish of Hayton contains the townships of Hayton and Beilby; the Parish of Pocklington contains the townships of Pocklington, Owsthorpe, and Meltonby; the Parish of Humbleton contains the townships of Humbleton and Danthorpe. On the other hand it is quite exceptional to find the name of the parish ending in *-thorpe* or *-by*, and the subsidiary townships in *-ton* or *-ham*. The explanation seems to be that the township which gave a name to the parish was the original Anglian settlement, while the later Danish immigrants settled on outlying waste lands, where they established a separate community, which has preserved its independent rights of local self-government and taxation. It is curious to note that in many cases the townships in *-ton* and *-ham* are the property of a single squire, while the townships in *-by* and *-thorpe* are owned by a number of small freeholders.

There are a few parish names from which intimations as to ancient tenures or hidation may be gathered. In some cases the names bear witness to the number of hides at which they were assessed. Some contained only a single hide, such as Huish Episcopi in Somerset, which means the Bishop's Hide, *huish* being a later form taken by the A.S. *hiwisc*, a 'hide of land.' The name of the owner also appears in the name of Hardenhuish in Wilts, which was the Hide of Heregeard, as is proved by the Anglo-Saxon name *Heregeardingc Hiwisc*. Huish Champflower in Somerset acquired the name of its owner at a later period, as in Domesday it is called simply *Hiwys*, 'the Hide.' Another place in Devon, called *Hewis* in Domesday, is now known as South Huish, and Rodhuish in Somerset is in Domesday *Radehewis*. While these parishes contained only a single hide, the names of others testify to a higher assessment. Fifehead, a parochial name as common as Huish, signifies that the parish contained five hides. Thus Fifehead Neville in Dorset has been identified with a place which we learn from Domesday contained five hides, and was called *Fifhide*. Sydling Fifehead, also in Dorset, is called *Sidelence* in Domesday, the second name, acquired since the date of

Domesday, being explained by the statement that it contained five hides. There is also a Fifehead Magdalen in Dorset, and a Fiveheads in Somerset, called *Fihida* in Domesday. Fifield, Essex, is *Fifhide* in Domesday. Sometimes the hidage was much larger. A manor on the River Piddle in Dorset, and hence called *Pidre* in Domesday, contained, we are told, thirty hides, which explains the fact that it now goes by the name of Piddletrenthide, to distinguish it from other places taking their names from this river.

Land was also measured by the quit rent paid—often an ounce of silver, or a pennyweight, or a farthing. Thus in North Uist we have a place called Unganab, the 'abbot's ounce,' the abbot receiving a rent of an ounce of silver. The places named Ayre or Eyre, when not corruptions of *Eyjar*, 'islands,' or of *Eyri*, a 'spit of land,' may be explained as *Eyrir* or *oers*, 'ounce lands,' either eighteen or twenty pennylands making an *oer*, or ounce land. We have also cases of pennylands. Penninghame, near Newton-Stewart, was a ham or enclosure held at the rent of a silver penny. Pennymuir, Pennytown, Pennyghael, Pennycross, and Penmollach, in Scotland, Pennymoor and Pennycross in Devon, and Pennyplatt in Wilts, may also be cited as penny lands, so called because the homestead paid a silver penny as scot.

The name of Sixpenny Handley in Wilts, already mentioned, may have arisen in a similar way. Farthingland and Farthinghoe in Northants were probably lands which paid a farthing scot, or possibly were the feórthlings or fourth parts of an estate in culture. At Galton in Dorset we have an undefined rent, the Domesday name *Gaveltone* pointing to the A.S. *gavel* or *gafol*, 'rent' or 'tribute.' Gidley in Devon is called in a charter *Gifle*, meaning probably a 'gift-lea' or pasture. Oundle, Northants, A.S. *on Undalum* and *Undala* was 'undealt' or undivided land. Unthank, the name of three places in Cumberland and two in Northumberland, denotes a piece of ground on which some squatter had settled 'without leave' of the lord. (See p. 284.) Offenham and perhaps Hovingham, may signify an *Of-nam*, or piece of land 'taken off' a larger tract still uninclosed. There is an old deed which describes an *of-nam* which was given from the lord's outlands (*de utlandis.*) There are twenty-eight places called Buckland. Four of these, in Berks, Dorset, Kent, and Somerset, appear in extant charters as *Bócland*, which is explained as Book-land, or land held by a charter, from *bóc*, a book or writing. But Boughton, A.S. *Bóctun*, is more probably from *bóc*, a beech-tree, while names like Buckley, Buckhurst, Buckholt, or Buckden, may be referred to *buc*, a stag or buck.

Theale, near Reading, called *Le Thele* in the Hundred Rolls, apparently takes its name from the *telga* or *telia* (German *zelge*), which denoted the third part in a three-field system of culture. Tilsworth, Beds, formerly *Telgasworth*, is from the same source. But Tiley in Dorset is called in an A.S. charter *Tigelleáh*, the 'potter's field' (A.S. *tigel*, a tile, brick, or pot). There are a number of places, mostly hills, whose names imply that on them watch or ward was kept. To the A.S. *weard* (m.), gen. *weardes*, a warden or watchman, or to *weard* (f.), gen. *wearde*, guard, watch, vigilance, we may refer such names as Warborough, Oxon, called in charters *Weardesbeorh* and *Weardburg*, Warden in Kent, A.S. *Weard-dún*, Warboys, Hunts,

A.S. *Warde - busc*, and Warburton, doubtfully identified with an A.S. *Weardburh*.

Warkton, Northants, in A.S. *Weargedún*, may be explained either as wolf hill, or robbers hill, from A.S. *wearg* or *wearh*, a villain, and hence a wolf, and Warley, Essex, A.S. *Wærleáh*, may be from the same source. Wareham, Dorset, called *Werham* in the Chronicle, is explained by the A.S. *wǽr* or *wér* a weir or dam, whence probably Warehorne, A.S. *Werhornas*, and Ware in Hertfordshire. Warminster, Wilts, in A.S. *Worge mynster*, Domesday *Guerminstre*, was identified by Camden with the Roman *Verlucio*. This is probably erroneous, as well as the derivation from the A.S. *weorc*, or *worc*, work. Warminster stands on the Willy where it is joined by a small stream now called the Were, and most probably is the minster on the Were.

§ 5. *Towns and Townships*

While *-chester*, *-cester*, and *-caster*, dialectic forms of the A.S. *-ceaster*, as explained on p. 33, are the characteristic suffixes which mark sites of Roman occupation, the A.S. *burg*, *buruh*, or *burh*, whence the modern forms *-bury*, *-burgh*, or *-borough*, ordinarily distinguishes defensible places, either of Teutonic foundation, or occasionally earlier pre-Teutonic earthworks like Amesbury, Avebury, Masbury, Ogbury, Egbury, or Yarnbury. The word *burg* or *burh*, which afterwards came to mean a town or city, primarily denoted an earthwork, or sometimes merely the house of the powerful man, defended by a ditch with a bank of earth or sods, as contrasted with the *tún*, which was the enclosure of the peasant, surrounded by a simple hedge. The modern forms of *burg* or *burh*, especially when derived from the oblique cases, often become identical with derivatives from *beorg* or *beorh*, a 'hill,' an ambiguity which also attaches to their German equivalents *burg* and *berg*. The A.S. *burg*, *buruh*, or *burh* (f.), a 'town,' makes the genitive *burge* and the dative *byrig* and *byrg*, while *beorg* or *beorh* (m.), a 'hill,' makes the genitive *beorges* and the dative *beorge*. In Middle English we have *burghe* and *borge* for a town, and *berghe* or *bergh* for a hill. Hence, when the earlier forms are unknown, the sources of the modern names are frequently undistinguishable. An instance of this ambiguity is seen in the Yorkshire names Knaresborough and Riseborough, the first of which is from *burg*, and the second from *beorg*, as appears from the Domesday forms *Chenaresburg* and *Risberg* or *Rysbergh*. In the case of Aldbrough and Brechenbrough, the one was *Aldeburgh*, the 'old town,' and the other was *Brachenbergh*, 'bracken hill.'

The chief modern forms of *burg* or *burh* are *bury* and *borough*, forms which are also assumed by *beorg* or *beorh*. A notable circumstance, which seems hitherto to have escaped due attention, is that in those districts where *bury* means a town, *borough* usually denotes a hill, and *vice-versa* where *borough*, *burgh*, or *brough* usually denotes a town, *bury* means a hill. Thus in the heart of 'Wessex we have Salisbury, Amesbury, Heytesbury, Shaftesbury, Westbury, Melbury, Badbury, Spettisbury, Tisbury, Whichbury, Tetbury, Ramsbury, Newbury, and Kintbury, all of which are from *byrig*, the dative of *burh*; while in the same region we have Wanborough, Farnborough, Bagborough, Brokenborough, Risborough, Rodborough, Charborough, Chelborough, and Crowborough, all from *beorh*, a 'hill,' as well as Stowborough, Dorset (D. B. *Stanberge*), and Felborougħ, Kent (A.S. *Feldbeorh*), 'the hill on the plain.' Willesborough, Kent (A.S. *Wifelesbeorge*), may be 'beetle hill.' An apparent exception to the rule is the town name of Marlborough; but here *Mærlebeorh*, the A.S. name, shows that Marlborough originally denoted a hill and not a burgh. On the other hand, where *borough*, *burgh*, or *brough* is normally from *burg*, a town, the names in *-bury* are from *beorh*, a 'hill.' Thus in Yorkshire Conisborough, Goldsborough, Mexborough, Kexborough, Guisborough, and Hemingborough are all from *burg*, while the names in *-bury*, such as Horbury, Sedbury, Welbury, Almondbury, and Burythorpe, are from *beorg*, represented in Domesday by *bergh*, *berg*, *berge*, or *berie*. Where *bury* means a town, it is derived from *byrig*, the dative of *burh*. For example, in Anglo-Saxon documents Sidbury, Devon, appears as *Sydebirig*, the 'burgh on the Sid'; Kintbury, Berks, as *Cynetanbyrig*, the 'burgh on the Kennet'; Shaftesbury and Abbotsbury, in Dorset, as *Sceaftesbyrig* and *Abbodesbyrig*, the 'abbot's burgh'; Littlebury, Essex, as *Lytlanbyrig*; Sudbury, Suffolk, as *Suthbyrig*; and Bury St. Edmunds, as *Eadmundesbyrig*. While in the south *bury* is usually from *byrig*, the dative of *burh*, the forms *burgh* and *borough* are usually from the nominative *burh* or *buruh*, as is well shown in the case of Peterborough, where, as we learn from the Chronicle, after Abbot Kenwulf had built a wall round St. Peter's Abbey at Medehamstead, the place obtained the new name of *Burh* or *Buruh*, whence the modern name of Peterborough (see p. 221). It will be noticed that the form *bury*, from *byrig*, prevails in the Saxon and Mercian districts, where the Saxon inflexions were familiar, while in the Anglian and Danish counties *borough*, from *buruh*, is usual, *burgh* being found in Northumberland and Scotland. Thus in the South, Canterbury, Tilbury, Sudbury, Aylesbury, Banbury, Newbury, Salisbury, Glastonbury, Bibury, Tenbury, Malmesbury, Tewkesbury, Ledbury, Shrewsbury, and others already enumerated, are from *byrig*, names in *borough*, as Wanborough, Crowborough, or Marlborough, being from *beorh* or its dative *beorge*, while in the Danelagh and Northumbria Peterborough, Gainsborough, Conisborough, Guisborough, Hemingborough, Sprotborough, Goldsborough, Knaresborough, Scarborough, and Flamborough are from *buruh*, the names in *bury* being from *beorh*. Further north we have Dunstanburgh, Bamburgh, Roxburgh, Jedburgh, Dryburgh, and Edinburgh, where the spelling shows that Edinborough, the present pronunciation, is of recent date.

Though the normal forms are *bury* and *borough*, sundry variants and anomalies occasionally occur. For instance, Barugh in Yorkshire, and two places called Bargh, all pronounced Barf, are represented in Domesday by *Berg*. A hill is sometimes *-berry*, as Berry Pomeroy, Devon, or Greenberry and Roseberry in Yorkshire. Both *burh* and *beorh* may become *bur* or *ber* in modern names. Thus Burford, Oxon, called *Beorgeford* in the Chronicle, and *Berghford* in a charter of 685, is the 'hill ford'; another place, which has been identified with Burford in Salop, appears in a charter as *Buruhford*, signifying a ford near a *burh* or earthwork. Burbage, Leicestershire, A.S. *Burhbeca*, is a beck near a *burh* ; and Burstead, Essex, is the A.S. *Burgestede*. The A.S. *burh* becomes *ber* in Bramber, Sussex ; while Limber and Sowber are *Limberge* and *Solberge* in Domesday. Great Berkhamstead, Herts, is from the A.S. *Beorh-hamstede*, the homestead on the hill ; Berstead, Sussex, is probably the *Berg-hamstyde* of a late charter, and Berwick-upon-Tweed was formerly *Beor-wic*. Bourton in Berks and Gloucestershire both represent an A.S. *Burgtún* ; and Burley, Yorkshire, though spelt *Burgelai* in Domesday, is probably the 'hill pasture.' In the case of Hoborough, Lincolnshire (D.B. *Haburne*, H.R. *Haburg*), and Loughborough, Leicestershire (D.B. *Lucteburne*, H.R. *Lutherburg*), the Domesday record is probably in error, *burg* being misheard or miswritten as *burn*. Carisbrooke, on the other hand, is a corruption of *Wihtgaraburg* (see p. 84). Another curious form is seen in Bridgewater, Somerset, which is a M.E. corruption of Burgh Walter. A curiously assimilated name is Scorborough, in the great Deira wood, near Beverley, called in Domesday *Scogerbud*, signifying a 'forest hut' (O.N. *bud*, a booth or hut, and *skógr*, a wood or forest). We have also the forms *borrow* and *barrow*, as in two places in Yorkshire called Borrowby, which are both *Bergebi* in Domesday, while Barrowby, Lincolnshire, is also *Bergebi* in Domesday. But Barrowcote or Barwardcote, in Derbyshire, is from a proper name, meaning Beorweard's cottage, as appears from the Domesday form *Berverdescote*.

But as a rule *barrow* is from *bearwe*, the dative of *bearu* or *bearo*, a wood, wooded hill, or swine pasture. Thus Barrow-upon-Humber, Barrow in Rutland, Gloucestershire, and Leicestershire, are all *Bearwe* or *Barwe* in charters, and Barrow, Derbyshire, is *Barewe* in Domesday. Sedgebarrow, Worcestershire, was *Secgesbearwe*, and Mapleborough, Warwickshire, was *Mapelesbarwe*. Wigborough, Essex, is a doubtful name, as we have the two forms, *Wigberga* and *Wigberwe*, of which the second might be a late form of the other. While *bearwe* is the dative singular of *bearu*, the dative plural is *bearwum*, which may explain Barum, the local designation of Barnstaple (see p. 62). From the nominative *bearo* or *bearu* we get *ber*, *bere*, and *bear*, in the same way that we get dene and dean from *denu*, and tear from *tearu*. Hence we may probably explain the names of Pamber Forest, of the Forest of Bere and the Hundred of Bere Regis (D.B. *Bera*), and Beerhackett in Dorset, as well as some thirty Devonshire names, such as Beer, Beerferris, Bear Alston, Loxbear, Rockbeare, Kentisbeare, Shebbear, and Aylesbere.

In such names as Burford or Burton, we have seen that the prefix may be a corruption of either *burh* or *beorh*. In the case of Burton it is frequently from the A.S. *búr* (bower), a storehouse, chamber, or sleeping-place, Burton signifying a *tún* or enclosure containing such a building (see p. 79). The A.S. word *búrcote* also denoted a chamber or sleeping-place, whence the name Burcott in Somerset (A.S. *Búrcot*), and other places of the same name. Burtoft, in Lincolnshire (A.S. *Búrtoft*), must have been a toft containing a *búr* or bower. Burham, in Kent, called *Burham* in a charter, would be a *ham* or enclosure containing a *búr* or dwelling. This does not exhaust the possible significations of this troublesome prefix, since Burdale, Yorkshire

(D.B. *Breddale*), is the 'broad dale'; while Burstock, Dorset (D.B. *Burewine-stoch*), and Burcombe, Wilts (A.S. *Brydancumb*), are from personal names.

The suffixes *-ton* and *-ham* are especially characteristic of English townships. It will be noticed that while the names in *-ham* seldom agree in the prefix, the contrary is the case with names in *-ton*, which mostly consist of large groups of homonyms. The cause of this difference is not difficult to discover, the first element of a name in *-ham* being commonly the personal name of the settler who first made the place his *hám* or 'home'; while a name in *-ton*, which signifies a farmstead, is commonly preceded by an adjectival term descriptive of the situation or character of the place.

Among the more usual names Newton heads the list with 129 examples, without counting such names as Newnton or Newington, which [retain a survival of the sign of the dative case. More than 300 names refer to the points of the compass, among which Sutton (73 examples) comes first, followed by Norton (65) and Weston (55). The comparative rarity of Easton (24) is explained by the fact that the A.S. *East-tún* usually becomes Aston (66), just as *Eastleá* and *Eastcot* are now represented by Astley and Ascot. In 32 cases the A.S. *Middeltún* has retained the longer form Middleton, but it frequently becomes Melton or Milton, as in the instances of Melton-Mowbray, or Milton near Sittingbourne (see pp. 192, 194). Relative elevation is a common distinction, as well as relative position, Hampton (25 names) being normally from *Heántúne*, the 'high tun' (see p. 141), and Upton (33) and Overton (13) being generally the 'higher tun,' though Overton is sometimes from A.S. *ófer*, a 'shore.' Eaton (31) is the 'tun by the river' (A.S. *eá*), Seaton (16) the 'tun by a lake or sea,' Marton (26) one by a mere or pool (A.S. *mære*), Marston (25) is sometimes from *mæres*, the genitive of *mære*, or the 'tun by a marsh' or fen (A.S. *mersc*). Merton (5) is the 'tun by a boundary,' Morton (36) a 'tun on or by a moor' (A.S. *mór*), and Fenton (12) by a fen. Dalton (17) is a 'tun in a dale,' Denton (16) one in a den, dean, or wooded valley, Compton (32) in a combe (p. 96), Hopton (10) in a hope or recess in a hillside, Litton (6) and Letton (4) on a slope (*hlith* or *hlid*), and Halton (15) on a *healh* or slope. This may also be the meaning of Holton (9) when it is not a tun in a hollow. Haughton (11) is a tun on a *halgh* or river flat (p. 143), but Houghton (24) (when not, as in South Yorkshire, from *healh*), as well as Hooton (4) and Hutton (33) is a tun on a *hoo* or projecting heel of land (A.S. *hóh* or *hó*), as explained on p. 151. Clifton (21) is a tun near a cliff, Reighton on a ridge, Broughton (44), as well as Brockton (6), Brotton and Brocton signify a tun by a brook (A.S. *Bróctún*), Brunton one by a burn, Beighton (3) and Bickton (4) one by a beck. Welton (9) or Wilton (10) is by a well, and Chilton (15) by a spring. Ditton (8) or Deighton (6) is a tun by a dike or ditch, and Walton (25) one by a wall or bank, or occasionally by a wood (*weald*), but this is more often Wootton (30), while Grafton (14) is a tun by a grove (see p. 137). Bampton (8) is usually a tun by a tree, Acton (27) by an oak, Thornton (29) by a thorn, Ashton (28) by an ash, Appleton (12) by an apple-tree, and Brompton (12) among broom. Leighton (9) is a tun on a woodland pasturage or thicket, and Leyton usually a tun on fallow or untilled land, Felton (6) is on a plain or open field, Hatton (12) on a heath, Stretton (17) and Stratton (13) being on a street or Roman road (see p. 266). Frampton (10) may be the firm or strong tun, Langton (17) the long tun, Witton (17) is usually the wide tun, and Whitton the white tun. Littleton (16) is the small tun, Drayton (24) the dry tun, and Hortun (19) either the dirty tun (A.S. *horu*, filth) or the hoar tun (A.S. *hár*, hoar, grey). Stockton (12) refers to logs, Stapleton (7) to posts, Stanton (24) to stones, Clayton (12) to clay, Gretton to grit (A.S. *greót*), Santon to sand, Garston to grass or meadow land, and Riston to brushwood (*hris*). Among the commonest names are Burton (60), Barton (45), and Bolton (22), elsewhere explained. A priest must have lived at Preston (49), farm servants at Carlton (40), Charlton (29), Chorlton (8), and Hinton (27), sheep were kept at Shipton and Skipton (see p. 257), wethers at Hambleton, bucks or goats at Boughton, and swine at Swinton. Oxton in Cheshire (A.S. *Oggodestún*) is, however, from a personal name. Another curious disguise is Dutton, Cheshire, called in Domesday *Duntune*, the ' hill tun.'

A noticeable thing about this suffix *-ton*, so universal in England as to have supplied the names of town and township, is that it is not found in Germany, Altona, an apparent exception, being from another source. The same is the case with the suffix *-don*, A.S. *dún*, a hill, which is undoubtedly a loan-word from the Celtic (see p. 113). That these suffixes *tún* and *dún*, so common in England, should be unknown in Germany, is an argument supporting a theory now in favour, that the first is a doublet of the second, but on the other hand it is difficult to understand why, if *tún* is derived from *dún*, or closely related to it, it should have a wholly different signification, agreeing with that of *zaun*, its phonetic equivalent in German, both meaning a place surrounded by a hedge, whereas *dún* signifies a hill, the Celtic *-dunum*, frequent in continental names, meaning a hill fort. The difficulty may to some extent be explained by assimilation, and as a matter of fact we find the suffixes *-don* and *-ton* are frequently interchanged with each other as well as with den and stone. Thus Headington, Oxon, was *Hedyndon*; Staunton, Notts, was *Staundon*; Bampton, Devon, was *Bedmdún*; and Bishampton, Worcestershire, was *Biscopes dún*, the ' bishop's hill.' Again Braydon, Wilts, was *Braden*, while Marden, Wilts, was *Meredún*, the ' hill by the mere.'

Next to *-ton* the commonest English suffix is *-ham*, which occurs in the names of insignificant hamlets, and even of isolated farms, as well as in those of great cities such as Birmingham, and of towns like Durham, Nottingham, Buckingham, Northampton, and Southampton, so important as to have given their names to shires or counties. The manifold difficulties which attend its discussion are shown by the fact that while the syllable *-ham* in Durham, Southampton, and Northampton arises from assimilation or corruption, it does not represent the same Anglo-Saxon word in Cheltenham and in Nottingham. When *-ham* is the final syllable of a name there are two chief sources to which it can generally be referred. When the first element is a personal or family name, as in the case of Rainham, Meopham, Lewisham, Rockingham, Collingham, or Effingham, the vowel as a rule was long, and *-ham* represents an A.S. *hám*, denoting the house or 'home' of an early settler. This

corresponds to the -*heim* so common in Germany, as in Mannheim or
Rüdesheim. But when the vowel was originally short, it is from the A.S.
ham, also written *hom*, which denotes an enclosure of some kind, and not
necessarily a place of habitation. Such hams or enclosures existed at Aston
as late as 1657, when mention is made of the Hayward's Ham, the Water
Steward's Ham, the Grass Steward's Ham, the Constable's Ham, the Smith's
Ham, the Herd's Ham, the Bull Ham, and the Penny Ham, most of which
were garths or closes appropriated as a recompense for the services of the
various village officials. In many places the reeve had a close called either
ref-ham, *ref-mede*, or *reve-lond*, and in the Abingdon Chronicle certain
enclosures for sheep are called *sceap-hammas*, and others for flax are
flax-hammas.

The two A.S. words from which the modern suffix -*ham* is derived were
distinguished, as we have seen, by the length of the vowel. This distinction,
which is marked in good early MSS., was unfortunately lost before the time of the
Norman conquest, as is shown by the mention of Buckingham in the Chronicle
(A.D. 918). One MS. has *to Buccingahamme*, where the doubled consonant
shows that the vowel must have been short, while another MS. has *to
Buccingaháme*, where the vowel is expressly marked as long. But as the
names in documents are usually in an oblique case, the distinction can often
be detected owing to the fact that *hám*, meaning a 'home,' makes the genitive
hámes and the dative *háme*, whereas *ham*, an 'enclosure,' has *hammes* in the
genitive and *hamme* in the dative. Among the names which the forms in
early charters prove to be from *ham*, an 'enclosure,' are Farnham, Surrey,
A.S. *æt Fearnhamme*, 'at the enclosure among the ferns'; Cheltenham,
A.S. *Celtanhomme*, the 'enclosure on the Chelt'; Culham, Oxon, A.S.
Culanhom, as well as Evesham, Chippenham, and Twickenham. It may be
noted that when *ham* means a 'home,' it usually occurs in combination with
a family or personal name, and there appears to be no clear and certain case
of -*ham* having this signification when it is not associated with a personal
name, or when it occurs as the initial or medial syllable of a word, as in the
instances of Hampton, Wolverhampton, or Carhampton, or when it stands by
itself as a village name. Thus three villages called Ham, in Kent, Sussex,
and Wilts, all appear in charters in the dative case as *Hamme* or *æt Hamme*,
and Ham, in Surrey, is called *Hom* in a charter, which is equally significant.
Another source of names in -*ham* is the word *ham*, *hom*, or *hamm*, which,
unlike the other two, is feminine, making both genitive and dative in *e*. It
means primarily the ham or knee of an animal, and seems to be also used to
denote the bend or curve of a river. When in the bends of a winding river,
like the Ouse near Bedford, we find a number of villages with names ending
in -*ham*, which are hemmed in by the successive curves of the stream, there is
a presumption that this may be the meaning. This may also be the case
with Hampton in Middlesex, which is inclosed by a great bend of the Thames,
and may perhaps be identified with a place called *Homtune* in a charter.
Hampton in Herefordshire is also called *Homtun* in a charter. But -*ham* is
often merely an assimilated form. In the names of Welham and Howsham
it has arisen, as we have seen, from the assimilation of -*um*, the suffix of the

dative plural, and in the case of Durham it is a corruption of *holm* (see p. 114). In other cases it is a corruption of the genitive singular in *-an*, or of *-ing*, the patronymic suffix, or it may be due to a river name. On the other hand, the suffix is obscured in such cases as Cheam (A.S. *Cegham*) or Epsom (A.S. *Ebbesham*). Hampton (see p. 141), whether alone or in composition, is usually a corruption of *Heántune*, 'high tún,' and Hampstead of *Heánstede*, the 'high place.' When we have no guidance from documents earlier than Domesday it is wiser to avoid speculation as to the meaning of this perplexing syllable. The A.S. *héma*, or *hǽma* (gen. pl.) means 'those of a *ham*' (p. 142).

The English *-ton* is usually replaced in Germany by *hof*, a word of nearly the same meaning, which occurs, usually as *hoven*, in more than 300 ancient German names. It is curious that though the Anglo-Saxons possessed the word *hof*, a 'house,' it should be so rare in England. We have, however, Hove in Sussex (D.B. *Hov*), Howden, Yorks (D.B. *Hovedene*), Hoveton, Norfolk (H.R. *Hoveton*), and other places of the same name.

From *bótl*, an abode or house, we have the names Newbottle and New-battle. Nobottle Hundred in Northants is a curious corruption of *Neubotle*, the form in the Hundred Rolls. Beadlam, Yorkshire, formerly *Bodelum* (D.B. *Bodlun*), is from the dative plural of *bótl*. Bolton, the name of 22 places in the northern counties, signifies a *tún* or enclosure containing a *bótl*, or house (see p. 71). The eight Yorkshire Boltons are all called *Bodelton* in Domesday. There are two names in the south, Kimbolton in Hunts, and Chilbolton in Hants, which are apparent exceptions to the rule that Bolton is found only in the north, but the old forms show that these are both from the personal names Cynebald and Ceolbald (p. 163). Bolton, Derbyshire (D.B. *Boletune*), may be referred to the O.N. *ból*, a farm, whence also Claypole, the farm on the clay, and the name Belton. Ten places are called Newbold (D.B. *Newebold*), which, as well as Newbald, is explained by the A.S. *bold*, which means a building, usually of timber. Bothwell is the A.S. *bótlwela*, a village or collection of houses, literally 'house wealth.'

The A.S. *cot* or *cott* denoted a thatched cottage with walls of loam or mud. It usually appears in the names of insignificant places. Draycott, Somerset (D.B. *Dregcota*), is the 'dry cottage'; Woodmancote, Hants (A.S. *Wode-manecote*), was a woodman's cottage. Burcott is a doubtful name. Cotting-with, Yorkshire (D.B. *Cotewid*), is the wood by the cottage. As already explained, Coatham, Cottam, and Cotton are from the dative plural *cotum* or *cottum*, 'at the cottages.' Seal in Kent (A.S. *Seale*), Seal in Worcestershire (A.S. *Sele*), and probably Zeal, Devon ; Seal, Surrey ; Selworthy, Somerset; Selborne, Hants, and a few similar names may be referred to the A.S. *sele*, a 'dwelling.' A few names such as Chiltern and Whithorn (p. 294), anciently *Hwit-ern*, translated *candida casa*, are from the A.S. *-ærn* or *-ern*, a place or habitation. Mintern, Dorset, A.S. *Minterne*, may have been at a place overgrown with wild mint.

The suffix *-hall*, usually represented by *heal* in A.S. charters, and by *hala* or *hale* in Domesday, was supposed by Kemble and Leo to denote a stone house (A.S. *heall*, 'aula'). More recent researches have shown that it usually represents the West Saxon *healh*, a slope, which is the old Northern *halc*, *halch*, or *halgh*, the source of the modern Northumbrian and Lowland Scotch *haugh* or *hauch*, locally used to denote a steep hill or bank, a meaning supported by the O.N. equivalent *hallr*, a hill or slope, and by an A.S. charter in which *Balwineshealh* is explained as *petrosum clivum*. Moreover, it is difficult to believe that halls or stone houses were so numerous at the time when the names were given as to account for the prevalence of this suffix, and there are many names in which hall would be an impossible translation of *heal* or *healh*. For instance, Ticknall, Derbyshire, called *Ticenheal* in an A.S. charter, would be the goat's rock or slope (A.S. *ticcen*, a goat or kid) ; and Tickenall, Staffordshire, is *Ticenheale* in a charter. Holton, Somerset, A.S. *Healhtún*, and Halton, Bucks, A.S. *Healtún*, would be the tun on a slope ; and Rushall, Yorks, was *Rischale*, the rushy slope. In charters *healh* occurs repeatedly, as in *Cymedeshealh*, *Puttanhealh*, and *Iddeshealh*, which is probably Iddinshall in Cheshire. Among other names we have Ludgershall, Wilts, A.S. *Lutegaresheal*; Buxhall, Suffolk, A.S. *Bucyshealæ* and *Bocceshale*; and Breadsall, Derbyshire, A.S. *Bregdeshale* or *Brægesheal*. Willenhall, Staffordshire, is called in a charter *Willanhalch*, the slope of Willa. Sheriff Hales in Salop is called in Domesday *Halas*, ' the slopes,' from *halas*, plural of *healh*, the prefix being due to its having been owned in the eleventh century by Rainold Bailgiole, Sheriff of Shropshire. From Domesday we also learn that Willingale Spain in Essex, called *Ulingehala*, was owned by a Norman adventurer from Spain, Hervey de Ispania, whence the distinctive affix. In the Yorkshire Domesday Crakehall is *Crachale*, Sicklinghall is *Sidingale*, Strensall is *Strensale*, Cattal is *Cathale*, Birdsall is *Briteshala*, Upsall is *Upeshale*, Ricall is *Richale*, Roall is *Ruhale*, and Elmsall is *Ermeshala*. But *healh* may become *hill* or *ill*: *Picala* or *Pichale* being now Pickhill, *Wifleshale* being now Wilsill, *Snachehale* being now Snaygill, and *Steineshale* being now Stancill, while -*hall* may be from other sources, such as the A.S. *scylfe*, a shelf or ledge of land ; Bashall, Yorks, being *Bascelf* in Domesday. The cognate Northumbrian word *haugh* or *hauch*, which signifies a slope or plot of ground near a river, must not be confounded with *heugh* or *heuch*, another Northumbrian dialect word supposed to be cognate with *hôgh* or *hôh* (see p. 151), which denotes an inland bluff, as in Keyheugh or Ratcheugh (see p. 143). We have *haugh* in Hawick, in Kirkhaugh, Northumberland (formerly *Kirkhalgh*), in Chartershaugh on the Wear in Durham, and in Great Haughton and Little Haughton in Durham, called respectively *Halctona* and *Halghtona* in the Boldon Book. A Domesday *Halctun* is now Haighton in Lancashire. It is often confused with *haw*, the normal descendant of the West Saxon *haga*, genitive *hagan*, which signifies pasture land surrounded by a hedge, and hence a small estate, whence Hagley, Worcestershire, A.S. *Haganled*; Haworth, Yorks, D.B. *Hageneworde*; Haynes, Beds, D.B. *Hagenes*; and the Lincolnshire Haugh or Hough, as in Hough-on-the-Hill, D.B. *Hag* and *Hage*. Haydon, Somerset, A.S. *Hægdun*; and Higham Ferrers, Beds, A.S. *Hegham*, may be from *hege*, a hedge, or possibly from *heg*, hay.

At Church Minshull, Cheshire, the church was served by monks from Combermere Abbey. The name appears in a charter of 1130 as *Munsculf*, the 'monk's shelf.' This suffix is often found with hardly any change, as at Raskelf, Yorkshire, Scutterskelfe (D.B. *Codrescelf*), or Hunshelf (D.B. *Hunescelf*). Shelton and Skelton usually signify a tun on a shelf or ledge, as at Shelton, Beds, called *Scelftún* in a charter of 792. Shelley, Suffolk, is *Scelfledge* in a will of 972. But Shelford is either the shallow ford, or a ford with large bivalves.

The British trackway, called the Ridgeway (A.S. *Hrycweg*) is from the A.S. *hrycg*, a 'back' or 'ridge.' Petridge, Surrey, was A.S. *Pédanhrycg*, and Cotheridge, Worcestershire, was *Coddanhrycg*. The word *hrycg* usually becomes *ric* in Domesday. Thus in Dorset Kimmeridge is *Cameric*, Boveridge is *Boveric*, and Pentridge is *Pentric*. In Yorkshire Askrigg is *Ascric*, the 'ash ridge,' and Reighton, near Bridlington, which stands on the escarpment of the chalk, is *Rictone*, the 'ridge-tun.' The A.S. *díc* (m.), a dike, and *díc* (f.), a ditch, are difficult to distinguish except in the oblique cases, the genitive of the first being *díces*, and of the second *díce*. Ditcheat or Dicheat in Somerset, A.S. *Dicesgat* or *Dichesgate*, D.B. *Dicesget*, was a place at a gate or gap in a dike, and Deighton, Yorkshire, D.B. *Diston*, may be a corruption of *Dícestún*. Ditton and Fen Ditton in Cambridgeshire are both *Dictún* in charters. Dogdike, Lincolnshire, was *Donnesdýk* ; Ditchford, Worcestershire, was *Dícford* ; Walditch, Dorset, is *Waldic* in Domesday ; and Ditchampton, Wilts, was *Díchæmatún*. The great earthwork in Wilts called the Wansdyke is a corruption of A.S. *Wodensdyk*. Berwick Prior, Oxon, is a curious assimilation, appearing as *Beridic* in a charter. Walton is sometimes from *Weald-tún*, the tun by the wood, but generally from *weal*, a wall, as at Walton, Northants, A.S. *Wealtún*. Several Waltons take their name from being near a wall or dyke erected for defence against enemies or the sea. Some of these names have been enumerated on p. 291. Wallasea, Essex, is an island surrounded by a sea-wall or embankment, and at Wallbury, Essex, there is a great camp or earthwork enclosing thirty acres.

The O.N. *hlid*, A.S. *hlíth*, a 'slope,' being a fertile source of Icelandic names, we should expect to find it in English topography. To this, or to the A.S. *hlyt*, *hlýt*, or *hlét*, a lot or portion, we may refer Litton, Somerset, and Lydd, Kent, which are called respectively *Hlyt-tun* and *Hlid* in charters. Litton in Derbyshire and in Yorkshire appear in Domesday as *Litun* and *Litone*. Lythe and Leatham are both *Lid* in D.B., Ledsham and Ledstone are *Ledesham* and *Ledestune*, and Lead is *Led*, *Lede*, and *Lied*. But Ledbury, Herefordshire, is on the river Liddon, and Litton Cheney, Dorset, A.S. *Lidentun*, is on the river Lidden. To *hlidgeat*, a swing-gate, we may refer Lidgate, Suffolk, as well as Leadgate in Durham and Cumberland, and the five places called Lydgate, and two called Lydiate.

In local names *field* (A.S. *feld*) does not mean a small enclosure like our present fields, but any flat unwooded land, such as the common open field or tillage ground of a village community, or the plain of a river valley : Mansfield, for instance, being on the plain of the Maun, and Sheffield on the plain of the Sheaf. In the same neighbourhood we have Macclesfield, Chesterfield, Wakefield, Huddersfield, Lichfield, Driffield, Duffield, and

Hatfield. Small enclosures, such as our present fields, went by other names, generally *garth*, as in Aysgarth, or *acre*, as in Sandiacre. A few names, such as Wetwang, Yorkshire, and Wenghale or Winghill, Lancashire, may be referred to the A.S. *wang* or *wong*, O.N. *vangr*, an enclosed field. More usual is the A.S. *hangra*, a meadow, grass plot, or village green, whence Birchanger, Essex, A.S. *Birchanger*; Moggerhanger, Beds, formerly *Morhanger*, the moor-field; Clehonger, Herefordshire, and Clayhanger in Devon, Staffordshire, and Suffolk, the last of which appears in A.S. charters as *Clæghangre* and *Clæighangra*. Ongar in Essex is called in Domesday *Angra*, and *Aungre* in a late charter. To these names we may add Tittenhanger and Panshanger in Herts, Ostenhanger in Kent, Goldhanger in Essex, and Shelfanger in Norfolk. The word *worth* or *worthig* denoted a small estate or plot of ground, as in the places called Hanworth. Tamworth is the estate by the river Tame; Wandsworth the estate on the Wandle; and Bosworth an estate with a boose or ox stall (see p. 72). Worthy, Hants, called *Worthig* in a charter, exhibits the form preserved in Woolfardisworthy, Devon. In Mercia *weorthig* usually becomes *wardine*, as Ingwardine, Shrawardine, or Wrockwardine, the 'estate near the Wrekin,' in Salop.

There are thirty-two places called Leigh, and others called Leighton, Leyton, Lee, and Lea, while *-leigh*, *-ley*, and *-lea* are common suffixes. They are often assimilated, but are from distinct sources. The A.S. *leáh* (m.), genitive *leáges* or *leás*, usually found in the dative singular as *led*, denotes a fallow or lea, untilled land or pasturage, while *leáh* (f.), making *leáge* in the genitive and dative, is cognate with the O.H.G. *lôh*, a thicket, or rough woodland pasture, whence Waterloo and Hohenlohe. Local names being usually from the dative, *leá*, dative of *leáh* (m.), is normally the source of the suffix *-ley* and such names as Leyton or Lee, while *leáge*, dative of *leáh* (f.), is the source of Leigh, Leighton, and *-leigh*, though *-ley* and *-leigh* are often confused in modern names, *-leigh* lapsing into *-ley*: Moseley and Bradley in Worcestershire being *Moseledge* and *Brádanlég* in charters, and Bromley in Kent and Staffordshire being *Bromledge*. This is often shown by the Domesday forms: in Derbyshire Bentley being *Benedlege*, Bramley being *Branlege*, while Hanley is *Henlege*, Rowsley is *Reuslege*, and Tansley is *Taneslege*; in Yorkshire Yearsley is *Everslage*, Stokesley is *Stocheslage*, and Womersley is *Wilmereslege*. Domesday sometimes has *-lac* instead of *-lage*, Pockley being *Pochelac* (in the twelfth century *Speokelegh*); while Helmsley is *Elmeslac*, Osmotherley is *Asmundrelac*, and Beverley is *Beverlac* (see, however, p. 68). While *leáge* is represented by a Domesday *lege* or *lage*, or even by *lac*, *leá* is represented by *lei*, *lie*, *leie*, or *lai*, Ripley and Stanley, for instance, being *Ripelie* and *Stanlei*. When we find *-leigh* in the modern name it is always from *leáge*. Thus Leigh-upon-Mendip, Somerset, is *Leáge* in a charter; Bickleigh, Devon, is A.S. *Bicanleáge*; Butleigh, Somerset, is A.S. *Buddecleighe*; and Hadleigh, Suffolk, was *Hedláge* in 972. Upper Leigh, Staffordshire, is A.S. *Lege*, and Leigh, Dorset, is *Lege* in Domesday. In the North *leigh* sometimes becomes *-laugh*, as at Healaugh, Yorkshire, D.B. *Hailaga* and *Helage*. In many instances *-ley* can be traced to an A.S. *leá*. Thus Berkeley, Gloucestershire, is A.S. *Beorcleá*; Wembley, Middlesex, is *Wembaleá*; Beckley, Sussex, is *Beccanleá*;

and Oakley, Staffordshire, is *Acled*. Though Leighton is normally from *Ledhtún*, Leighton Buzzard, Bedfordshire, is commonly identified with the *Lygetún* of the Chronicle ; but as *Lygetún* must mean the *tún* on the river *Lyge* or Lea, *Lygetún* must be Luton. Leyton, Essex, A. S. *Lygeantún*, is also on the Lea ; and the *Lygeanbyrig*, taken by Cuthwulf in 571, must be Lenbury or Lenborough, at the source of the Lea, near Buckingham. Loughton, near Epping Forest, was formerly *Loketon* or *Luketone*, probably from *locu*, a fold for cattle. Lees or Leese would be from the A.S. *lés*, pasture, of which the nominative plural *léswa* would give Leasow, a common name in Salop.

In the old forest districts, chiefly in the weald of Kent, Sussex, and Hants, we find numerous names in *-den*, which must have denoted woodlands suited for the pasturage of swine and goats, the number to be kept being regulated by a Court called the Court of Dens. The A.S. words *den* (n.), *dene* (m.), and *denu* (f.), formerly believed to be loan-words from the Celtic, denoted these wooded valleys or lowlands. Hence we may explain the name of the forest of Dean, and probably of the forests of Bra-den and Ar-den, and several villages called Dean, all in wooded valleys. Besides Dean we have Rotting-dean and Marden in Sussex, with numerous names in Kent, such as Tenterden, Cowden, Hazleden, or Romden, which appear originally to have referred to swine-pastures, answering to the Devonshire names in *bere* or *bear*. In Hants we have Chidden, A.S. *Cittanden*, 'kite valley'; and Surrenden, A.S. *Swithrædingdæn*. In Domesday Tincleton, Dorset, is *Tincladene*, evidently from a personal name ; and Silsden, Yorks, is *Siglesden*. On the skirts of Epping Forest we find Theydon, formerly *Taindena*, perhaps the thane's den. The South-Eastern *den* is replaced in the North by the Scandinavian *dale* (German *thal*), and in the South-West by *combe*. Thus the seventeen places called Dalton range with thirty-two called Compton and sixteen called Denton. Combe was an early loan-word from the Celtic, appearing as *cwm* in modern Welsh names, such as Cwm Bechan, and in Strath Clyde taking the form *cum*, as Cumwhitton and Cumdevock, both in Cumberland. It is not, however, confined to these districts, as we have Combe in Surrey and High Wycombe in Bucks. Winchcombe in Gloucestershire is called in a charter *Wincelcumb*, glossed *in angulo vicus* (A.S. *wincel*, a corner). Comb is found in Wessex charters in the eighth century, and then vanishes from English literature till 1578. A combe is usually a hollow in a hill side, and corresponds in meaning to *hope*, a word which takes its place in certain Northern and Mercian districts. In O.N. *hóp* denoted a small bay or inlet, whence the Scotch hope, a haven, as St. Margaret's Hope, a bay in South Ronaldshay, one of the Orkneys. Stanford-le-Hope, Essex, called The Hope by seamen, is near a bay or pool. In the Fen districts *hop* means a pool in a moor or marsh. Elsewhere it is a local term, probably unrelated, usually denoting a semicircular recess in a hill side, in which sense it is very common in Weardale, Durham, and in Yarrow and Ettrick, Selkirkshire. In Yarrow almost every farmhouse is sheltered in a recess or hollow of the hills, and the names in *-hope* are correspondingly numerous, as, for instance, Kirkhope, Dryhope, Whitehope, Levinshope, Sundhope, Bowerhope, and Ladhope, more than twenty in all.   In Upper Weardale, Durham, we find another cluster of these names, such as Stanhope, Burnhope, Westen-hope, Wellhope, Harthope, Swinhope, Rockhope, and Bollehope, the mean-ing of which is mostly transparent, though the names are sometimes dis-guised, as at Ryhope, Durham, which appears in the Boldon Book as *Refhope*, probably the 'reeves hope.' At Cassop, Durham, called *Cazhope* in the Boldon Book, we find the change from *-hope* to *-op*, which is usual in Mercia.   Ratlinghope, Salop, preserves the older form, but the contracted form is seen in Alsop, Derbyshire, D.B. *Elleshope*, which contains the same personal name which we have in Ellesmere.   Heslop and Glossop in Derby-shire, Worksop in Notts, and Middop in Yorkshire appear in Domesday as *Hetesope*, *Glosop*, *Werchesope*, and *Mithope*.   Skellingthorpe in Lincolnshire (D.B. *Scheldinehope*) has been assimilated to the neighbouring names in *-thorpe*.   An outlying name of the same class is Gattertop, Herefordshire, a corruption of *Gatterede-hope*.   To the same source we may refer the ten places which go by the name of Hopton.

The suffix *-gale*, like *-hope*, denotes a place in the hollow of a hill.   It is the Scotch *gill* and the O.N. *geil*, pronounced *gale*.   It is common in the Lake district, where it denotes a ravine or narrow lane, as Buttergill or Ormsgill.   Fingal in Yorkshire (D.B. *Finegala* and *Finegal*) may be the woodpecker's hollow (*fina*, a woodpecker).   In some cases, however, such as Repingale, Lincolnshire, called *Repinghale* in Domesday, Boningale in Salop, or Edingale in Staffordshire, the suffix is more probably from *healh*, a slope.

It is difficult to determine the meaning of the suffix *-wick* or *-wich*, which may be from the A.S. *wíc*, a 'dwelling-place,' cognate with the Latin *vicus*, or from *wíc*, a bay, as in the case of Sandwich, Kent, appropriately named the 'sandy bay.'   Alnwick was the dwelling on the Aln, Berwick the dwelling on the hill, and Norwich the northern dwelling.   Greenwich, A.S. *Gréne-wíc*, may be the green dwelling-place, or may refer to a bay or reach of the Thames, the name Woolwich, called *Wulewíc* in a charter, referring to the adjacent reach.   Wick in Dorset and Worcestershire are called *Wíc* in charters, and Wick Episcopi in Worcestershire was *Wican*, while Wickford in Essex and Worcestershire were *Wícford*.   There are twenty-one places called Hardwick, usually from *heorde*, a herd or flock.   Thus Hard-wick in Northants and in Warwickshire are called *Heordewic* in charters, and in the Boldon Book Hardwick, Durham, is *Herdewyk*, the station or abode of the herd.   In a charter the word *wíc* is glossed *mariscus*, a 'marsh,' but the corresponding modern names are difficult to distinguish. Sometimes the nature of the ground may determine the meaning, as in the case of Wykeham in the North Riding, which stands on the edge of an old morass.

Thorpe, the distinctive Danish designation of a township or a hamlet, corresponds to the O.H.G. *dorp*, now *dorf*, and is cognate with the Gaelic *tref*, Irish *treb*, Breton *trev*, and Welsh *tre*, a dwelling, and with the Latin *tribus*, appearing also in *A-treb-ates* and other Celtic tribe-names.   It is common in the Danish shires of York, Lincoln, Nottingham, Derby, Northampton, Norfolk, and Suffolk.   The prefix is frequently a personal name, as in Langthorpe, Yorks (D. B. *Lambetorp*), Haisthorpe (D.B. *Aschiltorp*), Tholthorpe (D.B. *Turulfestorp*), and Kettlethorpe. Places appearing simply as *Torp* in Domesday have usually acquired a distinctive suffix, generally from the name of a later owner, as Thorpe Bassett, Thorpe Bulmer, Thorpe Arch, Thorpe Mandeville, and Thorpe Abbots, or from the patron saint, as Thorpe Constantine, or from situation, as Thorpe By-Water, Thorpe-in-Balne, Thorpe-in-the-Street, Thorpe-on-the-Hill, Thorpe Underwood, or Thorpe-sub-Montem.

The commonest Scandinavian suffix, notably in Yorkshire and Lincolnshire, is *-by*, as in the names Kirby, Whitby, or Grimsby. It is the O.N. *bær*, *bœr*, or *byr*, Norwegian *bo*, Swedish and Danish *by*, from the root *búa*, to dwell, whence *bú*, a house. It originally denoted a building or dwelling, then a farmstead, and afterwards a village or town. Some names show that it was applied to a single house or hut. Thus Skidby, Yorkshire (D.B. *Schitebi*) must have denoted a log hut, or a building constructed of shingles or split wood (A.S. *scide*, O.N. *skid*, a billet of wood).

The suffix *-thwaite* is characteristic of the districts settled by the Norwegians rather than by the Danes. It is common in Norway in the form *-thweit*. The root is seen in the A.S. *thwítan*, 'to chop.' The Frisian *tved* means a place cleared of wood, and this seems to have been the original signification of *thwaite* in England, though the O.N. *thveit* denotes an outlying cottage with its paddock. This suffix occurs chiefly in the Lake district, being found more than a hundred times in Cumberland alone, as Thornthwaite, Thornythwaite, Applethwaite, Rosthwaite, Finsthwaite, Smaithwaite, Shoulthwaite, Satterthwaite, Legberthwaite, Ormathwaite, and Langthwaite. These thwaites are mostly on high ground, and apparently denoted 'clearings' on the Fells. The Norwegian colony extended into the adjacent parts of Yorkshire, where we have Gristhwaite, Staithwaite, Folithwaite, and Braithwaite. Elsewhere the word is rare, but there are two places in Norfolk and one in Suffolk called Thwaite, and a Thwaite Hall in Lincolnshire.

The suffix *-ville*, so common in France, does not seem to have been introduced into England, names apparently containing it being really from other sources. Thus Cheney Longville in Salop is an assimilated form from *Langefeld*, the 'long field,' with a prefix derived from the Cheney family, who in the fourteenth century owned the manor. Yeovil in Somerset is the modern form of *Givel*, the name of the river on which it stands. Melville and a few other names are attributed to Norman adventurers.

Villages must not be regarded as coming into existence as villages, but rather as townships gradually growing up round the *tún* or dwelling of the first settler, whose abode either bore the owner's name, or was distinguished by some local characteristic, such as position, colour, form, or frequently from some neighbouring natural object, a cliff, a brook, a wood, or frequently from the tree which shaded it. Trees of peculiar formation may account for such village names as Tiptree in Essex, Heavitree in Devon, Wavertree in Lancashire, Picktree in Durham, and Harptree in Somerset, while Bartestree, Herefordshire, A.S. *Bartholdes-*

treu, Austry, Warwickshire, A.S. *Adulfestreow*, 'Ealdulf's tree,' and Manningtree in Essex are plainly from personal names. The A.S. *treó* or *trebw* gives tree in modern English, just as *cnebw* gives knee. But in local names we have such abraded forms as Austry, Coventry, and Oswestry, or archaic spellings, such as Toltingtrough in Kent, Gostrow in Sussex, Oaktrow (D.B. *Wochitreu*) in Somerset, where also we find such names as Hallatrow and Wanstrow. Sometimes *treó* becomes *der*, *dur*, or *dore*, as in the case of Mappowder, Dorset, a curious form which represents an older *Mapulder* (D.B. *Mapledre*), the 'maple-tree.' Mapperton or Maplerton in Dorset, and Maperton in Somerset, are the A.S. *Mapelder-tún* (D.B. *Mapledre-tone*), the tun by the maple-tree, and Mapledurham, Oxon, is the A.S. *Mapulderham*, 'Maple-tree-ham,' like Appledurcombe in the Isle of Wight, which is the Appletree combe. A place in Kent, called in the Chronicle *æt Apuldre*, 'at the apple tree,' afterwards became *Apulder* or *Apolder*, the 'apple tree,' and is now Appledore. Appledram, Sussex, is a corruption of *Appelder-ham*, and Salterford, Notts, D.B. *Saltreford*, must be the ford at the sallow tree (A.S. *sealh*, a sallow). Hills and other natural features of the land were often named from trees, as in the case of such names as Onetreehill, Sevenoaks, or Fourashes. A.S. charters show that Bampton, Devon, was *Beámdún*, 'the tree hill,' and that Benfleet, Essex, was *Beám-fleót*, 'tree creek.'

From *ellen*, the elder tree, we have Allington, Wilts, A.S. *Ellendun*, 'elder tree hill.' In the north of England it is called the baw-tree or burtree, which has locally become 'buttery.' Butterley in Salop, called in Domesday *Butrelie*, is probably the elder-tree pasture, and a single elder-tree may have given a name to Bawtry, Yorkshire, formerly *Bautre*. Butterwick, a township in the East Riding, called *Butrvid* in Domesday, is evidently *Buirtre-vidr*, or 'elder-tree wood' (O.N. *vidr*, a wood). Butterwick in Lincolnshire and in the North Riding, both called *Butrvic* in Domesday, may, however, be from the proper name Buttr or Budar, or from *bud*, a booth or hut. The name of Buttermere in Westmoreland is also ambiguous.

The ash appears oftenest in local names. Some two hundred places are called Ashton, Ashby, Ashstead, Ashworth, Ashwick, Ashcot, and the like. Askrigg, D.B. *Ascric*, is a northern form answering to the southern Ashridge, Asquith, D.B. *Askvid*, is the Ash-wood, and Askham, D.B. *Ascam*, 'at the ashes,' appears to be a dative plural. Ashmansworth, Hants, is a corruption of *Æscmeresweorth*, either from a personal name, or the estate by the ash-tree mere. Ashton must not be confounded with Aston, which is usually the East tún. An isolated ash, which forms a sort of landmark in English history, must have crowned the summit of the Ridgeway in Berks, since Ashdown, A.S. *Æsces-dún*, the 'hill of the ash tree,' was the spot where Alfred and Ethelred gained their first victory over the Danes. If not from the personal name *Æsc*, isolated ashes may also have given names to Ashton in Wilts and Ashbury, Berks, called in charters *Asces-dún* and *Æsces-byrig*.

The oak and the thorn are nearly as common in local names as the ash. There are twenty-seven places called Acton, twenty-nine called Thornton, and twenty-eight called Ashton. Ockley in Surrey and Oakley in Hants appear in A.S. documents as *Acleáh* or *Acleá*, the 'oak lea,' and the curious name of Ugley in Essex appears to be a corruption of Oakley or Ockley. In D.B. Aughton, Yorkshire, is *Actun*, Oakford, Dorset, is *Acford*, and Oakover, Staffordshire, is the A.S. *Acofre*, the oak bank. Notable thorns appear at two places called Cawthorne, the leafless or 'callow thorn'; and at Cropthorne, Worcestershire, A.S. *Cropponthorn*, and Glapthorne, Northants, A.S. *Glapthorn*, were thorns with bunches or burrs. Hatherton in Staffordshire is the A.S. *Haguthorndun*, 'hawthorn hill.' Thornton is a name as common as Acton. There are sixteen in Yorkshire, all called *Torentun* in Domesday. Several places are called Thornbury, Thornborough, and Thornbrough, which usually appear in old records as *Thornebergh*, 'thorn hill.' Thornford in Dorset and Thornhaugh in Northants are also from the thorn. Thornholme in Yorks is *Thirnon* in Domesday, evidently a corruption of the dative plural *Thyrnum*, 'at the thorns.'

We find the elm at Elm, Cambridgeshire, A.S. *Ælm*; at Elmley, Worcestershire, A.S. *Elmleáh*; at Elmham, Norfolk, A.S. *Ælmham*; but such names are rare. Much more common is the birch, which gives names to more than fifty places, as Berkeley, Gloucestershire, A.S. *Beorcleá* and *Bercleá*, or Barkham, Berks, A.S. *Beorcham*. Birkin, Yorkshire, D.B. *Berchige*, is the 'birch isle.' Lindridge, Worcestershire, A.S. *Lindrycg*, may be from the lime-tree, but Linton in Gloucestershire and Cambridgeshire, both called *Lintún* in A.S. charters, Lindon, Dorset, A.S. *Lindun*, and Lincomb, Worcestershire, A.S. *Lincumb*, are from *lin*, flax. Apps, Surrey, is the A.S. *Æpse*, the 'aspen,' and Apsley Guise, Beds, and Apsley, Surrey, are from the same tree. An alder (A.S. *alr*, gen. *alres*), must have grown at Alresford, Hants, A.S. *Alrford* and *Alresford*, while Ellerton, Yorks, D.B. *Elreton*, is explained by the O.N. *elri*, an erle or alder tree. From the maple, in addition to Mappowder, Mapledurham, and Mapperton, already mentioned, we have Maplebeck in Notts; Maplestead, Essex, A.S. *Mapulderstede*, 'maple-tree place'; and Mapleborough, Warwickshire, A.S. *Mapelesbarwe*, which was a barrow with a maple-tree. The apple-tree is a fertile source of names, such as Appleton, Appleby, Applethwaite, and Applegarth. Eppleby was anciently *Apelby*. Appletree Hundred in Derbyshire is called *Apeltreu* in Domesday. Plumtree Hundred in Notts is a similar name, and Plumstead, Kent, is A.S. *Plumstede*. From the pear, A.S. *pirige*, we have Pirtun, Worcestershire, and Parton, Wilts, both called *Pirigtún* in charters. Purfleet, Essex, was *Pirigfleót*, and Pirbright, Surrey, was *Pirifrith*. The scarcity of names referring to the pine or the fir bears out, to some extent, Cæsar's assertion as to its absence from Britain, the few existing names being chiefly confined to the Northern region, which was not visited by Cæsar. The A.S. *gyr* or *gyrtreów*, a fir tree, explains Gartree Hundred in Leicestershire, and the lost Wapentake of Gartree in Lincolnshire (formerly *Gayrtree*, *Geyrtree*, and *Gairtree*). We have also a Garford in Berks, with Garforth and Gargrave (D.B. *Gereford* and *Geregrave*) in Yorkshire. Sefton may be from *sæppe*, fir. We find the hazel at Haslemere, Surrey, A.S. *Héselmæresgraf*, 'hazel mere grove,' and at Haselbury-Bryan, Dorset, A.S. *Héselberi*.

Nuthurst, Warwickshire, was *Hnuthyrst*, but Nutford, Dorset, and Nut-bourne, Sussex, are assimilated names, as appears from the Domesday forms *Nortforde* and *Nordborne*, while Notgrove, Gloucestershire, is the A.S. *Nætan gráfas* and *Natan grafum*. Widford, Gloucestershire, A.S. *Withig-ford*; Withycombe, Somerset, A.S. *Withicumb*; and Widley, Hants, A.S. *Withigled*, are from the A.S. *withige* or *withie*, a willow or osier, but without ancient forms such names are doubtful, many being from *wíd*, wide, or *hwít*, white, or from personal names, such as Willoughby from Willa, or Willerby from Wilgard.

Broom, heather, fern, sedge, grass, and rushes, are the source of names like Bromley, Hatley, Farnley, Sedgeley, Bentley, which denoted rough pastures overgrown with such vegetation. Bromley, a common name, is *Brómledge* or *Brómled* in charters, and there are twelve places called Brompton. To the A.S. *hæth*, heath, we may refer twelve places called Hatfield, A.S. *Hæthfeld*. Hadleigh is *Hæthledge*, and Hatton, Hadley, or Hatley are common names. Some forty places take their names from fern ; among them Farleigh, A.S. *Fearnledge* ; Farndon, A.S. *Fearndun* ; Farnborough and Farmborough, A.S. *Fearnbeorh*. Farnham, Surrey, called *Fearnhamme* in 893, is the enclosure in the fern, but Farnsfield, Notts, D.B. *Franesfeld*, must be from the per-sonal name Fræne. Brackenholm and Brechenbrough in Yorkshire, formerly *Brachenholm* and *Brachenbergh*, are from *braccan*, nom. pl. of *bracce*, fern or bracken. *Linghœse*, as Hayes, Middlesex, is called in a charter, shows that the O.N. word *ling*, heather, must have existed in A.S. Of the fourteen places called Bentley, four appear in charters as *Beoneı-ledge*, and others in Domesday as *Benedlage*, signifying pastures overgrown with bents or bennet grass (A.S. *beonet*). From the A.S. *gærs*, grass, or from *gærstun*, a grass meadow, we have several places called Garston and Garsdon, A.S. *Garstun* and *Gersdun*. Turvey, Beds, D.B. *Torveia*, would mean the turf isle. Rushmere, Rusholme, and Rushden may be referred to the A.S. *risc*, a rush, and Rushall, Staffordshire, A.S. *Hrischalh*, would be the rushy slope, or, like Princes Risborough, Bucks, A.S. *Hrisbeorh*, may be from the O.N. *hrís*, brushwood. Crowle, Worcestershire, A.S. *Crohled*, is from *croh*, meadow saffron ; Minety, Wilts, A.S. *Mintig*, is the 'mint isle '; and Humbleyard Hundred, Norfolk (H.R. *Humilyerd*) is from earth overgrown with bindweed (A.S. *hymele*), whence also Himbleton, Wor-cestershire, A.S. *Hymeltún*. We have nettles at Nettlestead, Kent, A.S. *Netlesstede* ; and at Netswell, Essex, A.S. *Nethleswel*. Names from reeds are common, as Redmarley, Worcestershire, A.S. *Reódmæreley* ; Rod-bourne, Wilts, A.S. *Reódburne* ; and Redbridge, Hants, A.S. *Reódford*. Soham, near Cambridge, A.S. *Sægham*, is appropriately named from sedge, as well as Sedgley, Staffordshire ; Sedgeberrow, Worcestershire ; and Sedg-moor, Somerset. Wedmore, Somerset, A.S. *Weódmor* ; Weedon, in Bucks and Northants, A.S. *Weódun* ; and many more are explained by the A.S. *weód*, herb, grass, or weed.

Wootton is generally from the A.S. *Wudutún*, the tun by the wood. In Theydon Bois the affix may be Norman French, but Warboys, Hants, is A.S. *Wardebusc*. The suffix *-hurst* is very common in the Weald of Kent and Sussex, as Midhurst, Maplehurst, or Lamberhurst. The A.S. *gráf*, a grove, must be distinguished from *græf*, a grave or ditch. Thus Broomsgrove, Worcestershire, is A.S. *Bremesgráfan*; Notgrove, Gloucestershire, is *Nætangráfas*; Boxgrove, Sussex, is *Bosgrave* in Domesday ; while Mulgrave, Yorks, is *Grif* in Domesday ; Falsgrave is *Wallesgrif*, and Stonegrave is *Stanegrif*. There are several villages called Holt, from the A.S. *holt*, a 'wood,' which is not uncommon in charters. Part of Bere forest is called Alice holt. Bagshot in Windsor forest, like Aldershot and Oakshot in the great Andred forest, may also be from *holt*, which in Belgium becomes *hot* and *hoat*. But since Whapshot, Surrey, is *Wopshete* in a charter, and Bramshott, Ludshot, and Empshot are *Brambresete, Lidesete*, and *Hibesete* in Domesday, apparently from *seáta, seóta*, or *séta*, plural forms of *seótu*, meaning open commons or cattle pastures, it is not impossible that the names may have been assimilated. Aldersholt and Oaksholt, on the one hand, and Brembresete and Lidesete, on the other, having lapsed into the common forms Aldershot, Oakshot, Bramshott, and Ludshot. Northolt, Middlesex, is not the North holt, but the North *healh* or slope, as appears from the Domesday form *Northala*. Monksilver, Somerset, called *Selva* in Domesday, may be from the Latin *silva*.

From animals two counties, Oxfordshire and Hertfordshire, and an important town, Gateshead, derive their names. There are many names of the same class, some bearing witness to the former existence of animals now extinct. Barbourne, Worcestershire, called *Beferburn* in a charter of 904, and Bevere, near Worcester, formerly *Beverie*, the beaver isle, besides Beverley, Yorkshire, testify to the diffusion of the beaver. The wild boar is found at Yearsley, Yorks (D.B. *Everslage*); Eversley, Hants (A.S. *Everslea*); Everleigh, Wilts (A.S. *Eburleáge*) ; Everdon, near Daventry, called *Eferdune* in 944 ; Evercreech, Somerset, A.S. *Evercric*, the 'boar's creek '; and Eversholt, Beds, D.B. *Evreshot*, ' the boar's wood.' The existence of the elk, called *ealh* in the Southern, and *elch* in the Northern dialect, has been inferred from the name of Alkborough, Lincolnshire, called *Alke-barue*, 'elk-wood' in a charter, and Elksley, Notts (D.B. *Elchesleig*). On a river island, near Winchester, called Wolvesey, the Welsh in the reign of Edgar had to deposit their annual tribute of wolves' heads. Woolpit, Suffolk, is one of several places called *Wulfpyt* or *Wulpit* in charters, and two charters mention wolf-pits as existing at Wolley, anciently *Wolfelay*, the 'wolf field,' in Yorkshire. Woolstone, Ulverstone, and Woolhead in Lancashire may also be referred to the wolf, the last being a name of the same class as Gateshead (see p. 132). Similar names, which are not uncommon, may have originated in the practice of erecting on a post the head of some animal as a boundary mark or a tribal emblem. The curious name Thickhead (A.S. *Tykenheved*) means the kid's head (A.S. *ticcen*, a kid), and Consett in Durham, called in the Boldon Book *Conekesheved*, is the coney's or rabbit's head. Farcet, Hunts, called *Fearresheafod* in a charter and *Faresheved* in the Hundred Rolls, is the bull's head, to which we may add Osnead and Neatishead in Norfolk, Hartshead in Lancashire and Yorkshire, Sheepshead in Leicestershire, Swineshead in Lincolnshire, called *Swineshedfod* in a charter, and a Swineshead Hundred in Gloucestershire (H.R. *Swinesheved*). The name Swineshead occurs also in Worcestershire and Hunts.

The A.S. *stód*, a stud, or herd of horses, whence *stódfald*, a horse-fold, explains the name of Stotfold in Beds and Yorkshire (D.B. *Stodfald*), as well as Stottesden, Salop. Studley in Oxon, Wilts, and Warwickshire, and Studley Royal and Studley Roger in Yorks were 'stud pastures.' Studham in Beds, called *Stodham* in a charter of Oswulf, with Stutton in Suffolk and Yorkshire (D.B. *Stutune*) were enclosures for horses, or possibly from the A.S. *studu*, a post or pillar. Fawley, Hants, A.S. *Falethleá*, was a pasture containing a cattle fold, but Fawley, Herefordshire, A.S. *Fæliglæh*, is the yellow, or 'fallow lea,' and Fawsley, Northants, A.S. *Fealuwesleá*, is the lea of the fallow (A.S. *fealwes*, genitive of *fealu*, fallow ground).

One of the commonest elements in English names is *stead* (A.S. *stede*), which means simply a 'place.' There are 1200 names in *stede* to be found in Kemble's collection of charters. It answers to the German *stadt*, which originally meant a place, but has now come to signify a town. Some of the Hampsteads may denote a 'homestead,' but Hampstead, Middlesex, formerly *Heámstede*, is probably from the dative *heán-stede*, 'at the high place.' Greenstead, Essex, A.S. *Grénstede*, is the 'green place,' and Ringstead, Norfolk, A.S. *Ringstede*, was a place enclosed by a ring. Felsted, Essex, anciently *Feldested*, is the place in the field or open country, and Stisted, Essex, was *Stigestede*, a place with a *stig*, either a path, or perhaps a sty or wooden enclosure. The A.S. *stów* also meant a 'place'; it then came to signify a dwelling-place, and ultimately a town, like the German *stadt*. Ely, for instance, was called a *stów*. The word *stoc* or *stóc*, which has now become Stoke, is used almost interchangeably with *stów*, which is possibly only a weak form of *stoc*. The primary meaning of *stoc* seems to have been a stem or stump of a tree, a stock, log, or stake. Possibly *stoc* may have been originally used to denote a place near the stump of a tree in a half cleared forest. In addition to seventy places called Stoke, some of which appear in charters as *Stoc*, we have Basingstoke and Tavistock (A.S. *Tafingstoc*). Stockwith in Notts and Lincolnshire seemingly denoted a wood where the stumps were left standing. Stokesley, Yorkshire (D.B. *Stocheslage*), was probably a pasture containing such a stump. One of the twelve places called Stockton appears in a charter as *Stoctún*, meaning either a *tún* near a stump, or an enclosure formed of logs ; Stockbridge, Hants, being a plank bridge or bridge of logs, and Stalbridge, Dorset (D.B. *Staplebrige*), a trestle bridge. Besides *stoc* and *stapul*, there are a few words of the same class, as *studu*, a post or pillar, dative *styde*, whence the word studded, which means literally 'set with posts.' This may explain the names of Great Stukeley, Hunts, called *Stivecleáh* in a charter, of two places in Yorkshire called Steeton, of Stewton in Lincolnshire, and Stittenham, Yorkshire, in Domesday *Stidnun*. From *swer* or *swir*, a column or pillar, we have Swyre, Dorset, A.S. *Sueire*, D.B. *Suere*. To *sceaftes*, genitive of *sceaft*, a pole, or the shaft of a spear, we may refer Shaftesbury, Dorset, called *Sceaftesbyrig* in the Chronicle. Stickford, Lincolnshire, D.B. *Stichesforde*, is explained by the O.N. *stik*, a pile or stick, and Stixwold, Lincolnshire, would be a field (*völlr*) marked by a post. To the A.S. *píl*, a stake, whence the word pile, or to *pill*, a local variant of pool, we may refer Pilton, Somerset, A.S.

Piltún, and other places called Pilton ; and from *pál*, whence pale and pole, we have Palgrave, Suffolk, A.S. *Palegraf.*

Names like Huntroyd and Ormerod may be explained by a northern dialect-word, which in the Huddersfield glossary is said to signify a clearing in a forest, corresponding to the Swaledale word *ridding*, which we have in the name Ben Rhydding, a hydropathic establishment at Ilkley, so called because it was erected on a piece of ground called in the title deeds, 'the bean ridding.' The O.N. *ruth* or *rud* means a clearing in a wood, and in Hesse, the Hartz, and other German forest districts, names in *reut, ried*, and *rode* are numerous, signifying forest clearings, or places where the trees have been 'rooted' out. Routh, in Holderness, D.B. *Rute* and *Rutha*, may have been such a clearing. In German names *slad* also denotes a forest clearing, probably cognate with the A.S. *sléd* or *sléd*, which is very common in charters, and survives as a dialect-word in the form *slade*, which usually means a strip of green sward between two woods, or between two breadths of ploughland, and is also used to denote strips of marshy ground in valley bottoms, also a valley or strath. In A.S. charters we have *Wulfslæde, Barfodsléd, Fearnhylles slæd*, as well as *Fearnslæd*, Worcestershire, and *Fúgelsléd* in Hants, none of which have been identified. Among modern names we have Slade in Gloucestershire, Waterslade in Somerset, and in Yorkshire, Slaidburn (D.B. *Slateborne*), Slaithwaite and Sledmere (D.B. *Slidemare*). Sleights may be from the O.N. *sléttr*, level. Snaith, in Yorkshire, called *Esnaid* in Domesday, may be referred to the A.S. *snéd*, or *snád*, which seems to have denoted a portion of land, usually a clearing in a forest, of defined limits, but unfenced, the boundaries being marked by incisions on trees (A.S. *snithan*, to cut or prune trees). A charter of 822 mentions a *Snadhyrst*, near Kemsing, in Kent, which seems to have been a portion of a larger wood. Whipsnade, a royal manor in Bedfordshire, is a corruption of *Wibbasnade*, and we know that Wibba, King of the Mercians, had a palace at Berkhamstead, two or three miles distant. The word *frith*, which is not uncommon in field names, and also occurs in village names, is derived immediately from the A.S. *firth* or *fyrth*, supposed to have meant a forest or sheep-walk, which is the meaning of the Welsh loan-word *fridd* or *frydd*, pronounced frith. Chapel-en-le-Frith, Derbyshire, is the Chapel in the Forest, a name analogous to that of Kirby Frith in Leicestershire. There is a township called Frith in the Parish of Forest, Durham, and a place called Fritham in the New Forest, a Frithstock or Frithilstock in Devon, and Frith-with-Wrenbury in Yorkshire. Holmfirth, in the West Riding, is the Forest on the River Holme. In the Craven dialect the word frith is still vernacular, signifying a tract enclosed from the mountain, usually for a plantation or woodland.

Such Celtic names as survived the Teutonic conquest are those of conspicuous hills, like Helvellyn or the Wrekin, fragments of the Celto-Roman names of important cities, as Winchester or Gloucester, or the names of large rivers like the Severn, the Thames, or the Avon. So far as any elements in our village names can be referred to Celtic speech, it is usually because these Celtic river names were incorporated by the Teutonic invaders into the names they gave to their own settlements : Tamworth, for instance, being the estate on the Tame, and Mansfield the plain beside the Maun. When a town or a village bears the name of a river, pure and simple, it is usually due to some portion of an earlier compound having disappeared. Thus the proper name of Hull is Kingston-upon-Hull, and Frome was formerly Minster-on-Frome. Thame was *at Tame* or *Tamu-villa*, Neath was *ad Nidum*, the station where the Roman road crossed the Neath. Such Roman names usually exhibit the suffix *ceaster*, Lancaster being on the Lune, Ribchester on the Ribble, Towcester on the Tove, Brancaster on the Bran, Grantchester on the Granta, Alcester on the Alne, Colchester on the Colne, Doncaster on the Don, Exeter on the Exe. In many cases the modern name is derived not directly from the river name but from the Roman town or station on the river, Cirencester being from *Corinium*, the town on the Corin, now the Churn, and not immediately from the river.

In Devon and other South-Western counties, owing probably to the more gradual character of the Saxon conquest, the Celtic names of the rivers must have become known to the invaders before the settlements on their banks were made, and consequently the village names are derived, more frequently than elsewhere, from the names of the rivers on which they stand. In Devon we have Plymton, Plymstock, and Plymouth on the Plym ; Teignton and Teignmouth on the Teign ; Dartington and Dartmouth on the Dart ; Tavy and Tavistock on the Tavy ; Torrington on the Torridge ; Otterton and Ottery on the Otter ; Culmstock, Cullompton, and Culm on the Colomb ; Crediton on the Crede ; Colyton on the Coly ; Ermington on the Erme ; Yealmpton on the Yealme ; Walkhampton on the Walcomb ; Tamerton on the Tamar ; Tawton and Tawstock on the Taw ; Sidbury and Sidmouth on the Sid ; six Clists on the Clist ; as well as five names from the Exe and two from the Axe. In Dorset seven villages take their names from the Piddle, eight from the Tarrant, three from the Cerne, and two from the Iwerne. In Somerset there are three from the Parret ; Taunton is on the Tone ; Chewton and Chew on the Chew ; Ilchester, Ilminster, Yeovilton, and Yeovil on the Ivel ; and Frome on the Frome. In Gloucestershire four places are named from the Churn, three from the Coln, two from the Leche, and Cheltenham is on the Chelt. Elsewhere we have Wilton on the Willy ; Led-bury on the Liddon ; Sturminster on the Stour ; Charminster and Charmouth on the Char ; Kintbury on the Kennet ; with two Leamingtons on the Leam ; Itch-ington on the Itchen ; Lenton on the Leen ; Tenbury on the Teme ; Coleshull or Coleshill on the Cole. In Surrey we have Weybridge, Wandsworth, and Molesey ; in Kent Maidstone, Tunbridge, Dartford, Darenth, Lenham, and Crayford ; in Essex Chelmsford, Colchester, and Stortford, with Panfield on the Blackwater, formerly the Panta ; in Suffolk Yarmouth, Aldeburgh, and Orford ; in Norfolk Thetford, Lackford, and Narborough ; in Lincolnshire, Louth (D.B. *Ludes*) is on the Lud, Sleaford on the Slea, and Market Rasen on the Rase. In the North there are a few well-known names from rivers, such as Sheffield, Rotherham, Mansfield, Rochdale, Kendal, and Alnwick.

The names of the larger rivers are, as a rule, of Celtic origin, only the smaller streams bearing Teutonic names, usually from *bróc*, a brook ; *burne* or *brun*, properly a rapid stream or torrent ; *bec*, a beck ; *lade*, a channel ; *ríth* or *ríthe*, a runlet ; *cric*, a creek ; and *fleót*, a flow of water, often a tidal flow. From these words we obtain many village names, since settlements were made where water was procurable. Of the forty-four places called Broughton, a large number are proved by documents to be from *Bróctún*, the 'tun by the brook,' whence also Brotton in Yorkshire, and several places called Brockton and Broxton, while Cornbrough is *Corlebroc* in Domesday, and Greasbrough is *Gersebroc*. From *burne* or *brun* we have Bourn, Lincolnshire, D.B. *Brune*, and Nunburnholme, Yorkshire, D.B. *Brunham*. Sherbourne, Sherburn, or Shirburn (A.S. *Scíraburne*), is the clear or bright burn ; Woburn in Wilts, and Wobourn in Surrey, are both *Wóburne* in charters (A.S. *wó* or *wóh*, bent, crooked). Woburn in Beds and Bucks, and Oborne, Dorset (D.B. *Wocburne*) are doubtless the same name. Winterbourn (A.S. *Winterburne*) is a common name, denoting streams which are dry in summer. Washbourne, Gloucestershire and Worcestershire, are *Wassanburne* and *Wasseburne* in charters (A.S. *wase*, dirt, mud). From *bec*, a beck, we have Beighton, Derbyshire, A.S. *Bectún* ; Burbage, A.S. *Burhbeca* ; several Beckleys, the Yorkshire Sandbeck, and the Mercian Sandbach and Comberbatch. Evercreech, Somerset, is the 'boar's creek,' from *cric*, a creek, whence Creech in Somerset and Derbyshire (D.B. *Cric* or *Crice*). Crixea, Essex, anciently *Crixheth* and *Kryxhithe*, is the landing-place in a creek, and Cricklade, Wilts, was the A.S. *Crecca-geláde*, where *geláid* signifies a collection of lodes or water-courses, from *láld*, a lode or channel, whence Evenlode, Whaplode and Lechlade. Linchlade (A.S. *Hlincgeláld*) is from *hlínc*, a bank. From the A.S. *ríth* or *ríthe*, a small stream, which still survives as a dialect-word, we have Childrey, A.S. *Cillaríth*, and Letherhead, A.S. *Leodríth* (see p. 170). Shottery, near Stratford-on-Avon, where Shakespearean pilgrims go to see Ann Hathaway's cottage, is called in a charter *Scotta-ríth*, which might be the 'trout-beck,' *sceóta* meaning a small trout, now called a *shot* or *shote* in some local dialects, or the 'quick stream,' from *sceót*, quick. Hendred, Berks, was *Hennaríth*, a stream frequented by water-hens (A.S. *henna*), and Eelrithe by eels. From the A.S. *fleót* or *fliét*, which signifies a place where vessels can float, and hence an estuary, tidal inlet, bay, channel, or running stream, we have Northfleet, Southfleet, and Purfleet on the Thames, and half a dozen villages called Fleet. Fleet Street obtained its name from the navigable tidal portion of the Holborn. Swinefleet, near Goole, and Adlingfleet (D.B. *Adelinges fluet*), a few miles lower down at the old mouth of the Don, are inlets which sheltered the ships of Sweine and Edgar the Atheling while their armies marched inland and took York.

Names from wells are extremely numerous. We have the town of Wells in Norfolk, and the city of Wells in Somerset, the latter being translated *Fontanetum* in an early Latin charter. In Domesday Wool, Dorset, is *Welle*, 'at the well'; Welham, Yorkshire, is *Wellun* (dative plural), 'at the wells'; Welton, Yorkshire, is *Welleton* ; Warmwell, Dorset, is *Warmewelle*, 'at the warm well'; and Caldwell, Yorkshire, is *Caldewelle*, 'at the cold well.' There are eight places called Bradwell, the 'broad well,' the variant form Braithwell appearing as *Bradewelle* in Domesday. In A.S. charters Whitwell, Derbyshire, is called *æt Hwítewylle*, 'at the white well'; Brightwell, Oxon, is *Beortanwyle*, and Brightwell, Berks, is *æt Brihtanwylle*, both meaning 'at the bright well'; Banwell, Somerset, is *Bananwyl*; Runwell, Essex, is *Runawell*, the magic or secret well; Barwell, Leicestershire, is *Barwell*, the bare well; and Chigwell, Essex, is *Cingwelle*. Wells were also named from their shapes. Thus Wherwell, Hants, A.S. *Hwærwelle* and *Hwerwillon*, is explained by the A.S. *hwer*, an ewer or kettle, and is equivalent to Kettlewell, Yorkshire, or Potwell, Hants. Holwell, Beds, A.S. *Holewel*, and Holwell, in Dorset and Devon, A.S. *Holanwyl*, are from *holan*, genitive of *hole*, a hole; and Cromwell is the 'crooked well.' Hordle, Hants, A.S. *Hordwelle*, and Hordwell, Berks, A.S. *Hordwyl*, denote wells holding a horde or store of water. Feltwell, Norfolk, A.S. *Feltwell*, may be the well in the field; Woldswell, Gloucestershire, A.S. *Waldeswel*, the well in the wood; and Saltwell, Worcestershire, A.S. *Saltwell*, the salt well. Bakewell, Derbyshire, A.S. *Badecan wiellan*, is from a personal name.

The A.S. word *cýle* also signifies a well, whence Yarkhill in Herefordshire, a curious corruption of the A.S. *Geard-cylle*. Kildwick Percy in the East Riding is in Domesday *Chilwic* or *Chillewinc*, probably the dwelling by the well; and Kilham, also in the East Riding, where the river Hull rises from springs in the chalk wolds, is called in Domesday *Chillun*, and afterwards *Kyllum* and *Killum*, apparently the dative plural *cýlum*, 'at the springs.' The word *keld*, which denotes in northern English a gathering of water bursting forth in a strong stream from a hill side, is from the O.N. *kelda*, or the A.S. *celd*, genitive *celdes*, dative *celde*. Hence the name of the Halikeld Wapentake in the North Riding, so called from the village of Hallikeld, where there is a celebrated 'holy spring.' Bapchild, near Sittingbourne, is a curious corruption of a name appearing in a charter of 697 as *Baccancelde*, and afterwards as *Bæccacild* and *Bachanchilde*, which denotes a 'beck source,' or a spring supplying a stream. Kildwick in Yorkshire, D.B. *Childewic*, the 'village at the source,' may throw light on the name of Child's Wickham, Gloucestershire. Wheldale, Yorkshire, with its well-known collieries, is in Domesday *Queldale*, the dale with a spring. From the A.S. *séath*, which denotes a spring which seethes or bubbles up, we have Roxeth, near Harrow-on-the-Hill, A.S. *Hróces séath* (A.S. *hróc*, a jackdaw, rook, or raven, genitive *hróces*). So Sittingbourne, in Kent, formerly *Sedyngburne*, may be from a seething or bubbling burn. At Nafferton, in the East Riding, numerous springs bubble up over more than an acre from small holes the size of a pea, which are locally called 'naffers.'

The A.S. words *funt* and *funta*, found in many local names, though not in A.S. literature, meant a fountain or spring, being probably derived through the Welsh from the Latin *fontem* and *fontana*. Havant, Hants, called in an early charter *Hamanfunta*, and afterwards *Hafunt*, is the cricket's spring (A.S. *hama*, a cricket, genitive *haman*). Fovant in Wilts, and Favant in Hants, A.S *Fobbefunt* and *Fobbefunta*, may be explained either as the ebbing fount, or from *fob*, a southern dialect-word, possibly ancient, which means foam or froth. Mobrisfont, Hants, and Chalfont, Bucks, A.S. *Ceadeles funta*, are from proper names. Fonthill, Wilts, is in A.S. *Funtgeal, Funtgeall*, and *Funtial*, whence the change to Fonthill is easy. The suffix *geal* or *gale* means a ravine or gill, or *Funt-ial* may be the Welsh *ffwnt-ial*, the clear fount. Fontlow, Surrey, in A.S. *Fontanhlew*, is the grave mound at the spring. Fontmell, Wilts, is the A.S. *Funtamel* or *Funtemal*.

There are sixteen places called Seaton, most of which, as well as Seamer, are from the A.S. *sæ*, a lake or sea. Many names with this suffix are accommodated forms, as in the case of Hornsea, Pevensea, Whittlesea Mere, Chelsea, or Mersea. This suffix is frequently from the A.S. *íg* or *ég*, usually found in the dative, *íge* or *ége*, which denoted a watery place, hence an island, or a place beside water, such as a river bank or a sea coast, as in Portsea, Anglesea, and Battersea. Two villages called Mersea stand on Mersea Island, A.S. *Meresíge*. The usual form of the suffix is *-ey*, as in Surrey, or Cholsey, Berks, A.S. *Ceólesíge*, from *ceól* (genitive *ceóles*), a ship or keel. Sheppey, Kent, A.S. *Sceápíg*, is the 'sheep island'; Ramsey, Hunts, A.S. *Ramesíge*, the ram's island; Hanney, Berks, A.S. *Hanníge*, the isle of [water] hens; Hinksey, Berks, A.S. *Hengestesige*, the horse's island. From personal names we have Dauntsey, Wilts, A.S. *Domeccesíge*; Kempsey, Worcestershire, A.S. *Cymesíge*; and Chertsey, A.S. *Ceortesíge*. The suffix may dwindle down to *y*, as at Ivory, 'Ivar's Island' in Lincolnshire, or Ely, the isle of eels. The word is used by itself at Eye, Northants, A.S. *Ége*, or as a prefix, as in Egham, A.S. *Egeham*, a village on the Surrey shore of the Thames.

From the A.S. *mære* or *mere*, a pool or mere, we have Cranmore, Somerset, A.S. *Cranmere*; Ozlemere, Staffordshire, A.S. *Oslanmere*; and Livermere, Suffolk, A.S. *Leuuremer*, all from water-birds. Tadmarton, Oxon, was the A.S. *Tadmærtun*, the tun by the frog-pool. Ashmore, Dorset, is A.S. *Æscmere*; Ashmansworth, Hants, is A.S. *Æscmeresweorth*; Haselmere, Surrey, was *Héselmæresgraf*; and Redmarley, Worcestershire, was *Reódmæreleáh*; while of the twenty-five places called Marston, several have been identified with places called *Merstun* in charters, though others may be from *mersc*, a marsh, which explains the name of Murston, Kent, A.S. *Mersctún*, and Middlemarsh, Dorset, A.S. *Middelmærsc*. From *wáse*, a swamp or wash, we have Hopewas, near Tamworth, anciently *Hopewaes*, the swamp in the valley; Alrewas, anciently *Alrewasse*, the alder swamp; and Buildwas in Salop. The common names Morley, Morton, and Morden are usually from *mór*, a moor, heath, or fen. Thus Morden, Surrey, is A.S. *Mórdún*; Morley and Morton, Derbyshire, are A.S. *Mórleáh* and *Mórtún*.

The A.S. *ófer* and *óra*, which mean the shore of a sea or river, usually appear as *-or* or *-ore* in modern names, as in Windsor and Cumnor (see pp. 296, 102). Eastnor, Herefordshire (D.B. *Astenofre*), is the eastern shore; Edensor, Derbyshire (D.B. *Ednesovre*), is Eadnoth's shore; and Esher, Surrey, A.S. *Æscore*, is the ash-tree shore. In Domesday Codnor, Derbyshire is *Cotenovre*; Ower, Dorset, is *Ora*; Owram, Yorkshire, is *Ovre*; and Hunsingore is *Holsingovre*. Radnor, Cheshire, was *Readenora*; and Rowner, Hants, was *Rugenora*. Wardour, Wilts, whence Wardour Street and the title of Lord Arundel of Wardour, was *Weardora*.

The fact that five shires and ten county towns take their names from fords, while Bristol is the only city whose name bears witness to the existence of a bridge, affords a curious testimony to the want of facilities for travel at the time when our local names originated. A river as large as the Severn had to be forded at Hereford, and we do not find a bridge before we come to Bridgenorth. The Thames had to be forded at Wallingford, Halliford, and Oxford, the Ouse at Bedford, and the Lea at Stratford. Cambridge, Bridgewater, and Redbridge cannot be reckoned among towns with bridges, since they are corruptions of earlier names, while at Tunbridge and Weybridge the streams are small. Several fords are named from the rivers they cross : Chelmsford being on the Chelmer, Stortford on the Stort, Dartford on the Darent, Brentford on the Brent, Sleaford on the Slea, Thetford on the Thet, Lidford on the Lid, Eynford on the Eyn, Colyford on the Coly. Others are from personal names, as Bedford, A.S. *Bedicanford*; Charford, A.S. *Cerdicesford*; Kempsford, A.S. *Cynemæresford*; Otford, A.S. *Ottanford*; Ugford, A.S. *Ucganford*; Snarford, A.S. *Snardesford*; Daylesford, A.S. *Degilesford*. Others are descriptive, named from a tree or other object on the bank : Ashford from an ash, Thornford from a thorn, Alresford from an alder, Widford, A.S. *Withigford*, from a willow, Salford from a sallow, and Garforth from a fir tree. Burford, A.S. *Berghford*, was near a hill, Clifford near a cliff, Woodford near a wood, Upford was the upper ford, and Bradford a broad ford. The fifteen Stanfords, Stamfords, or Stainforths were paved with stones, Coggleford with large round stones locally called coggles. The nine Staplefords were protected by piles or staples. The twenty-two Sandfords or Sampfords had a sandy bottom, Greatford had a bottom of grit or gravel, and Fulford is the foul or muddy ford. The fourteen Stratfords were fords on Roman roads, Fenny Stratford and Stony Stratford in Bucks being, for instance, fords on Watling Street, and Erminford, A.S. *Earmingaford*, and Chesterford on the Earming Street. Names like Streatham, Streatley, Street-field, and the thirty places called Stretton or Stratton, also mark the lines of Roman road, Church Stretton, in Salop, for instance, being on the Roman road from Kenchester to Wroxeter, while the direction of the Fosseway is disclosed by Stretton-under-Fosse and Stretton-on-the-Fosse, both in Warwickshire, and by Stratton-on-Fosse in Somerset (see p. 266). The A.S. *wæg* or *weg*, a road or way, sometimes becomes *wick*, Powick, Worcestershire, being the A.S. *Pohweg*, while Stanwick, Northants, A.S. *Stanweg*, Stanwick, Yorkshire, D.B. *Stenwege*, are the stone way.

The secular character of English names as compared with those elsewhere is very marked. In Ireland about 2700 names have the ecclesiastical prefix *Kil*, often followed by the name of a saint, and in Wales there are nearly 500 saint names with the prefix *Llan*, while in England places bearing the names of saints, such as St. Austel, St. Just, St. Agnes or St. Michael, are found chiefly in Cornwall, which long remained Welsh. Elsewhere a few names, chiefly of monastic sites like St. Albans, St. Neot's, St. Ives, and St. Bees, are all we have to show against some 315 villages and towns in France which bear the names of patron saints. Kirby, 'church village,' occurs thirty-five times in the Scandinavian districts, where also we have Kirkdale, Kirkham, Kirkstead, Kirton, and the like. The corresponding English forms, such as Bonchurch, the 'church of St. Boniface,' Boston, the 'town of St. Botolph,' Whitchurch, or Christchurch, are curiously rare, and the few that exist are often disguised, as in the case of Chirbury, Salop, the *Ciricbyrig* of the Chronicle, where Ethelfreda, the Lady of Mercia, built a church. Chritchell, Dorset, D.B. *Circel*, may be the 'little church,' and Chreshall, Essex, is called *Christeshalla* in a charter of Stephen's reign. From *ecclesia*, the source of such Welsh and Scotch names as Ecclefechan, the church of St. Fechan, the Vigeanus of the Scottish calendar, we may probably explain the names of Eccles in Norfolk and Lancashire, Ecclesfield and Eccleshill in Yorkshire, and five places called Eccleston. Exhall, Warwickshire, was the A.S. *Eccleshalc*, the church slope, and Eccleshall in Staffordshire has long been the residence of the Bishops of Lichfield.

The 644 religious houses which existed in England at the time of the dissolution have left numerous traces of their existence, often by the suffix minster, from *monasterium*, which we have in Westminster or Kidderminster. In the seventh century nunneries were founded at Minster in Thanet and Minster in Sheppey, and there was another at Nunminster, Hants, A.S. *Nunnan-minster*. Axminster, Ilminster, Sturminster, Charminster, and Warminster take their names from the rivers Axe, Ivel, Stour, Char, and Were on which they stand. Pitminster, Somerset, A.S. *Pipingminster* and *Pypmynster*, may be from the A.S. *pip*, a pipe or flute. Beaminster, Dorset, takes its name from St. Bega. There were monasteries at Bedminster, Dorset; Newminster, Northumberland; Minster Lovell, Oxon; Kirkstead, Lincolnshire; and at Kirkstall, Kirkham, and Kirklees in Yorkshire. At Abbotsbury, Dorset, a monastery was founded in the reign of Canute, and at Monkton Farley, Wilts, there was a convent of Cluniac monks. At Monks Kirby, Warwickshire, a Benedictine priory was founded in 1077, and there were monasteries at Monks Horton in Kent, and at Monk Bretton in Yorkshire. Nuneaton, Warwickshire, was a priory founded at Eaton by Robert, Earl of Leicester, for nuns of the order of Fontevrault. In Yorkshire, Nunburnholme, Nunmonkton, and Nunkeeling were Benedictine nunneries; while Nunappleton and Nunthorpe were Cistercian. Such names may only indicate monastic ownership. Thus Nunriding, Northumberland, belonged to the nuns of Hallystone (Holy Stone), a Benedictine priory near a large sacred stone which still bears the older name of the Drakestone (Dragon Stone). Abbots Ann, near Andover, belonged to Hyde Abbey, Winchester; Abbotside, Yorkshire, belonged to Jervaulx Abbey; and Abington, Cambridgeshire, to St. Mary's Abbey at York. Stapleford Abbots, Essex, belonged to the Abbey of Bury St. Edmunds; Abinghall, Gloucestershire, formerly called Abbenhall, was a residence of the abbots of Flaxley. Monkton, Durham, belonged to the monks of Jarrow; and Monkseaton, Northumberland, to the monks of Tynemouth. Monkland, Herefordshire, was a Benedictine cell; and Monkhill, near Pontefract, was a grange of St. John's Priory.

Several monastic houses show by their French names that they were founded by Norman nobles. Among them are Belvoir, with its wide outlook over the plains of Lincolnshire, a Benedictine priory founded by Robert de Todeni in 1076; Beauchief Abbey, Derbyshire, founded in 1183 for Premonstratensian canons; and Beaulieu, Hants, a Benedictine house founded by King John in 1204. We may add Beauvale in Notts and Beaudesert in Staffordshire and Warwickshire. Jervaulx and Rievaulx, the great Cistercian abbeys in the valleys of the Ure and the Rye, retain a suffix which is a corruption of *Vallibus*. We have an Abbas de Rivallibus at Rievaulx, Clairvaux in Anjou being mentioned in 1130 as *de claris vallibus*.

Survivals from the heathen period are few, the most notable being Lydney (p. 179). The numerous Holywells, rare in the east of England, but more frequent as we approach the Welsh border, are survivals of a Celtic cult, which at Holywell in Flintshire has been transferred to St. Winifred. Among survivals of Teutonic heathendom we may attribute to Woden names like the Wansdyke, Wednesbury (p. 292), and Wednesfield (A.S. *Wodnesfeld*). From *god*, an idol, genitive *godes*, we have Godshill, Isle of Wight, A.S. *Godeshyl*, the 'idol's hill'; and perhaps Godney, Somerset, A.S. *Godenei*, and Gadshill in Kent. Harrow-on-the-Hill (see p. 142) is from the West Saxon *hearg* or *hearh*, Mercian and Northumbrian *herg*, a heathen altar, or idol temple, which is the same word as the O.N. *hörgr*, a sacrificial stone. From *hearges*, the genitive singular, or *heargas*, the nominative plural of this word, we have Arras in Yorkshire, formerly spelt *Herghes* or *Erghes*, and from *hörgum*, the O.N. dative plural, we have Airyholme or Eryholme, called in Domesday *Ergun*; Erghum, D.B. *Ergone*; Airsholme or Ayresome, formerly *Arsum*; Arram, also in Yorkshire, formerly *Argun*; Arkholme, Lancashire, D.B. *Ergune*; and probably Averham in Notts, formerly *Argum* and *Aigrum*. Mr. Bradley has collected several instances in which this word forms the final syllable of the name. Grimsargh, a chapelry in the parish of Preston, Lancashire, D.B. *Grimesarge*, would be 'at the temple of Grîmr' or Odin. Goosnargh, a township in the parish of Kirkham, Lancashire, D.B. *Gusanarghe*, he interprets as *gudhsins hörgi*, 'at the idol's temple.' Mansergh, a chapelry in the parish of Kirby Lonsdale, Westmorland, D.B. *Manzserge*, might be a corruption of *Mânanshörgi*, 'at the temple of the moon.' The names Sizergh and Brettarg, also in Westmorland, and Kellamergh in Lancashire, are probably from the same word, which is only found in the North, except at Harrow, and at Pepperharrow in Surrey. The word was transferred to Christian shrines, as in the case of Anglezargh or Anglezarke, in the parish of Bolton, Lancashire, which may be explained as *Eingils-hörgr*, the angel's temple, while Golcar in the parish of Huddersfield was formerly *Gudlagesarc*, St. Guthlac's chapel or temple. As landmarks, charters frequently make mention of a *byrgels*, which signified a heathen burial-place. None of these have been identified, but Burghill, Sussex, called *Burgelstaltone* in Domesday, must have been a tún near the place of a burgels.

BIBLIOGRAPHY

Birch, *Cartularium Saxonicum.*
Blackie, *Dictionary of Place-Names.*
Boyd, *Indian Local Names.*
Bradley, *English Place-Names* (Sheffield Literary Society).
Buttmann, *Die Deutschen Ortsnamen.*
Cocheris, *Origine et Formation des Noms de Lieux.*
Crawford, *Descriptive Dictionary of the Indian Islands.*
Edmonston, *Shetland and Orkney Glossary.*
Egli, *Nomina Geographica.*
Ellis, *Domesday Book* (D.B.).
Esser, *Beiträge zur gallokeltischen Namenkunde.*
Förstemann, *Altdeutsches Namenbuch.*
    ,,   *Die deutschen Ortsnamen.*
Freeman, *Historical Geography of Europe.*
Gatschet, *Ortetymologische Forschungen.*
    ,,   *Quelques Noms Géographiques.* (*Revue de Linguistique,* vol. xv.)
    ,,   *Promenade Onomatologique sur les Bords du Lac Léman.*
    ,,   *Localbenennungen aus der Berner Oberland,* and other works.
Glück, *Die bei C. J. Cæsar vorkommenden Keltischen Namen.*
Grandgagnage, *Étude sur quelques Noms anciens de Lieux situés en Belgique.*
    ,,   *Mémoire sur les anciens Noms de Lieux dans la Belgique Orientale.*
Hamilton, *Indian Names.* (Transactions of Nebraska State Historical Society, vol. i.)
Hayden, *Ethnology of Indian Tribes.* (Transactions of American Philosophical Society, vol. xii.)
Holder, *Alt-Celtischer Sprachschatz.*
Houzé, *Noms de Lieux en France.*
Hundred Rolls (H.R.).
Hunter, *Imperial Gazetteer of India.*
Johnston, J. B., *Place-Names of Scotland.*
Joyce, *Irish Names of Places.* (Two Series.)
Jubainville, d'Arbois de, *Noms de Lieux en France* (Revue Celtique, vols. viii. and ix.), and other papers.
Kemble, *Codex Diplomaticus Ævi Saxonici.* (C.D.)
    ,,   *Saxons in England.*
Kornmesser, *Französische Ortsnamen Germanischer Abkunft.*

Leo, *Die angelsächsischen Ortsnamen.* (Rectitudines Singularum Personarum.)
„   *Local Nomenclature of the Anglo-Saxons.* (Translated by B. Williams.)
Lucas, *Historical Geography.*
Maxwell, Sir Herbert, *Scottish Land-Names.*
Miklosich, *Etymologisches Wörterbuch der Slawischen Sprachen,* and other works.
Moore, A. W., *Surnames and Place-Names of the Isle of Man.*
Müller, Ff., *Allgemeine Ethnographie.*
Payne, *History of the New World called America.*
Peschel, *Geschichte des Zeitalters der Entdeckungen.*
Redhouse, *Turkish Dictionary.*
Rhys, *Celtic Heathendom.* (Hibbert Lectures.)
„   *Studies in the Arthurian Legend.*
„   *Early Ethnology of the British Isles.* (Rhind Lectures.)
„   *Celtic Britain,* with other works.
Sibree, *Malagasy Place-Names.* (Journal of R.A.S. vol. xv.)
Skene, *The Four Ancient Books of Wales.*
„   *Celtic Scotland.*
Streatfield, *Lincolnshire and the Danes.*
Sweet, *Oldest English Texts.*
Thorpe, *Diplomatarium Anglicum.*
Trumbull, *Indian Names of Places in Connecticut.*
Yule, *Cathay and the Way Thither.*
„   *Marco Polo.*
Yule and Burnell, *Hobson-Jobson, an Anglo-Indian Glossary.*
Zeuss, *Grammatica Celtica.*
„   *Die Deutschen und die Nachbarstämme.*

Many valuable papers by d'Arbois de Jubainville, Dr. Horatio Hale, Mr. Powell, Dr. Brinton, Dr. Whitley Stokes, Prof. Skeat, Mr. Henry Bradley, Mr. Mayhew, Mr. Stevenson, Mr. Duignan, and others are hidden away in various Periodicals and Transactions, such as *The American Anthropologist, The Journal of American Folklore, The Magazine of Western History,* the *Revue Celtique,* the *Revue de Linguistique, The Journal of the Royal Asiatic Society, The Transactions of the Philological Society, The Antiquary, The Academy, The Athenæum, Notes and Queries,* Bezzenberger's *Beiträge, The Calcutta Review,* and Publications of the Smithsonian Institution (Bureau of Ethnology).

INDEX TO NAMES IN ENGLAND

399

Selwood, 254.
Selworthy, 371.
Settrington, 363.
Sevenoaks, 255, 378.
Severn, 255.
Sewerby, 351.
Shaftesbury, 256, 365, 366, 382.
Shebbear, 367.
Sheepshead, 381.
Sheepwash, 257
Sheffield, 256, 373, 384.
Shelfanger, 374.
Shelford, 373.
Shelley, 373.
Shelton, 373.
Sheppey, 257, 387.
Shepton, 257.
Sherbourne, 385.
Sherburn, 15, 385.
Sheriff Hales, 372.
Sherwood, 257.
Shields, 257.
Shiplake, 89.
Shipton, 5, 369.
Shirburn, 257, 385.
Shireoaks, 257.
Shitlington, 352.
Shoeburyness, 257.
Shoreham, 257.
Shottery, 385.
Shoulthwaite, 377.
Shrawardine, 374.
Shrewsbury, 257, 366.
Shropshire, 258.
Sibbertswold, 351.
Sicklinghall, 372.
Sidbury, 366, 384.
Sidlesham, 353.
Sidmouth, 384.
Silchester, 33, 258.
Silksworth, 349, 353.
Silsden, 375.
Singlecross, 359.
Sittingbourne, 386.
Sixpenny Handley, 10, 361, 364.
Sizergh, 390.
Skellingthorpe, 376.
Skelton, 373.
Skidby, 377.
Skipton, 5, 15, 369.
Skye, 27.
Skyrack, 359.
Slade, 383.
Slaidburn, 383.
Slaithwaite, 383.
Slaughter, 359.
Sleaford, 260, 384, 388.
Sledmere, 383.
Sleights, 383.
Smaithwaite, 377.
Smeaton, 357.
Smethcot, 357.
Smethick, 357.
Smisby, 357.
Smithdon, 362.
Snarford, 388.
Snaith, 383.
Snaygill, 372.
Sodor, 261.
Soham, 380.

Solent, 262.
Solway, 262.
Somerby, 357.
Somerleyton, 357.
Somersby, 357.
Somerset, 13, 262.
Southampton, 263, 369.
Southend, 263.
Southfleet, 385.
Southill, 299.
Sowber, 367.
Sparkenhoe, 361.
Speen, 264.
Speeton, 264.
Spelhoe, 361.
Spelthorne, 359.
Spettisbury, 365.
Sprotborough, 366.
Spurn, 264.
Stafford, 264.
Stalbridge, 357, 382.
Stamford, 265, 388.
Stancill, 372.
Stanford, 388.
Stanford-le-Hope, 375.
Stanford Rivers, 350.
Stanhope, 376.
Stanley, 374.
Stanton, 369.
Stanton Drew, 266.
Stanton-Harcourt, 350.
Stanwick, 388.
Staincross, 359.
Staine, 360.
Staines, 265, 340.
Stainforth, 388.
Staithwaite, 377.
Staple, 359.
Stapleford, 357, 388.
Stapleford Abbots, 389.
Stapleton, 357, 369.
Staploe, 361.
Start, 265.
Staunton, 369.
Steeton, 382.
Stepney, 265.
Stewton, 382.
Steyning, 353.
Stickford, 382.
Stisted, 382.
Stittenham, 382.
Stixwold, 382.
Stockbridge, 382.
Stockport, 227.
Stockton, 369, 382.
Stockwith, 382.
Stoke, 382.
Stokesley, 374, 382.
Stone, 360.
Stonegate, 341.
Stonegrave, 381.
Stonehenge, 266, 341.
Stortford, 384, 388.
Stotfold, 382.
Stottesden, 382.
Stour, 266.
Stourminster, 266.
Stourmouth, 266.
Stowborough, 266, 366.
Stratford, 266, 388.
Stratton, 369, 388.
Streatfield, 388.

Streatham, 266, 388.
Streatley, 388.
Streatly, 267.
Strensall, 372.
Stretton, 257, 369, 388.
Strood, 267, 341.
Stubhampton, 142.
Studham, 382.
Studley, 382.
Stukeley, 382.
Sturminster, 384, 389.
Stutton, 382.
Sudbury, 366.
Suffolk, 268.
Sundhope, 375.
Surrenden, 375.
Surrey, 268, 387.
Sussex, 13, 269.
Sutton, 28, 368.
Swanage, 270.
Swanborough, 361.
Swanton, 270.
Swinefleet, 385.
Swineshead, 381.
Swinhope, 376.
Swinton, 369.
Swyre, 382.
Sydling Fifehead, 363.

TADCASTER, 33.
Tadmarton, 387.
Taingoe, 362.
Talk-on-the-Hill, 271.
Tamerton, 272, 384.
Tamworth, 272, 374, 384.
Tansley, 374.
Tarrant, 280, 384.
Tarring, 354.
Taunton, 273, 384.
Tavistock, 273, 382, 384.
Tavy, 384.
Tawstock, 384.
Tawton, 384.
Tebworth, 352.
Teddington, 273.
Teignmouth, 384.
Teignton, 384.
Temple, 274.
Tenbury, 366, 384.
Tenby, 274.
Tenterden, 375.
Terling, 354.
Tetbury, 365.
Tewkesbury, 366.
Thame, 7, 384.
Thames, 275.
Thanet, 275.
Theale, 10, 364.
Thedwestry, 359.
Thetford, 275, 384, 388.
Theydon, 375, 380.
Thickhead, 381.
Thingoe, 361, 362.
Thingwall, 276.
Thirkleby, 351.
Tholthorpe, 351, 377.
Thornborough, 379.
Thornbury, 379.
Thornford, 379, 388.
Thornhaugh, 379.

Thornholm, 34, 348, 379.
Thornthorpe, 351.
Thornthwaite, 377.
Thornton, 368, 378, 379.
Thorpe, 29, 363, 377.
Thorpe Arch, 350, 377.
Thorpe Bassett, 377.
Thorpe Bulmer, 377.
Thorpe By-Water, 377.
Thorpe Constantine, 377.
Thorpe-in-Balne, 377.
Thorpe-in-the-Street, 377.
Thorpe le Soken, 362.
Thorpe Mandeville, 377.
Thorpe-on-the-Hill, 377.
Thorpe-sub-Montem, 377.
Thorpe-Under-Wood, 377.
Threo, 361.
Thurlstone, 351.
Thurstable, 359.
Thwaite, 377.
Tibbaldstone, 360.
Tickenall, 372.
Tickhill, 361.
Ticknall, 372.
Tilbury, 366.
Tiley, 364.
Tilsworth, 364.
Tincleton, 375.
Tintinhull, 361.
Tipnoak, 359.
Tiptree, 377.
Tisbury, 365.
Tittenhanger, 374.
Tiverton, 278.
Tockenham, 352.
Todenham, 352.
Toltingtrough, 359, 378.
Toltingtrow, 359.
Tooting, 353.
Torrington, 353, 384.
Torquay, 278.
Totsmanslow, 360.
Towcester, 32, 279, 384.
Tredegar, 339.
Trent, 280.
Treo, 361.
Triplow, 360.
Troston, 354.
Truro, 281, 339.
Tunbridge, 384, 388.
Turvey, 380.
Twickenham, 282, 370.
Twining, 282.
Twizel, 282.
Twyford, 278.
Twyneham, 346.
Tyningham, 170.
Tynwald, 276.

UGFORD, 388.
Ugley, 379.
Ulverston, 381.
Unthank, 284, 364.